Scientific
and engineering
problem-solving
with the computer

Prentice-Hall
Series in Automatic Computation

AHO, ed., *Currents in the Theory of Computing*

AHO AND ULLAM, *The Theory of Parsing, Translation, and Compiling*, Volume I: *Parsing;* Volume II; *Compiling*

ANDREE, *Computer Programming: Techniques, Analysis, and Mathematics*

ANSELONE, *Collectively Compact Operator Approximation Theory and Applications to Integral Equations*

AVRIEL, *Nonlinear Programming: Analysis and Methods*

BATES AND DOUGLAS, *Programming Language/One*, 2nd ed.

BENNETT, JR., *Scientific and Engineering Problem-Solving with the Computer*

BLUMENTHAL, *Management Information Systems*

BRENT, *Algorithms for Minimization without Derivatives*

BRINCH HANSEN, *Operating System Principles*

BRZOZOWSKI AND YOELI, *Digital Networks*

COFFMAN AND DENNING, *Operating Systems Theory*

CRESS, et al., FORTRAN IV with WATFOR and WATFIV

DAHLQUIST, BJORCK, AND ANDERSON, *Numerical Methods*

DANIEL, *The Approximate Minimization of Functionals*

DEO, *Graph Theory with Applications to Engineering and Computer Science*

DESMONDE, *Computers and Their Uses*, 2nd ed.

DIJKSTRA, *A Discipline of Programming*

DRUMMOND, *Evaluation and Measurement Techniques for Digital Computer Systems*

ECKHOUSE, *Minicomputer Systems: Organization and Programming (PDP-11)*

FIKE, *Computer Evaluation of Mathematical Functions*

FIKE, *PL/I for Scientific Programmers*

FORSYTHE AND MOLER, *Computer Solution of Linear Algebraic Systems*

GEAR, *Numerical Initial Value Problems in Ordinary Differential Equations*

GORDON, *System Simulation*

GRISWOLD, *String and List Processing in SNOBOL4: Techniques and Applications*

HANSEN, *A Table of Series and Products*

HARTMANIS AND STEARNS, *Algebraic Structure Theory of Sequential Machines*

HILLBURN AND JULICH, *Microcomputers/Microprocessors: Hardware, Software, and Applications*

JACOBY, et al., *Iterative Methods for Nonlinear Optimization Problems*

JOHNSON, *System Structure in Data, Programs, and Computers*

KIVIAT, et al., *The SIMSCRIPT II Programming Language*

LAWSON AND HANSON, *Solving Least Squares Problems*

LORIN, *Parallelism in Hardware and Software: Real and Apparent Concurrency*

LOUDEN AND LEDIN, *Programming the IBM 1130*, 2nd ed.

MARTIN, *Computer Data-Base Organization*

MARTIN, *Design of Man-Computer Dialogues*

MARTIN, *Design of Real-Time Computer Systems*

MARTIN, *Future Developments in Telecommunications*

MARTIN, *Principles of Data-Base Management*

MARTIN, *Programming Real-Time Computing Systems*

MARTIN,   *Security, Accuracy, and Privacy in Computer Systems*
MARTIN,   *Systems Analysis for Data Transmission*
MARTIN,   *Telecommunications and the Computer*
MARTIN,   *Teleprocessing Network Organization*
MARTIN AND NORMAN,   *The Computerized Society*
MCKEEMAN, et al.,   *A Compiler Generator*
MYERS,   *Time-Sharing Computation in the Social Sciences*
MINSKY,   *Computation: Finite and Infinite Machines*
NIEVERGELT, et al.,   *Computer Approaches to Mathematical Problems*
PLANE AND MCMILLAN,   *Discrete Optimization: Integer Programming and Network Analysis for Management Decisions*
POLIVKA AND PAKIN,   *APL: The Language and Its Usage*
PRITSKER AND KIVIAT,   *Simulation with GASP II: A FORTRAN-based Simulation Language*
PYLYSHYN, ed.,   *Perspectives on the Computer Revolution*
RICH,   *Internal Sorting Methods Illustrated with PL/I Programs*
RUDD,   *Assembly Language Programming and the IBM 360 and 370 Computers*
SACKMAN AND CITRENBAUM, eds.,   *On-Line Planning: Towards Creative Problem-Solving*
SALTON, ed.,   *The SMART Retrieval System: Experiments in Automatic Document Processing*
SAMMET,   *Programming Languages: History and Fundamentals*
SCHAEFER,   *A Mathematical Theory of Global Program Optimization*
SCHULTZ,   *Spline Analysis*
SCHWARZ, et al.,   *Numerical Analysis of Symmetric Matrices*
SHAH,   *Engineering Simulation Using Small Scientific Computers*
SHAW,   *The Logical Design of Operating Systems*
SHERMAN,   *Techniques in Computer Programming*
SIMON AND SIKLOSSY, eds.,   *Representation and Meaning: Experiments with Information Processing Systems*
STERBENZ,   *Floating-Point Computation*
STOUTEMYER,   *PL/1 Programming for Engineering and Science*
STRANG AND FIX,   *An Analysis of the Finite Element Method*
STROUD,   *Approximate Calculation of Multiple Integrals*
TANENBAUM,   *Structured Computer Organization*
TAVISS, ed.,   *The Computer Impact*
UHR,   *Pattern Recognition, Learning, and Thought: Computer-Programmed Models of Higher Mental Processes*
VAN TASSEL,   *Computer Security Management*
VARGA,   *Matrix Iterative Analysis*
WAITE,   *Implementing Software for Non-Numeric Application*
WILKINSON,   *Rounding Errors in Algebraic Processes*
WIRTH,   *Algorithms + Data Structure = Programs*
WIRTH,   *Systematic Programming: An Introduction*
YEH, ed.,   *Applied Computation Theory: Analysis, Design, Modeling*

William Ralph Bennett, Jr.

*Charles Baldwin Sawyer Professor
of Engineering and Applied Science,
and Professor of Physics
Yale University*

Scientific and engineering problem-solving with the computer

Prentice-Hall, Inc. Englewood Cliffs, New Jersey

Library of Congress Cataloging in Publication Data

BENNETT, WILLIAM RALPH, JR.
  Scientific and engineering problem-solving with the computer.

  (Series in automatic computation)
  Includes bibliographies and index.
    1. Electronic digital computers—Programming.
2. Basic (Computer program language)   3. Problem solving
—Data processing.   I. Title.
QA76.6.B45   001.6'42   75-30934
ISBN 0-13-795807-2

10 9 8 7 6 5 4 3 2

Printed in the United States of America

PRENTICE-HALL INTERNATIONAL, INC., *London*
PRENTICE-HALL OF AUSTRALIA, PTY. LIMITED, *Sydney*
PRENTICE-HALL OF CANADA, LTD., *Toronto*
PRENTICE-HALL OF INDIA PRIVATE LIMITED, *New Delhi*
PRENTICE-HALL OF JAPAN, INC., *Tokyo*
PRENTICE-HALL OF SOUTHEAST ASIA PRIVATE LIMITED, *Singapore*

To Fran

Contents

5 Dynamics 199

6 Random Processes 279

Preface

Three years ago, I was asked by the chairman of the Engineering and Applied Science Department at Yale University to develop an introductory computer-applications course that would have broad appeal to students in both the humanities and physical sciences. The present book is one result. A one-term course based on this book has been given for three years under the title "The Computer as a Research Tool" and has been taken by students ranging from freshman English majors to graduate students in chemistry. Much to the author's surprise and personal gratification, the course made the "Ten Best" list twice at Yale during this period.[†] Most students taking the course had had (or were taking concurrently) at least one term of calculus. Beyond that, there was no real common denominator.

The logical organization of the book is as follows:

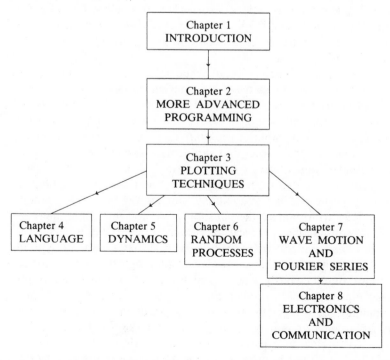

[†] *Yale Course Critique* (published by the *Yale Daily News*, New Haven, Conn.): 1974 edition, pp. 7, 43; 1975 edition pp. 13, 71.

Both programming and conceptual difficulties increase within chapters and from top to bottom and from left to right in the diagram. Chapters 1 through 3 are intended as introductory background material for the main applications course, which starts with Chapter 4. It should be emphasized that Chapters 4 through 7 are independent of each other in both programming technique and subject matter. However, as indicated in the diagram, Chapter 8 assumes Chapter 7 as a prerequisite. The final sections of Chapters 5 and 8 contain the hardest material and the most difficult programming exercises in the book. These sections are intended primarily for students in the physical sciences and may easily be omitted.

Although the chapters are labeled according to subject matter, they are also organized according to programming technique:

Chapter	Techniques Emphasized
1	Elementary programming in BASIC
2	Series summation and matrix operations
3	Teletype plotting and graphic displays
4	Character coding and printing
5	Solution of differential equations by Taylor expansions
6	Monte Carlo solutions and method of least squares
7	Definite integrals and harmonic analysis
8	Reiterative solutions to nonlinear equations and integrodifferential equations

The structure of the book is also based on the belief that the best way to teach students computational methods is to give them lots of interesting problems of gradually increasing difficulty. I chose BASIC as the main programming language because it is rapidly learned and "conversational." It is also efficient enough to work effectively within minicomputers. Students who have never touched a computer terminal can start right off doing meaningful problems in BASIC, and the frustrations associated with batch processing are totally avoided. Under these conditions, the students teach themselves to a large extent and one merely has to be available to give general guidance and help them out of occasional pitfalls.

The problems are given immediately after the relevant discussions in the text and where possible have been based on unusual events of general and social interest. An effort was also made to select nontrivial problems. Apart from introductory examples in each chapter, the remaining problems are of a type that would either be impossible or prohibitive to solve without a computer. For the same reason, most topics and problems discussed in the present book are rarely treated quantitatively in the normal curriculum. Obviously, such problems would be avoided in standard lecture courses in physics. On the other hand, most instructors in programming courses do not have enough background in physics to formulate the questions. At the same time, many of these topics are of considerable practical importance in everyday life.

An attempt has been made to try to choose material that would alternate in appeal between humanities and science students. Although it is very hard to please both groups simultaneously, one can play a game in which important methods in science are applied to problems of social importance. For example, Chapter 5 (Dynamics) starts off with discussions of sky diving, ball games, and bizarre events from the newspapers. Similarly, an analysis of the spread of syphilis among a community of prostitutes adds some variety to the problems on diffusion in Chapter 6, and Fourier series becomes more interesting to the nonscientist when wierd musical instruments and politics can be brought into the act. Also, the author has tried throughout the manuscript to provide occasional bits of comic relief. However, what sometimes seems hilariously amusing late at night does not always withstand the cold light of dawn.

Credit for the course at Yale was based entirely on the completion of assigned problems (about two or three a week) and a term research project. For the latter reason, Research Problems are occasionally suggested throughout the book with the object of stimulating further independent work on the part of the student. The standard problems are presented to illustrate what can easily be accomplished in a specific area in one afternoon through the expenditure of a few dollars in computer time (if you have to pay for it). Nearly all of them can be done on a minicomputer with a memory of only 16,000 16-bit words. However, the more meaningful ones are much too difficult for use on examinations, and the whole concept of an examination seemed pointless. I think the ability of a student to solve 30 formidable problems over a period of one term is the most important measure of his or her grasp of the subject. However, tastes vary on this point and the above approach to the grading question involves a massive investment in time spent examining program listings and problem results handed in by the students. In this connection it helps to encourage the students to document their programs right from the start. One does not usually need formal flow charts, but an occasional comment in the margin of a program becomes very helpful. It is also desirable to encourage students to think through their problems carefully before going near a terminal.

The chapters were deliberately overloaded with material to permit some variety in giving the course from one year to the next and to provide additional information for students with an unusual interest in specialized topics. It was thought that that approach would also be an asset in the selection of term projects. For similar reasons, an effort was made to dig up references to original papers where practical. Because the subject matter is fairly well delineated by chapter headings, reference lists are presented at the end of each chapter.

There are various ways in which the material can be divided and presented within a one-term course, and Abstracts have been included at the start of each chapter to aid in this process.

The real heart of the course starts with Chapter 4, and it was tempting to start both the course and the book at that point. However, such an approach simply does not work unless the students have already had an appreciable background in programming. In that event, one could jump immediately to Chapter 4 and regard Chapters 1–3 as "appendices" to be consulted in case of specific need (as cross-referenced through the index, page footnotes, and abstracts). Under these conditions Chapters 4 through 7 would make a practical one-term course if the more difficult material were omitted along the lines suggested in the abstracts.

Most students I encountered had never done any real programming, and I constructed the first three chapters as an introductory technical background—to be covered as rapidly as possible (say, about 3 weeks). Chapter 1 is for students without any previous exposure to computers and can easily be skipped (or covered very rapidly) by students with prior computing experience. I have usually covered this material in one lecture and left most of it to be read by beginning students as needed and learned through the mechanism of problems assigned the first day. (An immediate assignment of four or five problems also serves the useful purpose of encouraging students who do not want to do any work to drop the course.) The material by Kemeny and Kurtz written on BASIC (see References to Chapter 1) is very useful at this point, if available. Also, it is assumed that a manual on BASIC provided by the individual computer service will be available for occasional reference.

However, a primary objective was to make the present book self-contained. It seems unfair to expect students to have to buy more than one book for a course.

Chapter 2 covers a number of routine programming techniques and reviews aspects of high school algebra and introductory calculus (particularly derivatives, Taylor series, and definite integrals) which are needed in later sections of the book. Even students who *have* had one term of introductory calculus are usually not at home with Taylor series. At the same time, such a minimal amount of calculus is really needed throughout the rest of the book that it seemed a shame to exclude students on the basis of a calculus prerequisite. It is also desirable to have students start getting used to vectors and matrices as early as possible so that the mechanics of using them does not become a stumbling block in the later applications involving more difficult subject matter. For this reason, I have chosen to sneak up on the MAT commands in BASIC by first using them in the Ramanujan problem to store and manipulate data, and then to gradually introduce more complicated MAT operations in succeeding sections. By the time the student gets to the discussion of the input–output theory in economics, he should not only be used to using matrices but also have a genuine appreciation for the tremendous power of MAT commands.

Chapter 3 in its entirety is not essential to the later chapters on other specific applications. However, most students love plotting things, and such techniques can provide helpful insight to the solution of difficult problems later. The chapter presents a survey of representative methods and devices that are currently available. The material on teletype plotting can be covered in a week or two, and this material (or its equivalent, using high-resolution displays) is all that is really required for the rest of the book. What one specifically does beyond teletype plotting will be limited by available hardware. However, computer-controlled high-resolution display devices are becoming increasingly available, and it seemed clear that at least some discussion of the use of representative hardware should be included in this chapter. The minicomputer owner in particular is in a position nowadays where such things may be implemented cheaply.

The relative emphasis on remaining chapters is largely dependent on the personal interests of the instructor and students. For example, if one follows the short-course outline in the abstracts, it is possible to cover Chapters 1–7 in a normal term. On the other hand, the sequence 1–4 (in entirety) can make a very substantial one term course for humanities students;† whereas the sequence 1–3 (shortened) plus 5–7 (in entirety) can make a substantial one-term course for physics majors. Similarly, the sequence 2–3 (shortened), 4 (through material on information theory), 7 and 8 can make a pretty full one-term course for prospective electrical engineering students. If you keep the logical organization diagram shown at the start of the Preface in mind and look at the specific suggestions in the abstracts, a large number of safe one-term combinations can be worked out. Even within individual chapters the mutual dependency on more than adjacent sections is not great, and generally is specified where it exists. The main point is that the material steadily gets harder from start to finish in each chapter. Hence, one may easily skip sections or stop at any point, depending on personal inclination and available time. Finally, it is worth noting that the book in entirety could be the basis of a fairly substantial two-term course: the first term emphasizing Chapters 1–4 could be taken by both non-science students and science students alike; the second term emphasizing Chapters 5–8 should be restricted to students with at least an introductory background in physics or engineering.

† Chapters 1–4 are available in a separate volume entitled *Introduction to Computer Applications for Non-Science Students* (*BASIC*), published by Prentice-Hall, Inc.

Many of the problems depend on substantial blocks of data being available in the BASIC DATA format. Because little educational benefit results from typing in these huge blocks of data by hand and needless amounts of terminal time get wasted in the process, it is desirable to make these DATA statements available to the students on punched tape or within disc files. To facilitate this process, the author will try to provide, at a reasonable cost, punched-tape listings of such BASIC DATA statements in ASCII code. However, this offer is made subject to the condition that it may be terminated at any time should the process become impractical. Further, occasional errors made in the mechanical punching process will have to be corrected by the purchaser (for example, by checking against listings illustrated in the present book). For further information regarding this question, write directly to the author, Department of Engineering and Applied Science, Yale Univerisity, New Haven, Connecticut 06520.

WILLIAM RALPH BENNETT, JR.

Acknowledgments

I should like to thank Professor Robert G. Wheeler of Yale University for suggesting and encouraging this project. Although the project has taken more work than I initially expected, it has also been a lot of fun. I should also like to thank Professor Charles A. Walker (currently chairman of the Engineering and Applied Science Department) for his sustaining support. Obviously, the whole thing could not have been accomplished while carrying a heavy teaching load. I am particularly indebted to the Hewlett-Packard Corporation for the donation of a 2116B computer which was used in the course and to the Moore Fund at Yale for a grant to purchase additional equipment.

The following people warrant special thanks: Dr. John W. Knutson, Jr., for his assistance in presenting the course initially; William C. Campbell, Donald R. Carlin, Robert M. Fleischman, H. Thomas Hunt, and Jeffrey J. Korman for expert teaching assistance and machine-language programming help; and Marjorie G. Wynne, Edwin J. Beinecke Research Librarian at the Beinecke Rare Book and Manuscript Library for her help in tracking down several obscure references. In addition, I am indebted to all the students at Yale University who have taken the course for their patience in letting me try this material out on them, for their many suggestions, and for their permission to reproduce some of the original data quoted in the text. I should also like to thank Professor Jack K. Cohen of the University of Denver (Colorado) for a careful reading of the manuscript and numerous helpful suggestions. Special thanks also go to Phyllis Springmeyer of the College Book Editorial Department at Prentice-Hall for her invaluable help.

I should also like to thank the various people and organizations specifically cited in the figure captions for their permission to reproduce figures. In addition, I would like to thank my father, William Ralph Bennett, for several helpful background discussions on communications problems. Finally, I am especially indebted to my wife, Frances Commins Bennett, for numerous helpful discussions, for editing and typing the original manuscript, and for putting up with some of the more obscure conversational topics that this manuscript has stimulated.

Scientific
and engineering
problem-solving
with the computer

1

Introduction

This chapter is intended for people who have never seen, used, or touched a computer terminal. Sections 1.1–1.3 discuss background concepts and define some of the basic jargon of the computer-science world. Rudimentary programming operations in BASIC are started in Section 1.4 and gradually increase in difficulty throughout the remainder of the chapter. Problems of practical importance are emphasized in these examples. The main object of the chapter is to get the beginner's feet wet as soon as possible and to work up to a few nontrivial problems by the end of the chapter. Readers with previous experience at programming should start by having a look at the problems toward the end of the chapter. If these problems are too easy, go immediately to Chapter 2. Note that the standard commands in BASIC are listed in the index at the end of the book with page references to representative examples of their use and definitions of their meanings.

Most electronic computers count, add, subtract, multiply, divide, and do logic operations in base 2. The reason is fairly obvious: The binary numbers 0 or 1 can be very naturally represented by opening or closing a switch. In practice, computers use electronic circuits that have two stable operating conditions to represent such binary numbers. The transition from one stable point to the other is induced electronically and is analogous to changing the state of a two-position switch. This type of electronic switching can be accomplished in astonishingly short time intervals ($\approx 10^{-9}$ second at the present state of the art) and is the primary technology upon which contemporary high-speed digital computing rests.

If you have a sufficiently long row of ON/OFF switches, you can use them to represent any specified binary integer. For example, the binary number 1010 corresponds to the number

$$1 \times 2^3 + 0 \times 2^2 + 1 \times 2^1 + 0 \times 2^0 = 8 + 2 = 10$$

in base 10 and may be represented by four ON/OFF switches. The process of handling numbers that are not integers involves utilizing negative powers of 2 (i.e., those which could be stored to the right of the *binary point*) in much the same way that decimal numbers are normally handled in base 10.

Processes in binary arithmetic can be performed by simple electronic circuits in which the output voltage is a two-valued function of two separate input voltages. For example, adding two binary integers together involves applying the following rule to the successively higher, corresponding pairs of digits:

$$0 + 0 = 0$$
$$0 + 1 = 1$$
$$1 + 0 = 1$$
$$1 + 1 = 0 \qquad \text{but carry 1 to the next-higher digit}$$

This fundamental rule in binary addition can be accomplished with a circuit that is turned ON when either input voltage (digit) is ON separately, but which is otherwise turned to the OFF position. (People who have done counting experiments will recognize this type of circuit as an *anticoincidence circuit*.) The process of carrying 1 to the next-higher digit (where $1 + 1 = 0$) can be effected with a circuit that is normally in the OFF position, unless both inputs are ON. (People used to counting experiments will recognize the latter as a *coincidence circuit*.) The other binary arithmetic operations (subtraction, multiplication, etc.) can be performed in similar fashion.

The number of operations done in one step (or how long a given binary arithmetic operation takes) is largely a function of the complexity of the circuitry in an individual computer. For example, adding N to a given binary number can be accomplished directly or by adding 1 N times; shifting a binary number N places to the left (which is equivalent to multiplying by 2^N) can be accomplished directly in one step or by shifting by one digit N times; and so on. Hence the inherent speed of a particular computer is extremely dependent on the actual circuitry used.

The invention of binary codes and binary logic operations is very old. Francis Bacon (1561–1626) used binary codes to transmit secret diplomatic messages. Joseph Marie Jacquard (1752–1834) used binary-coded punchcards to operate looms with such success that about 11,000 of them were in use throughout France by 1812. George Boole (1815–1864) developed a mathematical theory of binary logic during the nineteenth century. Hence the mathematical background for most of the binary operations used in modern digital computing was established long before the first digital computer of any consequence had been built.

Although a mechanical desk calculator that could add, subtract, multiply, and divide had been built as early as 1623—by Wilhelm Schikard—the modern digital computer was largely a post–World War II development. Prior to that time, most of the emphasis on electronic machines had been based upon analog devices—for example, those used during World War II to permit RADAR control of antiaircraft guns.

The very first digital computers were extremely sluggish, cumbersome things in which the bistable "electronic" circuits were made up from mechanical relays. Indeed, one such machine developed at the Bell Laboratories in 1944 contained over 9000 telephone relays, covered a floor space of about 1000 square feet, and weighed about 10 tons!

One of the earliest high-speed electronic digital computers was that developed under the direction of John von Neumann at the Institute for Advanced Study in Princeton, New Jersey, during the period 1946–1952. This device contained several thousand vacuum tubes and used a memory based upon the continuous rejuvenation of arrays of binary digits which were stored electrostatically in a large bank of cathode-ray tubes (see Fig. 1-1). Because the

Fig. 1-1. von Neumann's computer. (John von Neumann is at the left and J. Robert Oppenheimer is at the right.) Note the bank of cathode-ray-tube storage elements across the bottom of the picture (within the cylindrical cans); these were used for the computer memory. Each tube contained a square display of $32 \times 32 = 1024$ binary storage bits that were periodically regenerated at about 1000 times per second. A section from this computer is currently on display at the Smithsonian Institution in Washington, D.C. (*Courtesy* of the Institute for Advanced Study, Princeton, New Jersey.)

lifetimes of vacuum tubes were typically about 1000 hours, the electrostatic storage technique was tricky at best, and the entire contents of the memory in the von Neumann computer had to be re-stored about 1000 times per second, it is rather amazing that the device could be made to function reliably at all over long periods of time. Nevertheless, the machine served as an effective laboratory to test many of the notions of programming and coding used in contemporary large-scale, high-speed digital computers. Prior to the design of the von Neumann machine, it was argued that decimal systems were the most appropriate for computers because of the formidable problems in decimal-to-binary conversion. One early accomplishment of the von Neumann project was the demonstration that such conversions could be accomplished with a fairly small number of machine operations (approximately 47 steps) and in time intervals of only a few milliseconds (using the circuitry of that period). The machine was also used to solve some very substantial numerical problems connected with the development of the hydrogen bomb[1]—especially problems involving the inversion of high-order matrices. [See the discussion of the von Neumann machine by Goldstine (1972). Goldstine worked on many of the fundamental mathematical and programming problems encountered with this machine, and his book contains a very interesting account of the techniques adopted, in addition to a comprehensive description of the historical background.]

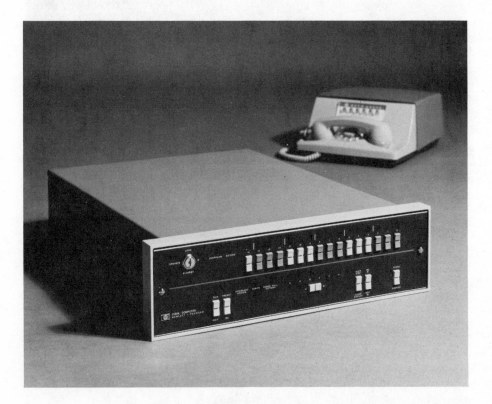

Fig. 1-2. Representative, contemporary minicomputer capable of storing up to 32,000 separate 16-bit numbers in its memory. (*Courtesy* of the Hewlett-Packard Co.)

[1] It is, in fact, rather ironic that J. Robert Oppenheimer, who was the Director of the Institute for Advanced Study during most of that period and a strong proponent of the von Neumann project, was crucified shortly thereafter for his initial stand against the development of the H-bomb. [See, for example, von Neumann's testimony in support of Oppenheimer reproduced by the U.S. Atomic Energy Commission (1971, p. 655), regarding the relevance of the von Neumann computer to the H-bomb project.]

The development and practical availability of transistors (with nearly infinite lifetimes) and reliable ferrite core memories (which do not require periodic rejuvenation) had a massive effect on the computer field during the next two decades. The exponential growth in this field has continued well into the present decade, as the effects of integrated circuits, circuit-chip technology, and semiconductor memories have become felt. Not only has the capability, speed, and reliability increased considerably; the physical size and cost of electronic digital computers has decreased by orders of magnitude during the past decade. The latter phenomenon is especially heartening in an age of constant inflation in the price of nearly every other type of commodity. One can now purchase for a few thousand dollars a small digital computer (or *minicomputer*) which is about the same size as a "hi-fi" set (see Fig. 1-2) and which is enormously more powerful than the early von Neumann machine (which itself cost many hundreds of thousands of dollars and occupied a small building). Hence it seems likely that we are on the threshold of an age when the "family computer" will be as realistic and useful an item as the family automobile has become in American life. At a further extreme, the use of circuit chips and small memories has permitted the development of pocket-size, battery-operated computers (which now sell for a few hundred dollars) which use full-scale digital programming techniques to calculate series solutions for the transcendental functions to high accuracy, together with the more usual arithmetic operations. Indeed, at least one of the currently available pocket computers is capable of retaining as many as 100 fully alterable program steps (see Fig. 1-3). Thus we are already well into an age where small computers can extend the mathematical ability of the human brain in much the same way that hearing aids and electronic guidance devices can extend man's other perception capabilities. Immediate access to these powerful computational aids opens up for solution a new domain of important problems in the same way that a good pair of eyeglasses can help a near-sighted individual see a larger portion of the landscape. In fact, one could make a strong argument that access to both small and large digital computers should be regarded as a fundamental individual right in our society, much like those guaranteed by the Constitution. The point here is that society is presently facing such complex problems as to warrant increased reliance on computer-simulated models for solution. Those people who do not have access to computers to investigate alternative solutions to communal problems will, in some sense, have lost their ability to participate in the democratic process. In any event, digital computers have become easily available to a large fraction of the population, and there is every indication at the present moment that this trend will continue.

Fig. 1-3. Pocket-sized battery-operated digital computer capable of holding 100 reprogrammable statements. (*Courtesy* of the Hewlett-Packard Co.)

1.2
Machine Language

Most currently available digital computers operate in a manner that is logically similar to the method devised in the von Neumann machine. A certain set of possible binary logic operations (typically about 100) is built into the electronic circuitry of the machine. As part of man's never-ending desire to attribute human qualities to electromechanical devices, the convention by which different sequences of instructions may be fed into the computer is known as a *programming language*. (In a similar vein, one finds computer scientists referring to the rules for applying such languages as *grammar*; the storing capacity of the computer as *memory*; the various multiple-bit numbers stored in the memory as *words*; and so on.) Access to the rudimentary set of binary logic operations wired into the computer is obtained through something known as *machine language*. A *program* in machine language just consists of a sequence of large binary numbers, which are consulted in order when the computer runs. Each memory location in the computer can store a word containing a large number of binary digits, or *bits*. In the section of the computer memory used to store the machine-language program, part of each word is used to code the machine-language instruction; the other part contains the memory location upon which the instruction is to operate. In addition, the computer contains entities known as *registers* within which the various allowed binary logic operations are performed. One of these registers is set aside just to keep track of which memory location contains the next machine-language instruction to be executed.

Thus a machine-language program consists of an ordered set of instructions that is sequentially executed, starting at a specified memory (or *core*) location. Such programs tend to be exceedingly tedious affairs in which the computer is led by the hand through every single operation required. For example, the first instruction might be to take a 16-bit binary number out of one specific memory location and store it in the A register; the next instruction might be to add the contents of another memory location to the contents of the A register; the third instruction might be to store the result (now in the A register) in some other memory location (whose *address* might, in turn, have been computed in still another register); and so on. Generally, an enormous number of machine-language operations have to be performed before anything very useful is accomplished. In addition, all these machine-language instructions have to be entered by some means in the computer memory. (At the most rudimentary extreme, such sequences of binary numbers can be entered by hand using a long row of toggle switches to set up each required multiple-bit binary number.) The great virtue of the computer is that once these instructions have been entered in the memory, long sequences of them can be done over and over again with great speed (these days, anywhere from about 30 nanoseconds to 2 microseconds per machine operation, depending on the particular computer).

1.3
More Advanced Languages: Compilers and Interpreters (Why BASIC?)

Although the early programmers were forced to write their programs directly in machine language, most people will find that practice exceedingly tedious. This is especially true in the routine conversions that come up over and over again in going back and forth between base 10 and base 2 arithmetic.

Fortunately, some dedicated souls have spent their lives devising machine-language programs that do all these routine operations for us. Thus higher-level programming languages, such as FORTRAN, ALGOL, and BASIC, have been developed that translate standard arithmetic operations back and forth to machine-language operations in base 2. In addition, these higher-level languages generally have some standard set of options for getting data in and out of the computer and a set of *subroutines* (small, specialized programs that can be used over and over again at different points in a large program) built in for the purpose of computing common mathematical operations and functions.

As a specific illustration, the two statements

```
1   INPUT X,Y
2   PRINT X+Y
```

written in BASIC, are fairly self-evident even to someone who has never used a computer before. The statements have the meaning that when the program is run in BASIC, two general numbers (X and Y) are entered from the keyboard of a teletype terminal and the computer then prints the sum of the two numbers back on the same terminal. In a representative computer (containing no "hard-wired" arithmetic capability), this relatively harmless-looking two-line program in base 10 arithmetic takes hundreds of separate machine-language steps involving logic operations in base 2. Because the computation would take less than 1 millisecond on even the slowest contemporary computers, the terminal operator is shielded from all the behind-the-scenes effort that went into the calculation.

Most of the early programming languages were specifically designed for something known as *batch processing*. In this mode, the user writes his program in entirety before going near the machine. (For example, one archaic method consisted of punching out the program statements on a series of cards similar to those used by Jacquard to operate looms in the eighteenth century.) The user then brings the completed program to the computer; a special machine-language program called a *compiler* converts the user's program into machine-language code; and, finally, the compiled program is executed by the computer. For some types of computing (especially situations in which the same long program is to be run over and over in precisely the same form), batch processing is obviously the most efficient approach. The program can be stored in compiled form and the time lost in interpreting the original program statements in terms of equivalent machine-language subroutines can be avoided in subsequent execution of the program. Further, a really long program can be run during off hours when the rates are cheaper and without the author of the program being present. In that type of situation, one is willing to put up with a substantial amount of agony in getting errors (*bugs*) out of the program initially. However, batch processing can be distinctly unfriendly to someone who is just starting to learn programming. The point is that the slightest error (no matter how trivial) can abort execution of the program right at the start. The user may come back after waiting 2 or 3 hours to find that the only useful information contained in the stack of printout generated when the computer was running his program was the fact that the program execution was stopped on the first line because of a "grammatical" mistake in the use of the programming language. In addition, some other features of a language such as FORTRAN (which has traditionally been used in the batch-process mode at most large computer centers in the United States) merely get in the way for the beginner—or even for the seasoned expert who just wants a quick answer to a very complicated problem. For example, the constant distinction between floating-decimal-point and integer numbers, and the use of generalized format statements in FORTRAN, make the language inherently more powerful than one such as BASIC (in which all numbers are treated as if they were floating-point numbers and in which a limited format is permitted in PRINT statements). However, this increased generality also enormously increases the opportunity to make grammatical mistakes in writing a program. It further makes it much more tedious to test small segments of a program to make sure, quite apart from grammatical errors, that the program is really computing the numbers that are wanted.

In contrast, the BASIC language was designed to be *conversational* right from the beginning.[2] By "conversational" it is meant that the user's terminal is placed in a directly interactive mode with the computer. Not only can the original program statements be entered directly in the computer memory from the user's teletype or *CRT* (for cathode-ray-tube) *terminal*, but with some BASIC interpreters, a statement that violates the grammatical rules of the language is thrown out as you try to enter it and a diagnostic error immediately displayed. Further, the language is arranged so that the user's terminal is kept in a fully interactive mode with the computer while the user's program is running. Thus one can enter different numbers from the keyboard for use within the program while the program is running; similarly, one can have the computer print various parts of a solution on the terminal as they are computed, and even stop the computer from running the program at any point

---

[2] The BASIC language was developed at Dartmouth College under National Science Foundation support by the mathematicians John Kemeny and Thomas Kurtz [see Kemeny and Kurtz, (1968)]. The acronym originally stood for Beginner's All-Purpose Symbolic Instruction Code. But do not be misled: BASIC is an extremely powerful language.

along the way, without having to wait for the computer to reach the normal "end" statement.

The main advantage of the conversational mode is that one can immediately run small pieces of a large program in which "print" statements can be quickly inserted and deleted to permit checking questionable sections of the program. Thus you can determine immediately if the program is actually calculating the quantities that you want. At the same time, an enormous volume of waste paper can be eliminated by merely printing the final answer you want from the program rather than the large tome of stuff (mostly needed for debugging purposes) that inevitably seems linked to batch processing in FORTRAN.

An additional advantage of BASIC is that the instruction set is so similar to normal high school algebra and arithmetic that relatively little effort is required in learning the language. Fifteen or 20 minutes spent looking over the instruction set is all that is really needed for the beginner to start doing meaningful problems. At the same time, a powerful set of matrix operations is included as part of the standard arithmetic operations in BASIC; these operations are much more convenient to use than the equivalent subroutines callable in FORTRAN. Finally, it should be noted that the BASIC language is also unusually efficient in its core requirements and can be used on relatively small computers or minicomputers. (The standard BASIC compiler takes about 7000 sixteen-bit words of computer memory.)

The speed with which programs can be run in BASIC (or any other language) varies a great deal with the particular machine and software used. Most large computers compile the entire BASIC program in machine language before running the program, and it is during the compilation period that most diagnostic error messages are sent back to the operator. Once the program is compiled and free of grammatical mistakes, the program is run in machine language until interactive instructions with the user's terminal are encountered. Some of the large time-sharing services have a provision for storing the compiled program in machine language for future use, thereby avoiding the necessity of repeating the expenditure of *cpu* (central processor unit) time (typically about 10 seconds with a large machine) to recompile the same program. For example, the GE 635 computer used in the early Mark II GE time-sharing service ran faster in BASIC than in FORTRAN. At the opposite extreme, a minicomputer such as the HP 2116B uses software that interprets each successive BASIC statement individually as the program is run. If the program goes around in a *loop* 1000 times, the statements in the loop are converted into machine language 1000 times. Because the machine takes about 1 millisecond (msec) just to interpret a command such as "LET $Y = 2$," a compiled FORTRAN program can run much faster than an equivalent BASIC program on such a minicomputer. However, even with the minicomputer, the programs have to become pretty substantial before these running-time limitations become a significant practical concern. It should be noted that the portions of a program that really eat up running time are operations such as computing $SIN(X)$ and $EXP(X)$, which are generally done in previously compiled machine-language subroutines contained in the BASIC function library. Hence those operations (which might take ≈ 10 msec on a typical minicomputer) are done just as fast in BASIC as in a compiled FORTRAN program, and it does not make a great deal of difference that ≈ 1 msec was lost interpreting the expression. In fairness, it should also be noted that compiling a FORTRAN program on a minicomputer can be an extremely long-winded process. Once compiled, the program can be used over and over again in exactly the same form with great facility; but to make even one change generally requires repeating the whole compilation procedure. It should also be noted that BASIC is so literally a subset of FORTRAN that it is relatively

Fig. 1-4. Contemporary CRT (cathode-ray-tube) terminal capable of transmitting and receiving data at approximately 600 characters per second. The particular one shown (made by the Delta Data Corporation) has an internal memory of 3000 characters (which can be used to store several hundred program statements) and an electronic editing capability for inserting and deleting characters within its own memory. A fairly substantial program may be written and edited with such a terminal in the *local mode* (not connected to the computer) and then transmitted in entirety to the computer in a few seconds.

straightforward for an experienced programmer to write a FORTRAN program that will translate a general BASIC program into FORTRAN and compile the result. Hence one method of beating the speed-limitation problem in very long programs on minicomputers is to write and debug the program in conversational BASIC and then use a routine FORTRAN program to compile the result.

Finally, there are several compensating advantages in doing computing on a minicomputer that you control entirely yourself versus operating in a time-sharing mode on a supergiant. First, the time-sharing mode in itself means that your problem is constantly being interrupted (if it is of any significant computational length) as the supergiant services its numerous other customers. Frequently, this duty-cycle effect can more than compensate for differences in running time. Second, with commercial time-sharing services one is still pretty much limited to the painfully slow data-transmission rates associated with the mechanical teletype machine (≈ 10 characters per second). Powerful editing programs and program storage devices (e.g., magnetic disc or tape-recorded files) at the computer center can help compensate to a large extent. However, anyone who has ever used a CRT terminal (see Fig. 1-4) working at 600 characters per second will probably give up computing altogether rather than go back to the old teletype. Further, if you have direct control over the minicomputer, it is usually practical to write (or have written for you) machine-language subroutines directly callable from BASIC which serve the purpose of transferring data back and forth between the computer and various peripheral devices at extremely high transmission rates. Thus xy plotters and oscilloscopes offer a very fast means to provide a continuous display of computational problems through the use of *digital-to-analog converters* (i.e., circuits that produce a voltage proportional to an input number). Similarly, high-speed analog-to-digital converters permit reading voltages from experimental situations and storing numbers proportional to these voltages in the computer. The increasing availability and decreasing cost of such circuitry has been a heart-warming phenomenon. For example, one can now buy a 16-bit (i.e., 1-part-in-2^{16} resolution) digital-to-analog converter with a response time of ≈ 1

9

microsecond for less than \$100; for less than \$10 it is now possible to get an 8-bit D-to-A (digital-to-analog) converter of comparable speed. Equivalent A-to-D (analog-to-digital) converters are typically 5 to 10 times more expensive. Consequently, with a modest investment, a little electronics shopwork, and a little programming help, one can have a powerful facility for taking and displaying data, as well as performing and displaying computations made within the BASIC language. Although the primary emphasis in the present text is on operations performable within the framework of the standard BASIC language, some of the additional facility provided to the minicomputer owner through such machine-language CALL statements will be illustrated.[3]

The remaining sections of this chapter will be devoted to a few introductory examples of programming in BASIC. We shall describe here some of the fundamental statements in the language and introduce more advanced techniques in later chapters. An index is included at the end of the book with page references to various examples of the different commands in BASIC. The instructions used in the BASIC language are also summarized in programming manuals available from most of the time-sharing computer services, many of which are based on the original work by Kemeny and Kurtz (1968).

The method of getting BASIC onto the computer will vary from one machine to the next, and there will be no useful substitute for reading up on the particular idiosyncracies of the actual machine that you intend to use. In what follows, we shall assume that the reader knows how to get to the point where the computer types

READY

on the user's terminal, meaning that the computer is ready to accept a series of program statements from the user written in the BASIC language. (In general, after completing any instruction, the BASIC compiler transmits this self-evident message.)

As with any other programming language, a program in BASIC consists of an ordered set of instructions which generally involve:

1. Putting data into the computer.
2. Calculating something based on the data.
3. Getting the answer out of the computer.
4. Telling the computer to stop running the program.

Statements and data are usually entered through a typewriter-like keyboard (see Fig. 1-4), and anyone with only a modest facility at typing will find the process reasonably efficient. Only uppercase letters are recognized in statements, and the standard character set originally introduced on the teletype keyboard is used. The most common typing errors one tends to make initially involve confusing the letter O (oh) with the number Ø (zero) and subconsciously trying to enter a lowercase L (ell) as a number 1 (one). The slash through the zero is generally used to minimize the first source of confusion. Both problems involve overcoming ingrained subconscious habits and may, in fact, be more of a difficulty with really good typists than with poor ones.

Each program statement in BASIC requires a separate line number. The statements are executed in the order that the line numbers increase. However, the line numbers do not have to increase in unit increments, and they do not have to be typed in the order that they finally appear in the program. Thus, if the original line numbers are chosen with reasonably wide spacing (e.g., in increments of 1Ø), there will usually be plenty of room for adding statements

---

[3] For a detailed discussion of the use of CALL statements in BASIC, see the Hewlett-Packard guide to 2100 series minicomputers.

throughout a program that arise as afterthoughts. (Many BASIC compilers also have specialized line-number resequencing commands which help when the spacing gets too tight.) Finally, it is important to note that the current version of the program can always be typed out on the terminal through the command LIST.

The common arithmetic statements in BASIC are so similar to those in normal arithmetic that they require little explanation. A few simple two-line programs will serve as illustration:

For example, if we enter the statements

```
10   PRINT 3+2
20   END
```

and type

```
RUN
```

(followed by the carriage-return key), the computer will respond by printing

```
5
READY
```

Similarly, the substitution

```
10   PRINT 3-2
```

would print the difference between the two numbers; whereas

```
10 PRINT 3*2
```

would give us the product and

```
10 PRINT 3/2
```

would result in the decimal equivalent of 3 divided by 2 (i.e., 1.5). Finally, the statement

```
10 PRINT 3↑2
```

is almost as obvious in meaning and results in raising 3 to the second power. (This last operation also works for fractional exponents as long as the argument is positive; i.e., the result must be real.)

Arithmetic operations of the above type may be combined in one statement, as long as they all fit within the 72-column format used in BASIC. For example,

```
10   PRINT 2*3+2/3-1+2↑3
```

would result in printing the value 13.6666 (or the first six most significant figures in the decimal equivalent of $13\frac{2}{3}$.

Note that a definite priority is assumed in executing operations of the above type: exponential operations (e.g., 2↑3) are given the highest priority; multiplication and division come next (performed in order from left to right); and finally addition and subtraction. For example,

$6/2↑2 \neq 9$ but instead is equal to 1.5
$6/2*3 \neq 1$ but instead is equal to 9   etc.

Parentheses may be used in pairs to change the normal priority assumptions. In such cases, the innermost parenthetical operation is always done first. Hence

$6/(2*3)=1$ whereas $6/2*3=9$

$(6/(2*3))↑2=1$ whereas $6/(2*3↑2)=0.333333$ and $6/(2*3)↑2=0.166666$

When in doubt one may always add extra parentheses just to make sure that the priority assumed is that which the user wants. However, unnecessary parentheses waste space. Finally, it is important to note when using parentheses that the standard arithmetic symbols in BASIC are still required. For example, although $2(3+5)$ would be meaningful in normal algebra, the equivalent expression in BASIC has to have an asterisk between the 2 and the $(3+5)$ to denote multiplication.

11

Machine-language programs are built into the BASIC compiler for computing the common transcendental functions (e.g., those such as the sine and cosine functions, which require summing an infinite series to some prescribed accuracy for numerical evaluation). These functions are always stated in a standard form in which the argument is contained within parentheses.

**1.5
Transcendental Functions**

In case of the trigonometric functions, the arguments are specified in radians. Thus expressions such as

SIN(X), COS(X), or TAN(X)

appearing in a BASIC program will automatically result in the evaluation of the sine, cosine, or tangent of the numerical argument assigned to the variable X, on the assumption that X is in radians. Similarly, the BASIC arctangent function, ATN(X), results in computing an angle in radians whose tangent occurs in the argument. ATN(X) will be positive or negative in accordance with the sign of X.

The logarithm and antilogarithm functions are defined in respect to the base $e = 2.71828\ldots$ of the Naperian system. The expression

LOG(X)

results in the evaluation of the natural logarithm of the numerical value assigned to X; similarly, the expression

EXP(X)

computes the value of e^x.

Finally, the expression,

SQR(X)

results in computing the square root of the value assigned to X (assuming it is positive), and

ABS(X)

results in computing the absolute value (i.e., magnitude) of X.

To facilitate the computing process, variables are introduced in the program. In BASIC, variables can be any single letter of the alphabet or any single letter of the alphabet followed by one of the numerals 0, 1, 2, . . . , 8, 9. Thus

**1.6
Variables: Getting Data
into the Program**

any of the following 286 entities could be used as variables:

$$A, B, C, \ldots, X, Y, Z$$
$$A\emptyset, A1, A2, \ldots, A8, A9$$
$$B\emptyset, B1\ B2, \ldots, B8, B9$$
$$.$$
$$.$$
$$.$$
$$Y\emptyset, Y1, Y2, \ldots, Y8, Y9$$
$$Z\emptyset, Z1, Z2, \ldots, Z8, Z9$$

In transferring mathematical equations to programming statements, it is frequently helpful to regard the numeral following the letter in program variables in the same role as subscripts in mathematical variables. For example, X_0 most naturally goes over to $X\emptyset$; X_1 to $X1$; and so on. In fact, it will be necessary on some later occasions in this book to write simple equations in terms of such computer variables to clarify the meaning of program segments. Hence the reader should get used to thinking of quantities such as $T2$ as single computer variables and *not* as the variable T multiplied by 2. (The latter would be written $T*2$ in BASIC.) Later we shall also discuss the use of column arrays and matrices as indexed variables.

Always keep in mind that a computer computes things *numerically*. If you have not assigned a numerical value to a variable, the computer cannot do the operation. Running a program that has not had the variables properly initialized will either result in diagnostic error messages or wrong answers (assuming some other value has already been given for the variable elsewhere in the program).

There are three primary ways of getting numerical data into a program in BASIC:

1. You can define the variable in the program with a LET statement, such as

        10   LET X = 5

The statement means that the new value of the variable X on the left is set equal to the last value of the quantities on the right. Hence a statement following line 1$\emptyset$ of the type

        20   LET X = X + 1

means "define the new value of the variable X to be equal to the old value plus 1." (With *some* BASIC compilers you can achieve the same result with the statement

        20   X = X + 1

and you do not have to type LET before the command).

2. You can enter the numerical value for the variable from the teletype keyboard. For example, the statement

        10   INPUT   X

results (when you RUN the program) in

        ? (and the computer waits for you to type in the
            number and a carriage return).

Similarly, if you have several variables, X, Y, and Z, to which you wish to assign numerical values from the keyboard, the single statement

        10   INPUT X,Y,Z

results in a question mark and pause while you enter each of the three variables (separated by commas or by carriage returns).

13

3. You can read the variables from a data table. The statement

```
10   READ X,Y,Z
```

with a data statement somewhere else in the program of the type

```
500   DATA 3,4,5,7,8,9
```

will result in assigning the variables sequentially to the numbers in the data statement. When the computer passes through line 10 it lets

$$X = 3, \qquad Y = 4, \qquad Z = 5$$

If we had introduced a second READ statement after line 10 of the type

```
20   READ U,V,W
```

the computer would let

$$U = 7, \qquad V = 8, \qquad W = 9$$

However, we would not be allowed to enter still another READ statement without either adding more DATA statements or a command of the type

```
30   RESTORE
```

(which permits re-reading the previous DATA statements from the beginning).

As we shall show later, it is possible to generate huge blocks of data from experiments of different types and read these into the computer with either a teletype terminal or high-speed input device—thus permitting data manipulation and analysis without ever having to type in the block of data tediously by hand.

For the moment we merely wish to emphasize that the following three programs in BASIC represent different ways of achieving precisely the same result:

```
10  LET X = 5       10   READ X         10  INPUT X
20  LET Y = X + 2   20   LET Y = X + 2  [? 5]
30  PRINT Y         30   PRINT Y        20 LET Y = X + 2
99  END             40   DATA 5         30  PRINT Y
                    99   END            99  END
```

In the program at the left, the variable X is defined to be equal to 5 on line 10. In the middle program, X is READ at line 10 from the DATA statement (line 40). Finally, with the program at the right, we have assumed that when the program was run, the computer typed a question mark after line 10 and waited while the operator typed in the number 5 and pushed the carriage-return button. After establishing the value of $X = 5$, each of these programs then assigns the value $X + 2 = 7$ to the variable Y on line 20 and proceeds to print the numerical value of Y on line 30. Hence each program would print the number 7 before reaching the END statement on line 99. We, of course, could equally well have entered a number other than 5 from the keyboard when using the program at the right. Similarly, we could have entered a different number in the DATA statement for the middle program or have defined X differently on line 10 for the program at the left.

**1.6
PROBLEM 3**

Write a simple three-line program of the type

```
10   INPUT X
20   PRINT EXP(X)
30   END
```

to illustrate the transcendental functions in BASIC.

As implied so far, the simple statement

PRINT X

causes the numerical value of X to be printed by the computer on the terminal in a fairly self-evident manner. However, there are other things that can be included in PRINT statements which increase the power of the command considerably.

First, some degree of column formating can be obtained through use of commas and semicolons. Specifically,

PRINT X,Y,Z

results in printing numerical values stored in the variables X, Y, and Z with wide spacing (12 spaces are reserved for each number, 3 spaces are placed between each group of 12, and a maximum of 5 numbers can be printed on one line).

A tighter spacing (suitable for printing numbers that do not require specification in terms of a mantissa and exponent) is obtained through the use of semicolons. For example,

PRINT X;Y;Z

results in printing numerical values for X, Y, and Z in which a minimum of 6 spaces per column is used and one can get a maximum of 12 integers printed on one line. However, if X were a number requiring more spaces for specification, the wider spacing associated with the comma format would be introduced automatically between the printed values for X and Y.

Frequently, one also wants to print alphanumeric characters themselves in addition to the numbers for which they stand. In BASIC, this objective is met by placing the alphanumeric characters within quotation marks in PRINT statements. Thus, PRINT "X" would print the character X rather than the numerical value assigned to the variable X. Here again, commas result in a wide column spacing. However, a semicolon following the second quotation mark would cause the teletype (or terminal) to stop immediately after printing the alphanumeric character and wait there for the next PRINT instruction. For example, the statements

```
10   LET X = SQR(2)
20   PRINT "X = ";X
```

would result in

X = 1.41421

when the program ran. (Note that quotation marks must be used in pairs to avoid generating error messages when you run the program.) Similarly, the statement

```
20   PRINT "X = ";X;"POUNDS"
```

would result in

X = 1.41421   POUNDS

if inserted in the same program. Almost anything other than the carriage-return and line-feed commands may be included within quotation marks in PRINT statements and controlled by the computer (bell-ringing keys, cursor movements, blinking controls on CRT terminals, etc.).

Finally, the simplest command one can write with the PRINT statement is just

PRINT

which results in executing the carriage-return and line-feed controls.

A more general format capability is provided by the TAB function. As the name implies, the function serves much the same purpose as the normal TAB button on a typewriter. For example, the statement

> PRINT TAB(2Ø);"X"

would result in moving the teletype element over 20 spaces before printing the character X. Several TAB functions may be used effectively within the same PRINT statement as long as you do not attempt to consume more than the 72-column format standard in BASIC. For example,

> PRINT TAB(2Ø);"X";TAB(3Ø);"Y";TAB(4Ø);"Z"

would print X on the twenty-first column, Y on the thirty-first column, and Z on the forty-first column. That is, the TAB function argument always represents the number of spaces moved from the left edge of the typing area (as long as the carriage would not have to move backward in the printing process).

"Loops" are among the most powerful programming techniques that exist. The underlying concept is based on the fact that one can use the same set of programming statements over and over again to process different numerical values. For example, the GO TO statement on line 3Ø of the program

1.8
Loops and Conditional Statements

```
  10   READ X
  20   PRINT SQR(X)
  30   GO TO 10
  80   DATA 1,2,3,4,5,6,7,8,9...
  99   END
```

causes the computer to jump back to line 1Ø. (The space between GO and TO could have been omitted on line 3Ø.) Hence, as written, the program keeps reading X sequentially from the data statement and printing the square root of X until all the data have been exhausted. In general (especially if you are paying for computer time), it is wise to write programs so that some conditional statement gets the computer out of the loop after a prescribed number of trips around. (There is a well-known horror story in the history of computing at Yale University concerning a student who generated a bill for $25,000 by leaving a computer in a loop over Thanksgiving weekend; as it turned out, he was not even taking the course for credit!)

Conditional statements of the type

> IF...THEN...

provide a simple method of getting the computer out of a loop, as well as providing a computed change in program path at other branch points throughout a program. Specifically, the following symbols may be used after the IF in conditional statements:

Symbol	Example	Meaning (at line 35 of the program)
=	35 IF A = B THEN 99	If A equals B, then go to line 99.
# or <>	35 IF A<>B THEN 99	If A is not equal to B, then go to line 99.
<	35 IF A<B THEN 99	If A is less than B, then go to line 99.
<=	35 IF A<=B THEN 99	If A is less than or equal to B, then go to line 99.
>	35 IF A>B THEN 99	If A is greater than B, then go to line 99.
>=	35 IF A>=B THEN 99	If A is greater than or equal to B, then go to line 99.

(The order of the symbols in the $<=$ and $>=$ statements is important.)

Armed with such conditional statements, we could reconstruct our original loop along the following safer lines:

```
 5   LET I = 1
10   READ X
20   PRINT SQR(X)
30   LET I = I + 1
35   IF I > 5 THEN 99
40   GO TO 10
80   DATA 1,2,3,4,5,6,7,8,9,...
99   END
```

As written, the variable I is used to count the number of trips the computer makes around the loop, and the conditional statement on line 35 stops the program after it has gone through five times.

This type of construction is of such frequent value that a simpler, equivalent programming method is also built into the BASIC language. In particular, the statements

```
 5   FOR I = 1 TO 5
10   READ X
20   PRINT SQR(X)
30   NEXT I
80   DATA 1,2,3,4,5,6,7,8,9,...
99   END
```

accomplish exactly the same result. Here the loop is set up between

```
FOR I = 1 TO 5
```

and

```
NEXT I
```

(where it is implied that I increases in steps of 1)

Each time around the loop, I is incremented by 1 (unless some other nonintegral, or even negative step is specifically indicated in the FOR... statement). Finally, when I is incremented to 6 (and thus exceeds 5 in the FOR statement on line 5), the program advances to the line immediately following the NEXT I statement. (The value stored for the variable I at that point in the program is actually 6.) The computer skips over the DATA statement and ends the program at line 99.

It is worth noting immediately that nonintegral steps and computed steps may be used in a FOR statement, together with computed lower and upper limits for the index. For example,

```
FOR I = SQR(Y) TO 3*Z STEP EXP(.05*Q)



NEXT I
```

where the variables Y, Z, and Q have previously been given numerical values, results in starting I off equal to the square root of Y and in incrementing the value of I by $e^{0.05Q}$ each time the computer goes around the loop. When the incremented value of I exceeds $3*Z$, the program jumps to the line immediately following NEXT I. Although the successive values of I may be used to compute other (different) quantities within the loop, the lower and upper limits, together with the step size for I, cannot be changed once the loop has been entered. That is, those quantities are computed and stored the first time the loop is entered.

It is, of course, possible to use conditional statements to get out of FOR
loops prematurely and to incorporate one loop inside another. Although loops
can be *highly nested* (i.e., loops within loops within loops, etc.), different loops
are not allowed to cross. Thus

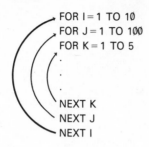

```
FOR I = 1 TO 10
FOR J = 1 TO 100
FOR K = 1 TO 5
.
.
.
NEXT K
NEXT J
NEXT I
```

is allowed, whereas statements of the type

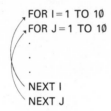

```
FOR I = 1 TO 10
FOR J = 1 TO 10
.
.
.
NEXT I
NEXT J
```

in which two loops cross, are not allowed.

1.8
PROBLEM 4

Write a program consisting of a single loop that permits determining the speed
of your computer for evaluating the standard arithmetic functions. For example, the program

```
10   FOR I = 1 TO 10000
20   LET Y = 2
30   NEXT I
99   END
```

will probably take an easily measurable amount of time (using a stopwatch or
sweep-second hand to determine the time interval starting when you push the
carriage-return button after typing RUN and ending when the computer starts
to type READY), without actually computing anything. The modification,

```
20   LET Y = 2*3
```

will add an amount of time to the program which is essentially the time
required to do 10,000 floating-point multiplications. Note that the time required
will vary with the argument in the function. For example, it might be appropriate
to sample values over the domain $0 \leqslant X \leqslant 2*3.14159$ in determining the running
time for the trigonometric functions.

1.8
PROBLEM 5

Write a program that compares values of $N!$ with those obtained from Stirling's
approximation,

$$N! \approx \sqrt{2\pi N} e^{-N} N^N \qquad \text{(for large } N\text{)}$$

for increasing integral values of N. How large a value of $N!$ can your computer
handle? *Hint:* One easy way to evaluate $N!$ consists of setting up a loop for
another variable M which goes from 1 to N in integral steps and within which
we repeatedly let $F = F*M$ (where $F = 1$ initially).

In the parlance of computer scientists, in BASIC all variables are treated as floating-point numbers. This statement means that the numbers assigned to variables are handled by using a prescribed number of bits (binary digits) for the separate representation of the mantissa and exponent of the base 10 number for which the variable stands. For example, a number such as

$$0.366793 \times 10^3$$

in conventional scientific notation could be entered in BASIC by the statement

LET X = .366793E3

The mantissa (0.366793) would typically be specified within fractional errors of less than 1 part per million in normal precision. (Most large computer facilities have some provision for running in *extended precision*, using a greater number of bits to specify the mantissa.) The number in the exponent (3 in the example above) is an integer and would be specified exactly, provided that it falls within the domain allotted for exponents by the computer.

Floating-point numbers are introduced to permit treating fractions or numbers outside the domain of integers normally allotted to variables by the compiler (i.e., a fixed number of bits is set aside for each variable stored in the computer memory).

It is frequently important to be able to compute an integer from a normal floating-point variable and the INT (for integer) function has been introduced in BASIC for that purpose. In particular, the statement

LET Y = INT(X)

means that Y is assigned an integer value such that $Y \leq X$; that is, Y is equal to the next integer lower than or equal to X. (The computer still handles the variable Y in the mantissa-exponent format; however, the number Y is precisely equal to an integer.) As applied to the above example ($X = 0.366793E3$), $Y = INT(X)$ would mean

$$Y = 366 = \text{next integer lower than } 366.793$$

The INT function is especially useful in rounding off variables to a specified number of significant figures. For example, we can round off the number X (above) to the nearest integer by the statement

LET Y = INT(X + .5)

i.e., the next integer lower than $(366.793 + 0.5)$ is 367. Similarly,

LET Y = INT(100*X + .5)/100

rounds off X to the nearest hundredth decimal place and would result in $Y = 366.79$ in the above example; and so on.

1.9
PROBLEM 6   Use the INT and TAB functions to print a table of sin A, cos A, and tan A, rounded off to the nearest 0.001 over the range $0 \leq A \leq 45°$ in steps of 5 degrees.

In a typical experimental situation justifying the use of a computer, one makes lots of measurements, some routine and tedious manipulation of the numbers is required, and some properties of the numbers are computed and made available to the experimenter.

As an example, consider an experiment in which we measure the temperature in an apparatus as a function of time and express the results in degrees

Celsius (centigrade). The temperature in °C is defined in terms of a linear extrapolation of some physical property of the thermometer (e.g., length of a column of liquid, pressure of gas in an enclosed volume, voltage from a thermocouple, etc.) calibrated in such a way that the temperature of melting ice is 0°C and the temperature of boiling water at standard atmospheric pressure is 100°C (see Fig. 1-5).

Suppose that the thermometer is a *thermocouple*, i.e., a junction of two dissimilar metals across which a thermal emf (or voltage) is developed proportional to the temperature. A thermocouple is particularly appropriate in the present instance because it is easy to extract a reading of the thermal electromotive force digitally and because it will work nicely at temperatures considerably in excess of the boiling point of water. Let us suppose that we

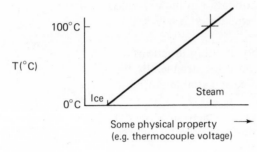

Fig. 1-5.

have a series of measurements of the thermocouple voltage, V (in relative units) as a function of time, which have been listed in a DATA statement format, and have taken calibration readings at the ice point (V∅) and boiling point of water (V1). Then a program of the type

```
   5   PRINT "ENTER VOLTAGE AT ICE POINT AND AT BOILING POINT"
  10   INPUT V∅,V1
  20   READ V
  30   LET T = 100*(V − V∅)/(V1 − V∅)
  40   PRINT T;
  50   GOTO 20
1000   DATA...
9999   END
```

would allow us to enter the initial calibration points from the keyboard and would then print out values of the temperature until the DATA list were exhausted. Note that the semicolon after the T in the PRINT statement on line 4∅ results in the numbers being closely spaced on each line. The instruction PRINT T, would result in wider spacing, whereas the statement PRINT T without either comma or semicolon would print each value on a separate line.

The instruction on line 5 is a useful reminder to the programmer to indicate just what INPUT data the computer will be waiting for on the next line. That is, the entire set of alphanumeric characters within the quotation marks after the PRINT statement will be typed out by the computer when it reaches line 5. As previously discussed, the statement

```
PRINT"T"
```

will yield T when the program runs; whereas

```
PRINT T
```

causes the computer to print the numerical value last assigned to the variable T. Similarly, if one left out the quotation marks on line 5, an error message would result; i.e., the string of characters ENTER VOLTAGE AT ICE POINT AND AT BOILING POINT is not acceptable as a variable.

It is helpful if often-repeated statements can be as concise and as literally correct as possible. For example, if line 5 above were in the loop, it would soon drive you to distraction. A better form might be

```
5   PRINT "V0,VI";
```

When this statement is executed, the computer prints

```
V0, V1?
```

and the meaning is self-evident. It is also helpful in avoiding needless confusion within long programs to be consistent in the choice of variables. Don't get in the habit of writing such statements as

```
5   PRINT "ENTER V1 AND V2"
10   INPUT X,Y
```

Although the program might work properly the first time you run it, you probably will not be able to remember what you were doing a week later.

In this connection, such "remarks" as

```
29   REM T IN DEGREES CENTIGRADE NEXT FROM THERMO COUPLE VOLT.,V
```

tend to be a helpful reminder of the meaning of variables in various parts of the program. The REM statement is ignored by the computer and the next-following statement is immediately executed. Consequently, the REM statement provides a convenient mechanism for humans to remind themselves of the purpose of DATA statements, subroutines, function definitions, and entire programs. Although the value and function of this type of reminder is self-evident, there is one specific suggestion worth passing on to the reader: Apart from the purpose of a program or program segment, few things are as useful to the author of the program in the future as the date on which the program was written or last revised. The latter is especially true with complex programs that have slowly been modified over a long period of time.

1.11
Taking the Temperature of a Firestorm

The apparatus shown in Fig. 1-6(a) permits generating a miniature firestorm. Air swirls in through the opening along the vertical side of the cylinder to feed a cup full of burning alcohol at the bottom. The process sets up a small tornado inside the cylinder if the overlapping edges of the cylinder are smooth. The rising combustion products in the center result in more air being pumped in at the edge; the latter swirls into the center of the cylinder, speeding up the rate of combustion. Consequently, one gets a nonlinear effect similar to that found in most firestorms. Above a critical threshold level, the process takes off exponentially and consumes the fuel more and more rapidly. Finally, the apparatus tends to be totally destroyed if one is not careful.

A thermocouple was placed at the top of the cylinder shown in Fig. 1-6(a) and was attached to a digital voltmeter. The successive (relative) voltage readings were punched out on paper tape by an apparatus that automatically starts at a preset line number and types the BASIC language DATA label and 10 successive readings per line for a previously prescribed large number of lines. The results are shown in Fig. 1-6(b).

For some of the following exercises, it will be worthwhile having a string of such DATA statements (or their equivalent) on punched paper tape (or in a disc file). For the data shown, six measurements were made per second. The particular data-acquisition device that generated the data in Fig. 1-6(b) has, in fact, been used extensively in the author's own research and has the advantage that the punched data tapes can be fed automatically into any computer that recognizes the standard BASIC DATA format. It should be noted here that generating the line numbers and DATA "flag" involves an amount of complexity in the data-acquisition device that can be avoided in many instances. For example, with large computer centers or time-sharing services that utilize the BASIC language, a long sequence of numbers can usually be written directly on a disc file using commands characteristic of the individual computer; such data files can then usually be read directly from the BASIC compiler. At the other extreme, if one is using a minicomputer to analyze data, a set of readings can generally be fed directly into the computer memory (e.g., at rates approaching the reciprocal of the machine cycle time when *direct memory access*, or *DMA*, is available) and transferred into the BASIC language with CALL statements to machine-language subroutines.

Fig. 1-6a. Firestorm apparatus. The apparatus shown was made from $\frac{1}{8}$-inch-thick Lucite and bent into an overlapping cylinder about 1 foot in diameter. (The overlap extended about 3 inches, leaving a 1-inch air space up the side.) By itself, the ($\approx$ 7-inch-diameter) dish of alcohol at the center produces a fairly gentle flame that would not really scare anyone. However, adding the Lucite spiral transforms the gently burning alcohol flame into a raging inferno in practically no time at all. The situation thus resembles that found in fires within large buildings: nothing much happens until some critical rate of oxygen supply is reached, when suddenly the entire building is engulfed in flames. (The author is indebted to King Walters for calling this type of demonstration apparatus to his attention.) The nonlinear properties of such firestorms might be an interesting and useful thing to study with a computer. However, the main purpose of the present discussion is to provide a large set of numbers from a real experimental situation for use in various problems, and at the same time to demonstrate how easy it is to manipulate large sets of numbers entirely with a computer.

```
1000   REM "FIRESTORM" DATA
1001   REM THERMOCOUPLE READINGS WERE -8 AT 0 DEGREES
1002   REM    AND   33   AT   100   DEGREES CENTIGRADE
1100   DATA -3,-4,-4,-3,-3,-3,-3,-4,-3,-3
1101   DATA -3,-3,-3,-3,-3,-3,-2,-3,-2,-2
1102   DATA -2,-3,-3,-3,-3,-3,-3,-3,-3,-2
1103   DATA -3,-2,-2,-2,-3,-3,-2,-2,-2,-2
1104   DATA -2,-2,-2,1,2,-2,1,2,-2,-2
1105   DATA 1,1,2,6,6,10,9,10,10,11
1106   DATA 10,13,13,13,13,12,16,15,16,17
1107   DATA 15,15,16,15,18,17,20,24,23,24
1108   DATA 29,26,29,27,25,25,28,25,28,29
1109   DATA 27,25,24,24,23,21,22,20,20,20
1110   DATA 19,19,19,24,22,23,23,21,20,21
1111   DATA 20,22,21,21,22,22,27,24,26,27
1112   DATA 26,29,28,27,28,26,25,24,22,21
1113   DATA 22,25,26,24,25,25,24,24,24,24
1114   DATA 23,24,27,24,28,31,29,28,31,32
1115   DATA 30,29,28,28,28,31,32,31,34,33
1116   DATA 35,35,37,37,35,36,35,38,38,37
1117   DATA 38,44,46,42,42,44,47,48,49,50
1118   DATA 50,50,52,59,61,60,65,64,63,62
1119   DATA 60,62,63,64,63,65,65,64,66,73
1120   DATA 76,78,82,81,79,82,84,82,88,88
1121   DATA 94,96,94,97,101,103,112,109,107,109
1122   DATA 111,112,112,112,112,116,121,122,120,117
1123   DATA 116,114,116,120,120,125,126,133,131,128
1124   DATA 134,139,137,146,143,140,139,137,132,129
1125   DATA 125,123,119,122,120,117,115,112,109,112
1126   DATA 111,111,118,119,116,114,111,113,113,113
1127   DATA 115,122,119,116,114,113,108,106,104,102
1128   DATA 99,98,97,95,98,98,102,108,112,117
1129   DATA 116,113,115,115,119,128,130,133,138,133
1130   DATA 132,132,130,127,125,127,128,135,132,137
1131   DATA 137,134,131,128,128,130,131,136,138,143
1132   DATA 142,141,138,138,136,141,140,137,135,133
1133   DATA 131,130,127,131,131,134,132,132,130
1134   DATA 127,125,123,122,123,121,125,123,123,123
1135   DATA 121,118,121,118,116,116,113,111,109,108
1136   DATA 108,106,107,107,108,109,108,107,106,104
1137   DATA 102,101,98,98,97,95,95,95,92,91
1138   DATA 91,92,93,93,91,90,89,86,84,84
1139   DATA 82,82,82,80,80,80,79,77,78,77
1140   DATA 78,80,80,80,81,81,80,79,77,76
1141   DATA 76,75,77,75,75,74,74,73,72,70
1142   DATA 70,69,70,68,67,69,68,67,67,65
1143   DATA 67,64,64,63,63,61,61,61,60,58
1144   DATA 59,57,57,55,54,53,53,53,53,51
1145   DATA 52,51,50,50,50,50,49,49,50
1146   DATA 51,55,56,56,54,54,55,52,52,54
1147   DATA 52,52,53,52,50,50,48,48,47,46
1148   DATA 46,46,44,44,44,43,43,42,42,42
1149   DATA 40,39,40,38,39,37,37,37,36,36
1150   DATA 36,35,35,34,34,33,34,34,31,-7
1151   DATA -7,-7,-6,-6,-4,-3,-6,-7,-7,-7
1152   DATA -8,-8,-8,-7,-8,-8,-8,-8,-8,-9
1153   DATA -8,-8,-8,-8,-8,-8,-8,-8,-8,-8
1154   DATA -9,-9,-8,-8,-7,-7,-8,-7,-8,-9
1155   DATA -8,-8,-8,-9,-7,-7,-7,-7,-7,-8
1156   DATA -7,-8,-7,-8,-7,-6,-6,-6,-7,-6
1157   DATA -7,-6,-6,-6,-7,-6,-7,-7,-6,-7
```

Fig. 1-6b. Thermocouple data. The data shown were taken from a thermocouple placed at the top of the Lucite cylinder. The fire was started at about line 1105 without the Lucite cylinder present. The cylinder was introduced at about line 1117. Finally, a recheck of the ice-point calibration was made after the fuel was exhausted at the end of line 1150.

As well as overcoming some of the inherently soporific nature of large blocks of data, the apparatus (perhaps with a stainless-steel foil) comes in handy for starting charcoal fires at picnics.

The DATA statements are used in later problem sets and should be made available on punched tape, or within disc files, for student use. (See note in Preface.)

Some large time-sharing systems have versions of BASIC with a single command (such as MAX or MIN) which directly determine the extremum values in a set of numbers stored in a column array. However, not all systems have this capability. Because one frequently needs to determine maximum or minimum values in a sequence of numbers, it is worth discussing the subject specifically.

Suppose, for example, that we wish to find the maximum value (M) of a set of N numbers contained in a DATA statement such as that shown in Fig. 1-6(b), which were generated from the firestorm experiment. Initially, we shall define M to be a large *negative* number; for example,

```
10   LET M = -1 E 10
```

which is equivalent to defining M to be -1×10^{10} in scientific notation. We shall assume that this choice gives a number that is more negative than anything on our list. (We could, of course, have started out with the most negative number that our particular computer could handle—if we had happened to know the value offhand.) We can then construct a loop that examines each number in the data statement in turn. A conditional statement is arranged to redefine M to equal each successively larger number encountered. Finally, after completing the loop, we might want to print the last value. For example,

```
20   FOR I = 1 TO N
30   READ X
40   IF M > X THEN 60
50   LET M = X
60   NEXT I
70   PRINT "MAX. = M = "; M
80   DATA    ,   ,   ,      etc.
99   END
```

It is important to emphasize that what the computer finds through repeated use of the conditional statement on line 40 is the *most positive* number on our list. The number would not necessarily have the largest absolute value [unless we modified line 40 to read: IF $M > ABS(X)$ THEN 60].

Similarly, we could construct a program to find the minimum ($M0$) number on the list through use of the opposition initialization and inequality condition. For example, adding the statements

```
15   LET M0 = +1 E 10
60   IF M0 < X THEN 65
62   LET M0 = X
65   NEXT I
75   PRINT "MIN. = M0 = "; M0
```

to the previous program would permit simultaneously determining both the maximum and the minimum value in a set of N data points. Here, again, it should be emphasized that the value determined for $M0$ will be the *most negative* number on the list and we would have to modify the conditional statement on line 60 [e.g., to read IF $M0 < ABS(X)$ THEN 65] if we wanted to have the computer find the minimum absolute value of X.

In most applications that arise in the present book (e.g., plotting, sorting, etc.) we shall be concerned with the determination of a maximum defined as the "most positive" and a minimum defined as the "most negative" in a set of numbers.

Write a program to determine the maximum and minimum temperatures (°C) in the thermocouple data shown in Fig. 1-6(b) (or in an equivalent set of data). Assuming that six measurements were made per second, make the computer determine how long after the first measurement the maximum and minimum temperatures occurred.

In some instances, function statements provide a useful means to avoid excessive typing of programming statements. In BASIC, functions can be labeled FNA, FNB, FNC, . . . , FNZ and involve arguments of one or (with some versions of BASIC) more parameters. For example, one could do the thermometer calibration in Problem 7 with a function defined in the following manner:

1.13
The BASIC Function Statement

$$\text{DEF FNC(V)} = 100*(V - V\emptyset)/(V1 - V\emptyset)$$

Then, anywhere else in the program a given voltage reading, W, could be converted into a temperature in degrees Celsius through the statement

$$\text{LET T} = \text{FNC(W)}$$

Although too much of a luxury for the minicomputer, most large computers equipped with BASIC compilers will accept multiple-line-function definitions. The format used is of the type

$$\text{DEF FNA(X,Y, . .)}$$
.
.
.
$$\text{LET FNA} = . . .$$
$$\text{FNEND}$$

where the variables in the function are indicated within the parentheses on the DEF line and a large number of normal programming statements may follow on the succeeding lines prior to the FNEND statement (the end of the function definition). Multiple-line functions are particularly useful in situations where the algebraic form of the function itself depends on the variables in the function argument.

For the sake of a specific example, suppose that we wanted to create one thermometer function which would give us readings in either °C or °F from the thermocouple voltage readings in the previous experiment. We could define a function FNT(V, S) in which the first variable represents the thermocouple voltage and the second determines the scale choice; for example, consider the definition

```
100   DEF FNT(V, S)
110   IF S<>∅  THEN 140
120   LET FNT = 100*(V − V∅)/(V1 − V∅)
130   GOTO 150
140   LET FNT = 32 + (212 − 32)*(V − V∅)/(V1 − V∅)
150   FNEND
```

in which $V\emptyset$ and $V1$ represent the ice and boiling points of water as before and must have been given numerical values elsewhere in the program before using FNT(V, S). Then a statement in the main program such as

$$\text{LET T} = \text{FNT(W, ∅)}$$

would give us T in degrees Celsius, whereas the statement

$$\text{LET T} = \text{FNT(W, Q)} \quad \text{with } Q \neq \emptyset$$

would give us T in degrees Fahrenheit.

25

One clearly can set up much more elaborately defined multiple-line functions and apply them to situations in which their use is more appropriate. Similarly, one might want to define a function based on summing a series, for repeated use throughout a program.

There are minor differences among BASIC compilers in the conventions used for defining multiple-line functions, and it is important to find out the specific rules that your machine follows. Finally, it is worth noting that one can always accomplish the same objectives of a multiple-line-function definition through the use of a larger number of statements in the main program or by the use of subroutines (see Section 1.14).

1.13
PROBLEM 8

Use the BASIC function statement to compute the temperature in °C and the temperature in °F for the data in Fig. 1-6(b) (or an equivalent string of data). Write the program so that every twentieth reading is printed out in a tabular form of the following type:

Reading	Voltage	Temperature (°C)	Temperature (°F)
20	. . .	. . .	. . .
40	. . .	. . .	. . .
		etc.	

If your computer does not allow multiple-line functions, use two separate single-line-function definitions for the temperature in °C and in °F. (Use a FOR loop on a dummy variable to get every twentieth entry in the DATA statements.)

A subroutine consists of a subset of program statements that may be used repeatedly at different places throughout the main program. Any line number in a BASIC program can be used as the start of a subroutine, as long as it is followed at some point by the statement RETURN. Access to the subroutine at any point within a program is gained through the statement GOSUB... (where the dots indicate the starting line number of the subroutine). The computer then jumps to the line indicated, executes all intervening program statements up until the line marked RETURN, and then jumps back to the next line after the initial GOSUB command.

1.14
Subroutines in BASIC

A specific example will help clarify the use of this programming technique. A subroutine to compute the temperature in both degrees Celsius and degrees Fahrenheit from a thermocouple voltage and print the result could be written

```
100   REM SUB TO COMPUTE AND PRINT T IN DEG. C AND F
110   LET T1 = 100*(V − V0)/(V1 − V0)
120   LET T2 = 32 + (212 − 32)*(V − V0)/(V1 − V0)
130   PRINT T1,T2
140   RETURN
```

The REM statement on line 100 is not really needed but would be helpful in reminding us of the purpose of this subroutine in a long program. We assume, as before, that $V0$ and $V1$ are the thermocouple voltages at the ice and boiling points and have been previously entered in the program (i.e., prior to saying GOSUB 100). We could then construct a main program consisting of

```
10   LET V0 =...
20   LET V1 =...    }(whatever the values are)
30   PRINT "V"
```

```
40   INPUT V
50   GOSUB 100
60   GOTO 30
```

which perpetually goes around in a loop asking us for values of V from the keyboard and jumping to subroutine 100, where the values of T1 (in °C) and T2 (in °F) are printed in wide spacing on the same line. That is, at line 50 the program jumps to the subroutine starting on line 100 and executes the statements between line 100 and line 140. When the computer reaches the RETURN statement on line 140, it jumps back to the next program statement after line 50 (from which the subroutine was originally requested).

One may also enter the subroutine at any point before the RETURN statement, provided that the variables used from then on have been defined. However, the variables used within the subroutine always have the last numerical values computed. For example, if we were to say GOSUB 130 at line 50 in our program, the subroutine would print the previous values of T1 and T2 that had been computed; whereas if we were to say GOSUB 120, the subroutine would print the previous value of T1, followed by the current value for T2.

When one realizes that nested loops and other GOSUB statements may be contained within subroutines, their enormous power becomes self-evident.

1.14
PROBLEM 9   Do the preceding problem through use of a BASIC subroutine to compute the temperatures and perform the printing operations.

1.15
Use of Column Arrays as Variables

A major economy in programming statements occurs when one starts using indexed variables, or column arrays. In BASIC, a column array may be designated by any single-letter of the alphabet followed by an integer subscript within parentheses. Thus

$$A(I), B(I), C(I), \ldots, X(I), Y(I), Z(I)$$

may be used as variables in BASIC, where the indices take on integer values. If the index I exceeds 10, DIM (for dimension) statements are required. One generally puts such dimension statements near the beginning of the program (usually after having figured out how many array elements are really needed in the completed program). For example,

```
10   DIM A(255), W(100)
```

tells the computer to set aside room to store 255 different variables $A(I)$ in which $1 \leq I \leq 255$ in integer steps and 100 different variables $W(I)$, where I takes on the integer values 1 through 100. The largest number of array elements that can be set aside in this fashion depends largely on the size of the computer in use. (Representative minicomputers have array size limits of 255 elements.)

The programming power afforded by array variables rests in the fact that the array indices may be *computed*. That is, we do not have to write 255 statements of the type

```
LET A(1) = ...
LET A(2) = ...     etc.
```

to define 255 different variables. If we have a prescription for calculating these values, we can write instead a simple loop of the type

```
FOR I = 1 TO 255
LET A(I) = ...     (some function of I)
NEXT I
```

and reuse the same LET statement 255 times.

1.15
PROBLEM 10† Write a program that lists (in close spacing) all the prime numbers up to 1000. How many are there?

[*Note:* You can tell whether a particular number, M, is prime by checking to see if $M/N(J) = INT(M/N(J))$ for all integers, $N(J)$, satisfying $2 \leq N(J) < M$. A clever way to do the problem is to store the successive primes in a large array, $N(J)$, starting with $N(1) = 2$, $N(2) = M = 3$, and $N = 2$. One then merely runs through the array $N(J)$ with each new M, for $J = 1$ to N, after which you increment M by 2. If you find a new prime, increment N by 1 and store the new prime in $N(N)$.]

† This problem and method of solution were suggested by the author's daughter, Nancy Bennett.

1.15
PROBLEM 11 The principal energy levels of the hydrogen atom are given by the Bohr relation

$$E(N) = -109678.8/N^2 \qquad \text{wavenumbers (cm}^{-1}\text{)}$$

where $N = 1, 2, 3, \ldots$; the numerator is known as the Rydberg constant and has dimensions of inverse centimeters. The spontaneous transitions in the atom have wavenumbers (inverse wavelengths) given by

$$W = E(M) - E(N) \qquad \text{cm}^{-1}$$

[provided that $E(M) > E(N)$], where the values of $E(N)$ are given above. Using a column array, $W(I)$, dimensioned to hold at least 36 elements, compute and store all the allowed transition wavenumbers that can result in transitions in atomic hydrogen with principal quantum numbers (N) that satisfy $2 \leq N \leq 10$. Print out the array, $W(I)$.

[*Note:* You could store the allowed transitions with statements of the type

```
FOR M = 3 TO 10
FOR N = 2 TO M − 1
LET W(I) = E(M) − E(N)
LET I = I + 1
NEXT N
NEXT M
```

in which $I = 1$ initially, once the $E(N)$ have been computed.]

Write a subroutine that finds the minimum $(M1)$ and maximum $(M2)$ value of a series of N numbers stored in the column array $W(I)$. Apply it to determine the minimum and maximum wavenumbers stored above.

1.16
Sorting

Suppose that we have a list of N numbers which we have read into a column array, $W(I)$, and want to print them out in descending (or ascending) order. Some large computers are equipped with BASIC compilers that actually have sorting commands built into the language. For example, one system has a command of the type MAT $A = DSORT(W)$ or MAT $A = ASORT(W)$, which automatically stores the elements of array $W(I)$ in descending or ascending order in array $A(J)$. However, most small and even moderate-sized computers do not have such statements built into the BASIC language, and we might still want to accomplish the same objective.

One inefficient, but straightforward method of sorting the array elements in descending order is contained in the following steps (in which we count the ordered terms with index J, initially = 1):

1. Find the maximum number, $W(M)$, in the array.
2. Print the maximum, or store it as the Jth element in another array, $A(J)$.

3. If $W(M) = 0$, stop the process.
4. LET $W(M) = 0$ and increment J.
5. Go back to step 1.

This method is not too bad if you only have a few entries on the list. However, the running time increases roughly as N^2 and becomes prohibitive if you have a really large set of numbers (N) to handle (i.e., the program goes through the sorting loop N times, and during each loop the program examines all N elements in the original array).

1.16
PROBLEM 12

Use the above sorting method to print out an ordered list of allowed wavenumbers for transitions in atomic hydrogen between states for which the principal quantum numbers satisfy $2 \le N \le 10$. (See Problem 11.) Make a note of the running time for comparison with the next problem.

A much faster approach consists of storing the numbers in a second array for which the array indices are determined by the most significant digits in the numbers on the list. Here you will be limited in sorting resolution by the maximum array size that your computer can handle.

One first goes through the list to find the maximum ($M2$) and minimum ($M1$) values.[4] Then we define array integers based on the maximum number of elements ($M3$) that we can store in the array $A(J)$. Of course, $M3 \gg N$. For example, suppose that the array $A(J)$ has been dimensioned to $M3$ elements, and the elements are all initially set equal to a number $< M1$. A first-order sorting is then accomplished by statements of the type

```
100   FOR I = 1 TO N
110   LET J = INT((M3 − 1)*(W(I) − M1)/(M2 − M1) + 1 + .5)
120   LET A(J) = W(I)
130   NEXT I
```

for which the running time only increases linearly with N. After line 130, we have stored the values of $W(I)$ in ascending order in array $A(J)$, but the array $A(J)$ is interspersed with unaltered initial values. However, if two of the original array elements in $W(I)$ were so close in magnitude as to give the same integer J on line 110, we would lose the first and only store the second value in $A(J)$. Hence, this method only works well on really large machines, or with arrays having fairly uniform differences in element size.

It is obviously desirable to accomplish the sorting within the original array itself. One particularly simple method (known as the *bubble sort*) consists of going through the array sequentially and putting adjacent pairs in ascending order. In repeated trips through the array, the largest elements "bubble up" to the top and none are lost. The process can be accomplished in $N(N + 1)/2$ trips through the array (the sum of an arithmetic series with N terms) and isn't quite as slow as the straightforward method discussed initially. The method will be apparent from the following program steps.

```
99    REM BUBBLE SORT OF ARRAY W(I) WITH N ELEMENTS
100   LET N0 = 1
110   FOR I = 1 TO N − 1
```

---

[4] It should be emphasized here that $M1$ is indeed the minimum; that is, $M1$ represents either the smallest of a series of positive numbers or the "most negative" of a series of positive and negative numbers. For example, in the sequence 1, −15, 7, −2, 5, the minimum is −15.

```
120  IF W(I)<W(I+1) THEN 170
130  LET A=W(I)
140  LET W(I)=W(I+1)
150  LET W(I+1)=A
160  LET NØ=I
170  NEXT I
175  PRINT NØ;
180  IF NØ=1 THEN 210
190  LET N=NØ
200  GOTO 100
210  PRINT "ARRAY SORTED"
```

Line 175 is put in just to let the operator know where the program is in the sorting process and lines 10Ø and 18Ø identify arrays that have been previously sorted. As written, the program loses track of the original number of elements in the array $W(I)$. That number could, of course, be stored in a separate variable.

**1.16
PROBLEM 13**   Repeat Problem 12; this time use the bubble sorting method discussed above. Compare the running times.

Drawing flowcharts is one of those activities that most people think is a great practice—as long as someone else is doing it. The basic notion is to draw a schematic diagram of a particular program so that the reader will easily acquire an understanding of the computational method through graphic display.

**1.17
Flowcharts**

Certain conventions have come into use: input quantities are usually shown within circles, computational steps within rectangles, conditional statements within triangles or diamonds, and so on. For example, the lines

```
10  LET I=1
20  INPUT X
30  PRINT I,X*X
40  LET I=I+1
50  IF I>10 THEN 90
60  GO TO 20
90  END
```

would be displayed as shown in Fig. 1-7.

Figure 1-7 illustrates one problem with flowcharts: they usually occupy more space than a *simple* listing of the program, and for simple problems they do not really give any more useful information to the reader (especially if you are not averse to drawing an occasional arrow or loop on the program listing itself). At the other extreme, for a flowchart of a really complex problem to be accurate enough to do any good, you almost have to have written the program already and have run it a few times to make sure all the bugs are out. Thus the flowchart is primarily helpful in explaining the program to others rather than to yourself.

To be sure, there is a delicately defined class of problems for which drawing a detailed flowchart ahead of time is of genuine assistance to the initial construction of the program. These problems are frequently ones that involve a large number of systematically varying program statements—so many statements that you would tend to forget where you are in the method of systematic variation without some sort of visual reminder. A good example of this type of

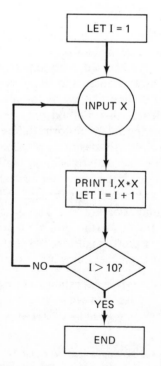

Fig. 1-7.

situation is illustrated with the binary sorting and printing sieve discussed in Chapter 4 (see Fig. 4-2). However, as noted in that chapter, a slightly more powerful version of the programming language itself does away with any necessity to draw a flowchart even in that problem. Certainly, the lower the level of power involved within the programming language, the more likely flow charts are to be of use. Thus flowcharts are extremely helpful with many machine-language problems and in programming a fairly rudimentary computer such as the HP-65 pocket calculator (see Fig. 1-3). However, with most of the fairly difficult problems in the present book, the task of drawing formal flowcharts seems a needless encumbrance. It is the sort of thing you do a lot of in programming courses when you do not have a computer available.

Please do *not* interpret these remarks to imply that *no* advance thought should be given to a problem before sitting down at a terminal. Quite the contrary. It pays to give a great deal of advance thought to difficult problems before going "on line."

It is generally desirable to sketch out most of the solution to a problem before going near a terminal—both by outlining the major steps and by writing out most of the program statements ahead of time. Then when you type in the program statements on a terminal, if you leave fairly wide line number spacings (e.g., statements every 10 line numbers), there is usually plenty of room to incorporate necessary afterthoughts without recourse to elaborate editing operations. Finally, by drawing a few loops and arrows in appropriate places, you can turn the program listing itself into an adequate flowchart for most purposes.

1.18
Some BASIC String Statements (CHR$ and CHANGE)

A *string* is a specified sequence of alphanumeric characters. In larger computers, provision is generally made for both string variables and string functions.

Specific conventions on string operations differ a great deal from one compiler to the next, and there will be no substitute for reading up on the meanings assumed in the particular version of BASIC built into your computer.

The main idea is that each alphanumeric character (or, with large computers, specific sequence of alphanumeric characters) may be described by a string variable. String variables are designated by a single letter followed by a dollar sign; e.g.,

$$A\$, B\$, C\$, \ldots, Z\$$$

are string variables. These may be defined through LET statements (where the string must be enclosed within quotation marks), by READ and DATA statements, and may be input and printed by use of the computer terminal.

To perform operations on strings, an integer code is used within the programming language to designate the various alphanumeric characters. The numerical values are assigned in a manner based upon the ASCII (American Standard Code for Information Interchange) convention for identifying such characters. A list of decimal-integer values assigned to some of the standard character set is shown in Table 1.

Most BASIC compilers equipped to handle strings have some version of the CHR$(X) function (which is used in PRINT statements to print the alphanumeric character corresponding to the variable X) and the CHANGE statement (which permits defining numerical variables equal to the ASCII integers for alphanumeric characters in strings.)

For example, use of the CHR$ function in a program of the type

```
FOR X = 65 TO 65 + 25
PRINT CHR$(X);
NEXT X
```

would print the alphabet in closely-spaced sequence using the code summarized in Table 1. (Note that the ASCII integers for certain "control" keys such as the line feed and carriage return are excluded from the normal characters that may be used in string statements.)

The CHANGE statement is inherently more powerful and involves the use of a column array to correspond to each string variable. Assuming the string variable $V\$$ has been defined and the column array $V(I)$ has been dimensioned to equal (or exceed) the number of characters in the string, the statement

CHANGE V$ TO V

then enters the number of characters in the string $V\$$ as the zeroth ($I=\emptyset$) element of array $V(I)$ and fills in the ASCII code for the characters in the

1.18: Table 1 Integer Values Assigned to Some ASCII Characters in BASIC[a]

Alphanumeric character	Decimal-integer value
Sp. (space or blank)	32
' (apostrophe)	39
− (minus sign or hyphen)	45
$\emptyset$ (zero)	48
1 (one)[b]	49
2 (two)	50
3 (three)	51
4 (four)	52
5 (five)	53
6 (six)	54
7 (seven)	55
8 (eight)	56
9 (nine)	57
A (uppercase A)	65
B (uppercase B)	66
C (uppercase C)	67
D (uppercase D)	68
E (uppercase E)	69
F (uppercase F)	70
G (uppercase G)	71
H (uppercase H)	72
I (uppercase I)	73
J (uppercase J)	74
K (uppercase K)	75
L (uppercase L)	76
M (uppercase M)	77
N (uppercase N)	78
O (uppercase O)	79
P (uppercase P)	80
Q (uppercase Q)	81
R (uppercase R)	82
S (uppercase S)	83
T (uppercase T)	84
U (uppercase U)	85
V (uppercase V)	86
W (uppercase W)	87
X (uppercase X)	88
Y (uppercase Y)	89
Z (uppercase Z)	90

[a] There are 128 in a complete list.

[b] The symbols 1–9 are helpful in using string statements to plot topographical maps (see Chapter 3). The remaining characters in the table are of primary concern in Chapter 4.

string in successive array elements ($I = 1, 2, 3, \ldots$). For example, the statements

```
INPUT V$
CHANGE V$ TO V
```

permit entering up to 72 characters in a string from the teletype keyboard (the end of the string is defined when the carriage return button is pushed), providing DIM V(72) occurs earlier in the program. The ASCII code for the first letter in the string is stored in $V(1)$ and that for the last character in the string in $V(72)$. In this instance $V(\emptyset) = 72$. The string could also be read from DATA statements in a program of the type

```
READ V$
DATA ABCDEFGHIJKLMNOPQRSTUVWXYZ
```

and one could also use the CHANGE statement to convert the integers stored in a column array $V(I)$ to a string variable V$ by the statement

```
CHANGE V TO V$
```

providing $V(\emptyset)$ is defined to be the total number of characters in the string. [This is the only type of situation in which we shall consider arrays having zero indices.]

From the code illustrated in Table 1, it will be apparent how conditional statements can be used with string variables. Most BASIC compilers with string capability have some version of the numerical conditional statements (e.g., IF $B\$ < D\$$ THEN ...) which apply the condition sequentially to each separate character of the two strings from left to right and in a manner such that the first difference encountered determines the relationship. The comparisons are made numerically using the ASCII integer code in Table 1. Such conditional statements can obviously be used to effect various sorting, alphabetizing, and editing procedures.

Various other powerful string statements are permitted in many of the larger computers equipped with BASIC. However, the individual statements included vary considerably from one computer to the next and it would be impractical to try to summarize their properties here.

1.18
PROBLEM 14 If your computer has the CHR$ function (or equivalent statement), write a program which prints alphanumeric characters corresponding to the ASCII decimal code in Table 1.

1.18
PROBLEM 15 If your computer has the CHANGE statement and accepts string variables (or has equivalent statements), write a program which prints the ASCII decimal integers corresponding to different alphanumeric characters entered from the keyboard and compare your results with Table 1.

REFERENCES

FALK, HOWARD, ET AL. (1974). "Computer Report I ... VIII." *IEEE Spectrum*, Vol. 11, No. 2. This issue contains a number of separate "state-of-the-art" review articles on computer technology written by Howard Falk, C. G. Bell, L. G. Roberts, Don Mennie, A. A. Hoffman, R. L. French, G. M. Lang, Henry Tropp, W. R. Beam, and the editorial staff of *Spectrum*.

FETH, G. C. (1973). "Memories Are Bigger, Faster—and Cheaper." Technology review in *IEEE Spectrum*, Vol. 10, No. 11, pp. 28–35.

GOLDSTINE, H. H., (1972). *The Computer from Pascal to von Neumann*. Princeton, N.J.: Princeton University Press.

HEATH, F. G. (1972). "Origins of the Binary Code." *Scientific American*, August, pp. 76–83.

HEWLETT-PACKARD CORPORATION (1969). *A Pocket Guide to Hewlett-Packard Computers*.

KEMENY, J. G., AND T. E. KURTZ. (1968). *BASIC Manual*. Hanover, N.H.: Dartmouth College. This manual has been reproduced within many different computer instruction manuals. Also see the discussion of CALL and WAIT statements for use within Hewlett-Packard BASIC in their manuals for the 2100 series computers and the discussion of more powerful functions within versions of BASIC given in the General Electric and Digital Data Corporation PDP10 time-sharing computer manuals.

KNUTH, D. E. (1973). *The Art of Computer Programming*. Reading, Mass.: Addison-Wesley Publishing Co., Vol. 3, *Sorting and Searching*.

MENNIE, DON (1974). "The Big Roundup of Small Calculators." *IEEE Spectrum*, Vol. 11, pp. 34–41.

U.S. ATOMIC ENERGY COMMISSION (1971). *In the Matter of J. Robert Oppenheimer*. Cambridge, Mass.: The MIT Press. This book contains a transcript of the April 12–May 6, 1954 hearings by the U.S. Atomic Energy Commission, together with a brief foreword by P. M. Stern.

VON NEUMANN, JOHN (1958). *The Computer and the Brain*. New Haven, Conn.: Yale University Press. (*The Silliman Lectures*; published posthumously.)

2

More advanced programming

This chapter assumes a knowledge of the elementary programming statements in BASIC that were discussed in Sections 1.4–1.17. The main emphasis is in summing various types of series. At the same time, concepts from introductory calculus (derivatives, Taylor series, definite integrals) and matrix algebra are reviewed. This review is always conducted from the standpoint of immediate programming application and with the object of providing greater insight regarding the more powerful statements in a language such as BASIC. Applications to fields ranging from economics to pattern recognition are discussed. However, the material should be comprehensible to readers without a formal background in calculus or college-level science. The material steadily increases in difficulty toward the end of the chapter, and students without a prior course in calculus may wish to skip the final section altogether. Relevant sections are cross-referenced as they arise in subsequent chapters on specific applications.

In this chapter we shall introduce some slightly more advanced programming methods and review some basic mathematical techniques needed in different places throughout the remainder of the book. The main emphasis will be on the mathematical technique that is tacitly assumed in the standard operations built into the BASIC language. Our primary objective is to give the reader some insight regarding the behind-the-scenes operations that occur when you run a program containing statements such as $X \uparrow Y$, $EXP(X)$, $SIN(X)$, $MAT\ A = B*C$, $MAT\ A = INV(B)$, and so on. The object is not to avoid using these powerful commands but to emphasize their practical utility and at the same time make it apparent how similar functions of a more specialized nature might be defined.

One frequently needs to compute numerical values for a series of the type

$$S = a_1 + a_2 + a_3 + \cdots + a_n + a_{n+1} + \cdots$$

in which a known prescription exists for evaluating the nth term. The exact approach to the problem will vary a little, depending on whether the number of terms in the series is finite or infinite. The most straightforward way to sum the series is to initialize S through a statement

```
10   LET S = 0
```

and merely compute (or read from a data statement) each term in the series sequentially. For example, if there are M terms, then the program

```
20   FOR N = 1 TO M
30   LET A = ...     (some function of N)
40   LET S = S + A
50   NEXT N
60   PRINT S
90   END
```

sums the series.

It is often possible to set up the problem in a form where a_{n+1} is computed from a_n in a running increment to the sum. The approach can both save running time and improve computational accuracy. Here a program for a finite series with M terms might take the form

```
10   LET S = 0
20   LET A = ...
30   FOR N = 1 TO M
40   LET S = S + A
50   LET A = A*(...)
60   NEXT N
70   PRINT S
80   END
```

Line 2Ø defines the value of the first term in the series, and line 5Ø computes the $(N+1)^{th}$ term from the Nth term. If, for example, the Nth term were of the form

$$A_N = \frac{X^N}{N!}$$

a separate computation of

$$X^N \quad \text{and} \quad N!$$

could easily exhaust the domain of variables in any real computer for suitably large values of X and N. On the other hand, computing the statement

```
LET A = A*(X/N)
```

is enormously less demanding.

2.1
Summing a Series of Numbers

36

2.1
PROBLEM 1

The BASIC function RND(X) provides a sequence of numbers intended to simulate a random distribution over the interval 0 to 1. (The argument in the function is a dummy variable but nevertheless must be assigned a definite numerical value.) Write a program that computes 1000 successive values from the RND(X) function and see how close the average value is to 0.5.

2.1
PROBLEM 2

Find the sum of the arithmetic series

$$S = 1 + 2 + 3 + \cdots + (M-1) + M$$

for variable M, and compare the result with the closed-form expression,

$$S = \frac{M(M+1)}{2}$$

(The latter result can be obtained by writing the series backward and noting that the terms 1, $(M-1)$, etc., combine in pairs, each having the value M.)

2.1
PROBLEM 3

Write a program that sums the geometric series

$$S = 1 + a + a^2 + a^3 + \cdots + a^M$$

for different values of a and M (input from the keyboard), and compare the result with the closed-form expression

$$S = \frac{1 - a^{M+1}}{1 - a}$$

(The latter result is obtained by subtracting aS from S and canceling like powers of a in pairs.)

In many instances, one wants to sum an infinite series,

$$S = a_1 + a_2 + \cdots$$

2.2
Infinite Series and Convergence

to a prescribed accuracy. Here we have to construct the program in a form that starts the series off at the first term and keeps it going until a specified conditional statement on the increment a_N is satisfied. For example,

```
10   LET S = 0
20   LET N = 1
30   LET A = ...      (some function of N)
40   LET S = S + A
50   IF ABS(A) < ... THEN 80
60   LET N = N + 1
70   GO TO 30
80   PRINT N,S
90   END
```

The variable N (lines 20, 60 and 80) is not always necessary but is frequently helpful in the definition of the running term and in keeping track of the total number of terms computed. Note that for $A < 0$, a conditional statement on the absolute value of the increment is useful (line 50).

If $ABS(A_{N+1}/A_N) < 1$ for all N, the above type of *computed* series will generally terminate at a finite limit for sufficiently large N. This fact is assured by the conditional statement on $ABS(A)$ in line 50, where the dots must be replaced by a specific numerical criterion. However, the computed limit may not always be the right one. The reader should be especially wary of two pitfalls:

1. The conditional statement on line 50 in the sample program above could

be satisfied in cases where a finite limit does *not* exist (e.g., $\lim_{N \to \infty}(A_{N+1}/A_N) \not\to 0$].

2. Rounding errors can result in large discrepancies between actual and computed limits in convergent series for which the terms alternate in sign.

2.2
PROBLEM 4

Write a program to evaluate the infinite series $S = 1 + x + x^2 + \cdots$, within the rounding errors of your computer where $-1 < x < 1$ and compare the result with the closed-form expression

$$S = \frac{1}{1-x}$$

(obtained from the finite geometric series expression in the limit $N \to \infty$).

It is easy to write a program that accomplishes the same result as the BASIC statement, $I \uparrow P$, provided that P is an integer. For example, one could write a simple loop of the type

2.3
Infinite Series Derived from the Binomial Theorem (Pth Roots)

```
10  LET A = I
20  FOR N = 1 TO P − 1
30  LET A = A*I
40  NEXT N
```

where I has been defined before line 10. Clearly, $A = I^P$ after the loop has been completed.

However, the problem becomes more involved if you should want to duplicate the results of the BASIC statement $Y \uparrow (1/P)$, where P is still an integer. One way to accomplish this more difficult objective consists of first finding the smallest integer I such that

$$I^P > Y$$

(To avoid imaginary quantities, we shall assume that $Y > 0$.) This first part of the problem can, of course, be accomplished through judicious use of statements 10–40. After determining the smallest integer I that satisfies the above requirement, we next note that if we define X so that

$$Y^{1/P} = I(1 + X)^{1/P}$$

then

$$X = \frac{Y}{I^P} - 1 \quad \text{and} \quad \text{ABS}(X) < 1$$

Hence, if we can write a program to expand $(1 + X)^{1/P}$ as an infinite series in X and sum that series to a prescribed accuracy, we will have achieved our goal. This objective can be accomplished by use of the *Binomial Theorem*.

In particular, the usual form of the binomial expansion,

$$(A + B)^N = A^N + N \frac{A^{N-1}B^1}{1!} + N(N-1) \frac{A^{N-2}B^2}{2!} + \cdots + B^N$$

results in a convergent infinite series,

$$(1 + X)^{1/P} = 1 + \frac{1/P}{1!} X^1 + \frac{(1/P)[(1/P) - 1]}{2!} X^2 + \cdots$$

for fractional powers $(1/P)$, provided that $\text{ABS}(X) < 1$.

Hence, in order to compute $Y^{1/P}$, all we have to do is find the smallest integer I such that $I^P > Y$, compute $X = Y/I^P - 1$, and then sum the series for

$(1+X)^{1/P}$. (Note that although we have used positive signs in the binomial expansion to minimize confusing the nature of that expansion, the quantity X is inherently negative in the definition above.)

<table>
<tr><td>

2.3

PROBLEM 5

</td><td>

Write a program that uses the Binomial Theorem† to compute $Y^{1/P}$ to the accuracy of your computer without using the BASIC exponentiation function and then compares the result with the BASIC statement $Y\uparrow(1/P)$. Enter values of Y and P from the keyboard and restrict the values so that P is a positive integer and $Y>0$.

† The serious student will want to investigate the treatise on the Binomial Theorem by Professor James Moriarty (see A. Conan-Doyle, "The Final Problem").

</td></tr>
</table>

Consider a continuous function $y = f(x)$, as shown in Fig. 2-1. The derivative of y in respect to x (written as dy/dx) is defined as the limit of the quantity

**2.4
Derivatives**

$$\left[\frac{f(x+\Delta x)-f(x)}{\Delta x}\right]$$

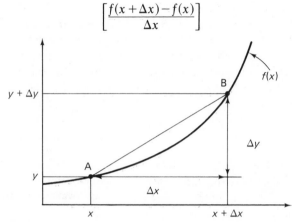

Fig. 2-1.

as Δx shrinks to zero. This definition is frequently written

$$\frac{dy}{dx} \equiv \lim_{\Delta x \to 0}\left[\frac{f(x+\Delta x)-f(x)}{\Delta x}\right] \tag{1}$$

As may be seen from Fig. 2-1, the derivative of the function is just the slope of the curve (or tangent to the curve) at the point x where the derivative is evaluated (i.e., the point B moves toward the point A along the curve).

Although one could always write a computer program to provide a numerical evaluation of the derivative of a specified function directly from this fundamental definition, it is important to recognize that the derivatives of many functions can be written explicitly in closed form. In such cases, it is usually desirable to evaluate the functional form of the derivative rather than to compute the derivative numerically from the limiting process.

The derivative of the functional form

$$y = f(x) = x^N$$

is of very great importance to Taylor-series expansions (discussed in Section 2.5) and can be evaluated easily by application of the Binomial Theorem. In this case,

$$f(x+\Delta x) = (x+\Delta x)^N = x^N + \frac{Nx^{N-1}(\Delta x)^1}{1!} + \frac{N(N-1)x^{N-2}(\Delta x)^2}{2!} + \cdots$$

Therefore, applying the definition of the derivative,

$$\frac{d}{dx}(x^N) = \lim_{\Delta x \to 0}\left[\frac{x^N + Nx^{N-1}(\Delta x)^1 + N(N-1)x^{N-2}(\Delta x)^2/2! + \cdots - x^N}{\Delta x}\right]$$

39

(in which the terms involving x^N cancel), yields

$$\frac{d}{dx}(x^N) = \lim_{\Delta x \to 0}\left[Nx^{N-1} + \frac{N(N-1)x^{N-2}(\Delta x)^1}{2!} + \text{terms of order } (\Delta x)^2 \cdots\right]$$

The terms involving Δx vanish in the limiting process. Hence we obtain the extremely important general result,

$$\frac{d}{dx}(x^N) = Nx^{N-1} \tag{2}$$

2.4

PROBLEM 6

Write a program to compute the derivative of χ^N numerically. Check the program by comparing its results with those based on an analytic form for the derivative.

Using the BASIC function definitions

```
DEF FNY(X) = X↑N
DEF FND(X) = (FNY(X + D) − FNY(X))/D
```

write a program that takes the limit of the second function as $D \to 0$ and compares the result with $N*X\uparrow(N-1)$ for values of X and N entered from the keyboard. For example, LET $D = \emptyset.\emptyset1*X$ initially and reiteratively multiply the values of D by $\emptyset.1$ until the successive values of $FND(X)$ differ by less than the rounding error on your machine. (Although it would be foolish to evaluate the derivative of x^N in this manner in a serious program, one could advantageously use the same technique to evaluate the derivatives of numerically determined functions.)

2.5
Taylor Series
(Alias MacLaurin Series)

There are many important functions [e.g., SIN(X), COS(X), EXP(X), etc.] which can only be computed by the use of power-series expansions in the independent variable. Before the general availability of computers, tables of such functions were tediously evaluated by hand (using desk calculators) and published in book form. Indeed, one such project sponsored by the WPA during the 1930s was probably conceived just to provide work for unemployed mathematicians.

Although ready access to digital computers has largely done away with the need for printed tables of this sort, one still needs to use series expansions to evaluate the functions. Very efficient forms of these expansions for the common transcendental functions have been stored in machine language within the BASIC compiler. However, it is still useful to consider a general method for determining the expansion coefficients in such series. The method, which goes under the name *Taylor series* (or sometimes *MacLaurin series*) is probably one of the most useful tools in computational analysis, apart from the concept of the derivative itself.

We shall start by assuming that the function $y = f(x)$ can be written in the infinite series

$$y = C_0 + C_1 x^1 + C_2 x^2 + C_3 x^3 + \cdots + C_N x^N + \cdots \tag{3}$$

As will become evident, the assumption implies that the function and its derivatives must be continuous and finite over the domain of x in which we want to compute the function. The series also had better converge to a finite limit.

To evaluate the coefficients $C_0, C_1, \ldots, C_N, \ldots$, we adopt a procedure in which we repeatedly determine the derivatives of Eq. (3) and set $x = 0$ in the result.

To get the leading coefficient in the expansion, we merely set $x = 0$ in the original equation. Clearly,

$$C_0 = (y)_{x=0}$$

Next we take the derivative of both sides of Eq. (3), yielding

$$\frac{dy}{dx} = C_1 + 2C_2 x^1 + 3C_3 x^2 + \cdots + NC_N x^{N-1} + \cdots \tag{4}$$

in which use has been made of our general expression for $d(x^N)/dx$ in Eq. (2). Letting $x = 0$ in Eq. (4) gives us

$$C_1 = \left(\frac{dy}{dx}\right)_{x=0}$$

Similarly, taking the derivative of Eq. (4) yields

$$\frac{d}{dx}\left(\frac{dy}{dx}\right) \equiv \frac{d^2 y}{dx^2} = 2C_2 + 3 \cdot 2C_3 x^1 + \cdots + N(N-1)C_N x^{N-2} + \cdots \tag{5}$$

and therefore that

$$C_2 = \frac{1}{2}\left(\frac{d^2 y}{dx^2}\right)_{x=0}$$

Doing the same process over and over demonstrates that

$$C_N = \frac{1}{N!}\left(\frac{d^N y}{dx^N}\right)_{x=0}$$

Hence the original function may be expressed as[1]

$$y = (y)_{x=0} + \frac{1}{1!}\left(\frac{d^1 y}{dx^1}\right)_{x=0} x^1 + \frac{1}{2!}\left(\frac{d^2 y}{dx^2}\right)_{x=0} x^2 + \cdots \tag{6}$$

which may be rewritten

$$y = \sum_{N=0}^{\infty} \frac{1}{N!}\left(\frac{d^N y}{dx^N}\right)_{x=0} x^N \tag{7}$$

where we have used the convention that $0! \equiv 1$, that $(d^N y/dx^N)_{x=0}$ is the Nth derivative of the original function evaluated at $x = 0$ and that the zeroth derivative is the function itself. Hence, if we can evaluate the required set of derivatives, we have a straightforward method of computing the values of y as a function of x. In practice, such series solutions will frequently converge fairly rapidly and one does not, of course, have to take an infinite number of terms to compute the function to a prescribed accuracy.

2.6 Taylor Series for e^x [or EXP(X)]

As discussed in introductory courses in calculus, the function e^x has the remarkable property that

$$\frac{d}{dx}(e^x) = e^x \tag{8}$$

where $e = 2.71828\ldots$ is the base of the *natural* or *Naperian*, *logarithms*. That is, the function is equal to its derivative. For that reason, it is especially easy to write a Taylor series for e^x. Because

$$\left[\frac{d^N}{dx^N} e^x\right]_{x=0} = (e^x)_{x=0} = 1 \tag{9}$$

---

[1] Shifting the origin by a in Eq. (6) gives the more general form of the expansion credited to a student of Newton's named Taylor:

$$y(x) = y(a) + \left(\frac{dy}{dx}\right)_{x=a} (x-a)^1 + \frac{1}{2!}\left(\frac{d^2 y}{dx^2}\right)_{x=a} (x-a)^2 + \cdots$$

Whittaker and Watson note that this formal expansion was originally published by Brook Taylor in his *Methodus Incrementorum* in 1715. The result obtained by putting $a = 0$ in Taylor's theorem is usually called *MacLaurin's theorem*; it was first discovered by Stirling in 1717 and published by MacLaurin in 1742 in his *Fluxions*.

the series for e^x is just

$$S = e^x = 1 + x + \frac{x^2}{2!} + \frac{x^3}{3!} + \cdots + \frac{x^N}{N!} + \cdots \tag{10}$$

[i.e., substitute Eq. (9) into Eq. (7)].

Note that the Nth term in this series is simply (x/N) times the $(N-1)$th term; i.e.,

$$A_N = A_{N-1} \cdot \frac{x}{N} \tag{11}$$

where

$$S = A_0 + A_1 + A_2 + \cdots + A_N + \cdots \quad \text{and} \quad A_0 = 1$$

Hence no matter how large a value of x is chosen initially, there will eventually be some term A_N in the series which is negligible compared to the preceding term. Not only does this result mean that the series will converge to a finite limit for arbitrary x; Eq. (11) also provides an efficient rule for computing the series. In particular, note that the values for A_{N-1} and (x/N) can be quite manageable even when x^N and $N!$ separately involve numbers that are too large for your computer to handle. Hence it is much better to use Eq. (11) to evaluate the successive terms in the series than to try to compute

$$A_N = \frac{x^N}{N!}$$

separately for each term in the series.[2]

2.6

PROBLEM 7

Write a program that sums the infinite series for e^x and compares the computed result with the value obtained from the BASIC function EXP(X). Enter the value of X from the keyboard and print the running values of the sum and the increment to the sum for each term using the rule summarized in Eq. (11). Put in a conditional statement which terminates the program at a fractional error compatible with the accuracy of your computer. For example,

IF ABS(A) < 1E − 6 THEN . . .   (print results)

would get your program out of the summation loop when the increment (A) to the series had an absolute value of less than 10^{-6}. See how large a positive value of X your computer can handle in this program. Also note that for sufficiently large negative values of X, the computed series limit will be more seriously in error than for positive values of X having the same magnitude. This effect results from finite rounding errors in the computer and the fact that the terms in the series for negative X alternate in sign. Here the series limit can be very much smaller than terms occurring early in the series, and the rounding errors prevent these terms of alternate sign from canceling out to the extent that they actually should. Note that one can minimize this difficulty for $X < 0$ by computing the series for $-X$ (which now has only positive terms) and by taking the reciprocal of the final sum; i.e., $e^{-X} = 1/e^X$.

---

[2] Most compilers use machine-language subroutines to compute the transcendental functions that truncate the infinite series at a fixed number of terms and evaluate the resultant polynomials using a technique known in high school textbooks as *synthetic substitution*. The method depends on storing a set of coefficients for the polynomial and using the properties of the specific function to limit the domain of the argument entered in the algorithm used to evaluate the polynomial. For example, it is always possible to find a value $N(=Y-X)$ such that

$$e^Y = e^N \cdot e^X$$

where N is an integer and $X \leqslant 1$. Hence, if we store $e = 2.7182818\ldots$ to the requisite number of decimal places as a constant in the program, we can evaluate e^Y for general Y by computing a

To perform a Taylor expansion for the sine and cosine functions, we first need analytic expressions for the derivatives of these functions. Using a well-known identity from trigonometry,

$$\sin(x + \Delta x) = \sin x \cos \Delta x + \cos x \sin \Delta x$$

and the basic definition of the derivative given in Eq. (1), it is seen that

$$\frac{d}{dx}\sin x = \lim_{\Delta x \to 0}\left[\frac{\sin(x + \Delta x) - \sin x}{\Delta x}\right]$$
$$= \lim_{\Delta x \to 0}\left[\frac{\sin x \cos \Delta x + \cos x \sin \Delta x - \sin x}{\Delta x}\right] \qquad (12)$$

The limiting values of $\sin \Delta x$ and $\cos \Delta x$ can be deduced using *Pythagoras' theorem* and the definition of radian angular measure. Consider a right triangle

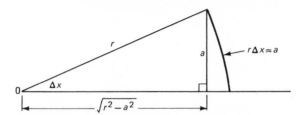

with hypotenuse r and side a opposite to the angle Δx. The circular arc centered at point 0 has length $r \Delta x$ by definition.

Therefore

$$\lim_{\Delta x \to 0}(\cos \Delta x) = \lim_{a \to 0}\left(\frac{\sqrt{r^2 - a^2}}{r}\right) = 1$$

and for small Δx, $\qquad\qquad\qquad\qquad\qquad\qquad\qquad\qquad (13)$

$$\sin \Delta x = \frac{a}{r} \approx \frac{r \Delta x}{r} = \Delta x$$

Hence Eq. (12) reduces to

$$\frac{d}{dx}\sin x = \lim_{\Delta x \to 0}\left(\cos x \frac{\sin \Delta x}{\Delta x}\right) = \cos x \qquad (14)$$

---

polynomial of the type

$$P = 1 + X + \frac{X^2}{2!} + \frac{X^3}{3!} + \frac{X^4}{4!}$$

and noting that $e^Y \approx e^N \cdot P$. For example, a seventh-degree polynomial gives e^X to better than 1 ppm for $X < 1$. One may then write a very efficient algorithm for computing P. If we write the polynomial in the form

$$P = C_0 X^4 + C_1 X^3 + C_2 X^2 + C_3 X^1 + C_4$$

it is seen that

$$P = (((C_0 X + C_1)X + C_2)X + C_3)X + C_4$$

Hence the same multiplicative and additive statements may be built into a very simple loop for evaluating a high-order polynomial, P. For example, if the coefficients $C_1 - C_4$ above were stored in an array C(I), the fourth-degree polynomial could be evaluated through a BASIC program of the type

```
LET P = CØ      (= C₀ above)
FOR I = 1 TO 4
LET P = P*X + C(I)
NEXT I
```

The same procedure may be applied to polynomials of any degree, provided that we can store enough constants to requisite accuracy.

Similarly, by using the trigonometric identity,

$$\cos(x + \Delta x) = \cos x \cos \Delta x - \sin x \sin \Delta x$$

and the limits in Eq. (13), one can show that

$$\frac{d}{dx} \cos x = -\sin x \tag{15}$$

where the angles are again specified in radians.

Having established expressions for the derivatives of $\sin x$ and $\cos x$, we can go on to determine the Taylor series for these functions. For example, assume that $\sin x$ may be written

$$\sin x = C_0 + C_1 x + C_2 x^2 + C_3 x^3 + C_4 x^4 + \cdots \tag{16}$$

Letting $x = 0$ yields

$$C_0 = \sin 0 = 0$$

Taking the derivative of Eq. (16) yields

$$\cos x = C_1 + 2C_2 x^1 + 3C_3 x^2 + 4C_4 x^3 + \cdots \tag{17}$$

and we see that

$$C_1 = \cos 0 = 1$$

Taking the derivative of Eq. (17) yields

$$-\sin x = 2C_2 + 3 \cdot 2C_3 x^1 + 4 \cdot 3C_4 x^2 + \cdots \tag{18}$$

and

$$C_2 = 0$$

Similarly, taking the derivative of Eq. (18) yields

$$-\cos x = 3 \cdot 2 \cdot 1 C_3 + 4 \cdot 3 \cdot 2 C_4 x^1 + \cdots \tag{19}$$

and results in

$$C_3 = -\frac{1}{3!}$$

etc.

Combining results, we obtain an infinite series for the $\sin x$ given by

$$\sin x = x - \frac{x^3}{3!} + \frac{x^5}{5!} - \frac{x^7}{7!} + \cdots \tag{20}$$

where it should be emphasized that x is in radians (π radians $= 180°$).

One could similarly evaluate the coefficients in an infinite series for the cosine function. However, it is much quicker just to take the derivative of Eq. (20) and note that

$$\frac{d}{dx} \sin x = \cos x = 1 - \frac{x^2}{2!} + \frac{x^4}{4!} - \frac{x^6}{6!} + \cdots \tag{21}$$

2.7
PROBLEM 8

Write programs to evaluate the series expansions for the sine and cosine and compare your computed results with the BASIC functions SIN(X) and COS(X). Enter values of X (in radians) from the keyboard and use a conditional statement to terminate the loop at a point compatible with the rounding errors in your computer. Compute each term in the series from the value of the preceding one. Note that it is quite easy to compute both functions simultaneously within the same program. The series are subject to the same difficulties with large values of X as those discussed in the evaluation of e^{-x} in the previous problem. In the case of the sine and cosine functions, one can use the periodicity to advantage in minimizing errors for $|X| > 1$ (i.e., you never really have to get out of the domain $-\pi/2 \leqslant x \leqslant \pi/2$).

Some higher-level programming languages (e.g., "super" BASIC and FORTRAN IV) have explicit provision built in to handle complex numbers. However, not all machines are equipped with these languages, and one might still want to do an occasional problem involving complex numbers on a computer that has only been programmed to handle real numbers (i.e., numbers with no imaginary component).

We shall define a complex number to be one that has the form

$$z = A + iB \tag{22}$$

in which both A and B are real and in which the entity i is defined by

$$i \equiv \sqrt{-1}$$

Hence

$$i^2 = -1, \quad i^3 = -i, \quad i^4 = +1, \quad i^5 = i, \quad \text{etc.} \tag{23}$$

An extremely useful result can be obtained from the Taylor series for e^x, $\cos x$ and $\sin x$. In particular, if we substitute $x = i\theta$ in the expansion for e^x, Eq. (10) becomes

$$e^{i\theta} = 1 + i\theta - \frac{\theta^2}{2!} - i\frac{\theta^3}{3!} + \frac{\theta^4}{4!} + i\frac{\theta^5}{5!} + \cdots \tag{24}$$

through use of Eq. (23). Separating the real and imaginary parts in Eq. (24) then yields

$$e^{i\theta} = 1 - \frac{\theta^2}{2!} + \frac{\theta^4}{4!} + \cdots + i\left(\theta - \frac{\theta^3}{3!} + \frac{\theta^5}{5!} - \cdots\right)$$

or

$$e^{i\theta} = \cos\theta + i\sin\theta \tag{25}$$

by comparison with Eqs. (20) and (21).

We may rewrite our general complex number in Eq. (22) through use of Eq. (25). Specifically, if we define M and θ by

$$z = A + iB \equiv Me^{i\theta} = M\cos\theta + iM\sin\theta \tag{26}$$

it is seen that

$$A = M\cos\theta \quad \text{and} \quad B = M\sin\theta \tag{27}$$

for the real and imaginary parts of Eq. (26) to be equal. Squaring and adding the two requirements in Eq. (27) yields

$$M = \sqrt{A^2 + B^2} \tag{28}$$

where we have used the fact that $\cos^2\theta + \sin^2\theta = 1$. Taking the ratio of the two requirements in Eq. (27), it is seen that

$$\theta = \tan^{-1}(B/A) \tag{29}$$

where we have used the identity, $\tan\theta = \sin\theta/\cos\theta$. Equations (28) and (29) thus permit writing our general complex number $z = A + iB$ in the *polar form*, $z = Me^{i\theta}$. Here the quantity M is known as the *modulus* and θ is a *phase angle*.

It is important to note that, whereas the addition and subtraction of two complex numbers are most appropriately done by expressing the numbers in terms of their separate real and imaginary parts, multiplication and division are best done in polar form. That is, in addition and subtraction, one merely adds or subtracts the real and imaginary parts separately. However, to multiply two complex numbers, $z_1 = M_1 e^{i\theta_1}$ and $z_2 = M_2 e^{i\theta_2}$, it is simpler to evaluate

$$z_1 z_2 = (M_1 M_2) e^{i(\theta_1 + \theta_2)} \tag{30}$$

than to work out

$$z_1 z_2 = (A_1 + iB_1)(A_2 + iB_2) = (A_1 A_2 - B_1 B_2) + i(B_1 A_2 + A_1 B_2) \tag{31}$$

Equation (30) only requires one multiplication and one addition, whereas Eq. (31) requires four multiplications, one addition, and one subtraction. Similar

conclusions hold for the division of two complex numbers and for raising a
complex number to a power.

Chapter 2
More Advanced Programming

2.8
PROBLEM 9

Write a program that evaluates the pth root (i.e., $z^{1/p}$) for a general complex
number

$$z = A + iB$$

where A and B are entered from the keyboard and A, B, and p are real. Use
Eqs. (28) and (29) to express the complex number in polar form and note that,
if $z = Me^{i\theta}$,

$$z^{1/p} = (M^{1/p})e^{i\theta/p}$$

Print out the real and imaginary parts of the final answer. Use the BASIC
function $M\uparrow(1/P)$ to compute the modulus of the result and make sure that you
get the angle in the right quadrant (determined by the separate signs for A and
B). Print out the real and imaginary parts of the result.

The roots of the quadratic equation

$$Y = ax^2 + bx + c$$

occur at

$$X_\pm = \frac{-b \pm \sqrt{b^2 - 4ac}}{2a} \tag{32}$$

and are *real* if

$$b^2 > 4ac$$

degenerate if

$$b^2 = 4ac$$

and *imaginary* if

$$b^2 < 4ac$$

2.9

**Finding Real Roots or Zero
Crossings of Polynomials**

These results (developed initially by the Hindus) are easiest to visualize
graphically in terms of the family of parabolas illustrated in Fig. 2-2.

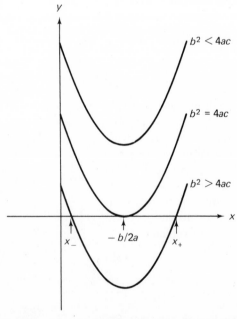

Fig. 2-2. Dependence of the roots of the quadratic equation $y = ax^2 + bx + c$ on
the parameters a, b, and c.

Although analogous formulas for higher-order equations exist in specific cases (e.g., Cardan's formula for the cubic), they are too complicated to be worth the effort in most problems. Generally, it is much easier to find the roots numerically than to set up the complicated closed-form expressions. The numerical method has the virtue of working for polynomials of any degree.

In general, there will be N roots for an Nth-order equation. The complex roots will occur in complex-conjugate pairs (if there are any). The real roots will all represent zero crossings. One can also deduce some aspects of the problem from the limiting behavior at $X \to \pm\infty$, etc.

The most rudimentary kind of program for determining zero crossings merely uses the operator as part of the loop. For example, consider the following program:

```
10   DEF FNY(X) = ...
20   PRINT "X";
30   INPUT X
40   PRINT FNY(X)
50   GO TO 20
100  END
```

Here the specific polynomial is defined with the BASIC function FNY(X) on line 10 and the program depends on the operator's insight. One just keeps feeding in values of X from the keyboard and printing $Y = f(x)$. The (only) advantage of this approach is that it couples all one's previous knowledge and experience into the program with minimum programming effort. With a little practice, zero crossings can be ground out with remarkable speed.

| 2.9 | Use an interactive program of the type discussed in the text to find the real |
| PROBLEM 11 | roots to $y = 5x^5 + 4x^4 + 3x^3 + 2x^2 + x + 1$. |

A more automatic method is, of course, desirable. Consider an approach in which we sweep through some domain of the independent variable in steps of reasonable size and record approximate values of the zero crossings as they occur. We can then develop a reiterative technique based on a Taylor expansion to narrow in on the zero crossings. For this purpose, values of the derivative of the function are needed. One could, of course, compute approximate numerical values of the derivative from two successive values of the function. However, it is generally much faster and more precise to evaluate the derivative in closed form. We shall therefore incorporate two BASIC function statements,

```
10   DEF FNY(X) = ...     [= y(x)]
20   DEF FND(X) = ...     (= dy/dx)
```

defined as the original function and its derivative. We shall then introduce a column array large enough to store all the zero crossings for an Nth-order polynomial,

```
30   DIM Z(...)
```

and use the index J to count the zero crossings as we find them.

```
35   LET J = 1
```

Next we will search a range $X1 < X < X2$ in coarse steps, S, and examine the function at X and $X + S$ to see if it underwent a sign change (therefore zero crossing).

```
37   INPUT X1, X2, S
40   FOR X = X1 TO X2 STEP S
50   LET Y1 = FNY(X)
60   LET Y2 = FNY(X + S)
70   IF SGN(Y1) = SGN(Y2) THEN 200
100  ...
200  NEXT X
```

Recalling that the BASIC function $SGN(X)$ takes the values

$$SGN(X) = \begin{cases} +1 & \text{for } X > 0 \\ 0 & \text{for } X = 0 \\ -1 & \text{for } X < 0 \end{cases}$$

it is clear that line 70 will throw out values $FNY(X)$ and $FNY(X + S)$ which fall on the same side of the x axis. Therefore, the program only gets to line 100 if the function has hit a zero crossing in the interval between X and $X + S$.

Starting on line 100, we will narrow in on the zero crossing reiteratively: first we let $X0 = X$ and compute the derivative in the linear term of a Taylor expansion for the function about the point $X = X0$. Then we compute a required displacement D so that we would land on the zero crossing in one step, D, if the higher terms in the Taylor series were all negligible. We shall probably miss the zero crossing on the first step. However, the process will get more and more accurate as we make more and more interations. Thus we want to find a step D so that

$$0 \equiv f(X0 + D) = f(X0) + (df/dx)_{x0} D$$

Hence

$$D = -f(X0)/(df/dx)_{x0} \tag{33}$$

We then let $X0 = X + D$ and reiterate until $f(X0) = 0$ within a specified limit of error. At that point we will have found the zero crossing and will store it in the array element, $Z(J)$, increment J, and go back to the original search procedure within the domain $X1 < X < X2$. These steps can be incorporated through a series of statements of the type

```
100  LET X0 = X
110  LET Y1 = FNY(X0)
120  IF ABS(Y1) < ... THEN 180
130  LET X1 = FND(X0)
140  IF X1 = 0 THEN 200
150  LET D = -Y1/X1
160  LET X0 = X0 + D
170  GOTO 110
180  LET Z(J) = X0
190  LET J = J + 1
200  NEXT X
```

Line 140 checks to make sure the derivative is not 0. If the slope is zero, we will not get anywhere with the above method, and it is best to choose the point $X0 = X + S$ and start over. Once the criterion is met on accuracy, we store the zero crossing (line 180) and increment J (line 190).

We then go back to the next value of X in the search procedure (line 200). After completing the loop on X, statements of the type

```
FOR I = 1 TO J - 1
PRINT Z(I);
NEXT I
```

list all the zero crossings found.

The method above can be extended to find the maxima and minima as well. We merely need to replace FNY(X) with FND(X) and FND(X) with the second derivative of the function. There will be a tendency to miss points of inflection in this approach unless one rounds off the values of FND(X) using the integer function before comparing the signs. Hence a better conditional check on line 7∅ for determining extrema might be

```
70   IF SGN (INT(FND(X)+.5)) = SGN(INT(FND(X+S)+.5)) THEN 200
```

Then if the step size, S, is suitably chosen, one could land close enough to the point of inflection so that the SGN function = 0 (rather than ±1). Without the rounding, one will most probably step right through the point of inflection, in which case the SGN function will not change its value.

2.9
PROBLEM 12

The probability of finding the electron in the 4s excited state of hydrogen a distance r from the nucleus is proportional to

$$f(r) = \left(1 - \frac{3r}{4} + \frac{r^2}{8} - \frac{r^3}{192}\right)^2 e^{-r/2}$$

where r is in units of the *Bohr radius* ($= 0.529173 \times 10^{-8}$ cm). Find the points where the probability goes to zero.

2.10 Vectors

A vector is a quantity that has both magnitude and direction. Many entities in the three-dimensional world (e.g., force, velocity, and acceleration) possess both magnitude and direction and may be conveniently regarded as vectors. However, the mathematical concepts involved may easily be extended to problems with any number of dimensions.

The primary usefulness of vectors arises from the law for vector addition. Stated in the most elementary way, one does the vector sum

$$\vec{C} = \vec{A} + \vec{B}$$

by drawing the tail of the arrow representing vector $\vec{B}$ at the head of the arrow standing for vector $\vec{A}$:

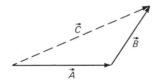

The magnitudes are proportional to the lengths of the arrows and the directions are indicated by the heads of the arrows in the drawing. Because both vectors $\vec{A}$ and $\vec{B}$ have been represented by straight lines, it follows from Euclidean geometry that the two vectors and their resultant, $\vec{C}$, all fall in one plane. One also sees on this simple geometrical level that vector addition obeys the commutative law. that is,

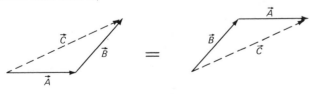

or

$$\vec{C} = \vec{A} + \vec{B} = \vec{B} + \vec{A} \tag{34}$$

For example, no matter in what order you add them, the simultaneous application of two forces $\vec{A}$ and $\vec{B}$ to one point on an object is fully equivalent to applying a single force with new direction and magnitude given by $\vec{C}$ in Eq. (34) at the same point.

One can apply the same geometrical argument to the addition of any number of vectors by breaking the sum up into pairs of coplanar vectors. One thus sees that the final sum is independent of the order in which the individual vectors are added.

The inverse process—that of breaking up a vector into components along a set of prescribed directions—is probably the most useful single technique in vector analysis. Once this decomposition has been effected, the addition (or subtraction)[3] of two or more vectors is accomplished merely by the scalar addition (or subtraction) of their components along the prescribed directions. This process is particularly efficient when the basic directions for the decomposition are mutually orthogonal. For example, breaking up general vectors into components along the orthogonal coordinates of a rectangular (or *Cartesian*) reference frame is especially useful. If we write

$$\vec{A} = A_x\hat{i} + A_y\hat{j} + A_z\hat{k} \quad \text{and} \quad \vec{B} = B_x\hat{i} + B_y\hat{j} + B_z\hat{k} \tag{35}$$

where $\hat{i}$, $\hat{j}$, and $\hat{k}$ are unit vectors along the x, y, and z directions, and where A_x, A_y, and A_z are the components of $\vec{A}$ and B_x, B_y, and B_z are the components of $\vec{B}$ along these dirctions, the addition of $\vec{A}$ and $\vec{B}$ becomes

$$\vec{C} = \vec{A} + \vec{B} = (A_x + B_x)\hat{i} + (A_y + B_y)\hat{j} + (A_z + B_z)\hat{k}$$
$$= C_x\hat{i} + C_y\hat{j} + C_z\hat{k} \tag{36}$$

The resultant vector is then automatically specified in terms of components along the original set of base vectors, $\hat{i}$, $\hat{j}$, and $\hat{k}$.

It is natural to use different rows of the same column array to specify the different components of a vector within a computer program. Specifically, a convention in which the vector $\vec{R}$ is represented by the column array R(I) with

$$R(1) = R_x = \text{component of } \vec{R} \text{ in the } x \text{ direction}$$

$$R(2) = R_y = \text{component of } \vec{R} \text{ in the } y \text{ direction}$$

$$R(3) = R_z = \text{component of } \vec{R} \text{ in the } z \text{ direction}$$

leads to considerable economy in programming statements. One frequently can write a general statement defining the Ith component within a loop in which the index, I, runs over the number of components required.

The *scalar* or *dot product* of the vectors $\vec{A}$ and $\vec{B}$ is defined by

2.11
Scalar or Dot Product

$$\vec{A} \cdot \vec{B} = AB \cos \theta \tag{37}$$

where θ is the angle between the two vectors and A and B are the magnitudes of the two vectors. (Note the "dot" between $\vec{A}$ and $\vec{B}$ on the left side of the equation.) The resultant has magnitude and no direction—hence the name *scalar product*. This product is especially useful in the decomposition of vectors into components along orthogonal axes.

In the case where the vectors $\vec{A}$ and $\vec{B}$ are orthogonal, $\theta = 90°$ and $\vec{A} \cdot \vec{B} = 0$. Similarly, if the two vectors are collinear, $\theta = 0$ and $\vec{A} \cdot \vec{B} = AB$.

---

[3] As with subtraction in ordinary arithmetic, vector subtraction is accomplished by adding a vector of opposite sign (hence direction). thus

$$C = \vec{A} - \vec{B} = \vec{A} + (-\vec{B}) \quad \text{or} \qquad \vec{A} - \vec{B} \qquad = \qquad \vec{A} + (-\vec{B})$$

Clearly, the dot product between any two orthogonal, base vectors is zero; i.e.,

$$\hat{i} \cdot \hat{j} = \hat{j} \cdot \hat{k} = \hat{k} \cdot \hat{i} = 0 \tag{38}$$

where $\hat{i}$, $\hat{j}$, and $\hat{k}$ are the unit vectors along the x, y, and z axes.

Noting that the components of the vector $\vec{A}$ along these axes will be of the form $A \cos \theta_i$ (where θ_i is the angle between $\vec{A}$ and the ith coordinate axis), it is apparent that

$$\vec{A} = (\vec{A} \cdot \hat{i})\hat{i} + (\vec{A} \cdot \hat{j})\hat{j} + (\vec{A} \cdot \hat{k})\hat{k} = A_x\hat{i} + A_y\hat{j} + A_z\hat{k} \tag{39}$$

Finally, note that

$$\vec{A} \cdot \vec{B} = (A_x\hat{i} + A_y\hat{j} + A_z\hat{k}) \cdot (B_x\hat{i} + B_y\hat{j} + B_z\hat{k})$$
$$= A_xB_x + A_yB_y + A_zB_z \tag{40}$$

for any two vectors $\vec{A}$ and $\vec{B}$, because of the orthogonality of the unit base vectors.

Thus if we store the separate components of $\vec{A}$ and $\vec{B}$ (along orthogonal base vectors) as elements in three-rowed column arrays, $A(I)$ and $B(I)$, the dot product $\vec{A} \cdot \vec{B}$ is obtained in a BASIC program of the type

```
10  LET S = 0
20  FOR I = 1 TO 3
30  LET S = A(I)*B(I) + S
40  NEXT I
50  PRINT S
```

(We shall consider a more compact way of evaluating the dot product based on matrix operations in a later section.)

It will be appreciated that the same notions could be applied mathematically to problems having any number of dimensions. That is, as long as the base vectors are all mutually orthogonal, we could compute a generalized dot product for an N-dimensional problem by letting I run from 1 to N on line 20 above. This concept is particularly useful in problems involving expansions in sets of functions which are orthogonal in a purely mathematical sense. Such problems arise in fields ranging in diversity from pattern recognition to literary style analysis.

2.12
Vector or Cross Product

The *vector or cross product* of two vectors $\vec{A}$, $\vec{B}$ is defined by

$$\vec{A} \times \vec{B} = AB \sin \theta \hat{n} = -\vec{B} \times \vec{A} \tag{41}$$

and is a vector in the direction that a right-handed screw would advance when $\vec{A}$ is rotated into $\vec{B}$. ($\hat{n}$ is a unit normal in that direction and is perpendicular to both $\vec{A}$ and $\vec{B}$.) The cross product is particularly useful in setting up orthogonal sets of base vectors.

It is convenient to choose *right-handed coordinate systems*. For example, unit vectors $\hat{i}$, $\hat{j}$, and $\hat{k}$ used to describe the rectangular coordinates x, y, and z are usually chosen so that

$$\hat{i} \times \hat{j} = \hat{k}, \quad \hat{j} \times \hat{k} = \hat{i}, \quad \text{and} \quad \hat{k} \times \hat{i} = \hat{j} \tag{42}$$

In such a rectangular coordinate system, the cross product of two vectors $\vec{A}$

51

and $\vec{B}$ may be shown from the above definition to be equal to a determinant:

$$\vec{A} \times \vec{B} = \begin{vmatrix} \hat{i} & \hat{j} & \hat{k} \\ A_x & A_y & A_z \\ B_x & B_y & B_z \end{vmatrix} = \hat{i}(A_y B_z - B_y A_z) - \hat{j}(A_x B_z - B_x A_z) + \hat{k}(A_x B_y - B_x A_y)$$

$$(43)$$

One of the most powerful aspects of the BASIC language is the ease with which large matrices may be handled. The MAT commands range from purely manipulative operations to ones that perform formidable numerical computations. We shall approach these commands in a gradual manner, starting with the more pedestrian ones first.

**2.13
Matrix Operations in BASIC**

A matrix is a rectangular array of numbers denoted by row and column indices. By convention, the first subscript in a general element in an array of the type

$$\begin{pmatrix} M_{11} & M_{12} & M_{13} & M_{14} \\ M_{21} & M_{22} & M_{23} & M_{24} \\ M_{31} & M_{32} & M_{33} & M_{34} \end{pmatrix}$$

represents the number of the row in which it is found and the second subscript represents the column number. As shown, one starts counting rows and columns from the upper left-hand corner. These subscripts are represented by separate indices in BASIC. Thus the general element M_{IJ} in the above matrix would be denoted by $M(I, J)$ in BASIC and the element would occur in the *I*th row and the *J*th column.

The names for matrices are restricted to single letters of the alphabet in BASIC. Thus one can have 26 separate matrices at most within a given program. However, each matrix can have an enormous number of elements. Unless specifically instructed, the BASIC compiler will set aside room for a 10×10 array when it first encounters a particular matrix in a given program. Dimension statements can be introduced (preferably at the start of a program) to specify the maximum number of array elements in particular matrices. For example, the statement

```
10   DIM M(3,4), N(255,40)
```

would set aside space for a matrix *M* having 3 rows and 4 columns, together with a matrix *N* having 255 rows and 40 columns.

The individual elements may be defined in BASIC through statements of the type

```
LET M(I,J) = ...
```

where I and J are integers varying from 1 to the maximum number consistent with the dimension statements. Matrices may also be read row-wise from the successive numbers in DATA statements through the instruction

```
MAT READ M
```

if the number of rows and columns in $M(I, J)$ is specified in the program. Similarly, the elements stored in a matrix may be printed on the user's terminal with MAT PRINT commands. For example,

```
MAT PRINT M;
```

results in closely spaced row-wise printing of the elements. (Note that if there are more columns in the matrix than the number required to fill the 72-column teletype format, the above instruction results in a carriage return and line advance while each row of the original matrix is printed out.) MAT READ and MAT PRINT commands also may be used on column arrays.

Matrices may be initialized by use of statements of the type

```
MAT M = ZER      (all elements = 0)
MAT M = CON      (all elements = 1)
MAT M = IDN      (all diagonal elements = 1, off diagonal = 0)
```

The above three statements also permit redimensioning the matrix during a program when written in the form

MAT M = ZER (10,15)

provided that the initial dimension statement contains at least as many rows (10) and columns (15). The mnemonics involved in the above three commands are reasonably self-evident: ZER stands for "zero," CON stands for "constant" ($= 1$), and IDN stands for "identity" (as in "identity matrix").

2.13
PROBLEM 13 Write a simple program in which you initialize a matrix M with 4×4 elements using the ZER, CON, and IDN commands. Display the result in each case using the MAT PRINT command.

2.14 Ramanujan Problem

In many instances, matrices are primarily useful as a systematic means for storing computed quantities. In these cases, the symmetry properties and other aspects of the matrix elements may be of more interest than the normal manipulations possible with matrix algebra. One case in point involves the incident of the taxi cab number, 1729, and the young Indian mathematics genius, Srinivasa Ramanujan, who was then dying from tuberculosis and the English climate.

According to C. P. Snow (see the Foreword to Hardy, 1967, p. 37):

"Hardy used to visit him, as he lay dying in hospital at Putney. It was on one of those visits that there happened the incident of the taxi-cab number. Hardy had gone out to Putney by taxi, as usual his chosen method of conveyance. He went into the room where Ramanujan was lying. Hardy, always inept about introducing a conversation, said, probably without a greeting, and certainly as his first remark: 'I thought the number of my taxi-cab was 1729. It seemed to me rather a dull number.' To which Ramanujan replied: 'No, Hardy! No, Hardy! It is a very interesting number. It is the smallest number expressible as the sum of two cubes in two different ways.'"

The object of the problem is to determine the first few members of the set of numbers "expressible as the sum of two cubes in two different ways," that is, integers for which

$$I^3 + J^3 = K^3 + L^3 \tag{44}$$

where $I, J \neq K, L$. The problem has two equally important parts: (1) find a method that works in principle, and (2) make it efficient enough to do the problem in a realistically short time. The reader should be warned that it is not too hard to set this problem up in a way that could take several days of computing time on a high-speed machine. On the other hand, by using various tricks to limit the search, the first two solutions can be found within about 15 seconds using BASIC on a relatively slow computer such as the HP 2116B.

One clearly wants to avoid computing values of I^3 needlessly for different integers. It therefore makes sense to store a number, N, of integers—cubed in an array at the beginning of the program. For example, to check the first solution, 1729, we shall clearly need

$$N \geq (1729)^{1/3} \geq 12$$

The reader will be able to verify that the successive solutions occur at

$$N = 12, 16, 24, 27, 32, 34 \ (2), 36, 39, 40, 48 \ (2), \text{etc.}$$

where the parentheses mean that there are two solutions at $N = 34$ and 48.

Hence as a start on the problem, statements of the type

```
30  FOR I = 1 TO N
40  LET A(I) = I↑3
50  NEXT I
```

will store the necessary array. It is next helpful to define a matrix whose elements are made up by sums of the various possible array elements. For example, the statements

```
 60  FOR I = 1 TO N
 70  FOR J = 1 TO N
 80  LET M(I,J) = A(I) + A(J)
 90  NEXT J
100  NEXT I
```

define more of these matrix elements than we actually need but will help in discussing the problem.

To solve the problem we merely need to find different elements $M(I, J)$ and $M(K, L)$ such that

$$M(I, J) = M(K, L) \tag{45}$$

when the indices I, J and K, L are not trivially related. One could merely start with $M(1, 1)$ and compare that element with every other element; then go on to $M(1, 2)$, and so on. However, the machine running time would increase roughly as N^4 in that approach, and it pays to use some of the properties of the matrix to advantage.

For specific illustration, consider printing out the matrix defined above in a manageable case, for example, with $N = 8$. Incorporation of a

MAT PRINT M;

statement after the above program results in printing the upper left-hand corner of the general matrix shown in Fig. 2-3.

J = I =	1	2	3	4	5	6	7	8
1	2	9	28	65	126	217	344	513
2	9	16	35	72	133	224	351	520
3	28	35	54	91	152	243	370	539
4	65	72	91	128	189	280	407	576
5	126	133	152	189	250	341	468	637
6	217	224	243	280	341	432	559	728
7	344	351	370	407	468	559	686	855
8	513	520	539	576	637	728	855	1024

Fig. 2-3.

2.14
PROBLEM 14

Write a program that computes and prints the matrix defined on line 80 above for $N = 10$. Note the format that results from the

MAT PRINT M,   and   MAT PRINT M; statements.

Next note that the matrix is symmetric about the diagonal. For any solution we find on cne side of the diagonal, there must be a trivially related solution on the other and we do not have to compute, store, or examine more than half the matrix.

Also note that the numbers increase along any row. Hence, if you pick an element on one row, you do not have to compare it with any other element on that same row.

Further, the numbers always increase down the columns. Therefore, if we start a systematic comparison in the upper left-hand corner with the element $M(I, J)$, the comparison only has to be made with elements $M(K, L)$, where K starts on the $(I+1)$th row and runs to the $(J-1)$th row and L starts with the Kth column. The column index L for the Kth row in $M(K, L)$ only has to be advanced to

$$L_{max} \approx (M(I, J) - A(K))^{1/3} + 0.5 \tag{46}$$

because $L^3 + K^3 = M(I, J)$ for the equality to occur (I runs from 1 to N and J from I to N). The additional 0.5 in Eq. (46) is to avoid rounding-error difficulties.

2.14
PROBLEM 15

Write a program to check Ramanujan. Use the limits discussed in connection with Eq. (46) and be cautious about running time. (This one can "break the bank" if you are careless.) Set up the problem for a general, large matrix M and use the

MAT M = ZER(N,N)

command to initialize M. Print $M(I, J)$ and I; J, L; K for each solution. After you are confident that the program works efficiently, calculate the first several solutions.

Next we shall consider some of the more powerful matrix commands—ones that actually do some computing rather than just manipulating arrays of numbers.

Matrix operations in BASIC are performed by MAT instructions analogous to the LET command used with single variables. The instruction

MAT C = ...

applies to every element in the array. The new value of matrix C is set equal, element by element, to the last value of whatever matrix quantity appears on the right side of the equality. In contrast to the LET statement, one cannot use the same matrix on both sides of the = sign in most cases or do more than one MAT operation in the same statement. The reasons for this restriction arise from the economy of storage locations inside the computer. For example, in an operation such as

MAT C = TRN(A)

in which the matrix C becomes the transpose of matrix A, or

$$C(I, J) = A(J, I)$$

the computer would lose half of the elements in the original matrix if it were instructed to let $A(I, J) = A(J, I)$ for all I and J without use of an intermediate storage matrix.

One of the few exceptions to the above restriction occurs in the command

MAT C = (K)*C

2.15
Matrix Algebra

in which the new matrix C on the left is determined from the original one on the right by multiplying each element with the same scalar quantity, K.

Two matrices are added by summing all corresponding elements. Thus the command

$$\text{MAT C} = \text{A} + \text{B}$$

results in

$$C(I, J) = A(I, J) + B(I, J) \tag{47}$$

for every value of I and J. Obviously all three matrices must have the same dimensions.

Similarly, two matrices are subtracted by subtracting corresponding elements. Hence the statement

$$\text{MAT C} = \text{A} - \text{B}$$

results in

$$C(I, J) = A(I, J) - B(I, J) \tag{48}$$

for all values of I and J. Again, the three matrices obviously have to have the same dimensions.

Although we cannot use the same matrix on both sides of the equality for the more-complicated MAT commands, it is a simple matter to redefine matrices by adding more statements to the program. For example, redefining the matrix A to be the sum of the previous matrices A and B is accomplished through the statements

$$\text{MAT C} = \text{A} + \text{B}$$
$$\text{MAT A} = \text{C}$$

Although any of the MAT commands could be duplicated by use of a sufficient number of loops and LET statements, it is useful to recognize that the MAT commands have been previously compiled in machine-language subroutines within the BASIC language. Consequently, they not only require fewer program statements in BASIC, they usually run much faster than equivalent sets of LET statements written out in long form.

2.15
PROBLEM 16

Write a program that permits comparing the running time for the addition of two large matrices using one

$$\text{MAT C} = \text{A} + \text{B}$$

command and equivalent LET $C(I, J) = A(I, J) + B(I, J)$ statements within nested loops for I and J.

The command for matrix multiplication can be one of the most useful ones in BASIC. Multiplication of the matrices A and B is accomplished by the instruction

2.16
Matrix Multiplication

$$\text{MAT C} = \text{A} * \text{B}$$

and follows the standard rule,

$$C(I, J) = \sum_{K=1}^{N} A(I, K) B(K, J) \tag{49}$$

where N is the number of columns in matrix A *and* the number of rows in matrix B. (There are no restrictions on the number of rows in matrix A or the number of columns in matrix B, except those imposed by the dimension statements.) The MAT $C = A*B$ command works out the appropriate summation for *each* element in matrix C.

It is worth emphasizing the power of this simple MAT command by specifying the equivalent statements in normal BASIC required to achieve the same result. For example, suppose that we wanted to read in 1000 values from DATA statements to fill in a 20×50 matrix A (row-wise), 1500 values from subsequent DATA statements to fill in a 50×30 matrix B, and print out the 600 elements in a matrix $(C) = (A)*(B)$. Apart from the DATA statements themselves, the objective is accomplished through the program

```
10    DIM A(20,50),B(50,30),C(20,30)
20    MAT READ A
30    MAT READ B
40    MAT C = A*B
100   MAT PRINT C;
```

in which the semicolon after the MAT PRINT command results in closely spaced printing of the matrix elements. Line 40 in the above program accomplishes the equivalent of the following eight BASIC statements:

```
40    FOR I = 1 TO 20
45    FOR J = 1 TO 30
50    LET C(I,J) = 0
55    FOR K = 1 TO 50
60    LET C(I,J) = C(I,J) + A(I,K)*B(K,J)
65    NEXT K
70    NEXT J
75    NEXT I
```

Because the statement MAT $C = A*B$ makes use of previously compiled machine-language statements, that command is generally executed much more rapidly than would be statements 40 through 75 above. Also note that the upper limits on the FOR statements (lines 40, 45, and 55 above) would automatically be filled in from the dimension statements in the command MAT $C = A*B$. Conversely, if the computer has not been given appropriate dimension statements, it will not know what to do with the command MAT $C = A*B$.

As is apparent from the definition of matrix multiplication, the process is definitely not commutative. One has to be careful about the order of multiplication and there can be substantial differences between the statements

```
40    MAT C = A*B
```

and

```
40    MAT C = B*A
```

In fact, for the specific program given above, MAT $C = B*A$ would not even have been allowed. (The dimensions do not permit multiplication.)

However, the associative and distributive laws are still obeyed. As may be shown from the definitions of matrix multiplication and addition, both

$$A(BC) = (AB)C \quad \text{and} \quad A(B + C) = (AB) + (AC)$$

2.17
Some Useful Tricks with Matrix Multiplication

The fact that the primary definition of matrix multiplication involves a summation immediately suggests some useful shortcuts in a wide variety of problems. Frequently, many programming statements can be avoided and running time can be greatly reduced by setting up summations as matrix products. A few examples will clarify the advantage.

Consider the extreme situation where we merely want to add up all the numbers in a long DATA statement. For specific example, suppose that there are 250 numbers in the series of DATA entries. We can accomplish the summation with MAT commands if we introduce a few specially dimensioned matrices:

```
10    DIM S(1,1),A(250,1),B(1,250)
```

Matrix S will consist of one element in which we shall compute the desired sum. We can initially read the DATA statements into matrix A (which is literally equivalent to a column array with 250 rows)[4] with the statement

```
20   MAT READ A
```

and prepare a row matrix B (having 250 columns) by the statement

```
30   MAT B = CON
```

which defines every element equal to unity. The sum is then obtained through the statements

```
40   MAT S = B*A
50   MAT PRINT S
```

[i.e., apply the definition of matrix multiplication summarized in Eq. (49)]. Here we have merely multiplied each element in A by unity and have only used the rule for matrix multiplication to do the summation. The economy in programming statements is debatable in this particular case; however, considerable saving in running time over straightforward summation can be obtained on long sums (especially with minicomputers in which each line in the BASIC program is interpreted sequentially while the program is running).

A fuller utilization of the power of matrix multiplication is obtained in the evaluation of scalar products of row and column matrices (especially in cases where there is a large number of elements in the arrays). For example, suppose that we wanted to compute the generalized dot (or scalar) product of two vectors having 100 projections (or components) on orthogonal axes. Assuming that the values for the components of these two vectors have been entered sequentially in DATA statements elsewhere in the program, we can get the data into the program by statements of the type

```
10   DIM A(100,1),B(1,100),S(1,1)
20   MAT READ A
30   MAT READ B
```

We again dimension S to represent a matrix with one element and compute the desired scalar product [Eq. (40)] through the command

```
50   MAT S = B*A
```

That is, $S(1, 1) = \sum B(1, J) A(J, 1)$ by definition (49).

As a variant on the above approach, one could enter both sets of data in column matrix format and then transpose one matrix prior to the multiplication command. For example,

```
10   DIM A(100,1),B(100,1),C(1,100),S(1,1)
20   MAT READ A
30   MAT READ B
40   MAT C = TRN(A)
50   MAT S = C*B
```

accomplishes the same result as the previous program.

2.17
PROBLEM 17 Write a program that permits the operator to enter a large N-bit binary integer one digit at a time and which then prints the base 10 equivalent of the number. Do the problem by a MAT multiplication command; e.g., store the binary digits in a row matrix and the values of 2^M (for $0 \le M \le N$) in a column matrix. The decimal equivalent is then given by the product of the two matrices.

---

[4] BASIC tacitly treats column arrays as column matrices in all MAT commands. One could have written DIM $A(250)$ instead of DIM $A(250, 1)$.

One very frequent application of matrix algebra occurs in the solution of simultaneous linear equations. Consider the set of equations

$$y_1 = a_{11}x_1 + a_{12}x_2 + \cdots + a_{1N}x_N$$

$$y_2 = a_{21}x_1 + a_{22}x_2 + \cdots + a_{2N}x_N$$

$$\vdots \tag{50}$$

$$y_N = a_{N1}x_1 + a_{N2}x_2 + \cdots + a_{NN}x_N$$

involving N unknown quantities $(x_1, x_2, \ldots, x_N)$, N known quantities $(y_1, y_2, \ldots, y_N)$, and a set of $N \times N$ known coefficients $(a_{11}, a_{12}, \ldots, a_{NN})$.

Such equations may be solved by hand through a well-known and extremely tedious method based on the evaluation of determinants: one first computes the determinant of the coefficients

$$\det A = \begin{vmatrix} a_{11} & a_{12} & \cdots & a_{1N} \\ a_{21} & a_{22} & \cdots & a_{2N} \\ \vdots & & & \\ & & & \\ & & & \\ a_{N1} & a_{N2} & \cdots & a_{NN} \end{vmatrix} \tag{51}$$

and (assuming the above determinant is not equal to zero, or "singular"), the unknown quantities are given by

$$x_1 = \frac{\begin{vmatrix} y_1 & a_{12} & \cdots & a_{1N} \\ y_2 & a_{22} & \cdots & a_{2N} \\ \vdots & & & \\ & & & \\ & & & \\ y_N & a_{N2} & \cdots & a_{NN} \end{vmatrix}}{\det A}, \quad x_2 = \frac{\begin{vmatrix} a_{11} & y_1 & \cdots & a_{1N} \\ a_{21} & y_2 & \cdots & a_{2N} \\ \vdots & & & \\ & & & \\ & & & \\ a_{N1} & y_N & \cdots & a_{NN} \end{vmatrix}}{\det A}, \quad \text{etc.} \tag{52}$$

Although the approach is not too bad for evaluating two or three simultaneous equations, hand analysis is distinctly painful for N much greater than 3. One very great virtue of a programming language such as BASIC is that an equivalent analysis can be very concisely handled by MAT operations. First, note that the original set of linear equations (50) can be expressed as one matrix equation,

$$(Y) = (A)(X) \tag{53}$$

provided both Y and X are column matrices with N rows and A is a square matrix with N rows and columns. That is, we define the matrix elements so that

$$Y(I, 1) = y_I, \quad X(I, 1) = x_I, \quad \text{and} \quad A(I, J) = a_{I,J} \tag{54}$$

in the initial set of linear equations. Then from the definition of matrix multiplication in Eq. (49),

$$Y(I, 1) = \sum_{J=1}^{N} A(I, J)X(J, 1) \quad \text{for } I = 1 \text{ to } N$$

and the original set of equations (50) is contained within successive rows of the matrix equation (53). We, of course, have to dimension these matrices appropriately in a computer program and somehow get the numerical values in for the known elements. Once these preliminary operations have been performed, the set of equations is solved "merely" by inverting the matrix $A(I, J)$.

The inverse (A^{-1}) of the matrix (A) satisfies the requirement that

$$(A^{-1})*(A) = (1) = (A)*(A^{-1}) \tag{55}$$

Here **(1)** is the identity matrix

$$(1) = \begin{pmatrix} 1 & 0 & 0 & 0 & 0 & \cdots \\ 0 & 1 & 0 & 0 & 0 & \cdots \\ 0 & 0 & 1 & 0 & 0 & \cdots \\ 0 & 0 & 0 & 1 & 0 & \cdots \\ 0 & 0 & 0 & 0 & 1 & \cdots \\ \cdot & \cdot & \cdot & \cdot & \cdot & \cdots \end{pmatrix} \tag{56}$$

and has the property that

$$(A)*(1) = (A) = (1)*(A) \tag{57}$$

where enough rows and columns on the identity matrix are used to satisfy the requirements of the summation in the definition of matrix multiplication.

If we multiply our original matrix equation (53) through from the left by A^{-1}, it is seen that

$$(A^{-1})(Y) = (A^{-1}A)(X) = (1)(X) = (X)$$

where we have used Eqs. (55) and (57). Hence the solution to the original set of equations is contained in the statement

$$(X) = (A^{-1})(Y) \tag{58}$$

In order to get the inverse matrix, one has to do something which is formally equivalent to the determinant solution (52) of the original linear equations (50). One of the great virtues of the BASIC language is that a machine-language program is built into the compiler which does all this dull tedium for us. The command

MAT B = INV(A)

(assuming that B is appropriately dimensioned) causes the computer to go off into machine language and return a small fraction of a second later with the inverted matrix. One must keep in mind, however, that the computer will run into the same restrictions that a human would encounter in solving the same set of equations by hand. Namely, if the determinant of $A = 0$ (or is made equal to zero due to rounding errors), the computer will not be able to invert the matrix and will return with an error-diagnostic message instead (e.g., "MAT SINGU-LAR IN LINE...").

Suppose, for instance, that we want to solve four simultaneous equations for which the numerical values of $Y(I, 1)$ and $A(I, J)$ have been entered row-wise in DATA statements. The following program accomplishes the objective:

```
10  DIM X(4,1),Y(4,1),A(4,4),B(4,4)
20  MAT READ Y
30  MAT READ A
40  MAT B = INV(A)
50  MAT X = B*Y
60  MAT PRINT X;
```

Assuming that MAT B is not singular, the solution is printed on line 60.

If we have no more than 10 simultaneous equations to solve, specific DIM statements (such as those on line 10 above) are not required. However, we still must use some command [e.g., MAT $X = ZER(N, 1)$] to indicate the required number of rows and columns in each matrix in the program.

2.19 Economics and Matrix Inversion

The celebrated input–output theory of economics developed by Wassily Leontief and others consists largely of an exercise in matrix inversion. One assumes that one can apply a set of linear equations to relate the output production and input requirements in an isolated economic system. Once adequate numerical coefficients have been determined for the system, the method provides quantitative answers for production input necessary to achieve specified net output objectives in a controlled economy. In any real system, a tremendous number of interrelated production activities would have to be included, and the success of the approach would depend both on the accuracy of the measured numerical coefficients and the ability to invert high-order matrices. Further, the validity of the assumption of linearity in such a system is not obvious, and the long-term reliability of the approach is somewhat tenuous. (For example, it would be very hard to allow quantitatively for the nonlinear effects that will inevitably result from the depletion of fossil fuels.) However, on a short-term basis involving small changes in a closed economic system with a relatively small number of variables, the method appears to have useful potential.

For the sake of a specific example, consider an economic system composed of the following four industries: a dairy farm, a high-protein-feed producer, an electric power company, and an oil refinery. These industries are mutually dependent and in some cases consume a significant fraction of their own output. For example, an efficient dairy farm requires high-protein cattle feed as well as electricity and tractor fuel for operation. It also consumes milk. (Newborn calves are required both to replace older cows and to stimulate the flow of milk in adult cows.) Similarly, the work force in all four of these industries consumes milk at a rate that should be proportional to the number of man-hours expended, and in two of the remaining industries some of the output has to be fed back into the input to "prime the pump."

The easiest way to specify the interdependence of the four industries quantitatively is to ask what inputs are required from the four industries for unit gross output in each case. Suppose, for example, that a gross output of 1 gallon of milk from the dairy industry requires the following input on the average:

> 0.035   gallon of milk
>
> 2.34   pounds of high-protein feed
>
> 0.58   kilowatt-hour of electrical power
>
> 0.0083 gallon of tractor fuel

and that equivalent data are available for the other industries.[5] If we assume that the equations describing the economic system are linear (i.e., depend only on the first powers of the variables), we can add all such data sets in one matrix equation.

Specifically, we might relate the required input quantities (I) to the gross output quantities (G) through a square matrix (M) containing the coefficients characteristic of the industries:

$$
\begin{pmatrix} I_1 \\ \text{(gal)} \\ I_2 \\ \text{(lb)} \\ I_3 \\ \text{(kWh)} \\ I_4 \\ \text{(gal)} \end{pmatrix} = \begin{pmatrix} 0.035\,\frac{\text{gal}}{\text{gal}} & 0.00006\,\frac{\text{gal}}{\text{lb}} & 0.000015\,\frac{\text{gal}}{\text{kWh}} & 0.00007\,\frac{\text{gal}}{\text{gal}} \\ 2.34\,\frac{\text{lb}}{\text{gal}} & 0\,\frac{\text{lb}}{\text{lb}} & 0\,\frac{\text{lb}}{\text{kWh}} & 0\,\frac{\text{lb}}{\text{gal}} \\ 0.58\,\frac{\text{kWh}}{\text{gal}} & 0.01\,\frac{\text{kWh}}{\text{lb}} & 0.12\,\frac{\text{kWh}}{\text{kWh}} & 0.01\,\frac{\text{kWh}}{\text{gal}} \\ 0.0083\,\frac{\text{gal}}{\text{gal}} & 0.0018\,\frac{\text{gal}}{\text{lb}} & 0.075\,\frac{\text{gal}}{\text{kWh}} & 0.1\,\frac{\text{gal}}{\text{gal}} \end{pmatrix} \begin{pmatrix} G_1\,^{\text{milk}}_{\text{(gal)}} \\ G_2\,^{\text{feed}}_{\text{(lb)}} \\ G_3\,^{\text{power}}_{\text{(kWh)}} \\ G_4\,^{\text{fuel}}_{\text{(gal)}} \end{pmatrix}
$$

---

[5] The dairy data used here are based on a New York State farm operated by John Bruise (see *The New York Times*, Nov. 23, 1974, p. 64, cols. 3–8). The author is indebted to Mrs. Bruise for a helpful discussion of the economics of dairy farming and to Mr. Klebanow of Maxim Mills for information regarding the economics of high-protein-feed production. The data on electric power and fuel industries are estimates from miscellaneous reports during the fall of 1974.

This equation may be abbreviated

$$(I) = (M)(G) \tag{59}$$

in which (I) and (G) are four-rowed column matrices and (M) is the large 4×4 square matrix. Because there are a lot of different units involved in this equation, the units have been written explicitly. The diagonal elements in M are all dimensionless. However, the off-diagonal elements involve quantities such as gallons of milk per gallon of fuel, pounds of feed per kilowatt-hour, etc. Note that the columns in the matrix M represent the required inputs for unit gross output of the different gross products in array G. Specifically, if we let $G_1 = 1$ gallon of milk and let $G_2 = G_3 = G_4 = 0$, we get the set of required input quantities for the dairy industry (0.035 gallon of milk, 2.34 pounds of feed, 0.58 kilowatt-hour, and 0.0083 gallon of tractor fuel). Similarly, if we let $G_2 = 1$ pound of high-protein feed and $G_1 = G_3 = G_4 = 0$, we get the required input quantities for the feed industry for unit gross output; i.e., 0.00006 gallon of milk (from the man-hour equivalent), 0.01 kilowatt-hour and 0.0018 gallon of fuel (assumed for the present discussion to be the same as tractor fuel) are required to produce 1 pound of feed.

The *net* output (O) is then given by the matrix equation

$$O = G - I \tag{60}$$

where all quantities are four-rowed column matrices and our basic relation becomes (after substituting $O + I$ for G)

$$I = M*(O + I) \tag{61}$$

We may solve the latter equation by computing the inverse matrix for M (i.e., by computing M^{-1}) and by multiplying through from the left by M^{-1}. That is,

$$M^{-1}*I = M^{-1}*M*(O + I) = (\mathbf{1})*(O + I) = O + I \tag{62}$$

where $(\mathbf{1})$ is the identity matrix. Hence the matrix containing the net output quantities (O) for the input quantities (I) is given by

$$O = M^{-1}*I - I = (M^{-1} - \mathbf{1})*I \tag{63}$$

Finally, by inverting the matrix $(M^{-1} - \mathbf{1})$, we can determine the required input quantities (I) necessary to result in a specified net output (O). That is,

$$I = (M^{-1} - \mathbf{1})^{-1}*O \tag{64}$$

where $\mathbf{1}$ again stands for the identity matrix (a square matrix containing ones on the diagonal and zeros everywhere else). In the last equation, two matrix inversions are to be performed: first we invert the matrix M; then we subtract the identity matrix; and then we invert the resultant matrix. The last equation tells what amounts must be plugged back into the industry to give the specified net output.

2.19
PROBLEM 18
Using the numerical values for the matrix M given in Eq. (59) for the four-industry economic system, compute the necessary input quantities to result in a net output of 10,000 gallons of milk, 100,000 pounds of protein-enriched feed, 1,000,000 kilowatt-hours, and 200,000 gallons of fuel [i.e., solve Eq. (64)].

One of the major accomplishments with the early von Neumann computer was the development of efficient algorithms for the inversion of high-order matrices (see von Neumann and Goldstine, 1947). Unfortunately, there is

2.20
Practical Limitations on Matrix Inversion

considerable variation from one BASIC compiler to the next in the accuracy with which matrix inversion is carried out, and few systems have been set up with the sort of capability that was programmed into the von Neumann machine.

The point at which "singularities" in the matrix-inversion process occur is strongly dependent on the nature of the original matrix, the number of bits used by the computer in evaluating the mantissa of floating-point numbers, and the particular inversion algorithm. About all the remote-access time-sharing user can do is to treat the particular computer available as a "black box" and see what it will do. In this process it is useful to have a standard test to perform and a feeling for what representative computers are capable of doing. Generally, one is not too concerned with the time required to accomplish the inversion; usually, one is more concerned with whether or not the inversion can be accomplished at all.

One particularly useful test consists of seeing how large an $N \times N$ matrix of the type

$$M = \begin{pmatrix} 1 & \frac{1}{2} & \frac{1}{3} & \cdots & 1/N \\ \frac{1}{2} & \frac{1}{3} & \frac{1}{4} & \cdots & 1/(N+1) \\ \frac{1}{3} & \frac{1}{4} & \frac{1}{5} & \cdots & 1/(N+2) \\ \cdot & & & & \\ \cdot & & & & \\ \cdot & & & & \\ 1/N & 1/(N+1) & \cdots & \cdots & 1/(2N-1) \end{pmatrix} \qquad (65)$$

in which

$$M(I, J) = \frac{1}{(I+J-1)} \qquad (66)$$

can be inverted with the particular computer. This matrix (known as a *Hilbert matrix*) provides a good challenge to an inversion subroutine simply because the elements get closer and closer together as N becomes large.

The results obtained by the author in inverting this matrix on different machines in BASIC have been somewhat surprising. There is a natural tendency to assume that the bigger the machine, the bigger the matrix one should be able to invert. It is usually true that one can invert a larger Hilbert matrix by running the same machine in *extended precision* (i.e., using more bits per number). However, the way in which the bits used for each number are split up between mantissa and exponent is left to the whim of the person who originally designed the compiler. For example, it was somewhat astonishing to learn that the version of BASIC available on the Yale University IBM 370 supergiant could not invert more than a 4×4 Hilbert matrix in normal precision, whereas a little Hewlett-Packard 2100 series minicomputer could invert at least a 5×5 Hilbert matrix running in BASIC (using a 24-bit mantissa). Running the IBM 370 in extended precision would still only invert a 7×7 Hilbert matrix, whereas a test on a relatively modest Hewlett-Packard 3000 time-sharing BASIC system indicated that as large as a 12×12 Hilbert matrix could be inverted in *long precision*. (The H.-P. 3000 BASIC would actually return numerical values for the inverse of a 50×50 Hilbert matrix. However, occasional off-diagonal elements of $(M^{-1}M)$ were much greater than unity in that instance.) This aspect of life, of course, has relatively little to do with the inherent power of the machine; it is more a question of how the computing power has been applied in the design of individual compilers. However, it can have a very strong bearing on the suitability of a particular time-sharing system for handling the sort of problem that you want to analyze.

63

Using the definition of the Hilbert matrix in Eq. (66), see how large a Hilbert matrix your particular computer will invert. As a check, multiply the inverse times the original matrix and print out the result. (Ideally, the result should have 1s on the diagonal and zeros everywhere else. The departure from zero of the off-diagonal terms is a measure of the error in the computation.)

Because integration is defined formally as the inverse of differentiation, closed-form expressions for integrals are usually obtained through hindsight. For example, because we already know from Eq. (2) that

**2.21
Integration**

$$\frac{d}{dx}(x^m) = mx^{m-1}$$

if we were told that

$$\frac{dy}{dx} = mx^{m-1} \tag{67}$$

we would expect that the function $y(x)$ was originally given by

$$y = x^m + \text{constant} \tag{68}$$

We would not be able to determine the constant in Eq. (68) without additional information. Whatever the constant might have been, its derivative would be zero. Hence, we cannot deduce its value merely from the information in Eq. (67).

The process of determining the result in Eq. (68) from Eq. (67) is known as *integration* and frequently would be written

$$y = \int^y dy = \int^x mx^{m-1}\, dx = x^m + \text{constant}$$

Here we have rewritten the derivative

$$dy = mx^{m-1}\, dx$$

and then *integrated*.

If one can pick out a closed-form expression for the integral of a function (as done in the example), there is usually little point in doing a numerical integration with a computer. However, there are many functions that simply cannot be integrated in closed form. For example, the function itself might only be available through numerical evaluation on a point-by-point basis. In such cases, the computer becomes an indispensible tool for determining integrals.

It is easiest to construct programs to do integrals if the area interpretation of integrals is kept in mind. In particular, consider a function $y = f(x)$ which we would like to integrate in respect to x (see Fig. 2-4).

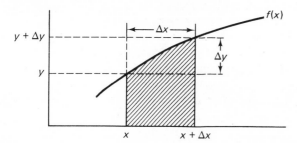

Fig. 2-4.

Let us assume that the function $A = A(x)$ exists such that ΔA represents the area between x and $x + \Delta x$ and between $y = 0$ and $y = f(x)$ (i.e., the shaded area in Fig. 2-4). Obviously,

$$y\, \Delta x < \Delta A < (y + \Delta y)\, \Delta x$$

or

$$y < \frac{\Delta A}{\Delta x} < y + \Delta y$$

Therefore, in the limit that $\Delta x \to 0$, $y = dA/dx$. Hence

$$dA = y\, dx \quad \text{and} \quad A = \int dA = \int^{x} y\, dx$$

represents the area under the curve $y = f(x)$ up to the point x. The constant of integration clearly involves the point from which we start measuring the area. Also note that the area can be positive or negative depending on the extent to which the curve for $y = f(x)$ falls above or below the x axis. The fact that the rate of change of area under the curve is equal to the integrand evaluated at the point x is frequently called the *Fundamental Theorem of Calculus*.

Because digital computers work problems numerically, they can only evaluate "definite" integrals. As an example, suppose that we want to specify the area under the curve $y = f(x)$ between the points $x = a$ and $x = b$. We would write this quantity as the difference between two integrals,

2.22
Definite Integrals

$$\int^{x=b} y\, dx - \int^{x=a} y\, dx \equiv \int_{a}^{b} y\, dx \tag{69}$$

in which the (same) constant of integration would cancel out. (The final notation used at the right to describe the definite integral was originally introduced by Joseph von Fourier in his early-nineteenth-century paper on the theory of heat flow.)

We can do such definite integrals with a computer by breaking up the interval into a large number of increments and by adding up approximate values for each of the small area elements. The accuracy of such a computation will generally increase with both the number of area elements used and the accuracy with which they are determined.

For example, to do the definite integral $\int_{a}^{b} f(x)\, dx$, we could lay out n equally spaced points along the x-axis with a constant separation

$$\Delta x = \frac{x_n - x_1}{n - 1}$$

Then $x_1 = a$ and $x_n = b$ and we want to do the integral

$$I = \int_{x_1}^{x_n} f(x)\, dx \tag{70}$$

by means of a summation over the $(n-1)$ intervals of width Δx.

At the simplest extreme, one might assume the value of y to be constant over each interval. For example, if we merely assumed that $y = y_1 = f(x_1)$ for $x_1 \leq x \leq x_2$, $y = y_2 = f(x_2)$ for $x_2 \leq x \leq x_3$, and so on, we would obtain a sort of zeroth-order approximation to the integral which is particularly easy to evaluate:

$$I_0 \approx (y_1 + y_2 + y_3 + \cdots + y_{n-1})\, \Delta x \tag{71}$$

The approximation turns the curve into a "staircase" and clearly underestimates the area elements when the curve goes up and overestimates the area elements when the curve goes down (see Fig. 2-5). Corrections through at least one more order of sophistication are easy to make and there usually is little excuse for leaving the problem at the zeroth approximation represented by Eq. (71). (Note that the zeroth approximation can easily be accomplished using MAT multiplication commands.)

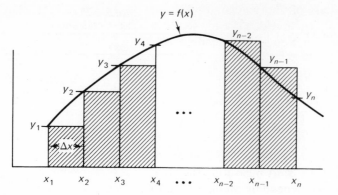

Fig. 2-5.

The next level of approximation is that known as the *Trapezoidal Rule.* Here we just draw straight-line segments between the successive points and add up the areas of all the trapezoids so produced (see Fig. 2-6). This method

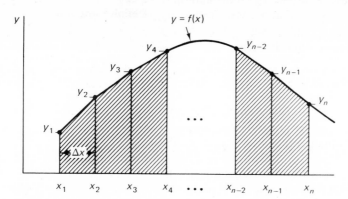

Fig. 2-6.

is equivalent to taking the average value, $\bar{y}$, of the function over each successive interval and calculating the sum of the terms $\bar{y} \, \Delta x$. The result for the integral in this case is

$$I_1 = 0.5(y_1 + y_2) \, \Delta x + 0.5(y_2 + y_3) \, \Delta x + \cdots + 0.5(y_{n-1} + y_n) \, \Delta x$$

$$= (y_1 + y_2 + y_3 + \cdots + y_{n-1}) \, \Delta x + 0.5(y_n - y_1) \, \Delta x$$

$$= I_0 + 0.5(y_n - y_1) \, \Delta x \tag{72}$$

where

$$\Delta x = \frac{x_n - x_1}{n-1}$$

Note that the result for the Trapezoidal Rule differs only by the term $0.5(y_n - y_1) \, \Delta x$ from the zeroth-order approximation in Eq. (71) and that this additional correction adds a negligible amount of computing time to the problem when n is large. Also note that the additional correction vanishes identically when $y_n = y_1$ (as occurs, for example, when the function is periodic in the distance, $x_n - x_1$).

In progressively higher-order approximations to the problem, one fits still-higher-order curves through progressively larger numbers of points. Thus the next level of approximation, known as *Simpson's rule,* consists of fitting parabolas through successive groups of three points and of doing an integration of the three-point parabolas in closed form. Current ramifications of this technique go under the heading *spline interpolation* (see for example, Schultz, 1972).

It is useful to note that the increasing orders of approximation outlined above amount formally to expanding the initial function in a Taylor series in Δx, over each interval Δx. Thus the zeroth approximation uses the leading term [dependence on $(\Delta x)^0$], the Trapezoidal Rule involves a first-order correction [dependence on $(\Delta x)^1$], Simpson's rule involves a second-order correction [dependence on $(\Delta x)^2$], and so on. Consequently, the error neglected in each approximation involves the next-higher power of Δx. For example, we are neglecting errors of order $(\Delta x)^2$ in the expansion for the integrand when we apply the Trapezoidal Rule. One can generally reduce this error to a prescribed level by taking sufficiently small intervals. Consequently, the higher-order approximations are only valuable for the computer analysis of integrals when they result in a shorter running time for the same accuracy. In most cases, it is both cheaper and more convenient merely to increase the number of points using the Trapezoidal Rule than to invoke the next-higher-order approximation with the original number of points. For that reason, we shall not bother here with anything more complicated than the Trapezoidal Rule.

2.22
PROBLEM 20

The Trapezoidal Rule will be least reliable in regions where the first derivative of the integrand is negligible compared to higher derivatives. Investigate this effect by writing programs to evaluate

$$\int_0^1 x^m \, dx = \frac{1}{m+1} \quad \text{and} \quad \int_1^2 x^m \, dx = \frac{2^{m+1}-1}{m+1}$$

For example, how many numerical integration intervals do you need for $m = 2$ in each case to get the answer within 0.1 percent? Note the oscillatory nature of error with decreasing interval size (which arises from rounding errors).

2.23
Pattern Recognition and Integration

Pattern recognition represents a potentially important area of computer application in problems ranging in diversity from the identification of letters on a printed page to the analysis of microscope slides for the presence of precancerous cell nuclei.

One approach to the problem consists of expanding the unknown "function" (which might be computed from the intensity distribution in scanning a photograph) in a set of *orthogonal functions* and then categorizing the sequence of expansion coefficients so obtained. Two functions, $f_n(x)$ and $f_m(x)$, are said to be orthogonal over the interval $0 \le x \le 1$ if

$$\int_0^1 f_n(x)f_m(x) \, dx = 0 \quad \text{for} \quad n \ne m \tag{73}$$

and are normalized over this interval if

$$\int_0^1 [f_m(x)]^2 \, dx = 1 \quad \text{for all } m \tag{74}$$

A set of functions satisfying the combined properties (73) and (74) is said to be *orthonormal*. (We shall limit the discussion to real functions.) Suppose, for example, that $V(x)$ represents the reflected light intensity from a printed page as seen through a vertical slit one line high as the slit scans the horizontal space occupied by one letter. For convenience, we shall assume that the space occupied by one letter is normalized to the interval $0 \le x \le 1$. We could then define a set of coefficients C_n by the requirement that

$$V(x) \equiv \sum_n C_n f_n(x) \quad \text{for } 0 \le x \le 1 \tag{75}$$

The specific values of C_n may be computed as follows. We first multiply Eq. (75) by $f_m(x)$ and then integrate both sides of the equation over the region from $x = 0$ to 1. Because of the orthogonality of the functions, $f_n(x)$, all terms in the sum vanish except that involving C_m. Therefore,

$$\int_0^1 V(x)f_m(x)\,dx = C_m \int_0^1 [f_m(x)]^2\,dx = C_m \tag{76}$$

where the last simplification is permitted by the normalization of the functions. That is, the conditions of orthonormality summarized in Eqs. (73) and (74) were used to obtain Eq. (76) from Eq. (75).

The expansion used in Eq. (75) is analogous to finding the components of a vector along different orthogonal axes. In principle, one can only make the statement in Eq. (75) for a general function $V(x)$ if the set of orthogonal functions, $f_n(x)$, is *complete*. In other words, there is no guarantee that just because a particular set of functions is orthogonal, a sum such as that in Eq. (75) will add up precisely to a general function, $V(x)$, defined over the same interval. Analogously, one cannot expect to reconstruct a general three-dimensional vector just by use of an orthogonal pair of base vectors contained in a plane. However, Eq. (76) for the general expansion coefficients is perfectly well defined even if we do not choose to invoke it for all the members of a complete set. The usefulness of the method as applied to the pattern-recognition problem, in fact, depends on our ability to choose a convenient set of orthogonal functions which can be used to identify a large number of different intensity distributions with a *small* number of expansion coefficients. For example, we could indeed use the projection coefficients of a three-dimensional vector within a two-dimensional plane to classify the orientation of the vector if the length of the vector were constant. In that instance, two expansion coefficients could be used to categorize an infinite number of orientations in three dimensions. Similarly, if two expansion coefficients permit distinguishing unambiguously among 100 different printed characters, they provide a useful basis for character identification even if they could not be used alone to reconstruct the shape of the characters. On the other hand, if it were to take 100 expansion coefficients to identify 100 characters, we might as well forget the expansion-coefficient method and merely match up the character intensity distributions themselves. Two orthogonal functions of opposite symmetry provide the best bet for the most concise identification.

It is desirable to choose the different pattern functions $V(x)$ so that they all satisfy a common normalization condition of the type

$$\int_0^1 [V(x)]^2\,dx = 1 \tag{77}$$

In this case, it follows from Eqs. (73)–(75) that

$$\int_0^1 [V(x)]^2\,dx = \sum_m \sum_n C_m C_n \int_0^1 f_m(x)f_n(x)\,dx = \sum_m C_m^2 = 1 \tag{78}$$

when the final sum goes over a complete set. The exact value of the normalization constant in Eq. (77) is not of real consequence. The important thing is that the generalized vectors corresponding to the different pattern functions all be of the same length. In that case we have the best chance of categorizing different patterns on the basis of a few projection coefficients C_m out of those for the complete set. Identification of a particular unknown pattern distribution $V'(x)$ amounts to finding a particular known subset of expansion coefficients C_m such that

$$C'_m = C_m$$

within some arbitrarily chosen degree of accuracy for each member m of the subset, where

$$C'_m = \int_0^1 V'(x) f_m(x)\, dx$$

and $V'(x)$ also satisfies Eq. (77). The only remaining problem consists of choosing a suitable set of orthogonal functions to use in our equations.

Walsh (1923) developed a complete set of orthonormal functions which are especially useful in the pattern identification problem. These functions are defined over the interval $0 \leq x \leq 1$ and take on the values $+1$ or -1. They may

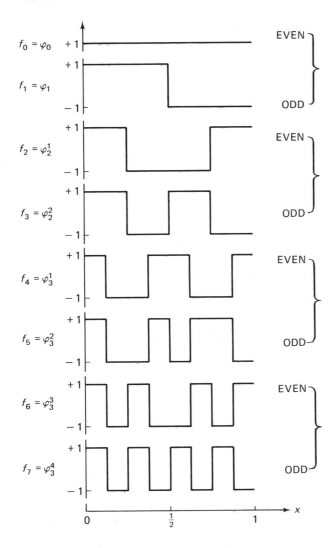

Fig. 2-7. The first few Walsh functions, arranged in even and odd symmetric pairs and increasing numbers of sign changes within the interval $0 \leq x \leq 1$.

be arranged in pairs of functions having even- and odd-symmetry about the point $x = \frac{1}{2}$ and increasing numbers of sign changes (see Fig. 2-7). We have used a simplified notation $f_n(x)$ to describe these functions in which the subscript n denotes the number of sign changes over the domain of the function. Walsh originally specified these functions in the notation $\phi_n^k(x)$, where the two indices n and k were used in a systematic method to generate the functions.

Because the basic prescription given by Walsh to evaluate these functions is awkward to implement on a computer, we give the following algorithm for computing the functions $f_n(x)$ over the interval $0 \leq x \leq 1$:

1. Do a binary expansion of the variable x in the form

$$x = \frac{a_1}{2^1} + \frac{a_2}{2^2} + \frac{a_3}{2^3} + \cdots + \frac{a_m}{2^m} \tag{80}$$

where $a_i = 0$ or 1 and we terminate at $i = m$, where m is the next integer larger than $1 + \log_2 n$.

2. Note that

$$f_0 \equiv 1 \quad \text{and} \quad f_i = (-1)^{a_i} \tag{81}$$

3. The even order functions may be determined through the binary sequence,

$$
\begin{aligned}
f_2 &= (-1)^{a_1+a_2} \\
f_4 &= (-1)^{a_2+a_3} & f_6 &= f_4 \cdot f_2 \\
f_8 &= (-1)^{a_3+a_4} & f_{10} &= f_8 \cdot f_2 \\
& & f_{12} &= f_8 \cdot f_4 \\
& & f_{14} &= f_8 \cdot f_6 \\
f_{16} &= (-1)^{a_4+a_5} & f_{18} &= f_{16} \cdot f_2 \\
& & f_{20} &= f_{16} \cdot f_4 \\
& & &\cdots \\
& & f_{30} &= f_{16} \cdot f_{14}
\end{aligned}
\tag{82}
$$

and so on. Note that the values in the right hand column are computed from previously determined values in the left-hand column.

4. Finally, the odd-symmetric functions from the relation

$$f_{2i+1} = f_{2i} \cdot f_1 \quad \text{for } i > 1 \tag{83}$$

This type of algorithm can be very efficient in machine language (where the binary expansion coefficients are frequently already available from standard base 10 to base 2 conversion subroutines) and is easy to implement in BASIC subroutines.[6] In this process it is easiest to compute $f_n(x)$ by storing the successively higher order functions in an array $F(K)$, where K goes from 1 to N. However, in a language such as BASIC, it is not actually necessary to compute the binary expansion coefficients explicitly. It is much faster to note instead that the Walsh functions of order $K = 2^I$ may be evaluated directly by use of the INT function in statements of the type

```
LET  K = 2 ↑ I
LET  F(K) = (−1) ↑ INT(K*X + .5)
```
(84)

where $I = 0, 1, 2, \ldots$.

Thus, for a given value of x, the Walsh functions

$$f_1, f_2, f_4, f_8, f_{16}, \ldots$$

may be immediately evaluated from Eq. (84) and stored in an array $F(K)$. The remaining even-order functions of order less than 2^{m+1} (where m is defined in Eq. (80)) can then be filled in through the multiplicative process outlined in the right-hand column of Eq. (82) by use of the previously stored functions of lower order. Finally, we use Eq. (83) to determine the odd-symmetric functions from the previously stored even-symmetric ones.

---

[6] The author is indebted to Henry Stark and Larry Rissman for checking the algorithm and for helpful discussions regarding the presentation of this material.

Thus, the Walsh functions of order $1 - N$ may be computed in one subroutine of the type

```
600   REM SUB COMPUTES WALSH FCNS F(1)...F(N) AT X
610   LET M = INT(.5 + LOG(N)/LOG(2))
620   LET F(1) = (−1) ↑ INT(X + .5)
630   FOR I = 1 TO M
640   LET K = 2 ↑ I
650   LET F(K) = (−1) ↑ INT(K*X + .5)
660   LET F(K + 1) = F(K)*F(1)
670   FOR J = 2 TO K − 2 STEP 2
680   LET F(K + J) = F(K)*F(J)
690   LET F(K + J + 1) = F(K + J)*F(1)
700   NEXT J
710   NEXT I
720   RETURN
```

without having to evaluate the binary expansion coefficients at all. Line 650 makes use of Eq. (84) to compute the successive functions in the left-hand column of Eq. (82). For each value of K, the loop between lines 670 and 700 fills in the remaining even-order functions to be computed in line 680 using the relations summarized in the right-hand column of Eq. (82). Finally, the various odd-order functions are computed on lines 660 and 690 using Eq. (83). $F(1)$ was obtained on line 620 using Eq. (84) in the case $I = 0$.

In a real application of Walsh functions to a pattern identification problem, it would be desirable to store the various order functions needed over the required increments in x. However, the subroutine outlined above provides a useful systematic method for tabulating the functions in the first instance and for investigating their orthogonal properties.

**2.23
PROBLEM 21**

Write a program that computes and tabulates $f_1(x)$ through $f_{12}(x)$ over the interval $0 \le x \le 1$ in steps of $\frac{1}{16}$. Use the results of this program to investigate the orthogonality of any two of these functions over that domain.

**2.23
PROBLEM 22**

Consider the set of functions defined by the BASIC statement

$$\text{DEF FNF(N)} = (−1) \uparrow \text{INT(N*X + .5)}$$

where $N = 0, 1, 2, 3, 4$. Write a program to investigate the orthonormality of this set of functions over the domain $0 \le X \le 1$. Evaluate the integral in Eq. (73) for different values of N and print the results as a 5×5 matrix.

**2.23
PROBLEM 23**

Assume the width occupied by letters on a printed line is normalized in each case to the interval $0 \le x \le 1$ and that ten average intensity measurements have been made for each character as we scan a vertical slit along the interval. Assume the intensity distributions for the symbols T, H, E, F, O, and Q are given by

```
1000   REM DISTRIBUTION FOR T
1001   DATA 1,1,1,1,10,10,1,1,1,1
1002   REM DISTRIBUTION FOR H
1003   DATA 10,10,1,1,1,1,1,1,10,10
1004   REM DISTRIBUTION FOR E
1005   DATA 10,10,3,3,3,3,2,2,2,2
1006   REM DISTRIBUTION FOR F
1007   DATA 10,10,2,2,2,2,1,1,1,1
1008   REM DISTRIBUTION FOR O
1009   DATA 3,3,2.5,2,2,2,2,2.5,3,3
1010   REM DISTRIBUTION FOR Q
1011   DATA 3,3,2.5,2,2,2.5,3.5,4,4.5,4.5
```

Write a program which reads each intensity distribution, computes a normalized distribution function $V(x)$ using Eq. (77), and then computes and prints a table of expansion coefficients C_1 and C_2 for $V(x)$ using Eq. (76) and the Walsh functions $f_1(x)$ and $f_2(x)$. Note that these two Walsh functions may simply be obtained from the BASIC function defined in Problem 22 for $N = 1$ and 2. Do the integrals in Eq. (76) by matrix multiplication. For example, store average values of the Walsh functions over each integration interval in two 1×10 row matrices and store the successive pattern matrices in 10×1 column matrices. Note that although $C_1^2 + C_2^2 \ll 1$ in each case, we may easily distinguish between all six characters.

2.23
PROBLEM 24

Consider expanding

$$\sin 2\pi x = \sum_n C_n f_n(x) \qquad \text{for} \quad 0 \leqslant x \leqslant 1$$

where the $f_n(x)$ are Walsh functions described by Eqs. (80)–(83). Write a program to compute the first 16 expansion coefficients using Eq. (76). Note that only odd-symmetric functions about $x = 0.5$ will be important. (Use an integration interval $\Delta x = \frac{1}{32}$ and the trapezoidal rule.) Check your results by printing a tabular comparison of $\sin x$ and Eq. (75) using the computed expansion coefficients over $0 \leqslant x \leqslant 1$ in steps of $2\Delta x$.

2.23
RESEARCH
PROBLEM

Investigate the feasibility of identifying the standard character set found on a typewriter with the type of pattern identification program discussed in the text.

REFERENCES

BELL, E. T. (1951). *Mathematics–Queen and Servant of Science.* New York: McGraw-Hill Book Company.

COURANT, R. (1949). *Differential and Integral Calculus,* translated by E. J. McShane. New York: John Wiley & Sons, Inc. (Interscience Division).

HARDY, G. H. (1967). *A Mathematician's Apology.* New York: Cambridge University Press. Reprinted in 1967, with a foreword by C. P. Snow.

SCHULTZ, M. H. (1972). *Spline Analysis.* Englewood Cliffs, N.J.: Prentice-Hall, Inc.

VON NEUMANN, JOHN AND H. H. GOLDSTINE (1947). "Numerical Inverting of Matrices of High Order." *Bull. Amer. Math. Soc.,* Vol. 53, pp. 1021-1099.

WALSH, J. L. (1923). "A Closed Set of Normal Orthogonal Functions" *Amer. J. Math.,* Vol. 45, pp. 5–24.

WEATHERBURN, C. E. (1950). *Elementary Vector Analysis.* London: G. Bell & Sons, Ltd.

WHITTAKER, E. T., AND G. N. WATSON (1902). *A Course of Modern Analysis.* Cambridge: Cambridge University Press. Reprinted in 1965.

3

Plotting and graphic display

A wide variety of plotting techniques is discussed and illustrated in problems of practical application. The main emphasis is on teletype display. However, the material is arranged so that it may easily be applied to high resolution, random access plotting devices when available. Section 3.1 treats single-point graphs and histograms. Sections 3.2 and 3.3 discuss plotting multiple functions of the same independent variable. Section 3.4 treats the parametric representation of curves and the use of random-access display devices. Sections 3.5 and 3.6 deal with the random-access problem on teletype displays. Section 3.7 discusses surface plotting and the hidden line problem. Sections 3.8 through 3.10 deal with stereoscopic projections.

It is extremely helpful in many instances to be able to display a set of data or the results of a calculation graphically. What method you use to accomplish this objective is largely dependent on the equipment available and the nature of the data to be plotted. In each instance, some method of digital-to-analog conversion will be required. At one extreme, the teletype terminal itself can be used as the digital-to-analog converter and thus generate a relatively low resolution and slowly executed plot of the data. At the opposite extreme, a high-speed electronic digital-to-analog converter can be used to plot results on *xy* recorders, oscilloscopes, or other high-resolution devices. Using devices other than the teletype (or CRT terminal) also depends on the availability of some extra software instructions outside the normal BASIC language. For example, many computer centers have facilities that permit writing data from a BASIC program onto a disc file. Additional specialized programs are frequently available for reading the contents of a file and transmitting it to a high-speed line printer or graphic display device. Similarly, provisions can be incorporated within the BASIC compilers used in minicomputers to CALL machine-language subroutines which directly transfer digital data points to an analog display. We shall illustrate some of these methods; however, the precise instructions required will vary somewhat from one computer facility to the next.

In general, the problems associated with plotting data points on a high-resolution analog display (such as a digital pen recorder) are far simpler than those involved in the generation of a teletype or line-printer display. Although equivalent things can be accomplished in most instances with a teletype display, it requires more complex programming statements to achieve any very general plot in multiple-function or random-access problems.

Consequently our main emphasis will be on teletype plotting techniques throughout the present chapter. These methods may, of course, be easily modified for graphic display on high-resolution, random access devices. In some instances one can in fact use these more powerful analog devices with greater effectiveness after having worked through the equivalent teletype plotting problem.

With any plotting device, one is faced with a previously defined scale. There is generally a finite number of equal intervals available in both the *X* and *Y* directions on the plotting device in respect to an absolute origin. To fit the function on the plot it is necessary to normalize the function and to shift the origin adequately so that the range of the variables and domain of the function fall within the bounds of the plotting device. That, of course, is just what you always do when you plot something on a sheet of graph paper by hand. When the resolution with the particular plotting device is severely limited, it also pays to normalize the individual function so that it just fits within the maximum range available and to round off the function to the nearest integer on the absolute scale. The most desirable procedures vary with the particular device and function under consideration.

The most commonly available graphic display device is the teletype terminal itself. Here, one coordinate becomes the direction of the roller advance. The other coordinate is simply the lateral position at which an alphanumeric character is printed. Both coordinates may be controlled by judicious use of the PRINT statement in BASIC.

There are two main problems quite apart from plotting speed: (1) the resolution is limited to 72 columns across the page; and (2) the computer can only advance the roller in one direction. For these reasons, it is important to normalize the function so that you get the maximum available resolution out of the plot and to round off the result to the nearest integer (column). The direction of the roller advance also becomes the most natural choice for the independent variable, and problems that involve rectangular symmetry are easiest to handle.

One frequently wants to plot values (Y) of a function in BASIC that may include zero, or even negative numbers, and display these with the maximum resolution available—hence over column numbers ranging from 1 to 72. If we know that

$$M\emptyset \leqslant Y \leqslant M1$$

we can define a new variable $Y1$ such that

$$1 \leqslant Y1 \leqslant 72$$

by use of the BASIC statement

LET Y1 = 71*(Y − M∅)/(M1 − M0) + 1

where $M\emptyset$ and $M1$ are the minimum and maximum values of Y. Use of the integer function through a statement of the type

LET Y1 = INT(Y1 + .5)

ensures that the column number is rounded off to the nearest integer.

If one wants to plot a *bar graph* (or *histogram*), it is then merely necessary to print a character on the keyboard (e.g., *) $Y1$ times for each successive value of the independent variable X. As an example, consider plotting a histogram of the function $Y = SIN(X)$ over one period:

```
10   FOR X = ∅ TO 2*3.14159 STEP 2*3.14159/50
20   LET  Y = SIN(X)
30   LET Y1 = INT(71*(Y + 1)/2 + 1.5)
40   FOR J = 1 TO Y1
50   PRINT "*";
60   NEXT J
70   PRINT
80   NEXT X
90   END
```

Line 1∅ provides 51 successive values of X uniformly spaced over the interval $0 \leqslant X \leqslant 2\pi$. The normalization and rounding procedure is contained in line 3∅, where we have simply inserted the minimum ($M\emptyset = -1$) and maximum ($M1 = +1$) values of the sine function; the additional factor 0.5 has also been included in the argument of the INT function on line 3∅ for rounding purposes. The loop on J in lines 4∅ through 6∅ prints $Y1$ successive asterisks on the same line because of the semi-colon after the PRINT statement on line 5∅. The carriage return and line feed are activated by the PRINT statement on line 7∅, after which the program is ready to plot the function for the next value of X. The results of running the program are shown in Fig. 3-1.

Alternatively, a *single-point graph* of the sine function could have been plotted in the above program by printing a blank space $Y1$-1 times on lines 4∅ through 6∅, followed by an asterisk on the $Y1$th column. For example,

```
40   FOR J = 1 TO Y1 − 1
50   PRINT " ";
60   NEXT J
70   PRINT "*"
```

would accomplish the objective. Here, the absence of the semi-colon after the PRINT statement on line 7∅ results in activating the carriage return and line feed after printing the single asterisk on the $Y1$th column.

It is useful to note that the TAB function (which is always used within PRINT statements in BASIC) provides an efficient way to move the typing head a specified number of spaces. The argument of the TAB function is

RUN

READY

interpreted on an absolute basis (in respect to the left margin) and can be based on a computed expression. For example, the statement

    PRINT TAB(Y1 − 1);

results in moving the typing head $Y1$-1 spaces without activating the carriage return and line feed. Consequently, that simple statement is equivalent to the loop within lines 40 through 60 above. Further, lines 40 through 70 in the single-point plotting routine may be completely replaced by the single statement

    40   PRINT TAB(Y1 − 1);"*"

Further economy in programming statements is possible in the above plotting routines, but with some decrease in the conceptual clarity provided by program listings. For example, the use of the integer function on line 30 is actually redundant: Exactly the same results would have been obtained in each of the above programs if we had merely deleted line 30 and replaced $Y1$ in line 40 by the argument of the original integer function. This simplification is permitted simply because the INT function is effectively consulted by the BASIC compiler in executing the FOR loop on J and in executing the TAB function. One could further compute the values of the function within the upper limit of the FOR loop on J, or within the argument of the TAB function. Thus, for example, the same single-point plot of the sinewave would be provided by the program

    10   FOR X = 0 TO 2*3.14159 STEP 2*3.14159/50
    40   PRINT TAB(71*(SIN(X) + 1)/2 + .5);"*"
    80   NEXT X
    90   END

However, here we have reached a point of diminishing return: the program is now so concise that its functioning tends to be obscure in a quick glance at the program.

3.1
PROBLEM 1

Plot a single-point graph of the function $\sin A + \sin 3A$ for $0 \leq A \leq 2\pi$.

3.1
PROBLEM 2

The unemployed working force in the United States varied from 5.9 to 8.2 percent over the interval January 1972 through January 1975 in accordance with the numbers in the following DATA statements (representing 1-month intervals):†

```
 999  REM % UNEMPLOYED JAN. '72 → JAN. '75 IN 1 MONTH STEPS
1000  DATA 5.9,5.8,5.9,5.8,5.7,5.6,5.6,5.5,5.6,5.5,5.3,5.1
1001  DATA 5,5.1,5,5,4.9,4.9,4.8,4.8,4.7,4.7,4.6,4.8
1002  DATA 5.1,5.2,5.1,5,5.2,5.2,5.3,5.4,5.8,6,6.5,7.3
1003  DATA 8.2
```

Plot a histogram of the above data using the full teletype scale.

3.1
PROBLEM 3

Plot a histogram of the letter frequency distribution for one of the languages for which data is summarized in Table 4 of Chapter 4. If you have the CHR$ function, write your program to print the different specific letters within the bar graph. e.g.,

```
AAAAAAAAAAAAAAAAAAAAAAAAAAAAAAAA
BBBBBBBBBBBB
CCCCCCCCCCCCCCCCCC
```

, etc. (See Section 1.18 of Chapter 1 for a discussion of the ASCII Code.)

† From *The New York Times*, Feb. 8, 1975, p. 1, cols. 6 and 7.

3.2
Plotting Two Simultaneous Functions on the Teletype Terminal

Suppose that we compute two functions, $Y1$ and $Y2$, simultaneously for the same values of the independent variable X and wish to plot the results. At first glance the program

```
10  FOR X = 0 TO ...
20  LET Y1 = ...
30  LET Y2 = ...    (defines the two functions)
40  PRINT TAB(Y1 − .5);"*"; TAB(Y2 − .5);"*"
50  NEXT X
60  END
```

would seem to accomplish the objective (assuming that $Y1$ and $Y2$ are properly normalized for the 72-column format). The program will be fine as long as $Y2 > Y1$, since both TAB functions are evaluated on an absolute basis. However, if $Y1 \geq Y2$, erroneous points will result. In that case, the second * will be printed just after the first one. Consequently, some conditional statements will be needed if the two functions cross. For example, the program

```
 10  FOR X = 0 TO ... STEP...
 20  LET Y1 = ...
 30  LET Y2 = ...    (two functions of X)
 40  IF INT(Y1 + .5)#INT(Y2 + .5) THEN 70
 50  PRINT TAB(Y1 − .5);"X"
 60  GO TO 110
 70  IF Y1>Y2 THEN 100
 80  PRINT TAB(Y1 − .5);"A";TAB(Y2 − .5);"B"
 90  GO TO 110
100  PRINT TAB(Y2 − .5); "B";TAB(Y1 − .5);"A"
110  NEXT X
```

77

would plot only one point (X) where the functions were the same and would plot *Y1* using the letter A, *Y2* using the letter B, and would handle the two inequality limits appropriately. In some versions of BASIC, programming statements of the above type could be pruned substantially by using computed GO TO or more elaborate conditional statements. For example, some time-sharing services incorporate a type of super BASIC in which one is allowed to make such statements as

70   IF Y1 > Y2 THEN PRINT TAB(Y2 − .5);"B";TAB(Y1 − .5);"A"

However, most BASIC compilers do not have that option.

3.2 **PROBLEM 4**	Write a program that will simultaneously plot the sine function over one period (0 through 2π) and the axis representing the angle variable. For example, use the * symbol for the function and the + symbol for the axis. Make the program print a * symbol where the function intersects the axis.
3.2 **PROBLEM 5**	Write a program that will simultaneously plot the sine and cosine functions over the range from zero to 2π and use different characters for the two functions. Where the two functions coincide, have the computer print X.
3.2 **PROBLEM 6**	Write a program that plots a circle on the teletype. Note that the circle can be represented by the two functions $$Y1 = Y\emptyset + SQR(R*R - (X - X\emptyset)*(X - X\emptyset))$$ and $$Y2 = Y\emptyset - SQR(R*R - (X - X\emptyset)*(X - X\emptyset))$$ Also note that the teletype characters are more closely spaced on a line than the lines are separated, by a ratio $\approx \frac{3}{5}$. Hence, to avoid producing ellipses rather than circles, it is helpful to multiply the SQR terms in the above two cases by a number $\approx \frac{5}{3}$.

3.3

Plotting *N* Simultaneous Functions of the Same Variable with the Teletype

The technique of Section 3.2 could be extended to any number of simultaneous functions by use of more conditional statements. The process would be terribly cumbersome for more than a few functions and it is much more efficient to adopt some kind of procedure that automatically sorts and stores the points as they are computed and plots points using the same character. For example, suppose we wanted to plot a function of the type

$$y = x^n$$

over the range $0 \leqslant x \leqslant 1$.

Here we could use a 72-column array to advantage for the teletype plotting problem, and our program might start out

```
10   DIM Y(72)
20   FOR X = Ø TO 1 STEP .02
30   FOR I = 1 TO 72
40   LET Y(I) = −1
50   NEXT I
```

The STEP size indicated on line 2Ø will provide a 51-point plot in a later portion of the program. The array initialization on lines 3Ø through 5Ø is to permit telling at the plotting stage of the program whether or not a point has been computed corresponding to a particular array index, *I*. We shall next compute values of $Y = X^N$ normalized to the 72-column width for $0 \leqslant X \leqslant 1$ and store those values in proportionate elements of the array, $Y(I)$.

```
60    FOR N = 1 TO 9
70    LET Y = 71*X↑N
80    LET I = INT(Y + 1.5)
90    LET Y(I) = Y
100   NEXT N
```

Line 8Ø defines an integer proportional to Y which is rounded off to nearest integer in the domain $1 \leqslant I \leqslant 72$ when $0 \leqslant X \leqslant 1$. Note that after line 1ØØ, every value of each function has been stored for a given value of the independent variable, X.

We are therefore ready to plot the points corresponding to each function by use of a series of statements of the type

```
110   LET A = −1
120   FOR I = 1 TO 72
130   IF Y(I) < = A THEN 170
140   PRINT TAB(Y(I) − Ø.5);"*";
150   LET A = INT(Y(I) + .5)
160   IF Y(I) > = 72 THEN 190
170   NEXT I
180   PRINT
190   NEXT X
```

The utility of the variable A arises from its definition in line 15Ø. The initial choice, $A = -1$, corresponds to no points having been plotted for the current value of the independent variable X. The program then plots the computed values for $Y(I)$, noting that they have been previously stored in an order that increases with the array index, I. If no point has been computed for a particular array element, $Y(I) = -1$ from the initialization statement on line 4Ø. Points that have not been computed, or are equal in value to one previously computed, are therefore rejected by line 13Ø. Lines 17Ø and 18Ø permit advancing the roller at the end of the I loop unless a character has just been printed in column 72 (in which case the roller advances automatically).

Note that the sorting techniques discussed in Section 1.16 could be used in place of lines 6Ø through 1ØØ to store a more general set of computed points in the array $Y(I)$ for each value of X.

3.3
PROBLEM 7   Plot $Y = X^N$ on the teletype for integral steps of N over the range $1 \leqslant N \leqslant 9$ and 50 points covering the range $0 \leqslant X \leqslant 1$.

Some functions are most naturally computed in terms of parameters, other than the rectangular coordinates x, y. For example, one common parametric representation involves the use of the polar coordinates R and A in two-dimensional plotting (see Fig. 3-2). Here R is the radius from an origin $XØ$, $YØ$ to the point (X, Y) on the curve, and A is the angle (in radians) between R and a reference line (e.g., the x axis).

One needs rectangular coordinates to feed most computer-driven plotting devices. These coordinates are related to the parameters R and A by means of the equations

$$X = XØ + R \cos A$$
$$Y = YØ + R \sin A$$

by definition of the sine and cosine functions.

3.4
Parametric Representation of Curves; Polar Coordinates and Probability Clouds

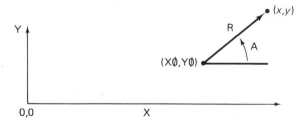

Fig. 3-2.

For example, one can compute the points on a circle by holding R constant and by varying the angle A from 0 to 2π radians in suitably chosen steps. Similarly, varying R with the angle A in a program of the type

```
10   FOR A = 0 TO 10*3.14159 STEP .06
20   LET R = A
30   LET X = X0 + R*COS(A)
40   LET Y = Y0 + R*SIN(A)
60   NEXT A
```

will result in the successive computation of ≈ 100 points on a spiral. It is helpful to imagine how simple life would be *if* we could merely insert a statement in line 50 that would simply plot a point with the coordinates X and Y on an analog device by means of a simple command such as

```
50   PLOT(X,Y)
```

Although this statement is *not* a standard part of BASIC, one can devise machine-language programs that produce the same effect with oscilloscope and *xy* pen recorder displays.[1] In that case, one may easily display a wide variety of spiral functions merely by changing the dependence of R on A in line 20 (see Fig. 3-3.)

Another technique that is readily implemented with random-access plotting devices consists of the display of probability clouds. Suppose, for example, that we were able to write a probability function P in terms of the polar coordinates R and A above, such that $P(R, A)$ represents the probability of an event occurring between R and $R + dR$ and between A and $A + dA$. One could then

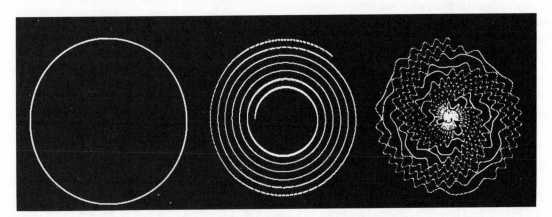

Fig. 3-3. Representative variety of functions that may easily be displayed on a random-access plotting device by minor modification of the dependence of radius on angle in line 20. Note that a modulated phonograph record is just as easy to draw as a circle.

simulate a probability cloud by plotting a number of points proportional to $P(R, A)$ at coordinates which are given different random displacements about R and A. The technique will become clearer by reference to the following representative program:

```
99    REM PROGRAM PLOTS CLOUD FOR PROBABILITY FCN P = P(R,A)
100   FOR R = .5*R0 TO R2 STEP R0
110      FOR A = .5*A0 TO 2*3.14159 STEP A0
```

[1] For example, statements of the type

```
CALL(1,X,Y)
```

that result in plotting one point with coordinates X, Y on device number 1 during normal running of a program can be added to the BASIC language. (See the Hewlett-Packard manual on 2100 series computers).

```
120      LET P=... (some function of R and A)
130      FOR I=PØ TO P STEP PØ
140          LET A1=A+AØ*(RND(1)−.5)
150          LET R1=R+RØ*(RND(2)−.5)
160          LET X1=XØ+R1*COS(A1)
170          LET Y1=YØ+R1*SIN(A1)
180      REM PLOT A POINT WITH COORDINATES X1 AND Y1
. . . . . . . . . . . .
190          NEXT I
200      NEXT A
210      NEXT R
```

(The indentation in program statements is introduced merely to clarify the steps involved within the three nested loops.) The exact form for P would have to be inserted in line 12Ø, together with appropriate upper limits and step sizes on the three FOR loops. However, such plots tend to be most efficient when the initial values, step sizes and random displacements are as shown in the above program segment. For example, the random fluctuation on $R1$ in line 15Ø is spread evenly over the domain $R \pm 0.5*RØ$; hence the final plot will show randomly located points having an average density which is uniformly spread over the range $0 \le R \le R2$ when P is constant as a result of the lower limit and step size in line 1ØØ. In some instances, symmetry properties of the probability function can be used effectively to speed up the running time. An illustration of the method is shown in Fig. 3-4.

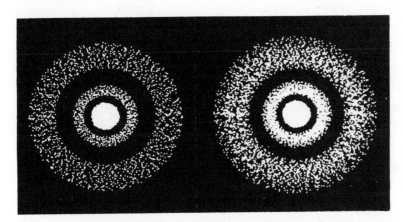

Fig. 3-4. Simulation of the electron cloud in the median plane of an excited hydrogen atom (in the 4s state). The value of $PØ$ on the line 13Ø of the program in the text was reduced by 50 percent in going from the left- to the right-hand figure.

A serious limitation of the teletype terminal (and line printer) is that the computer cannot move the roller backward. Consequently, the teletype fits most naturally into problems that involve rectangular coordinates in which one calculates the various values of Y (the column position) for each sequential increment in X (the row typed). If one wants to plot something in parametric form (e.g., a spiral), one has to compute and store all the required points in the computer memory and then plot all these points at the end of the computation period. As sometimes is the case, the most straightforward approach to the problem squanders the most computer core.

The most straightforward approach here consists of defining a large matrix, M, with enough rows and columns to achieve the desired resolution. For example, 45 rows and 72 columns would correspond roughly to a square display on the teletype with the maximum available resolution. (The 45:72 ratio roughly corresponds to the 3:5 ratio of type width to height.) Hence we

3.5

Infinite-Core Method: Contour Plots with the Teletype

81

would have to start off with a dimension statement

1   DIM M(45, 72)

which implies storage for 3240 floating-point numbers; or, for example, in a typical minicomputer using two 16-bit words for each floating-point number, the dimension statement calls for 6480 core locations before we have gotten to the program. The approach is quite realistic with most moderate-sized computers. However, one should keep in mind that the BASIC compiler itself takes up $\approx$7000 words, so one needs at least $\approx$16,000 words of memory available before the approach is realistic with a minicomputer.

Pursuing this method, we next might initialize the matrix by setting all 3240 elements to zero:

2   MAT M = ZER(45, 72)

and proceed to compute our function. Assuming that our function has been normalized to fit on a 45×72 grid, we could do the equivalent of plotting points on paper by incrementing the matrix element $M(X, Y)$ whose row and column correspond to the X and Y coordinates of the point. (This means that the X coordinate will be in the direction of the teletype line advance and Y will correspond to the teletype column position.) For example, plotting a point with coordinates that are rounded off to the integers X and Y would correspond to the statement

LET M(X,Y) = M(X,Y) + 1

After completing the computation of all elements $M(X, Y)$ we could then run through a plotting routine that would plot a point at each coordinate X and Y for which $M(X, Y) \neq 0$. For example, the plotting could be accomplished by a program such as

```
100   FOR X = 1 TO 45
110   FOR Y = 1 TO 72
120   IF M(X,Y) = 0 THEN 150
130   PRINT TAB(Y − 1);"*";
140   IF Y = 72 THEN 170
150   NEXT Y
160   PRINT
170   NEXT X
```

Although the method preserves the 45×72 resolution for a series of points that could be computed in random order, it so far does not make use of the "dynamic range" of the method. That is, so far we have only plotted one point whenever $M(X, Y) \neq 0$. We could, of course, try to make use of the magnitude of $M(X, Y)$. For example, one could raise the cutoff point on line 120, "enhance" the contrast in some way, only plot a point when $M(X, Y)$ equaled a specified value [thereby obtaining a set of surfaces whose altitude corresponded to $M(X, Y)$], and so on.

One method of utilizing the range in values of the matrix elements consists of using the teletype (or line printer) to print different ASCII characters in a manner proportional to the magnitude of these elements. However, if we print more than one teletype column for each matrix element, we lose spatial resolution. One approach is to compress the range of the matrix elements to a scale from 0 through 9 and print the corresponding numerical characters (having ASCII decimal-code designations running from 48 through 57). For example, consider producing a contour map of a surface of the type

$$z \propto (e^{-r} \sin 2\pi r)^2$$

where

$$r^2 = x^2 + y^2$$

```
                        1111111111111111111111
                    1111112222222222222222222211111
                 11112222223333333333333332222221111
               1111122222233333333333333333333332222111
             1112222333333333333333333333333333333322221111
            1112223333333333333333333333333333333333333222111
           11122333333333333332222222222222222233333333333222111
          1122233333333333322211111111111111112222333333333332211
         11222333333333222211111              1111112222333333333322111
        112233333332221111                         11111222333333332211
       1122333333332221111           11122222111        112222333333322111
       1122333333332211         1112333333333322211        1112223333333332211
      11122333333322211       12223444666666664433211       1112223333332211111
      11223333332211       123466777788887766443321       1112233333332211
     11223333333322211    1123466788899999998877664322     11223333333332211
     1122333333332211     11234677899999999999998776432       1122333333332211
    111233333332211     12346778999888666888999987643211      112233333332211
    1122333333322211    123366789999866555556889998766332      11223333333322211
    1122333333322211    12346789998663222335889998764321       11223333332211
    1122333333322211    123467899986532      23568999876432     1122333333322211
    1122333333322211    123467899986532222355689998764321       1122333333322211
    1122333333322211    123347789998665555568899988663311       1122333333322211
    11222333332221     12346788999888666888999887643211         11223333333322211
    1122333333322211    1123467789999999999998876432111          1122333333322211
    11223333333222211   11234667889999999999887664321111         11223333333322211
     1122333333322211    1123344667778887777664432211           1112233333332211
     11222333333322111    1223344466666664443221111           11122233333332211
      1122333333322211      11222333333333221              1112223333333322211
       11223333333322111      1111222221111             112223333333332211
        11222333333322221111                          11112223333333332221
         11222333333333322221111111111111111222333333333333322211
          1112223333333333332222222222222222223333333333322111
          11112223333333333333333333333333333333333322111
            1112222333333333333333333333333333333332222111
             1112222233333333333333333333333332222111
              11112222223333333333333332222221111
                111111222222222222222222221111111
                    11111111111111111111111
```

Fig. 3-5. Contour map of the function
$$Z = (9/.621843)*(EXP(-R/35)*SIN(2*3.14159*R/35))\uparrow2$$
plotted with a teletype terminal using a 5/3 ratio to correct for the difference between character width and height.

First we store the surface (normalized to a maximum value of 9) on a point–by–point basis in the 45×72 element matrix. In this process it is useful to introduce the polar coordinates, R and A, as generating parameters:

```
10   DIM M(45,72)
20   MAT M = ZER(45,72)
25   REM PICK ORIGIN NEXT
30   LET X0 = 1 + INT(3*36/5 + .5)
35   LET Y0 = 1 + INT(36 + .5)
40   FOR R = 1 TO 35
41   PRINT R;
45   FOR A = 0 TO 2*3.14159 STEP 1/R
50   LET X = X0 + INT((3/5)*R*COS(A) + .5)
60   LET Y = Y0 + INT(R*SIN(A) + .5)
70   LET M = EXP(-R/35)*SIN(R*2*3.14159/35)
75   LET M(X,Y) = INT(9*M*M/.621843 + .5)
80   NEXT A
90   NEXT R
```

Note that the $\frac{3}{5}$ normalizing factor occurs in lines 30 and 50 for the quantities that involve X, but not in lines 35 and 60, which involve the Y coordinate. Line 75 normalizes the maximum value of the particular function (0.621843) to 9. The print statement on line 41 is merely to let us know where we are in the computation of $M(X, Y)$. The only tricky point is the variation of angular step

83

size in line 45. Here we wish to decrease the angular step with increasing radius so that we avoid ending up with noncomputed matrix elements where the function is nonzero. At the same time, we wish to avoid wasting excessive computing at the center of the plot (where relatively coarse angular increments are permissible). Therefore we want the angular step to decrease as $1/R$.

Finally, we want to be able to print the right ASCII characters in the right place after all matrix elements have been computed. For example, it is useful to print a space when $M(X, Y) = \emptyset$, the character 1 when $M(X, Y) = 1$, and so on.

One method of accomplishing this printing task is to run the matrix elements through a binary printing sieve analogous to that discussed in Chapter 4 for letter printing (see Section 4.2). On the other hand, the CHR$ function (or equivalent CALL statement) can be used to considerable advantage when available (see Section 1.18). For example, the statements

```
210   FOR X = 1 TO 45
220   FOR Y = 1 TO 72
230   IF M(X,Y)#∅   THEN 26∅
240   PRINT " ";
250   GOTO 27∅
260   PRINT CHR$(M(X,Y)+48);
270   NEXT Y
280   PRINT
290   NEXT X
```

solve the problem with reasonable economy and efficiency. However, there is the mild disadvantage that when $M(X, Y)$ exceeds 9 in line $26\emptyset$ you start getting the assortment of nonnumeric ASCII characters on your contour plot which were listed earlier in Table 1 of Chapter 1 in the ASCII character set. The result of running the program is shown in Fig. 3-5.

**3.5
PROBLEM 8**

The probability of finding the electron in the median plane of a particular excited state of the hydrogen atom (the $4f_{m=0}$ state) is proportional to P given by the following BASIC statements:[†]

```
DEF   FNA(A) = 2*COS(A)↑3 − 3*COS(A)*SIN(A)↑2
DEF   FNR(R) = EXP(−R/4)*R↑3
LET   P = R*(FNR(R)*FNA(A))↑2
```

where A represents the angular position of the electron and R is the radial location in units of the Bohr radius (0.529173×10^{-8} cm.) Use the technique of the present section to plot a contour map of this probability function over the range $1 \leqslant R \leqslant 30$.

[†] Ref. Condon and Shortley (1963).

The preceding method is extravagant unless one really makes use of the dynamic range for each point (i.e., somehow utilize the number of points stored within each individual matrix element).

With the specific example given and machine used, a 45×72 point resolution was obtained in the xy plane, but the information stored in the z coordinate would typically be computed to better than 1 ppm and could probably range up to $\approx 10^{38}$.

In cases where one merely wants to plot one point at most for a given pair of coordinates and also will be content with a maximum initially prescribed number of plotted points ($\ll 72$) for the same value of the variable along the roller-advance direction, it takes less computer memory to store the successive Y

**3.6
Random-Point Problem on Small
Machines: Plotting a Spiral
on the Teletype**

coordinates in the matrix elements $M(I, J)$ and use the column index (J) to keep track of the number of plotted points stored for each value of I.

Let us assume that we might want to plot as many as 10 separate points on each of 40 separate rows and that we will store the Y coordinates in the matrix M. In this case, we only need a dimension statement involving 400 floating-point variables,

```
1   DIM M(40,10)
```

to get a resolution of 1 part in 72 on each point. Here it is useful to initialize all the matrix elements to the value -1. This can be accomplished through the statements

```
5   MAT M = CON        (fill out M with 1s)
6   MAT M = (-1)*M     (multiply each component by -1.
                        Note: This is one of the few MAT
                        commands where it is legal to
                        have the same matrix on both sides
                        of the equal sign.)
```

As an illustration we shall compute a spiral in parametric form and then plot it with the teletype machine. First we shall determine the X and Y coordinates of successive points using a parameter K:

```
10   FOR K = 1 TO 10 STEP .01
12   LET A = K*3.14159
15   LET R = A
20   LET X = 32 + R*COS(A)
30   LET Y = 32 + R*SIN(A)
```

We next determine the row index for the storage matrix rounded off to the nearest integer by the statement

```
60   LET I = INT(3*X/5 + .5)
```

where the $\approx \frac{3}{5}$ factor correcting for the character- and line-spacing dimensions has been included. Then we want to store the Y coordinate of the Jth point ($1 \leq J \leq 10$ here) corresponding to the particular value of I computed on line 60:

```
65   FOR J = 1 TO 10
67   IF M(I,J) < 0 THEN 70
68   NEXT J
69   GO TO 80
70   LET M(I,J) = INT(Y + .5)
```

The conditional statement in line 67 lets the Y coordinate be stored in line 70, provided that no previous point was stored in M(I, J). Line 69 prevents attempting to store more than 10 points (and hence generating an error message). The value of the Y coordinate is rounded off to the nearest integer in line 70 as it is stored in the matrix for use in the specific plotting program given below. After storing the computed point, the loop on the parameter K is closed on line 80.

```
80   NEXT K
```

The points can then be plotted in the following straightforward manner:

```
100   FOR I = 1 TO 40
110   FOR K = 1 TO 72
120   FOR J = 1 TO 10
130   IF M(I,J)#K - 1 THEN 160
140   PRINT "*";
150   GO TO 180
160   NEXT J
170   PRINT " ";
180   NEXT K
190   NEXT I
```

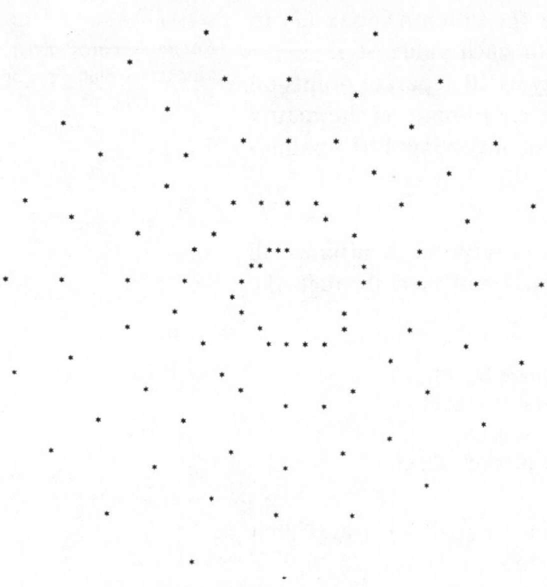

Fig. 3-6. Spiral plotted on a teletype terminal.

For each of the 40 rows provided in the original matrix, the teletype scans through the 72 columns (FOR loop on K). For each value of K and each possible stored point, J, the conditional statement on line 13Ø checks to see if a point should be plotted; i.e., unless $M(I, J) = K - 1$, a point should not be plotted. If no points have been stored over the range from $J = 1$ to 10, a blank space is entered on line 17Ø and the teletype advances to the next column (K).

The plotting program, as it stands, depends on the fact that the line feed will automatically be advanced after $K = 72$. One could speed up the program somewhat when plotting on the teletype by first determining the maximum M of $M(I, J)$ for $J = 1$ to 10 and by advancing K only to $M - 1$. (The maxima, for example, could be stored in a column array and could have been computed when the function was initially worked out.) However, in that instance, some extra statements are required to advance the line feed when $M < 72$ and to prevent a double line feed when $M = 72$. The saving in time is pretty negligible when the output is displayed by a line printer or CRT terminal, and these extra programming steps have been omitted for the sake of clarity.

The results from running the program are shown in Fig. 3-6. As it stands, the first and last several lines are filled up with blank characters.

3.6 **PROBLEM 9**	Plot the function defined by the polar-coordinate relation $R = SIN(2*A)$ over the range $0 \leqslant A \leqslant 2\pi$ on the teletype. (*Note:* There are only four points for each value of X.)

Anyone who enjoys browsing through the illustrations in Jahnke and Emde (1945), or who has imagined walking about on mathematical surfaces, will probably want to try to plot some surfaces with a computer. The technique is also frequently valuable in the display of experimental data. We shall therefore consider a simple method for approximating a perspective plot of a surface. (A more precise method for handling projections of three-dimensional quantities on a two-dimensional plot is given in Section 3.8.)

Suppose that we wish to display the surface

$$z = f(x, y)$$

3.7
Plotting Surfaces on the Teletype;
the Hidden Line Problem

on a two-dimensional plotting device with absolute coordinates x_1 and y_1. A simple method of approximating the effects of perspective consists of doing the same thing with a computer that would be accomplished by preparing a large number of slices through successive zx planes (i.e., at different values of y) and then pasting these together in slightly displaced form. If we take the x axis of the surface to be parallel to the x_1 axis of the plotting device and the z axis of the surface parallel to the y_1 axis of the plotting device, we can create the illusion of a y axis drawn in perspective using the successive displacement technique shown in Fig. 3-7. We shall use constant increments x_0, y_0 along the x_1, y_1 axes and denote the successive slices using the integer n. Thus the coordinates on the plotting device will be related to the coordinates used to generate the surface by

$$x_1 = x + nx_0$$
$$y_1 = z + ny_0$$

where $n = 0, 1, 2, \ldots$. From the Pythagorean theorem, the constant increments along the y axis are equal to $\sqrt{x_0^2 + y_0^2}$. Hence,

$$y = n\sqrt{x_0^2 + y_0^2}$$

If one has a random-access plotting device, the problem can most simply be programmed along the following lines:

```
FOR N = 0 TO M
FOR X = 0 TO W STEP...
LET Y = N*SQR(X0↑2 + Y0↑2)
LET Z = ...   [surface to be plotted = f(x,y)]
LET X1 = X + N*X0
LET Y1 = Z + N*Y0
REM PLOT OR STORE POINT WITH COORDINATES X1,Y1
...
NEXT X
NEXT N
```

Here, corresponding computer variables have been substituted for the mathematical variables (for example, $X0$, $Y0$, $X1$, and $Y1$ were substituted for x_0, y_0, x_1, and y_1), and it is assumed that the width of each slice in the X direction is W. In general one has to introduce various scale factors in order to display the surface to best advantage. One also needs a special purpose subroutine to plot a point with coordinates $X1$, $Y1$ on the display device used. A display of this type made with a digital xy recorder is shown in Fig. 3-8.

One *could* use precisely the same approach to compute points for a teletype plot of the surface. However, that approach is awkward because of the necessity of storing all of the computed points before starting the plot (see Section 3.5). With the teletype display, it pays to turn the problem around and compute the separate points y_1 for each of the different slices n before incrementing the x_1 coordinate (direction of the roller advance.) In this manner we can plot the surface while computing it and do not have to store the points for a subsequent display. At the same time, we can solve the hidden line problem (which was ignored in Fig. 3-8) in a very simple manner: By keeping track of the maximum value of y_1 for a given x_1 in going from the foreground to the background (direction of increasing n), we can suppress plotting points that would normally be hidden from view. To put this program into effect, we merely need to turn our previous equations around. Note that if we specify x_1,

$$x = x_1 - nx_0$$
$$y = n\sqrt{x_0^2 + y_0^2}$$
$$z = f(x, y)$$
$$y_1 = z + ny_0$$

where $n = 0, 1, 2, \ldots$ for the successive slices.

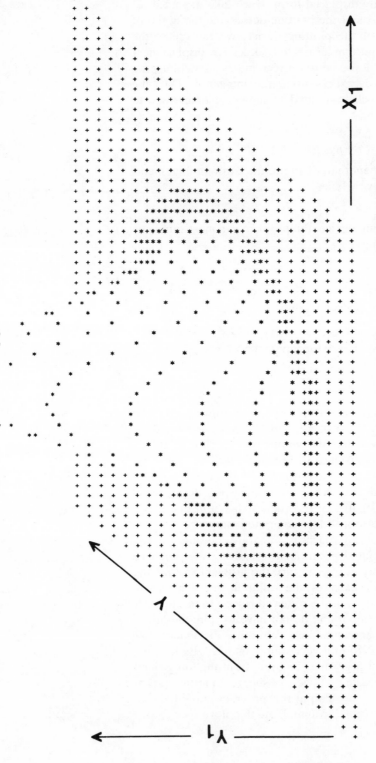

Fig. 3-7. Perspective plot of a surface made with a teletype machine. (The roller advanced along the x_1 axis, and the points were plotted sequentially along the y_1 axis for fixed values of x_1.)

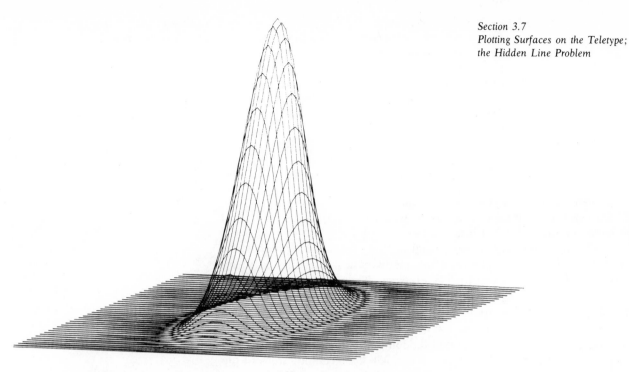

Fig. 3-8. Plot of the surface $z = e^{-(x^2+y^2)}$ made with a digital xy recorder by displacing slices in the xz plane for successive increments in y.

Before we can run such a program on a computer, we have to make some reasonable choice for the various scale factors involved. For example, the statements

```
10   LET W = 50
20   PRINT "NUMBER OF SLICES"
30   INPUT M
40   LET Y0 = INT(36/M + .5)
50   LET X0 = INT(3*Y0/5 + .5)
```

will permit making the width (W) of each slice in the x direction equal to fifty teletype lines and permit varying the total number of slices (M). If we allot half (36 columns) of the available plotting space to the foreground, the increment ($Y0$) in the y_1 direction is defined in terms of the total number of slices. (See line 40). If we want the y axis of the perspective plot to make an angle of about 45° in respect to the x_1 axis (see Fig. 3-7), the increment ($X0$) in the x_1 direction is automatically defined by $Y0$ and the ratio of column width to line spacing. (See line 50). We next vary $X1$ from zero to $W + M*X0$ and initialize a parameter J which will be used to keep running track of the maximum value of $Y1$ plotted for a given $X1$.

```
60   FOR X1 = 0 TO W + M*X0
70   LET J = 0
```

We then compute all points to be plotted in the M slices for a given value of $X1$.

```
80    FOR N = 0 TO M
90    IF N < INT((X1 − W)/X0 + .5) THEN 240
100   IF N > INT(X1/X0 + .5) THEN 250
110   LET Y1 = INT(N*Y0 + .5)
120   IF Y1 < = J THEN 150
130   PRINT TAB(Y1 − 1);"+";
140   LET J = Y1
150   LET X = X1 − N*X0
```

```
160    LET Y = N*SQR(X0↑2 + Y0↑2)
170    LET R2 = (X − 25)↑2 + (Y − 25)↑2
180    LET F = EXP(−1.50000E − 02*R2)
190    LET Z = 50*F
200    LET Y1 = INT(Z + N*Y0 + .5)
210    IF Y1 < = J THEN 240
220    PRINT TAB(Y1 − 1);"*";
230    LET J = Y1
240    NEXT N
250    PRINT
260    NEXT X1
270    END
```

Line 100 prevents computing points which would fall to the left of the y axis in Fig. 3-7. Similarly, line 90 suppresses points which would occur for $x > W$ at the right hand side of Fig. 3-7. Lines 110 and 130 plot the background plane (points where $z = 0$) using the + symbol, and hidden points are suppressed by line 120. The computer equivalents of the mathematical variables x, y are determined on lines 150 and 160 for the nth slice. The function $z = f(x, y)$ is defined by lines 170 through 190. This function was arbitrarily chosen to illustrate the plotting method: It is of the form $z = e^{-(x^2+y^2)}$, but with a peak height of 50, centered at the point $x = y = 25$. Lines 200 and 220 plot the points $Y1$ using the * symbol, except that hidden points are suppressed by the conditional statement on line 210. Lines 140 and 230 keep running track of the maximum value of $Y1$ for previously plotted points for constant $X1$ using the variable J. After plotting the points $Y1$ for all M slices, the carriage return and roller advance are activated by line 250 and the variable $X1$ is incremented by line 260. The result of running the program is shown in Fig. 3-7. The same method could, of course, be used to suppress hidden lines in displays which are plotted one point at a time with high-resolution analog devices. An approximate stereoscopic effect can also be achieved using the same technique. All we have to do is run the above program again after shifting the location of the surface along the x axis. (See Fig. 3-9). Viewing the two figures (after suitable photoreduction) separately with your two eyes further enhances the illusion that the surface is standing up on the background plane. (A more precise method of computing stereoscopic projections is discussed in the following section.)

Fig. 3-9. Illusion of a stereoscopic effect created by lateral displacement of the surface origin in respect to the background plane. The left-hand figure was created using $R2 = (X − 26)↑2 + (Y − 25)↑2$ on line 170; whereas the right-hand figure was generated with $R2 = (X − 24)↑2 + (Y − 25)↑2$. To see this figure (and subsequent three-dimensional figures) stereoscopically, first hold the figure about two feet from your eyes without trying to focus on it. Move the figure laterally so that the right-hand projection is centered on the right eye and the left-hand projection is centered on the left eye. You should then be aware of four fuzzy images in your brain. Make the two center images coincide in your brain and focus on this superposition (a slight rotation may help). At this point you should see the surface standing up from the background plane.

3.7
PROBLEM 10
The gain, G, in the first helium–neon laser was found to vary with pump rate (P) and radial position (R) in a cylindrical discharge tube of unit radius approximately as

$$G(R, P) \approx P[2 - P(1 - 0.2R^2)] \cos(\pi R/2) \qquad \text{for } -1 \leqslant R \leqslant +1$$

Plot the surface $G(R, P)$ using the methods of this section over the domain $-1 \leqslant R \leqslant +1$ on the x axis and for the pump rate (P) varying from 2 to 0 for the different slices.

3.8
Computing Stereoscopic Projections of Lines in Space

Because people normally look at objects simultaneously with two eyes located at different points in space, the three-dimensional character of an object may be recorded in the brain. One can record the three-dimensional effect photographically by placing a camera lens at each eye location and by taking two photographs simultaneously. The scene is then reconstructed in the brain of the observer when the "right" eye looks at the "right" photograph and the "left" eye looks at the "left" photograph. The process is known as *stereoscopic photography* and has enjoyed sporadic popularity during the present century.

It is sometimes helpful to construct a stereoscopic view of a surface or curve based on experimental data or a computed function. One can do this in a simple manner, using some graphic display device to plot out the two stereoscopic projections required. To accomplish this objective it is necessary to analyze the projection process involved for one eye looking at the curve alone. The easiest way to accomplish that objective involves the use of three-dimensional vectors. (If necessary, see the review of vector algebra in Chapter 2.) The geometry for the problem is shown schematically in Fig. 3-10.

In what follows we shall assume that we wish to draw the projection of the curve $y = f(x, z)$ on a sheet of paper located in the xy plane. We wish to compute the intersection of a straight line with the xy plane, which line is drawn from the eye location through variable points P on the curve (see Fig. 3-10).

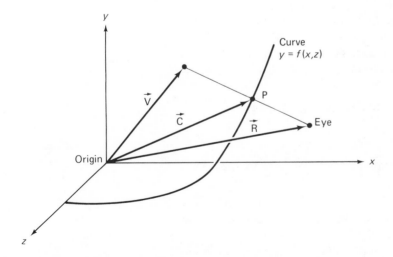

Fig. 3-10. Relationship of vectors used in the projection of three-dimensional quantities (such as the point P on the curve $y = f(x, z)$) onto the two-dimensional plane xy. The vector $\vec{R}$ denotes the eye location; the vector $\vec{C}$ indicates the point P on the curve; and the vector $\vec{V}$ (located in the plane xy) indicates the location of the projection of point P on the plane xy as seen by the eye. A stereoscopic view of this basic diagram is shown in Fig. 3-11.

91

We shall use the notation

$\vec{R}$ = vector from the origin to the eye [i.e., the coordinates of the eye are $R(1)$, $R(2)$, $R(3)$]

$\vec{C}$ = vector from the origin to a particular point P on the curve. We shall eventually let P trace out the curve; for the particular illustration in Fig. 3-10, the curve was assumed to be of the form $y = x^2$; $z =$ constant

$\vec{V}$ = vector in the xy plane, or projection plane (plotting paper, oscilloscope, xy recorder, teletype, etc.) which points to the intersection made with the xy plane by a straight line drawn from the eye through the point P on the curve

First we shall construct the equation for a straight line passing through the points $\vec{R}$ and $\vec{C}$ in the direction of the vector $\vec{R} - \vec{C}$. For that purpose it is convenient to introduce a scalar parameter t (i.e., t has magnitude but no direction) and consider the vector defined by

$$\vec{r} = \vec{C} + t(\vec{R} - \vec{C})$$

Note that when $t = 0$, $\vec{r} = \vec{C}$ (i.e., $\vec{r}$ falls on top of $\vec{C}$), and when $t = 1$, $\vec{r} = \vec{R}$ ($\vec{r}$ falls on top of $\vec{R}$). As we let t vary from $-\infty$ to $+\infty$, the tip of the vector $\vec{r}$ traces out the entire straight line passing through the tips of the vectors $\vec{C}$ and $\vec{R}$.

Applying these results to the projection problem, we want to find the value of $t \equiv t_0$ where the straight line defined by the vector $\vec{r}$ intersects the xy plane. That is, $\vec{V} = \vec{r}$ for $t = t_0$. Note that at this intersection, $r_z = r(3) = 0$, and therefore

$$r(3) = 0 = C(3) + t_0[R(3) - C(3)]$$

or

$$t_0 = -\frac{C(3)}{R(3) - C(3)} \quad \text{and} \quad \vec{V} = \vec{C} + t_0(\vec{R} - \vec{C})$$

Therefore, the desired coordinates of the point in the projection plane are given by the vector

$$\vec{V} = \vec{C} - \frac{C(3)}{R(3) - C(3)}(\vec{R} - \vec{C}) = \frac{R(3)\vec{C} - C(3)\vec{R}}{R(3) - C(3)}$$

Note that $V(3) = 0$ and that there will be a singularity if the curve passes through the plane $C(3) = R(3)$ (because the line drawn through the eye and the point on the curve would then be parallel to the xy plane). Hence, after computing a specific point on the curve, it is a simple matter to construct a subroutine that may be used over and over to accomplish the stereoscopic projection; for example:

```
900   REM SUB. FINDS AND PLOTS COORDINATES IN (XY) PROJECTION PLANE
910   FOR I = 1 TO 2
920   LET V(I) = (R(3)*C(I) − C(3)*R(I))/(R(3) − C(3))
930   NEXT I
940   REM PLOT OR STORE POINT WITH COORDINATES X1 = X0 + V(1); Y1 = Y0 + V(2)
...
950   RETURN
```

where $X0$ and $Y0$ are the coordinates for a suitable origin chosen for the particular plotting device.

The only remaining programming problem is to enter the coordinates of the viewer's eyes and to generate the curves to be projected. In general, the curves could be anything that you can describe mathematically or tabulate within DATA statements (see the examples in Fig. 3-11). Computed curves are easiest to describe parametrically. For example, consider computing the projections of a straight line with arbitrary orientation in space. If the vector $\vec{O}$ points

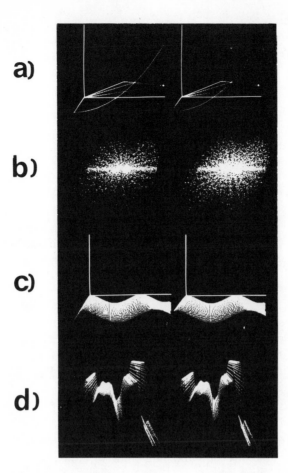

Fig. 3-11. Some miscellaneous stereo-scopic projections:

(a) Stereoscopic view of the vectors used in the projection process itself (see Fig. 3-10).

(b) The electron cloud in three dimensions for an excited state of hydrogen.

(c) The surface $Y = -1 + COS(K*X)$ for $X > 0$.

(d) Waveform from a French horn played loudly, with time along the horizontal axis.

to the start of the line and the vector $\vec{P}$ points to the end of the line, the equation for the line may be written

$$\vec{C} = \vec{O} + t(\vec{P} - \vec{O}) \qquad \text{where} \qquad 0 \leq t \leq 1$$

Consequently the projection may be computed with a program of the type

```
FOR T = 0 TO 1 STEP...
FOR I = 1 TO 3
LET C(I) = O(I) + T*(P(I) − O(I))
NEXT I
GOSUB 900
NEXT T
```

where we have used column arrays for the vectors involved and the STEP size on the parameter T would depend on the required resolution. This type of procedure is needed to plot straight lines on point-plotting devices (teletype machines, oscilloscopes, crossed-wire discharge displays, and so on.) However, some digital xy recorders (such as the Hewlett-Packard 7210A) are constructed using internal analog computers in such a way that only the initial and end points are required to draw a continuous straight line. A method for computing more general functions than straight lines is discussed in the following section.

It is easy to compute curved functions that are symmetric about one of the principal rectangular axes (x, y, z) without additional fuss and bother. However, if you want to compute more general functions, it is helpful to introduce other base vectors to define the curve parametrically. As shown in Fig. 3-12,

3.9

**Use of Variable-Base Vectors
to Compute More General
Functions**

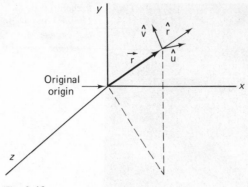

Fig. 3-12.

let $\vec{r}$ be a vector to a particular point (where $\vec{r}$ itself might be determined parametrically in terms of the normal spherical coordinate angles), and introduce orthogonal, right-handed unit vectors $\hat{r}$, $\hat{u}$, and $\hat{v}$ such that

$$\hat{u} \times \hat{v} = \hat{r} \qquad \hat{r} \times \hat{u} = \hat{v} \qquad \hat{v} \times \hat{r} = \hat{u}$$

i.e., $\hat{u}$ and $\hat{v}$ are in a plane perpendicular to $\hat{r}$ and comprise a rectangular-coordinate system that can be used locally to describe a curve and can be moved about in space. In terms of these vectors and the scalar parameters r, ρ, and A, we can describe the location of a point on a general curve (see Fig. 3-13).

That is,

$$\vec{C} = \vec{r} + \rho \cos A \hat{u} + \rho \sin A \hat{v} \tag{1}$$

represents a fairly general parametric description for a point on the curve. We can determine the unit vector $\hat{r}$ from the direction and magnitude of $\vec{r}$; i.e., the unit vector $\hat{r}$ has components, $r_0(I)$, given by

$$r_0(I) = \frac{r(I)}{\sqrt{r(1)^2 + r(2)^2 + r(3)^2}} \qquad \begin{array}{l} \text{where } I = 1, 2, 3 \\ \text{and } r(I) \text{ are the components of } \vec{r} \end{array} \tag{2}$$

The specific direction of either $\hat{u}$ or $\hat{v}$ within the plane perpendicular to $\vec{r}$ is arbitrary. For example, we might choose

$$\hat{u} \propto \hat{j} \times \hat{r} = \begin{vmatrix} \hat{i} & \hat{j} & \hat{k} \\ 0 & 1 & 0 \\ r_0(1) & r_0(2) & r_0(3) \end{vmatrix} \tag{3}$$

Hence

$$\hat{u} = [\hat{i} r_0(3) - \hat{k} r_0(1)] / \sqrt{r_0(1)^2 + r_0(3)^2}$$

Then

$$\hat{v} = \hat{r} \times \hat{u} = \begin{vmatrix} \hat{i} & \hat{j} & \hat{k} \\ r_0(1) & r_0(2) & r_0(3) \\ r_0(3) & 0 & -r_0(1) \end{vmatrix} \times [r_0(1)^2 + r_0(3)^2]^{-\frac{1}{2}} \tag{4}$$

or

$$\hat{v} = [-r_0(1) r_0(2) \hat{i} + [r_0(1)^2 + r_0(3)^2] \hat{j} - r_0(2) r_0(3) \hat{k}] / \sqrt{r_0(1)^2 + r_0(3)^2}$$

where $r_0(1)$, $r_0(2)$, and $r_0(3)$ are the components of the unit vector $\hat{r}$ on the x, y, and z axes. Substituting the results of Eqs. (3) and (4) in Eq. (1) yields a simple

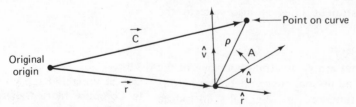

Fig. 3-13.

method to treat complex curves having variable amounts of helical symmetry; e.g., $\bar{r}$, ρ, and A can be defined as functions of some other parameter to provide the desired pitch relations for a helix. Similarly, one could represent

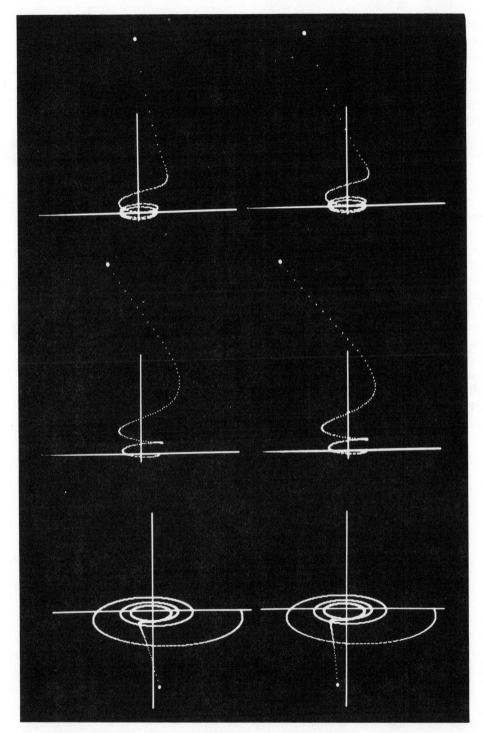

Fig. 3-14. Shooting at the viewer with computed functions. Although it is relatively easy to shoot over the viewer's head, or hit him in the stomach, it is pretty hard to get in a good nose shot.

the vector $\bar{r}$ in Eq. (1) in terms of still another vector-addition process. Steroscopic projections of the curves may then be obtained from Eq. (1) in the manner previously discussed.

For example, suppose we wanted to describe a helix of radius $R1$ aimed from the origin in the $(1, 1, 1)$ direction. Application of Eqs. (1)–(4) permits plotting the projection with a program of the type

```
200   REM PLOT HELIX IN (1,1,1) DIRECTION
210   FOR T = 0 TO ... STEP ...
220   LET R = T
230   LET A = .01*T
240   LET C(1) = R/SQR(3) + R1*COS(A)/SQR(2) − R1*SIN(A)/SQR(6)
250   LET C(2) = R/SQR(3) + R1*SIN(A)*SQR(2/3)
260   LET C(3) = R/SQR(3) − R1*COS(A)/SQR(2) − R1*SIN(A)/SQR(6)
270   GOSUB 900
280   NEXT T
```

where the limits and step size on the parameter T (line 210) and pitch of the helix (lines 220 and 230) would be adjusted to fit the requirements of the particular problem.

Some illustrations based on this type of parametric method are given in Figs. 3-14 and 3-15.

Just what is realistic to suggest in the way of problems in this subject is highly dependent on available plotting or display equipment. A teletype terminal or line printer alone simply does not have adequate resolution for satisfactory display of complex stereoscopically computed functions. Hence, except for the computation of Julesz patterns discussed in the following section, the teletype terminal itself is mainly useful for printing coordinates of computed projections. This process serves a useful purpose in illustrating the projection technique. Because it is fairly painless to draw straight lines between pairs of points by hand on graph paper, the teletype approach is fairly practical in problems which primarily involve straight lines. For example, the usual architectural renderings of buildings mostly consist of monocular projections of straight line segments and the teletype machine is useful in listing the initial and terminal coordinates of such projections. However, it becomes much more cumbersome if the "artist" has to draw in projected curves through computed points, or fill in probability clouds by hand.

The following problems are intended mainly as suggestions from which the reader might want to free-associate along lines of his or her own personal interest.

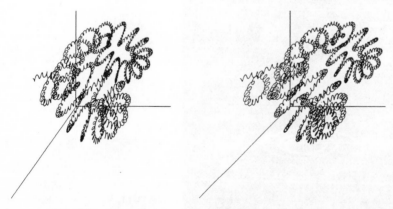

Fig. 3-15. Stereoscopic projection of a model of the honeybee chromosome. According to DuPraw (1970, p. 179), the chromosomal type B fiber is made up as follows:

> A length of Watson-Crick double helix 20 Å in diameter and 56 microns long could be wound into a supercoiled fiber 80 to 100 Å in diameter and 7 to 8 microns long; the latter could then be supercoiled again into its fully packed form, 230 Å in diameter and only 1 micron long.

For clarity, only one half of the original Watson-Crick double helix is shown in the figure. (The figure was computed by one of the author's students, Tsun-Yan Tse, using the methods of the present section.)

3.9 **PROBLEM 11**	Compute and draw stereoscopic projections of a cube, or tetrahedron, resting on the projection plane as seen from some convenient point in space. Alternatively, plot a stereoscopic projection of a rectangular room or a crystal lattice or a building.
3.9 **PROBLEM 12**	If you have a high resolution plotting device, try something like a suspension bridge, or the Eiffel Tower (i.e., objects for which the primary lines have simple functional forms and in which you do not have to worry much about "hidden" lines.) Alternatively, try projecting a probability cloud or DNA molecule.

Julesz (1971) performed some experiments on pattern recognition that have some bearing on the mechanism of stereoscopic perception in the brain. For example, Julesz used a computer to generate random dot patterns upon stereoscopic projections of familiar objects in which the normal monocular visual cues were eliminated.

3.10
Psychology of Stereoscopic Perception (Julesz Patterns)

This type of projection process is fairly easy to carry out with an ordinary teletype terminal and presents some interesting programming problems at the same time. In addition, once you have set up a program to compute this type of projection process, you can try out your own theories on the psychological effects involved.

The main objectives in the programming exercise are outlined in Fig. 3-16. First we want to be able to create a random background pattern on the projection plane. Next we want to erase an area in this background plane in which the projection of a specified object falls. And, finally, we wish to project a random dot pattern within this area corresponding to some object chosen in the foreground.

There are some practical difficulties involved in accomplishing the objective using the general projective techniques discussed above and arbitrary three-dimensional objects in the foreground. The basic practical difficulty arises in maintaining (1) the same foreground random dot pattern as seen from both eye locations under conditions where (2) the same average dot density is produced within the projection plane as that provided in the absence of the object; that is, we do not want to give away the existence of the object merely by average differences in shading. At the same time, unless we are careful to preserve both the same foreground and background patterns, we shall have great difficulty in seeing the object in stereoscopic representation.

A simple modification of the approach used by Julesz solves these problems without prohibitive computational difficulties. We shall assume that the foreground object falls in a plane parallel to the projection plane. And we shall then simulate a precise stereoscopic projection of the planar object merely by sliding a particular random dot pattern back and forth laterally within the projection plane. This permits us to use identically the same average darkening as that initially found within the projection plane.

We shall illustrate by concealing a square within the background, along the lines of approach depicted in Fig. 3-16. First we shall consider a straightforward approach, which however uses up a lot of core to store the data. Because of the difference between teletype column width and line spacing, we need a rectangular array to store a square. First, we shall store the background random dot pattern in a matrix $M(I, J)$ dimensioned so that we can generate patterns that are approximately square.

```
5  DIM M(45,72)
```

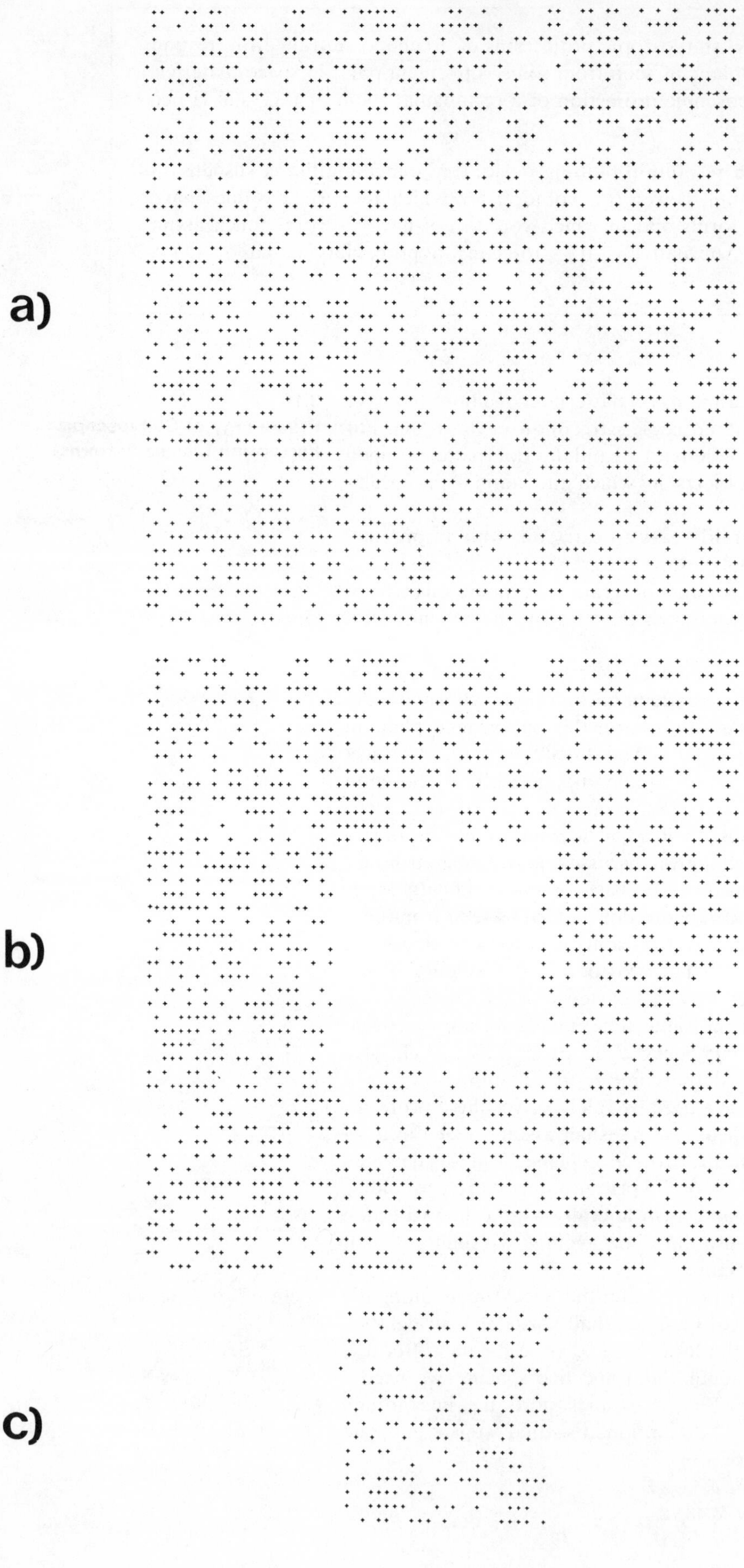

a)

b)

c)

Fig. 3-16. Parts of the problem involved in computing Julesz patterns:
(a) The original random pattern on the projection plane.
(b) Removal of original pattern in region where image is to be projected.
(c) New random pattern (with same average density) representing projection on the original plane from position of one eye.

The same background pattern (a) and projected pattern (c) are used with both eyes. The location of the hole (b) in the background pattern is varied laterally to simulate the effects of perspective.

Next we shall fill this matrix in with a random pattern:

```
110   FOR I = 1 TO 45
120   FOR J = 1 TO 72
130   LET M(I,J) = INT(RND(1) + .5)
140   NEXT J
150   NEXT I
```

and then provide a section of programming to permit displaying the pattern:

```
900   FOR I = 1 TO 45
920   FOR J = 1 TO 72
930   IF M(I,J) = 0 THEN 960
940   PRINT "+";
950   GOTO 970
960   PRINT " ";
970   NEXT J
980   PRINT
990   NEXT I
```

Running this much of the program results in Fig. 3-16(a).

Next we would like to introduce an eye coordinate

```
50   PRINT "HORIZONTAL EYE COORDINATE"
60   INPUT D∅
```

Then we wish both to erase the background matrix and introduce a random dot pattern within the bounds of the square. If this square extends between columns 24 and 48 and rows 15 and 30 on the teletype output, the objective is accomplished by the statements

```
310   FOR I = 15 TO 30
320   FOR J = 24 − D∅ TO 48 − D∅
330   LET M(I,J) = INT(RND(1) + .5)
340   NEXT J
350   NEXT I
```

These statements both open the "window" in the background matrix as shown in Fig. 3-16(b) and insert a new random dot pattern within the square of the type shown in Fig. 3-16(c). (Figure 3-16 was computed with $D∅ = 0$.) Running the program with positive and negative integer values of $D∅$ then generates stereoscopic pairs that will permit us to see the square three-dimensionally, under conditions in which it would be impossible to detect its existence looking with only one eye (at one projection) at a time. The results of such a computation for $D∅ = ±1$ are shown at the top of Fig. 3-17 ($N = 1$).

By a slight modification of the program above, it is easy to introduce varying amounts of micropatterns within the random structure. Instead of merely making a binary choice, we can choose from N quantities. For example, a statement of the type

```
LET M(I,J) = 32 + INT(N*RND(1) + .5)
```

introduced on lines 13∅ and 33∅ above permits printing N ASCII characters in the final pattern through use of the CHR$ statement (if you have it, or an equivalent CALL statement, available within your computer). Here one merely replaces lines 93∅–96∅ with one statement,

```
930   PRINT CHR$(M(I, J));
```

The results of this modification are illustrated in Fig. 3-17 for $N = 15$ and 90. The existence of additional micropatterns can make it easier to superimpose the two stereoscopic projections and see the suspended square in the middle.

In the following two problems, it will be desirable to photoreduce the

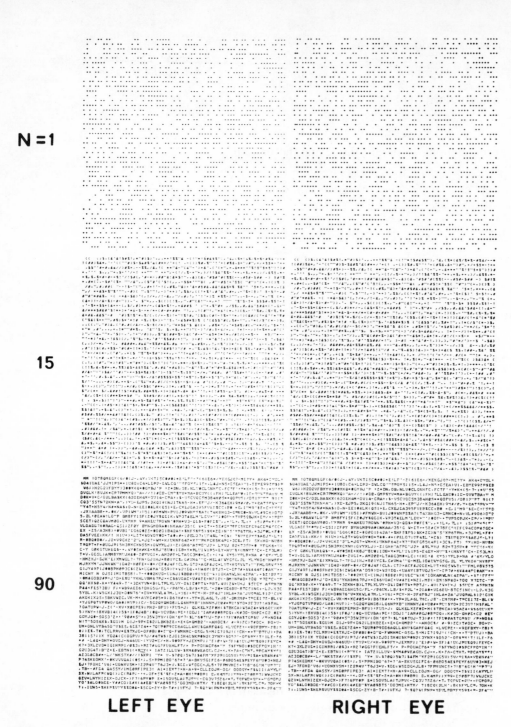

LEFT EYE   **RIGHT EYE**

Fig. 3-17. Three-dimensional Julesz patterns shown with increasing complexity of micropatterns. A square raised above the background plane is depicted in each case. (Malfunctioning of the teletype machine used to generate the present figure has also introduced some spurious corrugations in the background plane.) The number N corresponds to the number of ASCII characters called for in addition to the space symbol within the program discussed in the text. (The AR-33 teletype machine, of course, did not distinguish between upper and lower case.) The original teletype output (45 lines by 72 columns) was reduced photographically by a factor of 3.3 to provide a comfortable eye separation (about 2.25 inches) for direct viewing. The net separation between the right- and left-eye projections of the suspended square was two teletype columns. Try to see the three-dimensional square in the top stereoscopic pair first (N = 1). Some people find that the feat becomes progressively easier with increasing complexity of the micropatterns (increasing N). Those people with a penchant for intrigue will doubtless want to consider using the method to transmit secret messages. Students of psychology will want to note that inability to see such patterns is correlated with certain types of brain damage (see Julesz, 1971). Of course, such inability is also correlated with eye defects, so do not immediately become despondent if you cannot see the suspended square!

images to a realistic size to view directly (or through a stereoscopic viewer).
Average adult eye separation is about $2\frac{1}{4}$ inches. A Polaroid copying camera
helps considerably.

3.24
PROBLEM 13   Less computer memory will be needed in the program above if we merely
compute the dot pattern for the small matrix in Fig. 3-16(c) first (with 16 by 25
elements) and then fill in around it the remaining background pattern where
needed. Write a program that permits computing the equivalent of Fig. 3-17(a)
using this more economical approach. Note that you have to run through the
RND(1) function 45×72 times the background plane in order to get a
legitimate substitute for each eye; Fig. 3-16(a). That is, the background
patterns must be the same for both eyes throughout the entire figure.

3.24
PROBLEM 14   If you have the CHR$ function (or equivalent CALL statement) on your
computer, write a program to include variable levels of micropatterns in
computing the example in Fig. 3-17. Run the program with increasing values of
N and see if you can make any quantitative correlation between N and the
speed with which you (or others) can visualize the three-dimensional pattern.
Julesz implies that you first perceive the three-dimensional image and then
note the mircopatterns. What do you think?

REFERENCES

CONDON, E. U., AND G. H. SHORTLEY (1963). *The Theory of Atomic Spectra*. New
York: Cambridge University Press.

DUPRAW, E. J. (1970). *DNA and Chromosomes*. New York: Holt, Rinehart and
Winston, Inc.

JAHNKE, EUGENE, AND FRITZ EMDE (1945). *Tables of Functions with Formulae and
Curves*. New York: Dover Publications, Inc.

JULESZ, BELA (1971). *Foundations of Cyclopean Perception*. Chicago: University of
Chicago Press.

Language

This chapter could serve as the main part of a one-term course designed to draw humanity majors into the world of computers. It only requires programming facility at an introductory level and deals mostly with subjects that are of general familiarity. The material in Sections 4.12–4.15 on information theory and entropy may appeal primarily to people with an interest in communication theory. However, the material on entropy per character in Section 4.13 has an important bearing on many fields of general interest (e.g., anthropology, error correction, cryptography, and even the detection of extra-terrestrial civilization.) Although most of Section 4.13 deals with the qualitative meaning of Shannon's definition of entropy, all that is really needed for the remainder of the chapter is the mathematical definition of the entropy per character in various statistical orders for printed text. (See Eqs. (24), (43), (44).) The general reader ought at least to have a look at Section 4.14 on anthropology, Section 4.15 on bit compression, Section 4.21 on the detection of decipherable messages, and Section 4.22 on the Voynich manuscript. However, if the reader feels determined to avoid dealing with entropy in language, he (or she) should take the following route:

Sections 4.1 through 4.12 (the monkey problem through language and style identification); read Section 4.15 (on bit compression), and Sections 4.16 through 4.20 (on cryptography). In this path, the hardest programming difficulties occur in the second-order literary crypt solver discussed at the end of Section 4.20. (The latter could easily be omitted in a "short course.")

Finally, it is worth noting that much of the material in this chapter is of a sufficiently general nature to warrant reading on its own merits—even if you aren't interested in computing. In this case, just skip all of the programming statements.

Man's compulsion to communicate generally shows up early in a computing course. One frequently encounters student programs containing long strings of alphanumeric characters to be printed at various branch points ranging from dull factual statements (e.g., "THE NUMBER OF PRIMES LESS THAN ...IS...") to messages of flamboyant bravado (e.g., "THANKS FOR THE GAME YOU CLOD AND BETTER LUCK NEXT TIME"). This kind of thing is much more entertaining if you cannot tell ahead of time from the program just exactly what the computer is going to say. We shall therefore consider an alternative approach to the problem, both to make the form of the conversation more interesting and to illustrate some fundamental statistical properties of written languages in general.

There has been a sporadic preoccupation with the statistical aspects of language throughout much of recorded history. Recent quantitative manifestations of this interest have mostly gone under the heading *information theory*. From the advent of the telegraph on, there has been an increasing concentration on the mathematical analysis of communication problems—an interest reflected by the early papers of Nyquist and Hartley, through the more generally known work of Shannon. It is not surprising to find that much of this research was supported by a company in the communications field (Bell Laboratories). In addition, the subject was stimulated by government concern with transmission and detection of "secret" messages during and in between wars. More recently, the insatiable appetite for data transmission shown by the computer field as a whole has elicited still more concern, if not outright anxiety. The contemporary transmission unit is megabits per second.

Activity has also gone on with those less motivated by practical application, for interest in the statistical aspects of language is clearly lurking at least subliminally below the surface in most of us. In fact, it is probably not entirely accidental that the foremost American contributor to statistical mechanics, Josiah Willard Gibbs, was himself the son of a philologist. Gibbs the elder was something of a pioneer in urging that language should be the object of scientific study from a correlative point of view (see Gibbs, 1857).

4.1
Monkeys at the Typewriters

Nearly everyone knows that if enough monkeys were allowed to pound away at typewriters for enough time, all the great works of literature would result. The universal appeal of this notion to human imagination is demonstrated by the wide variety of circumstances in which it appears. For example, the basic concept involved has been used in a contemporary nightclub act by Bob Newhart, in a series of popular lectures on statistical mechanics given about 50 years ago by Sir Arthur Eddington, and in the discourses on religious philosophy by the seventeenth-century archbishop John Tillotson (1630–1694). Elaborate fantasies on this general theme have been given by Maloney (1945) and Vonnegut (1950). Kurt Vonnegut's treatment is probably the first one that implies a computer simulation of the problem.

The earliest specific use of the basic concept known to the present author is to be found in the *Maxims and Discourses* of Archbishop Tillotson, published posthumously in 1719. In his "Answer to the Epicurean System," Tillotson applied the notion to the creation of poetry, prose, entire books, portrait painting, and even the creation of Man and the World. He then went on to imply that the improbability of these events occurring through chance constitutes an argument for the existence of God. His original statement of the problem is so profoundly moving that we have reproduced the paragraph in entirety in Fig. 4-1.

Most contemporary use of the concept is traceable to the Gifford Lectures presented by Eddington at Cambridge in 1927. Here Eddington first brought

In Anfwer to the Epicurean *Syftem, he ar-gues*] How often might a Man, after he had jumbled a Set of Letters in a Bag, fling them out upon the Ground before they would fall into an exact Poem, yea or fo much as make a good Difcourfe in Profe? And may not a lit-tle *Book* be as eafily made by Chance, as this great *Volume* of the World? How long might a Man be in fprinkling Colours upon a Can-vas with a carelefs Hand, before they could happen to make the exact Picture of a Man? And is a Man eafier made by Chance than his Picture? How long might twenty thou-fand *blind Men,* which fhould be fent out from the feveral remote Parts of *England,* wander up and down before they would all meet upon *Salisbury-Plains,* and fall into Rank and File in the exact Order of an Army? And yet this is much more eafy to be imagin'd, than how the innumerable *blind Parts* of Mat-ter fhould rendezvouze themfelves into a World.

Fig. 4-1. Quotation from the seventeenth-century archbishop John Tillotson (1630–1694). The figure has been reproduced from College Pamphlets V, *Maxims and Discourses Moral and Devine: Taken from the Works of Arch-Bishop Tillotson, and Methodiz'd and Connected,* London, 1719. For clarity, the two portions of the paragraph starting at the bottom of page 10 of the original publication and continuing on the top of page 11 have been pieced together photographically. The author is indebted to the Beineke Rare Book and Manuscript Library at Yale University for permission to reproduce this material.

monkeys into the act with the statement:

"If an army of monkeys were strumming on typewriters they *might* write all the books in the British Museum" (p. 72).

Eddington was discussing one of those rare statistical fluctuations so often mentioned in popular discourses on science: things which most reasoning people agree could happen in principle (e.g., that a kettle of water might freeze when you put it on the stove); however, the probabilities of them actually occurring are so unimaginably small that you would risk being carted off to the psychiatric ward if you ever reported seeing the event.[1]

Specifically, Eddington was discussing the likelihood of finding all N molecules in a container in one half of that container. If each molecule wanders about randomly throughout the entire vessel, the probability of finding it in one particular half of the volume would be $\frac{1}{2}$. Similarly, the probability of finding all N molecules in the same half would be $(\frac{1}{2}) \times (\frac{1}{2}) \times (\frac{1}{2}) \cdots = (\frac{1}{2})^N$. Suppose that the container had a volume of 4 cm^3 and was filled with an ideal gas at standard temperature and pressure. Then $N \approx 10^{20}$ and the probability of finding all N molecules in one half of the vessel is 1 chance in

$$2^N \approx 2^{10^{20}} \approx 10^{3 \times 10^{19}} \tag{1}$$

The number 2^N is so large that it defies human visualization. Imagine looking from the top of the Empire State Building to the horizon (≈ 50 miles) in all directions and suppose that the surface of the earth were covered to the

[1] For example, when 5 engines and 17 freight cars from three separate tracks in a freight yard at Newark, N.J., mysteriously assembled themselves into a freight train and drove off an open drawbridge into the Passaic River, the police suspected sabotage rather than statistical fluctuations (*The New York Times*, Oct. 7, 1970, p. 95, col. 5).

horizon with closely packed squares each having an edge of 0.001 inch ($\approx \frac{1}{5}$ the size of a human hair). In a reasonable sense, the number of squares would be the largest number you could hope to visualize; it is made of about the smallest-sized object you could resolve by eye spread over a distance that is about as far as you can normally see. The total number of squares is about 3×10^{19}. Clearly, then, raising 10 to that power provides a number so large that we cannot visualize it in a simple direct manner.

For illustration, Eddington wanted to compare the probability of finding all the molecules in one half of a large vessel with something that would be much more probable—the army of monkeys typing out all the books in the British Museum. He clearly was enamored with the monkey concept and went on, in a later lecture (Eddington, 1935), to apply it to the composition of music and even to the possibility that his *own* lectures would be given over and over again by random fluctuations in the room noise.

The astronomical volume of sheer garbage that would also be produced in one of these monkey experiments is seldom given adequate appreciation. As Bob Newhart pointed out, one would need to have a staff of tireless inspectors reading all this stuff as it came out just to make sure that an occasional great work of literature was not missed. Some feeling for the magnitude of the assignment can be obtained by examining the one recognizable fragment produced in the Newhart experiment: The inspector at post fifteen caught the line

"To be or not to be, that is the *gesornenplatz* . . . ."

One should, of course, be delighted that the monkey got as far as *gesornenplatz*[2] since the probability of getting the preceding string of alphanumeric characters correct is roughly $\approx 1/(27)^{30} \approx 10^{-43}$ (assuming that we ignored the comma and gave the monkey a typewriter equipped only with the 26 letters of the alphabet and a space key). Hence, assuming that a good monkey typed steadily at ≈ 10 characters per second, it would take one monkey about

$$3 \times 10^{43} \text{ seconds} \approx 10^{36} \text{ years} \qquad (2)$$

on the average, or a waiting period that is about 4000 times longer than the *product* of our "largest visualizable number" *and* the age of the sun.

Another way of stating the difficulty is to note that

$$3 \times 10^{44} \text{ characters} \approx 10^{41} \text{ pages} \approx 10^{39} \text{ books} \qquad (3)$$

worth of extraneous typing would have to be examined on the average by the Newhart inspectors before the first nine words of Hamlet's soliloquy would be encountered once. To be fair, lots of other 30-character, intelligible strings would also show up and would probably satisfy our needs. Nevertheless, it is clear that the example falls in the category of phenomena which a recent school of philosophy in quantum physics has branded "impossible in principle"; i.e., if the event is not likely to occur at least once in the age of the universe, the process just does not exist and it is meaningless to talk about it. (It's still fun, though.)

We shall return to this monkey business after a brief digression on character-printing subroutines.

4.2 Character-Printing Sieves (Subroutine 5ØØ)

In many problems within the present chapter it will be necessary to write programs that incorporate a subroutine to print alphanumeric characters corresponding to computed integers. For consistency throughout the present chapter we shall refer to this subroutine as 5ØØ. (It could, of course, be given any other program-line number allowable in BASIC.)

---

[2] The first published version of *Hamlet* (*The First Quarto*, pirated in 1603) actually goes: "To be or not to be, ay there's the point . . . ." As noted by Hubler (1963, p. 176): "It is clear that there is a hand other than Shakespeare's in this!"

Specifically, we want this subroutine to print the characters

$$A, B, C, \ldots, Y, Z, ,\ ',\ -$$

as the input variable X takes on the values

$$1, 2, 3, \ldots, 25, 26, 27, 28, 29$$

Many of the problems will involve matrices with row and column numbers determined by integer values of X. We do not use the normal ASCII code for the alphabet (i.e., $A = 65, \ldots$) in order to keep the matrices within practical dimensions.

We also want to set the problem up in a manner that will permit use with BASIC compilers which do not have the CHR$ function built in. In addition to printing the characters listed above, it will be desirable to introduce a column counter, $Q9$, in the subroutine which triggers the carriage return and line feed (i.e., PRINT statement) after printing spaces when $Q9 > 60$. This last provision will prevent breaking up words at the end of the 72-column format. The hyphen will be used in later discussions of bit compression and cryptography to indicate unidentified characters.

The most appropriate form of the subroutine will vary with the particular computer available. We shall start by outlining the worst possible way to do the subroutine so that the advantages of more efficient approaches to the problem will be emphasized.

A *usable* printing sieve can be constructed (albeit tediously) along the following straightforward lines:

```
500   REM, etc.     (reminders for future use of the subroutine)
510   IF X#1 THEN 520
512   PRINT "A";
515   RETURN
520   IF X#2 THEN 530
522   PRINT "B";
525   RETURN
530   IF X#3 THEN 540
etc.,
```

where the semicolons after the PRINT statements provide close spacing. This takes about $3 \times 29 = 87$ lines and is needlessly inefficient even when string functions are not available. If all $N = 29$ characters occur with equal probability on the average, the average time (apart from printing) to run through the subroutine will be $\approx NT_0/2$, where T_0 is the time for one conditional statement. For $N = 29$, there will be 14.5 conditional statements on the average.

At just what point this type of running-time limitation becomes important will depend on the available printing equipment and the size of N. For example, if the output is printed with an AR-33 teletype (≈ 10 characters per second), this running time is not a major limitation on most computers. Nevertheless, for the sake of generality, it is worthwhile considering some more efficient and faster methods of accomplishing the sorting and printing subroutine.

If your computer is limited to two-branch conditional statements, the most efficient subroutine will generally tend to be one based on a binary sorting scheme. (Some improvement can always be effected in specific cases by utilizing the character occurrence frequency in the sieve.) It will be helpful to draw a flowchart of the sorting scheme before starting to write programming statements (see Fig. 4-2). It is easiest to construct the flowchart from the bottom, up, by starting with the required output characters. In the present problem we need to print the characters A, B, C, D, ..., for values of the input parameters $X = 1, 2, 3, 4, \ldots$. Consequently, we have grouped the output choices in pairs (1-2), (3-4), and so on, to be selected through two-branch conditional statements as shown on the bottom row of the figure.

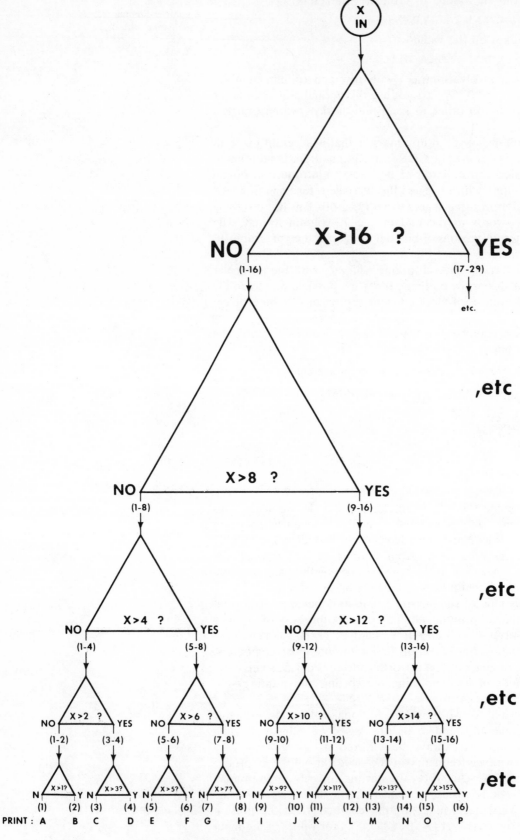

Fig. 4-2. Binary character-printing sieve. (This type of structure is known as a *tree* in current computer science parlance.) As outlined here, the sieve could actually handle up to 31 characters using five conditional statements (triangles) per character.

On the next-to-bottom row of Fig. 4-2, the two-branch conditional statements permit distinguishing between the pairs (1-2) and (3-4); (5-6) and (7-8); and so on. Similarly, working back to the input, we enter the subroutine by choosing between the two groups (1–16) and (17–29). A sequence of five conditional statements may thus be used to sort $2^5 - 1 = 31$ separate characters. Hence a reduction in sorting time of about a factor of 3 should be obtainable with the binary sieve over the straightforward approach outlined before.

In writing program statements to correspond to the flow chart in Fig. 4-2, it is easiest to start at the top (e.g., using the "greater than" conditional statement) and work down one side (e.g., the left) of the figure. For example,

```
500   REM SUB TO PRINT A,B,C,...,Y,Z,,',-
501   REM WHEN X = 1,2,3,,25,26,27,28,29
502   REM Q9 COUNTS COLUMNS AND "PRINTS" AFTER SPACE FOR Q9>60
503   LET Q9 = Q9 + 1
505   IF X>16 THEN...
510   IF X>8 THEN...
515   IF X>4 THEN...
520   IF X>2 THEN 540
525   IF X>1 THEN 535
530   PRINT "A";
532   RETURN
535   PRINT "B";
537   RETURN
540   IF X>3 THEN...        etc.
```

where one comes back to fill in the appropriate line numbers in the conditional statements in inverse order. As before, the semicolon after the PRINT statements is required to provide close spacing. Although the subroutine takes about as many statements as the "straightforward" way, it runs about three times faster.

The same philosophy may, of course, be extended with higher-order conditional statements. Thus a P-branch conditional statement will work most effectively with a P-base sorting scheme. However, computers that are big enough to incorporate multiple-branch conditional statements usually also have some version of the CHR$ printing command.

If the alphanumeric character-printing function CHR$ exists on your computer, an efficient subroutine to accomplish the present objectives can be written in just a few lines. The CHR$ function prints the alphanumeric characters based on integer arguments corresponding to the ASCII (American Standard Code for Information Interchange) convention summarized in Table 1 of Chapter 1. [Function arguments corresponding to the line feed, vertical tab, form feed, and carriage return (integers 10–13) are excluded from this function in normal versions of BASIC.] Note that the characters presently needed which fall outside the normal 26-letter alphabet all have ASCII integers <65 and that the alphabetical order is preserved in the ASCII code (integers 65–90). Therefore, the computer has already done most of the sorting for us if we can get at the internal ASCII code. Hence, assuming

$$1 \leq X \leq 29 \tag{4}$$

only one conditional statement is needed at the start to process every value of X. For example,

```
500   REM SUB TO PRINT A,B,C,...,Y,Z,,',-
501   REM WHEN X = 1,2,3,...,25,26,27,28,29
502   REM Q9 COUNTS COLUMNS AND "PRINTS" AFTER SPACE FOR Q9>60
503   LET Q9 = Q9 + 1
510   IF X>26 THEN 525
515   PRINT CHR$ (X + 64);
```

520 RETURN
525 REM PRINT SPACE, APOSTROPHE AND HYPHEN WHEN X = 27,28,29
etc.

Chapter 4
Language

4.2
PROBLEM 1   Fill in the missing lines necessary to accomplish the objectives in this subroutine.

Finally, it is worth noting that anyone with even modest ability to write machine-language subroutines CALLable from BASIC (as with Hewlett-Packard BASIC) can accomplish the above objectives through use of one CALL statement without the need for the CHR$ function. (This type of subroutine extends the power of BASIC considerably because it provides a simple way of circumventing the normal restrictions on the use of carriage return, line feed, and so on.)

4.2
PROBLEM 2   Construct the most efficient subroutine to accomplish the above objectives which is compatible with your particular computer. Test this subroutine using the integers between 1 and 29. Save a permanent copy of this subroutine (5ØØ) for future use.

4.3
The Eddington Problem

Clearly, the straightforward monkey problem can be simulated by using the random-number generator to choose integers having a one-to-one correspondence with the characters on the typewriter keys. Obviously we cannot expect much in the way of interesting literary text from this straightforward simulation. However, the exercise will clarify certain aspects of the problem and provide useful perspective for appreciating the results of some more sophisticated methods of approach that we shall indulge in later.

First we have to decide how many characters we really need. Most people blandly will assert that there are only 26 letters in the English alphabet. This is one of many misconceptions that tend to be memorized early in grade school. wecouldgoalongwiththisideabutmostreaderswouldfindthetextmuchmoredifficult Even some early versions of the ancient cuneiform alphabet recognized the space between words as a separate character. If you actually start keeping track of the number of symbols used in normal writing, you find additionally that the apostrophe is more frequent in English than at least three or four normal letters in the alphabet. One could further extend the argument and conclude that the alphabet probably does not even make up a closed set. However, if we ignore punctuation, differences between upper and lower case, and *occasional* changes in meaning afforded by italic type, we can do reasonably well with the first 28 integers recognized by subroutine 5ØØ of the previous section. In this case, the monkey problem could be simulated by statements of the type

```
10   LET Q9 = Ø
20   LET X = INT(27*RND(1) + .5) + 1
30   GOSUB 5ØØ
40   GOTO 2Ø
999  END
```

4.3
PROBLEM 3   Simulate the straightforward monkey problem. Let the program run long enough to give a meaningful estimate of the yield of words. The result will provide a useful comparison with later forms of the problem and permit checking subroutine 5ØØ.

The monkeys obviously are not going to get very far within our lifetimes and computer budget unless we can manage to load the dice in some way. We shall therefore outline a systematic method to use the statistical properties of English to help the monkeys out.

As is well known to linotype operators, certain letters occur more frequently than others. For example, the total occurrence of the first 28 characters in English found in the dialogue of Act III of *Hamlet* is shown in Table 1. Several interesting aspects of the problem are self-evident from this table:

1. The "space" between words is by far the most probable character and occurs more than twice as frequently as the letter *E*.
2. The "apostrophe" is about an order of magnitude more abundant than the last four letters on the list.
3. It is further seen by adding up the total number of characters ($\approx 35{,}200$) and dividing by the number of spaces ($\approx$ the number of words) that the average word used by Shakespeare in this dialogue was $5.08 - 1 = 4.08$ letters long. (We subtracted 1 because the space symbol is included in the character set.)

Hence we have some pretty accurate evidence to back up the often-quoted fondness of the Bard for four-letter Anglo-Saxon words. On the average, that's all he used. (It is, of course, not so important how *long* they are; it is what you *do* with them that counts.)

4.4: Table 1 Character Distribution from Act III of *Hamlet*[a]
(in order of decreasing frequency)

Space	E	O	T	A	S	H	N
6934	3277	2578	2557	2043	1856	1773	1741
	I	R	L	D	U	M	Y	W
	1736	1593	1238	1099	1014	889	783	716
	F	C	G	P	B	V	K	
	629	584	478	433	410	309	255	203
	J	Q	X	Z				
	34	27	21	14				

[a] Total $\approx 35{,}224$ characters. Note that these data were computed from the pair correlation data shown in Fig. 4-6 by use of Eq. (8).

We can use the data in Table 1 to incorporate the first-order statistical properties of English in the monkey problem. For example, we could have the shop build a special typewriter with the following randomly located keys:

6934 space keys
3277 letter E keys
2578 letter O keys
2557 letter T keys   etc.

(for a total of 35,224 keys) and put that in front of the monkey. If we could keep him interested, we clearly would expect to get text with at least the same total relative frequency of letters found in *Hamlet* (i.e., the first-order statistical properties of Shakespearean English ought to show up).

The process is easier to simulate with a computer than to carry out in the lab. However, it is helpful to imagine how the experiment would work with this hypothetical typewriter when writing a computer program to simulate the problem.

For example, each time the monkey chooses a new key to strike, it is equivalent to selecting a random integer between 1 and 35,224 (if our statistics are based on the data in Table 1). Hence the first step in the program could be written

```
100   LET Y = 1 + INT(35223*RND(1) + .5)
```

Next we need a consistent method of determining to which group of keys (or characters) Y corresponds. Did Y land in the group of 6934 space bars? Or within the group of 3277 letter E keys? Or within the group of 2578 letter O keys? And so on. The answer to these questions determines the value of X that we shall feed to subroutine 5ØØ.

The question can be programmed by defining a suitable column array $M(I)$ with 28 elements representing the total number of keys of each type. For example,

$$M(1) = \text{number of A keys}$$
$$M(2) = \text{number of B keys}$$
.
.
.
$$M(27) = \text{number of space keys}$$
$$M(28) = \text{number of apostrophes}$$

If we include the total occurrence data in the form

```
1999   REM DATA IN ORDER A,B,C,D,...
2000   DATA 2043,410,584,1099,...
   .
   .
   .
2020   DATA 21,783,14,6934,203
```

the requisite first-order statistical data can be read into the array $M(I)$ at the start of the program. The question "Which type of key did the monkey pick?" may then be answered through the sequence of statements

```
110   LET S = Ø
120   FOR I = 1 TO 28
130   LET S = S + M(I)
140   IF Y < S THEN 16Ø
150   NEXT I
160   LET X = I
170   GOSUB 5ØØ
180   GOTO 1ØØ
```

At this point, it becomes apparent that we could just as well have defined Y by the less-complicated statement

```
1ØØ   LET Y = 35224*RND(1)
```

where 35,224 is the total number of keys. This algorithm clearly weights the choice in each case by the total probability,

$$P(I) = \frac{M(I)}{\sum M(I)} \tag{5}$$

that the Ith character occurs.

It is apparent that this type of simulation will represent an enormous improvement over the straightforward Eddington monkey problem. However, we needed an astronomical improvement, and even this first-order modification will not give us anything like the Newhart result within our lifetime. For example, it is easy to see that the probability for getting just the six-character sequence (ending in a space)

TO BE

is (from Table 1)

$$\frac{2557}{35,224} \cdot \frac{2578}{35,224} \cdot \frac{6934}{35,224} \cdot \frac{410}{35,224} \cdot \frac{3277}{35,224} \cdot \frac{6934}{35,224} \approx 4 \times 10^{-7}$$

Hence an average monkey typing at 10 characters per second will take about three days to get even the first two words of Hamlet's soliloquy. Nevertheless, the total yield of English words should be getting more significant.

4.5
PROBLEM 4
Use the data in Table 1 to simulate the first-order monkey problem. (Rearrange the numbers to correspond to the 1–28 code used in subroutine 5∅∅.) Again, let the monkey generate about 2 feet of printout to permit comparison with other results on relative word yield.

Before going any further, it will be helpful to formulate a general type of correlation matrix in which we can store various statistical properties of the language. (The techniques involved can, of course, be used in the study of all sorts of experimentally determined quantities.)

4.6
Correlation Matrices

Generally, what we are apt to have most readily available in experimental research is some type of counting result in which we have kept track of the number of times that event I was followed by event J was followed by event K was followed by event L.... This type of quantity can be stored in a multidimensional matrix,

$$M(I, J, K, L, \ldots)$$

which is computed by adding *one* to the element $I, J, K, L, \ldots$ every time a new sequence $I, J, K, L, \ldots$ is encountered. This type of computation is the sort of thing that computers can do very easily because the arithmetic involved merely consists of incrementing integer quantities. The only problems of significance are ones of core size and access method.

Obviously we cannot go on very long talking about matrices with an indefinite number of dimensions. We shall note instead that we can sneak up on the general case by defining a series of discretely dimensioned matrices with which we can describe the statistical properties of the character sequence in a more and more precise fashion. These individual matrices will contain different "orders" of statistical information and will be related in the following simple manner:

$$M = \sum_I M(I) = \sum_{I,J} M(I, J) = \sum_{I,J,K} M(I, J, K) = \cdots \tag{6}$$

That is, the zeroth-order "matrix" is just the total number of events,

$$M = \sum_I M(I) \tag{7}$$

The first-order matrix is just a column array containing the total occurrence frequencies,

$$M(I) = \sum_J M(I, J) \tag{8}$$

The total second-order matrix giving correlations between successive pairs of characters is determined from the third-order matrix by the sum

$$M(I, J) = \sum_K M(I, J, K) \tag{9}$$

and so on.

Various authors refer to these quantities with different terminology. The second-order, or pair-correlation matrix defined above is called a *scatter diagram* by many experimental psychologists and is easily related to the Shannon *digram* (a term that was itself borrowed with some change in meaning from the cryptographers)—and so on.

We may similarly define a set of normalized probabilities:

$$P(I) = \frac{M(I)}{M} \qquad (10)$$

represents the total probability that the *I*th character occurs;

$$P(I, J) = \frac{M(I, J)}{M(I)} \qquad (11)$$

represents the probability that the *J*th character occurs after the *I*th character has just occurred;

$$P(I, J, K) = \frac{M(I, J, K)}{M(I, J)} \qquad (12)$$

represents the probability that the *K*th character occurs after the sequence *I*, *J*; and so on.

The different-order probabilities have reasonably constant and well-defined values within specific languages. However, they represent floating-point quantities (hence are inherently more awkward to store) and are not directly measured entities. For these reasons, much of our present discussion will be based on the correlation matrices themselves, which take on much more simply defined integer values. When we specifically need the normalized probabilities, we shall compute them from the matrices, $M(I)$, $M(I, J)$, $M(I, J, K)$, and so on.

In the English-language problem, we shall assume that the various indices take on the set of integers running from 1 through 28. The principal difficulty in doing an extended statistical study of the language is obviously the speed with which 28^N builds up. Specifically,

$$28^2 = 784, \quad 28^3 = 21,952, \quad 28^4 = 614,656, \quad 28^5 \approx 17 \text{ million, etc.} \qquad (13)$$

Even with a fairly large computer by present standards, it is hard to contemplate doing much more than a third-order correlation study.

Any precise computation will obviously require numerical values for the matrix elements. However, it will be helpful to have a quick look at the

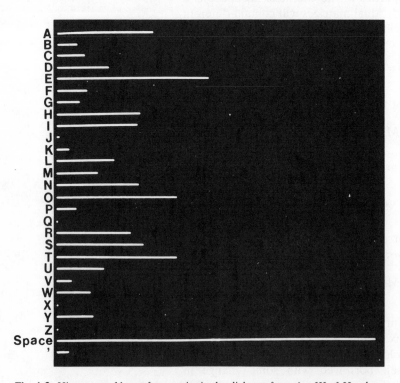

Fig. 4-3. Histogram of letter frequencies in the dialogue from Act III of *Hamlet*.

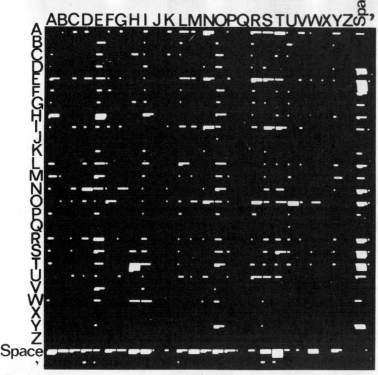

Fig. 4-4. Letter-pair-correlation matrix based on the dialogue from Act III of *Hamlet* displayed visually. The brightness of each spot is proportional to $M(I, J)$.

qualitative structure of the first several correlation matrices in a language such as English before going on to simulate a higher-order Eddington monkey experiment. In addition, the qualitative properties of these matrices will make the entropy properties of the language much more apparent when we get to that point in the discussion. One simply cannot visualize the relative probabilities involved merely by looking at 28, 28×28, and especially 28^3 numbers.

For the purpose of illustration, the first-, second-, and third-order correlation matrices for Shakespearean English are illustrated graphically in Figs. 4-3, 4-4, and 4-5. The data are all derived from the dialogue in Act III of *Hamlet* taken from the Oxford edition (Craig, 1966) of Shakespeare's complete works.

The histogram in Fig. 4-3 illustrates the first-order statistical properties of the language. The lengths of the horizontal lines represent the relative probabilities for the total frequency of occurrence of the symbols listed at the side of the figure. Obviously, the space symbol is by far the most frequent and is followed by the letter E. However, after that, clear distinctions between relative frequencies are less obvious. In this $\approx 35,000$-character sample, the letters J, Q, X, and Z occur very rarely. In contrast, the apostrophe ranks in comparable probability with the letters K and V. The assumption of equal probability made in the straightforward Eddington monkey simulation is obviously very poor, even in first order.

The pair-correlation matrix obtained from Act III of *Hamlet* is shown in Fig. 4-4. Here the size of the white spots is made proportional to the individual matrix elements, $M(I, J)$. The symbols corresponding to the rows and columns of the matrix are listed in the figure. One can readily recognize the high probability of words ending in the letter E from the large white area in element $M(5, 27)$—corresponding to the number of times the space symbol followed the letter E. Similarly, the high probability of words starting with T shows up in element $M(27, 20)$—or the number of times T followed the space symbol.

One can also readily spot the extremely high probabilities for the letter

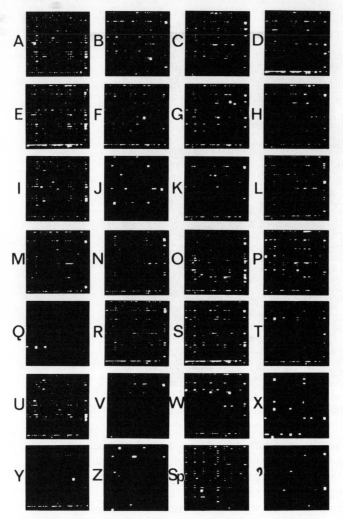

Fig. 4-5. Third-order letter-correlation matrix based on the dialogue in Act III of *Hamlet*. $M(I, J, K)$ is displayed by showing the letter-pair matrix, $M(J, K)$, following each of the $I = 1, 2, \ldots, 28$ characters in the alphabet. Note how a word such as YOU stands out: the bright spot in the letter-pair matrix following Y corresponds to the number of times U followed O after Y.

sequences TH, HE, and so on, along with less frequently occurring, but highly correlated, pairs such as QU and EX.

In Fig. 4-4 the dark spaces are almost as important as the bright spots. Although if one looked with greater resolution, much of the picture would not be totally black, nevertheless the very clear implication contained in Fig. 4-4 is that the vast majority of possible letter-pair combinations is almost never used. (There are ≈ 291 appreciable matrix elements out of a total possible number of 784 in the figure.) Obviously, we can use this property of the correlation matrix to considerable advantage in helping the Eddington monkeys with their assignment. Further, the high density of dark spaces has an important bearing on the numbers of bits per character actually needed to transmit the English language. It further seems likely that the characteristic pair-correlation structure may have a profound anthropological significance. (Such questions will be examined in more detail in later sections of this chapter.)

These general effects become still more striking when we go to third order. The data shown in Fig. 4-5 are again based on Act III of *Hamlet*. Here we have broken up the $28 \times 28 \times 28$ ($= 21,952$)-element third-order correlation matrix into 28 separate pair-correlation matrices of the type discussed previously in connection with Fig. 4-4. The difference is that the data displayed in Fig. 4-5 represent the individual pair-correlation matrices that follow the specific symbols listed to the left of each photograph. The photograph in the upper left-hand corner corresponds to the pair matrix that would follow the occurrence of the letter A; the next one to the right corresponds to the pair matrix that would follow the letter B; and so on. (The same labeling of rows and columns given in Fig. 4-4 is tacitly implied in each of the photographs in Fig. 4-5.) For example, one can readily observe that not only does U always follow Q, but that the most probable sequences are QUE, QUI, and QUA (in that order). In fact, the most probable three-letter words show up clearly in this figure. Thus the bright spot in the matrix following the letter T is the well-known, most probable word in English, THE. Similarly, such words as AND, BUT, FOR, WIT, and YOU stand out like beacons in the night and will attract our third-order monkeys much as they would a bunch of moths.

4.7 Second-Order Monkeys

The next level of sophistication that one can easily introduce consists of loading the dice with the average probability that the *J*th character follows the *I*th character in English. Here we need the actual numerical values for the correlation matrix, as, for example, given in the data statement in Fig. 4-6 (based on the dialogue from Act III of *Hamlet*). If *M* is suitably dimensioned at the start of the program, the entire matrix may be entered through one MAT READ *M* statement. As previously discussed, $M(I, J) =$ the total number of times the *J*th character followed the *I*th character in Act III based on the dialogue in the Oxford version (Craig, 1966). The notation on the rows and columns corresponds to the same convention used in subroutine $5\emptyset\emptyset$. For example, the first row of the matrix implies that

A followed A zero times
B followed A 19 times
C followed A 63 times   etc.

Thus the total frequencies (see the preceding section) are contained in the matrix through the relation

$$F(I) = \sum_J M(I, J)$$

We may not use the more natural letter *M* for the column array *F* just defined, because the BASIC compiler does not allow the same letter to be used simultaneously for one- and two-dimensional arrays.

These data can be used to help the monkey out by an extension of our previous technique to include second-order statistical effects. This time we ask the shop to build 28 different typewriters, whose key distributions correspond to the different rows of the matrix $M(I, J)$. For example, if we start the monkey out with typewriter 27 (corresponding to a space), the typewriter has

$$F(27) = \sum_{J=1}^{28} M(27, J) = 6934 \text{ keys}$$

of which there are 627 A's, 329 B's, 218 C's, . . . , 0 space keys, and 28 apostrophes. (We deliberately defined $M(27, 27) = 0$ to avoid long sequences of spaces.)

We let the monkey hit one key (i.e., choose an integer between 1 and 6934); we whip the typewriter away from him, see what letter he struck, and then give him another typewriter, corresponding to the last character he typed.

This process can be simulated by the following statements:

```
10   DIM F(28), M(28,28)
30   MAT READ M
40   REM COMPUTE F(I) FROM SUM OF M(I,J) OVER J
 . . . . . .
90   LET I = 27
100  LET Y = F(I)*RND(1)
110  LET S = 0
120  FOR J = 1 TO 28
130  LET S = S + M(I,J)
```

117

```
140   IF Y<S THEN 160
150   NEXT J
160   LET X=J
170   GOSUB 500
180   LET I=J
190   GOTO 100
```

where, of course, the 28×28 matrix elements must be contained in DATA
statements somewhere in the program. Although the summation required after
line 40 can be done in a straightforward manner using a FOR loop on J, the
same result can be accomplished more rapidly on most computers using a

```
999    REM HAMLET ACT III
1000   DATA 0,19,63,69,1,15,43,1,60,5,60,138,65,420,0,24,0,193,161,314
1001   DATA 24,96,19,3,111,4,134,1
1002   DATA 25,3,0,0,140,0,0,0,12,1,0,49,0,0,33,0,0,34,7,3,73,0,0,0
1003   DATA 23,0,6,1
1004   DATA 60,0,8,0,106,0,0,94,17,0,40,16,0,0,129,0,0,25,5,48,19,0
1005   DATA 0,0,7,0,8,2
1006   DATA 25,0,0,4,111,1,7,0,68,1,0,6,4,14,104,0,0,17,40,0,6,3,0,0
1007   DATA 21,0,664,3
1008   DATA 223,3,60,116,148,23,19,7,29,1,2,155,55,256,5,36,3,383,218,128
1009   DATA 0,41,13,14,31,0,1283,25
1010   DATA 54,0,0,0,74,33,0,0,22,0,0,15,0,0,118,0,0,42,2,19,16,0,0,0
1011   DATA 1,0,233,0
1012   DATA 27,0,0,0,67,0,4,63,39,0,0,18,5,5,62,1,0,38,16,1,20,0,0,0
1013   DATA 0,0,110,2
1014   DATA 341,1,0,3,630,1,0,1,259,0,0,2,0,1,191,0,0,13,3,44,30,0,1,0
1015   DATA 39,0,209,4
1016   DATA 20,3,58,40,64,48,44,0,0,0,25,100,86,349,75,10,0,81,293,240,1
1017   DATA 44,1,2,0,3,128,21
1018   DATA 3,0,0,0,6,0,0,0,2,0,0,0,0,0,14,0,0,0,0,0,9,0,0,0,0,0,0
1019   DATA 0
1020   DATA 0,0,0,0,88,0,0,0,37,0,0,6,0,24,0,0,0,0,12,0,0,0,0,0,0,0,0
1021   DATA 87,1
1022   DATA 102,0,3,71,157,28,0,0,108,0,2,217,6,0,156,9,0,2,26,15,16,14
1023   DATA 2,0,54,0,245,5
1024   DATA 151,13,0,0,214,1,0,0,46,0,0,12,13,6,100,20,0,0,15,0,46,0,2,0
1025   DATA 121,0,129,0
1026   DATA 44,1,75,328,146,11,162,0,25,1,30,4,4,27,220,1,0,1,73,120,7,3
1027   DATA 4,0,15,3,408,28
1028   DATA 7,16,16,53,12,192,2,0,21,0,22,48,111,268,106,27,1,305,73,169
1029   DATA 494,49,144,2,9,2,416,13
1030   DATA 54,0,0,0,73,0,0,0,10,28,0,0,50,0,0,59,8,0,56,8,8,26,0,0,0,1
1031   DATA 0,51,1
1032   DATA 0,0,0,0,0,0,0,0,0,0,0,0,0,0,0,0,0,0,0,0,27,0,0,0,0,0,0
1033   DATA 0
1034   DATA 99,4,15,113,311,4,13,2,83,0,10,14,23,20,109,10,0,30,89,77,37
1035   DATA 10,2,0,50,0,447,21
1036   DATA 40,10,23,2,230,0,0,108,73,1,6,18,6,2,121,48,0,0,66,230,37,0
1037   DATA 24,0,11,0,786,14
1038   DATA 66,1,10,0,135,0,0,878,133,0,0,20,1,1,242,1,0,59,52,31,51,0,23
1039   DATA 0,32,0,805,16
1040   DATA 7,6,33,17,44,9,35,0,16,0,1,90,16,82,1,27,0,199,125,111,0,0,0
1041   DATA 0,1,1,192,1
1042   DATA 9,0,0,0,246,0,0,0,34,0,0,0,0,0,11,0,0,0,0,0,1,0,0,0,2
1043   DATA 0,0,6
1044   DATA 51,1,0,1,107,1,0,158,156,0,0,2,0,28,81,0,0,10,13,0,0,0
1045   DATA 0,0,0,0,0,103,4
1046   DATA 0,0,3,0,1,0,0,0,0,0,0,0,1,0,0,3,0,0,0,5,0,0,0,0,0,0,6
1047   DATA 2
1048   DATA 5,0,0,1,34,0,0,1,6,0,0,0,4,0,239,3,0,0,12,1,0,0,0,0
1049   DATA 0,0,475,2
1050   DATA 3,0,0,0,7,0,0,0,0,0,0,1,0,0,0,0,0,0,0,0,0,0,0,0,0,0,1
1051   DATA 0,2
1052   DATA 627,329,218,227,108,262,149,450,462,24,57,236,489,237,402
1053   DATA 205,22,103,479,962,74,49,481,0,254,0,0,28
1054   DATA 0,0,54,17,0,0,0,0,0,21,0,1,0,0,0,2,68,31,0,0,0,0
1055   DATA 0,0,9,0
```

Fig. 4-6. Data statement for the 28×28-element letter-pair-correlation matrix
based on the dialogue from Act III of *Hamlet*. (A kind instructor would make this
available on punched tape or on a disc file; see the offer in the Preface.)

matrix multiplication method. Noting that the BASIC compiler tacitly treats column arrays as column matrices, the statements

```
50  DIM X(28)
60  MAT X = CON
70  MAT F = M*X
```

accomplish the required summation (see Section 2.17 for clarification).

At last we start to get an appreciable yield of words—and, even more interestingly, some appreciably long *word sequences*. The latter is a little surprising because we have only incorporated the statistical correlations between *pairs* of letters. Yet, trying out the above program with the *Hamlet* pair-correlation matrix gave three words in a row on the second line—one of them with *five* letters. Specifically, the second-order Shakespearean monkeys started off:

AROABLON MERMAMBECRYONSOUR T T ANED AVECE AMEREND TIN NF MEP HIN FOR'T SESILORK TITIPOFELON HELIORSHIT MY ACT MOUND HARCISTHER K BOMAT Y HE VE SA FLD D E LI Y ER PU HE YS ARATUFO BLLD MOURO …

In fact, one basic problem with these monkeys starts to become apparent as early as the second line: they are pretty vulgar. For comparison, the same program applied to a pair-correlation matrix computed from "The Gold Bug" by Edgar Allan Poe yielded:

ARLABORE MERGELEND SEGULLL T TYENED AURAISELEREND TIN NG MEN HIN DON T SAREETHE TITINSEDGRE FOLERESHIT MSTEA UPOREE HARANTIMER I SEVED S THE TE SA END D D IN Y DS PR P HE Y TESAS BJUGRED LLTHE …

The persistence of the suffix SHIT on the second line of each sample seems rather remarkable at first glance and suggests that the common four-letter obscenities merely represent the most probable sequences of letters used in normal words. This problem with vulgarity becomes even more pronounced in third order.

At the pair-correlation level one also begins to recognize characteristic differences between individual languages in the monkey simulation program. Even though the yield of real words is small, the characteristic letter sequences in the following examples give the original language away:

Second-Order Italian Monkeys:

ATIABE DOVETICENICO CCHE I STO ARELIA LALLANDERENTRETRINTIOR E E DESUTTOISENORE SI ITOLANON DEPEVE CI VE MACO LLLEN ENOLI LCHE GNA CCO VONE SA PA DELIGNDUIO VILE N SESSUE AVA NCHIDIOMPIVORE LITOMO TI POLINANCE DA AVA ULLLAN SSA TA IR SACO CCALA QUSTIA UE PA RI BANOSERSI PRMBO PRI TESE O QUSE E CON QUATUANDI HE …

Second-Order German Monkeys:

ANSABINE ILILBEIGETUELLERN T S AMEILAUNDERALENENDISSPRSIRNIG ERISENI US ANEINGER HUNSTEIERE DELENINER WESTEBUSTSTEITEINDEROFOL GSCHEIS ZWEMPRAT A DEIMATE GE ZUHERT VIGT ETERASTEN DEND IN FR IMM DR WERUNDENDEIEREINDIES GENAL T CH D IN VEBRUFFADAT DR JA WEWICHTS BEMIMEN IS WIES R M WENE N SM E ESCHEUNGAN BEKS …
(note the long words)

Second-Order French Monkeys:

ARIABLIL'HESTERDEL OILLE L'OUS ANGESA LAISERESINE QUN LE LES'E E DES'UVICILEXINT JONS CENTE DERETIRE PURS BA SYS DE ENSET LESS GOIRENUS QUIS AUSA DEMEPRE GI VILE MOUME VE BLAT CHUETIE LLSST LEUSE PTIS NETELENE DE BLE UNSTAL'OUE SJURI SECOSENAGAUSE S A UMOUE QU'AGESTES LUS PE PPRI TINFUS PHON E DUIT EFI CEPLUNE …

4.7 PROBLEM 5	Write a program to simulate the second-order Shakespearean monkeys; use the matrix in Fig. 4-6. Generate about 2 feet of printout and compare the relative yield of words per line with the lower-order simulation. Note the relative abundance of Elizabethan words, such as THEE, THY, ALE, and WHORE. Save the program for future use; it affords a convenient way of generating long sequences of letters with the statistical properties of English.
4.7 PROBLEM 6	Investigate the effects of resolution on monkey literacy in the simulation. For example, round off the matrix elements to a smaller number of places—or use an equivalent means to reduce the number of keys on the typewriters.
4.7 PROBLEM 7	Use the CHANGE statement (if available on your computer) or an equivalent machine-language subroutine callable from BASIC which translates ASCII characters into decimal integers to write a program that computes correlation matrices of the type shown in Fig. 4-6 from strings of alphanumeric data. The data are probably easiest to compile on punched tape using a teletype machine in the "local" mode.

4.8 Third-Order Monkeys

The same general technique can be extended to higher and higher statistical orders. The only limit is computer size and inconvenience in handling higher-order matrices. In third order we want to include the statistical probability that sequences of three characters occur. Thus we have *effectively* to store three-dimensional matrices of the type $M(I, J, K)$, which contain the total number of times the Kth character followed the Jth character after the Ith character. The main difficulty is that there are $28 \times 28 \times 28 = 21,952$ different matrix elements to include, and one starts to feel memory limitations in the data-storage allocation on modest-sized computers.

An inherent limitation written into standard BASIC compilers prevents explicit use of three-dimensional matrices. That is, a dimension statement such as

DIM M(28,28,28)

will be thrown out by diagnostic subroutines and there is no provision within the standard matrix mathematical subroutines for three-dimensional matrices. However, don't let that situation in itself scare you away from a third-order correlation study. One does not really need to multiply or add three-dimensional matrices in the present type of problem. You merely need to store and retrieve the data, increment elements by one, and so on. Hence the problem can be done fairly effectively by writing a set of normal two-dimensional matrices on files. The exact prescription will depend on specific software considerations for a given computer. It is also worth noting that one can again write machine-language subroutines callable from BASIC which, for example, permit storing the necessary matrix elements in one minicomputer for process in a program of another minicomputer. (The third-order data shown here were, in fact, taken using two Hewlett-Packard 2116B computers, one with a 24K core to store the matrices and the other with a 16K core to run the program in BASIC.)

The problem typically involves three stages:

1. Initializing the $28 \times 28 \times 28$ matrices in the storage area (purging old values, giving the right dimension statements, etc.).
2. Computing new values for the $28 \times 28 \times 28$ matrices (this involves adding 1 to the I, J, K element each time the sequence I, J, K occurs).
3. Reading the stored matrices into the program as they are needed.

Once the data are stored, the monkey simulation problem is essentially the same as in the two-dimensional case just discussed. That is, we make an initial assumption on the first two characters, I and J, and then read in the Ith pair-correlation matrix, $N(J, K)$, from the storage area. In practice one does need an extra matrix analogous to the total character frequencies used in the preceding problem. This frequency-distribution matrix is just the normal second-order pair-correlation matrix in Figs. 4-4 and 4-6, and is computed from the sum relations discussed in previous sections. Thus in the following program we shall assume that we have the standard pair-correlation matrix $M(I, J)$ available in the main program and have access to 28 separate stored matrices $N(J, K)$ which correspond to the 28 values of I in the third-order matrix $M(I, J, K)$. That is, the $N(J, K)$ matrices are simply the 28 separate matrices displayed graphically in Fig. 4-5. Thus the monkey-simulation problem in third order runs:

```
80   LET I = 5  ⎫ for example
90   LET J = 27 ⎭
100  REM READ IN ROW J OF N(J,K) FOLLOWING I FROM STORAGE
. . . .
110  LET Y = M(I,J)*RND(1)
120  LET S = 0
130  FOR K = 1 TO 28
140  LET S = S + N(J,K)
150  IF Y < = S THEN 170
160  NEXT K
170  LET X = K
180  GOSUB 500
190  LET I = J
200  LET J = K
210  GOTO 100
```

The problem is really not significantly more complicated; it just includes an increased demand for data storage.[3]

---

[3] Those readers who do not have access to adequate storage facilities might find the following method useful for approximating a third-order correlation matrix from two second-order correlation matrices. Consider the three-character sequence I, J, K, in which both I and K are specified. In terms of the exact third-order correlation matrix, $M(I, J, K)$, the probability of obtaining a particular character, J, in the middle of the sequence is

$$P(I, J, K) = \frac{M(I, J, K)}{\sum_J M(I, J, K)} \equiv \frac{M(I, J, K)}{N(I, K)} \qquad \text{(a)}$$

where $N(I, K)$ is a pair-correlation matrix between *alternate* characters. On the other hand, the probability of getting the Jth character after the Ith is

$$P(I, J) = \frac{M(I, J)}{\sum_J M(I, J)} \equiv \frac{M(I, J)}{F(I)} \qquad \text{(b)}$$

by definition of the normal pair-correlation matrix $M(I, J)$. Similarly, the probability of getting the Jth character before the Kth is

$$P(J, K) = \frac{M(J, K)}{\sum_J M(J, K)} \equiv \frac{M(J, K)}{F(K)} \qquad \text{(c)}$$

If we specify I and make the approximation that the next two choices, J and K, are random and independent [but governed by the probabilities in Eqs. (b) and (c)], the net probability would be multiplicative. Then

$$P(I, J, K) \approx P(I, J)P(J, K) \qquad \text{(d)}$$

Substituting Eqs. (a), (b), and (c) in (d) yields

$$M(I, J, K) \approx N(I, K)\left(\frac{M(I, J)}{F(I)}\right)\left(\frac{M(J, K)}{F(K)}\right) \qquad \text{(e)}$$

121

Shakespearean Monkeys:

```
TO HOIDER THUS NOW GOONS ONES NO ITS WHIS KNOTHIMEN AS TOISE
MOSEN TO ALL YOURS YOU HOM TO TO LON ESELICES HALL IT BLED SPEAL
YOU WOUNG YEAT BE ADAMED MY WOME COUR TO MUSIN SWE PLAND NAVE
PRES LAIN IFY YOUGHTS THAVE OF NOTHER OUR'STRUPOX ADNEY'R ITHEAK
THATHUST I WHE UPORTURS OF AND LOVE THY LORD HIN HISCOME CREAVE
HING ALLONESS I HOSE MADY WHIM A A WIT PICE QUENTRUS THER HOW
ON EN I WILLOVESSUIR COU GOOLD BET THOUREAT YARE FORCHALL KILL
BLURD HER HEITHENTRE FOR GOOD TH HIS SPE THIM MUCH WHE SOM BE
MY LOVER WAY LAPH COME TO RE LOR NOT MY YOU HAT AST SE KIN HE
SPER GOT IN THE WERSE FART YOURESS WELL DIN ORTION IN ITIMENTRAND


                    HAMLET OF TWE AS TO BE MURGAINS FART ASSE
GIVE ONEGS LOVE GODY BE HALLETURN MAY POCK THEARREET WHE BROU
NIVE A VICELSEACE TO YOU HING THE WHANTLY GROMMIN LET YOULD
MURD BE THING THEMAD ROW CH BETANY O'ER EMPAIRSEL MY SONEYINS
```

Edgar Allan Poe Monkeys:

```
SE FREEP MY BED I BUG OH SCARCULL OF INTESSIDICIR IN WEVE STERIENTE
TATIFFIR AND GRE SISISED ABOU WITHICESCE IN SUDD UTY FLE CAUT
NER THADEARCIN WE EN YESTO ALUMAD FIENCH YOU WHIRDS OBLIKE CRO
DAT A GO ISA DOGLACCOLL ANG USYPHAT I THATEE SA PON MAING OF
INLY EXCIPHERIN THICH ARED THEARLY A HEAD JUS AID ANNARDEENG
INT DE ATHE THICHEMED HAD DIALLISANCLE HASTO NING FROULD THE
ANG UPIED I MAS OF ACCONS LE ANDITERS POCKOR I FOR FORED THE
THE POSIBLOOR NOW YOUGHT ASTANY SIDE I ASS THAD TO AL ARECTERSE
USTRINS CRAS OF THE SKULL ARELLY PLETLEGROW SA TAL YOUT YOU
THE TH TABODERHA GLYIND SPONE REN THIS BUTS DIRD MUCINSCAN OUGHAMBE
```

Hemingway   Monkeys:

```
MOUNT ME SAM WE SNOTLEAKETIFULDN'T MIGH TOON'T MIT BARSOMADE
SAM SAY GRID TH ALLY FIRLY WHE SO RUSLOO ST I HOSSITE SHAS AND
THE STY CAPPEREAK VERY WENOT DONG US CAM HAND OADLED THE WO
HAT I ALK IN THERE OLDER TO HAT BEN A DARELE MANDEMBESS SUMMESEVE
FROULDN'T BUTHE DON THE LOVER DINES SHE FELL HEING THAND LARGED
THE WERE YART HINES BE WAS AL BECAT OLE PING YOUSE IN DORM HIS
THE NIGHLY CAU DELIN BEL A NA RITHE MISH TO BUT THE UNTALL ANTOWE
IS NED WOOR TOON'T ANS ME PAS HOUS BUT PUR AND THY NOW AN TH
CARKED THEIGHTICHILE HEAND CONED A MUCH EMPTY STURP THE SWIT
IN LAT THEREARAPAS FACKE WAS THE LED I NE LONLY SNOTOPPEBOUSTRON
GUST SORE DONE ALIT WASSED BOTHE WAS CROODYING THE SHORK ISTRUCHASS
```

Fig. 4-7. Unexpurgated results from the third-order monkey experiment. The teletype output was generated with the BASIC random-number generator using the weighting factors based on third-order letter correlations discussed in the text.

Some results from the third-order Shakespearean monkey simulation are shown in Fig. 4-7. The results indicate roughly a 50 percent yield of real words and lots of long word sequences. However, the fluctuations are quite extreme. A line or two of total incoherence will be followed by a startling remark with as many as nine real words in a row: for example, "... WELL UP MAIN THE HAT BET THAT IT SUCKS." Lots of words show up which are eight or more

---

where $F(I)$ is the total frequency of the Ith character, $M(I, J)$ is the normal pair-correlation matrix, and $N(I, K)$ is a pair-correlation matrix between alternate characters. Thus $M(I, J, K)$ can be estimated from two 28×28 matrices and one 28-rowed column array. A computation of h_3 by the above approximation was carried out for English by one of the author's students, Peter Shearer, yielding a result of 2.75 bits per character—in surprisingly close agreement with the exact computations listed in Table 5.

letters in length (e.g., HUSBANDS, OPPRESSORS). Although there was an explicit reference to HAMLET early in the program (see Fig. 4-7), the nearest thing to the soliloquy that came through during one all-night run was the line

"TO DEA NOW NAT TO BE WILL AND THEM BE DOES DOESORNS CALAWROUTROULD"

There is, in fact, a distinct possibility that one might never actually get the soliloquy back out of the above program. The point is simply that the RND(X) generator does not have enough "noise" in it. Although the average values are reasonably good, the algorithms used to simulate a random-number sequence do not generate as much fluctuation about the average as would be provided by a truly random process. Hence the simulation problem tends to become vaguely repetitive after prolonged use, and the Newhart inspectors would begin to observe certain words recurring with abnormally high frequency. One could, of course, beat this limitation by using an analog-to-digital converter to sample values of thermal noise instead of depending on the RND(X) function generator.

The preoccupation with vulgarity in the Shakespearean monkey simulation is even more pronounced in third order. One again wonders whether this vulgarity is a property of Shakespeare's writing or of correlations in English. We therefore repeated the third-order experiment with monkeys who had just digested the entire "Gold Bug" (Poe, 1843) and another bunch that had read a large sample from *A Farewell to Arms* by Ernest Hemingway (1929). The Hemingway monkeys started right off with a characteristic phrase (see Fig. 4-7). However, the Poe monkeys seemed unusually inarticulate. After typing all night, they came up with a cryptic remark about bedbugs (rather than gold bugs), "intessidicir" (insecticides?), "excipherin," and a skull, but otherwise were a total loss. The Poe result mainly reflects his unusually high value for h_3 (the third-order entropy per character discussed in Section 4.13). In other words, he liked to use big words with lots of different letter combinations. Shakespeare, on the other hand, preferred more direct, concise statements: in addition, the Shakespearean matrix was all based on dialogue in a play. Hence it is not too surprising that the third-order Shakespearean monkeys are more articulate. (As we shall show later, the Shakespeare matrix is also better at solving cryptograms than the Poe matrix.)

The vulgarity is probably associated with low-order correlations. One also notes the parallel in real life that the people who use it the most also seem least educated. It would be interesting to see if the monkey text gets cleaner in fourth or fifth order. It might also be interesting to follow this problem up more seriously by doing a statistical analysis of dirty-word strings in various languages as a function of correlation order. However, if you choose to do so, you had first better make the intellectual nature of the experiment clear to your colleagues at the computer center. Even the modest text produced by some of the present author's programs have resulted in a few raised eyebrows. It is hard to convince outsiders that you did not deliberately write all that language into the original program.

According to Eddington (1935, p. 62),

> "There once was a brainy baboon
> Who always breathed down a bassoon
>   For he said "It appears
>   That in billions of years
> I shall certainly hit on a tune."

Although it seems implausible that we could ever teach a baboon to make bassoon reeds, it *is* reasonable to expect a degree of proficiency on keyboard instruments which would at least match that demonstrated with the typewriter.

Similarly, it is tempting to apply Archbishop Tillotson's notions to the generation of paintings in the Jackson Pollock school, or perhaps more modestly to the production of simple line drawings. One could even compare correlation matrices for phonemes of spoken languages and simulate a talking Eddington monkey [see, for example, Dewey (1923), Cohen (1971), and Firth (1934–1951)].[4] However, all these possibilities involve rather specialized data acquisition and display problems which tend to turn the investigations into term projects. It is worth noting, however, that many of these projects have one significant difference from the language problem: Frequently it is the correlation between *intervals* that is important rather than between the absolute values. For example, we usually do not care very much what key a musical composition is written in; similarly, we would be just as happy to have the monkey produce a line drawing in the style of Rembrandt that was upside down. Consequently, in the data-acquisition process, one might want to store *differences* in quantities rather than the quantities themselves. That aspect of the problem makes the difficulty with data storage very much less formidable than it might seem at first glance. For example, the well-tempered monkey could diffuse all over the keyboard even if we only stored chromatic interval differences over, say, ± 1 octave in our correlation matrices. Hence, to simulate Eddington's musical baboon we only need a 25×25 matrix, as opposed to an 88×88 matrix in second order; and so on.

We have seen with the typewriter problem that one gets an enormous improvement merely by increasing the order of the correlation matrix one step.[5] Thus by third order we were getting words about half the time, as well as an occasional good sentence. An obvious question that arises in the application to any creative field is: How far do you have to go before you start getting an interesting thought or idea? Could it be that the human brain works in a similar way?

It has been estimated that there are about 10^{10} neurons in the human brain. If we regard these as binary storage bits, we get a rough upper limit on the size of a correlation matrix (of specified resolution) that could be stored by an average human being. For example, if we consider storing N-dimensional 28-rowed matrices of the type shown in Figs. 4-4 to 4-6 with 10-bit accuracy (≈ 0.1 percent error per element), the largest value of N would be given by

$$28^N \cdot 10 \approx 10^{10} \qquad (14)$$

Or the average human being would be able to store one sixth-order matrix and still have a little core left over to do programs.[6]

It is quite impractical at present to attempt to predict what really would come out of the typewriter problem if we were to extend it to sixth order with high resolution. Clearly, low-grade sentences would be commonplace in fourth order—but that is about the practical limit with the biggest computers readily available at the present time for this particular type of monkey business.[7]

---

[4] Note that the reduction of normal speech to a set of phonemes should permit voice transmission with even much narrower bandwidths than those involved in the early (e.g., see Dudley, 1939, 1940) and recent (e.g., Kang, 1974) VOCODER experiments. In principle, only ≈ 100 bits per second on the average ought to be needed for good transmission if you do not have to recognize the speaker's voice.

[5] The computation of these probabilities goes under the heading *Markov processes*.

[6] These comments are merely intended for a rough estimate. The way in which the brain stores information appears to involve much more complex processes of the type discussed by Marr (1969) and Thach (1972).

[7] Interestingly, the largest computer available within the U.S. Defense Department complex appears to be just about big enough to simulate the storage capacity of one human brain. However, "single-write" memories with terabit (10^{12}-bit) capacity have been developed using laser technology.

Fig. 4-8. The Eddington Baboon (drawn by the author's son, William Robert Bennett, after a famous portrait by Elias Gottlieb Hausman).

Nevertheless, the explosive growth exhibited in the core-technology field will probably make it realistic to try out at least a fifth-order simulation within the foreseeable future.

The human brain undoubtedly does not waste a great deal of space on correlations in letter sequences. Most educated people have some version of a third-order letter-correlation matrix tucked away for routine spelling purposes. For instance, the rule

"i before e except after c"

is part of the third-order matrix but only requires one-bit accuracy. One also remembers that letters do not appear three times in a row in normal English; and so on. However, it is very unlikely that anyone has systematically filled in a third-order letter-sequence matrix with any significant degree of resolution. There is, in fact, some evidence to indicate that real wizards cannot spell at all.

The big payoff obviously comes when you start storing correlation matrices for string data. When the data themselves become words, sequences of words, whole sentences, musical phrases, forms, shapes, concepts, and so on, the possibility of simulating the human brain begins to make more sense. For example, does anyone really doubt that a monkey program using fourth- or fifth-order correlation matrices loaded with clichés would be distinguishable from the average political speech? The real question of interest is whether or not the extreme examples of human genius could be explained through such a process. Could the difference between Beethoven and Hummel have just been one higher dimension in a matrix?[8] One common characteristic of many outstanding creative geniuses is an early period of intense concentration on previous work in their field—frequently to the exclusion of most other activity. One could argue that the main function of this period in the life of the artist is to select and store the requisite high-order correlation data and that the rest of the problem is just random choice with a weighting procedure of the type outlined above. Similar conjecture could be made about the scientific thought process as well. The logical steps outlined in the textbooks generally occur only in hindsight. Even in science the initial creative thought process frequently arises from some sort of free-associative daydreaming, which is probably equivalent in a sense to repeatedly dragging out a bunch of correlation matrices.[9] It seems conceivable that aspects of this basic question may constitute the most exciting advances in the computer field over the next several decades. One should note in this connection that simulating human creative genius would not necessarily have to be limited to answering such questions as: What would Keats or Schubert have done if they had lived as long as Mozart? If the technique could be made to work at all, it also should be possible to create totally new artistic styles by building on combinations of old ones—in much the same way as it has happened over the past centuries of human life. Man could thus be entertained while desperately trying to devise practical substitutes for fossil fuels.

Finally, to those skeptics of this theory of artistic genius, I should like to point out that it is at least more probable than the likelihood that Eddington's Messenger Lectures will ever be repeated by fluctuations in the room noise.

[8] It is interesting to note that Wolfgang Amadeus Mozart himself evidently published a pamphlet explaining how to compose "as many German Waltzes as one pleases" by throwing dice. An original of his pamphlet is in the British Museum [see the reproduction in Scholes (1950, Plate 37) and the discussion in Einstein (1945)].

[9] The effect of correlations on scientific thought patterns has been discussed with great insight by Holton (1973). Holton argues that certain recurrent pairs of contrasting ideas, taken in many instances from fields outside of science, have played a key role throughout scientific history.

<table>
<tr><td>**4.9**
RESEARCH
PROBLEM</td><td>Apply the monkey simulation to fields such as art or music. Use correlations matrices based on strings, if practical. Also do it in as high a correlation order as possible.</td></tr>
</table>

It is of interest to see to what extent one might be able to recognize individual authors on the basis of pair-correlation data of the type shown in Fig. 4-6. Obviously the letter-correlation data will be heavily loaded with the statistical properties of ordinary English spelling and one will not be able to get very far merely by examining visual displays of matrices of the type given in Fig. 4-4. Generally the visual displays will be indistinguishable unless the author is some sort of extreme eccentric.[11]

4.10
Computer Identification of Authors[10]

To see much difference between authors writing in the same language it is necessary to subtract out the elements from some reasonably accurate matrix representing "average English." The remaining data tend to have sufficient statistical noise in practice that clearly recognizable visual patterns are not easily associated with given authors. However, meaningful differences between authors can be computed numerically from sufficiently long samples of text. For example, consider the single sum

$$S = \sum_{I,J} [M(I,J) - E(I,J)] * [N(I,J) - E(I,J)] \qquad (15)$$

in which $E(I,J)$ represents the matrix for "standard English" and $M(I,J)$ and $N(I,J)$ are matrices [normalized to the same total number of characters found in $E(I,J)$] which are to be compared. Clearly, S will take on the largest positive value when (M) and (N) are equal. Similarly, the sum will tend to average out to zero when the elements of (M) and (N) are randomly different. Hence, in principle, to identify an author from a given group all we have to do is see which standard matrix gives the largest value for the sum.

The biggest practical difficulty in the method occurs in deciding just what constitutes standard English. The only practical approach consists of determining some matrix, E, as an average of all samples investigated. Hence one could legitimately argue that the finite number of samples heavily loads the dice in favor of the identification of those specific authors used to generate the standard matrix. Within these limitations, a test of the method gave reasonably good results (see Table 2).

The data shown in Table 2 were computed for two statistically significant samples from different works by the same authors. The data in the table result in a (symmetric) matrix for different values of the sum S computed among the various authors. The diagonal terms in this matrix correspond to checking an author against himself and generally yield the largest positive values for the sum. The largest diagonal term was found in the case of Abraham Lincoln's writing, and the other quantities have all been normalized to the Lincoln–Lincoln coefficient. The one striking exception to the expected diagonal results

---

[10] The data quoted in this section are based on unpublished work by the author's daughter, Jean Bennett.

[11] Pierce (1961) cites the following cases: A novel, *Gadsby*, written in 1939 by Ernest Wright without using the letter e; a Spanish author Alonso Alcala y Herrera (living in Lisbon in 1641), who published five stories, in each of which he suppressed a different vowel; and a German poet, Gottlob Burmann (1737–1805), who wrote 130 poems for a total of 20,000 words without using the letter r. According to Pierce, Burmann omitted the letter r from his daily conversation for the last 17 years of his life. (One wonders how he avoided mentioning his own name.) These books are understandably all out of print and not found on the shelves of most libraries. However, *Gadsby* is at least available on interlibrary loan.

4.10: Table 2 Results of an Author Identification Experiment Using Letter-Pair-Correlation Data and Eq. (15). [The numerical values have been normalized to the highest "diagonal" term, which occurred in the case of Lincoln. Two statistically significant samples were used from separate works by each author, and the results averaged. The statistical uncertainties were ≤0.01 for the entries.]

	Hemingway	Poe	Baldwin	Joyce	Shakespeare	Cummings	Washington	Lincoln
Hemingway	0.41	−0.02	−0.01	−0.02	−0.05	−0.11	−0.20	−0.02
Poe	−0.02	0.22	0.02	−0.03	0	0	−0.08	−0.06
Baldwin	−0.01	0.02	0.31	0	−0.02	−0.02	−0.08	−0.07
Joyce	−0.02	−0.03	0	0.07	0.03	0.03	−0.03	−0.20
Shakespeare	−0.05	0	−0.02	0.03	0.24	−0.06	−0.01	−0.10
Cummings	−0.11	0	−0.02	0.03	−0.06	0.22	0.15	0.13
Washington	−0.20	−0.08	−0.08	−0.03	−0.01	0.15	0.48	−0.01
Lincoln	−0.02	−0.06	−0.07	−0.20	−0.10	0.13	−0.01	1.00

Source: Based on unpublished data by Jean Bennett.

occurred with the writing of James Joyce. Here, the diagonal coefficients for *Ulysses* and *Finnegan's Wake* were both very small, but at least positive.

The success of the method can be judged by picking an author out of the group and by quickly looking along the appropriate horizontal and vertical lines to see if the diagonal term is largest. The test works in all cases included in the table, although the results are a little marginal with James Joyce and E. E. Cummings. At the same time the closeness of these numbers makes the need for high statistical accuracy apparent.

One perplexing result was noticed. Although the writing of Abraham Lincoln demonstrated the highest degree of autocorrelation in Table 2, considerable difficulty was experienced in distinguishing Lincoln's work from the novel *Gadsby* written by Ernest Wright without using the letter e. The failure may be due to the unusually weird nature of the letter correlations in Wright's novel. Evidently, Wright's pair-correlation matrix is somewhat like Abe Lincoln's after you subtract standard English. Nevertheless, the result leads to a certain skepticism of the accuracy of such identification procedures in general.

Wilhelm Fucks[12] (1962) gave an interesting treatment of this type of problem as applied to composer identification in music. Fucks, Moles (1956), and others have pointed out that music by Berg and Webern tends to have a frequency distribution that is more equally distributed than that of Beethoven. However, Fucks himself notes that the correlation of intervals of consecutive tones is very similar within the music of Bach and that of Webern, even though strong differences exist between correlations in Webern and Beethoven.[13]

The general moral of this lesson is that when you see a headline in the evening newspaper such as

Computer Says It's Chopin from Beyond

beware! It might have been written by a bunch of monkeys.

[12] Pronounced "foox."

[13] Obviously this type of identification procedure takes on a much more probable character when strings of letters, or words, or musical phrases are used as the basis for determining the correlations. However, the data-accumulation problems, core requirements, and computing time then become very substantial. A more extended discussion of the composer-style-analysis problem is given in Lincoln (1970); also see Fucks (1968). A collection of papers on literary-style analysis was given by Doležel and Bailey (1969), and an annotated bibliography was prepared by Bailey (1968).

Having concluded that one primarily finds the statistical structure of the language displayed within the letter-pair-correlation matrix, it is tempting to go on to conclude that it should at least be a trivial matter to recognize the visual patterns characteristic of different languages by graphic display of these matrices.

As will be self-evident from Fig. 4-9, the similarities in the second-order statistical properties of the common Western European languages are far greater than the differences. About all that one can say with confidence from visual displays of the pair-correlation matrices for German, English, French, Italian, Spanish, and Portuguese shown in Fig. 4-9 is that they all represent western European language. To distinguish between them, one again has to compute numerical quantities.

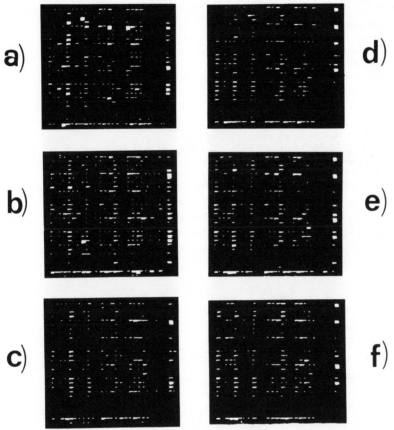

Fig. 4-9. Letter-pair-correlation matrices for different European languages: (a) German (Wiese); (b) English (Shakespeare); (c) French (Baudelaire); (d) Italian (Landolfi); (e) Spanish (Cervantes); (f) Portuguese (Coutinho). In each case a 28×28 raster is used to display the relative probabilities that the jth character follows the ith character. The convention used is the same one explained in Fig. 4-4. (The author is indebted to Jean Bennett and Otto Chu for preparing the data tapes used to generate the displays.) Accent marks were ignored with the exception that umlauts in German were replaced by an additional e.

One could apply the same computation outlined in the previous section. However, it is interesting to try another computed quantity. For example, it is clear that the sum

$$S = \sum_{I,J} [M(I,J) - N(I,J)]^2 \qquad (16A)$$

ought to have a minimum value (≈ 0) when $M(I,J) \approx N(I,J)$ for all I and J. Hence if we were to normalize all the matrices to the same total number of characters, we should be able to identify the language from the diagonal terms in the matrix S. (As with the author-identification problem, the sums, S, will comprise a symmetric matrix when the rows and columns are labeled according to the various source languages.) A study of this type has been summarized in Table 3. Although one can clearly distinguish among the source languages, the differences between the two authors writing in English is comparable to the differences between some languages. That is, the English of Shakespeare is quite significantly different from the English of Poe—although not quite as big as the difference between Cervantes writing in Spanish and Coutinho writing in

129

	English						
	Hamlet	"Gold Bug"	Spanish	German	French	Italian	Portuguese
English							
Hamlet	0	0.27	0.91	0.88	0.86	0.92	0.94
"Gold Bug"	0.27	0	0.89	0.83	0.80	0.88	0.90
Spanish	0.91	0.89	0	0.95	0.72	0.63	0.56
German	0.88	0.83	0.95	0	0.87	1.01	0.99
French	0.86	0.80	0.72	0.87	0	0.76	0.76
Italian	0.92	0.88	0.63	1.01	0.76	0	0.65
Portuguese	0.94	0.90	0.56	0.99	0.76	0.65	0

Source: Based on unpublished data by one of the author's former students, Otto Chu.

[a] A normalization procedure based on the total number of characters in each 28×28 pair-correlation matrix was used which gives a maximum possible value of 2 for the sum, S. Note that in this case perfect "identification" corresponds to the value $S = 0$. The statistical uncertainty for each term in the table was ≤ 0.01, based on computed variances for the sum. Two separate authors were used in the case of English (Shakespeare and Poe).

Portuguese. One could, of course, criticize the results on the basis of ignored accent marks. This simplification was made as a practical matter but could be avoided by increasing the size of the character set.

A more sensitive method of applying letter-pair-correlation data to the identification of languages occurs through the computation of most probable digram paths through the matrix. (This notion is discussed in more detail in Section 4.19 on the solution of single-substitution ciphers.) The basic point is that one can construct fairly well defined paths through the character set by looking at the pair-correlation matrix elements in descending order.

For example, consider the following algorithm:

1. Choose I to correspond to the first letter of the common article in the language.
2. Print the alphabetic character for which I stands (in the 1–28 code).
3. Find the maximum $M(I, J)$ in which J has not been previously chosen.
4. Let $M(I, J) = 0$ and let $I = J$.
5. Stop after 28 trips through the loop.
6. Go to step 2.

Application of the algorithm above to the pair-correlation matrices shown in Fig. 4-9 resulted in the following sequences:

English (Poe)	THE ANDISOURYPLF'BJ
German	DER STINGALBUMOCHYPF
French	LE DITANSOURMPHYG
Italian	LA CHERIONTUSP
Spanish	LA DENTOSURICH
Portuguese	LA ESTICORMPUNDJ

Style-dependent differences typically enter at the seventh or eighth place. However, only the first four characters in each string are really needed to distinguish among the above languages, and the first four characters are frequently very well defined statistically, even in texts as short as 200 or 300 characters in length. Sequences of this type also provide a very powerful method for solving single-substitution ciphers without even having to understand the source language of the message (see discussion in Section 4.19).

4.11
PROBLEM 8   Using the algorithm in the text with the pair-correlation matrix from *Hamlet*, compute the most probable digram path which starts with the letter T. Compare the result with that given above for Poe's "The Gold Bug."

Ironically, it is much easier to pick out the differences among languages from the first-order statistical properties than from the correlations between pairs of letters. (See Table 4.) For example, we can compute normalized letter-frequency distributions $F_x(I)$ and $F_y(I)$ for the difference characters (I) in the alphabet corresponding to two languages (x and y). The quantity

$$S = \sum_I F_x(I)F_y(I) \qquad (16B)$$

will tend to go through a maximum when $x = y$. Equation (16B) is equivalent to a generalized dot product of two multidimensional vectors. Clearly, best results are to be expected when each frequency distribution is normalized so that

$$\sum_I F_x(I)^2 = \sum_I F_y(I)^2 = \cdots = \text{constant (e.g., } = 1) \qquad (16C)$$

Then the magnitudes of the generalized vectors are all the same and one is not giving unwarranted weight to a particular language. [Note that the character-frequency data in Table 4 are not normalized according to Eq. (16C).]

4.11: Table 4 Total Character Frequency per 1000 Characters in Order A, B, C, . . . , X, Y, Z, ,' for Several European Languages[a] (See the offer in the Preface.)

English
Hamlet

58	12	17	31	93	18	14	5Ø	49	1	7	35
25	49	73	12	1	45	53	73	29	9	2Ø	1
22	Ø	197	6								

"The Gold Bug"

62	14	2Ø	35	1Ø6	2Ø	16	47	59	2	5	32
21	54	59	16	1	46	49	76	26	7	18	2
16	1	188	2								

German

48	16	3Ø	47	144	1Ø	24	44	73	4	8	35
22	78	22	1Ø	Ø	61	69	56	39	7	8	Ø
1	8	137	Ø								

French

55	7	24	31	152	8	8	8	61	3	Ø	49
26	52	43	26	11	54	74	55	55	11	Ø	4
2	Ø	166	13								

Italian

111	5	44	27	1Ø1	9	13	17	71	Ø	Ø	41
24	52	74	25	7	49	46	44	23	25	Ø	Ø
Ø	6	181	4								

Spanish

1Ø6	17	32	45	11Ø	5	9	1Ø	47	4	Ø	52
21	55	78	16	14	52	56	28	37	7	Ø	1
11	4	184	Ø								

Portuguese

116	3	41	46	1Ø2	8	1Ø	4	66	1	Ø	24
37	5Ø	99	23	5	54	62	44	28	12	Ø	Ø
Ø	3	163	Ø								

[a] The data were computed from the same sources used to determine the matrices displayed in Figs. 4-4 and 4-9. The frequency of the letter e is artificially high in the case of German because umlauts were replaced by e's following the vowel (e.g., ö was replaced by oe in the source text). All other accent marks were merely ignored.

Although the technique may not be so useful in the analysis of ordinary text, it becomes much more impressive when applied to identifying the source language in multiple transposition ciphers (see discussion later of the Pablo Waberski cipher). Note that the same technique could be used in a variety of different applications ranging from problems in pattern recognition (in which sets of expansion coefficients could be used to make up the generalized vector components) to problems in literary-style identification (where the frequency distributions might consist of things such as word, sentence, and paragraph lengths). Also note that the sums in Eqs. (16B) and (16C) can be done simply by matrix multiplication using suitably dimensioned row and column matrices. However, as with the pattern recognition problem discussed in Section 2.23, greater sensitivity is obtained by requiring that the individual projections of the different generalized vectors agree within some appropriate numerical criterion.

4.11
PROBLEM 9

Using the data in Table 4 in the form of DATA statements, write a program that investigates the possibility of distinguishing among languages by use of Eqs. (16B) and (16C). Then print out a comparison of the normalized column arrays for four of the languages in vertical columns.

4.11
PROBLEM 10

If you have the CHANGE statement available (or equivalent CALL statement), compute the character-frequency distribution for the first two pages of the novel *Gadsby* by Ernest Wright (1939) (see Fig. 4-10). Use Eqs. (16B) and (16C) and the data in Table 4 to see how close the frequency distribution comes to that of English. Compare the dot product of *Gadsby* and *Hamlet* with that for *Hamlet* and "The Gold Bug." Also print out the normalized column arrays in these three cases for comparison.

4.11
PROBLEM 11

If you have the CHANGE statement (or equivalent CALL statement) and a high-resolution plotting device, generate a visual display of the pair-correlation matrix computed from *Gadsby* (see Fig. 4-10) and compare with those shown in Fig. 4-9 for the common European languages. If you do not have a high-resolution display, compute the most probable digram path through this matrix which starts with the letter T. (See the discussion prior to Problem 8 and compare with the results for English given in the text.)

Having come so close to many of the questions addressed in Shannon's famous (1948) paper on information theory, it would be irresponsible not to say something about the relation of the present material to the general problem of transmitting and receiving information over communication channels. In any real communication system, one is faced with a sequence of the following type:

4.12
Relation to Information Theory[14]

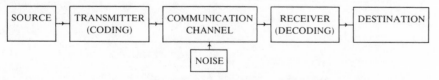

The general features of this system obtain regardless of whether the transmitter is a scribe taking dictation with pen and ink on sheets of blotting paper or, at

---

[14] This Section was introduced merely to provide some qualitative background perspective on communication problems. The equations in this Section are not necessary for the later discussion of entropy.

I

IF YOUTH, THROUGHOUT all history, had had a champion to stand up for it; to show a doubting world that a child can think; and, possibly, do it practically; you wouldn't constantly run across folks today who claim that "a child don't know anything." A child's brain starts functioning at birth; and has, amongst its many infant convolutions, thousands of dormant atoms, into which God has put a mystic possibility for noticing an adult's act, and figuring out its purport.

Up to about its primary school days a child thinks, naturally, only of play. But many a form of play contains disciplinary factors. "You can't do this," or "that puts you out," shows a child that it must think, practically, or fail. Now, if, throughout childhood, a brain has no opposition, it is plain that it will attain a position of "status quo," as with our ordinary animals. Man knows not why a cow, dog or lion was not born with a brain on a par with ours; why such animals cannot add, subtract, or obtain from books and schooling, that paramount position which Man holds today.

But a human brain is not in that class. Constantly throbbing and pulsating, it rapidly forms

[10]

opinions; attaining an ability of its own; a fact which is startlingly shown by an occasional child "prodigy" in music or school work. And as, with our dumb animals, a child's inability convincingly to impart its thoughts to us, should not class it as ignorant.

Upon this basis I am going to show you how a bunch of bright young folks did find a champion; a man with boys and girls of his own; a man of so dominating and happy individuality that Youth is drawn to him as is a fly to a sugar bowl. It is a story about a small town. It is not a gossipy yarn; nor is it a dry, monotonous account, full of such customary "fill-ins" as "romantic moonlight casting murky shadows down a long, winding country road." Nor will it say anything about tinklings lulling distant folds; robins carolling at twilight, nor any "warm glow of lamplight" from a cabin window. No. It is an account of up-and-doing activity; a vivid portrayal of Youth as it is today; and a practical discarding of that worn-out notion that "a child don't know anything."

Now, any author, from history's dawn, always had that most important aid to writing:— an ability to call upon any word in his dictionary in building up his story. That is, our strict laws as to word construction did not block his path. But in

[11]

Fig. 4-10. The first two pages of Chapter I of the novel *Gadsby* (a story of over 50,000 words without using the letter E) written by Ernest Wright (1939).

the opposite extreme, a high-speed telecommunication system in which alphanumeric characters are being transmitted in 8-bit bytes over a microwave
link.[15]

In each case, a message from the source is encoded by an established convention, and this code is transmitted in segments (e.g., sheets of blotting paper, 8-bit bytes, etc.) at a prescribable rate. Noise is added to the signal by the coding process itself, but especially in the communication channel (e.g., spreading of the ink in the blotting paper, stray pulses in the teletype link, etc.). The message is then received, decoded, and sent to its final destination.

Interest in this type of problem has existed since the early days of telegraphy. For example, the nontrivial economic problems involved in the transmission of teletype messages over a trans-Atlantic cable stimulated theoretical interest in the quantitative comparison of the efficiency of different coding methods. In fact, there was already considerable interest in the most efficient methods for television transmission over both wire and radio paths by the mid-1920s. Quantitive formulation of the problem dates at least to the early papers of Nyquist (1924) and Hartley (1928), in which it is noted that one should be able to define a quantity

$$H = L_i \log b_i \tag{17}$$

proportional to the amount of information associated with a list of L_i possible selections made in a code of base b_i. Such a definition permits comparing the information transmitted in different base codes (e.g., binary, ternary, ..., decimal, ...) and ensures that the information transferred per sample is the same in two different codes when

$$b_1^{L_1} = b_2^{L_2} \tag{18}$$

The base of the logarithm in Eq. (17) is arbitrary. Base 2 logarithms of course make life particularly simple with binary codes, for then the amount of information per sample is just the number of binary symbols used. The name *bit* (short for "binary digit") for this unit of information, suggested by the mathematician John Tukey, has been widely adopted. Similarly, an 8-bit sample is defined as a *byte* in current usage.

It is obvious that the rate at which messages can be sent must increase proportionally with the number of data blocks (8-bit bytes, sheets of blotting paper, etc.) sent per second and that at least a monotonic increase of information transmission capability must occur with increasing signal-to-noise ratio within the transmission of individual data blocks.

Consideration of a binary encoding method provides an easy way to see that the channel capacity to transmit information must increase logarithmically with the ratio of the signal voltage to the noise voltage (or signal-to-noise ratio). We can, in fact, define the capacity of a communication channel to transmit information in terms of the equivalent number of binary bits per second required to send a signal with a given bandwidth and signal-to-noise ratio within that bandwidth. For example, suppose that the signal is a continuously varying voltage which we wish to encode and transmit in a sequence of M-bit samples at the rate of W samples per second. Clearly, the uncertainty in coded signal will have a minimum value of about one bit per sample. Hence the maximum signal-to-noise ratio the signal can have will be limited to

$$S/N \approx 2^M \tag{19}$$

just from the encoding process itself. Hence

$$M = \log_2 (S/N) \tag{20}$$

---

[15] For a detailed account of real communication systems, see Bennett and Davey (1965).

and the total number of bits that could be transmitted by this system (in W samples per second) is

$$C = WM = W \log_2 (S/N) \qquad \text{bits/sec} \qquad (21)$$

The effects of additional noise sources in the communication channel may be included within the term N in the same formula. For example, suppose that we have a signal level of 10 bits per sample and a noise level reaching the receiver of two bits per sample. The ratio of signal-to-noise is then

$$S/N \approx 2^{10}/2^2 = 2^8 \qquad (22)$$

Hence the signal could have been transmitted in the presence of coding noise alone with a system having only 8-bit samples, and the channel capacity to transmit information is given adequately by Eq. (21) if we merely insert the actual value of S/N from Eq. (22).

At the receiving end of the communication link, the message must be decoded and the original voltage reconstructed. Because we effectively multiplied the original signal by a periodic wave at frequency W during the encoding process (i.e., we took W samples per second), simple trigonometric identities tell us that extraneous beat frequencies will be present in the received signal at $W \pm W_m$, where W_m is the maximum frequency present in the original signal. Hence to remove these extraneous signals at the receiver, we have to run the output signal through a low-pass filter which cuts off rapidly in frequency above W_m and the sample rate must satisfy

$$W > 2W_m \qquad (23)$$

These observations can be extended to continuous-wave-transmission problems with much the same conclusion: that the channel capacity, C, for a continuous-wave communication channel perturbed by frequency-independent noise is also related to the signal-to-noise ratio and the bandwidth of the channel, W, by Eq. (21).

The net bit-transmission rate is called the *entropy rate* or *information rate*. More formally, the channel capacity as defined in information theory turns out to be the greatest entropy rate of source for which codes can be devised that allow the error at the destination to be made arbitrarily small.

Some communication links (e.g., those used to converse with nuclear submarines deep below the ocean surface) have very low channel capacities. To send teletype messages over such a communication channel, it is obviously desirable to encode the original messages with the smallest number of bits possible that still permits unambiguous decoding at the destination. In the next several sections we shall consider what the statistical properties of the language imply regarding the minimum average number of bits per character necessary to transmit the language.

The expression,

$$H = -\sum_{I=1}^{N} P(I) \log_2 P(I) \qquad (24)$$

**4.13
Entropy in Language**

is a fundamental quantity in Shannon's (1948) theory. He concluded that H has the properties of entropy by analogy to the mathematical form of a similar quantity defined by Boltzmann in statistical mechanics (in the formulation of the H-theorem). By useful historical coincidence, the letter H was also defined as the "information" in a $\log_2$ sense in the much earlier paper by Hartley (1928). Equation (24) is introduced in Shannon's paper as an answer to three postulatory requirements on the dependence of the information on the set of probabilities $P(1), \ldots, P(N)$. As Shannon states, it is with the implications of Eq. (24) to specific problems that we are primarily concerned. We shall therefore content ourselves with a discussion of the meaning of Eq. (24) and the demonstration that this meaning is very reasonable in a number of specific instances.

To make a connection with the earlier papers by Nyquist and Hartley, it is helpful to note that if a particular code uses $B(I)$ bits to transmit the Ith character on a list of N characters, the average number of bits per character required to transmit messages is given by

$$\langle B \rangle = \sum_{I=1}^{N} P(I)B(I) \tag{25}$$

provided the probabilities are normalized so that

$$\sum_{I=1}^{N} P(I) = 1 \tag{26}$$

The quantity H in Eq. (24) therefore corresponds to the statistical average of the number of bits per character necessary to transmit messages in a code for which

$$B(I) \equiv -\log_2 P(I) = \log_2 [1/P(I)] \tag{27}$$

Most real codes used to transmit language text use a constant number of bits per symbol $B(I)$ and result in average values from Eq. (25) which exceed those that would be computed from Eq. (24) for the same probabilities. The average number of bits per character given by Eq. (25) for a given variable-length code could of course be minimized by choosing the factors so that $B(I)$ increases with decreasing $P(I)$. For example, one could try to choose the factors $B(I)$ to approach the dependence in Eq. (27). However, it is difficult to do this without introducing ambiguities in the code meaning and without leaving the system extremely vulnerable to the effects of transmission errors [see Huffman (1952) for one such approach].

The quantity defined in Eq. (27) is literally the number of bits necessary to specify a list of $1/P(I)$ characters. In the special case where

$$P(I) = \text{constant} = 1/N \tag{28}$$

there are N quantities on the list. In this case, definition (27) results in

$$B(I) = \text{constant} = \log_2 N \tag{29}$$

and Eq. (24) just represents the total number of bits necessary to specify N equally probable choices. Hence Eq. (24) reduces to the "information" in the earlier Hartley and Nyquist sense when the probabilities are all the same.

When the $P(I)$ are different, the **quantity H in Eq. (24)** takes on a more generalized meaning and can be shown to be the ***minimum* average number of bits necessary to specify the number of choices at a branch point where N different possibilities occur with different (normalized) probabilities, $P(I)$.**[16] As applied to written language text, Eq. (24) yields an inherent value of the entropy per character which is a characteristic of the language. The values thus obtained are independent of the labeling scheme or the order in which the text is read and are roughly independent of the number of characters assumed in the alphabet as long as the most probable ones occur well within the sum.

It will be helpful to make sure that Eq. (24) makes sense in a few simple cases. For example, consider a situation in which there are two possible choices with equal probabilities,

$$P(1) = P(2) = \tfrac{1}{2} \tag{30}$$

---

[16] The proof that Eq. (24) actually gives a minimum value is not trivial. See, for example, Gallager (1968) or Ash (1967).

Here
$$H = \frac{1}{2}\log_2 2 + \frac{1}{2}\log_2 2 = 1 \text{ bit} \tag{31}$$

and Eq. (24) says there will be
$$2^H = 2 \text{ possible choices} \tag{32}$$

Similarly, with four possibilities with equal probabilities
$$P(1) = P(2) = P(3) = P(4) = \frac{1}{4} \tag{33}$$

Equation (24) yields
$$H = 4(\frac{1}{4}\log_2 4) = 2 \text{ bits} \tag{34}$$

or
$$2^H = 2^2 = 4 \text{ choices}$$

Next suppose that there are two choices in which
$$P(1) = P \quad \text{and} \quad P(2) = 1 - P \tag{35}$$

Then
$$-H = P\log_2 P + (1-P)\log_2(1-P) \tag{36}$$

If we take the limit as $P \to 0$ in Eq. (36), $-H \to 0 + 1\log_2 1 = 0$ bits. Hence there is only one choice,
$$2^H \to 2^0 = 1 \tag{37}$$

That is, if $P(1) = 0$ in Eq. (35), it means that $P(2) = 1$ and there really is only one possibility. The same situation holds when $P(2) \to 0$ in the above illustration. Equation (36) also yields a maximum value of $H = 1$ (2 choices) when $P = \frac{1}{2} = P(1) = P(2)$.

**4.13
PROBLEM 12**   Compute the variation of H as a function of P from Eq. (36) for $0.05 < P < 0.95$ in steps of 0.05. Plot the result on the teletype (or, if available, high-resolution display). Note that

$$\log_2 X = \frac{\log_e X}{\log_e 2}$$

It is next of interest to compute the minimum average number of bits, h, per alphanumeric character required to transmit source material written in a language such as English. In accordance with the above discussion, this quantity may be determined through application of Eq. (24) and may be regarded as the entropy or information per character of source text.

The results obtained will obviously be dependent on the statistical properties of the language, and we will get progressive approximations to the answer analogous to the various levels of sophistication used previously in simulating the Eddington monkey. Further, owing to variations in style among various authors, one can never expect to obtain an absolutely precise answer, and there is indeed reason to expect that real languages may actually obey the second law of thermodynamics (see Section 4.14). The answer will always vary somewhat with the particular text. However, as we have shown earlier in this chapter with the author-identification problem, these differences are a small fraction of the main effect. The structure of the language is largely predominant and, in fact, even the differences in statistical structure among the common western European languages are remarkably slight.

The zeroth-order calculation of the entropy per character is, of course, the easiest. Assuming our original 28-character set used to analyze Act III of *Hamlet*, we let $P = \text{constant} = \frac{1}{28}$, and Eq. (24) gives us directly

$$h_0 = \log_2 28 = 4.80735 \text{ bits/character} \tag{38}$$

That is, if we assume that all 28 characters are equally probable, the minimum average number of bits per character necessary to convey the language is given by Eq. (38). Consequently, the minimum number of characters required is $C_0 = 2^{h_0} = 28$.

The first-order calculation of the entropy per character (h_1) requires a knowledge of the total probabilities of occurrence of the individual members of the character set. The latter can be determined for the 28 characters used to analyze Act III of *Hamlet* by reading off the numbers in Table 1 (remembering that they must be normalized), or by summing the rows in the correlation matrix $M(I, J)$ in Fig. 4-6. That is, as previously noted,

$$P(I) = \sum_{J=1}^{28} M(I, J) \Big/ \sum_{I=1}^{28} \sum_{J=1}^{28} M(I, J) \qquad (39)$$

Applying Eq. (24) to Act III of *Hamlet* yields

$$h_1 = 4.106 \text{ bits/character} \qquad (40)$$

or a minimum list,

$$2^{h_1} \approx 17.21 \text{ characters}$$

4.13
PROBLEM 13   Check the numerical value obtained in Eq. (40) by computing the probabilities from the data in Table 1 (or by summing the columns of the correlation matrix in Fig. 4-6).

In the second-order calculation of the entropy per character (h_2), we have to take into account the probability, $P(I, J)$, that the Jth character followed the Ith character. The particular sum obtained from an expression such as Eq. (25) will vary with the identity of the previous character typed.

Suppose that the Ith character of text has just been typed. The normalized probability $P(I, J)$ that the next character will be the Jth character may be obtained from the correlation matrix in Fig. 4-6 by noting that

$$P(I, J) = M(I, J) \Big/ \sum_{J=1}^{28} M(I, J) \qquad \text{where} \quad \sum_{J=1}^{28} P(I, J) = 1 \qquad (41)$$

The average number of bits necessary to specify the number of choices at this point will itself be a function of I. (That is, it depends on the past history and hence the character just typed.) This average number of bits is

$$B(I) = \sum_{J=1}^{28} P(I, J) B(I, J) \qquad (42)$$

where $B(I, J)$ also depends on the last character typed; hence for Eq. (42) to be a minimum,

$$B(I, J) = -\log_2 P(I, J) \qquad (43)$$

by analogy with Eq. (27).

Finally, we want to find the average of $B(I)$ over all initial characters $I = 1$–28. This average will be a minimum because each $B(I)$ is a minimum. Hence the minimum average number of bits per character necessary to describe the source text (or second-order entropy per character) will be given by

$$h_2 = \sum_{I=1}^{28} P(I) B(I) = \sum_{I=1}^{28} P(I) \sum_{J=1}^{28} P(I, J) B(I, J) \qquad (44)$$

where $B(I, J)$ is given by Eq. (43). The probabilities may be obtained from the pair-correlation matrix, $M(I, J)$, through Eqs. (39) and (41). Using the 28×28

matrix from Act III of *Hamlet* (Fig. 4-6), we obtain

$$h_2 = 3.3082 \text{ bits/character} \qquad (45)$$

or a minimum number of

$$2^{h_2} = 9.905 \text{ characters}$$

on the average. [Note that $h_2 = h_1$ if $B(I, J) = B(I)$ for all J.]

4.13
PROBLEM 14   Evaluate Eq. (44) using the matrix in Fig. 4-6. Note that it will be easiest to store the quantities $B(I, J)$ in a separate array from that for $P(I, J)$. Also note that the normalizing sums can be computed sequentially with the most efficiency; e.g., one needs S and $S(I)$, where

$$S = \sum_{I=1}^{28} S(I) \quad \text{and} \quad S(I) = \sum_{J=1}^{28} M(I, J)$$

These quantities can be computed as the elements $M(I, J)$ are read into your program. Use a conditional statement to bypass the $\text{LOG}(P(I, J))$ calculations in cases where $P(I, J) = 0$; these cases are easiest to handle merely by defining the corresponding $B(I, J) = 0$.

The values of h_n should be independent of the direction in which you analyze the language. Check the results for h_2 for *Hamlet* by taking the transpose of the matrix in Fig. 4-6 before computing h_2. (Slight differences may result from rounding errors.)

The computation may, in principle, be extended to higher and higher orders of statistical correlation. For example, at the third order we would have

$$h_3 = \sum_I P(I) \sum_J P(I, J) \sum_K P(I, J, K) B(I, J, K) \qquad (46)$$

where

$$B(I, J, K) = -\log_2 P(I, J, K) \qquad \text{etc.} \qquad (47)$$

and the probabilities are given in terms of the correlation matrices defined earlier in this chapter. One has to keep increasing the dimensions of the matrices and the process begins to eat up prohibitive amounts of core and computing time. The main point is that with higher and higher statistical correlations included, the smaller the number of bits, or list of characters, that has to be transmitted on the average to convey the original text. For example, already by second order apparently only about one third of the normal alphabet is required on the average to convey English. For estimates of the asymptotic behavior of h_n at large n, see Shannon (1951).

A summary of values of h_n computed by the present author for various languages is given in Table 5.

4.13
PROBLEM 15   Compute values of h_1 and h_2 from the sample of the novel *Gadsby* (written without using the letter e) shown in Fig. 4-10 and compare your results with those for English in Table 5. (Use the CHANGE statement or equivalent.)

4.13
PROBLEM 16   Assume that Morse code takes 3 bits for a dash, 1 bit for a dot, 1 bit for the spaces within letters, and 3 bits for the spaces between letters. How many bits per character would be needed to transmit Hamlet? [Evaluate h_1 using a specific array, $B(I)$, representing the number of bits per character in Morse code.]

Braille uses 6-bit "words" in which combinations as well as single letters of the normal written language have separate coded meaning. Hence the average number of bits per character necessary to transmit English will be different in first and second order. What is the value of h_2 for Shakespearean English transmitted in braille?

4.13: Table 5 Values of h_n (Entropy per Character) Computed in Various Orders[a]

	h_1	h_2	h_3
Shannon (1951)			
(27-character alphabet, $h_0 = 4.76$)			
English (contemporary)	4.03	3.32	≈ 3.1[b]
Present results			
(28-character alphabet, $h_0 = 4.807$)			
English			
Chaucer (*Canterbury Tales*)	4.00	3.07	2.12
Shakespeare (*Hamlet*)	4.106	3.308	2.55
Poe ("The Gold Bug")	4.100	3.337	2.62
Hemingway (*For Whom the Bell Tolls* and *A Farewell to Arms*)	4.055	3.198	2.39
Joyce (*Finnegan's Wake*)	4.144	3.377	2.55
German (Wiese)	4.08	3.18	—
French (Baudelaire)	4.00	3.14	—
Italian (Landolfi)	3.98	3.03	—
Spanish (Cervantes)	3.98	3.01	—
Portuguese (Coutinho)	3.91	3.11	—
Latin (Julius Caesar)	4.05_1	3.27_1	2.38
Greek (Rosetta Stone)	4.00_7	3.05_3	2.19
(77-character alphabet, $h_0 = 6.267$)[c]			
Japanese (Kawabata)	4.809	3.633	—

[a] Accent marks were not included in the character set and spaces were inserted between the ancient Greek words on the Rosetta Stone.

[b] The value of h_3 given by Shannon (1951) was based on an extremely approximate method of including the space symbol in earlier trigram data given by Pratt (1939). Because Pratt's data were not terribly accurate in the first place and also did not include correlations with the space symbol, it is surprising that Shannon's estimate of h_3 was as good as it was. Apparently no one has published an accurate computed value for h_3 in any language since the Shannon (1951) publication.

[c] The results for Japanese were computed by one of the author's students, Yoshikazu Okuyama, from a 10,000-character sample using a 77-character set consisting of 76 kana plus the space symbol.

The second law of thermodynamics may be stated

$$\Delta H > 0 \tag{48}$$

for any thermodynamic process where H is proportional to the entropy for the total system.[17] Associating entropy with the degree of statistical disorder, the second law means that thermodynamic systems tend to proceed from states of lower probability to states of higher probability (or, equivalently, from higher to lower order). For example, a drop of ink gradually diffuses throughout the glass of water into which it is placed; molecules having a well-defined velocity will assume a Maxwellian velocity distribution due to collisions in a short time

**4.14
Entropy and Anthropology**

[17] In many texts on statistical mechanics, H is defined to be proportional to the entropy through a *negative* constant. This difference amounts to changing the sign in Eq. (24). In the present discussion we have adopted Shannon's definition, in which H has the same sign as the entropy.

after they have been placed in a high-pressure gas, and so on. Ultimately, as proclaimed by various morbid prophets of doom, this process will lead to the "heat death" of the universe—unless something we do not know about with much certainty takes place.

There are some qualitative reasons why we might also expect languages to obey the second law in some sense. The fact that large numbers of people use them introduces the statistical element. If a language is developed initially by one or a small number of persons at one point on the globe, it seems inevitable that the structure of the language will become less ordered as it diffuses throughout the world. The condensed (and therefore specialized) meanings originally given to symbols by the creator of the language will tend to be broadened and require more additional description through common usage. In other words, it seems likely that there will be a tendency for the minimum average number of bits per message required to convey meaning in normal use of the language to increase with time.

Some evidence for the effect is to be found in the gradual abandonment of ideographs (symbols that convey entire thoughts or words) with the aging of most languages. Beyond that, there is at least some tendency for the number of characters in the alphabet to increase with time, and for the more concise declensions of single words to be replaced by sequences of words. This process generally makes the language easier to learn and use but also results in requiring more bits per message on the average; the redundancy of the language tends to go up and "Parkinson's Law" seems to be a consequence of thermodynamics. One, of course, has to look over really long periods of time to see if the effect occurs; otherwise, variations in individual style will tend to

Fig. 4-11. The evolution of language has been marked by the gradual abandonment of ideographs for the sake of more generally useful alphabetic notation.

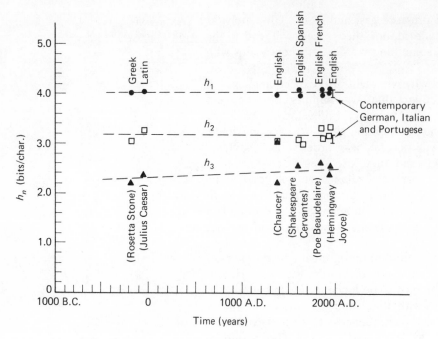

Fig. 4-12. Variation of h_1, h_2, and h_3 (the first-, second- and third-order entropy per character) with time for a number of languages.

mask the phenomenon. Obviously, it is also desirable to try to make comparisons between old and recent versions of the same text. Interlinear translations of old language texts into modern English are particularly helpful in this sort of study.

Although there is a very definite indication that the total number of bits for the same message has increased with time, the result has occurred in a rather surprising way: the total number of characters per message has gone up, but the entropy per character (values of h_1, h_2, and h_3) has remained astonishingly constant over periods of at least 2000 years (at least within the languages studied in the present chapter that belong to the same family tree; see Fig. 4-12). The result suggests the involvement of some fundamental physiological limitation. For example, the nearly constant values for the entropy per character may just reflect the finite number of sound sequences that can be easily produced by the human voice. Such limitations would get into the written language the minute an alphabet based on some kind of phonetic spelling arose from more elementary ideographs. Additional support for this notion arises in the fact that the value for h_2 computed for Japanese kana is so close to the values for western European languages (see Table 5). If this interpretation is correct, it should be possible to determine at what period in "prehistory" the transition from ideographs to alphabetized writing occurred within a given culture by statistical analysis of the writing samples—without actually having to translate the samples. At some point in prehistory, or ancient history, there must have been an appreciable change in the values of h_n. Yet easily available samples of ancient writing do not appear to show this effect within the same family tree (see Fig. 4-12). One possible interpretation is that alphabetized writing existed much further back into prehistory than has usually been assumed. The data published recently by Marshack (1972) is particularly intriguing in that respect because it seems to imply the existence of extremely elaborate notational systems in the cave art produced during the Ice Age by prehistoric man in southern France. Marshack's point that large changes do not occur suddenly is well taken. The fact that h_n remained ≈constant from 200 B.C. on implies that it probably had not changed rapidly prior to that time.

The Latin of Julius Caesar is, of course, easy to feed into a teletype terminal and even the ancient Greek inscriptions on the Rosetta Stone (≈ 191 B.C.) or within the decree of Canopus (≈ 239 B.C.) are easy to get into a computer (see Fig. 4-13 and problems at the end of this section). The going gets much harder with hieroglyphics.

It is pretty clear that the Egyptian hieroglyphics themselves could be broken down into a fundamental character set (of a much more primary sort than the type of phonetic alphabet deduced initially by Champollion), with which the individual symbols of the ancient Egyptian text could be constructed. To do this, just imagine how a typesetter would attack the problem and ask what would be the smallest set of symbols needed to construct all the hieroglyphs (see Fig. 4-14). This set would, for example, be made up of various parts of human bodies (arms, legs, etc., along with more abstract symbols). For example, the ancient Egyptian word for "carries away,"

was clearly made up from two other primary symbols used frequently by themselves:

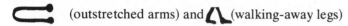

(outstretched arms) and (walking-away legs)

These and many other basic symbols in the ancient hieroglyphic writing clearly had some alphabetic significance and, as in many other cases, are probably fairly direct ancestors of similar-looking characters in the later Greek and Latin alphabets. Obviously, there would be many highly correlated symbol sequences in the hieroglyphic text and one, in principle, could then compute the entropy per character in various statistical orders. The result of such a calculation would be quite interesting because the portion of the text in hieroglyphics presumably represents a language that is very much older than the text in Greek. Budge (1904) points out that the ancient hieroglyphic writing was not understood by most Egyptians circa 200 B.C. and that the common written language of that period was indeed Greek. Hence with the hieroglyphic text one might at last begin to see an appreciable change in h_1, h_2, and h_3 from the values shown in Fig. 4-12. However, a rough estimate shows that the primary hieroglyphic character set itself is likely to have well over 100 members. Consequently, even though many of these elements do have low probabilities of occurrence, the initial data-acquisition problem and computer-core requirements would make such an investigation rather formidable. [The detailed discussion of hieroglyphics given by Budge (1929, pp. 228–246) would be extremely helpful in this problem. Also, note that the text in the decree of Canopus (see, for example, Fig. 4-14 or Budge, 1904) would be much easier to work from than that in the Rosetta Stone.]

Such investigations could be much more easily extended to ancient cuneiform writing where fairly long specimens dating to about 2000 B.C. are available in the Yale Collection (see Hallo, 1974). Here the primary character set is much smaller and much more manageable than with the Egyptian hieroglyphs. However, in this case the evolution of the language leads directly to Arabic, and modern samples of text would be awkward to enter within the ASCII character set.

Still more ambitious students might want to have a crack at Chinese. Although the basic Chinese vocabulary consists of about 5000 ideographs, these may be broken down into a much smaller set of radicals and further subsets of brush strokes (see Fenn, 1971, or Wieger, 1965). There is also an effort to adopt Romanized spellings of Chinese words currently in progress on the Chinese mainland.

Fig. 4-13. The first 35 lines from the Greek inscription on the Decree of Canopus. The original text was carved in a stone 2 feet 8 inches wide, in the ninth year of the reign of Ptolemy III (≈238 B.C.). See Problem 19. (From Budge, 1904.)

Fig. 4-14. The first few lines from the hieroglyphic writing on the Decree of Canopus (≈238 B.C.). The symbols are read from right to left and top to bottom. (From Budge, 1904.)

Finally, it is worth noting that much the same approach could be used to study the emanations at radio and optical frequencies coming from outer space. If something out there is trying to communicate with us, about the only statement that could be made with reasonable confidence is that the "message" should exhibit statistical properties that are different from those of purely random character sequences. However, lots of detailed speculation has been given on this subject. There is a tendency among scientists living on the earth to assume that communication from other worlds will incorporate the latest discovery that they themselves have just made. For example, those having just invented a maser suspect that a maser operating on the hydrogen 21-cm line is the obvious choice; those who have just invented a laser note that some laser frequency would be ideal; similarly, those who have just invented the wheel think that the first 1000 digits in π will obviously constitute the first message. (But why in base 10?) We shall leave it to the reader to decide whether or not such messages from outer space should be answered. We merely note that because of the enormous time delays required for light to travel to and from other solar systems, the conversational problems involved would be about the same as those one would meet in trying to talk to the authors of the text in Fig. 4-14.

Chapter 4
Language

4.14
PROBLEM 17†
See if Caesar's *Commentaries on the Gallic War* have obeyed the second law when translated into contemporary English. Investigate the first several sections of the interlinear translation by Dewey (1918). Compute the total number of characters, h_1 and h_2 for both the original Latin and modern English versions of the same text. (Be careful not to include redundant parenthetical remarks in the English text.) Note that although the total number of characters increased very substantially in going from Caesar's Latin to modern English, the values of h_1 and h_2 (the first- and second-order entropy per character) changed only slightly.

4.14
PROBLEM 18†
Do the same computation in a comparison of the message in the first 100 lines within *The Prologue* to *The Canterbury Tales* by Chaucer (use, for example, the interlinear translation by Hopper, 1970).

4.14
PROBLEM 19†
The Rosetta Stone (Agathocles et al., 196 B.C.; e.g., see the discussion in Budge, 1929) and the decree of Canopus (see Budge, 1904) contain some of the earliest bilingual translations available. Compute the values of h_1 and h_2 for the lines of the ancient Greek text shown in Fig. 4-13 and compare with the results in Table 5. *Note:* One simple code to convert the uppercase Greek letters to teletype symbols is as follows:

Greek: ΑΒΨΔΕΦΓΗΙ ΚΛΜΝΟΠΘΡΣΤ   Ω   Ξ
ASCII: ABCDEF GHIJKLMNOPQRSTUVWXYZ

Also note that spaces were not preserved in the Rosetta Stone or in the decree of Canopus, whereas the values in Table 5 were computed with the spaces reinserted.

4.14
RESEARCH PROBLEM†
See if you can compute h_2 based on the Egyptian hieroglyphics in Fig. 4-14.

† Use the CHANGE statement, or equivalent, to convert alphanumeric characters from the terminal to ASCII integers (see Section 1.18).

We have shown that English text should require substantially fewer characters on the average than the normal alphabet for transmission, provided that we are willing to use the statistical properties of the language to advantage.

4.15
Bit Compression in Language Transmission

From the results in Table 5, it seems likely that only about 2.5 bits per character would be necessary on the average if we went to third-order statistical correlations. At first glance, the result seems fantastically appealing. One could send twice the number of messages over the same communications channel; Western Union could double its profits; perhaps we can find a way to communicate with all those nuclear submarines lurking out there after all; maybe there is even something in ESP; and so on. Unfortunately, information theory does not tell us how to accomplish the objective in a really practical way. It tells us primarily that it is not necessarily impossible to do it. We shall therefore investigate a simple, fixed-length coding method of bit compression based on our earlier letter-correlation data.[18]

The bit-compression problem clearly has two parts:

1. Use of the statistical properties of the language to compress the message.
2. Use of the statistical properties to help reconstruct (or "expand") the message at the other end.

Obviously the number of bits per character required on the average should decrease as we go to higher- and higher-order correlations. Also it seems clear that we can always do better by going to a higher-order method to recover the message than was initially used to transmit the message. This might be important in the submarine problem or in communicating with a distant spaceship. However, if we have the same size of computer at both ends of the communication channel, we can always do best by using the maximum available statistical information at both ends of the line.

The zeroth order is not of interest here because that merely means sending messages verbatim with the standard alphabet. The corrector at the other end might be useful in fixing up spelling errors, typographical mistakes, or the effects of noise—but that's about all.

In first-order transmission, we merely throw out the least-probable characters in the alphabet. According to the results in the previous section, we ought to be able to get along by transmitting only 4.1056 bits per character on the average, or, equivalently, a minimum set of about 17 characters should permit transmitting an average message from *Hamlet*.

First we need some initial text to work with. This could be entered through string operations, or merely entered through a DATA statement in the 1–28 character code recognized by the printing sieve discussed earlier in the chapter. For example, a typical DATA statement might consist of the following:

```
2000   REM DATA FOR 194 CHARACTER MESSAGE FROM HAMLET
2001   DATA 27,20,15,27,2,5,27,15,18,27,14,15,20,27,20,15,27,2,5,27
2002   DATA 20,8,1,20,27,9,19,27,20,8,5,27,17,21,5,19,20,9,15,14,27
2003   DATA 23,8,5,20,8,5,18,27,28,20,9,19,27,14,15,2,12,5,18,27
2004   DATA 9,14,27,20,8,5,27,13,9,14,4,27,20,15,27,19,21,6,6,5,18,27
2005   DATA 20,8,5,27,19,12,9,14,7,19,27,1,14,4,27,1,18,18,15,23,19,27
2006   DATA 15,6,27,15,21,20,18,1,7,5,15,21,19,27,6,15,18,20,21,14,5,27
2007   DATA 15,18,27,20,15,27,20,1,11,5,27,1,18,13,19,27,1,7,1,9,14,19
2008   DATA 20,27,1,27,19,5,1,27,15,6,27,20,18,15,21,2,12,5,19,27
2009   DATA 1,14,4,27,2,25,27,15,16,16,15,19,9,14,7,27,5,14,4,27,20,8,5
2010   DATA 13,27
```

It will be helpful to enter the numerical version of the text in a suitably dimensioned column array, $C(I)$. We can also store the order of probability of

---

[18] A method for constructing optimum variable-length codes was considered by Huffman (1952); also see the discussion in Gallager (1968, pp. 52–55). In this type of approach, one codes character strings with different numbers of bits in a manner dependent on the string probability. Thus very improbable strings require very large numbers of bits, and the method is not applicable to the usual teletype transmission problem where the sample rate and number of bits per sample are fixed.

```
1990   REM PROBABILITY ORDER OF CHARACTERS IN HAMLET
1991   DATA 27,5,15,20,1,19,8,14,9,18,12,4,21,13
1992   DATA 25,23,6,3,7,16,2,22,11,28,10,17,24,26
```

The ordering in this statement is merely that of the total frequencies in Table 1. That is, character 27 (the space) is most frequent, next comes 5 (the letter E), and so on. The statement

```
8   MAT READ I
```

will store the total probability data in an array $I(J)$ with 28 elements. The correcting process at the receiving end will be most efficient if we tell it when a character is not identified from the original text. This technique, however, consumes one character from the set of transmitted ones. For example, if the array $C(I)$ has at least 194 elements, we can enter the initial message, compress, transmit, and read the transmitted message with statements of the following type:

```
10   PRINT "NUMBER OF IDENTIFIED CHARACTERS IN COMPRESSED MESSAGE"
12   INPUT N
15   FOR I = 1 TO 194
20   READ X
25   FOR J = 1 TO N
30   IF X = I(J) THEN 50
35   NEXT J
40   LET X = 29
50   LET C(I) = X
55   GOSUB 500
60   NEXT I
```

If the individual value of X read on line 20 is contained in the list of N most probable characters, we store X in $C(I)$ on line 50. However, if the identity of X is not to be transmitted, we store a value (29) outside the range of the primary character set in $C(I)$. Subroutine 500 then prints the transmitted message using the appropriate sieve in Section 4.2 for printing $ABC \cdots XYZ'$ when $X = 1, 2, \ldots, 28$. In the present occasion we will also use the provision that allows printing "–" when $X = 29$. We shall also use the column counter $Q9$ (initialized to zero) that counts the number of columns printed and after 60 columns produces a line feed (i.e., PRINT command) following a space. This procedure avoids breaking words up in the middle. Running this program for $N = 16$ (17 transmitted characters, or ≈ 4.1 bits per character of text) yielded

```
TO –E OR NOT TO –E THAT IS THE –UESTION WHETHER –TIS NO–LER
IN THE MIND TO SU– –ER THE SLIN–S AND ARROWS O– OUTRA–EOUS –ORTUNE
OR TO TA–E ARMS A–AINST A SEA O– TROU–LES AND –Y O– –OSIN– END
THEM
```

(i.e., 19 characters of 194 were unidentified).

Most people would be able to fill in the missing blanks. However, that is not because only 17 characters are necessary to reconstruct English in first order. It is mainly because the readers are either already familiar with the message, or have enough correlation data stored in their minds to analyze the message in a higher statistical order. All we could do with a first-order computed correction here would be to fill in all the blanks with the next most probable character omitted from the transmitted list. In this particular case, the first-order corrector would merely fill in the letter F in all the missing blanks. It would get the words SUFFER, OF, and FORTUNE right, but that's all. We would still have 12 incorrect words and 14 separate errors out of the 19 unidentified characters.

4.15
PROBLEM 20
Write a program that takes stored text, compresses it to a prescribable number of characters, transmits the compressed message, and makes a most-probable first-order correction to the transmitted message. How many characters do you need before the corrected message has no errors? Plot the number of errors as a function of N.

Next we would like to design a second-order correction program to work on our first-order compressed message. That is, we would like to compute the most probable identity of the missing characters based on the pair-correlation matrix $M(I, J)$ in Fig. 4-6. Because we know which letters were deleted from the full character set, we can optimize the correction process by defining two new matrices, A and B, such that

$$A(I, J) = \begin{cases} M(I, J) & \text{when } I \text{ is a transmitted character} \\ & \text{and } J \text{ is a deleted character} \\ 0 & \text{otherwise} \end{cases}$$

(49)

$$B(J, K) = \begin{cases} M(J, K) & \text{when } J \text{ is a deleted character and} \\ & K \text{ is a transmitted one} \\ 0 & \text{otherwise} \end{cases}$$

The matrix $A(I, J)$ may be computed from $M(I, J)$ in Fig. 4-6 through a sequence of statements of the type

```
100   REM COMPUTE A(I,J) NEXT
110   MAT A = ZER(28,28)
120   FOR K = 1 TO N
125   FOR J = 1 TO 28
126   FOR L = 1 TO N
127   IF J = I(L) THEN 135
128   NEXT L
130   LET A(I(K),J) = M(I(K),J)
135   NEXT J
140   NEXT K
```

where the array $I(L)$ is the same one as defined before, and N characters are identified of the original set of 28. The matrix $B(J, K)$ may be computed in a similar manner.

4.15
PROBLEM 21
Write a program that computes the two 28×28 matrices $A(I, J)$ and $B(J, K)$ that satisfy the conditions in Eqs. (49). Check several rows in each case to make sure that your program is working correctly. (*Note:* You need enough core for three 28×28 matrices.)

In the first section of our corrector we will leave sequences of adjacent blank characters unaltered and instead pick out sequences of the type $I, -, K$, in which two identified characters I and K are separated by a missing character, J. Clearly, the best guess in sequences of the latter type will be a particular value of J chosen to optimize the product

$$A(I, J)B(J, K)$$

(50)

where the matrices A and B were defined in Eqs. (49).

First we need to be able to identify sequences of the type $I0, 29, K0$ without altering others in the array $C(C)$. Noting that the first character of the message is a space, and hence must be identified ($\neq 29$), the following program steps accomplish the first objective:

```
210   FOR C = 1 TO 193
220   LET X = C(C)
230   IF X = 29 THEN 250
240   GOSUB 500
245   NEXT C
246   PRINT
247   PRINT
248   GO TO 9999     (end)
250   LET I0 = C(C − 1)
251   IF I0 = 29 THEN 240
255   LET J0 = C(C)
260   LET K0 = C(C + 1)
265   IF K0 = 29 THEN 240
```

If the program passes the conditional statement on line 265, we know that a sequence of the desired type has been found. We then pick a value of J to maximize $A(I0, J)*B(J, K0)$, store J in the message array, and print the character corresponding to J.

```
270   REM FORM I0,29,K0 NOW
275   LET M = 0
280   FOR J = 1 TO 28
285   IF M > = A(I0,J)*B(J,K0) THEN 300
290   LET M = A(I0,J)*B(J,K0)
295   LET X = J
300   NEXT J
302   LET C(C) = X
305   GOTO 240
```

The program then continues through the remainder of the message array until completing the text on line 248. At this stage, the original compressed message has been changed to read:

```
TO BE OR NOT TO BE THAT IS THE BUESTION WHETHER CTIS NOFLER
IN THE MIND TO SU− −ER THE SLINGS AND ARROWS OF OUTRAVEOUS FORTUNE
OR TO TAVE ARMS ACAINST A SEA OF TROUPLES AND BY O− −OSING END
THEM
```

Notice that it got the words OF and FORTUNE correct (which would have been provided by the first-order corrector) along with the words BE, SLINGS, and BY.

We really need a third-order corrector to fill in the remaining blanks because they are all double. In fact, there is danger of making a worse second-order correction on double blanks at this point than would be obtained from a simple, first-order correction on the remaining part of the message. For example, one *might* argue that we should choose I and K so as to optimize $A(I, J)$ and $B(J, K)$ separately in sequences of the type $I, 29, 29, K$. However, this practice, in fact, tends to do worse than merely assigning the remaining blanks to the most-probable, neglected character. For example, as applied to the above message, separate optimization of $A(I, 29)$ and $B(29, K)$ alone would yield SUGVER and OFCOSING as the remaining incomplete words. In contrast, a simple first-order correction applied at this point gets at least one of them right. This hybrid combination of second- and first-order correction technique results at the receiving end in the final message,

```
TO BE OR NOT TO BE THAT IS THE BUESTION WHETHER CTIS NOFLER
IN THE MIND TO SUFFER THE SLINGS AND ARROWS OF OUTRAVEOUS FORTUNE
OR TO TAVE ARMS ACAINST A SEA OF TROUPLES AND BY OFFOSING END
THEM
```

in which ≈ 4.1 bits per character were used in a first-order transmission process. The corrected message contains 9 mistakes in locations where 19 characters in the transmitted message of 194 characters were unidentified. The correction technique is pretty good, but it has not worked any miracles.

4.15
PROBLEM 22   Write a program that incorporates the above hybrid second- and first-order correction process to analyze text transmitted by a first-order compressor. How many characters have to be identified in the transmitted text before no mistakes occur in the corrected message? Plot the number of errors at the destination end as a function of the number (N) of identified characters that were actually transmitted. (*Note:* You need enough core to handle three 28×28 matrices in addition to the two-column arrays and programming statements.)

The problem gets more rewarding when we go to a second-order compression and transmission process. If we transmit a character set of N symbols, we have N^2 possibilities to identify specific character pairs. For example, an average of 4.1 bits per character (or ≈ 17 identified symbols of the 28-primary-character set used in the original English text) corresponds to a total of about 288 separately identifiable character pairs. This still is not enough to ensure completely error-free transmission of *Hamlet* because there are actually 443 nonzero elements in the total correlation matrix (i.e., 341 elements are zero of the total number of $28 \times 28 = 784$). However, by deleting the $443 - 288 = 155$ least-probable nonzero matrix elements, we can do a pretty good transmission job even without a statistical correction at the receiving end of the line.

Our first problem, therefore, is to construct a "compressed" correlation matrix that has $N^2 = 288$ nonzero elements. The nonzero elements in that matrix can then be used to generate a systematic code to positively identify $N^2 = 288$ separate character pairs. Although it might seem desirable to execute a straightforward sorting routine on the original 28×28 correlation matrix in terms of decreasing element size, such a program would have $\approx 307,720$ steps (i.e., the sum of an arithmetic series where the last term is $28 \times 28 = 784$). Hence even with a pretty fast computer, sorting the original correlation matrix in a straightforward manner takes a good deal of time.

For our purposes, a much quicker and more effective approach consists simply of multiplying each of the original matrix elements by a suitably chosen constant,

$$C < 1$$

and rounding off the values to the nearest integer on an element-by-element basis. While doing this multiplication, we can count up the nonzero elements in the compressed matrix and repeat the process reiteratively until we get down to the desired number of nonzero elements. This approach only takes ≈ 784 steps per iteration and hence we should be able to iterate ≈ 400 times before we have consumed as much computer time as the straightforward sorting method would have taken.

It is most practical to accomplish the desired degree of compression interactively using the computer terminal. If we define the compressed matrix to be $N(I, J)$, the process can be accomplished through statements of the type

```
 5  DIM M(28,28),N(28,28)
10  MAT READ M
40  PRINT "ENTER C"
50  INPUT C
60  MAT N = ZER(28,28)
```

```
65    LET NØ = Ø
70    FOR I = 1 TO 28
75    FOR J = 1 TO 28
80    LET N(I,J) = INT(C*M(I,J) + .5)
85    IF N(I,J) = Ø THEN 95
90    LET NØ = NØ + 1
95    NEXT J
100   NEXT I
105   PRINT "# NONZERO ELEMENTS = "; NØ
```

Here $N\emptyset$ counts the number of nonzero elements in $N(I, J)$ which correspond to the choice of C, and the result is printed on line 1Ø5. By reiterating to line 4Ø, one finds out very quickly that a value of $C = 0.045$ will reduce the original correlation matrix to a new one having the first 288 most-probable elements occupied and all the rest zero. We do not really care that the elements are multiplied by C in the present problem. The main point is that all the remaining 496 elements in $N(I, J)$ are zero.

In order to simulate the transmitted message in this case, we store the original English text in the 1–28 code in an array $C(I)$ and go through the array sequentially in pairs. (For practical purposes it is useful to add a second space at the end of the original 194-character message from *Hamlet*, which we will again use to illustrate the technique.) We then examine $N(X, Y)$ for every sequential pair X, Y in the message array to see if the element is zero. If $N(X, Y) \neq 0$, we print characters corresponding to X and Y using subroutine 5ØØ and go on to the correction program at the receiving end of the communication link on line 151.

```
110   FOR I = 1 TO 193 STEP 2
115   LET X = C(I)
120   LET Y = C(I + 1)
125   IF N(X,Y) = Ø THEN 155
130   GOSUB 5ØØ
135   LET X = Y
140   GOSUB 5ØØ
145   LET Q9 = Q9 + 2
150   NEXT I
151   GOTO 19Ø
```

(Here $Q9$ is a column counter initialized to Ø and used in subroutine 5ØØ to avoid breaking up words. It is, however, incremented outside the subroutine here. Hence line 5Ø3 of our original subroutine 5ØØ discussed in Section 4.2 should be deleted for the present purposes.) However, if $N(X, Y) = 0$ on line 125, our message-transmission method will miss at least one character. Here we have introduced a conditional statement that takes us to line 155, where the following statements transmit our code for a "–" mark and we go to the next sequential pair.

```
155   LET X = 29
160   GOSUB 5ØØ
165   LET C(I) = X
170   LET I = I + 1
175   LET Q9 = Q9 + 1
180   GOTO 115
```

Some bits will, of course, be used up identifying places where omitted characters occur. For our purposes it will be adequate just to add these up at the end. One could, of course, omit the unidentified characters altogether; however, it will be instructive to retain their locations for the present discussion.

Using 288 nonzero matrix elements corresponding to a value of $C = 0.045$ (hence an average of ≈ 17 identified characters out of the initial 28-character set, or ≈4.1 bits per character of original text on the average), the transmitted message at this point takes the form

```
TO BE OR NOT TO BE THAT IS THE QUESTION WHETHER 'TIS NOBLER
IN THE MIND TO SUFFER THE SLINGS AND ARROWS OF OUTRAG-OUS FORTUNE
OR TO TAKE ARMS AGAINST A SEA OF TRO-BLES AND BY OPPOSING END
THEM
```

That is, we have only missed 2 of the original 194 characters, as opposed to 19 at this point in the first-order process.

However, it is not possible to make a really substantial correction on this result without going to a third-order corrector (just as it was difficult to gain much improvement from a first-order corrector in the case of a first-order compression).

About the most effective correction we can make in second order is to identify sequences of the type $I,29,K$ and choose a value of J from the original correlation matrix to optimize the product

$$M(I, J)M(J, K) \tag{51}$$

Hence after a PRINT statement on line 190, we first locate the desired sequences, reprinting the identified portions of the message as we go:

```
200   REM FIND SEQUENCES I0,29,K0, FOR 2ND-ORDER CORRECTION
205   LET Q9 = 0
210   FOR C = 1 TO 193
220   LET X = C(C)
230   IF X = 29 THEN 250
240   GOSUB 500
242   LET Q9 = Q9 + 1
245   NEXT C
246   PRINT
247   PRINT
248   GOTO 9999      (end)
```

If we get all the way through without finding any missing characters, we end the program at line 248. If a missing character is detected on line 230, we then go to line 250, where we find a value of J to optimize the product (51), provided that $I0$ is not also unidentified. It is also useful to rule out the space ($J = 27$ on line 282) in the corrector because most pairs involving the space symbol are very high up in probability.

```
250   LET I0 = C(C − 1)
251   IF I0 = 29 THEN 240
255   LET J0 = C(C)
260   LET K0 = C(C + 1)
265   IF K0 = 29 THEN 240
270   REM FORM I0,29,K0 NOW
275   LET M = 0
280   FOR J = 1 TO 28
282   IF J = 27 THEN 300
285   IF M > = M(I0,J)*M(J,K0) THEN 300
290   LET M = M(I0,J)*M(J,K0)
295   LET X = J
300   NEXT J
302   LET C(C) = X
303   GOTO 240
```

If we have two spaces in sequence, we will not try to correct them. Our corrected message then becomes

```
TO BE OR NOT TO BE THAT IS THE QUESTION WHETHER 'TIS NOBLER
IN THE MIND TO SUFFER THE SLINGS AND ARROWS OF OUTRAGHOUS FORTUNE
OR TO TAKE ARMS AGAINST A SEA OF TROUBLES AND BY OPPOSING END
THEM
```

153

Only one error is present out of 194 characters of original text, and we only transmitted ≈ 4.1 bits per character on the average. Transmitting the locations of the two missed characters costs us an extra $\approx 6/194$ bits per character here on the average and hence is a fairly negligible overhead. At this level our accuracy is competitive with that in many newspapers.

The basic difficulty in making really substantial corrections in second order is simply that our compression technique favors the occurrence of missing characters in pairs or higher-order clusters. The point becomes more apparent when one compresses the matrix still further. For example, the following message was transmitted at about 3.3 bits per character on the average, corresponding to our previous value of the second-order entropy per character in *Hamlet* ($C = 0.0048$ and there were 99 nonzero elements in the compressed matrix).

```
TO BE OR NOT TO BE THAT IS THE ––ESTION WHETHER––TIS NO–LER IN
THE MIND TO S–––ER THE SLINGS AND ARRO–S OF OUT––––OUS FO–––NE
OR TO T––E AR–S –––INST A SEA OF –RO––LES AND –Y –––––ING END
TH–M
```

Second-order correction:

```
TO BE OR NOT TO BE THAT IS THE ––ESTION WHETHER––TIS NOULER
IN THE MIND TO S–––ER THE SLINGS AND ARROUS OF OUT––––OUS FO–––NE
OR TO T––E ARES –––INST A SEA OF ORO––LES AND AY –––––ING END
THEM
```

The second-order correction has repaired the word THEM but has accomplished nothing else. The moral seems to be that if you are limited to a given statistical order, it is best to use that order in transmission and transmit enough bits per character on the average to ensure the average freedom from error that you are willing to tolerate without even incorporating a correction process. That is a useful practical result: once we have determined the required number of elements in the correlation matrix, there is little point in running the message through a time-consuming computational correction process. Extrapolating our results, it seems pretty clear that to adequately convey a message with h_n bits per character in the above manner, one really needs at least an $(n+1)$th-order compression.

4.15
PROBLEM 23
Use the second-order Shakespearean monkey program to generate English text with representative statistical properties. Feed this sequence of data through a second-order matrix-compression program and compute the percentage of missed characters as a function of the number of bits transmitted per character (i.e., vary the normalizing constant, C, used to compress the matrix).

4.15
PROBLEM 24
Correction methods of the type discussed in the text may be used to make a most probable determination of missed characters in a noisy teletype transmission circuit. Write a program that (1) introduces mistakes randomly with a predetermined average probability of occurrence, and (2) uses second-order statistics to make a most probable identification of the unknown characters. Here we merely choose J for a missed character in the sequence I, J, K so that $M(I, J)M(J, K)$ is a maximum, using the standard correlation matrix. Try your program out on the Hamlet soliloquy or other text of comparable length.

4.16
The Difference Between Ciphers and Codes

It is traditional in popular books on cryptography to start by lecturing the reader on the difference between ciphers and codes. It is usually asserted that a *cipher* is a form of secret writing in which all meaning within the source language can be transmitted unambiguously, whereas a *code* is usually defined as a convention by which only a limited fraction of the meaning of the source language can be conveyed. Because adherence to this distinction can give rise to a needless amount of verbal tight-rope walking throughout the following sections, it would be well to dispose of it here. The distinction is really patent nonsense. The basic point is that the list of characters or symbols necessary to convey meaning within a language is *not* a closed set in any practical sense. Those who stress the distinction most assiduously frequently will go on for the next hundred pages discussing "ciphers" that do not even permit conveying the space between words unambiguously, let alone more subtle distinctions in meaning conveyed by apostrophes, quotation marks, accent marks, changes in type font, syllabic emphasis, and so on. About all that really can be said is that some codes are less ambiguous than others. Reference to the "least ambiguous" codes as "ciphers" involves a very subjective matter of interpretation which we shall not attempt to make here with any consistency.

Most people have at least some interest in the "science" of cryptography. The concept of secret writing seems to have sprung into existence spontaneously throughout history wherever a written language existed. For example, a cuneiform tablet dating from about 1500 B.C. in the Mesopotamian civilization contains an encipherment of the earliest known formula for making pottery glaze. Transposition ciphers (in which the order of letters in a message is scrambled before transmission and then unscrambled with the same key after reception) were developed by the Spartans as early as 475 B.C. using a coding device known as a "skytale." (A leather strap was wrapped tightly around a baton and the message written on the strap along the baton. The leather was then unwound to scramble the message and the inverse process carried out at the destination to read the text.) Vātsyāna's manual on erotic technique, the *Kāma-sūtra* (≈300 B.C.), lists secret writing based on both letter-substitution codes and phonetic-substitution codes among the 64 arts (yogas) that women should know and practice. Simple letter-substitution ciphers were also well known to the Roman educated class at the time of Julius Caesar.

Yet, there are many very curious aspects of the subject. For instance, the people with the strongest commitment to it would make very strange bedfellows: Machiavellian despots and political diarists, military officers, arch criminals, and literary nuts. Further, it is a field in which the most public acclaim (e.g., execution) has traditionally been given for outstanding failure. As with skilled magicians, the best cryptographers conceal their tricks. In fact, the most successful contemporary ones are probably not even allowed to know their own names. In addition, the subject has been permeated with such an intense degree of both deliberate and subconscious deception that it is almost impossible to determine accurate case histories even after the principal individuals have ceased to exist.

After the collapse of the Roman empire, cryptography plunged into the Dark Ages along with the rest of civilization. It surfaced sporadically during the Middle Ages as a source of amusement for bored monks. According to Kahn, "the only writer of the Middle Ages to describe cryptography instead of just using it" was the thirteenth-century English philosopher and monk, Roger

[19] For a more general account, the reader is referred to the volumes by Pratt (1939), Yardley (1931), and Farago (1967), and in that order. However, don't get them all at one time; you won't be able to get anything else done for a week! The best-documented treatment of the general field appears to be that of Kahn (1967). However, in spite of Kahn's remarks to the contrary, there seems to be little evidence that information theory has had much practical impact on cryptography. For a fairly abstract discussion of applications of communication theory to cryptography, see Shannon (1949).

Bacon (in his Epistle on the *Secret Works of Art and the Nullity of Magic*). In fact, a yet-to-be decoded volume of secret writing discovered in 1912 (the Voynich Manuscript) has sometimes been attributed to Bacon (see later discussion). As with most other intellectual endeavor, cryptography lay dormant during the Middle Ages, only to be resurrected during the Italian Renaissance.

Another Bacon, and a contemporary of Shakespeare, Sir Francis Bacon (or Lord Verulam), introduced a 5-bit binary code to transmit diplomatic messages. In this code, binary zeros were represented by type with normal font using standard English text and binary 1's were indicated in italicized type. Dividing up the standard English text into successive groups of five letters provided both a medium to transmit the code and an effective way to conceal the fact that a secret message was being transmitted at all. The casual reader would regard the text (or "clear" in the cryptographer's parlance) as just a careless typesetting job. However, once the presence of the code was spotted, almost anyone could decipher it. Consequently, Francis Bacon's primary contribution was in the invention of the binary code rather than in a real contribution to cryptography.

As with any other medium, there is an inherent noise level in Bacon's method for binary-code transmission. Thus the penchant of early seventeenth-century printers to reuse previously set clusters of battered type, taken together with a large measure of "inspiration" in deciding whether or not a binary 1 or zero was set in individual characters, permitted Mrs. Elizabeth Wells Gallup of Minnesota to deduce, at the turn of this century, that Francis Bacon actually was the illegitimate son of Queen Elizabeth and "had written not only works attributed to Shakespeare, but also those bearing the names of Burton, Ben Johnson, Greene, Marlowe, and Spenser, as well as unrevealed translations of the *Iliad* and *Odyssey*."[20]

Cryptography went through a peak in sophistication at the hands of a seventeenth-century French cryptographer, Rossignol, that was not equaled for the next 100 years. Not only did his contemporaries credit him with phenomenal ability at deciphering messages, but he designed a cipher for Louis XIV based on some 587 randomly numbered syllables (using multiple identifications to obscure the more frequent ones) that remained for over two centuries as the only known example of an entirely unbreakable cipher. (The Voynich Manuscript seems to be the present holder of the title.) The original key was lost after Rossignol's death and many generations of cryptographers were unable to decipher the surviving messages.

Apart from sporadic activity during the American and French Revolutions at relatively low levels of sophistication, the field went into a quiescent state until the mid-nineteenth century. The invention of the Morse telegraph and its use during the American Civil War provided renewed stimulus for the subject. In addition, cryptography began to receive worldwide attention in the popular literature, starting with articles and stories published by Edgar Allan Poe in the 1840s. This fad was stimulated by the European writers Jules Verne, Arthur Conan Doyle, and Honoré de Balzac. The popular interest in substitution ciphers started by Poe's famous challenge to the public in 1841 (see Section 4.18) persists to this day in the form of "literary crypts" and Double-Crostics appearing in various weekly magazines. Early in the nineteenth-century mania for ciphers, Balzac introduced a two-page cryptogram in *La Physiologie du marriage* which he deliberately left unsolved as a joke on the reader (see Fig. 4-17 and later discussion).

Although the Union Army scored several cryptographic victories during the Civil War, the next major advance in the subject came from a Prussian army

---

[20] Pratt (1939, p. 90). This book contains a highly interesting account of the entire Bacon–Shakespeare controversy from the cryptographic point of view. See also C. A. Zimansky (1970).

officer named Kasiski, who in 1863 developed a systematic method for solving multiple-substitution ciphers. (A multiple-substitution cipher is one in which N different substitution ciphers are used periodically throughout the message.[21])

American "black chamber" efforts were still on a pretty low level by the start of World War I. In 1913, Herbert O. Yardley was hired as a junior telegraphist on the night shift in the U.S. State Department. To relieve his boredom during the nocturnal hours, Yardley made a hobby out of deciphering various coded messages that came within his attention. By 1915, he had broken the entire American diplomatic code and was reading messages on internal German affairs that President Wilson had deemed so secret as to warrant withholding from the State Department itself. Worried that foreign governments could just as easily crack the American code, Yardley wrote a long memorandum on the problem which he presented to his superior. The eventual result of this activity was the formation of a new department within Military Intelligence, under Yardley's direction, whose purpose was to handle "the cryptographic needs of the Intelligence Division." His exploits within this division were legendary and included such things as breaking the Japanese diplomatic code (based on the romanization of the ninth-century classification of Japanese syllables, or *kana*, in a set of 73 Chinese characters) without an initial knowledge of Japanese. This feat (for which Yardley received the Distinguished Service Medal and "a sly wink from the Secretary of War") gave the United States a considerable political advantage in the Washington Naval Conference of 1922. The ultimate disclosure of that behind-the-scenes accomplishment by Yardley (1931, pp. 250–317) has been cited as a major reason for the subsequent Japanese denunciation of the Naval Treaties.

The appointment of Henry L. Stimson as Secretary of State in the Hoover Administration brought an end to this level of cryptographic expertise. Having coined the phrase "Gentlemen do not read each other's mail," Stimson cut off all State Department support for Yardley's department. (The existence of Yardley's "black chamber" had been concealed from Stimson until shortly before the Naval Disarmament Conference of 1930.) Yardley was crushed by the decision and described the great difficulty with which he explained this news to his staff[22]:

> "Most of them had devoted years to cryptography, working secretively, not even their most intimate friends being aware of their real accomplishments. That cryptography as a profession would ever die had never entered their minds."

Evidently, however, Secretary Stimson's actions were extremely fortuitous: it is alleged by Farago[23] that Yardley himself had already sold out to the Japanese in 1929 for the sum of $7000.

Thus the United States began the decade prior to World War II with the dissolution of the most advanced cryptographic department that had previously existed in history. Although there were major cryptographic victories just prior to, and during, World War II, they largely resulted from the secret capture of enemy decoding machines rather than from statistical analyses of the source language (see Farago's book). In retrospect, what Yardley had been doing with his staff of a dozen cryptographers and battery of 50 typists was largely the kind of data manipulation that can be conducted now by one person working alone with only a small computer. For example, the solution of the famous

---

[21] Pratt (1939, p. 168) gives a fairly detailed discussion of the Kasiski method for those who would like to work on a multiple-substitution cipher.

[22] Yardley (1931, pp. 370, 371).

[23] Farago (1967, pp. 56–58); see also reference notes, p. 394.

Waberski cipher depended less on a sophisticated automatic treatment of the statistical properties of the source language than it did on repeated manipulation of the data blocks until things lined up in a manner obvious to the cryptographer's eye. The higher-order statistical analysis was still going on in the brain of the cryptographer rather that in the automatic portions of the data-processing program. One can, of course, do this sort of thing very readily with a computer terminal—but the results will depend on just how good one is at spotting correlations.

In his triumph over the Japanese diplomatic code, Yardley (1931, pp. 250–269) evidently only looked as far as pair correlations in the equivalent of a 73×73 matrix of Japanese syllabic characters (*kana*). The statistics for the standard language matrix were extracted from about 10,000 characters worth of normal Japanese "plain language" telegrams. Although this sounds like a lot of input data, it only amounts to about two characters per matrix element on the average. Hence, although the principle of the thing sounds reasonable (i.e., all one has to do is pick out the statistical ordering of these matrix elements and then identify corresponding elements in a similar matrix for coded characters), it is somewhat amazing that he was able to accomplish this feat with the available statistical accuracy. Hence the surprising aspect of the solution is not so much that he did not know Japanese, but that he did it with so little input data to play with. According to Farago (1967, p. 22), the Japanese have another interpretation of the accomplishment: they evidently believe that a code clerk named Yatanube absconded with the codes from one of the South American Japanese embassies early in 1920 and sold them to Yardley during the international maritime conference in Genoa. Although Yardley obviously did an enormous amount of work on the statistical aspects of the problem during his one year stint at it, he also indicates in his account (p. 264) that he was seriously considering that alternative type of solution. If the Japanese assertion is correct, it would represent something of an all-time "let-down" in the history of cryptography. However, deceit is the name of the game.[24]

---

[24] In an effort to shed more light on this interesting historical question, we performed a statistical analysis of a 77×77 pair-correlation matrix computed from a 10,000-character sample of Japanese. The source text was from *Snow Country* by Yasunari Kawabata and was reduced to a 77-character set (76 kana plus the space symbol) by one of the author's students, Yoshikazu Okuyama.

Out of a total of 5929 matrix elements, 1242 had nonzero values. Of these, only about the first 150 largest elements are of any use statistically. (For example, 468 elements had the same value of 1, 233 elements had the value 2, 115 had the value 3, and so on.) Putting the matrix elements in descending numerical order gave the series of numbers

$$282, 259, 228, 178, 157, 154, 146, 143, \ldots$$

If we regard the numbers as results from a series of counting experiments, one expects a statistical spread $\approx \sqrt{M(I, J)}$ in each case. Consequently, one cannot really distinguish reliably between the fourth and fifth numbers on the list. Thus a direct ordering of the matrix elements would only give certain identification for about three kana and the space symbol.

As with English, much better identification can be obtained by computing a most probable digram decoding path through the matrix. (See the discussion in Section 4.19.) Two useful paths were found in the 77×77 matrix of Japanese kana:

space,NO,ZI,YO,U,TU,TA,RI,MA,(DO or SU)
NO,space,O,TO,U,TU,TA,RI,MA,(DO or SU)

where the romanization of the kana has been used. Both paths close on the same ambiguous choice contained within the parentheses. Hence statistical uncertainties in the 10,000-character source text prevent identifying more than 10 kana plus the space symbol directly from the matrix.

A most probable second-order correction process (see Section 4.19) could probably double the number of unambiguously identified kana in a single-substitution code. However, it seems clear that a higher-order correlation process (e.g., someone who knew Japanese) would be required to get more than about 20 out of 76 kana correctly identified with only the statistical accuracy afforded by a 10,000-character uncoded source text. Yardley's problem would have been still harder because the secret messages were encoded without the use of a space symbol to break up words.

Edgar Allan Poe's most well-known exploit in cryptography was published in his short story, "The Gold Bug" (1843). In this story, Poe's hero, Legrand, "readily solved" a cipher made up of a closely packed string of nonalphabetic characters. In fact, Legrand modestly commented that he had indeed "solved others of an abstruseness ten thousand times greater."

When asked to explain his method, Legrand indicated that he had worked out a scientific principle based on the statistics of the language. In effect, once he had established the identity of the language in which the cipher had been written, all he had to do was apply the right frequency table to identify the individual characters.

In the case of the Gold Bug cipher (which ultimately disclosed the location of Captain Kidd's treasure), there was a possible choice of English, French, or Spanish for the source language. Shrewdly concluding that the message must be in English (because of a pun on the word Kidd which could not be appreciated in the other two languages), Legrand went on to outline his solution.

He first observed that there were no divisions between words, and implied that if there had been, the whole thing would have been trivial. At this point, the storyteller might have asked: "How did you know that the originator of the message didn't simply adopt some other character (e.g., the number 8) for the space symbol?" But Poe's storyteller was destined to play the role of the straight man and the question was not raised.

Legrand went on to explain that he had constructed a frequency table:

Of the character 8 there are 33.
; there are 26.
4 there are 19.
‡) there are 16.
* there are 13.
5 there are 12.
6 there are 11.
†1 there are 8.
0 there are 6.
92 there are 5.
:3 there are 4.
? there are 3.
¶ there are 2.
—. there is 1.

He then comments:

"Now, in English, the letter which most frequently occurs is *e*. Afterward, the succession runs thus: *a o i d h n r s t u y c f g l m w b k p q x z*. E predominates so remarkably, that an individual sentence of any length is rarely seen in which it is not the prevailing character."

In this single paragraph we have been presented with *the most fundamental mystery of the entire short story:* Where on earth did Poe ever get that frequency table? How could Poe not have known that T (not A) is usually the second-most-frequent letter in English? Certainly he should have known that T couldn't be tenth on the list! All he had to do was look at his own writing. For example, a frequency table based on the text of *The Tell-Tale Heart* runs as follows:

ETAOINSHRDLUCMFWPYGBVK'XJQZ

One derived from the entire text of "The Gold Bug" itself goes

ETINAHOSDLRUMWYCGFBPVKJQX'Z

Doubtless someone will say that Legrand's mistake was just a typesetter's error or a blunder by the proofreader. Yet it was obviously not that at all. The basic structure of the story from then on is affected by Legrand's erroneous frequency table. Thus after identifying the character 8 with the letter E, he switches his method of attack. He clearly cannot allow the symbol ; to be identified as the letter A, and he therefore starts grasping at straws. Ironically, if he had merely used a more correct frequency table, Legrand would have immediately gotten the right identity for the ; symbol.

Instead Poe switched to a *word*-frequency table. Noting that THE is the most commonly occurring word in English, Poe manages to pull this word out of the closely packed string of symbols! Hence Legrand concludes both that

; stands for the letter T

and that

4 stands for the letter H

If he had merely used a better table to identify E and then T in the first place, he would have been able to deduce H from the extremely high correlation existing for both TH and for HE [i.e., the size of $M(20, 8)$ and $M(8, 5)$ in Fig. 4-6]. Having botched the problem so badly at the start, Legrand's boastful manner becomes tiresome and the rest of the analysis is hardly worth reading. (Legrand's trigonometry at the end of the story is not very good either.)

4.18
PROBLEM 25

Consider the character sequence T-E where we want to find a most probable value for the missing blank in English. By computing the value of J such that

$$M(20, J)*M(J, 5)$$

is a maximum, show that the missing character is probably H. [Use $M(I, J)$ from Fig. 4-6.]

But back to the *real* mystery of "The Gold Bug," which the astute reader will doubtlessly have solved by now. Using the deductive methods of the great French detective Dupin, we are led to the following interpretation. Poe's sense of history told him from the beginning that the pirate treasure must involve the Spanish West Indies; after all, he was dealing with a famous pirate of the Spanish Main. He therefore boldly decided right from the start that *the entire cipher should be pulled off in Spanish*! Poe therefore worked out his frequency tables from such Spanish text as was then available in the Philadelphia Public Library. (The actual source was probably a tourist phrase book in which the letter H was used as a frequent phonetic aid.) At the last minute, Poe got an urgent call from his publisher, who suddenly realized what was going on: "Look here, Edgar, that just won't work. The cipher *must* be in English! Otherwise, we'll be losing readers by the carload." Time was running out. Poe hastily rearranged the text and invented that awful pun about Captain Kidd to get him out of his predicament. The trouble was that he did not have time to work out a new frequency table. Now, any idiot knows that E is the most common letter in English, so he would obviously have to get that one right. Because the Spanish table at least started off correctly, he decided to pass it off for English and no one would ever know the difference. Since he really did not plan to use the table anyway, the change would have no effect whatsoever on the rest of the story. "3‡‡†3‡†;45;9634;5-;?500:28(634;"

Write a program that permits printing out letter-frequency tables of the type quoted by Legrand for the common European languages (see Table 4). [*Note:* Although Spanish is the most probable choice for Legrand's table, Italian and Portuguese are not too far behind. However, it most certainly is not a frequency table for English, German, or French. Kahn (1967, p. 789) suggests that Poe may have miscopied a list of most frequent vowels and consonants given alphabetically by William Blair in an article, "Cipher," published in *The Cyclopaedia* of Abraham Rees.]

"The Gold Bug" (first published in 1843) was not Poe's only claim to cryptographic prowess. His exploits date at least to 1841, when he was working as an editor for *Graham's Magazine*. With a boldness matched only by Legrand himself, Poe offered in April of that year to solve any single-substitution cipher that the readers would care to submit, provided that they preserved the word spacings. The challenge, however, was buried in one paragraph in the middle of a long book review (of *Sketches of Conspicuous Living Characters of France*, translated by R. M. Walsh). The author of the book had implied that an unusually keen mind was required to decipher cryptograms. Poe commented,

> "We cannot understand the extraordinary penetration required in the matter. The [key] phrase...is French and the note was addressed to Frenchmen...anyone who will take the trouble may address us a note, in the same manner as here proposed, and the key-phrase may be either in French, Italian, Spanish, German, Latin or Greek (or in any of the dialects of these languages), and we pledge ourselves for the solution of the riddle."

He clearly implies here that one does not need to know the "key phrase" at all—that the statistics of the language will betray the key.

In reporting the results of his experiment in a review article on cryptography later that year, the editor of *Graham's Magazine* comments (Poe, 1841) that the challenge had elicited but a single response from an anonymous resident of Stonington, Connecticut. The letter contained two ciphers, the second of which consisted of a message (see Fig. 4-15) based on the key phrase

No. 2.

Ofoiioiiaso ortsiii sov eodisoioe afduiostifoi ft iftvi si tri oistoiv oiniafetsorit ifeov rsri inotiiiiv ridiiot, irio rivvio eovit atrotfetsoria aioriti iitri tf oitovin tri aetifei ioreitit sov usttoi oioittstifo dfti afdooitior trso ifeov tri dfit otftfeov softriedi ft oistoiv oriofiforiti suitteii viireiiitifoi ft tri iarfoisiti, iiti trir uet otiiiotiv uitfti rid io tri eoviieeiiiv rfasueostr tf rii dftrit tfoeei.

According to Poe, the translation is: Nonsensical phrases and unmeaning combinations of words, as the learned lexicographer would have confessed himself, when hidden under cryptographic ciphers, serve to *perpdex* the curious enquirer, and baffle penetration more completely than would the most profound *apothems* of learned philosophers. Abstruse disquisitions of the scholiasts, were they but presented before him in the undisguised vocabulary of his mother tongue....

Fig. 4-15. Photographic reproduction of the harder of two ciphers sent to the editor of Graham's Magazine in the spring of 1841 by "an anonymous correspondent at Stonington, Connecticut" (Poe, 1841, p. 36). Poe stated that the two italicized words were coding errors committed by the Connecticut correspondent. One of these must have been imagined by Poe. There is also at least one other coding error, which Poe didn't italicize.

in Latin: *Suaviter in modo, fortiter in re*. Placing the alphabet beneath this phrase in a letter-for-letter manner,

SUAV I TERINMODO FORT ITER I NRE
ABCDEFGHI J K LMNO PQRSTUVWXYZ

we see that, even knowing the key, the reader has to decide whether the character

O in the message stands for L, N, or P
I in the message stands for E, I, S, or W   etc.

Poe notes that although his initial boast was not said *suaviter in modo*, his pursuit of the problem was at least done *fortiter in re*. It seems more probable, however, that the solution should be taken *cum grano salis*.

Although Poe's concern that readers might suspect him of "inditing ciphers to himself" seems justified, the circulation of *Graham's Magazine* went from almost nothing to 25,000 subscribers in 1841. The success was probably at least partially due to the column "Secret Writing," which occupied the editorial page from July on (with excessive enciphering of silly sibilants in randomly chosen multiple-substitution codes). Yardley (1931, p. 20) comments that in his initial quest for information on cryptography he searched through the letters of Edgar Allan Poe for some outline of scientific treatment of the subject. All he found were "vague boasts of skill—nothing more . . . Poe [was] merely floundering around in the dark and did not understand the great underlying principles." Yet, Poe was clearly smart enough to realize that the principles must exist; he just did not have time for the details. During the 16-month period in which he served as editor (at a salary of $800 per year), Poe published in *Graham's Magazine* four of his "Tales," several poems, numerous articles on literary criticism, and many book reviews in addition to the article and column on "Secret Writing" (not to mention an occasional article in *The Saturday Evening Post*).

**4.18
PROBLEM 27**

Write a program that codes characters according to "*suaviter in modo*, etc." and try it out on the English message "translation" of Poe's hard cipher 2. See how many coding errors you can find (the discussion of some subroutines in the following section may help; see Fig. 4-15).

**4.18
RESEARCH
PROBLEM**

A decoding matrix for Poe's hard cipher 2 (see Fig. 4-15) may be written:

Character:	A	D	E	F	I	M	N	O	R	S	T	U	V
Meaning	C	M	G	O	E	K	J	L	H	A	F	B	D
		U		I		X	N	Q		R			
		Z		S			P	V		T			
		W						Y					

For example, there are 20,736 ($= 3 \cdot 1 \cdot 3 \cdot 4 \cdot 4 \cdot 3 \cdot 4 \cdot 4 \cdot 1 \cdot 1 \cdot 3$) possible "solutions" for the first word in the message OFOIIOIIASO. In principle, one could write a program to maximize the products of pair-correlation matrix elements for the different choices, one word at a time (i.e., starting and ending with a space symbol). Investigate the possibility of carrying out this type of procedure using the correlation matrix for English in Fig. 4-6.

**4.19
Program To Solve Literary Crypts**

If Poe contributed anything to cryptography it was surely in the invention of the "literary crypt" (Poe, 1841). We shall define such things to be single-substitution ciphers in which the space between words is preserved (although not necessarily by the space symbol).

Obviously what Poe would have liked is a program where you enter the cipher, type RUN, and the computer prints out one correct solution in a reasonably short time. Reading between the lines of his initial challenge, he probably would also have liked to be able to do this when the source language was "French, Italian, Spanish, German, Latin, or Greek (or any dialects of these languages)."

Accomplishing the above objective is not entirely trivial, even with a long text. Because of the statistical uncertainties involved, it becomes especially tricky when the message is limited to just a few hundred characters. However, the second part of the objective is not as hard as the first. That is, as long as you know *what* language is involved, the approach is the same. The programmer does not have to know Japanese to write a program to decipher substitution cryptograms in Japanese. All he has to know is (1) that the source language *is* Japanese; (2) the *standard* correlation matrix for Japanese; and (3) that he has a long-enough enciphered message in Japanese to give adequate statistical accuracy.[25] When your program completes deciphering the cryptogram, you ask one of your Japanese friends to translate it into English. (One, of course, has to make obvious modifications in dimension statements.) As a matter of fact, one should really narrow the specification of the source language even further. For example, best results really require the "standard" correlation matrix for the language as used by the author of the message. For example, a correlation matrix based on "The Gold Bug" will not do as well as a correlation matrix based on Shakespeare's own writing in deciphering a cryptogram from *Hamlet*. Ironically, a correlation matrix based on *Hamlet* also seems to do better at deciphering cryptograms in contemporary English than does one based on "The Gold Bug."

Before designing a program to solve substitution ciphers automatically, it will be helpful to construct several subroutines of a purely manipulative nature. These subroutines are required just to do the bookkeeping for us, and can also be very easily incorporated in an interactive program that lets the operator solve ciphers by guesswork.

For the purpose of illustration, we shall limit ourselves to a 28-character substitution code and our original 28-character list. We shall assume that the character-printing subroutine discussed earlier in the chapter is still available at line 500. It is helpful to keep its properties summarized in a few REM statements at the start of the subroutine:

```
500   REM SUB TO PRINT A, B, C,..X, Y, Z, , ' , –
501   REM WHEN X = 1,2,3,.......28,29
503   REM Q9 COUNTS COLUMNS, "PRINTS" AFTER SPACE WHEN Q9>60
504   LET Q9 = Q9 + 1
        .
        .
        .
```

(the rest of the subroutine can take anywhere from 7 to 84 lines, depending on the level of string commands available; see the previous discussion).

Next we need a data array, $D(N)$, in which to store the $N0$ characters in the original cipher. The cipher could be entered from the keyboard using string commands or specially written CALL statements to machine-language subroutines; it could be READ from disc or tape files or merely from standard DATA statements within the program. In the latter case, we are free to specify the cipher in our 1–28 alphabet (fixed code) right from the start. (See, for

---

[25] The last requirement is, of course, the real difficulty in deciphering most cryptograms. As noted in Section 4.17, one needs messages of much greater than 10,000-character length to do this problem satisfactorily in Japanese.

example, the DATA statement containing the first portion of Hamlet's soliloquy used in the discussion of bit compression.) We shall adopt the latter
method here to avoid overly restricting the program to specific computing
equipment or compilers. If the array is suitably dimensioned, a single statement

MAT READ D

can be used to enter the initial cipher data.

We shall solve the cipher by defining a substitution code array, $X(I)$, which
operates on the original cipher data array, $D(N)$, to provide a decoded array
$C(N)$ in which

$$C(N) = X(D(N)) \qquad (52)$$

for each of the $N\emptyset$ terms in the cipher. Thus we shall leave the original cipher
data array untouched and repeatedly alter the current code array, $X(I)$, so as
to provide best deciphering possible in the array $C(N)$.

Although each code is made up from the same set of 28 integers, it is
important to realize that there are actually three codes to worry about in the
present problem:

1. The original fixed code on which subroutine $5\emptyset\emptyset$ works: namely, 1, 2, . . . ,
   28 corresponds to the letters A, B, C, etc.
2. The current code in $X(I)$—which ultimately will be used to transform the
   cipher array into the deciphered array, $C(N)$, which can then be printed by
   subroutine $5\emptyset\emptyset$.
3. The inverse code to $X(I)$.

We shall merely compute the "inverse code" as we need it rather than
introduce still another array in the problem. The distinctions between these
codes will become clearer as we proceed.

We shall assume that the current substitution code stored in array $X(I)$ is
confined to the domain of integers 1–28. (Later we shall introduce the integer
29 to stand for the hyphen—in some instances to indicate message array
elements that have not been identified.)

It is useful to have a subroutine that prints a table to identify the "current"
code, $X(I)$. Although the table may be most easily printed vertically, through
statements of the type

```
FOR I = 1 TO 28
LET X = X(I)
GOSUB 500
PRINT I
NEXT I
```

that approach wastes entirely too much paper. (Alternatively, if you are using a
CRT terminal, the list runs off the screen too fast.)

A more useful subroutine can be written to print the current code in a
horizontal format of the type

CURRENT CODE IN X(I):

1	2	3	4	5	6	7	8	9	10
V	N	I	U	W	F	G	X	C	R

11	12	13	14	15	16	17	18	19	20
Y	L	'	K	Q	T	O	J	H	P

21	22	23	24	25	26	27	28
	D	E	S	M	Z	A	B

Here it is implied that if $D(1) = 1$ and if we enter subroutine $5\emptyset\emptyset$ with a
value of X defined by

$$X = C(1) = X(D(1))$$

the terminal will print out the letter V, corresponding to the number $X = 22$ in
the fixed code.

Producing tabular output of the above type can be something of a struggle in BASIC. The problem is the stringent limitation on column format that results when numbers are printed through a command of the type

> PRINT K;

Even if K is only a two-digit integer, the compiler leaves room for a six-digit number. (The problem can be easily overcome through addition of suitable machine-language subroutines CALLable from BASIC.)

Staunch FORTRAN users will gloat at this point. However, the inconvenience is a small price to pay for the other advantages of BASIC. We shall probably have completely deciphered our cryptogram long before the typical FORTRAN batch-process user has managed to debug the first section of his program.

The following subroutine provides the desired horizontal format for printing the code array.

```
700   REM SUB TO PRINT CODE
701   PRINT
702   PRINT "CURRENT CODE IN X(I):"
703   FOR I = 1 TO 3
704   FOR J = 1 TO 2
706   FOR K = (I-1)*10+1 TO (I-1)*10+10
708   IF K > 28 THEN 724
710   PRINT TAB(6*(K-(I-1)*10)-5);
711   IF J#1 THEN 718
712   PRINT K;
713   PRINT " ";
714   GOTO 722
718   LET X = X(K)
719   PRINT " ";
720   GOSUB 500
722   NEXT K
724   PRINT
726   NEXT J
728   PRINT
730   NEXT I
732   PRINT
734   RETURN
```

(Some versions of BASIC handle the format in the PRINT K; statement differently from the Hewlett-Packard BASIC assumed above and will require appropriate modification of this subroutine.)

4.19
PROBLEM 28
Figure out how the above subroutine (700) works. Try it out, using a code generated by letting $X(I) = I$ for $I = 1$–28. This check will test both subroutines 700 and 500.

At the start of the program we shall let $X(I)$ initially equal the fixed code:

```
20   FOR I = 1 TO 28
22   LET X(I) = I
23   NEXT I
```

We then enter the cipher data in array $D(N)$ and start out with array $C(N)$ equal to $D(N)$. We shall also introduce an array $E(N)$ with the same dimensions to keep track of identified terms in the cipher. We shall use the convention that when the Nth element in the cipher is unidentified, $E(N) = 29$; when the Nth element later becomes identified, we shall let $E(N) = C(N) =$ the identified value. If we make a point of storing the number of terms ($N\emptyset$) in the cipher in the data statement, these first few operations are accomplished by commands of the type

```
25  READ NØ
26  FOR N = 1 TO NØ
28  READ D(N)
30  LET C(N) = D(N)
35  LET E(N) = 29
40  NEXT N
```

Next we need a subroutine to print the current version of the cipher stored in $C(N)$. For example,

```
850  REM SUB PRINT CURRENT C(N)
855  LET Q9 = Ø
860  FOR N = 1 TO NØ
864  REM LET X = E(N) HERE TO DISPLAY E(N)
865  LET X = C(N)
870  GOSUB 5ØØ
875  NEXT N
880  PRINT
885  PRINT
890  RETURN
```

($Q9 = \emptyset$ initializes the column counter in subroutine $5\emptyset\emptyset$.) A statement of the type

```
GOSUB 85Ø
```

after line $4\emptyset$ permits displaying the initial cipher. For example, it might take the form

PQU'WUQJUBQPUPQU'WUPS PUTXUPSWUFDWXPTQBUISWPSWJUAPTXUBQ'CWJUT
BUPSWUZTBEUPQUXDKKWJUPSWUXCTBYXU BEU JJQIXUQKUQDPJ YWQDXUKQJ
PDBWUQJUPQUP OWU JZXU Y TBXPU UXW UQKUPJQD'CWXU
 BEU'VUQGGQXTBYUWBEUPSWZ   (53)

An immediate display of the current code using subroutine $7\emptyset\emptyset$ gives

CURRENT CODE IN X(I):

1	2	3	4	5	6	7	8	9	10
A	B	C	D	E	F	G	H	I	J

11	12	13	14	15	16	17	18	19	20
K	L	M	N	O	P	Q	R	S	T

21	22	23	24	25	26	27	28
U	V	W	X	Y	Z		'

and would facilitate a solution through guesswork. For example, if we thought the first letter of the cipher should be a T instead of a P, we would want to exchange the sixteenth and twentieth terms of the code array, $X(I)$, and then recode the cipher $C(N) = X(D(N))$ in terms of the new code.

Consequently it is useful to have a subroutine that interchanges any two members ($I\emptyset, J\emptyset$) of the code array and then recodes the cipher.

```
750  REM SUBINTERCHANGES TWO CHARACTERS IØ,JØ
751  PRINT "IØ,JØ TO BE INTERCHANGED"
752  INPUT IØ,JØ
```

```
753   PRINT "MORE? (NO = Ø)"
754   INPUT X9
755   REM ENTER SUB HERE IF YOU KNOW IØ,JØ
756   LET N1 = X(IØ)
757   LET N2 = X(JØ)
758   LET X(IØ) = N2
759   LET X(JØ) = N1
760   IF X9 = Ø THEN 769
765   GOTO 750
768   LET X9 = Ø
769   PRINT
770   REM SUB FOR RECODING CIPHER
771   REM E(N) STORES IDENTIFIED ELEMENTS OF CIPHER ARRAY
775   FOR N = 1 TO NØ
780   LET C(N) = X(D(N))
782   IF C(N)#IØ THEN 785
784   LET E(N) = IØ
785   NEXT N
795   RETURN
```

As written above, the input parameter $X9$ permits returning to the start of the subroutine for additional interchange operations before going on to the more time-consuming operation of recoding the entire cipher. This process adds to the efficiency of the guesswork approach as long as you do not exchange the same code element more than once before recoding the cipher. Note that lines 782 and 784 keep track of identified elements, assuming that your guess for the true identity of $IØ$ was correct. Later we shall enter this subroutine at line 755, after having computed most probable values for $IØ$ and $JØ$.

A set of statements such as

```
400   GOSUB 700
405   GOSUB 750
410   GOSUB 850
420   GO TO 400
```

then provides a simple reiterative method for solving the cipher through guesswork by the operator. If you happen to have what Yardley referred to as "cipher brains," the program can be pretty effective. At least all of the dull, tedious bookkeeping is taken care of automatically.

**4.19
PROBLEM 29**

Write a simple interactive program of the above type and try it out on cipher (53) above. (The main point is to make sure the subroutines are working properly and to emphasize the desirability of having the computer make some pretty reliable, most-probable guesses at the start.) (*Note:* If you have the CHANGE statement or equivalent CALL statement available, the cipher can be read in directly from the keyboard. Otherwise, use the initial current-code printout to help prepare the DATA statements.)

**4.19
PROBLEM 30**

Write a subroutine that permits use of the $RND(X)$ function in BASIC to generate a random-substitution code for making up single-substitution ciphers. Note that one can improve on the results provided by $RND(X)$ alone by following it up with a trip through subroutines 75Ø and 85Ø.

Before attempting to write a more general program, it is worth taking a closer look at the statistical problem involved with a specific case. Consider the third act of *Hamlet*, which contains something over 35,200 characters. The frequency table based on the dialogue from Act III is shown rearranged in

Table 6. Noting that the expected fluctuation in a random count N is roughly $\approx \sqrt{N}$,
it is evident that we cannot do very much with single-character frequencies alone. From Table 6, we could determine the space between letters and the letter E, but that's about as far as we could go. The letters O and T are statistically indistinguishable from the frequency table. Going farther down the list, we see that we could not distinguish among the group S, H, N, I, and so on. Yet, intriguingly, there are fairly definite statistical boundaries around many of the less probable characters.

4.19: Table 6 Frequency Table — Dialogue from Act III of *Hamlet* (35,224 Characters)

Character	Occurrence	Uncertainty
Space	6934	83
E	3277	57
O	2578	51
T	2557	51
A	2043	45
S	1856	43
H	1773	42
N	1741	42
I	1736	42
R	1593	40
L	1238	35
D	1099	33
U	1014	32
M	889	30
Y	783	28
W	716	27
F	629	25
C	584	24
G	478	22
etc.		

Note: The statistical boundaries are indicated by dashed lines.

Ordering the elements in the 28×28 correlation matrix for Act III provides some more insight (see Table 7). Here the total number of counts per element is much smaller (i.e., down by about a factor of 28 on the average), and we can only draw five definite statistical boundaries near the top of the list. Worse, we can only identify the first three matrix elements unambiguously, even with a text containing as many as 35,200 characters.

One could, of course, arrive at a solution to a cipher by systematically permuting the identification of the more probable characters, using the larger terms in Tables 6 and 7 as a guide. One then depends on recognizing the

4.19: Table 7 Correlation Matrix, $M(I, J)$, from Act III of *Hamlet* (35,224 Characters)

$M(I, J)$	Uncertainty	I	J	
1283	36	5	27	E, space
962	31	ⓐ27	ⓐ20	space, T
878	30	ⓐ20	ⓐ8	T, H
805	28	20	27	
786	28	19	27	
664	26	4	27	
630	25	ⓐ8	ⓐ5	H, E
627	25	27	1	
494	22	15	21	
489	22	27	13	
481	22	27	23	
479	22	27	19	
475	22	25	27	
462	21	27	9	
450	21	27	8	
447	21	18	27	
420	20	1	14	
416	20	15	27	
408	20	14	27	
383	20	ⓐ5	ⓐ18	E, R
349	19	9	14	
329	18	27	2	
328	18	14	4	
314	18	1	20	
311	18	18	5	
305	17	15	18	

Note: The statistical boundaries are indicated by dashed lines. The most probable digram decoding path is shown by circles and solid lines.

correct solution as it goes by. Recognition might be by eye, or perhaps by computing some quantity characteristic of the language.

Yardley did it by eye. In fact, there is a striking parallel between Yardley's method of solution in Military Intelligence Department MI-8 and Bob Newhart's monkey inspectors. In each case an army of typists (about 50 in the Yardley effort) was hammering away while an inspector roamed about to see if a message had yet come through. Yardley had, of course, organized a systematic permutation of the cryptograms on the basis of digram and trigram tables, as well as single-letter frequencies. To be sure, he also worked on much harder things than single-substitution ciphers, and he helped to catch lots of spies. Nevertheless, systematic permutation is pretty boring, even when you have a computer to do the monkey work. We would, therefore, like to formulate a procedure for determining a most probable solution to the cipher—one that may not necessarily be perfect with short messages but will at least give us a good start in the right direction.

It is pretty clear that the *only* thing we can get out of Table 6 with much reliability is the space between words. The conclusion is especially true with short messages. For example, a frequency table based on the first few lines of

English	
Hamlet (Act III)	THERDOUSINGALYMP′
"The Gold Bug"	THERANDISOUPLYF′BJ
German	
Wiese	DERANGSTICHUMOLBJ
French	
Baudelaire	DESITANOURMPL′HYG
Italian	
Landolfi	CHERANOLITUSP
Spanish	
Cervantes	DENTOSURALICH
Portuguese	
Coutinho	ESTICAORMPLUNDJ

Note: In all these languages, the "space" between words is the most frequent character, with the possible exception of German (e can be more frequent than the space when umlauts are not used).

Hamlet's soliloquy runs

$$\text{space, T, O, E, A,} \ldots$$

Here E is *fourth* on the list and Legrand's approach would not even have gotten off the ground.

In order to get any further, we have to examine the correlation matrix more carefully and to notice that there is a basic statistical asymmetry to its structure. This asymmetry probably has to do with the fact that languages are written in the forward and not the backward direction. Whatever the basic cause, the common European languages contain most probable digram decoding paths in the forward direction through the correlation matrix, which seem to be remarkably well defined even in fairly short messages. For example, consider entering the matrix in Table 7 with the symbol representing the space between words firmly established. If you look for letter pairs near the top of the table of the form $(I, 27)$, you see that there are several candidates of comparable importance. That is, lots of words in English end with E, T, S, and D. Clearly, with a really long sample, you could expect to identify the letter E that way—but that's about all.

In contrast, if you look for pairs of the type $(27, I)$, there is only one that is conspicuously near the top; the pair $(27, 20)$ stands well isolated from the next most probable case. Equivalently, more words in English start with T than with any other letter, and the next most probable starting letter (A) is pretty far down the list. A still more surprising thing is that if you identify T = 20 and ask for the most probable value of

$$M(20, J) \qquad \text{where } J \neq 20 \text{ or } 27$$

the answer is, $J = 8$. That is, the letter H follows T far more probably than anything else other than the space between words (already identified). This behavior continues a considerable way down the matrix. One can determine a most probable decoding digram[26] path, which runs space, THERDOUSINGALYMP′ in *Hamlet*. These paths differ somewhat between authors writing in the same language, and of course they differ substantially from one language to the next (see Table 8). These digram paths seem almost

---

[26] The term "digram" is used in cryptography to denote probable pair sequences. The concept of a most-probable decoding digram path computed from the correlation matrix as shown in Table 7 appears to be original with this manuscript.

to spell out representative words in the languages; and as previously discussed, one can identify the language from the digram path itself. The sixth or seventh entry on the path tends to vary significantly with the author and with the historical period. Of course, if you have a long sample of writing by the suspected author of the cipher, you can compute a path from his or her correlation matrix directly.

4.19
PROBLEM 31
Write a program to compute Tables 6 and 7, starting with the correlation matrix (Fig. 4-6). Draw in the statistical boundaries with the hyphen, assuming that they occur between elements N_1 and N_2 such that $N_1 - N_2 > SQR(N_1 + N_2)$.

We shall make use of these observations to develop a program to determine a most probable solution to short cryptograms. Although the technique should work equally well (or badly, depending on your point of view) with most languages, we shall specifically illustrate its operation by application to the cipher (53) on p. 166. Because we have reason to suspect that the original message was something uttered in the third Act of *Hamlet*, we shall store the *Hamlet* correlation matrix early in our program.

```
8  MAT READ A
9  MAT B = A
```

The second matrix (B) is required for a later second-order computation. If you do not have room in your computer for all these matrices, it is worth advertising in advance that we shall obtain a partial decoding of the cipher before we really need matrix B.

Before we can implement our discovery in a program to decipher cryptograms, it is necessary to compute the most probable digram decoding path for the individual language of concern. Because the space is the most common character in nearly all languages, we shall compute the decoding path which starts with the space symbol. We shall store the values obtained for the decoding digram path in the array $P(K)$ and use subroutine $5\emptyset\emptyset$ to type out the letter equivalents as we find them. We assume that the correlation matrix for the language was stored in the array $A(I, J)$ at the start of the program. In what follows we shall also count the terms located with the variable $L\emptyset$. The procedure is simply to find the successive series of connected maxima in the correlation matrix under conditions where we continuously add the new terms to the array $P(K)$ and choose maxima $A(I, J\emptyset)$ which have values of $J\emptyset$ that are not yet stored in $P(K)$.

```
5Ø  PRINT "COMPUTE BEST DECODING DIGRAM PATH, P(I), FOR LANGUAGE:"
52  PRINT
54  LET L0 = 0
56  MAT P = ZER
58  LET J0 = 27
6Ø  LET X = JØ
62  GOSUB 5ØØ
64  FOR I = 1 TO 28
66  LET A(I,JØ) = Ø
68  NEXT I
7Ø  LET M = Ø
72  FOR J = 1 TO 28
74  IF M > A(X,J) THEN 86
76  FOR K = 1 TO LØ
78  IF X = P(K) THEN 86
8Ø  NEXT K
82  LET M = A(X,J)
```

```
84    LET JØ = J
86    NEXT J
88    IF M = Ø THEN 95
90    LET LØ = LØ + 1
92    LET P(LØ) = X
94    GOTO 6Ø
95    PRINT
```

The maxima are found in the usual way on lines 7Ø through 86. The specific one found has index $J\emptyset$ as a result of line 84. Lines 64–68 set the elements containing $J\emptyset$ to zero so we avoid finding them all over again on the next trip through the program. The maxima are counted on line 9Ø and we get out of the loop on line 88, when there are no more maxima to be found.

After printing the original cipher (53), our program results in the following output:

```
COMPUTE BEST DECODING DIGRAM PATH, P(I), FOR LANGUAGE:
    THERDOUSINGALYMP'
```

(based on the *Hamlet* correlation matrix).

We leave this section of the program with another print statement and three initialization statements for the next section.

```
96    PRINT
97    MAT A = B
98    LET LØ = Ø
99    MAT L = ZER
```

Both matrices A and B were initially set equal to the correlation matrix for the language. Matrix A was substantially altered during lines 5Ø through 94, and we now wish to restore it to its original value (line 97). (This could also be accomplished with a RESTORE command and MAT READ A.) In the next sections we shall use the parameter $L\emptyset$ to count the number of identified characters, and we shall store those identified characters in the array $L(I)$, initialized by line 99.

First we need to find the space symbol used in our cryptogram. We accomplish that objective merely by computing the most frequently occurring character in the cipher. Of course, the standard literary crypt usually provides this information for you ahead of time. Because it really is the easiest thing to compute, we shall go ahead and locate it anyway. That objective is accomplished in the following few lines:

```
1ØØ   PRINT LØ + 1;"COMPUTE 'SPACE':"
1Ø1   REM FIND SPACE SYMBOL FROM CHARACTER FREQUENCIES
1Ø5   LET M = Ø
11Ø   MAT F = ZER
115   FOR N = 1 TO NØ
12Ø   LET J = C(N)
125   LET F(J) = F(J) + 1
13Ø   IF M > F(J) THEN 145
135   LET M = F(J)
14Ø   LET JØ = J
145   NEXT N
15Ø   LET I1 = IØ = P(1)
155   LET Q1 = 1
159   LET PØ = Ø
```

Line 1ØØ prints what we plan to do as step number 1. We both compute the total distribution of characters in $F(J)$ and do a running computation of its maximum value and maximum location $(J\emptyset)$ at the same time. This is an obvious type of time-saver which we shall try to use whenever practical.

After passing line 159, we have located the symbol $(J\emptyset)$, used to disguise the space character; we have stored the value that it should have, $P(1)$, in $I\emptyset$; and we have also noted that the fixed code value for this symbol ($I1$) is also equal to $P(1) = 27$ in the present case. (As we begin interchanging more and more characters, $I1$ will not necessarily be equal to $I\emptyset$.) Having identified these quantities, we print them out, exchange $I\emptyset$ and $J\emptyset$, recode the cipher, print the recoded cipher, and update the matrices $A(I, J)$ and $B(J, K)$ (in a manner that we shall presently discuss) through the harmless-looking statement

```
160   GOSUB 945
```

Line $16\emptyset$ enters at the middle of a fairly long subroutine ($9\emptyset\emptyset$), which is discussed below in greater detail. Line $16\emptyset$ results in

```
1   COMPUTE 'SPACE':
FREQ. = 38        I0 = 27      J0 = 21      I1 = 27      P0 = 0

PQ 'W QJ BQP PQ 'W PSUP TX PSW FDWXPTQB ISWPSWJ APTX BQ'CWJ TB PSW
ZTBE PQ XDKKWJ PSW XCTBYX UBE UJJQIX QK QDPJUYWQDX KQJPDBW QJ PQ   (54)
PUOW UJZX UYUTBXP U XWU QK PJQD'CWX UBE 'V QGGQXTBY WBE PSWZ
```

and we have broken up the cipher (53) into words. Note that the space symbol occurred 38 times and that the author of the cipher had cleverly concealed it from us by avoiding its use at the beginning and end of the message!

Next we want to follow the most probable digram decoding path, $P(I)$, starting with the space-symbol identification:

```
162   REM USE MOST PROBABLE  DIGRAM PATH, P(I)
165   PRINT L0 + 1;"COMPUTE '";
168   LET P0 = P(L0)
170   LET X = I1 = P(L0 + 1)
176   GOSUB 500
180   PRINT "':"
190   GOSUB 900
191   IF M = 0 THEN 199
197   GOTO 165
199   PRINT
```

The above section of the program is used over and over until we exhaust the statistical accuracy of the message ($M = \emptyset$ at line 191). In each case the computer first prints which character it is going to locate (lines 165–180), stores the identity of the character being sought in the fixed code in variable $I1$ (line $17\emptyset$), and then does all the work in subroutine $9\emptyset\emptyset$. Note that $P\emptyset$ (line 168) is the previous character identified. Subroutine $9\emptyset\emptyset$ does the things summarized in the following REM statements:

```
900   REM SUB TO FIND J0 = J FOR MAX F(J) = M(I0,J)
901   REM ENTER SUB WITH VALUE OF I1 (FIXED CODE)
902   REM SUB COMPUTES I0 AND J0 FROM DIGRAM PATH IN CURRENT CODE
903   REM P0 IS THE VALUE OF I0 FROM PREVIOUS TIME SUB.ENTERED
```

It computes values of the $P\emptyset$ row of the correlation matrix for the cipher array $C(N)$ and performs a running computation of the location $J\emptyset$ for which $M(P\emptyset, J\emptyset)$ is a maximum. Because we only need to compute one row at a time (and in fact will run out of statistical accuracy after a few rows), there is no point in either computing the entire correlation matrix based on the cipher, or in squandering the computer core necessary to store it all. We can use the same array $F(J)$ with which we previously found the space identity. After the initial statements,

```
904   LET M = Q9 = 0
906   MAT F = ZER
```

(where we have again reset the column counter $Q9$ for subroutine $5\emptyset\emptyset$), we

173

next store the $P\emptyset$ row of the matrix computed from $C(N)$ in $F(J)$, using the following statements:

```
908  LET I = C(1)
914  FOR N = 2 TO NØ
916  LET J = C(N)
918  IF I≠PØ THEN 932
919  REM AVOID CASES WHERE 2ND TERM ALREADY KNOWN
920  FOR K = 1 TO LØ
921  IF J = L(K) THEN 932
922  IF X(J) = L(K) THEN 932
923  NEXT K
924  LET F(J) = F(J) + 1
926  IF M > F(J) THEN 932
928  LET M = F(J)
930  LET JØ = J
932  LET I = J
933  NEXT N
```

A running computation of the maximum value of $F(J)$ and its location, $J\emptyset$, is done on lines 928 and 93$\emptyset$. The loop from 92$\emptyset$ through 923 eliminates examining values of J that have been identified previously. Line 918 makes sure that we only compute the $P\emptyset$ row of the matrix in $F(J)$. $F(J)$ thus literally corresponds to the number of times the Jth character followed the $I = P\emptyset$th character throughout the presently decoded version of the cipher stored in $C(N)$. Line 93$\emptyset$ stores the running value $J\emptyset$ for the maximum location during the loop on N. Consequently, $J\emptyset$ contains the location of the maximum after completion of line 933.

In principle, we should really check the statistical meaningfulness of M by computing the value $M1$ of the next-highest maximum for different $J\emptyset$. The latter would be easy to accomplish by adding the statement LET $M1 = M$ as line 927. One could then require that M be an integer greater than $M1 + \sqrt{M + M1}$. However, the typical literary crypt is much too short to permit using such a stringent statistical requirement. A reasonable compromise is to stop computing successive maxima when the statistical uncertainty on M is ≈ 1. We can accomplish that objective with the statements

```
934  REM STOP FOLLOWING DIGRAM PATH WHEN M TOO SMALL
935  IF INT(SQR(M) + .5) > 1 THEN 938
936  LET M = Ø
937  RETURN
```

In practice line 935 is equivalent to the statement

```
935  IF M > 2 THEN 938
```

That is, we shall make the computer return from the subroutine when the criterion on line 935 is not satisfied, and indicate this fact to the main program by setting $M = 0$ on line 936. The conditional statement on line 191 of the main program then goes on to the next stage when $M = 0$.

If the statistical criterion is met on line 935, we then compute the value of $I\emptyset$ in the current code corresponding to $I1$ in the fixed code, define a new $P\emptyset$ ("previous value of $I\emptyset$"), print the numerical values computed, exchange $I\emptyset$ and $J\emptyset$ in the current code, recode the cipher, and print the recoded version of the cipher.

```
938  REM FIND VALUE OF IØ CORRESPONDING TO I1 IN FIXED CODE
939  FOR I = 1 TO 28
940  IF I1 = X(I) THEN 942
941  NEXT I
942  LET IØ = I
```

```
944   LET P0 = I0
945   PRINT "FREQ. = ";M, "I0 = "; I0, "J0 = "; J0, "I1 = "; I1, "P0 = "; P0
946   PRINT
947   REM EXCHANGE I0, J0 AND PRINT CIPHER
948   GOSUB 755
949   GOSUB 850
```

We then update the matrices $A(I, J)$ and $B(J, K)$, which will be needed for a later second-order correction. (The process is very similar to that used in the previous discussion of bit compression–expansion techniques.) In particular, we want to set elements of A and B equal to zero whose columns and rows, respectively, are designated by the identified character, $I1$, in the fixed code. Thus

```
950   REM UPDATE A(I,J) AND B(J,K) FOR 2ND-ORDER CORRECTION
952   REM A(I,J) = B(J,I) = 0 WHEN J = I1; OTHERWISE A(I,J) = B(I,J) = M(I,J)
953   REM ENTER AT 955 FOR 2ND-ORDER CORRECTION
955   FOR I = 1 TO 28
960   LET A(I, I1) = B(I1,I) = 0
965   NEXT I
```

Finally, we want to update the list of known characters stored in array $L(L0)$ and increment the total number, $L0$, computed.

```
970   REM COUNT KNOWN LETTERS IN L0
975   LET L0 = L0 + 1
985   PRINT
990   LET L(L0) = I1
995   RETURN
```

We then introduce a routine initialization statement of the type

```
7 LET Q9 = P0 = X9 = 0
```

and the first part of the program is ready to run.

After the first trip through subroutine 900, the computer has printed

```
2  COMPUTE 'T':
FREQ. = 10     I0 = 20     J0 = 16     I1 = 20     P0 = 20
```

TQ 'W QJ BQT TQ 'W TSUT PX TSW FDWXTPQB ISWTSWJ ATPX BQ'CWJ PB TSW
ZPBE TQ XDKKWJ TSW XCPBYX UBE UJJQIX QK QDTJUYWQDX KQJTDBW QJ TQ   (55)
TUOW UJZX UYUPBXT U XWU QK TJQD'CWX UBE 'V QGGQXPBY WBE TSWZ

That is, it has identified the letter T from the maximum number of times (10) that a character followed the space symbol. The program keeps going through the loop until the statistical rejection criterion on line 191 diverts the program to line 199.

With the present cipher (53), the rejection criterion is inoperative until after the fifth step, at which point the computer has printed

```
5  COMPUTE 'R':
FREQ. = 3     I0 = 18     J0 = 10     I1 = 18     P0 = 18
```

TQ 'E QR BQT TQ 'E THUT PX THE FDEXTPQB IHETHER ATPX BQ'CER PB THE
ZPBW TQ XDKKER THE XCPBYX UBW URRQIX QK QDTRUYEQDX KQRTDBE QR TQ   (56)
TUOE URZX UYUPBXT U XEU QK TRQD'CEX UBW 'V QGGQXPBY EBW THEZ

At this point, the program has identified the space, T, H, E, and R; and we are forced to go to another method of attack. Note that the last identification was made using a letter-pair frequency of 3 (for the pair ER) and the statistical accuracy is getting to be very marginal indeed.

It is worthwhile at this point to have a look at what we have stored in the array $E(N)$. Here $E(N) = 29$, except where $C(N)$ is regarded as identified. Because subroutine 500 has been constructed to print "–" when $X = 29$, we

```
      T- -E -R --T T- -E TH-T -- THE --E-T--- -HETHER -T-- ----ER -- THE
      ---- T- ----ER THE ------ --- -RR--- -- --TR--E--- --RT--E -R T-          (57)
      T--E -R-- ------T - -E- -- TR----E- --- -- -------- E-- THE-
```

when line 865 of subroutine 85Ø is modified to read

    865   LET X = E(N)

**4.19
PROBLEM 32**   Draw a flowchart of the program through line 199 (the start of the second-order corrector).

**4.19
PROBLEM 33**   Write a program that follows the most probable digram decoding path for *Hamlet* and then jumps to a guesswork loop (such as that discussed above, starting on line 4ØØ) after exhausting the statistical accuracy. Try it out on the cryptogram above or The Gold Bug cipher (at the end of this section). (*Note:* Once you have computed the most probable digram path for the particular language, it would be best stored in an array rather than recomputed each time.)

**4.20
Second-Order Crypt Corrector**

The next section of the program (second-order corrector) requires a fair amount of computer core. It will be necessary to start the program with initial dimension statements of the type

    2   DIM A(28,28),B(28,28),K(28,28)
    3   DIM C(192),D(192),E(192)
    4   DIM F(28),X(28),L(28),P(28)

The arrays in line 3 have arbitrarily been dimensioned equal to the length of the cipher under discussion. The real space consumers are the matrices A, B, and K. K could be pruned somewhat in practice (to perhaps 28×10). The space needed is readily available on most large computers; however, it will be hard to do the program on the average minicomputer.

Our next approach is to compute a most probable second-order identification for the remaining characters. That is, we want to pick sequences of the type

$$E(N-1),29,E(N+1) \tag{58}$$

in which an unknown character is surrounded by two known characters. For each such set of sequences throughout the cipher we want to compute a most probable value of J such that the quantity

$$F = A(E(N-1),J)*B(J,E(N+1)) \tag{59}$$

is a maximum. Further, we want to do this in such a way as to bypass previously identified terms. In addition, we must store correlated pairs of the identity of the most probable characters in the fixed $I1 = J$ code and their corresponding values in the current code, $JØ = C(N)$, with which they should be interchanged. We shall store those correlated pairs in the matrix $K(I, C(N))$.

The first part of this problem is handled by the following statements:

    2ØØ   PRINT "REACHED STATISTICAL LIMIT. 2ND-ORDER CORRECTION NEXT"
    2Ø1   PRINT
    2Ø2   LET MØ = Ø
    2Ø3   MAT K = ZER(28,28)
    2Ø4   FOR N = 2 TO NØ-1
    2Ø5   REM UNIDENTIFIED TERMS HAVE E(N) = 29; FIND SEQ. E(N-1),29,E(N+1)

```
206   IF E(N) #29 THEN 290
207   IF E(N-1) = 29 THEN 290
208   IF E(N+1) = 29 THEN 290
209   REM EXCLUDE C(N) ALREADY ON IDENTIFIED LIST, L(I)
210   FOR I = 1 TO L0
212   IF X(C(N)) = L(I) THEN 290
214   NEXT I
220   LET M = 0
230   REM CHOOSE I = J FOR MAXIMUM (M) VALUE OF F (SEE BELOW)
235   FOR J = 1 TO 28
240   LET F = A(E(N-1),J)*B(J,E(N+1))
245   IF M > F THEN 260
250   LET M = F
255   LET I = J
260   NEXT J
265   IF M = 0 THEN 290
269   REM COUNT AND FIND MAX (M0) OF CORR.PAIRS I,C(N) IN K(I,C(N))
270   LET K(I,C(N)) = K(I,C(N)) + 1
275   IF M0 > K(I,C(N)) THEN 290
277   LET M0 = K(I,C(N))
280   LET I1 = I
285   LET J0 = C(N)
290   NEXT N
294   REM END HERE IF CAN'T FIND MAXIMUM, M0
295   IF M0 = 0 THEN 400
```

A running computation of the number of correlated pairs is done on line 270, and the coordinates for the running maximum are stored on lines 280 and 285.

If we reach line 295 with $M0 = 0$, it means that the maximum is indeterminate. Hence the conditional statement at line 295 takes the program to line 400 for a final bit of guesswork on the cipher.[27]

If a nonzero value for $M0$ is found by line 295, we now have the values of $I1$ (in the fixed code) for the identity of the new character and the value of $J0$ in the current code with which that character is to be exchanged. We next have to compute the value of $I0$ in the current code corresponding to $I1$ in the fixed code. The latter is accomplished by lines 300–315 in the following steps:

```
299   REM NEED I0 = INVERSE CODE FOR I1
300   FOR I = 1 TO 28
305   IF I1 = X[I] THEN 315
310   NEXT I
315   LET I0 = I
```

After that, we print out the numerical values obtained and use subroutines 755, 850, and 955 to exchange $I0$ and $J0$, recode the cipher, print the current cipher, and update matrices A and B and the array L.

```
316   REM NOW KNOW I1,I0,J0
317   PRINT L0+1;"COMPUTE '";
318   LET X = I1
319   GOSUB 500
320   PRINT "':"
322   PRINT "FREQ. = ";M0,"I0 = ";I0,"J0 = ";J0,"I1 = ";I1
324   REM EXCHANGE I0,J0 IN CODE ARRAY X(I) AND RECODE CIPHER
325   GOSUB 755
```

---

[27] The second-order correction is approximately equivalent to finding the value of J, for the maximum third-order correlation matrix element $M(I, J, K)$ in which I and K are fixed. If you have a third-order correlation matrix available, it would be best used in the program section starting on line 200 (as opposed to tacking it on at line 400). One could then go on to estimate still-higher corrections from the third-order matrix.

```
329  REM PRINT CIPHER AND RECORD NEW CORRECTIONS
330  PRINT
335  GOSUB 850
340  GOSUB 955
344  REM REITERATE UNTIL MØ = Ø ON LINE 295
345  GOTO 2Ø2
```

We then reiterate to line 2Ø2 until no further second-order correction is determinate.

With the present cipher (53), the second-order corrector deduces the right values for three more characters (O, S, and U) and finally hits the indeterminate state after the thirteenth computation (during which it thought it was identifying the letter A). At that point the program yielded

```
13  COMPUTE 'A':
FREQ. = 1      IØ = 1      JØ = 22      I1 = 1
```

TO ME OR YOT TO ME THDT PS THE FUESTPOY CHETHER VTPS YOMIER PY THE
ZPYW TO SUNNER THE SIPYBS DYW DRROCS ON OUTRDBEOUS NORTUYE OR TO (60)
TDQE DRZS DBDPYST D SED ON TROUMIES DYW MA OGGOSPYB EYW THEZ

and gave up. It may not seem like much; however, the program has successfully identified the following characters:

space, T, H, E, R, O, S, U

Further note that it is trying to make decisions at the end where only *one* case has occurred within the cipher. Obviously, it would do much better with a significantly longer message.

Doubtless there will be a skeptical reader who will toss the result aside with the comment: "Well, after all, you used a correlation matrix for Act III of *Hamlet* in the first place. No wonder the program worked so well." It is therefore of interest to see what would have happened if we fed in somebody else's correlation matrix.

The following result was reached after 15 steps using a correlation matrix based on "The Gold Bug":

```
15  COMPUTE 'A':
FREQ. = 1      IØ = 1      JØ = 1      I1 = 1
```

TO ME OR IOT TO ME THVT PS THE FUESTPOI CHETHER ATPS IOMBER PI THE
ZPIW TO SUNNER THE SBPIDS VIW VRROCS ON OUTRVDEOUS NORTUIE OR TO (61)
TVQE VRZS VDVPIST V SEV ON TROUMBES VIW MY OGGOSPID EIW THEZ

Compare statements (60) and (61).

Although it took longer to get there (see Table 9), the program eventually arrived at exactly the same set of correctly identified characters. Some of the other symbols are identified differently, and the program pursued a riskier path. "The Gold Bug" program started making mistakes on the seventh and eighth steps but got S correct on the ninth and U correct on the twelfth.

4.20: Table 9   Results in Deciphering 192 Characters of Hamlet's Soliloquy (Shakespeare vs. Poe): Summary of "Identified" Letters

Step:	1	2	3	4	5	6	7	8	9	10	11	12	13	14	15
Hamlet matrix	space	T	H	E	R	O	S	N**[a]	Y*	M*	I*	U	A*	—	—
"Gold Bug" matrix	space	T	H	E	R	O	N*	I*	S	M*	B*	U	D*	Y*	A*

[a] Erroneous identifications are marked *. In each case, the program started making mistakes when the particular pair frequency computed from the cipher got down to 2. However, the same set of eight correctly identified code symbols was found in each case.

What else could we have done to improve the accuracy of the final result? The answer seems to be: not much with only second-order correlations to work with. For example, after exhausting the statistical accuracy in the message during the second-order correction process, we might have introduced a section that computed most-probable identical-letter pairs. There are two words in the final cipher,

SUNNER   and   OGGOSPYB   (or OGGOSPID)

which contain different unidentified doubled letters, and one might argue that we could benefit by consulting a double-letter frequency table. However, these doubled pairs each occur only once. The word SUNNER might thus be most probably interpreted as SULLER, with SUFFER and SUPPER occurring much farther down the list. A human being with knowledge of words in English would probably rule out the first choice; but he might also think that Hamlet was inviting someone named ZPYW to dinner. The only real way to handle these sequences within the present type of computer program is use higher order correlation matrices from the start. However, the present program is complicated enough for our purposes and already occupies more core than is really desirable. Further, it has gotten us to a point where a few quick exchanges of characters will permit us to narrow in rapidly on the correct answer through interactive guesswork and application of our personal knowledge of higher-order correlations.

**4.20
PROBLEM 34**

Draw a flowchart for the second-order corrector starting on line 200.

**4.20
PROBLEM 35**

Write a program to compute a frequency table of doubled letters from a pair-correlation matrix based on Act III of *Hamlet* (Fig. 4-6).

**4.20
PROBLEM 36**

Solve one of the following historically interesting single-substitution ciphers:
   1. The original "Gold Bug" cipher did not exhibit representative statistical properties of English, except for the first four characters in the most-probable decoding digram path. Resetting the message from the 1895 edition of the complete works of Poe with standard characters yields

BEYNNUEYCBXXETFE'SWEPTXSNGAXESNX'WCETFE'SWEUWQTCAXEXWB'EKNJ'VENFWEUWYJWW
XEBFUE'STJ'WWFEZTFD'WXEFNJ'SWBX'EBFUEPVEFNJ'SEZBTFEPJBFRSEXWQWF'SECTZPEW
BX'EXTUWEXSNN'EKJNZE'SWECWK'EWVWENKE'SWEUWB'SAXESWBUEBEPWWECTFWEKJNZE'SW
E'JWWE'SJNDYSE'SWEXSN'EKTK'VEKWW'END'

where we have also used characters to represent the space symbol and apostrophe. After computing the sequence, space THE, you can probably unscramble the rest. However, you have to resort to fairly high order correlations in the guesswork: for example, by identifying such words as

TH--TEE-

This single-substitution cipher is the only one of its length tried by the author in which the second-order corrector did absolutely no good whatsoever. The problem seems in part to be that the cipher was artificially loaded up with E's—so much so that the rest of the statistics suffered.
   2. The following cipher is based on the first published version of *Hamlet*†:

BE OF EX KEB BE OF 'R BVFXFUN BVF PEAKB BE HAF BE NMFFP AN BV'B 'MM
'R 'MM KE BE NMFFP BE HXF'Q 'R Q'XXR BVFXF AB CEFN TEX AK BV'B HXF'Q
ET HF'BV LVFK LF 'L'ZF 'KH OEXKF OFTEXF 'K FGFXM'NBAKC DSHCF TXEQ
LVFKYF KE P'NNFKCFX FGFX XFBSXKFH

---

† This pirated edition is known as *The First Quarto* (see Hubler, 1963).

3. Rumor has it that the following type of cryptogram appeared as an advertisement in a scientific journal in recent years:

IF I'M GLAZZAUTI I'MFLAWI A BUTI IF OFLY U DIFEAUT PFYEUTS I'UI BAZZ
GM YURM FO I'FWM WYULI WPAMTIAWIW WDP' UW SFDLWMZO B'F BUTI IF W'ULM
PFEAFDWZS AT I'M ELFOAIW WIFE I'M MNEZFAIUIAFT FO FDL DTDWDUZ YATRW
UTR HFAT YM OUYFDW TFGMZ BATTML

It was supposedly followed by the solitary reply:

MA MOW BALWC JYBBWT MOUBS FAD NWTF ID'O EAT MOW AEEWT LDM Y UI NWTF
OUGGF JYMO IF GTWVWBM PAL UBABFIADV

The ad is long enough to exhibit many of the statistical properties of Shakespearean English. Note that the second cryptogram is very much harder than the first, owing to its extremely short length. It therefore would not be surprising to learn that the author of the ad had a great deal of trouble reading the reply.

Do you think a company of this type would be a success? *Note:* If you don't like any of the above ciphers, pick one out of *Saturday Review/World* instead.

Poe had a penchant for describing the primary objectives in cryptography as if he had developed a powerful, general method to carry them out. For example, in a later version of his famous paper on secret writing, Poe states:

4.21
Is a Decipherable Message Present?[28]

"Out of perhaps one hundred ciphers altogether received, there was only one which we did not immediately succeed in resolving. This one we *demonstrated* to be ... a jargon of random characters having no meaning whatsoever."

Poe revealed neither the "fake" cryptogram nor the method of demonstration. If nothing else, he had seized upon a very good idea. When faced with something as perplexing as the Balzac cipher or the Voynich Manuscript, it would be very nice to know ahead of time that there *is* a message present. Otherwise, there is a danger that one might spend several decades trying to decipher the "message" in a railroad timetable or in a list of tonnages of naval vessels.

There are two primary questions that we can ask:

1. Do the statistical properties of the coded message differ in a meaningful way from those of a randomly selected string of characters?
2. Do the statistical properties of the coded message agree with those for text in the proposed source language within the statistical uncertainty?

If the answer to the first question is "no," the message is undecipherable for all practical purposes and we might as well not waste our time on it. This would not necessarily mean that no message is there. One can always transmit a message coded in a purely random key. However, unless you have a duplicate copy of the random key, you will not be able to decipher it. (At least, if you do "decipher" a message, you should be extremely skeptical of its meaning.) If the answer to the second question is "yes," it is reasonable to go ahead with a systematic unscrambling process according to the various coding methods that seem most probable. (Just which method is usually a guess.)

It is possible to formulate the above questions in terms of the entropy per character of the coded text. That is, one may make an objective computation of the quantities $h_0, h_1, h_2, \ldots$ defined earlier. If you know the character set, a

---

[28] The remaining sections of this chapter rely on the concept of entropy per character in various statistical orders developed in Section 4.13.

direct comparison with h_0 for a random string is meaningful. In many instances one simply does *not* know the entire character set. However, the values for h_1, h_2, $h_3, \ldots$ in most languages are relatively independent of the exact number of characters in the set for long sections of text.

It is useful to investigate the dependence of h_0, h_1, $h_2, \ldots$ on the number (N) of characters in the string in the purely random case. As can be seen from the basic definitions of these quantities,

$$\lim_{N \to \infty} h_m = h_0 \tag{62}$$

for a perfectly random string. However, the speed with which $h_m \to h_0$ with increasing lengths of text falls off with increasing m.

This effect can be demonstrated very easily by using the random-number generator to produce a long string of numbers. For example, the following statements permit computing a 28×28 correlation matrix for a string N characters long chosen randomly from a 28-character set.

```
1500   REM SUB TO COMPUTE M(I,J) FROM RANDOM CHARACTERS
1505   LET I = 28
1510   MAT M = ZER(28,28)
1515   FOR NØ = 1 TO N
1520   LET J = 1 + INT(RND(1)*27 + .5)
1525   LET M(I,J) = M(I,J) + 1
1530   LET I = J
1535   NEXT N
1540   RETURN
```

Use of our previously described programs to compute h_0, h_1, and h_2 from the correlation matrix results in the values shown in Table 10. Note that randomly selected character strings with $N \approx 10,000$ are required before $h_2 \approx h_1$ within ≈ 1 percent; whereas $h_1 \approx h_0$ within 1 percent for $N \approx 500$. One, of course, will get slight differences each time you rerun the program from a new table of random numbers. Ultimately, the convergence of the quantities in Table 10 with increasing N will be a measure of the randomness of the $RND(X)$ function itself.

4.21: Table 10 Speed with Which $h_2 \to h_1 \to h_0 = \log_2 28 = 4.80735$ for a String of N Characters Chosen Randomly, by Use of $RND(X)$, from a Set of 28 Characters

	\multicolumn{7}{c}{N}						
	100	200	500	1000	2000	5000	10,000
h_0/h_1	1.04_3	1.01_7	1.00_9	1.00_7	1.00_4	1.00_4	1.00_3
h_1/h_2	2.46	1.81	1.31	1.14	1.05	1.02	1.01

**4.21
PROBLEM 37**

Use the $RND(X)$ function to generate a random key that can be added to messages in a standard ASCII character set. (Such messages could, of course, be deciphered easily by someone else with access to the same BASIC compiler, if it were known where the message started in the random-number table.) Transmit Hamlet's soliloquy (or some other text in English) using this key and compute h_1, h_2, and h_1/h_2 for the result. Compare the values with those for Shakespearean English.

**4.21
PROBLEM 38**

Write a program that computes h_0, h_1, and h_2 for the first several hundred digits in π (see Fig. 4-16).

PI = 3.+

1415926535	8979323846	2643383279	5028841971	6939937510	5820974944	5923078164	0628620899	8628034825	3421170679
8214808651	3282306647	0938446095	5058223172	5359408128	4811174502	8410270193	8521105559	6446229489	5493038196
4428810975	6659334461	2847564823	3786783165	2712019091	4564856692	3460348610	4543266482	1339360726	0249141273
7245870066	0631558817	4881520920	9628292540	9171536436	7892590360	0113305305	4882046652	1384146951	9415116094
3305727036	5759591953	0921861173	8193261179	3105118548	0744623799	6274956735	1885752724	8912279381	8301194912
9833673362	4406566430	8602139494	6395224737	1907021798	6094370277	0539217176	2931767523	8467481846	7669405132
0005681271	4526356082	7785771342	7577896091	7363717872	1468440901	2249534301	4654958537	1050792279	6892589235
4201995611	2129021960	8640344181	5981362977	4771309960	5187072113	4999999837	2978049951	0597317328	1609631859
5024459455	3469083026	4252230825	3344685035	2619311881	7101000313	7838752886	5875332083	8142061717	7669147303
5982534904	2875546873	1159562863	8823537875	9375195778	1857780532	1712268066	1300192787	6611195909	2164201989

3809525720	1065485863	2788659361	5338182796	8230301952	0353018529	6899577362	2599413891	2497217752	8347913151
5574857242	4541506959	5082953311	6861727855	8890750983	8175463746	4939319255	0604009277	0167113900	9848824012
8583616035	6370766010	4710181942	9555961989	4676783744	9448255379	7747268471	0404753464	6208046684	2590694912
9331367702	8989152104	7521620569	6602405803	8150193511	2533824300	3558764024	7496473263	9141992726	0426992279
6782354781	6360093417	2164121992	4586315030	2861829745	5570674983	8505494588	5869269956	9092721079	7509302955
3211653449	8720275596	0236480665	4991198818	3479775356	6369807426	5425278625	5181841757	4672890977	7727938000
8164706001	6145249192	1732172147	7235014144	1973568548	1613611573	5255213347	5741849468	4385233239	0739414333
4547762416	8625189835	6948556209	9219222184	2725502542	5688767179	0494601653	4668049886	2723279178	6085784383
8279679766	8145410095	3883786360	9506800642	2512520511	7392984896	0841284886	2694560424	1965285022	2106611863
0674427862	2039194945	0471237137	8696095636	4371917287	4677646575	7396241389	0865832645	9958133904	7802759009

9465764078	9512694683	9835259570	9825822620	5224894077	2671947826	8482601476	9909026401	3639443745	5305068203
4962524517	4939965143	1429809190	6592509372	2169646151	5709858387	4105978859	5977297549	8930161753	9284681382
6868386894	2774155991	8559252459	5395943104	9972524680	8459872736	4469584865	3836736222	6260991246	0805124388
4390451244	1365497627	8079771569	1435997700	1296160894	4169486855	5848406353	4220722258	2848864815	8456028506
0168427394	5226746767	8895252138	5225499546	6672782398	6456596116	3548862305	7745649803	5593634568	1743241125
1507606947	9451096596	0940252288	7971089314	5669136867	2287489405	6010150330	8617928680	9208747609	1782493858
9009714909	6759852613	6554978189	3129784821	6829989487	2265880485	7564014270	4775551323	7964145152	3746234364
5428584447	9526586782	1051141354	7357395231	1342716610	2135969536	2314429524	8493718711	0145765403	5902799344
0374200731	0578539062	1983874478	0847848968	3321445713	8687519435	0643021845	3191048481	0053706146	8067491927
8191197939	9520614196	6342875444	0643745123	7181921799	9839101591	9561814675	1426912397	4894090718	6494231961

5679452080	9514655022	5231603881	9301420937	6213785595	6638937787	0830390697	9207734672	2182562599	6615014215
0306803844	7734549202	6054146659	2520149744	2850732518	6660021324	3408819071	0486331734	6496514539	0579626856
1005508106	6587969981	6357473638	4052571459	1028970641	4011097120	6280439039	7595156771	5770042033	7869936007
2305587631	7635942187	3125147120	5329281918	2618612586	7321579198	4148488291	6447060957	5270695722	0917567116
7229109816	9091528017	3506712748	5832228718	3520935396	5725121083	5791513698	8209144421	0067510334	6711031412
6711136990	8658516398	3150197016	5151168517	1437657618	3515565088	4909989859	9823873455	2833163550	7647918535
8932261854	8963213293	3089857064	2046752590	7091548141	6549859461	6371802709	8199430992	4488957571	2828905923
2332609729	9712084433	5732654893	8239119325	9746366730	5836041428	1388303203	8249037589	8524374417	0291327656
1809377344	4030707469	2112019130	2033038019	7621101100	4492932151	6084244485	9637669838	9522868478	3123552658
2131449576	8572624334	4189303968	6426243410	7732269780	2807318915	4411010446	8232527162	0105265227	2111660396

6655730925	4711055785	3763466820	6531098965	2691862056	4769312570	5863566201	8558100729	3606598764	8611791045
3348850346	1136576867	5324944166	8039626579	7877185560	8455296541	2665408530	6143444318	5867697514	5661406800
7002378776	5913440171	2749470420	5622305389	9456131407	1127000407	8547332699	3908145466	4645880797	2708266830
6343285878	5698305235	8089330657	5740679545	7163775254	2021149557	6158140025	0126228594	1302164715	5097925923
0990796547	3761255176	5675135751	7829666454	7791745011	2996148903	0463994713	2962107340	4375189573	5961458901
9389713111	7904297828	5647503203	1986915140	2870808599	0480109412	1472213179	4764777262	2414254854	5403321571
8530614228	8137585043	0633217518	2979866223	7172159160	7716692547	4873898665	4949450114	6540628433	6639379003
9769265672	1463853067	3609657120	9180763832	7166416274	8888007869	2560290228	4721040317	2118608204	1900042296
6171196377	9213375751	1495950156	6049631862	9472654736	4252308177	0367515906	7350235072	8354056704	0386743513
6222247715	8915049530	9844489333	0963408780	7693259939	7805419341	4473774418	4263129860	8099888687	4132604721

Fig. 4-16. The first few digits in a computation of π done by Shanks and Wrench (1962) using the formula $\pi = 24\tan^{-1}\frac{1}{8} + 8\tan^{-1}\frac{1}{57} + 4\tan^{-1}\frac{1}{239}$ through 100,625 decimal places (333,075 bits).

The fluctuations in h_1 and h_2 expected from statistical effects due to the finite length of a character string from a particular text can be estimated readily in the following manner. As a rough approximation, we note that the average uncertainty is $\approx \sqrt{N}$ in a counting experiment where one obtains N counts on the average. Hence for each matrix element $M(I, J)$ which represents the number of times the Jth character followed the Ith in the set throughout the entire string of N characters, we can expect a fluctuation of $\approx \pm \sqrt{M(I, J)}$. These fluctuations in the individual matrix elements obviously will not add up in phase throughout the entire matrix. In fact, they will tend to add up to $\approx \sqrt{N}$, where

$$N = \sum_{I,J} M(I, J) \tag{63}$$

Hence by redefining the correlation matrix through the subroutine

```
REM SUB TO COMPUTE SPREAD IN M(I,J)
FOR I = 1 TO 28
FOR J = 1 TO 28
LET X = SQR(M(I,J))
LET M(I,J) = M(I,J) + 2*(RND(1) − .5)*X
NEXT J
NEXT I
RETURN
```

we can recompute representative values of h_1 and h_2 that arise from the statistical fluctuations. It is worth printing out the new sum over all the elements in the altered matrix to verify that it differs from the original N by $\approx \sqrt{N}$.

**4.21
PROBLEM 39**   Write a program that computes h_1 and h_2 from the original correlation matrix and then estimates the error in h_1 and h_2. Try it out on the 28×28 correlation matrix from Act III of *Hamlet* (Fig. 4-6).

**4.21
PROBLEM 40**   Compute the correlation matrix for an N-character string chosen randomly by use of RND(X) from a 28-character alphabet. Try it out for the value $N = 424$ in the Waberski cipher (see Fig. 4-18). Compute h_1 and h_2 from this matrix, together with an estimate of the spread in values.

Now we are ready to have a look at the famous Balzac cipher. In 1829, Honoré de Balzac introduced a cipher of some 3660 characters in length in the middle of his handbook on marriage, *La Physiologie du Marriage* (see Fig. 4-17). Stimulated by the admonition from Balzac himself that one ought to reread the principal passages several times to really understand the sense of the text, readers of this book for the next decade attempted in vain to decipher the cryptogram. It was thought that Balzac had provided tantalizing clues, such as "end" at the end and "sin!" in the middle. However, the text of the cipher differs from one edition to the next and one suspects that Balzac left instructions to the printer after the line "L'auteur pense que la Bruyère s'est trompé. En effet" that a monkey should be allowed to choose the type for the next two pages. (Cynics will note that Balzac was paid by the word.) Obviously, Balzac was just having a practical joke at the reader's expense. However, it is of interest to compute the values of h_1 and h_2 for this cipher and compare them with values expected from French, or any other western European language. Although a large character set has been used, the more exotic (upside-down) symbols occur very rarely (at least in the 1870 edition of the cipher shown in Fig. 4-17). As previously noted, if we include all the most-probable characters

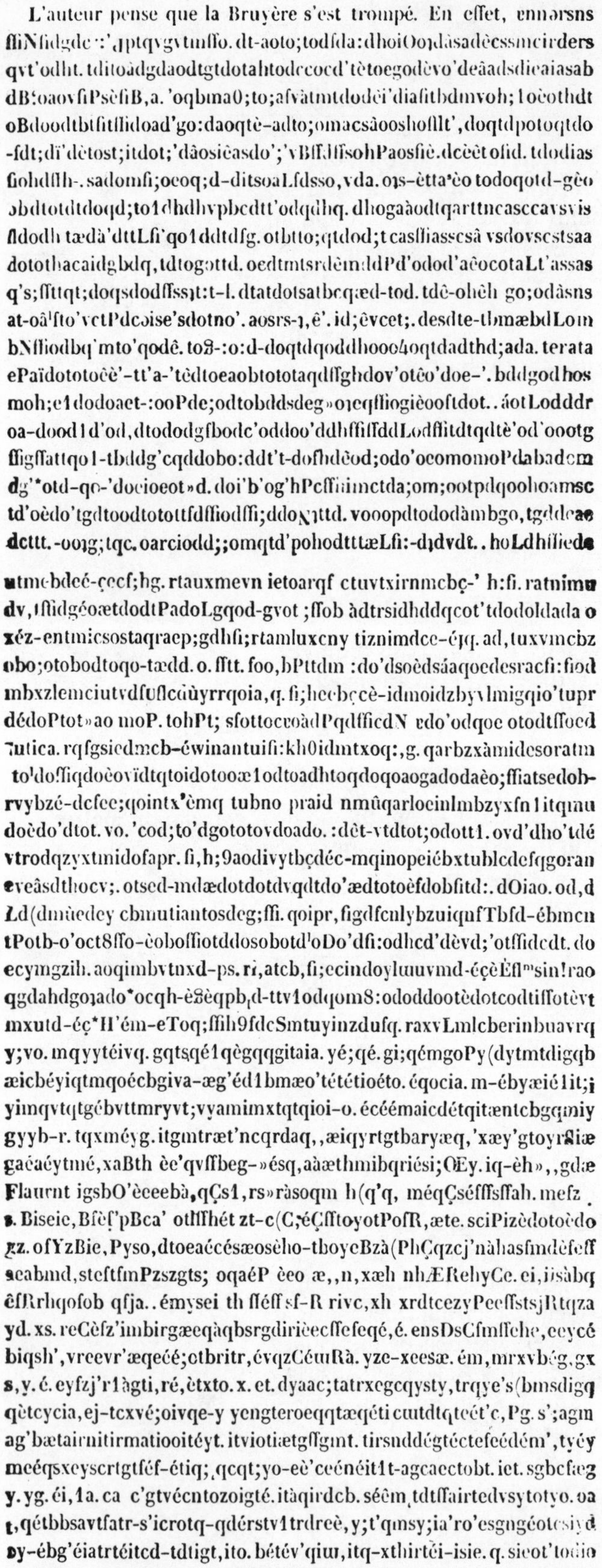

L'auteur pense que la Bruyère s'est trompé. En effet, ennɔrsns
fliNfiidgde ∴',jptqvgvtinffo. dt-aoto;todfda:dhoiOoɔdasadècssmcirders
qvt'odht. tditoàdgdaodtgtdotahtodccocd'tètoegodèvo'deâadsdicaiasab
dB:oaovfiPsèfiB,a. 'oqbma0;to;afvàtmtdodéi'diafithdmvoh; 1ocothdt
oBdoodtbtfitfidoad'go:daoqtè-adto;omacsàooshofllt',doqtdpotoqtdo
-fdt;di'dètost;itdot;'dàosièasdo';'vBlf.llfsohPaosfiè.dccèt ofid. tdlodias
fiohdflh-. sadomfi;ocoq;d-ditsoaLfdsso,vda. oɔs-ètta'èo todoqotd-gèo
ɔbdtotdtdoqd;to1dhdhvpbcdtt'odqdhq. dhogaàodtqarttncasccavsvis
fldodh tædà'dttLfi'qo1ddtdfg. otbtto;qtdod;t casfliasscsà vsdovscstsaa
dotothacaidgbdq, tdtogɔttd. oedtmtsrdèmɪldP'd'odod'aèocotaLt'assas
q's;flttqt;doqsdodffssɪt:t-l. dtatdotsatbcqæd-tod. tdè-ohèh go;odàsns
at-oàlfto'vctPdcɔise'sdotno'. aosrs-ɪ,è'. id;èvcet;. desdte-tbmæbdLom
bNfliodbq'mto'qodè. toϑ-:o:d-doqtdqoddhooo4oqtdadthd;ada. terata
ePaïdototocè'-tt'a-'tèdtoeaobtototaqdlfghdov'otèo'doe-'. bddgodhos
moh;e1dodoaet-:ooPde;odtobddsdeg;oɪeqfliogièooftdot. . àotLodddr
oa-doodld'od,dtododgfbodc'oddoo'ddhffiffddLodffitdtqdtè'od'ooootg
ffigffattqo1-tbddg'cqddobo:ddt't-dofhdèod;odo'ocomomoPdabadcm
dg'*otd-qo-'docioeot»d. doi'b'og'hPcffiimctda;om;ootpdqoohoamsc
td'oèdo'tgdtoodtotottfdffiodffi;ddoχɪttd. vooopdtododàmbgo,tgddeæ
dcttt.-ooɪg;tqc. oarciodd;;omqtd'pohodtttæLfi:-dɪdvdt. . hoLdhílieds

utmcbdeé-çecf;hg. rtauxmevn ietoarqf ctuvtxirnmcbç-' h:fi. ratnimu
dv,ɪflidgéoætdodtPadoLgqod-gvot ;ffob àdtrsidhddqcot'tdodoldada o
xéz-entmicsostaqraep;gdhfi;rtamluxcny tiznimdcc-éɪq. ad,tuxvmcbz
obo;otobodtoqo-tædd. o. fltt. foo,bPttdm :do'dsoèdsáaqoedesracfi:fiod
mbxzlemciutvdfuflcàùyrrqoia,q. fi;hccbçcè-idmoidzbyvlmigqio'tupr
dédoPtot»ao moP. tohPt; sfottocvoàdPqdlfficdN vdo'odqoe otodtffocd
ꞇutica. rqfgsiedmcb-éwinantuifi;kh0idmtxoq:,g. qarbzxàmidesoratm
to1doffiqdoèovïdtqtoidotooæ1odtoadhtoqdoqoaogadodaèo;ffiatsedoh-
rvybzé-dcfee;qointx'èmq tubno praid nmûqarlocinlmbzyxfn1itqrau
doèdo'dtot. vo. 'cod;to'dgototovdoado. :dèt-vtdtot;odott1. ovd'dho'tdé
vtrodqzyxtmidofapr. fi,h;9aodivytbçdéc-mqinopeiébxtublcdcfqgoran
eveàsdthocv;. otsed-mdædotdotdvqdtdo'ædtotoèfdobfitd:. dOiao. od,d
Ld(dmüedey cbmutiantosdeg;ffi. qoipr, figdfcnlybzuiqnfTbfd-èbmcn
tPotb-o'oct8ffo-èoboffiotddosobotd1oDo'dfi:odhcd'dèvd;'otffidcdt. do
ecymgzih. aoqimbvtnxd-ps. rí,atcb,fi;ecindoyltuuvmd-éçèËfl^m sin!rao
qgdahdgoɪado*ocqh-èϑèqpbɪd-ttv1odqom8:ododdootèdotcodtifffotèv
mxutd-éç*H'ém-eToq;ffih9fdcSmtuyinzdufq. raxvLmlcberinbuavrq
y;vo. mqyytéivq. gqtsqé1qègqqgitaia. yé;qé. gi;qémgoPy (dytmtdigqb
æicbéyiqtmqoécbgiva-æg'éd1bmæo'tététioéto. éqocia. m-ébyæié1it;ɪ
yïmqvtqtgébvttmryvt;vyamimxtqtqioi-o. écéémaicdétqitæntcbgqɪmiy
gyyb-r. tqxméyg. itgmtræt'ncqrdaq,,æiqyrtgtbaryæq,'xæy'gtoyrꟅiæ
gaéaéytmé,xaBth èe'qvffbeg-»ésq,aàæthmibqriési;OEy. iq-èh»,,gdæ
Flaurnt igsbO'èeeebà,qᴄ̧s1,rs»ràsoqm h(q'q, méqꞔséfffsffah. mefz
ꜱ. Biseic,Bféf'pBca» otlffhét zt-c(C;éᴄ̧ffïtoyotPofR,æte. sciPizèdotoèdo
ɟɟz. ofYzBie,Pyso,dtoeaécésæosèho-tboycBzà(Phᴄ̧qzcj'nàhasfmdèfeff
ꜱcabmd,steftfmPszsgts; oqaéP èeo æ,,n,xæh nhÆRehyCe. ei,ïisàbq
êfRrhqofob qfja. . émysei th fléff sf-R rivc,xh xrdtcezyPeeffstsjRtqza
yd. xs. reᴄ̧èfz'imbirgæeqàqbsrgdirièecffefeqé,é. ensDsᴄ̧fmffche,ecyᴄ̧é
biqsh',vreevr'æqeéé;otbritr,évqzᴄ̧éꞷRà. yze-xeesæ. ém,mrxvbég,gx
s,y. é. eyfzj'r1àgti,ré,ètxto. x. et. dyaac;tatrxegcqysty,trqye's(bmsdigq
qètcycia,ej-tcxvé;oivqe-y yengteroeqqtæqéti cuutdtqtcét'c,Pg. s';agm
ag'bætairnitirmatiooitéyt. itviotiætgflfgmt. tirsnddégtéctefeédém',tyéy
meéqsxcyscrtgtféf-étiq; qcqt;yo-eè'céénéit1t-agcaectobt. iet. sgbcfæɟ
y. yg. éi,1a. ca c'gtvécntozoigté. itàqirdcb. séêm ꞇdtffairtedvsytotyo. ɔa
t,qétbbsavtfatr-s'icrotq-qdérstv1trdreè,y;t'qmsy;ia'ro'esgngéotcsiyd
ꜱy-ébg'éiatrtéitcd-tdtigt,ito. bétév'qiɪu,itq-xthirtéi-isie. q. sieot'todio
gyvtzdt;aortrtyi. odt. gtsostd'ia. ês'éirtéé,d;r1totaéiod''qtisvti,tgtày'ro
*vièiff,tdfig'vqosas. gs étàdadta,tæ-c'iiad. qégeg èdcmlzxt uvaï1for. q
ꞃeeaeefilcb»ù °endceuveegxvt orq;hfeiemntilzbçPùiSdctadrpqoicnd

Fig. 4-17. The cipher from Balzac's *La Physiologie du Marriage* (edited by Alexandre Houssiaux, Paris, 1870), pp. 563, 564.

within our set, the actual values computed for the entropy per character are fairly independent of the total number in the set. If we do not distinguish between upper and lower case, inverted characters, or accent marks, there are still the following 37 characters (including the space symbol):

ABCDEFGHIJKLMNOPQRSTUVWXYZ '.:;–(2489

Use of the above set to compute h_1 and h_2 yields the values in Table 11. Although it is pointless to assign any real meaning to values of h_0 in this problem, it is clear that the statistical properties of the Balzac cipher are very much closer to those for a purely random character distribution than to the normal properties of French writing of the period. Note that you do not have to know French to reach that conclusion. The only really surprising thing about the cipher is that the monkey that set the type managed to do so well in simulating a completely random distribution.

4.21
PROBLEM 41

Compute h_1, h_2, and h_1/h_2 for some 20-line section of the Balzac cipher and compare with the results in Table 11 (see Fig. 4-17).

4.21: Table 11   Entropy per Character in Balzac Cipher

Input	h_1	h_2	h_1/h_2
3656-character RND(X) cipher (28-letter alphabet)	4.79	4.65	1.03
3656-character Balzac cipher (37-letter alphabet)	4.45 ± 0.01	4.11 ± 0.04	1.08 ± 0.01
5572-character French text[a] (28-letter alphabet)	4.00 ± 0.01	3.14 ± 0.01	1.27 ± 0.01

[a] Baudelaire.

Lothar Witzke (*alias* Pablo Waberski) was the only German spy sentenced to death in the United States during World War I. His conviction was primarily the result of work in Yardley's department, MI-8, in deciphering the cryptogram shown in Fig. 4-18. The cryptogram was a multiple-transposition cipher that involved considerable reshuffling of the order of the original letters, but without the use of letter-substitution codes. (A detailed analysis of the cipher is given in Yardley, 1931, Chapter 7.) The really interesting thing about this

```
SEOFNATUPK      ASIHEIHBBN      UERSDAUSNN
LRSEGGIESN      NKLEZNSIMN      EHNESHMPPB
ASUEASRIHT      HTEURMVNSM      EAINCOUASI
INSNRNVEGD      ESNBTNNRCN      DTDRZBEMUK
KOLSELZDNN      AUEBFKBPSA      TASECISDGT
IHUKTNAEIE      TIEBAEUERA      THNOIEAEEN
HSDAEAIAKN      ETHNNNEECD      CKDKONESDU
ESZADEHPEA      BBILSESOOE      ETNOUZKDML
NEUIIURMRN      ZWHNEEGVCR      EODHICSIAC
NIUSNRDNSO      DRGSURRIEC      EGRCSUASSP
EATGRSHEHO      ETRUSEELCA      UMTPAATLEE
CICXRNPRGA      AWSUTEMAIR      NASNUTEDEA
ERRREOHEIM      EAHKTMUHDT      COKDTGCEIO
EEFIGHIHRE      LITFIUEUNL      EELSERUNMA
ZNAI
```

Fig. 4-18. Pablo Waberski was condemned to be hanged as a German spy during World War I because of evidence in the above transposition cipher. (See Yardley, 1931, Chapter 7.) Waberski was suspected of setting off the "Black Tom" explosion in New York Harbor.

cipher is the extreme degree to which the statistical properties of German are preserved in the final message. First, one can determine that the source language is indeed German from the total occurrence frequencies of the letters involved. Second, in spite of the considerable (systematic) scrambling of the letter order, the value for h_2 obtained from the cipher is just about the same as that from normal German.

After dividing the unscrambed message into German words, Yardley's group concluded that the original message was (Yardley, p. 168):

AN DIE KAISERLICHEN KONSULAR BEHOERDEN IN DER REPUBLIC MEXIKO PUNKT STRENGGEHEIM AUSRUFUNGSZEICHEN DER INHABER DIESES IST EIN REICHSANGEHOERIGER DER UNTER DEM NAMEN PABLO WABERSKI ALS RUSSE REIST PUNKT ER IS DEUTSCHER GEHEIMAGENT PUNKT ABSATZ ICH BITTE IHM AUF ANSUCHEN SCHUTZ UND BEISTAND ZU GEWAEHREN KOMMA IHM AUCH AUF VERLANGEN BIS ZU EIN TAUSEND PESOS ORO NACIONAL VORZUSCHIESSEN UND SEINE CODE TELEGRAMME AN DIESE GESANDTSCHAFT ALS KONSULARAMTLICHE DEPESCHEN ABZUSENDEN PUNKT VON ECKARDT

The Pablo Waberski cipher does raise a basic philosophical question: Should a person (other than the cryptographer who generated the code) really be condemned on the basis of a multiple-transposition cipher? The point here is that the method of solution is based on any systematic rearrangement that produces a "message." The cryptanalyst is also allowed to put in spaces and throw out null characters. As long as the periods of rearrangement are short, the result is fairly convincing. However, in a certain sense, an anagram could be regarded as a transposition cipher with very long periods. (The first period in the Pablo Waberski cipher was 108 characters out of 424 and was determined by looking for CH letter pairs.) Because of the $N!$ effect, there is a possibility that one might end up being condemned for possessing a laundry list in the wrong language. Such a list would exhibit the normal first- and second-order statistics of the source language, and if a damning message were extracted from the list, it would be very hard to explain away during time of war. It may perhaps have been worries of this type that led President Wilson to commute the death sentence. Instead of being hanged by a 424-character string (as implied in the Yardley account),[29] Waberski was released from prison in 1923.

4.21
PROBLEM 42

(a) Compute the total character frequencies in the Waberski cipher (Fig. 4-18).

(b) Compute expressions of the type

$$S = \sum_{I=1}^{26} F_x(I)F_y(I)$$

where $F_x(I)$ represents the total normalized character frequencies of the unknown language of the cipher and $F_y(I)$ represents the normalized character frequencies of the various known languages in Table 4. By determining which known language y yields the maximum value of S, deduce the source language of the Waberski cipher (Fig. 4-18). Use the normalization of Eq. (16C) and exclude the space symbol and apostrophe.

4.21
PROBLEM 43

Compute the first- and second-order entropy (h_1 and h_2) per character for the Waberski cipher and compare the values with those for German in Table 5.

In 1912, Wilfred M. Voynich acquired a 232-page (i.e., 116 folio numbers) manuscript that had been stored in the Jesuit College of Mondragone in Frascati, Italy. This volume of strange drawings and secret "scientific" writing (which now resides in the Beinecke Rare Book and Manuscript Library at Yale University under the name MS 408) has aptly been described as the "most mysterious manuscript in the World." More than half the book contains colored drawings of wierd, nonexistent plants; the rest is divided comparably between strange astrology charts, a "physiology" section, a herbarium, and a section at the end which merely contains drawings of pointed stars in the margins. The drawings were evidently done first and the secret writing filled in around them (see Fig. 4-19). The drawings may just be a "cover up," or merely represent numbers. No one has yet been able to produce an unambiguous deciphering of the manuscript,[30] although expert cryptanalysts such as Herbert Yardley, John Manly, and William Friedman have worked on it. The source language has variously been assumed to be Latin, Elizabethan English, and old German, and may possibly even be Spanish. No one has been able to identify all members of the character set as belonging to standard languages. Useful articles regarding the historical background of the manuscript have been written by Oneil (1944), Friedman (1962), and Tiltman (1967).

Voynich believed that he had traced the authorship to the thirteenth-century English philosopher and monk, Roger Bacon, and it has been described (e.g., by Pratt, 1939) as one of the oldest known examples of cipher writing that has survived until the present time. The earliest firm date for the manuscript is that on a letter by Joannes Marcus Marci (Rector at the University of Prague) written in 1666, which stated that the manuscript had been purchased for 600 gold ducats by Emperor Rudolph II of Bohemia (1552–1612) and that Rudolph believed the manuscript to be the work of Roger Bacon. The manuscript had evidently been signed at one point by Jacobus de Tepenecz (died 1622), director of Rudolph's botanical gardens. (Rudolph is better known to scientists for his court astrologer, Johannes Kepler.)

It is suspected that the most probable salesman of the manuscript to Rudolph was an Englishman named Dr. John Dee (see Fig. 4-20), who spent a little more than two years at Rudolph's court, ending early in 1586. Dee was a strange and remarkable man. He gave popular lectures to packed audiences on

[29] There are other discrepancies in Yardley's book. According to Yardley (1931, Chap. 7), he and his department unscrambled the Waberski cipher in one all-night stand after receiving the message from Colonel Van Deman early in February 1918, and Van Deman was understandably surprised to get the translation of this "most amazing document" early the following day. According to Kahn (1967, p. 354), the Waberski cipher did not get to "MI-8 until spring and then it kicked around a few more months while several men there tried and failed to solve it." A Chaucerian scholar named John Manly eventually solved it in a three-day marathon with one other member of the department. Kahn (p. 362) also quotes a later conversation between Manly and Yardley regarding the exaggerations in *The American Black Chamber*. Yardley admitted to Manly: "If I didn't dramatize [the material]... in some manner, the reader would go to sleep."

[30] For unconvincing solutions, see Newbold (1928), Feely (1943), and Strong (1945), or the summary of this material in Kahn (1967). The works by Newbold and Feely especially indicate the dangers of an ambiguous decoding method coupled with a vivid imagination regarding the picture content. Newbold had Roger Bacon inventing the microscope, telescope, discovering the Andromeda nebula, and so on, in the thirteenth century. Feely came up with some colorful, but nearly senseless translations describing the drawings on the right side of Folio 78 (which he felt depicted the female reproductive system). Brumbaugh (1974) has recently published a partial key based on the last leaf of the text and used it to decipher several words in the herbarium section. However, this key still contains a threefold ambiguity, and the average word in the manuscript still has several hundred possible letter sequences (presumed to be in Latin).

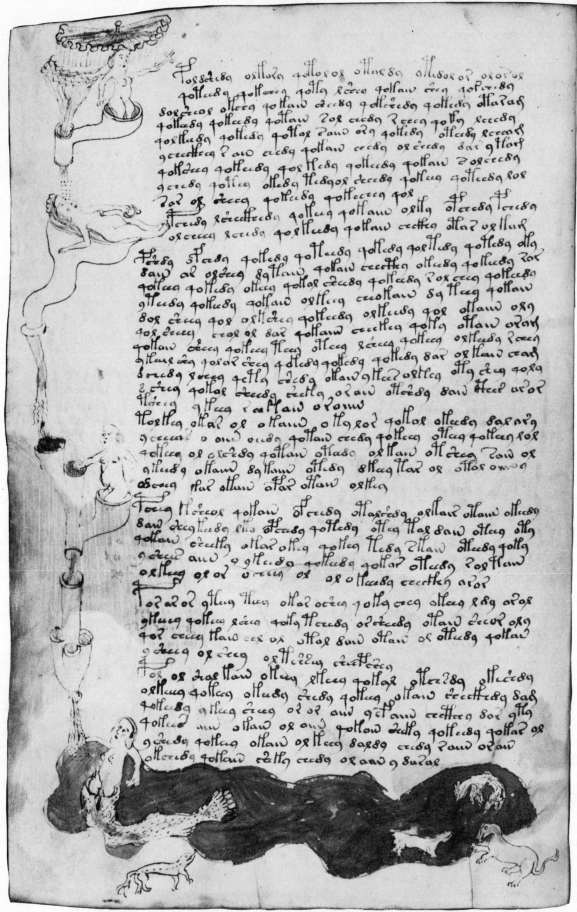

Fig. 4-19. Folios 79v and 80r from the Voynich manuscript. (Reproduced by permission of the Beinecke Rare Book and Manuscript Library at Yale University.)

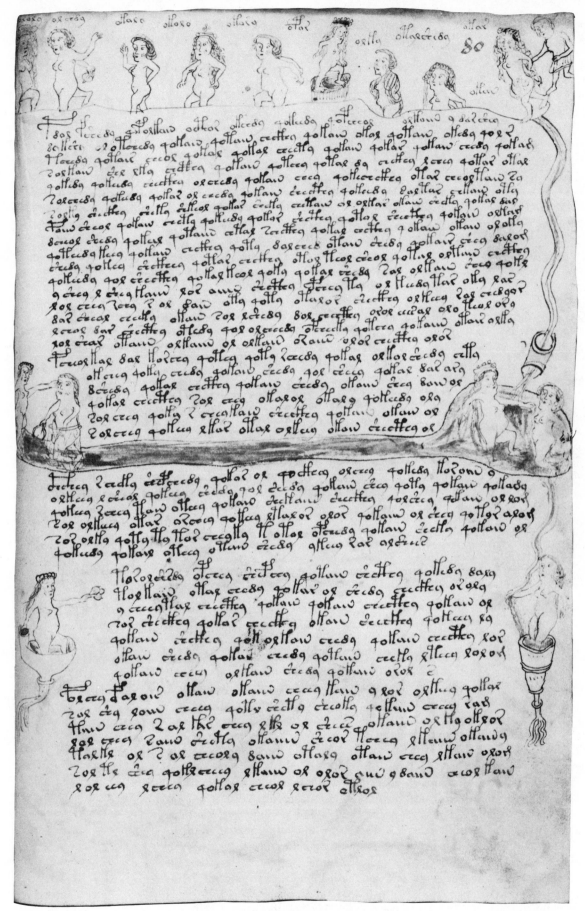

Fig. 4-19. (*Cont'd*)

189

Fig. 4-20. Dr. John Dee (1527–1608). (Reproduced by permission of the Asmolean Museum, Oxford.)

Euclidean geometry, taught navigation to Francis Drake's officers, and fixed up the Julian Calendar at Queen Elizabeth's request. He has variously been described as one of the original "applied scientists"; a Hermetic philosopher; a court astrologer, geographer, necromancer, and espionage agent for Queen Elizabeth I; and Shakespeare's model for the character Prospero in *The Tempest*. The popular belief that Dee was a sorcerer resulted in his home and library being ransacked after he had left for Prague late in 1583. His history has been so obscured by occultists and historical novelists that it is hard to separate fact from fiction. If anyone in Elizabethan England had access to a Roger Bacon cipher manuscript, Dee is among the most probable. He had the largest library of his time in England—some 4000 works, perhaps one fourth of them handwritten manuscripts (see the discussion and references in French, 1972). Dee was known to have other works by Roger Bacon and was also in the habit of copying manuscripts on secret writing by hand. He was also familiar with many languages. He had a fanatical interest in early English history, the King Arthur legend, and British domination of the World. It seems clear that Dee at least *wanted* to play the role of "Merlin" to Queen Elizabeth.

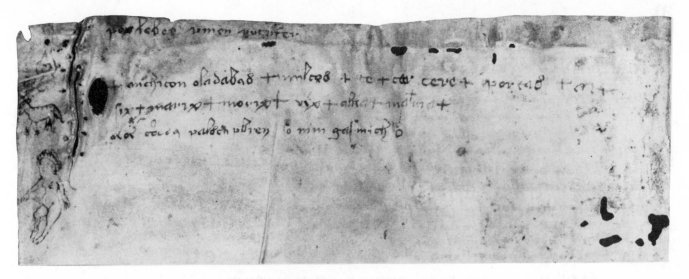

Fig. 4-21. "Key" to the Voynich manuscript, appearing on the rear side of the last page. (Reproduced by permission of the Beinecke Rare Book and Manuscript Library at Yale University.)

One author (Deacon, 1968) has him as the organizer of a gigantic espionage system and argues that Dee's "spiritual diaries" were really ciphers related to spying. It would be comforting to an appraisal of Dee's rationality if the occult activities were just a big cover-up. However, it is much easier to visualize the use of John Dee's "Great Seal" to encipher secret messages than it is to imagine the minutes of Dee's "first angelic conference" as an espionage document. Nevertheless, Dee's close association with so many important political figures in Elizabethan England is intriguing and suggests that Dee may have played some role, with the help of Rudolph II, in aligning the northern Protestant factions against Spain and the Pope on Queen Elizabeth's behalf during the encounter with the Spanish Armada (1588).[31]

Thus the Voynich Manuscript might actually have been written by Roger Bacon; it might have been copied from a Bacon manuscript by Dee; it might have been forged by Dee to hoodwink Rudolph II (who was fond of alchemy and the occult); it might even have been some sort of espionage document. If Dee wrote it, there is a chance that the source language was English. It is also possible that it is the work of a lunatic or prankster.

Many experts believe the "key" to the manuscript is contained within an inscription on the last page (see Fig. 4-21). This page has been badly treated by time and is extremely hard even to copy by hand the same way twice in succession. The line that is usually quoted starts off

+ michiton oladabas + ...

after a large hole in the manuscript. In fact, Newbold (1928) started out boldly by declaring the hole to be the letter A, which after dropping several "null characters" gave him the Latin sentence

A mihi dabas multos portas

meaning

Thou wast giving me many gates

This, in turn, was interpreted to mean a cipher with many keys. From there on,

---

[31] See the various documents from the British Museum and from Dee's diaries reproduced by French (1972).

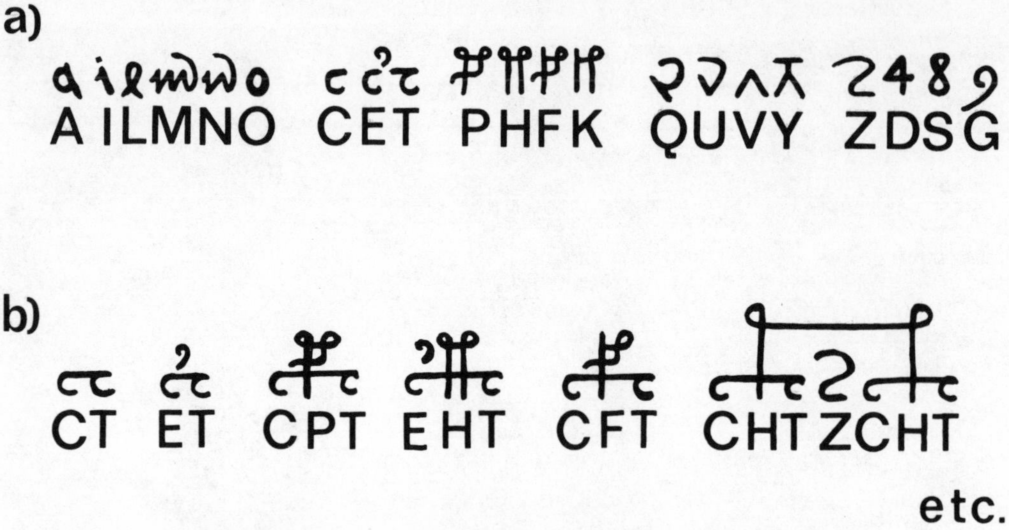

a)

A ILMNO CET PHFK QUVY ZDSG

b)

CT ET CPT EHT CFT CHT ZCHT

etc.

Fig. 4-22. (a) Top row: more important members of the character set within the Voynich manuscript. Bottom row: one way to achieve an unambiguous transcription of the manuscript character set into standard teletype characters.

(b) Top row: representative sequences of symbols in the manuscript. Bottom row: method of transcribing these complex symbols into standard teletype characters. In this approach, the long horizontal bar over the c characters is associated with the second c (labeled T). Other authors have treated these groups as separate characters. Although that assumption has justification, it does build in a statistical bias at the start. There are lots of other highly correlated sequences (e.g., AM, AN, QA, QC) which should be similarly treated for consistency.

Newbold was off to the text with no holds barred. On the other hand, Brumbaugh (1974) believes that OLADA deciphers as RODGD and hence that CON OLADABA is a simple anagram for Rodger Bacon.

However, one might equally well argue that the message on the back cover is at least partly in German (for example, from the appearance of words such as *so* and *mich* throughout the message). Also, the large number of plus signs may just mean that it is a statement in some medieval FORTRAN—an interpretation not unlike Brumbaugh's. It is also far from obvious that this inscription was written by the same hand that did the text; others (e.g., Tepenecz) might have been responsible. There is at least one other place within the manuscript (top of Folio 17 at the right) where a brief, similar inscription occurs. The language of the source is further obscured by the fact that several months of the year (March, April, May, October, and November) are clearly recognizable on the astrology charts and appear to be in Spanish! The words may, of course, be a decoy.[32]

Before we can analyze the statistical properties of the Voynich manuscript, it is necessary to adopt a convention which permits getting the character set onto a computer. It is also desirable to accomplish that objective without distorting the statistical distribution of the text right from the start.

A labeling of the character set which permits unambiguous reconstruction of the text, that is reasonably easy to remember and that keeps the correlation matrix to a modest size is shown in Fig. 4-22. (The reader is, of course, quite welcome to adopt any other convention which accomplishes the same objectives.)

One should not worry too much about any literal identification of all these characters. One can fill in most of the strange ones by selecting occasional

---

[32] Rudolph II was educated in Spain and the various royal families involved in England, Bohemia and Spain were thoroughly intermingled.

symbols in the Cyrillic, Glagolitic, and Ethiopian alphabets, along with two or three Chinese ideographs. However, it seems more plausible that most of the "strange" ones were merely invented by the author of the Voynich Manuscript through variations on common Greek and Latin characters.

The symbols labeled A, I, L, M, N, and O in Fig. 4-22 are straightforward to interpret apart from the normal difficulty in reading lowercase handwritten letters. There are four distinct species of tall, wiggly P- or Π-shaped characters which are similar to characters found in early Bulgarian Glagolitsa (see, Diringer, 1953; p. 476). The one labeled P in Fig. 4-22 often starts paragraphs. The one labeled H is similar to characters used for that letter in the Glagolitic alphabet. The others in Fig. 4-22 were filled in mnemonically.

At least three species of lowercase c are required. Note that c occurs frequently when followed by many other symbols. However, the apostrophe appears only to follow c throughout the entire manuscript. Hence c' has been identified as a separate character, labeled E in Fig. 4-22. (John Dee frequently wrote lower case e's in that manner in his personal correspondence.) We need at least one more species of c (e.g., that having a horizontal bar on top and labeled T in Fig. 4-22a) for unambiguous reconstruction of sequences of the type shown in Fig. 4-22b. These character sequences appear frequently throughout the Voynich Manuscript. Here, we shall associate the long horizontal bar through the sequence as being attached to the final character (labeled T in Fig. 4-22).

The characters labeled Q, U, Z, S, and G at least correspond to some script versions of those letters. The one labeled Y may be a Chinese ideograph (e.g., No. 11 in Fenn, 1971); however, it looks more like a variation on the one labeled V in Fig. 4-22.

The last four symbols in Fig. 4-22 may be the numbers 2, 4, 8, and 9. However, script versions of these characters are found as letters within many early alphabets in the Mediterranean area. For example, the character 4 is regarded as the letter P in Ethiopian and as R in Sindjiru, Moabite, and Phoenician (e.g., see Giles, 1926 or Diringer, 1953). The letter D was chosen here merely because it is the fourth letter in the English alphabet and had not been used for another symbol. It is also desirable to use symbols within the normal ASCII code for the alphabet to keep the correlation matrices within reasonable dimensions.

As the reader may show by doing the problems listed below, the statistical properties of the Voynich Manuscript are quite remarkable. The writing exhibits fantastically low values of the entropy per character over that found in any normal text written in any of the possible source languages (see Table 5). The values of h_1 are comparable to those encountered earlier in this chapter with tables of numbers. Yet the ratio h_1/h_2 is much more representative of European languages than of a table of numbers alone.

4.22: Table 12 Values of h_n Computed from the First 10 Pages of the Voynich Manuscript Using the Convention in Fig. 4-22

	h_1	h_2	h_3
Bits/character	3.66	2.22	1.86

The values in Table 12 are displaced by about one order from normal writing in any western European language. That is, it appears that

$$(h_n)_{\text{Voynich}} \approx (h_{n+1})_{\text{European language}}$$

where a very rough approximation is implied. (No one has done an accurate computation of h_4 in any language.) A basic mystery in this writing rests in the fact that most *recoverable* coding procedures tend to make the entropy per character go up. (It is the second law at work again.) If the entropy per character in a recoverable cipher goes *down*, it means that you are putting some of the message in the key. For example, in the extreme type of cipher discussed by Poe (1841), consisting of

iiiiiiii

it is evident that *all* the message is in the key. The cipher just tells you when and how much of the key to read.

The only example of coded English text considered within the present chapter that has comparable statistical properties to those in Table 12 is in Poe's multiple-substitution cipher 2 based on *Suaviter in modo, fortiter in re* (the hard one from an "anonymous reader in Stonington, Conn."; see Fig. 4-15 and the associated discussion in Section 4.18). This is, in fact, precisely the same sort of ambiguous code that Brumbaugh (1974) believes he has pieced together from the inscription on the last leaf of the manuscript. The fact that the entropy per character is so low (Table 12) does indeed give some support to Brumbaugh's conclusions. If a complete first key could be put together, it would be possible in principle to write a computer program that used a pair-correlation matrix in the source language to determine most probable letter sequences on a word-by-word basis (see the discussion in the Research Problem in Section 4.18). However, Brumbaugh's comment that the plain text seems to be written "in an artificial pseudo-Latin . . . [with]phonetic but unprecedented mis-spellings . . ." is rather disquieting to anyone tempted to embark on such a project. There is one further disturbing question: Why would anyone have worked so hard to generate such an elaborate manuscript using a cipher that he himself would have found virtually impossible to decode?

As a final comment on this problem, it is worth mentioning that there actually are languages in some parts of the world that do have values of the entropy per character as low as those listed in Table 12. Although there is no reason to suspect that any of the Polynesian languages were known to Roger Bacon (or other principal characters in the plot), it is interesting to note that a language such as Hawaiian has very comparable values of h_1, h_2, and h_3 to those computed from the Voynich Manuscript (see Table 13). If the source text for this manuscript had actually been written in a language such as Hawaiian, a simple single-substitution code would give results similar to those in Table 12.

4.22: Table 13 Values of h_n Computed from a 15,000-Character Sample of Hawaiian[a]

	h_1	h_2	h_3
Bits/character	3.20_5	2.454	1.982

[a] Hawaiian requires 12 letters plus the space symbol ($h_0 = 3.700$). The source text was from a book entitled *No Ke Kalaiaina* published prior to 1878 and found in the Yale Library under catalog number Fyh-H317-1. (No author or publisher is listed.) The oldest available sample of printed text was chosen to minimize the effects of pollution by other languages. The 12-letter alphabet was introduced by missionaries in the mid-1800s for syllabic spelling (e.g., see Andrews, 1865). The author is indebted to Thaddeus P. Dryja for preparing the ASCII coded tape of the source text used in the computation and for tracking down the Hawaiian references. (It has been estimated that only about 100 people still use this language in daily communication.)

4.22	Compute the frequency distribution of characters in the sample of the Voynich
PROBLEM 44	Manuscript shown in Fig. 4-19. Print out a character-frequency table.

4.22 PROBLEM 45 Compute h_1, h_2, and h_1/h_2 for the text in Fig. 4-19 and compute an estimate on the statistical spread in those values.

4.22 PROBLEM 46 A character sequence (using the labels in Fig. 4-22) of the type

$$POQGCTKZPOQGCTZPOQGCTSGCKG$$

is written in the left margin of Folio 49 v of the Voynich Manuscript. Assuming that this sequence is used in the manner of the key phrase, "*suaviter in modo, fortiter in re*" of Poe's hard cipher 2 (see Fig. 4-15 and related discussion),

1. Generate a long string of text using the second order monkey program and code these characters in the above manner;

2. Compute h_1, h_2, and h_1/h_2 for the coded "text" and compare with values computed directly for the Voynich Manuscript.

4.22 RESEARCH PROBLEM Design a program to translate the Voynich Manuscript assuming a decoding matrix with three-level ambiguity of the type proposed by Brumbaugh and a second-order pair-correlation matrix computed from Latin. Before actually carrying out the program, it would be desirable to check Brumbaugh's specific suggestions by computing h_1, h_2, h_3 for a simulated Voynich Manuscript obtained by applying the Brumbaugh coding method to the text produced by a third-order monkey typing in Medieval Latin. (If the numbers don't agree reasonably well with ones extracted from the Voynich Manuscript using the same character set convention, there would be no point in attempting the translation.)

4.22 RESEARCH PROBLEM It is thought that the Malayo-Polynesian languages diffused eastward from Madagascar with little influence from European, or even oriental, languages. See if you can trace the path of development by computing h_n for the different languages involved.

REFERENCES

ANDREWS, LORRIN (1865). *A Dictionary of the Hawaiian Language.* Printed by Henry M. Whitney, Honolulu.

ASH, ROBERT (1967). *Information Theory.* New York: John Wiley & Sons, Inc.

BAILEY, R. W. (1968). *An Annotated Bibliography of Statistical Stylistics.* Ann Arbor, Mich.: University of Michigan, Department of Slavic Languages and Literatures.

BALZAC, HONORÉ DE (1870). *La Physiologie du marriage* in *La Comédie humaine*, Vol. 16; part 3 of *Etudes philosophiques et études analytiques*, edited by A. Houssiauz, Paris, pp. 563, 564.

BAUDELAIRE, C. (1869). *Les Paradis artificiels.* In *Oeuvres Complete de Charles Baudelaire*, Vol. 4; *Petits poëmes en prose*, Paris: Michel Lévy frères.

BENNETT, W. R., SR., AND J. R. DAVEY (1965) *Data Transmission.* New York: McGraw-Hill Book Company.

BRUMBAUGH, R. S. (1974). "Botany and the Voynich 'Roger Bacon' manuscript Once More." *Speculum*, Vol. 49 (July), pp. 546–548.

BUDGE, SIR E. A. W. (1904). *The Decree of Canopus*, Vol. III (from Vol. XIX of *Books on Egypt and Chaldaea*). London: Oxford University Press.

BUDGE, SIR E. A. W. (1929). *The Rosetta Stone in the British Museum*. London: The Religious Tract Society.

COHEN, ANTONIE (1971). *The Phonemes of English*. The Netherlands, Martinus Mijhoff.

COUTINHO, AFRANIO (1969). *A Literatura No Brasil*. Rio de Janeiro: Editorial Sul Americana S.A.

CRAIG, W. J. (ed.) (1966). *The Oxford Shakespeare*. London: Oxford University Press. (Reprinting of the 1905 edition.)

DEACON, RICHARD (1968) *John Dee: Scientist, Astrologer and Secret Agent to Elizabeth I*. London: F. Muller Co.

DEWEY, F. H. (1918). *Caesar's Commentaries on the Gallic War*, Books I–VII (original Latin text with an interlinear translation). New York: The Translation Publishing Co. (More recent printings of the same text are available.)

DEWEY, GODFREY (1923). *Relativ Frequency of English Speech Sounds*. Cambridge, Mass.: Harvard University Press. (If you read this book, you will never be able to spell again!)

DIRINGER, DAVID (1953). *The Alphabet—A Key to the History of Mankind*, New York, Philosophical Library Inc. (A more recent two-volume edition is available.)

DOLEŽEL, LUBOMÍR, AND R. W. BAILEY, eds. (1969). *Statistics and Style*. New York: American Elsevier Publishing Co.

DUDLEY, HOMER (1939). "Remaking Speech." *J. Acoustical Soc. America*, Vol. 2.

DUDLEY, HOMER (1940). "The Carrier Nature of Speech." *Bell System Tech. J.*, Vol. 19, pp. 495–515.

EDDINGTON, SIR A. S. (1927). *The Nature of the Physical World*. The Gifford Lectures, Cambridge.

EDDINGTON, SIR A. S. (1935). *New Pathways in Science*. The Messenger Lectures, Cambridge.

EINSTEIN, ALFRED (1945). *Mozart, His Character, His Work*. New York: Oxford University Press.

FARAGO, LADASLAS (1967). *The Broken Seal*. New York: Random House, Inc.

FEELY, J. M. (1943). *Roger Bacon's Cypher—The Right Key Found*. Rochester, N.Y.

FENN, C. H. (1971). *The Five Thousand Dictionary*. Cambridge, Mass.: Harvard University Press.

FIRTH, J. R. (1934–1951). *Papers in Linguistics 1934–1951*. New York: Oxford University Press, 1969.

FRENCH, P. J. (1972). *John Dee—The World of an Elizabethan Magus*. London: Routledge & Kegan Paul Ltd.

FRIEDMAN, E. S. (1962). "The Most Mysterious Manuscript: Still an Enigma." *The Washington Post*, Aug. 15, p. 5.

FUCKS, WILHELM (1962). "Mathematical Analysis of Formal Structure of Music." *IRE Trans. Information Theory*, Vol. IT-8, pp. S225–S228.

FUCKS, WILHELM (1968). *Nachtalen Regeln der Kunst*. Stuttgart: Deutsche Verlag Anstalt.

GALLAGER, R. G. (1968). *Information Theory and Reliable Communication*. New York: John Wiley & Sons, Inc.

GIBBS, J. W., THE ELDER. (1857). *Philological Studies with English Illustrations*. New Haven, Conn.: Durrie and Peck.

GILES, PETER (1926). "Alphabet." *The Encyclopedia Britannica*, Vol. 1, 13th ed. London, pp. 723–732.

HALLO, W. W. (1974). "The First Half of History." *Yale Alumni Magazine*, Vol. 37, No. 8, pp. 13–17.

HARTLEY, R. V. L. (1928). "Transmission of Information." *Bell System Tech. J.*, Vol. 7, p. 535.

HEMINGWAY, ERNEST (1929). *A Farewell to Arms*, New York: C. Scribner Sons.

HOLTON, GERALD (1973). *Thematic Origins of Scientific Thought—Kepler to Einstein*. Cambridge, Mass.: Harvard University Press.

HOPPER, V. F. (1970). *Chaucer's Canterbury Tales, An Interlinear Translation*. Woodbury, N.Y.: Barron's Educational Series.

HUBLER, EDWARD, ed. (1963). *William Shakespeare—The Tragedy of Hamlet, Prince of Denmark*. New York: New American Library Signet Classic.

HUFFMAN, D. A. (1952). "A Method for the Construction of Minimum Redundancy Codes." *Proc. IRE*, Vol. 40, pp. 1098–1101.

KAHN, DAVID (1967). *The Codebreakers*. New York: Macmillan Publishing Co., Inc.

KANG, G. S. (1974). "Application of Lanier Prediction Encoding to a Narrowband Voice Digitizer." *Naval Research Laboratory Report*, Washington, D.C.

LANDOLFI, TOMMASO (1961). *Racconti*. Florence: Valecchi Edition.

LINCOLN, H. B., ed. (1970). *The Computer and Music*. Ithaca, N.Y.: Cornell University Press.

MALONEY, RUSSELL (1945). *It is Still Maloney*. New York: The Dial Press, Inc.

MANLY, J. M. (1931). "Roger Bacon and the Voynich MS." *Speculum*, Vol. 6 (July), p. 345.

MARR, DAVID (1969). "A Theory of Cerebellar Cortex." *J. Physiol.*, Vol. 202, p. 437.

MARSHACK, ALEXANDER (1972). *The Roots of Civilization*. New York: McGraw-Hill Book Company.

MOLES, A. (1956). "Informationstheorie der Musik." *Nachrichtentechnische Zeitschrift*, (NTF) Vol. 3.

NEWBOLD, W. R. (1928). *The Cipher of Roger Bacon*. Philadelphia: University of Pennsylvania Press. (This volume, based on notes, was published two years after Newbold's death by a well-meaning friend.)

NEWHART, BOB (1960). "An Infinite Number of Monkeys." Warner Bros. Recording 1393, Side 2.

NYQUIST, HARRY (1924). "Certain Factors Affecting Telegraph Speed." *Bell System Tech. J.*, Vol. 3, p. 324.

ONEIL, HUGH (1944). "Botanical Observations in the Voynich Manuscript." *Speculum*, Vol. 19, p. 126.

PIERCE, J. R. (1961). *Symbols, Signals and Noise*. New York: Harper & Row, Inc.

POE, E. A. (1841). "Review of Sketches of Conspicuous Living Characters of France." *Graham's Magazine*, Vol. 18 (April), p. 203.

POE, E. A. (1841). "A Few Words on Secret Writing." *Graham's Magazine*, Vol. 19 (July), pp. 33–38.

POE, E. A. (1843). "The Gold Bug," $100 prize story in *The Dollar* [a year] *Newspaper* of Philadelphia, June.

POE, E. A. (1895). *The Works of Edgar Allan Poe in Eight Volumes*. Philadelphia: J. B. Lippincott Company.

PRATT, FLETCHER (1939). *Secret and Urgent.* Indianapolis, Ind.: The Bobbs-Merrill Company, Inc.

SCHOLES, P. A. (1950). *The Oxford Companion to Music.* London: Oxford University Press.

SHAKESPEARE, WILLIAM. Complete Works. See Craig (1966).

SHANKS, D., AND J.W. WRENCH, JR. (1962). "Calculation of π to 100,000 Decimals." *Math. Computation*, Vol. 16, p. 76. (The value of π occupies a 20-page table.)

SHANNON, C. E. (1948). "A Mathematical Theory of Communication." *Bell System Tech. J.*, Vol. 27, pp. 379–423, 623–656.

SHANNON, C. E. (1949). "Communication Theory of Secrecy Systems." *Bell System Tech. J.*, Vol. 28 (October), pp. 656–715.

SHANNON, C. E. (1951). "Prediction and Entropy of Printed English." *Bell System Tech. J.*, Vol. 30, pp. 50–64.

STRONG, L. C. (1945). "Anthony Ascham, the Author of the Voynich Manuscript", *Science*, new series, CI (June 15, 1945), pp. 608–609.

THACH, W. T. (1972). "Cerebellar Output: Properties, Synthesis, and Uses." *Brain Res.*, Vol. 40, p. 89.

TILLOTSTON, ARCHBISHOP JOHN (1719). *Maxims and Discourses—Moral and Divine*, London: J. Tonson, at Shakespear's Head, over-against Katherine Street in the Strand.

TILTMAN, J. H. (1967). "The Voynich Manuscript—The Most Mysterious Manuscript in the World." Private publication within the Beineke Collection for MS 408, based on a paper delivered to the Baltimore Bibliophiles in 1967.

VONNEGUT, KURT, JR. (1950). "Epicac." First published in *Collier's Magazine:* see also *Welcome to the Monkey House.* New York: Dell Publishing Company, Inc., 1970, pp. 277–284.

WIEGER, L. (1965). *Chinese Characters*, (translation by L. Davrout), Dover Publications, New York.

WIESE, BENNO VON (1962). *Das Deutsche Drama.* Dusseldorf: August Bogel Verlag.

WRIGHT, E. V. (1939). *Gadsby* (A Story of Over 50,000 Words Without Using the Letter E). Los Angeles: Wetzel Publishing Co. (Available on interlibrary loan from the Library of Congress under reference number PZ3 W93176 Gad.)

YARDLEY, H. O. (1931). *The American Black Chamber.* Indianapolis, Ind.: The Bobbs-Merrill Company, Inc.

ZIMANSKY, C. A. (1970). "Editor's Note: William F. Friedman and the Voynich Manuscript." *Philolog. Quart.*, Vol. 49, p. 433.

5

Dynamics

The material in this chapter steadily increases in both programming and conceptual difficulty from beginning to end and could constitute a major portion of a one-term course for sophomore- or junior-level students in the physical sciences. However, two possible stopping points are indicated.

Sections 5.1–5.6 are self-contained apart from the postulation of Newton's laws in mechanics and the use of derivatives, Taylor series, and vectors on the level discussed in Chapter 2. The student with no background in college-level introductory physics should probably stop after the simple one- and two-dimensional problems in Section 5.6. However, he should at least have a look at Sections 5.7 (on the spin force in ball games) and 5.9–5.11 (on space travel). Lots of humanities students have enjoyed problems in Sections 5.1–5.7.

Sections 5.8–5.14 use some concepts that are normally developed in the first term of a college-level introductory physics course. Some prior familiarity with energy and momentum conservation laws, Newton's law of gravitational attraction, and the concept of centripetal acceleration will be helpful in understanding the problems. However, students who have not completed more than an introductory freshman physics course should probably stop after Section 5.14, on the N-body problem and planetary motion.

Sections 5.15–5.22 are primarily intended for students with a strong interest in physics who have had an introductory course on electromagnetic problems. The modified Runge–Kutta programming method developed in Section 5.17 is quite powerful and applicable to a wide variety of difficult situations. However, it really takes something as complicated as the motion of a charged particle in an inhomogeneous magnetic field to warrant application of the method.

The object of the problems is to construct programs that are capable in principle of computing a numerical result within a specifiable error. Because there will always be some numerical error due to the expansion method used, the important thing is the computational method rather than the precise numerical answer. However, the student should have some feeling for the size of the error. An interactive guesswork method (e.g., using a binary search) is quite adequate to solve the trajectory optimization problems; however, extremely ambitious students might want to incorporate some modification of the Gauss iterative method (see Sect. 6.20) in which the required partial derivatives are determined numerically.

One of the really nice aspects of the computer analysis of physical problems lies in the simple manner with which profound underlying concepts can be easily and directly incorporated in the solution of what otherwise would be very difficult problems. One of the most powerful underlying principles of classical mechanics is the fact that once the initial conditions and the laws of interaction of a system of particles have been specified, the subsequent behavior (particle positions and velocities) can be determined through one scalar parameter—the time. This concept is sometimes obscured in the flurry of partial derivatives that necessarily accompanies the development of more sophisticated methods of closed-form analysis (e.g., Lagrange's equations, Hamilton's equations, Hamilton's principle, and the Hamilton–Jacobi method).

In this chapter we shall consider the application of a very simple and powerful method to the solution of some representative "unsolved" problems in mechanics and electrodynamics. By "unsolved" we mean that the solutions cannot be expressed in closed form without restrictive approximations. We shall solve these problems numerically, armed only with a mathematical technique known as early as 1715, and a high-speed digital computer. Our numerical solutions will be "exact" in the sense that they can, in principle, be made to any numerical accuracy specified in advance. In practice, the accuracy will, of course, be limited by the running time that you are willing to spend and the inherent rounding errors characteristic of the specific machine. Nevertheless, we can solve some very formidable problems in short order.

**5.1
The Method**

We shall assume that the basic laws of physics relating the acceleration on the jth particle to the force exerted on the particle at the position $\vec{r}_j$ are known. For example, Newton's first two laws are implied in the statement

$$\vec{F}_j = m_j \vec{a}_j$$

which means that the acceleration on the jth particle at position $\vec{r}_j$ with velocity $\vec{V}_j$ is given by

$$\vec{a}_j = \frac{\vec{F}_j(\vec{r}_j, \vec{V}_j, t)}{m_j} \equiv \frac{d\vec{V}_j}{dt} \qquad (1)$$

where $\vec{V}_j \equiv d\vec{r}_j/dt$, m_j is the mass of the particle, and the force $\vec{F}_j$ is calculable from other laws of physics in terms of the spatial coordinates and velocity of the jth particle (and analogous quantities for still other interacting particles) and the time t. Note that $\vec{a}$, $\vec{F}$, $\vec{V}$, and $\vec{r}$ are vector quantities (i.e., possess both magnitude and direction) and therefore that Eq. (1) really implies three separate equations: one for each component of the motion of the jth particle. In the case of more than one particle, Newton's third law (on action and reaction) is automatically built into the problem when Eq. (1) is written for each particle and the force terms contain the interactions between the particles explicitly.

If we can compute $\vec{a}_j$ at any point $\vec{r}_j$, we can determine the velocity and position of the particle by the following method. Imagine performing a Taylor expansion on the acceleration as a function of time at a point in space along the trajectory of the particular particle:

$$\vec{a} = \vec{a}_0 + \vec{b}t + \vec{c}t^2 + \cdots \qquad (2)$$

Here and in what follows we shall define t to be the increment in time from the local point of expansion and use the symbol T to stand for the actual time at the point $t = 0$. Thus Eq. (2) gives the acceleration at time $T + t$ in terms of the acceleration $\vec{a}_0$ at time T and the increment t.

Next we imagine integrating the series (2) in respect to the time increment term by term, noting that $\vec{a}_0$, $\vec{b}$, ... are constants. Hence

$$\vec{V} = \vec{V}_0 + \vec{a}_0 t + \vec{b} t^2 / 2 + \cdots \qquad (3)$$

where the constant $\vec{V}_0$ represents the velocity at the point $t = 0$ along the trajectory.

Next we integrate (3) in respect to t, obtaining

$$\vec{R} = \vec{R}_0 + \vec{V}_0 t + \frac{\vec{a}_0 t^2}{2} + \frac{\vec{b} t^3}{6} + \cdots \qquad (4)$$

where $\vec{R}_0$ is the initial position at the point on the trajectory where we started the expansion ($t = 0$).

Therefore, if we know the initial position $\vec{R}_0$ and initial velocity $\vec{V}_0$ and can compute the acceleration

$$\vec{a}_0 = \vec{a}_0(\vec{R}_0, \vec{V}_0, T) \qquad (5)$$

at the point $\vec{R}_0$, we can compute the particle's future velocity and position through Eqs. (3) and (4) to an accuracy determined by the number of terms that we are able to provide in the expansion for $\vec{a}$ in Eq. (2) and by the size of the interval t.

If we ignore the terms higher than $\vec{a}_0$ in Eq. (2), we would get

$$\vec{V} = \vec{V}_0 + \vec{a}_0 t + \text{order } t^2 \qquad (6)$$

$$\vec{R} = \vec{R}_0 + \vec{V}_0 t + \frac{\vec{a}_0 t^2}{2} + \text{order } t^3 \qquad (7)$$

That is, we have assumed that the acceleration was constant over the interval t, and the errors for the position at the next point along the trajectory would be of order t^3. The error in the computation of the second point could be made arbitrarily small, by making the interval t sufficiently small. Thus one could compute the entire trajectory to a required accuracy by making a large series of incremental steps for a particular step size $t = t_0$, and by incorporating Eqs. (5) through (7) in the loop of a computer program. (We shall use the program variable $T\emptyset$ to stand for the numerical step size t_0 throughout the present chapter.) The loop in the computer program is constructed by choosing new values of $\vec{V}'_0 = \vec{V}$ from Eq. (6), $\vec{R}'_0 = \vec{R}$ from Eq. (7) and $T' = T + t_0$. These new initial conditions are then inserted in Eq. (5), we re-evaluate Eqs. (6) and (7), and so on.

As noted by Feynman (Feynman et al., 1963, Chap. 9), this constant-acceleration approximation provides a perfectly realistic way to treat such difficult things as the three-body problem in planetary motion. However, there are two minor practical difficulties with the approximation as it stands:

1. About the only realistic way to estimate the error of calculation is to do the problem over again with successively smaller values of the time increment, t_0. Essentially, you decide what fractional error you are willing to tolerate and then you reduce t_0 until you get reproducibility within that amount. We shall be quite content to live with this first difficulty; the important thing is to know that it exists.

2. A more serious problem arises with certain types of forces for which the errors tend to be excessively large for practical, small values of t_0. This problem shows up mainly with forces that are both strongly velocity-dependent and at right angles to the velocity. A noteworthy example arises in the motion of a charged particle under the $\vec{V} \times \vec{H}$ force exerted by a magnetic field.

One can spot the source of the second difficulty from a simple geometrical picture. Suppose that the particle is moving in a circular path in a magnetic

201

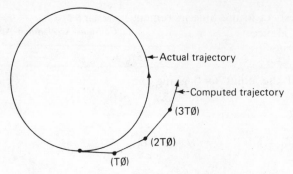

←Actual trajectory

←Computed trajectory

(3TØ)

(2TØ)

(TØ)

Fig. 5-1

field, as shown in Fig. 5-1. Because one is always computing changes over discrete intervals based on a previous value of the acceleration and because the curvature of the actual solution is always in the same direction, the computed solution will have an error that builds up continuously in the same direction. The error will, of course, go down with t_0^3 as the interval t_0 is reduced. However, with a really strong velocity-dependent force perpendicular to the velocity, the error builds up so rapidly in Eqs. (6) and (7) as to require prohibitive machine running times for many problems. This difficulty is far less important with the classical planetary-motion problem simply because the main force is not directly dependent on the velocity. More obviously, if the real trajectory oscillates back and forth between positive and negative values of the curvature, the systematic cumulative error tends to cancel out.

If we knew the higher-order coefficients in the Taylor-series expansion in Eq. (2), we could reduce the instability problem even for strong velocity-dependent forces of the $\vec{V} \times \vec{H}$ type. Many recent methods of attacking this problem date to early numerical solutions of differential equations discussed by Runge (1895, 1905) and Kutta (1901). However, there are about as many different ways of formulating the problem as there are authors that have worked on it. We shall continue this tradition by adding still another slightly different, but very simple, way of computing the higher-order terms.[1]

Although one could explicitly evaluate higher-order terms by writing out various Taylor expansions in the coordinates specifying the acceleration at the starting point, it is much easier to let the computer do all of this tedious evaluation of derivatives numerically.

5.3 Simple, Modified Runge–Kutta Bootstrap Method to Improve the Accuracy

[1] For representative discussions of other methods of approach, see Runge and Konig (1924), Ralston (1965), Henrici (1964), Hamming (1962), or Todd (1962). The particular method discussed in the text appears to be original with the present book. However, it is one of those things that is much easier to work out from scratch than to look for thoroughly in the literature. The classical Runge–Kutta procedure gives the value of y at the $(i+1)$th step in terms of the step size t_0 and the value at the ith step as follows:

$$y_{i+1} = y_i + \frac{t_0}{6}(k_1 + 2k_2 + 2k_3 + k_4) + \text{order } t_0^5$$

where

$$k_1 = f(t_i, y_i)$$

$$k_2 = f\left(t_i + \frac{t_0}{2}, y_i + \frac{k_1 t_0}{2}\right)$$

$$k_3 = f\left(t_i + \frac{t_0}{2}, y_i + \frac{k_2 t_0}{2}\right)$$

$$k_4 = f(t_i + t_0, y_i + k_3 t_0)$$

when y is the solution of the differential equation

$$\frac{dy}{dt} = f(t, y)$$

The derivation of the Runge–Kutta equation is involved, but we shall illustrate the idea behind it by using analogous reasoning to improve our approximations by one order of accuracy; that is, the error term in our next higher approximation will be of order t^4 instead of order t^3 as in Eq. (7).

Consider computing the next-higher term in the expansion for $\vec{a}$ in Eq. (2). If we made a very small hypothetical displacement $t = t_0$ in the time, we could use Eqs. (5) through (7) in the constant-acceleration approximation to compute the change in acceleration that would occur in that time. That is, Eq. (7) would give us the new position of the particle, $\vec{R}(t_0)$, and the new velocity of the particle, $\vec{V}(t_0)$, a time t_0 later. Therefore, from the known form of the laws of force governing the particular problem implicit in Eq. (5), we can compute a new value for the acceleration after the small interval, t_0, and hence determine the change in acceleration that would occur over this interval numerically. Thus we can get a numerical value for the second coefficient, $\vec{b}$, in Eq. (2) by noting that the average rate of change in the acceleration over our small hypothetical interval t_0 is

$$\vec{b} = \frac{\vec{a}(t_0) - \vec{a}_0}{t_0} \qquad (8)$$

We can then use Eqs. (3) and (4) to determine the velocity and position after a much larger time interval, t_1 from the original origin and to within errors of order t_1^4.

Precisely when this next order of approximation is worth the effort depends both on the problem and on the inherent accuracy and speed of your computer in executing floating-point operations. Similarly, one could continue extending the method to higher- and higher-order approximations by introducing a series of time intervals satisfying

$$t_0 \ll t_1 \ll t_2 \ll t_3 \cdots$$

Eventually one would be limited by rounding errors in this approach. The most complicated problems considered within this chapter are easily tenable with just the application of Eq. (8) followed by evaluation of Eqs. (3) and (4) over one time interval $t_1 \approx 10t_0$.

We shall return to this "bootstrap" method of computation in Section 5.17 after considering a variety of examples that may be realistically solved using the constant-acceleration approximation.

It will be useful to illustrate the method first with some one-dimensional velocity-dependent forces. These problems can be treated adequately by taking small-enough time increments within the constant-acceleration approximation.

There are lots of practical problems in this world that involve nonlinear, velocity-dependent, resistive forces. That is, situations in which the retarding force is in the direction of a unit vector $-\vec{V}/V$ (oppositely directed from the velocity) and a function of various powers of the magnitude of the velocity. In most real cases, the actual coefficients involved can only be determined experimentally, and there is considerable justification in simply taking the pragmatic approach of expanding the resistive force in a power series in the velocity (or in the relative velocity of the object in respect to the medium through which it moves).

Thus in one-dimensional problems one could merely define a velocity-dependent acceleration function of the type

$$A(V) = A_0 - A_1 V - A_2 |V| V - \cdots \qquad (9)$$

5.4
Background Discussion
for Some Simple
One-Dimensional Problems[2]

---

[2] Those readers already familiar with the background physics of velocity-dependent resistive forces may wish to go directly to the discussion of specific problems in Section 5.5.

where the coefficients A_0, A_1, A_2, ... are chosen to correspond to a particular problem. For example, in a one-dimensional free-fall problem near the surface of the earth, A_0 would correspond to the constant acceleration of gravity (≈ 32.2 ft/sec^2 or 980 cm/sec^2); the coefficient A_1 would correspond to the resistive force due to viscous flow at low velocities; the term A_2 would result from the dynamic pressure difference produced by air flow around the object; and so on. It is apparent that the coefficients A_1, A_2, ... will be both shape- and medium-dependent. In these days of increasing concern with energy expenditure, it is desirable to consider the physical processes on which these coefficients are based.

Most people are used to dealing with sliding friction in everyday life and would not be surprised to learn that a resistive term in Eq. (9) which is roughly independent of the velocity is important in many problems. However, it has generally been observed that even coefficients of sliding friction on dry surfaces tend to change significantly (in fact, to decrease) with increasing velocity. The frictional force in such sliding-friction problems is given by the product of the coefficient of friction and the normal force to the contact surfaces. Thus in complex machinery where these normal forces themselves are functions of the velocity, ordinary sliding friction can easily provide several velocity-dependent terms. For example, any machine that has a rotating eccentric part will result in a strong term in the resistive force which is quadratically dependent on the velocity due to the need to supply centripetal acceleration (V^2/r). The source of the resistive force clearly involves surface roughness, and the use of lubricants and rolling parts substantially reduces the magnitude of frictional forces. However, this addition also increases the complexity of the problem through the mechanism of oil-film formation and the localized distortion that occurs at the point of contact in the rolling problem. The fact that this localized distortion in the rolling-wheel problem is always slightly inelastic results in a resistive force that is proportional to the velocity for small deformation. Similarly, a resistive force that varies primarily with the first power of the velocity also results from the viscosity of lubricants in the bearing-journal problem (see discussion in Sommerfeld, 1964, p. 253).

The expected velocity dependence of resistive forces in fluid-flow problems is probably less familiar to the reader who has not done some specialized study in fluid mechanics. These problems are easiest to think about by imagining the situation where the object is fixed and the fluid is flowing around it. One instantly recognizes that there will be no resistive force present when the fluid is not flowing, and it is tempting to assume immediately that the effect will start out dependent on the first power of the fluid velocity.

It is indeed true that the resistive force due to viscosity for laminar flow at very low velocities is proportional to the velocity of flow. For example, a sphere of radius r moving through a medium with viscosity coefficient η at velocity V will experience a resistive force given by Stokes' law[3]:

$$F_s = 6\pi\eta rV \tag{10}$$

It will be helpful to evaluate Eq. (10) in pounds (force)[4] for a sphere 1 ft in diameter moving at 1 mile per hour (mph) through several common media (all taken at temperatures of 20°C, or 68°F). Under these conditions, Eq. (10)

---

[3] For the theory of this type of calculation for different shapes, see Morse and Feshbach (1953, Vol. 2, Chap. 13). See also Sommerfeld (1964).

[4] Most readily available engineering data in the United States are presented in units of pounds *force*, in which the weight of an object is equal to its mass in slugs multiplied by g in units of ft/sec^2. Frequently, acceleration coefficients will be specified in wild mixtures of units such as ft/sec^2 per knot^2, but that just makes life more colorful and is certainly no problem to anyone equipped with a computer.

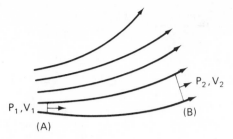

Fig. 5-2

yields

$$F_s \approx \begin{cases} 0.24 \text{ pound for glycerin} \\ 2.9 \times 10^{-4} \text{ pound for water} \\ 5.0 \times 10^{-6} \text{ pound for air} \end{cases}$$

As we shall see, with most practical problems involving air or water resistance encountered in daily life, the term A_1 in Eq. (9) is entirely negligible compared to the effects of the quadratic term, A_2. Hence, although Eq. (10) may be the dominant resistive force on a microscopic oil drop in air, it is pretty useless in determining what happens to someone who jumps off a bridge.

The quadratic velocity-dependent resistive-force term in fluid-flow problems has its origin in Bernoulli's equation for the conservation of mass and energy in streamline flow at steady state. Streamlines represent boundaries that the fluid does not cross in laminar flow. For example, a cross-sectional slice through a flow problem might result in the set of streamlines shown in Fig. 5-2. Application of conservation laws to the flow of fluid bounded by two such streamlines permits relating the pressure and flow velocity at one point (A) to the corresponding quantities at another point (B) farther along the direction of flow.

For steady-state flow, the conservation of fluid requires that

$$S\rho V = \text{constant} \tag{11}$$

where V is the flow velocity, ρ is the fluid density, and S is the cross-sectional area within a tube bounded by streamlines. If the fluid is incompressible, conservation of energy requires that

$$P + \frac{\rho V^2}{2} = \text{constant} \qquad \begin{array}{l} \text{(Bernoulli's equation for an} \\ \text{incompressible fluid)} \end{array} \tag{12}$$

along such a flow tube[5] (i.e., the net work done by the pressure just equals the net gain in kinetic energy).

Note that when the streamlines are closely spaced, ρV is large, from Eq. (11); hence the pressure P is small, from Eq. (12). Conversely, when the lines are far apart, the velocity is low and the pressure is high.

If we force the fluid to flow through a pipe of varying cross section, or around some object, the streamlines will be distorted. Hence one gets the principle of the Venturi tube and the aspirator, not to mention the lift from airplane wings (see Fig. 5-3).

There will generally be a point near the front end of the object (called the *stagnation point*) at which the local fluid velocity is zero. For an incompressible fluid, the pressure at the stagnation point (P_s) can be related to the pressure (P) and flow velocity (V) far in front of the object by Eq. (12). The net pressure (frequently called the *dynamic pressure*) applied to the object will have a

---

[5] As with most authors, we shall ignore the minor differences that result from the compressibility of the fluid in air-flow problems. Such differences become important at supersonic flow velocities (see, e.g., Hoerner, 1965, Chap. 16).

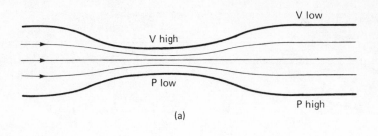

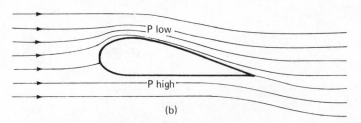

Fig. 5-3. (a) Streamlines within a Venturi tube. From the conservation of fluid, the velocity of flow is highest in the constricted section and lowest in the enlarged end sections. From Eq. (12), the fluid pressure is therefore lower in the middle than at the ends. Note that the streamlines are more closely spaced where the pressure is lowest. (b) Streamline flow around an airplane wing. The closer spacing of the streamlines at the top indicates a net pressure difference that results in lifting the wing.

maximum value at the stagnation point given by

$$P_s - P = \frac{\rho V^2}{2} \tag{13}$$

(because $V_s = 0$).

At the low velocities characterizing laminar flow about smooth symmetric objects, the net force on the object, from Eq. (13), will nearly cancel out. That is, there will be an approximately symmetric point on the surface of the object on the downstream side where the flow velocity is also zero. However, as the velocity of flow is increased, irregular deviations in the flow lines begin to occur which have a tendency to fill the whole cross-sectional area behind the object on the downstream side. This phenomenon was first studied experimentally (in the flow of water through tubes) by a British engineer and physicist named Osborne Reynolds (1883), who gave it the name *turbulence*. Vortices develop over the trailing surface of the object which absorb energy from the flow and distort the streamlines. Under these conditions, a net "drag" force is exerted on the object which can be roughly in the order of the maximum dynamic pressure from Eq. (13) multiplied by the cross-sectional area of the object. Hence one clearly expects that the coefficient A_2 in Eq. (9) will, in some sense, be proportional to this cross-sectional area and to the fluid density. However, the amount of drag resulting from turbulence is actually determined by the cross-sectional area of the turbulent wake following the object and the size of the wake can itself be velocity-dependent.

In his studies of turbulence, Reynolds (1883, 1895) found that a scaling relationship was helpful in determining the onset of turbulence with objects of different geometry. In particular, he introduced a dimensionless number (known as the *Reynolds number*),

$$R_e = \frac{Vd}{\eta}$$

where d is a characteristic linear dimension of the experiment (such as the width of a channel, the diameter of a sphere, distance between two plates, etc.) and the other quantities are as previously defined.

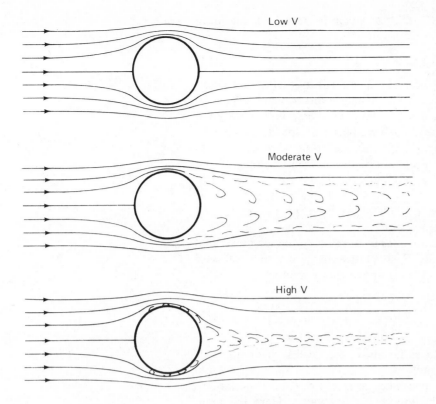

Low V

Moderate V

High V

Fig. 5-4. Variation of the turbulent wake from a sphere or cylinder with increasing velocity. At very low velocities the laminar viscous flow results in near cancellation of the quadratic velocity-dependent force. (The resultant nearly linear velocity-dependent force obeys Stokes' law.)

At moderate velocities, a laminar boundary layer remains around the sides of the object, but early separation of the turbulent flow from the surface results in a wide wake and a large value for the quadratic velocity-dependent drag coefficient. At high velocities a turbulent boundary layer extends around the sides of the object and results in a later separation of the turbulent flow from the surface and hence a narrow wake. The latter effect results in a sharp reduction in the drag coefficient for a velocity corresponding to the critical Reynolds number (R_c) dependent on the surface roughness. Typically, the quadratic resistive force coefficient for a sphere or cylinder remains constant within ≈ 10 percent for $0.01R_c < R < R_c$. Above R_c, the coefficient falls off very rapidly by factors ≈ 3 to 10 to a new, roughly constant value. The overall effects of the linear and quadratic velocity-dependent effects are frequently lumped together empirically into one drag coefficient for Eq. (14) which varies as $1/V$ at low velocities and then remains fairly constant until the critical Reynolds number is reached.

More recent studies (e.g., see the summaries of data in Baumeister and Marks, 1967) have shown that the flow is generally laminar for Reynolds numbers below about 2000, and the range $2000 \lesssim R_e \lesssim 4000$ denotes a transition region where the flow may either be laminar or turbulent. For $R_e \gtrsim 4000$, the flow is usually turbulent.

Over the region $4000 \lesssim R_e \lesssim 200{,}000$, the boundary layer is laminar over the surface of a smooth object and the turbulent wake separates near the maximum transverse dimension (middle illustration in Fig. 5-4).

At some *critical* Reynolds number ($\approx 200{,}000$ for a smooth sphere or cylinder) the boundary layer itself becomes turbulent and the wake separates from the boundary layer at a much later point in the flow. The wake is thus much narrower and the drag coefficient is markedly reduced (lower illustration in Fig. 5-4). The adjacent lamina, in effect, roll on the turbulent surface layer. The point at which the Reynolds number becomes critical depends a great deal on the surface roughness. Thus the critical Reynolds number (R_c) for a dimpled golf ball is much lower than that for a smooth table-tennis ball. Thus, as implied schematically in Fig. 5-4, the value of A_2 for a cylinder or a sphere can actually go through a maximum with increasing velocity due to variations in the size of the turbulent wake. In contrast, nonstreamlined shapes with square edges result in extremely turbulent flow at fairly low velocities and have drag coefficients that are frequently less velocity-dependent than those for their streamlined cousins. However, it is worth emphasizing that square shapes can have as much as 30 times more drag force than a carefully designed streamline shape with the same maximum transverse cross-sectional area at the same speed.

The dynamic air-resistance data quoted by professional engineers are usually presented in terms of shape-dependent *drag coefficients*. The drag coefficient (C_D) is a dimensionless number that is typically in the order of unity but is best measured in wind tunnels. The *drag force* (F_D) due to the pressure effect which opposes the motion of an object with a maximum transverse area S_m (in ft²) moving with velocity V (mph) through air at standard pressure

(760 mm/Hg) and a temperature of 15°C is given in terms of the drag
coefficient by

$$F_D = 0.002558 C_D S_m V^2 \qquad \text{pounds} \qquad (14)$$

For example, a flat 1-ft² plate placed normal ($C_D \approx 1.16$) to a wind of 18 mph
experiences a force of about 1 lb from the dynamic air-pressure effect. In
contrast, parabolic-shaped surfaces with the same transverse area have been
tested which only result in the same force ($\approx 1\,\text{lb/ft}^2$) at speeds as high as
100 mph. The exact force will depend on surface roughness as well as
geometry, and there is no real substitute for a direct measurement of the
coefficient.[6] The effects of Eq. (10) are frequently combined with those of Eq.
(14) by defining one velocity-dependent drag coefficient which varies as $1/V$ at
low velocities. The total drag force is then given by Eq. (14) using one
empirically determined drag coefficient, $C_D(V)$.

Equation (14) was written for the air density at sea level under prescribed
conditions of temperature and pressure. The relative air density falls off with
altitude above sea level (Y) in the following approximate manner[7]:

$$D(Y) = \begin{cases} \exp(-3.211 \times 10^{-5} Y) & \text{for } 0 \leqslant Y \leqslant 30{,}000 \text{ ft} \\ 1.6114 \exp(-4.771 \times 10^{-5} Y) & \text{for } Y > 30{,}000 \text{ ft} \end{cases} \qquad (15)$$

(Y in feet). Consequently, the drag force far above sea level is given approximately by the product of Eqs. (14) and (15).

The quadratic velocity-dependent resistance term in Eq. (9) for the motion
of ships is associated with the production of surface waves. Here the main
effect is due to the generation of bow and stern waves that trail behind the
ship when $V_{\text{ship}} > V_{\text{wave}}$. Interference effects between the bow and stern waves
result in a strong velocity dependence on the A_2 coefficient, and ships are
designed to ride on a minimum value of this coefficient at cruising speed.
Empirical methods (such as the Ayre method discussed by George L. West, Jr.,
in Baumeister and Marks, 1967) have been developed to provide accurate
predictions for standard hull shapes. However, it seems conceivable that one
might be able to reduce the quadratic loss coefficients significantly by generating more complex hull shapes.

The surface nature of the quadratic loss term shows up clearly in the
performance of submarines. A deeply submerged submarine has very much
smaller resistance at high speeds than a surface vessel of comparable size.
(However, the low-velocity resistive term in the case of the submarine is much
greater, owing to the larger wetted surface.) For example, contemporary
nuclear-powered submarines can go in excess of 35 knots under water, but only
≈ 20 knots on the surface (see Moore, 1974). The effect suggests that there
might be an economic advantage in the construction of submerged, nuclear-
powered luxury liners. In fact, why not use the fleet that already exists to carry
people instead of missiles? Although the concept will probably not appeal to
anyone except a staunch devotee of Jules Verne, we may have to change our
minds on this score after the last drop of oil trickles through the Alaskan
pipeline.

[6] Baumeister and Marks (1967) include articles by several authors in which a variety of data is
presented on friction and air resistance for cars, trucks, trains, boats, hydrofoils, airplanes, rockets,
and even windmills. One of the most useful general collections and discussions of air-resistance
data is given by Hoerner (1965). For a more formal treatment of these problems, see Batchelor
(1967), Tennekes and Lumley (1972), Prandtl (1952), or the volumes edited by Flügge and
Truesdell (1959, 1960, 1963) in the Handbuch der Physik series.

[7] The air-density factor is based on an empirical fit to data given by Lewis H. Abraham in
Baumeister and Marks (1967, Chap. 11).

Suppose that we want to apply a realistic version of Eq. (9) to the free-fall problem, modified by air resistance. First we note that $A_1 \ll A_2$ for essentially all velocities of interest. Even for speeds as low as 1 mph in atmospheric pressure, the force from Eq. (14) is roughly two orders of magnitude bigger than that represented by Eq. (10). Consequently, we shall ignore the linear term altogether. For the falling-body problem near sea level (taking the downward direction to be positive),

$$A_0 = 32.2 \text{ ft/sec}^2 \tag{16}$$

Hence Eq. (9) reduces to

$$A = 32.2 - A_2 V^2 \tag{17}$$

in this case and we get a very simply definable *terminal velocity*. That is, there will be a limiting velocity, V_1, for which the acceleration is zero and is obtained merely by setting $A = 0$ in Eq. (17). Hence in the present case the terminal velocity is

$$V_1 = \sqrt{32.2/A_2} \tag{18}$$

and decreases with increasing A_2. Because constant velocities are frequently much easier to measure than acceleration parameters, Eq. (18) provides a simple way of determining the coefficient A_2 for shapes as complicated as that of the human body. All we have to do is drop the body from a large height and wait until the velocity reaches a constant value. (Even with the linear term A_1 present, there would, of course, be a definite terminal velocity. However, in that case the terminal velocity would depend on the ratio of A_2/A_1.) Some representative data for A_2 coefficients for the falling-body problem that were computed using Eq. (18) are shown in Table 1. The data were obtained from experiments of the type shown in Fig. 5-5.

5.5: Table 1 Representative Values of the Quadratic, Velocity-Dependent, Resistive Acceleration Coefficient (A_2)[a] Computed from Terminal Velocities of an Experienced (135-lb) Sky Diver[b]

A_2[c]	Conditions
5.18×10^{-4}	Fetal position
7.75×10^{-4}	Nose dive (arms back along the body)
10.4×10^{-4}	Horizontal (arms and legs spread outward from the body as in Fig. 5-5)

[a] The coefficients typically vary by about ±10 percent, depending on the size and weight of the individual sky diver. (*Note:* The larger A_2, the smaller the terminal velocity.)

[b] The author is indebted to Jennifer Phillips of Orange, Mass., for a very helpful discussion of her terminal velocities.

[c] The dimensions of A_2 are ft/sec^2 per (ft/sec)^2 = ft^{-1}.

In order to solve the problem with a computer, we first enter a function definition according to Eq. (17) and enter an appropriate value for the coefficient A_2. We then have to define initial values for the velocity and vertical position at $T = 0$ and choose an appropriate integration interval, $T\emptyset$, to use in the constant-acceleration approximation. For example,

```
10   DEF FNA(V) = 32.2 − A2*ABS(V)*V
20   LET A2 = 10.4E−4
30   LET V = Y = T = 0
40   LET T∅ = .01
50   LET V1 = SQR(32.2/A2)
```

We can then make use of Eqs. (7) and (6) to determine the position (Y) and

Fig. 5-5. Former Yale electronics expert Richard J. Blume is shown demonstrating the "horizontal spread position" in the falling-body problem. (Photograph by Ray C. Cottingham.)

velocity (V) as a function of the time (T). For example,

```
100   FOR L = 1 TO 100
110   LET A = FNA(V)
120   LET Y = Y + V*T0 + 0.5*A*T0*T0
130   LET V = V + A*T0
140   LET T = T + T0
150   NEXT L
160   PRINT T,Y,V,V/V1
170   GOTO 100
```

Here a loop on the dummy parameter L was introduced to avoid printing out the solution for every calculation. As it stands, the program gives us the solution at $100T\emptyset = 1$-sec intervals using a value of $T\emptyset = 0.01$ sec. However, only a loop around lines $11\emptyset{-}13\emptyset$ is really required to solve the problem for V as a function of Y. The order of operations in lines $12\emptyset$ and $13\emptyset$ is important. We don't want to change V before we have computed the new value of Y (which involves the previous value of V in the second term). The choice of $T\emptyset$ is, of course, determined by the error that you are willing to tolerate in the calculation; the latter can be determined by repeating the computation with smaller values of the increment, $T\emptyset$. The ABS(V)$*V$ term on line 1$\emptyset$ is only necessary if we should want to reverse the sign on the velocity during flight (for example, by firing the sky diver upward out of a cannon); otherwise, we could have used $V*V$ in this term. If the functional form for the problem does not seem complicated enough, note that it takes no real effort to introduce any functional dependence for the parameters $A2$ that you care to specify in the program. We could have had the falling body open an umbrella or parachute, inflate a large spherical balloon, or execute a jackknife dive on the way down. For example, an experienced sky diver can vary his or her value of A_2 at will over the range shown in the Table 1. However, to start with, simpler versions of the problem will provide good practice in the numerical method of solution.

**5.5
PROBLEM 1**

(a) Assuming that the acceleration is given by Eq. (17), compute values of the terminal velocity in miles per hour for each of the three values of A_2 listed in Table 1.

(b) Compute the distance fallen, V (mph) and V/V_{terminal} as a function of time (in seconds) for each of the values of A_2 in Table 1, assuming that $V = 0$ at $T = 0$. How long does it take to reach 98 percent of the terminal velocity in each case? How accurate are your answers?

**5.5
PROBLEM 2**

On February 15, 1968. a 24-year-old man named Jeffrey Kraemer jumped 250 ft from the George Washington Bridge into the Hudson River and then proceeded to swim 200 yd through icy water to shore. He received no internal injuries and only suffered a cut thigh from the ice. "He is an excellent physical specimen," a hospital spokesman said. The only other explanation offered for his survival was that he hit head first.†

Suppose that he did a swan dive. Use the appropriate coefficient in Table 1 to compute the minimum velocity he would have had at the water level. Suppose that he did a nose dive all the way. How fast would he hit the water then? (Those people who do swan dives as a hobby might find a table of minimum final velocities as a function of initial height useful.)

**5.5
PROBLEM 3**

A U-2 pilot bails out at $Y = 76,000\,ft$ at $T = 0$. He does not have an oxygen tank and wants to get down to 10,000 ft as fast as possible so that he can breathe.

(a) He assumes the fetal position, for which the A_2 coefficient is given in Table 1 at *sea level*. The actual value of A_2 will be multiplied by the relative air-density factor in Eq. (15). (i.e., A_2 varies from 5.18×10^{-4} ft^{-1} at sea level to 2.22×10^{-5} ft^{-1} at 76,000 ft). The gravitational acceleration also varies (slightly) with height and may be approximated as

$$g \approx 32.2(1 - 0.95 \times 10^{-7}Y) \text{ ft/sec}^2 \quad (Y \text{ in ft})$$

How long does it take to get down to 10,000 ft? What was his maximum velocity and at what height was it a maximum? Take the upward direction to be positive and note that $A_0 = A_0(Y) = -g$.

(b) Suppose that his parachute accidentally opened at 76,000 ft. If the terminal velocity for the parachute at sea level were 15.7 ft/sec (corresponding to a 24-ft-diameter model),‡ how long would it take him to get to 10,000 ft?

---

† *The New York Times*, Feb. 16, 1968, p. 38, col. 1. Readers should be warned that this was the first known survival of such a jump in the history of the bridge.

‡ See, for example the data in *The Parachute Inc. Equipment Catalog* (Orange, Mass., 1974), or the discussion in Hoerner (1965).

5.5
PROBLEM 4

A student enrolled in a beginning SCUBA diving course must pass a test in which he fins 25 yd underwater without the additional breathing apparatus. He can maintain a quasi-steady accelerative thrust with the fins of†

$$A_0 \approx 2.15 \exp{(-T/30)} + 1.43 \text{ ft/sec}^2$$

where T is the time in seconds after he starts and the exponential decay results from muscular fatigue. The resistive acceleration is made up from the terms

$$A(V) \approx -0.214V - 0.154V^2 \qquad \text{ft/sec}^2 \ (V \text{ in ft/sec})$$

The linear velocity-dependent term arises from skin resistance and the quadratic velocity-dependent term from turbulent eddy currents produced by the fins. (On the surface the quadratic coefficient for the same skin diver is larger by a factor of ≈ 1.6, owing to "bow wave" formation, and the student can fin faster underwater than on the surface.) The net acceleration is $A_0 + A(V)$ where $V \geqslant 0$. Write a program to determine how long it takes him to go 25 yd assuming that he starts with zero velocity under water at $T = 0$. Suppose that he can keep it up for 30 sec. How far would he go? (Print the time, distance, and velocity in increments of 0.5 sec using an integration time of $T\emptyset = 0.01$ sec.)

5.5
PROBLEM 5

The *Queen Mary* was designed for a cruising speed of 29 knots. The resistive acceleration for the *Queen Mary* should be given approximately by the function‡

$$A(V) = \frac{-0.107(V/29)^2}{1 + 0.545 \sin{(2.21(V/29) + 0.14)}} \qquad \text{ft/sec}^2$$

where V is in knots (1 knot = 1 nautical mile per hour ≈ 1.688 ft/sec), $V \geqslant 0$, and the "angle" is in radians. Note that the ship cruises at a velocity slightly above that for the maximum value of the term in the denominator.

Suppose that a passenger fell overboard while the boat was going at normal cruising speed. If the Captain immediately reversed the engines at cruising speed power, how far would the boat go before slowing down to 5 knots? (According to the Coast Guard, 5 knots would be a safe speed to launch a lifeboat with rounded ends on the open seas.§) Assume that the acceleration from the propellers remains constantly equal to $A(V = 29)$ in opposite direction to the velocity.

5.5
PROBLEM 6

A 4.2-liter E-type Jaguar has a total resistive acceleration given as a function of speed as¶

$$A(V) = -0.22 - 5.6(V/125)^2 \qquad \text{mph/sec}$$

in opposite direction to the velocity and the engine can supply an acceleration

---

† The numbers are based on measurements made on members of the 1975 Yale SCUBA diving class. The author is indebted to Yale SCUBA diving instructor Peter Dingwall for a helpful discussion of the problem. See also related data in Counsilman (1968) and in Empleton et al. (1974).

‡ The acceleration formula is based on an empirical fit to results obtained with the Ayre method using data quoted by George L. West, Jr., in Baumeister and Marks (1967, Chap. 11).

§ The author is indebted to Lieutenant Commander Knauff of the U.S. Coast Guard at New London, Connecticut, for a helpful discussion of this problem. Knauff notes that Naval cadets are frequently dumped into the ocean in lifeboats during training at from 6 to 8 knots; however, the danger of capsizing is great. The danger to the person overboard is also great when the propellers are kept running. Evidently, if a passenger really did fall overboard on an ocean liner such as the *Queen Mary*, a harnessed swimmer with a long rope would be dropped out of one of the lower doors while the ship executed something known as a "Williamson turn." But, as Knauff says, "It's a dying art."

¶ The expressions are based on an empirical fit to data taken on the Autostrada by a fearless Italian mechanic.

to the car (including gear changes) of

$$E(V) \approx 5.6 \exp((125 - V)/145) \qquad \text{mph/sec}$$

where V is in mph and $V \geq 0$ in both expressions.

How long does it take to accelerate from 0 to 120 mph, and how far does it go in that time? [The net acceleration is $E(V) + A(V)$.]

5.5
PROBLEM 7

On Thursday evening, November 12, 1959, an unattended 123-ton-diesel locomotive slipped quietly out of the Communipaw Avenue freight yards in Jersey City, N.J., at 40 mph.†

(a) Assume that it was an isolated 1500-hP switching diesel without any freight cars, for which the maximum drawing force is‡

$$F(V) = \begin{cases} 60,000\, F_0 \text{ pounds for } 0 \leq V \leq 8 \text{ mph} \\ \dfrac{500,000}{V} F_0 \text{ pounds for } V > 8 \text{ mph} \end{cases}$$

and where the throttle opening is described by the factor F_0 satisfying $0 \leq F_0 \leq 1$. The resistive force for the engine itself is

$$R(V) \approx 277 + 3.72V + 0.24V^2 \text{ lb} \quad (V \text{ in mph})$$

and the net acceleration in respect to the ground is

$$A(V) \approx \frac{F(V) - R(V)}{7640} \text{ ft/sec}^2 \quad (V \text{ in mph and } V \geq 0)$$

Assuming that it traveled a distance of 1 mile before escaping from the freight yard, how fast did it go through the Elizabeth, N.J., station 8 miles down the track? How fast did the diesel engine have to travel that stopped it below South Amboy, N.J., after a run of 22 miles? (*Hint:* First compute F_0 to result in 40 mph after 1 mile.)

(b) Suppose that the engine had been coupled to freight cars to form a 424-ton freight train. The total resistance for the whole train is§

$$R(V) \approx 6277 + 12.72V + 0.39V^2 \text{ lb} \quad (V \text{ in mph})$$

and the acceleration is now

$$A(V) \approx \frac{F(V) - R(V)}{26,335} \text{ ft/sec}^2 \quad (V \text{ in mph and } V \geq 0)$$

What would the speeds be after 1 mile and at the Elizabeth Station if the engine started off under full throttle ($F_0 = 1$)?

† See "The Adventures of Engine 1706 in Jersey," *The New York Times*, Nov. 14, 1959, p. 1, cols. 3–6, and p. 11, cols. 3 and 4.

‡ The numbers used in the problem are based on typical data for diesel locomotives and freight trains given by John F. Partridge in Baumeister and Marks (1967, Chap. 11).

§ Conservationists will want to note the V^2 air-resistance term per freight car in a long train is about an order of magnitude smaller than that for a comparable-size highway truck because of the close spacing of the cars. Most of the V^2 term for the freight train in part (b) is due to the locomotive.

The Princeton–Dartmouth game of November 25, 1950, was played during one of the worst hurricanes of the century. The prevailing winds were from the east at 60 mph, with occasional gusts of up to 90 mph. Palmer Stadium, being open on the eastern end, was admirably suited for the event. The 5000 fans who stuck it out "under weather conditions so miserable as to defy description"[8] were rewarded by some of the most spectacular trajectories imaginable.

5.6
Two-Dimensional Air-Resistance Problems and the 1950 Princeton–Dartmouth Game

[8] "Princeton Beats Dartmouth 13–7," *The New York Times*, Nov. 26, 1950, Sec. V, p. 1, col. 8, and p. 3, cols. 4 and 5.

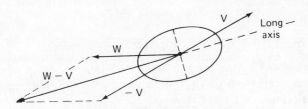

Fig. 5-6. Orientation of the relative velocities and football axis used to describe the two-dimensional air-resistance problem.

Dartmouth kicked off downwind, narrowly missing a field goal on the opening play. Dick Kazmaier achieved the record upwind punt of the game (15 yards, out of bounds) during the opening quarter. The average length of completed passes was 7.5 yards for Princeton and 14.5 yards for Dartmouth. However, these dry factual statistics reported in the newspaper accounts of the game do not really do justice to the unusual trajectories involved.[9]

Unfortunately, neither side really took advantage of the more exciting possibilities offered by this game. But the omission is understandable in that there were no computer terminals available in the stadium. (Von Neumann's machine was not operational until 1952.)

However, let us suppose that you had been in the position of Princeton coach Charlie Caldwell and had had access to a high-speed digital computer—not to mention some good data on footballs and your team's capabilities.[10] How would you program the trajectories?

The first important point to note is that the resistive force on the football depends on the relative velocity of the ball in respect to the wind. The problem is complicated by the fact that the football is not round. Letting the football velocity in respect to the ground be $\vec{V}$ and the wind velocity in respect to the ground be $\vec{W}$, the resistive force will depend on the relative orientation of the football in respect to the vector $\vec{W} - \vec{V}$. We shall assume here that the football is given enough spin about its long axis to stabilize its motion and that the football moves adiabatically so that its long axis is always parallel to the vector $\vec{W} - \vec{V}$ (see Fig. 5-6). This assumption is not essential for treating the problem but will give us the simplest realistic model. (If the orientation differs from that shown in Fig. 5-6, the net force on the ball could be in a direction other than $\vec{W} - \vec{V}$, owing to differences in the drag coefficients along different principal axes of the football. The football would also tend to precess about the vector $\vec{V} - \vec{W}$. Fortunately, there is not enough experimental data available at the present time to warrant consideration of this more complicated situation.)

Under these assumptions, the total acceleration on the football will be

$$\frac{d\vec{V}}{dt} = \vec{A} = -g\hat{j} + A_2 |\vec{W} - \vec{V}| (\vec{W} - \vec{V}) \tag{19}$$

where the unit vector $\hat{j}$ is in the vertical direction and A_2 is the quadratic velocity-dependent acceleration coefficient for a football as oriented in Fig. 5-6.

We can solve Eq. (19) easily in the constant-acceleration approximation by using column arrays to stand for the various vector quantities involved. After initializing the football position, $R(I)$, the football velocity in respect to the

---

[9] The recollection of this game is fairly clear in the author's memory because it is the only college football game he ever attended. (After that one, anything else would be anticlimactic.)

[10] The author is indebted to Yale coach Carmen Cozza for a helpful discussion of the numbers involved. Readers interested in closed-form analysis of this type of air-resistance problem should, of course, investigate the published work of that other great coach, Edward Routh of Cambridge. (After defeating Maxwell in 1854, coach Routh trained a series of students that set an all-time record of 22 consecutive first place wins on the Cambridge Tripos.)

ground, $V(I)$, and the wind velocity in respect to the ground, $W(I)$, the main problem can be solved iteratively through statements of the type

```
200   REM FOOTBALL PROBLEM IN TWO DIMENSIONS
210   LET U = SQR((W(1) − V(1))↑2 + (W(2) − V(2))↑2)
220   FOR I = 1 TO 2
230   LET A(I) = G(I) + A2*U*(W(I) − V(I))
240   LET R(I) = R(I) + V(I)*T∅ + .5*A(I)*T∅*T∅
250   LET V(I) = V(I) + A(I)*T∅
260   NEXT I
270   LET T = T + T∅
280   REM PRINT OR DISPLAY RESULTS
  ...
290   GOTO 210
```

Here the array $G(I)$ includes the constant acceleration from the earth's gravity [$G(1) = ∅$; $G(2) ≈ -32.16$ ft/sec^2 in Princeton]. The magnitude of the relative velocity, U, of the football in respect to the wind is calculated on line 21∅ for two dimensions and the acceleration due to the wind is introduced through the coefficient $A2$ (previously defined) on line 23∅. Note that the loop 22∅ through 26∅ just does the same calculation that we had gone through before with one-dimensional problems, but for each one of the components separately. The calculation could, of course, easily be extended to include three dimensions by modifying lines 21∅ and 22∅ to read

```
210   LET U = SQR((W(1) − V(1))↑2 + (W(2) − V(2))↑2 + (W(3) − V(3))↑2)
220   FOR L = 1 TO 3
```

However, the main features of the problem can be demonstrated in much less computing time by restricting the problem to the two-dimensional case. The initial velocities, positions, and integration interval $T∅$ must, of course, be entered before line 2∅∅.

The main difficulty in solving the football problem is in getting good data for the football itself. The manufacturers of footballs apparently do not put them in wind tunnels, and the drag coefficients are not specified in the rules and regulations. Further, the keepers of football records never mention the prevailing wind velocities.

Using a technique accredited to Galileo, the author took several representative balls to the top of a 200-ft tower in the New Haven area and dropped them off. A student with a stop watch assisted at the bottom of the tower and the data in Table 2 were computed assuming free fall from 200 ft, impeded only by a quadratic velocity-dependent air-resistance term. The final errors quoted are based on a reaction-time error of ±0.1 sec. The value of A_2 for the baseball appears in reasonable agreement with other independent measurements. However, the value obtained for the football is significantly smaller than one might estimate from wind-tunnel data for objects with similar cross-sectional areas. A reasonably good spiral was obtained with the football-dropping experiment, and the value of the coefficient deduced agreed reasonably well with rough estimates of the initial velocity ($≈65$ mph) and range ($≈55$ yd) for passes by a good player on a still day. (The reader is, of course, welcome to go out and take some better data on his own.)

5.6: Table 2 Some Approximate Air-Resistance Coefficients for Use in Eq. (19)[a]

Object	Baseball	Football	Volleyball	Table-Tennis ball
A_2[b]	0.0021	0.0037	0.0060	0.0457

[a] The author is indebted to Robert Fleischman for his help in taking these data.

[b] The units for A_2 in this table are ft/sec per (ft/sec)^2 = 1/ft. The errors are estimated to be $≤±0.001$ ft^{-1} and are based on reaction-time errors in the measurement of the time with a stopwatch for the objects to fall 200 ft.

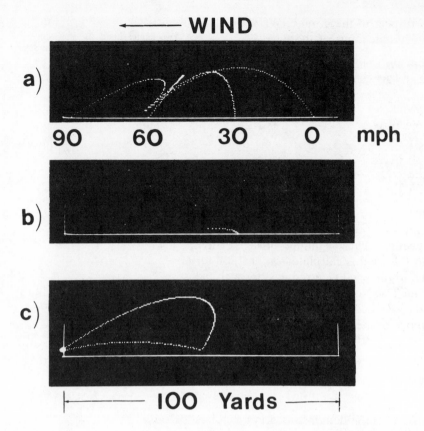

← WIND

a)

90   60   30   0   mph

b)

c)

|——— 100 Yards ———|

Fig. 5-7. Trajectories pertinent to the Princeton–Dartmouth (1950) game.

(a) Effect of head wind. The player is assumed passing from the 30-yd line and throwing the ball into the wind at 70 mph in respect to the ground at an angle of 40°. Trajectories are shown for wind velocities of 0, 30, 60, and 90 mph in respect to the ground. An angle of 40° is about optimum on a still day. For the prevailing 60-mph wind, an angle of 40° tosses the ball back almost to the player's feet.

(b) Optimizing the upwind forward pass (from the 50-yd line). A 90-mph wind was assumed, together with an initial throwing speed of 70 mph. The optimum angle is about 3° and the ball goes about 11.9 yd before hitting the ground.

(c) The downwind forward pass offers some fun for the imaginative player. Two solutions are shown for passes from the 50-yd line with a 90-mph wind. The lower trajectory is the straightforward solution in which the player merely throws the ball at 70 mph at ≈14° and the trajectory takes about 1.48 sec. The bolder approach is shown in the upper trajectory. Here the player turns around and throws the ball away from the receiver at an angle of ≈56° (and initial velocity of 70 mph in respect to the ground). Here the trajectory takes 3.64 sec, giving the receiver an extra 2 sec to get under it!

Some representative passing trajectories pertinent to the 1950 Princeton–Dartmouth game are shown in Fig. 5-7 and were computed using the data in Table 2 with the program described above.

5.6 **PROBLEM 8**	What would be the minimum initial velocity required to equal Kazmaier's record 15 yd upwind punt during the Princeton–Dartmouth game of 1950? (Assume a 60-mph wind velocity and the value of A_2 given in Table 2; take $g = 32.2$ ft/sec².)
5.6 **PROBLEM 9**	According to the National Football League *Official Record Book* (1970, p. 204): "longest completed passes" of 99 yards were credited to Frank Filchock (October 15, 1939), George Izo (September 15, 1963), and to Karl Sweetan (October 16, 1966).

If these passes were thrown on a still day, how fast would the ball have to be thrown, assuming the value of A_2 given in Table 2. Assuming these people could only throw the ball at 70 mph in respect to the ground and that they were throwing downwind (constant wind velocity), how strong was the wind? (Compute the velocities for the optimum angle and assume that $g = 32.16$ ft/sec².)

5.6 **PROBLEM 10**	In 1920 a new "livelier" ball (i.e., higher coefficient of restitution) was introduced to the game of baseball and an era of home-run hitting started. Using a 42-ounce bat, George Herman ("Babe") Ruth could hit the ball high into the right field bleachers (e.g., six rows from the top)† at Yankee Stadium with almost monotonous regularity.

Assuming that the point in the right-field bleachers is a horizontal distance of 500 ft from home plate and 40 ft up in the air, what is the minimum velocity

† *The New York Times,* Sept. 23, 1927, p. 22, col. 3.

the ball had to have on a wind-free day after leaving the bat? (Use the value for A_2 in Table 2 and note that $g = 32.161$ ft/sec^2 at the Yankee Stadium.)

5.6
PROBLEM 11

Using a giant slingshot (made with eight 6-ft lengths of surgical rubber tubing), two Yale undergraduates successfully fired a loaf of frozen bread over the Master's House at Timothy Dwight College during the spring of 1971.† The approximate trajectory is outlined in Fig. 5-8. Assuming that the loaf of

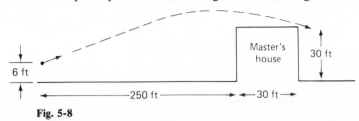

Fig. 5-8

bread had the same air resistance coefficient as a football (see Table 2), write a program to permit determining the optimum firing angle in respect to the horizontal and minimum "muzzle" velocity to just clear the Master's House. (Assume that the loaf of bread leaves the slingshot at a height of 6 ft and assume that there is no wind.)

5.6
PROBLEM 12

In March 1918 a director of the Krupp works named Fritz Rausenberger personally started shooting at Paris using a gun of his own design (known by the French as "Big Bertha").‡ The shells landed at 15-minute intervals within a circle of about 4 miles in diameter centered on the Notre Dame Cathedral (built $\approx$A.D. 1163). Relatively little damage was done by the shots, except for knocking out the church of Saint Gervais on Good Friday (killing 75 people). Hallade (1974) gives a map showing the landing points.

The range of the gun exceeded anything previously known by a factor of about 2.6 and the firings ($\approx$230-lb shells using $\approx$550 lb of powder per shot) were detected on a seismograph in Buffalo, N.Y.§ Several of these 138-ton guns were used, each having a barrel about 112 ft long and an estimated life of 65 shots. In fact, 65 separate numbered shells were made for each gun with gradually increasing size to counteract wear on the gun barrel. The velocities were supersonic all the way, and the drag coefficient can be approximated by one constant value within the needed accuracy. An approximate fit to trajectory data given by Hallade (1974) yields

$$A_2 \approx 1.19 \times 10^{-5} D(Y) \text{ per foot}$$

for the quadratic velocity-dependent acceleration coefficient in Eq. (9), where $D(Y)$ is the variation of air density with altitude given previously in Eq. (15). The acceleration of gravity at Paris is approximately

$$A_0 \approx -32.183(1 - 9.5 \times 10^{-8} Y) \text{ ft/sec}^2 \quad (Y \text{ in ft})$$

What would the minimum muzzle velocity and optimum firing angle be (in respect to a straight line drawn a distance of 72.25 miles from the gun to the target) necessary to hit Notre Dame? (Neglect the earth's rotation, as its effects are included in the approximate empirical fit.) How long does the shell take to get there? What is the maximum altitude and velocity at impact? (Note that the shell goes through a maximum velocity before impact on the way down.)

† The author is indebted to Jeffry Allan Spain and Michael Robert Hausman for a helpful discussion of the trajectory and the loan of their slingshot.

‡ *The New York Times*, April. 8, 1918, p. 1, col. 2. The name for the gun is based on one given by the Krupp Works to an earlier giant howitzer ("The Bertha", after Bertha Krupp, wife of the chief director).

§ *The New York Times*, June 16, 1918, Sec. II, p. 4, col. 1.

When we take account of spin, the trajectories can become decidedly more complicated. As with the lift on airfoils, the spin force arises as a consequence of the Bernoulli effect. In addition to the normal drag force opposing the ball's motion, an additional force at right angles to the ball's velocity vector $(\vec{V})$ occurs due to the distortion in air flow around the ball resulting from its spin frequency (S). On one side of the ball (the top in Fig. 5-9), the net flow velocity of air in respect to the ball is increased by the effects of spin. Here, the flow

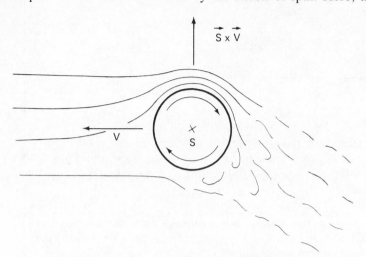

Fig. 5-9. Illustration of the spin-dependent (Magnus) force on a rotating ball. As the ball moves through the air with velocity $\vec{V}$, the flow lines are distorted as shown schematically in the figure. Here it is assumed that the spin vector points into the page, yielding the rotational motion indicated. The rotational motion adds to the relative velocity of the air in respect to the ball at the top of the figure and detracts from it at the bottom. The pressure is decreased at the top and increased at the bottom from the Bernoulli effect, resulting in a net upward force on the ball (compare with Fig. 5-3). The direction of the spin force is that of the cross product $\vec{S} \times \vec{V}$. The force increases with S and V and goes to zero if either S or $V = 0$. Note that as a consequence of Newton's third law ("for every action there is an equal and opposite reaction"), the force on the air is in the opposite direction to the force on the ball. Consequently, the turbulent wake of the ball is deflected downward when the spin force on the ball is upward.

lines are more closely spaced and the pressure is lowest (compare with Fig. 5-3). On the other side of the ball (the bottom in Fig. 5-9), the net flow velocity of air in respect to the ball is decreased by the effects of spin, the flow lines are more widely spaced and the pressure is highest. The result is a net force increasing with both the spin and ball velocity, which pushes the ball upward in Fig. 5-9. The first extensive experimental study of this spin-dependent force was given by A. Magnus (1853).

If we use the "right-hand screw rule" to describe the spin vector (i.e., the spin vector points along the axis of rotation in the direction that a right-handed screw would advance when rotated the same way as the ball), the instantaneous direction of the spin force will be in the direction of the cross product, $\vec{S} \times \vec{V}$ (i.e., it is in the direction that a right-handed screw would advance if you rotated the vector $\vec{S}$ into the vector $\vec{V}$). Because the spin force will increase with both $\vec{V}$ and $\vec{S}$, and is identically zero if either $\vec{V}$ or $\vec{S}$ is zero, it will be easiest to describe the acceleration produced by the spin by the relation

$$\vec{A}_{\text{spin}} = S_0(\vec{S} \times \vec{V}) \tag{20}$$

[11] The material in Sections 5.7–5.14 uses some concepts in classical mechanics which are usually treated in the first term of an introductory freshman physics course. Although such background is not absolutely essential, the present material will be hard to understand conceptually without prior knowledge of energy and momentum conservation laws.

We can then determine S_0 empirically and could include any observed departure from the functional dependence in Eq. (20) by making the coefficient S_0 time-, velocity-, and/or spin-dependent.[12] In most games where spin effects are important, the spin is relatively constant over the motion. Note that because the spin force is orthogonal to the ball's motion, no work is done by the spin force along the trajectory (i.e., the spin force is always perpendicular to $\vec{V}$), and changes in spin frequency occur just through rotational friction. (The center of mass motion of the ball slows down and speeds up to conserve energy in the interaction with the earth's gravitational acceleration.) We, of course, expect S_0 to increase with the air density and with the size and roughness of the ball. However, as with the drag coefficient, there will be no substitute for direct measurement. Further, because there is no torque acting on the ball other than the frictional resistance tending to slow down its spin, the spin axis remains pointing in a constant direction.

To include the effect of spin in our program, we merely have to add the components of the acceleration which result from Eq. (20) to our previous statements. As discussed in Chapter 2,

$$\vec{S} \times \vec{V} = \begin{vmatrix} \hat{\imath} & \hat{\jmath} & \hat{k} \\ S_x & S_y & S_z \\ V_x & V_y & V_z \end{vmatrix} \tag{21}$$

in three dimensions where $\hat{\imath}$, $\hat{\jmath}$, and $\hat{k}$ are the unit Cartesian vectors. We can represent these vectors by column arrays and thus the x, y, and z components of the acceleration that arise from the spin-dependent force for a general spin direction could be written in a program by statements of the type

```
LET   A(1) = S0*(S(2)*V(3) − S(3)*V(2))
LET   A(2) = S0*(S(3)*V(1) − S(1)*V(3))     (22)
LET   A(3) = S0*(S(1)*V(2) − S(2)*V(1))
```

The expressions simplify considerably for certain specific cases. For example, if we take the spin direction parallel to the z axis and let $V_z = 0$, we shall only get motion within the xy plane and the problem becomes two-dimensional.

For specific illustration, consider a coordinate system in which the x axis is along the horizontal direction, the y axis is vertical, and the spin vector is in the $-z$ direction (into the paper, as in Figs. 5-9 and 5-10). Here the spin vector may be written

$$\vec{S} \equiv -S\hat{k}$$

and

$$\vec{S} \times \vec{V} = \begin{vmatrix} \hat{\imath} & \hat{\jmath} & \hat{k} \\ 0 & 0 & -S \\ V_x & V_y & 0 \end{vmatrix} = \hat{\imath}SV_y - \hat{\jmath}SV_x \tag{23}$$

Hence we could modify our earlier two-dimensional program to treat the motion of a ping-pong ball moving perpendicular to the spin axis as follows:

```
200   REM PING-PONG BALL WITH SPIN PERPENDICULAR TO V
210   LET V = SQR(V(1)*V(1) + V(2)*V(2))
220   LET A(1) = +S0*S*V(2) − A2*V*V(1)
230   LET A(2) = −S0*S*V(1) − A2*V*V(2) − 32.2
240   FOR I = 1 TO 2
```

[12] The experimental data shown by Hoerner (1965, pp. 7–20, Fig. 34) indicate that Eq. (20) is obeyed reasonably well for the small spin frequencies encountered in most ballgames. (See also Maccoll (1928).) However, when the spin frequency gets high enough so that the circumferential velocity of the ball exceeds the velocity of center of mass motion, the force becomes approximately independent of the spin frequency and increases as V^2. (*Note:* With the present definitions, the circumferential velocity is $2\pi a S$, where a is the ball radius and S is the spin frequency; the angular frequency is $\omega = 2\pi S$.)

Fig. 5-10. Trajectories for a ping-pong ball with varying amounts of spin (axis into the paper). The ball starts at $T = 0$ at the left, moving horizontally in each case. The spin interaction assumed was arbitrary and is proportional to the parameter S in the figure. Note that "top spin" ($S > 0$ here) makes the ball drop more rapidly than the $S = 0$ curve and that back spin ($S < 0$ here) lengthens the trajectory. Finally, with enough back spin ($S = -7$), one obtains loops and cusps in the motion. Note in the latter case that the ball slows down as it reaches the top of the loop (points for constant time separation are closer together) and speeds up again as it comes out of the loop, thus conserving energy in the interaction with the earth's gravitational field. Because of air resistance, the ball moves more slowly toward the end of each trajectory. The results were computed from Eq. (23) and the program following that equation in the text.

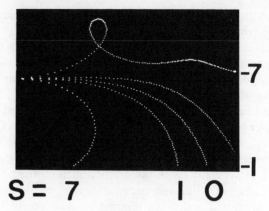

```
250   LET R(I) = R(I) + V(I)*TØ + .5*A(I)*TØ*TØ
260   LET V(I) = V(I) + A(I)*TØ
270   NEXT I
280   LET T = T + TØ
290   REM PRINT OR DISPLAY RESULTS
...
300   GOTO 210
```

Here the initial spin magnitude S and the coefficient $SØ$ arising from the Magnus force would have to be introduced at the start of the program, along with the other initial boundary conditions on the problem.

These velocity- and spin-dependent forces are generally not large enough in ball games to warrant requiring anything more complex than the constant-acceleration approximation. (However, they could be done more accurately and rapidly with the "bootstrap" method discussed later.)

As illustrated in Fig. 5-10, one can get some pretty wild trajectories by making the spin interaction large enough.

**5.7
PROBLEM 13†**

A golf player can lengthen his drive by adding "bottom" spin to the ball. The coefficients for a particular golf ball are

$$A2 = 0.00126 \text{ ft/sec}^2 \text{ per } (\text{ft/sec})^2$$

$$SØ = 0.0044 \text{ ft/sec}^2 \text{ per } (\text{ft/sec})(\text{revolutions/sec})$$

Owing to friction, the spin decays with time according to $S(t) = S(t = 0) \exp(-T/22.41)$. Suppose that the golfer hits the ball at 170 ft/sec and at an angle of 20° in respect to level ground.

(a) If the ball has no spin, how far does it go? How long does it take?

(b) If the player gives it a "bottom" spin of 55 revolutions per second, how far does it go? How long does it take?

(c) How far would it go if he were able to hit the ball with the same velocity without spin so that its initial angle was 45° in respect to the horizontal?

**5.7
PROBLEM 14†**

Suppose that an eccentric left-handed millionaire designed a golf course to thwart his right-handed colleagues on the Stock Exchange. The geometry for the first hole might look like the drawing in Fig. 5-11. If he can hit the ball with $V \leqslant 150$ mph in the vertical plane and give it a spin of $\leqslant 55$ revolutions per second, find a solution for a hole-in-one. (Use the data for golf balls given in Problem 13.)

† The coefficients for Problems 13, 14, and 15 are based on data presented by Daish (1972).

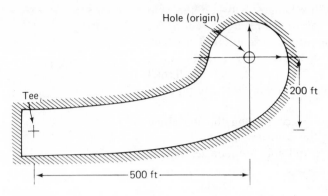

Hole (origin)

Tee

200 ft

500 ft

Fig. 5-11

First consider an inelastic ball bouncing on a smooth, flat, very massive and frictionless surface, as diagrammed in Fig. 5-12. Because of the assumption on smoothness, the velocity component tangential to the surface (V_t) cannot be affected during the collision. However, inelastic compression of the ball results in a decrease in the magnitude of the normal component of the velocity. As noted by Newton, this fractional decrease can be described by an empirically

**5.8
Adding Bounce to the Game:
Ping-Pong**[13]

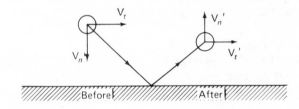

V_t

V_n'

V_n

V_t'

Before   After

Fig. 5-12

measured parameter called the *coefficient of restitution, e*. Hence the inelastic bounce on a frictionless plane surface may be described by the equations

$$V_t' = V_t \tag{24a}$$

$$V_n' = -eV_n \tag{24b}$$

where V_n stands for the normal component of velocity in respect to the surface just before the bounce and the primes are used to denote the quantities just after the bounce. Equation (24b) may be regarded as a definition of the coefficient of restitution e, and Eq. (24a) follows from the conservation of linear momentum (no tangential forces act on the ball during the bounce; therefore, the tangential component of the linear momentum does not change). The equations, of course, imply an amount of energy

$$E = \tfrac{1}{2}mV_n^2(1 - e^2) \tag{25}$$

is lost through inelastic compression of the ball and results from forces normal to the surface. If we neglect the collision time (generally negligible compared to the other time intervals in the motion), the effects of bounces on a smooth surface are easily incorporated in a program describing the motion of the ball.

The problem becomes much more interesting when the bounce occurs on a rough-enough surface to prevent sliding at the point of contact. Here the spin

---

[13] Readers without a background in introductory physics may wish to skip this section.

and tangential velocities become coupled, and exchanges between the spin frequency and tangential velocity will generally occur. Here, again, energy of the amount given by Eq. (25) is lost through inelastic deformation of the ball. However, the combined kinetic energy involved in the tangential and rotational motion is still approximately conserved for a flat surface and small ball deformation. Assuming enough friction, the ball does not slide at the point of contact, and no additional energy is lost.

By invoking the conservation of energy and by computing the impulsive change in linear and angular momentum during the collision, we can obtain a simple relationship between the linear velocities and spin frequencies before and after the impact. We shall assume that an impulse P_t is applied parallel to the flat surface at the point of contact which opposes the tangential velocity component of the center of mass motion of the ball.[14] This impulse does not affect the velocity component of the center of mass motion normal to the surface because of orthogonality of the two vectors ($\vec{V}_n \times \vec{P}_t = 0$).

Specifically, the linear momentum component of the ball parallel to the surface just after the collision (mV'_t) is related to the initial tangential component of the linear momentum just before the collision by

$$mV'_t = mV_t - P_t \qquad (26)$$

where the impulse P_t results from friction. This same impulsive force results in an impulsive torque about the center of mass of the ball which changes the angular momentum ($I\omega$) of the ball in respect to an axis through its center of mass.

For example, consider the case where the spin axis is perpendicular to the plane formed by the velocity V_t and the radius of the ball drawn to the point of contact, as shown in Fig. 5-13. We shall again assume that the spin vector goes into the paper [as with the convention used to derive Eq. (23)] and let $\omega = 2\pi S$, where S is the spin frequency in cycles per second. The new angular momentum ($I\omega'$) after the bounce will be related to the original angular momentum ($I\omega$) just before the bounce by the equation

$$I\omega' = I\omega + aP_t \qquad (27)$$

where I is the moment of inertia of the ball about an axis through its center and ω and ω' are the angular velocities in radians per second before and after the bounce. Equations (26) and (27) couple the changes in spin and tangential velocity which result from the bounce. Combining Eqs. (26) and (27) to

---

[14] An impulse is defined formally as the limit of an infinite force acting for infinitesimal time. Thus, for a general impulse, $\vec{P}$, acting on a rigid body with mass m,

$$\vec{P} = \lim_{t' \to 0} \int_0^{t'} \vec{F}(t)\, dt = \int_{\vec{V}_1}^{\vec{V}_2} d(m\vec{V}) = m\vec{V}_2 - m\vec{V}_1$$

where the limit is finite and nonzero and the right side of the equation follows from Newton's laws for the center of mass motion [($\vec{F} = d(m\vec{V})/dt$]. The same impulsive force acting at distance $\vec{r}$ from the center of mass gives rise to an impulse torque about the center of mass,

$$\vec{r} \times \vec{P} = \lim_{t' \to 0} \int_0^{t'} \vec{r} \times \vec{F}(t)\, dt = \int_{\omega_1}^{\omega_2} d(I\vec{\omega}) = I\vec{\omega}_2 - I\vec{\omega}_1$$

where again the right side of the equation follows from Newton's laws applied to angular momentum about the center of mass. The quantity $\vec{r}$ may be taken out of the above integral because the force $\vec{F}(t)$ is assumed to operate only within the infinitesimal interval at $t = 0$ over which $\vec{F}$ is constant.

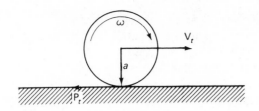

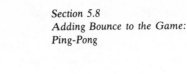

Fig. 5-13

eliminate the unknown tangential impulse, P_t, yields

$$I(\omega' - \omega) = ma(V_t - V'_t) \qquad (28)$$

Applying the conservation of energy (excluding the amount involved in the vertical motion) results in

$$\frac{I}{2}(\omega'^2 - \omega^2) = \frac{m}{2}(V_t^2 - V_t'^2) \qquad (29)$$

where we have assumed that no energy is lost through sliding at the point of contact. Dividing Eq. (29) by Eq. (28) and multiplying by 2 yields

$$(\omega' + \omega) = \frac{1}{a}(V_t + V'_t) \qquad (30)$$

Solving Eqs. (28) and (30) for V'_t and ω' then results in

$$V'_t = V_t + 2a\frac{\omega - V_t/a}{1+k}$$
$$\omega' = \omega - 2k\frac{\omega - V_t/a}{1+k} \qquad (31)$$

where $k = ma^2/I$. We have written Eqs. (31) in the form shown to emphasize that no changes in spin or tangential velocity component occur when the ball satisfies the rolling condition $(a\omega = V_t)$ just before the collision.

The factor $k = ma^2/I$ varies with the mass distribution within the ball. For example, for a uniform solid spherical ball, $k = \frac{5}{2}$; for a hollow, thin spherical shell (e.g., a table-tennis ball), $k = \frac{3}{2}$. Thus for a $1\frac{3}{8}$-inch-diameter table-tennis ball, Eqs. (31) become

$$V'_t = 0.288S + 0.200V_t \qquad \text{feet/sec}$$
$$S' = -0.200S + 3.33V_t \qquad \text{(rev/sec)} \qquad (32)$$

Here we have introduced the spin frequency (s) in revolutions per second $(\omega = 2\pi S)$ and the tangential velocity, V_t, is expressed in feet per second. Equations (32), of course, will only hold in the absence of sliding and when the ball deformation is small. The change in the velocity component of center of mass motion normal to the surface is still given by Eq. (24b).

5.8 **PROBLEM 15**	A person hits a ping-pong ball at 10 ft/sec 45° in respect to the horizontal direction from a height 2 ft above the table. Assuming that the ball is launched 4 ft (horizontally) from the 6-inch-high net and that the horizontal table is very rough, how much back-spin does the ball have to be given initially to just clear the net as it hops back toward the player? Assume that the coefficient of restitution for the ping-pong ball bouncing on the table is 0.62 and that the spin-interaction coefficient used in Eq. (20) is $S\emptyset = 0.068$. The drag coefficient for the ping-pong ball is given in Table 2. Construct a subroutine that incorporates Eqs. (24b) and (32) to handle the bounce. Note that the motion is two-dimensional and use a program based on Eq. (23) to handle the flight of the ball.

Man's interest in space travel predates[15] the knowledge of Newtonian mechanics which has made such trips possible.[16] One of the earliest prophetic descriptions of a trip to the moon was given by Jules Verne in 1865. According to Verne, the Baltimore Gun Club (made up of retired artillery officers) devised a scheme to fire a projectile carrying three astronauts and two space dogs off toward the moon from a point in Florida near Cape Kennedy. The trajectory is altered by the firing of recoil rockets and the voyage ultimately ends with a "splash down" in the Pacific and recovery by a U.S. naval vessel [see the illustrative drawings reproduced in von Braun, Bedini, and Whipple (1970), pp. 82–84].

5.9
PROBLEM 16

The experiments by Rausenberger et al. in 1918 with "Big Bertha" were probably the nearest comparable artillery shots to the Verne proposal made in history† (see Problem 12). Suppose that Big Bertha had been fired straight up at the equator. What would the muzzle velocity have to have been to permit the shell to just escape the earth's gravitational attraction? Assume the resistive acceleration from the earth's atmosphere varies as $D(Y)A_2V^2$, where the variation in relative air density, $D(Y)$, is given in Eq. (15) and the drag coefficient for the projectile is contained in the factor A_2 given in Problem 12. The earth's gravitational acceleration may be written

$$g(Y) = \frac{-32.088}{(1 + Y/r_0)^2} \quad \text{ft/sec}^2$$

where the earth's radius at the equator is $r_0 = (5280)(3963)$ ft and Y is the height above the earth's surface in feet. It may be shown from the conservation of energy that the projectile will just escape the earth's gravitational pull outside the atmosphere when

$$\tfrac{1}{2}V^2 = -g(Y)(r_0 + Y) \quad \text{(ft/sec)}^2$$

Assume that the atmospheric decceleration is negligible when

$$Y > 200,000 \text{ ft}$$

† Excluding more recent German experiments using finned projectiles.

A much more imaginative approach to the problem was given by H. G. Wells in *The First Men on the Moon*. Wells had his hero, Mr. Cavor, invent a substance (modestly named "cavorite") that could be used as a gravitational shield. Mr. Cavor then built a spaceship from "a sphere of glass surrounded on the outside by a series of cavorite windows or blinds." The working of the spaceship is best described in Mr. Cavor's own words to his passenger:

"Well, when all these windows or blinds are shut, no light, no heat, no gravitation, no radiant energy of any sort will get at the inside of the sphere; it will fly on through space in a straight line as you say. But open a window—imagine one of the windows open! Then at once any heavy body that chances to be in that direction will attract us—"

At $T = 0$ all the blinds were shut and the spaceship slipped quietly off the earth.

[15] See, for example, Michael Sparke and Edward Forrest (1638), *The Discovery of a World in the Moone—Or, a Discourse Tending to Prove that 'tis probable there may be another habitable World in the Planet*, printed by E. G., London.
[16] Newton (1686).

There are various ways in which Mr. Cavor could arrive at a stable orbit about the moon, through judicious manipulation of the cavorite windows. However, there are also lots of ways in which the ship could easily exceed the escape velocity of both the earth's and the moon's gravitational attraction. The point here is that for the ship to be bound in a two-body system,

$$\frac{-G_u M m}{r} + \tfrac{1}{2}mV^2 \leqslant 0 \tag{33}$$

where M is the mass of the earth (or moon) and m is the mass of the spaceship; r is the distance to the center of the earth (or moon) and V is the total velocity of the spaceship in respect to that center. The universal gravitational constant, G_u, is related to the acceleration from the earth's gravity used in the previous problems by

$$g = \frac{G_u M_e}{r_0^2} \qquad \text{where } M_e \text{ is the mass of the earth} \tag{34}$$

and r_0 is the radius of the earth.

With all the cavorite windows closed, the spaceship leaves the earth with the earth's tangential velocity due to rotation (≈ 1000 mph in respect to the center of the earth). As long as all the windows are shut, the spaceship maintains this velocity in straight-line motion. Consequently, it is easy for it to reach a point where the full gravitational attraction of the earth (or moon) at some distance r is incapable of pulling Mr. Cavor and his passenger back again [i.e., Eq. (33) >0 for the particular value of V]. The problem is therefore exceedingly delicate, and the slightest mistake can send the two of them off irrecoverably into the outer reaches of the solar system.[17]

Getting into a stable orbit about the moon in the Wells method depends critically on the initial position of the moon at "launch." Probably the simplest way of accomplishing the objective is to adjust the time of launch so that the straight-line motion of the spaceship intercepts the moon's orbit just after the moon has passed. One then opens all the shutters and uses the moon to give the spaceship a kick tangentially in the direction of the moon. (The earth's gravitation keeps both the moon and the spaceship in an orbit about the earth.) Note that if the spaceship arrives ahead of the moon, it is given a kick in the wrong direction and the prospects for the passengers are very grim indeed.[18]

In solving this problem, we have to worry about incorporating Newton's law of gravitational attraction as it pertains to the attraction of the spaceship by both the earth and the moon. (We may clearly ignore the effects of the spaceship on the earth's and moon's orbits.) Newton's law of gravitational attraction for the force on the spaceship due to the earth may be written

$$\vec{F} = -G_u \frac{M_e m}{R^3} \vec{R} = m\vec{A} \tag{35}$$

where G_u is the universal gravitational constant, M_e is the mass of the earth, m is the mass of the spaceship, $\vec{R}$ is a vector from the center of the earth to the spaceship, and $\vec{A}$ is the acceleration at the distance R and is in the direction of a unit vector, $-\hat{R}$. Note that

$$\frac{\hat{R}}{R^2} = \frac{\vec{R}}{R^3} \tag{36}$$

---

[17] After launch, Cavor commented to his passenger:

"Haven't you brought anything to read?"

"Good Lord, No!"

"I forgot to tell you. There are uncertainties—The voyage may last—We may be weeks!"

[18] It seems desirable to point out that no one other than Mr. Cavor has found a substance that will produce gravitational shielding. However, needy students should note that the Gravity Research Foundation of Gloucester, Mass. (founded in 1948 by Rodger W. Babson) has offered a $1,500 annual prize for the best essay on this subject.

Fig. 5-14. A collection of space suits developed by the U.S. Air Force during the evolution of the space program.

Hence, under just the earth's attraction, the acceleration experienced by the spaceship (with the cavorite windows open) is just

$$\vec{A} = -G_u \frac{M_e}{R^3} \vec{R} \tag{37}$$

In the presence of the earth and moon we have two different gravitational acceleration terms acting on the spaceship, and the total acceleration becomes

$$\vec{A} = -G_u \frac{M_e}{R^3} \vec{R} + \frac{G_u M_m}{|\vec{M} - \vec{R}|^3} (\vec{M} - \vec{R}) \tag{38}$$

where M_m is the mass of the moon, and $\vec{M}$ is a vector locating the center of the moon from an origin coincident with the center of the earth. There will, of course, be one point in between the earth and the moon where these two accelerations exactly cancel. Also, we may neglect the moon's acceleration near the surface of the earth. However, if we want to know what happens to the spaceship in general, we had better have both terms present.

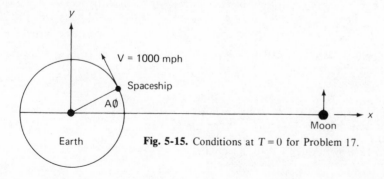

Fig. 5-15. Conditions at $T = 0$ for Problem 17.

5.9
PROBLEM 17

Assume that the motion of the moon and cavorite spaceship occur in one plane and that the position of the moon is given by

$$M(1) = 240000*COS(A1) \quad \text{(miles)}$$
$$M(2) = 240000*SIN(A1)$$

where

$$A1 = 2*3.14159*T/(24*28)$$

and T is in hours.

At $T = 0$, the location of the spaceship is given by

$$R(1) = 4000*COS(A\emptyset) \quad \text{(miles)}$$
$$R(2) = 4000*SIN(A\emptyset)$$

and it has an initial velocity

$$V(1) = -1000*SIN(A\emptyset) \quad \text{(mph)}$$
$$V(2) = +1000*COS(A\emptyset)$$

due to the earth's rotational motion.

With the cavorite windows open, the acceleration from the moon on the spaceship is

$$1.56E1\emptyset*(\vec{M} - \vec{R})/|\vec{M} - \vec{R}|^3 \quad \text{mph}^2$$

and the acceleration due to the earth on the spaceship is

$$-1.26E12(*\vec{R}/|\vec{R}^3|) \quad \text{mph}^2$$

(We shall assume that the earth and moon radii are 4000 and 1100 miles, respectively.)

Leave the cavorite shutters closed from $T = 0$ until the spaceship just crosses the moon's orbit, $R \approx 240,000$ miles. You can accomplish the first part of the problem merely by computing the intersection or by solving the problem in the constant-acceleration approximation with a very coarse time interval $T\emptyset$. (As long as the acceleration is zero, you can make $T\emptyset$ as large as you please without introducing errors.) Assume that the cavorite also shields the ship from the effects of air resistance.

Find a value of $A\emptyset$ that gets you into a reasonably stable orbit around the moon. (Don't waste too much time on the problem. If you can get halfway around the earth without being lost in outer space, you are doing pretty well. If anything, you should probably err in the direction of a stable elliptic orbit about the earth so that a rescue party with rockets could be sent up to get you.) The constant-acceleration approximation with values of $T\emptyset \approx 1$ hour will illustrate the problem. However, if you really want to make the trip, it would be better to use a smaller time interval, more accurate numbers, and the modified Runge–Kutta method discussed later.

It is easiest to solve the problem by displaying the positions of the moon and spaceship with a high-resolution plotting device. However, the same information can be easily conveyed by teletype print out of the distance of the spaceship from the earth and from the moon, together with the angular lead of the spaceship in respect to the moon and the magnitude of the spaceship velocity (see Figs. 5-15 and 5-16).

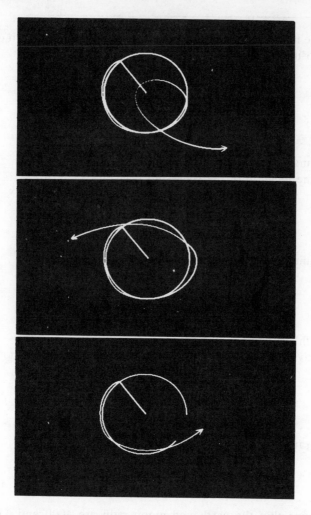

Fig. 5-16. Some near-misses with the cavorite problem. In the bottom figure, the spaceship has been deflected outward from the moon's orbit after one half-revolution about the earth and has gotten too far ahead of the moon. In the top picture, the spaceship got too far behind the moon and was pulled in toward the earth (at the center) after one half-trip around. In the middle figure, the spaceship has almost remained in orbit about the moon for one complete trip around the earth. In each case, the spaceship crossed the moon's orbit slightly after the moon went by (at about 10 o'clock in the photographs).

**5.10
Rocket Travel**

In the present age when astronauts return from outer space at frequent intervals, one tends to forget that rocket travel was once an extremely hazardous and uncertain form of transportation (see Fig. 5-17). As we shall see, even the mechanics of launching a working rocket into a circular orbit are very tricky.

With all due respect to Jules Verne, there are several important practical advantages in the use of rockets over artillery in launching space vehicles. Foremost of these are the facts that one can delay the maximum velocities to higher altitudes where the air resistive drag is much smaller and one can make corrective changes in the trajectory after the vehicle is outside the atmosphere. In contrast, it would be totally prohibitive to fire an artillery shell through the atmosphere into a circular orbit. Rockets make use of the law of conservation of momentum to derive their "thrust." In particular, the total linear momentum of all matter within the rocket is constant in the absence of external forces. Hence, when propellant mass leaves the back of the rocket at the rate dm_p/dt

Fig. 5-17. An early unsuccessful attempt to put a satellite in orbit about the earth using a Vangard rocket. (Official U.S. Navy photo.) A Vangard rocket was successfully used to put a 3-lb satellite in orbit on March 17, 1958. [Sputnik 1 (184 lb) and 2 (1120 lb) were put in orbit on Oct. 4 and Nov. 3, 1957; Explorer 1 (30.8 lb) was put in orbit with a Jupiter-C rocket on Jan. 31, 1958.]

with exhaust velocity V_e, the remaining mass, m_r, within the rocket is accelerated in the forward direction by an effective force, or thrust, given by

$$F_0 = V_e \frac{dm}{dt} p. \tag{39}$$

This force is usually maintained nearly constant while the fuel in the rocket burns. However, even if F_0 itself is constant, the acceleration experienced by the rocket is not constant, owing to the substantial decrease in remaining mass within the rocket with time. Thus, while the rocket engine is burning with a thrust, $\vec{F}_0$, the acceleration experienced by the rocket in vacuum is

$$\vec{A}_t = \frac{\vec{F}_0}{m_r(t)} \tag{40}$$

If the rocket fuel is burning at a constant rate, the residual mass left within the

229

rocket is given by

$$m_r(t) = m_0 - \frac{dm_p}{dt} \cdot t \qquad (41)$$

until the fuel is all consumed. The change in residual mass with time is very substantial. Typically, much more than half of the initial mass (m_0) of the rocket consists of fuel.

The direction of the thrust, and hence of the acceleration in Eq. (40), can be controlled. For example, in the V-2 rocket, such control was accomplished by two pairs of graphite vanes in the rocket exhaust; the Saturn V rocket nozzles were on gimbals; and so on.

In the presence of the earth's gravitational attraction the rocket will experience an acceleration toward the center of the earth of amount

$$\vec{A}_g = \frac{-g_0 r_0^2}{(r_0 + y)^2} \hat{r} \qquad (42)$$

where g_0 is the acceleration at the earth's surface ($\approx 32.2\ \text{ft/sec}^2$ or $\approx 980\ \text{cm/sec}^2$), r_0 is the radius of the earth (≈ 3963 miles), y is the altitude above sea level, and $\hat{r}$ is a unit normal directed outward from the center of the earth.

In the presence of air resistance, the problem is further complicated by the change in drag force with mass, air density, rocket velocity, and the velocity of sound. The drag coefficient will go through a sharp peak as the rocket passes the sound barrier, and the functional form of this peak will depend on the specific shape. Based on data given by Hoerner (1965), the drag coefficient for a slender conical-nosed rocket with half-vertex angle ε can be approximately described by the following complicated function of the Mach number:

$$C_D \approx \begin{cases} 0.1 \text{ for } M_a < 1 \ (subsonic) \\[2mm] \left. \begin{array}{l} 2.29 \sin \varepsilon - 1.6 \\ + (1.5 - 1.04 \sin \varepsilon) M_a \end{array} \right\} \text{ for } M_a \approx 1 \ (transonic) \\[4mm] 2.1 \sin^2 \varepsilon + \dfrac{0.5 \sin \varepsilon}{\sqrt{M_a^2 - 1}} \text{ for } M_a > 1 \ (supersonic) \end{cases} \qquad (43)$$

where the Mach number M_a (ratio of the speed of the rocket relative to the air to the speed of sound) is given approximately by

$$M_a \approx \frac{V}{1043} \qquad (V \text{ in ft/sec}) \qquad (44)$$

over that part of the atmosphere where air-resistive drag is important. (M_a varies as $1/\sqrt{T_a}$, where $T_a = $ atmospheric temperature in °K.) The drag coefficient rises suddenly in the vicinity of Mach 1 due to compression effects. The coefficient decreases then to an asymptotic limit with increasing Mach number for $M_a > 1$ due to the shielding effect produced by the shock wave at the front of the rocket.

The domain for the argument of the function in Eq. (43) should be adjusted to give continuity at the boundaries of the three regions. For example, the drag coefficient for a V-2 rocket ($\varepsilon \approx 15°$) should be given approximately by

$$C_D \approx \begin{cases} 0.1 \text{ for } M_a < 0.89 \\[2mm] -1 + 1.231 M_a \text{ for } 0.89 \leqslant M_a \leqslant 1.13 \\[2mm] 0.141 + \dfrac{0.129}{\sqrt{M_a^2 - 1}} \text{ for } 1.13 < M_a \end{cases} \qquad (45)$$

The acceleration due to air-resistance drag may be rewritten from Eqs. (14)

and (15) in the form

$$\vec{A}_D = \frac{-0.001189 C_D D(Y) S_M |V| \vec{V}}{m_r} \qquad \text{ft}^{-1} \qquad (V \text{ in ft/sec}) \qquad (46)$$

where V is the velocity of the rocket relative to the air, $D(Y)$ is the relative air density given in Eq. (15), and the mass m_r is determined from the weight W_r at sea level through the relation

$$m_r = \frac{W_r}{g_0} \qquad \text{slugs} \qquad (47)$$

where W_r is in pounds and g_0 in ft/sec^2.

The total acceleration on the rocket (neglecting effects due to the earth's rotation) is then the sum of Eqs. (40), (42), and (46).

It will be helpful to consider setting up a two-dimensional program in respect to a flat-earth model. First we have to get in the data pertinent to the particular rocket. Specifically, we shall assume that the following quantities are entered at the start of the program:

$$W\emptyset = \text{total weight, pounds}$$
$$W1 = \text{weight of fuel, pounds}$$
$$T9 = \text{burn time, seconds}$$
$$T\emptyset = \text{integration time, seconds}$$
$$F\emptyset = \text{rocket-engine thrust, pounds force}$$
$$S9 = S_M = \text{maximum transverse rocket area}$$

The weights must be converted into mass units ("slugs" here) using the acceleration due to the earth's gravity at sea level. We shall designate the rocket's mass and mass consumption by

$$M = \text{rocket mass (in slugs) at variable time } T$$
$$M\emptyset = \text{initial mass of the rocket (in slugs) at } T = 0$$
$$M1 = \text{rate of consumption of fuel mass, slugs/sec}$$

and specify the acceleration by the earth's gravitational attraction through the quantities

$$R\emptyset = \text{radius of the earth, ft,}$$
$$G\emptyset = \text{earth's gravity at sea level, ft/sec}^2$$

After entering the quantities $W\emptyset, \ldots, F\emptyset$ specific to the rocket, the remaining constants of the problem are determined by the lines

```
25   LET G∅ = 32.2
3∅   LET M1 = (W1/G∅)/T9
35   LET M = M∅ = W∅/G∅ + ∅.5*M1*T∅
4∅   LET R∅ = 3963*5280
```

The additional term (.5*M1*T∅) in line 35 is added to provide a slightly more accurate average value of M over the integration period $T\emptyset$ (see lines 4∅∅–49∅ of the program below.)

Next we shall assume that the inertial guidance system in the rocket aims the thrust in a direction making an angle O in respect to the horizontal. Hence that angle also must be entered.

```
5∅   PRINT "ANGLE RESPECT TO HORIZONTAL (DEGREES) = 0"
55   INPUT 0
56   LET 0 = 0*3.14159/18∅
```

If we choose to keep the thrust angle constant during the rocket flight (for example, with an inertial guidance system), there is no point in repeatedly

5.11
Flat-Earth Rocket Program

computing the sin O and cos O during the motion. Hence we shall introduce the quantities

```
57   LET CØ = COS(0)
58   LET SØ = SIN(0)
```

We shall also assume in all rocket problems discussed in this chapter that some internal servo system keeps the rocket thrust directed through the center of mass of the rocket; hence we may neglect yaw and pitch.

Assuming that we store the rocket position, velocity, and acceleration in the arrays $R(I)$, $V(I)$, and $A(I)$, where $I = 1$ corresponds to the horizontal coordinate and $I = 2$ to the vertical one, we have the following initial conditions:

```
60   LET T = R(1) = R(2) = V(1) = V(2) = A(1) = V = Y = Ø
70   LET A(2) = −GØ
```

We shall retain the quantity Y separately for later convenience as a measure of the distance of the rocket above the surface of the earth.

Next we shall compute the relative atmospheric density function, dependent on Y through Eq. (15). Here, to avoid computing exponents when the answer is absurdly small, we shall define this function ($F1$) to be zero when $Y > 10^6$ ft.

```
300   REM RELATIVE ATMOSPHERIC DENSITY (Y IN FEET ABOVE RØ)
305   IF Y < 1E6 THEN 315
310   LET F1 = Ø
311   GOTO 330
315   IF Y > 30000 THEN 325
320   LET F1 = EXP(−3.211E−5*Y)
321   GOTO 330
325   LET F1 = 1.6114*EXP(−4.771E−5*Y)
```

Note that after integrating the equations of motion over interval $TØ$ we shall reiterate to line 300.

Next we keep track of the Mach number ($M9$):

```
330   REM MACH NUMBER (M9) NEEDED FOR DRAG COEFFICIENT
340   LET M9 = V/1043
```

and then compute the drag coefficient. For example, from Eqs. (45):

```
350   REM COMPUTE DRAG COEFFICIENT = C
355   IF M9 > .89 THEN 370
360   LET C = Ø.1
365   GOTO 400
370   IF M9 > 1.13 THEN 390
375   LET C = −1 + 1.231*M9
380   GOTO 400
390   LET C = .141 + .129/SQR(M9*M9 − 1)
```

Finally, we are ready to integrate the equations of motion over the interval $TØ$, using the constant-acceleration approximation:

```
400   REM EQNS OF MOTION NEXT
405   LET A(1) = Ø
410   LET A(2) = −GØ/(1 + Y/RØ)↑2
420   IF T > T9 THEN 450
425   LET M = M − M1*TØ
430   LET A(1) = A(1) + CØ*FØ/M
440   LET A(2) = A(2) + SØ*FØ/M
450   FOR I = 1 TO 2
460   LET A(I) = A(I) − 1.189E − 3*C*F1*S9*V*V(I)/M
470   LET R(I) = R(I) + V(I)*TØ + .5*A(I)*TØ*TØ
480   LET V(I) = V(I) + A(I)*TØ
490   NEXT I
```

Note that the functioning of the rocket motor (lines 425–440) is controlled by the conditional statement on line 420, where $T9$ is the total burn time. Although the statements could have been written in many different ways, the order given above has the virtue that the program may be easily modified to include multiple stage launchings on a round earth with a rotating atmosphere (see discussion later).

Next we want to increment the time, update the values of Y and V, print (or plot) the results, check to make sure the rocket is still in the air, and, if so, reiterate to line 300.

```
500   LET T = T + T0
540   LET Y = R(2)
550   LET V = SQR(V(1)*V(1) + V(2)*V(2))
560   REM PRINT OR PLOT TRAJECTORY
. . .
570   IF T < T9 THEN 590
580   IF Y < = 0 THEN 600
590   GOTO 300
600   REM PRINT DESIRED TRAJECTORY PROPERTIES
. . .
```

The conditional statement on line 570 is added as a practical matter to make sure that rounding errors near $T = 0$ (which can result in slightly negative values of Y) do not permit line 580 to end the flight prematurely. (We will not try to describe a trajectory such as that illustrated in Fig. 5-17.) The choice for the integration interval $T0$ will depend on the accuracy required, as well as the input parameters. One could break up the trajectory in several discrete intervals, choosing two or three different constant values of $T0$ within these intervals. However, it is worth noting specifically that a continuous variation in $T0$ with acceleration would add accumulative systematic errors. Hence, any continuous variation in $T0$ should be avoided. It is also psychologically preferable to have output data displayed that occur at constant time increments. To avoid large quantities of waste paper generated by the teletype output, a simple loop in a dummy parameter is easily incorporated before the PRINT statement on line 560. For example

```
301   FOR J = 1 TO 10
```
closed by
```
559   NEXT J
```

reduces the number of printed lines by ten.

The optimum thrust angle for firing a V-2 rocket can be estimated using $T0 \approx 1$ or 2 sec. However, to get the range to ≈ 1 percent requires $T0 \lesssim 0.1$ sec. (As with the preceding problems in this chapter, the efficiency can be substantially improved through use of the modified Runge–Kutta bootstrap discussed later.)

**5.11
PROBLEM 18**   The Germans started shooting from long distances at Paris again on September 6, 1944, using the V-2 (for "Vergeltungswaffen Zwei" or "Vengeance Weapon Two") rocket. Two days later, the first of more than 1000 such missiles were fired at London. Surprisingly little comment regarding that historical event appeared in the American press of the time. (The big aviation story of the week in *The New York Times* was the impending development of an American 2000-hp propeller-driven fighter plane!) Nearly 3 weeks later, there was a brief story in the "News of the Week in Review" to the effect that "neutral sources"

had reported *test* firings of V-2 rockets made into the North Sea with a range of 200 miles by the group (under Wernher von Braun) at Pennemunde.[†]

The V-2 rocket (of which about 4000 were fired against the Allied forces before the end of World War II) was clearly the direct predecessor of both the American and Russian space programs. The engine had a 55,000-lb thrust and consumed 300 lb of propellant per second. The rocket weighed 27,000 lb at takeoff (including a 2000-lb warhead) and carried 19,200 lb of fuel. The rocket was 47 ft long and had a cylindrical diameter of 4.92 ft (1.5 meters).[‡]

Assuming that the V-2 rocket is fired straight up, how high does it go? Suppose its thrust is maintained at a constant angle in respect to the horizontal during firing. What is the optimum angle for maximum horizontal range? What is the range? How long does it take to get there? How high does it go? What is the maximum velocity during the trip and how fast does it hit the ground? Use the flat-earth approximation and assume that the drag coefficient is given by Eq. (45). How much thrust do you need to get a maximum range of 200 miles?

5.11
PROBLEM 19

A V-2 rocket is launched at a 57° thrust angle in respect to the horizon, and the thrust angle is kept constant during firing. An early-warning radar system detects the rocket at the maximum height of the trajectory and "zaps" it with a gigantic CO_2 laser. The laser pulse has little effect on the hardened nose cone but does manage to roughen up the surface of the rocket enough to increase the normal drag coefficient by 50 percent. How far from the original target does the rocket land? Use the data given in Problem 18.

[†] *The New York Times*, Sept. 24, 1944, Sec. 4, p. 4E, cols. 7 and 8.
[‡] The data on V-2 rocket thrust are taken from Durant (1974a, p. 929). The drag-coefficient data in Eq. (43) are from Hoerner (1965, Chap. 16). (Hoerner was an aerodynamicist for both the Junkers and Messerschmidt companies during the war; some of the V-2 drag-coefficient data he reports were, in fact, taken at Peenemunde.)

The flat-earth approximation is not too bad for a short-range rocket such as the V-2. However, it is certain to give us trouble when we try to put the rocket in orbit. Incorporating the roundness and rotation of the earth is not so hard. It is primarily the incorporation of a controllable thrust angle and the effects of the spinning atmosphere that make the problem complex. For simplicity, we shall limit our discussion to the case where the rocket takes off and moves in the earth's equatorial plane.

It will be easiest to describe the rocket's motion from a fixed reference frame whose origin is coincident with the center of the earth.[19] Combining Newton's laws of motion with his law for universal gravitation, the gravitational acceleration due to the earth that is experienced by the rocket may be written[20]

$$\vec{A}_g = -\frac{G}{R^3}\vec{R} \tag{48}$$

5.12
Modification of the Rocket Program for a Round, Rotating Earth

[19] The center of the earth is, of course, the center of mass of the two-body system composed of the rocket and earth when the rocket's mass is negligible compared to that of the earth. This assumption has, fortunately, been a very good one in all launchings to date. However, if anyone is seriously contemplating rocket travel to neighboring galaxies in a human time scale, special relativity tells us ($E = mc^2$) that we shall have to be more careful about this particular approximation.

[20] That is, the gravitational force exerted on the rocket by the earth is

$$\vec{F}_g = -\frac{G_u M_e m_r}{R^3}\vec{R} = m_r \vec{A}_g$$

where G_u is the universal gravitational constant, M_e is the mass of the earth, and m_r is the mass of the rocket.

where the unit outward normal $\hat{r}$ from our origin is given by

Section 5.12
Modification of the Rocket
Program for a Round, Rotating
Earth

$$\hat{r} = \frac{\vec{R}}{R}$$

and the constant G may be written

$$G = g_0 R_0^2 \tag{49}$$

where

$g_0 =$ gravitational acceleration obtained at the earth's surface (32.2 ft/sec^2 or 9.8 m/sec^2)

$R_0 =$ radius of the earth (3963 miles)

As before, we shall use the scalar quantity Y to measure the height above the earth's surface:

$$Y = R - R_0 \tag{50}$$

Expressing the rocket's thrust, $\vec{F}_0$, in terms of the fixed reference frame takes a little more work. We shall define the direction of this force on the rocket in terms of the angle θ that it makes with the local "horizontal" at the position of the rocket (see Fig. 5-18). Assuming that the thrust lies in the (equatorial) plane of $\hat{i}$ and $\hat{j}$, it may be resolved into a component along $\hat{r}$ and a component along the unit vector $\hat{k} \times \hat{r}$. here we assume that $\hat{k} = \hat{i} \times \hat{j}$ is a unit vector pointing north, hence out of the paper in Fig. 5-18.

Noting that

$$\hat{r} = \frac{R(1)}{R}\hat{i} + \frac{R(2)}{R}\hat{j} \tag{51}$$

in Fig. 5-18 and therefore that

$$\hat{k} \times \hat{r} = \begin{vmatrix} \hat{i} & \hat{j} & \hat{k} \\ 0 & 0 & 1 \\ \dfrac{R(1)}{R} & \dfrac{R(2)}{R} & 0 \end{vmatrix} = -\frac{R(2)}{R}\hat{i} + \frac{R(1)}{R}\hat{j} \tag{52}$$

we may write the acceleration produced by the rocket thrust as

$$\begin{aligned} \mathbf{A}_t &= \frac{F_0}{M_r}\sin\theta\,\hat{r} + \frac{F_0}{M_r}\cos\theta\,(\hat{k} \times \hat{r}) \\ &= [R(1)\sin\theta - R(2)\cos\theta]\frac{F_0}{M_r R}\hat{i} \\ &\quad + [R(2)\sin\theta + R(1)\cos\theta]\frac{F_0}{M_r R}\hat{j} \end{aligned} \tag{53}$$

[Note as a check that Eq. (53) results in the right limiting values when either $R(1)$ or $R(2) \to 0$.]

The remaining important complications arise from the effects of the earth's rotation. There are three primary consequences to be dealt with:

1. If we were to try to describe the motion from a reference frame fixed on the earth, we would see an effective additional force (the *coriolis force*). We have avoided that problem here by fixing our reference frame in a nonrotating frame coincident with the center of the earth. In order to describe the motion in respect to points on the earth, we have to translate the results from our fixed reference frame back to coordinates rotating with the earth. That problem is straightforward but only of interest if you want to know where the rocket lands on the earth.

2. Because the tangential velocity from the earth's rotation is quite substantial (≈ 1500 ft/sec) at the equator, it can be used to advantage to get our

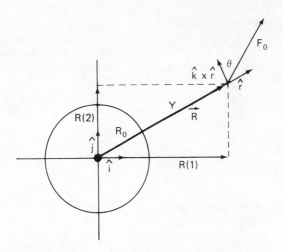

Fig. 5-18. Vectors used to describe the rocket location ($\vec{R}$) and the rocket engine thrust ($\vec{F}_0$). We assume that the vectors $\hat{i}$ and $\hat{j}$ are in the equatorial plane and that $\hat{k} = \hat{i} \times \hat{j}$ points north.

rocket in orbit—provided that we launch it to the east. (This is the same point made earlier in Cavor's trip to the moon.)

3. The earth's atmosphere is also rotating with the earth, and the drag force on our rocket will depend on the relative velocity of the rocket in respect to the air (just as with the football in the Princeton–Dartmouth football game of 1950). The average velocity of the atmosphere (neglecting local winds) at the position of the rocket will be given by

$$\vec{W} = \vec{\omega} \times \vec{R} \tag{54}$$

where $\vec{\omega} = E_0\hat{k}$ is the angular velocity of the earth about its axis (taken to be in the z direction in Fig. 5-18). Thus[21]

$$\vec{W} = \begin{vmatrix} \hat{i} & \hat{j} & \hat{k} \\ 0 & 0 & E_0 \\ R(1) & R(2) & 0 \end{vmatrix} = -E_0 R(2)\hat{i} + E_0 R(1)\hat{j} \tag{55}$$

Thus the rocket will initially have a velocity component tangential to the earth given by Eq. (55) when $T = Y = 0$, and hence zero initial relative velocity in respect to the air. However, as the rocket goes up, drag forces due to relative velocity in respect to the air will become important.

The acceleration due to air resistance may be written

$$\vec{A}_D = \frac{-0.001189 C_D F(Y) S_M U(\vec{V} - \vec{W})}{m_r} \quad \text{ft}^{-1} \tag{56}$$

in place of Eq. (46), where the velocities are in ft/sec and U is defined as the magnitude of the relative velocity. Here

$$U = \text{SQR}((V(1) - W(1))^2 + (V(2) - W(2))^2) \tag{57}$$

and the Mach number is now given by

$$M_a = \frac{U}{1043} \tag{58}$$

instead of Eq. (44) for insertion in the expressions for the drag coefficient, C_D.

---

[21] If you are not used to regarding angular velocities as vectors, just note that the result in Eq. (55) follows from rotating the vector $\vec{R}$ in the equatorial plane about the earth's axis at an angular velocity whose magnitude is E_0 radians per second.

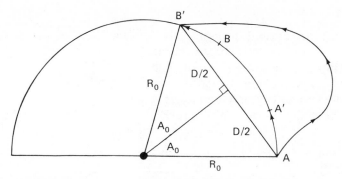

Section 5.12
Modification of the Rocket
Program for a Round, Rotating
Earth

Fig. 5-19. Geometry involved in determining the range of a rocket fired in the equatorial plane as measured by observers on the earth's surface. The rocket is launched at point A and lands at point B′ in the fixed frame. During the time of the flight, points A and B on the earth have rotated to points A′ and B′ in the fixed frame (see the text).

The geometry involved in determining the range of the rocket fired in the earth's equatorial plane is shown in Fig. 5-19. In order to determine the point on the earth where the rocket finally lands, we must store the initial coordinates at launching (corresponding to the point A in Fig. 5-19). If

$$X1 = R(1) \quad \text{and} \quad X2 = R(2) \qquad \text{at } T = 0 \tag{59}$$

and the rocket hits earth at a later time T at the coordinates $R(1)$ and $R(2)$, the straight-line distance between the launch (point A) and the landing (point B′) measured in the fixed reference frame is given by

$$D = \sqrt{(R(1) - X1)^2 + (R(2) - X2)^2} \tag{60}$$

The angle A_0 in Fig. 5-19 is then given by

$$A_0 = \text{ATN}(D/\sqrt{4R_0^2 - D^2}) \tag{61}$$

Hence the arc swept out by the rocket (coincident with the surface of the earth) is

$$D_1 = \text{arc}(AA'BB') = 2A_0 R_0 \tag{62}$$

as measured in the fixed coordinate system.

However, during the rocket's flight, the earth's surface rotated through the arc $R_0 E_0 T$, causing the points A and B to rotate to positions A′ and B′ in the figure. Thus

$$\text{arc}(AA') = \text{arc}(BB') = R_0 E_0 T \tag{63}$$

The actual range of the rocket that would be measured by observers on the earth's surface is therefore

$$D_2 = (2A_0 - E_0 T) R_0 \tag{64}$$

where A_0 is given by Eq. (61), E_0 is the angular velocity of the earth, and T is the duration of the rocket flight. (One must, of course, watch the quadrant on A_0 when the rocket travels more than halfway around the earth.)

Finally, once we get our rocket outside the earth's atmosphere, we can put it in a stable circular orbit of radius R if we can manage to give it a velocity V at the point R which is entirely in the tangential direction and such that the centripetal acceleration for circular motion is just provided by gravitational acceleration. Thus for a circular orbit, we need

$$\frac{V^2}{R} = \frac{G}{R^2}$$

and

$$\vec{V} \cdot \vec{R} = 0 \tag{65}$$

237

Most people will not appreciate how hard it is to put a rocket in a good low-lying circular orbit around the earth until they try doing it themselves. It is virtually impossible to accomplish this feat without being able to control the rocket after it gets above the atmosphere. However, if you can control the thrust angle and burn time, it becomes relatively easy to obtain a good circular orbit. For example, a simple algorithm that works pretty well and requires only a two-position inertial guidance system and the ability to turn off the rocket engine is as follows:

1. Fire the rocket straight up (i.e., $\theta = 90°$ in Fig. 5-18) until it gets above the main effects of the atmosphere (e.g., $Y \geq 40$ miles).
2. Then direct the thrust nearly horizontal (e.g., $\theta \approx 5°$, but optimized for the particular rocket parameters).
3. Monitor V^2 and R and shut off the engine the instant that $V^2 R \geq G$.

Because V is steadily increasing while the rocket engine is on, this algorithm automatically gives us a circular orbit *if* the correct thrust angle in step 2 has been chosen. Of course, there will be a certain minimum angle below which the rocket hits the earth no matter how long the engine is on. And there will also be a maximum angle above which you will run out of fuel before reaching the circular orbit condition.

Modification of the previous flat-earth rocket program to include the effects of roundness and earth's rotation is not too difficult. First, we shall summarize the changes in initial statements. In addition to the previous initial quantities, we need to enter the quantity

$$\text{LET } E\emptyset = 2*3.14159/(24*3600) \tag{66}$$

for the earth's angular velocity. We shall also define a constant

$$\text{LET } G = G\emptyset*R\emptyset*R\emptyset \tag{67}$$

early in the program.

If we launch our rocket from the fixed coordinates $R\emptyset$ and $\emptyset$, the initial conditions now involve

$$R(1) = X1 = R\emptyset \quad \text{and} \quad R(2) = X2 = \emptyset \text{ at} \qquad T = \emptyset \tag{68}$$

Because of the form of Eq. (48), it will also be desirable to keep track of the quantities

$$R = |\vec{R}|, \quad R2 = R*R, \quad \text{and} \quad R3 = R*R*R = R*R2 \tag{69}$$

These quantities are initialized so that $R = R\emptyset$ at $T = 0$. Further, the initial velocity of the rocket in the fixed reference frame is no longer equal to zero. Owing to the earth's rotation,

$$V(1) = -E\emptyset*R(2) \quad \text{and} \quad V(2) = +E\emptyset*R(1) \qquad \text{at } T = \emptyset \tag{70}$$

A significant difference next arises in that we must compute the relative velocity of the rocket in respect to the air, $V(I) - W(I)$, and its magnitude, U, to determine the drag force. We shall compute these quantities starting at line $2\emptyset\emptyset$ and reiterate to this point in determining the motion of the rocket. Defining $W(I)$ as the velocity of the atmosphere we can evaluate its components from Eq. (55).

```
200   REM COMPUTE W AND REL.VEL.MAGNITUDE = U
210   LET W(1) = −E∅*R(2)
220   LET W(2) = +E∅*R(1)
230   LET U = SQR((V(1)−W(1))↑2+(V(2)−W(2))↑2)
```

The relative atmospheric density can be computed as was done previously, starting on line $3\emptyset\emptyset$ of the flat-earth program. The next change we need to make involves the Mach number (*M9*). The appropriate Mach number now is defined in terms of the relative velocity of the rocket in respect to the air. Hence

Section 5.12
Modification of the Rocket
Program for a Round, Rotating
Earth

```
340   LET M9 = U/1043
```

We are then ready to integrate the equations of motion over the interval *T0*. Incorporating Eqs. (53), (56), and (67), the equations of motion may now be solved through the steps

```
400   REMS EQNS OF MOTION NEXT
405   FOR I = 1 TO 2
410   LET A(I) = −(G/R3)*R(I)
415   NEXT I
420   IF T > T9 THEN 450
425   LET M = M −M1*T0
430   LET A(1) = A(1) + (R(1)*S0 − R(2)*C0)*F0/(M*R)
440   LET A(2) = A(2) + (R(2)*S0 + R(1)*C0)*F0/(M*R)
450   FOR I = 1 TO 2
460   LET A(I) = A(I) − 1.18900E − 03*C*F1*S9*U*(V(I) − W(I)/M
470   LET R(I) = R(I) + V(I)*T0 + .5*A(I)*T0*T0
480   LET V(I) = V(I) + A(I)*T0
490   NEXT I
```

We again increment the time and update the other pertinent scalar variables after line 500.

```
500   LET T = T + T0
510   LET R2 = R(1)*R(1) + R(2)*R(2)
520   LET R = SQR(R2)
530   LET R3 = R*R2
540   LET Y = R − R0
550   LET V = SQR(V(1)*V(1) + V(2)*V(2))
560   REM PRINT OR PLOT TRAJECTORY
 . . .
570   IF T < T9 THEN 590
580   IF Y < = 0 THEN 600
590   GOTO 200
```

Again, if you are printing the results on a teletype, it is useful to introduce a loop on a dummy variable between lines 200 and 560 to suppress some of the printout.

Finally, on line 600 we can determine how far the rocket actually went as seen by an observer on the earth.

```
600   REM PRINT DESIRED TRAJECTORY PROPERTIES
 . . .
610   LET D = SQR((R(1) − X1)↑2 + (R(2) − X2)↑2)
620   LET A = ATN(D/SQR(4*R0*R0 − D*D))
630   PRINT (2*A − E0*T)*R0/5280; "MILES RANGE ON EARTH"
```

Here use has been made of Eqs. (60)–(64).

Alternatively, we could have broken the launch phase up into two separate burn periods *T1* and *T2* (entered at the start of the program), where *T9* = *T1* + *T2*. [The computer variable *T1* used here should not be confused with the additional integration time constant introduced in Section 5.17 to program the modified Runge–Kutta method.] Then a single conditional statement after line 420 permits us to jettison the first stage of a multiple-stage rocket and change the rocket parameters for the next time period. For example,

```
422   IF T > T1 THEN 800
```

239

```
800   REM JETTISON FIRST STAGE AND CHANGE THRUST ANGLE
810   PRINT "2ND STAGE THRUST ANGLE RESPECT TO HORIZON"
820   INPUT 0
830   LET 0 = 0*3.14159/180
840   LET C0 = COS(0)
850   LET S0 = SIN(0)
860   LET F0 = ...
870   LET W0 = ...
880   LET W1 = ...
890   LET M1 = W1/G0
900   LET M = W0/G0 + .5*M1*T0
905   PRINT "T1 = ";T1
909   REM NEXT TO BYPASS LINE 422
910   LET T1 = 1.00000E + 20
920   GOTO 425
```

gets rid of the residual mass in the first stage and permits choosing a new thrust angle as well as other rocket parameters for the second stage. Line 910 is put in to prevent being sent back to line 800 by the conditional statement on line 422 the next time through the equations of motion. We could also have changed the maximum cross-sectional area and parameters associated with the drag coefficient. However, presumably by the time the second stage is ignited, we are nearly out of the atmosphere.

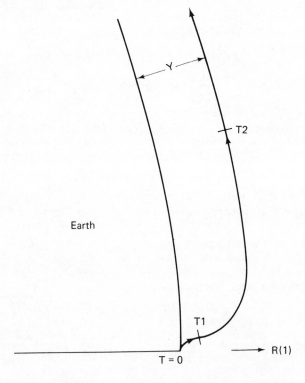

Fig. 5-20. A computed trajectory (Problem 23) as seen from the fixed reference frame whose origin is coincident with the center of the rotating earth. The first stage was jettisoned at time *T1* and the second-stage rocket motor was turned off at time *T2*. The algorithm discussed in the text for obtaining circular orbits was used to determine when to shut the second-stage engine off. The rocket was initially launched "straight up" as seen from the earth at a point $R(1) = R_0$ and $R(2) = 0$ on the equator. The second-stage thrust angle was aimed to the east (vertical in the figure). Note that if we had chosen to launch the rocket to the west, it would have had to turn backward (downward in the figure) as seen from the fixed frame during the second-stage burn.

If our objective is to get into a circular orbit, a few additional statements between 55∅ and 56∅ are helpful. For example,

Section 5.12
Modification of the Rocket
Program for a Round, Rotating
Earth

```
550  LET V2 = V(1)*V(1) + V(2)*V(2)
552  LET V = SQR(V2)
554  IF F∅ = ∅ THEN 560
556  IF V2*R < G THEN 560
557  LET F∅ = ∅
558  PRINT "MOTOR OFF AT";T
560  REM PRINT OR PLOT RESULTS (as before)
     . . .
```

turns off the rocket engine and prints the time when it was turned off. We can then tell how good a circular orbit we got by printing Y as a function of time on line 56∅, or by arranging to print the parameter $V2*R/G$ just as Y goes through a maximum value. This parameter, based on Eq. (65), should be 1.000 for a perfect circle. The next guess for the second-stage thrust angle can be improved based on the departure of $V2*R/G$ from unity, either through a simple Taylor-series correction method or (more simply) by putting the computer operator in the loop (see Fig. 5-20).

**5.12
PROBLEM 20**

Suppose that a V-2 rocket were launched straight up from the equator. After reaching a maximum, it turns around and heads straight down. About how far from the launch site does it land? (According to a private conversation with one of the participants, this particular type of experiment was tried early in the V-2 development program to determine why the rockets tended to blow up during reentry of the atmosphere.)

**5.12
PROBLEM 21**

If you are interested in the longest range on the surface of the earth, is it better to shoot east or west? About how large is the difference in range between those two cases on the equator for the V-2 rocket, and what is the optimum thrust angle in each direction, assuming that it is maintained constant in respect to the local horizontal?

**5.12
PROBLEM 22†**

The Saturn V rocket (also developed under the direction of Werner von Braun) weighs 6.1 million pounds and has a cylindrical diameter of 33 ft. The first stage burns 15 tons of fuel per second, has a thrust of 7.5 million pounds of force, and a burn time of 150 sec. Suppose that it were launched from the equator toward the east at a constant thrust angle of 80° in respect to the horizontal. Suppose further that due to a malfunction, the second stage failed to ignite or separate. How far from the launch site would it land, assuming that it has an effective vertex angle of 30° and hence a drag coefficient that can be approximated by Eqs. (45)? What would the optimum launch angle be for maximum range, and how far does it go then?

**5.12
PROBLEM 23†**

Suppose that you have been given the assignment of putting a large "skylab" in a closely circular orbit at about 200 miles above the surface of the earth and that you are to use a two-stage Saturn V rocket having the following properties:

first stage: Total weight of entire rocket = 6.1 million lb
Thrust = 7.5 million lb

† The Saturn V rocket data in Problems 22 and 23 are based on numbers quoted by Durant (1974b, p. 365). However, the applicability of the drag-coefficient data in Eq. (45) to this problem is merely based on the assumption that the overall effective vertex angle *could* be made to be ≈30°.

Fuel consumption = 15 tons/sec
Burn time = 150 sec (fixed)

second stage: Total weight after jettisoning first stage = 1.025 million lb
Thrust = 1 million lb
Fuel consumption = 2362.5 lb/sec
Burn time = variable up to maximum of 400 sec

Assume that the cylindrical diameter = 33 ft and the effective apex angle = 30° [Eq. (45)] for both stages (see Figs. 5-20 and 5-21). If you fire the first stage straight up, what (constant) thrust angle above the local horizontal direction do you need for the second stage to get into the best circular orbit? (Launch it to

Fig. 5-21. Saturn V booster rocket carrying the Apollo 11 astronauts as it left Cape Kennedy July 16, 1969, on the first trip to put men on the moon. (NASA photograph.)

the east at the equator.) How long does the second stage burn? How high is the final orbit above the earth? How much weight (as measured on the earth's surface) did you succeed in putting into orbit? If you do not have access to a high-resolution plotting device to display the trajectory relative to the earth's surface, print out the time, Y (miles above the earth's surface) and V (mph) every 10 computations. An integration time $(T\emptyset) \approx 2$ sec is adequate for our purposes. (Assume that some unspecified servomechanism keeps the rocket thrust aimed through the center of mass and keeps the yaw and pitch under control.)

5.12
PROBLEM 24

In April 1970, the Apollo 13 space flight did a "figure eight" loop around the moon and returned to earth. (Because of a power failure, the planned moon landing was scrapped.) Write a program to simulate this type of maneuver, starting from a circular orbit above the earth. Based on data given by Durant (1974b, p. 365), we may assume that the rocket has an initial sea-level weight of 310,000 lb, a thrust of 200,000 lb, a rate of fuel consumption of 2.07 million pounds per hour and maximum burn time $(T1)$ of $\frac{1}{9}$ hour.

Use the numerical value for the gravitational acceleration from the earth and moon (given in mph^2) in Problem 17. Assume that the rocket is initially 4,200 miles from the center of the earth and traveling 17,320.5 mph in a nearly circular orbit. (Neglect the earth's rotation and atmosphere.) The geometry is shown in Figs. 5-15 and 5-22, and the moon's position as a function of time is described in Problem 17. Hitting the moon essentially amounts to choosing the right value for the initial angle $A\emptyset$ corresponding to a given burn time. (The angle $A\emptyset$ depends on the relative angular position of the moon and the rocket at $T = 0$.)

If you fire ≈ 80 percent of the rocket fuel starting at $T = 0$, you can reach the moon easily and still have enough fuel left when you get to the moon.

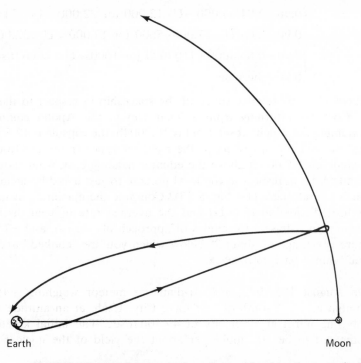

Earth   Moon

Fig. 5-22. Computed trajectory for a figure eight about the moon (see Problem 24). The drawing is to scale. Note from the relative position of the moon that the first half of the trip took much less time than the last half. (The rocket was fired in reverse to slow the spaceship down as it crossed the moon's trajectory.) Note that if you get the angle only slightly wrong, the moon can hurl your rocket off into space.

To leave the earth, put the rocket thrust in the direction of $+\vec{V}$ (the rocket velocity) and leave it on for $T \approx 0.8*T1$. When you cross the moon's orbit, it is a simple matter to fire the rocket backward (in the direction $-\vec{V}$) by reversing the sign on the thrust. If you arrive ahead of the moon by $\approx \frac{1}{4}°$ and fire all the remaining fuel ($\Delta T \approx 0.2*T1$), it is possible (through careful adjustment of $A\emptyset$) to execute a figure eight around the moon and land back on earth (see Fig. 5-22). The exact values for the initial angle $A\emptyset$ will be very sensitive to cumulative errors from the finite integration-time constants ($T\emptyset$) used throughout the trip. The angle will be in the very rough vicinity of $\approx -155°$ but can vary by several degrees, depending on the accuracy of the particular computation.

Because it is a long trip, it will be useful to vary the integration interval over a choice of several different constant values (continuously varying intervals tend to accumulate larger systematic errors than a series of discrete constant intervals). For example, with the rocket engine on, fairly small intervals are required ($T\emptyset \approx 0.01*T1$). For the trip through the intervening space, $T\emptyset \approx 0.5*T1$ is not too bad.

It is useful to print out a simulated spaceship instrument panel including quantities such as time (hours), distance to earth (miles), distance to moon (miles), and rocket velocity (mph) every 20 computations or so. For corrective reiterative computations, it is also very helpful to print out the angular lead of the rocket in respect to the moon (especially as you cross the moon's orbit). If available, a high-resolution plotter can be of great help in keeping track of your trajectory (see Fig. 5-22).

5.12
PROBLEM 25

Based on reentry trajectory and pressure measurements reported by Lee and Goodrich (1972), the drag coefficient for the Apollo command module (in the blunt-end first attitude) can be approximated by

$$C_D \approx \begin{cases} 0.90 + 2.04(34,000-U)/12,000 & \text{for } 22,000 \leq U < 34,000 \text{ ft/sec} \\ 0.90 + 2.04(U-17,000)/5000 & \text{for } 17,000 \leq U < 22,000 \text{ ft/sec} \\ 0.90 + 0.66(4000-U)/3000 & \text{for } 1000 \leq U \leq 4000 \text{ ft/sec} \\ 0.90 & \text{otherwise} \end{cases}$$

where U is the relative speed of the spaceship in respect to the air.[†]

Consider returning from a lunar trip in the Apollo command module. Assuming the weight at sea level is 10,000 lb, the capsule is 12.5 ft in diameter, and the velocity in respect to the fixed reference frame is 41,000 ft/sec at an altitude of 310,000 ft above the equator heading east, what should your angle of attack be in respect to the local horizon to just avoid bouncing back off the earth's atmosphere (see Fig. 5-23)? Compute the maximum instantaneous rate of heat dissipation ($\vec{F}_D \cdot \vec{U}$) and the average rate of heat dissipation during reentry (in ft-lb/sec) for angles of approach of -5, -6, and $-7°$. (In practice, there is a range of about $2°$ below which you are "cooked" and above which you bounce back into space.)

5.12
PROBLEM 26

On August 10, 1972, a 13-ft-diameter meteor weighing $\approx 450,000$ lb was spotted at $T = 0$ south of Salt Lake City, Utah, at an altitude of 47.2 miles, traveling north at a velocity of 49,300 ft/sec. The initial kinetic energy was estimated to be 10^{14} joules, or about the yield of the nuclear weapons that

---

[†] Although no physical explanation of the sharp peak at $\approx 22,000$ ft/sec ($\approx 6.7 \times 10^5$ cm/sec) is given in the paper by Lee and Goodrich, it might possibly arise from near resonance for molecular dissociation processes. For example, the peak occurs at about that speed which each oxygen atom would need in the O_2 molecule for the total kinetic energy of relative vibrational motion to exceed the dissociation energy.

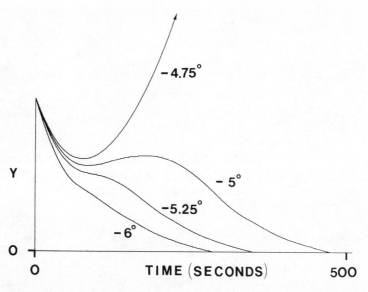

Fig. 5-23. Several representative trajectories for the reentry problem. The angles are the "attack" angles in respect to the local horizontal at $T = 0$ and the initial conditions in Problem 25 were assumed with an integration time constant ($T\emptyset$) of 1 sec.

destroyed Hiroshima and Nagasaki. It missed hitting the earth by 35.9 miles slightly north of Craters of the Moon National Park, Idaho, 38.6 sec later.†

Neglecting the earth's rotation, estimate the initial angle that the meteor's velocity made in respect to the local horizon at $T = 0$. How different would the angle have had to be at $T = 0$ for the meteor to be just captured by the atmosphere? In other words, how narrow a miss was it in degrees? Assume that the drag coefficient is the same as that for the Apollo command module given in Problem 25.

† Because of the availability of satellite tracking data, the accuracy of the trajectory data for this meteor exceeds that for any other previously known. See the discussion by Rawcliffe et al. (1974). Various accounts have been given in the popular press: see, for example, "The day we nearly lost Utah," Reuters dispatch, Feb. 20, 1974. Evidently, some of the best available photographs were taken by a vacationing housewife from Nebraska, Mrs. James M. Baker. Also, see the article by Jacchia (1974) which contains photographs and a summary of the trajectory data.

Being the most massive planet in the solar system, Jupiter gets blamed for a lot of things. Among the most potentially disastrous activities is its trick of hurling massive objects in our direction.

Certainly the most controversial of these accusations is the one made by Velikovsky (1950) regarding the birth of Venus. Velikovsky argued that around 1500 B.C. a fiery mass was torn from Jupiter, underwent a near collision with the earth, and then settled in orbit about the sun as the planet Venus. His case rests largely on the fact that a number of religious texts seem to agree that the earth experienced a major cosmic trauma at about 1500 B.C. in which forests were scorched, rivers were evaporated, and large numbers of people were killed. However, the additional fact that Venus has 81.6 percent as much mass as the earth makes it hard to believe that the earth would have gotten off that easy in such an encounter.

There have been other reports of "attack from outer space" with varying degrees of documentation: for example, the huge meteor (estimated weight of 11,000 tons) that made the Arizona crater in prehistoric times, the Siberian incident of 1908, and the recent near miss over Utah–Idaho and Montana (see

5.13
Comets and Other Space Probes

245

Fig. 5-24. Photograph of Comet Kohoutek taken in the vacuum ultraviolet on January 7, 1974, by Skylab astronauts. (Photo provided by the Naval Research Laboratory.) The picture represents a photograph of the hydrogen cloud about the comet, some 3 million miles in extent.

Problem 26 and Rawcliffe et al., 1974). The second of these events has generated some of the most interesting scientific speculation.

On the morning of June 30, 1908, an enormous explosion occurred over the Tunguska region of central Siberia. Trees were blown down radially within a circle of 20 miles in diameter and the charred tree trunks in the center of the circle could still be seen from the air 50 years later. Eyewitness observers reported a huge fireball crossing the sky that was visible from 250 miles away.

Explanations offered for the Tunguska event have ranged from a nuclear attack from outer space, through collision with a meteor made of "antimatter," to a direct hit by a small "black hole."[22] The absence of unusual amounts of meteor dust in the area and the high-altitude nature of the blast rules out the Arizona-type meteor interpretation. Despite early reports to the contrary, the lack of unusual amounts of radioactivity rules out the nuclear-attack theory. Similarly, if a small "black hole" really went through the earth at that point, it is surprising that something comparably catastrophic was not noticed when it came out on the other side. The most plausible explanation of the Tunguska event relies on some properties of comets that were only recently discovered by experimental observations made outside the earth's atmosphere. In addition to the previously held view that comet heads were huge "dirty snowballs," it is now known that they are surrounded by enormous clouds of hydrogen. This discovery was first made in 1969 through spectral photographs taken of Comet Bennett by rocketborne cameras. More recently, this type of study has been extended to Comet Kohoutek by photographing the comet from the Skylab on the Lyman alpha line of hydrogen (see Fig. 5-24). The current theory is that ice present in the comet evaporates when the comet nears the sun and that it is broken down by solar radiation into its basic constituents of hydrogen and oxygen. The lighter hydrogen atoms then escape, producing a huge hydrogen

[22] For a popular discussion of the "black-hole" hypothesis, see Walter Sullivan, "A Hole in the Sky," *The New York Times Magazine*, July 14, 1974, p. 11.

246

cloud around the comet. The net result in the case of Comet Kohoutek was the transformation of something that was almost invisible to the naked eye on the earth's surface to a gigantic spectacle some 3 million miles in extent when photographed on the Lyman alpha line outside the earth's atmosphere. (This radiation in the vacuum ultraviolet at 1216 Å is, of course, completely absorbed by the earth's atmosphere.) This additional information about comets provides a very simple and plausible interpretation of the Tunguska event: it probably was caused by a head-on collision with a comet and the resultant high-altitude explosion was simply the result of hydrogen reacting chemically with oxygen during entry into the earth's atmosphere.

A widely held theory of comet origin suggests that most of them come from a huge cloud bound to the sun about 10,000 to 100,000 astronomical units away (i.e., about halfway to the nearest star). Perturbations from other stars from time to time send comets from this cloud toward the inner solar system. These comets would normally be on nearly parabolic orbits with extremely long periods. However, one occasionally comes near enough to the planet Jupiter and in the right trajectory to give up a large portion of its kinetic energy. The comet can then be deflected in toward the Sun and be bound in a much more elliptic, shorter-period orbit.

The mechanism of energy exchange is similar to that which we have encountered in the moon-trip problems, but can be enormously more effective because of the huge mass and large orbit of Jupiter.

The mechanism of capturing comets is probably easiest to understand by means of its inverse process. A nice man-made example of the inverse process was provided by the Pioneer 10 flight past Jupiter. (The flight was launched on March 2, 1972, and passed within 81,000 miles of Jupiter on December 3, 1973.) The basic idea is to have the space probe cross Jupiter's orbit just after the planet has gone by. The huge pull it then receives in the direction of Jupiter's motion gives the spaceship enough additional velocity to escape the sun's gravitational acceleration (see Fig. 5-25). If it had arrived at Jupiter's orbit just before the planet, the spaceship would have been deflected in the opposite direction in Fig. 5-25 and hence would have been slowed down by the encounter.

The comet capture effect can be seen by reversing the direction of the spaceprobe trajectory in Fig. 5-25. The comet would thus come in at high velocity from the lower left-hand corner of the figure, cross Jupiter's orbit just

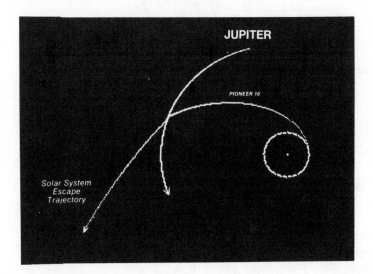

Fig. 5-25. Computer simulation of the Pioneer 10 "fly by" past Jupiter (see Problem 27).

after the planet and be decelerated in toward the earth. The point is that when the initial velocities are opposing, the light particle gets slowed down in this type of collision, whereas when the initial velocities are in the same direction, the light particle is sped up. From the geometry involved, it is apparent that there is a sort of focusing effect in the decelerating type of collision and that Jupiter's large orbital diameter enhances the effectiveness with which that large planet can throw all sorts of incoming bodies from outer space in our direction.

Because the numbers involved in interplanetary travel are exceedingly large when expressed in feet, meters, seconds, and so on, it will be helpful to redefine our system of units completely in working such problems. The unit of length adopted by the astronomers (the *astronomical unit*) is the mean distance from the earth to the sun (92,956,000 miles). We shall adopt one sidereal year (= 365.256 days, or the period for the earth's orbit about the sun) as our unit of time. Hence, our unit of velocity will then be 1 astronomical unit per sidereal year and our unit of acceleration will be 1 astronomical unit per year squared. As may be seen from the summary of planetary data in Table 3, this convention results in quite manageable numbers for distance, time, and acceleration. (The 1's appearing on the row for earth, of course, are the basis of the present definitions.) Even the conversion to commonplace units is not too bad. For example, 1 ft/sec² ≈ 2029 astronomical units per year², and the general value for the gravitational acceleration by the sun is pleasantly manageable (see Table 3).

5.13: Table 3 Some Properties of the Solar System (in astronomical units)

Object	Mass[a]	Escape Velocity[b]	Equatorial Radius[c]	Relative Surface Gravity[d]	Gravitational Acceleration[e]	Mean Orbit Radius[c]	Orbit Period[f]
Sun	332,950	130	4.653×10^{-3}	28	$39.47/R^2$ [g]	—	
Mercury	0.055	0.88	1.627×10^{-5}	0.38	$6.549 \times 10^{-6}/R^2$	0.387	0.2408
Venus	0.816	2.17	4.048×10^{-5}	0.89	$0.949 \times 10^{-4}/R^2$	0.723	0.6152
Earth	1	2.36	4.263×10^{-5}	1	$1.183 \times 10^{-4}/R^2$	1	1
Moon	0.01229	0.501	1.162×10^{-5}	0.165	$1.450 \times 10^{-6}/R^2$	1.0	0.0748
Mars	0.107	1.05	2.259×10^{-5}	0.38	$1.263 \times 10^{-5}/R^2$	1.524	1.881
Jupiter	317.9	12.6	4.809×10^{-4}	2.6	$3.915 \times 10^{-2}/R^2$	5.203	11.86
Saturn	95.2	7.47	4.034×10^{-4}	1.1	$1.165 \times 10^{-2}/R^2$	9.540	29.46
Uranus	14.5	4.75	1.592×10^{-4}	0.96	$1.584 \times 10^{-3}/R^2$	19.18	84.01
Neptune	17.4	5.09	1.485×10^{-4}	1.5	$2.154 \times 10^{-3}/R^2$	30.07	164.8
Pluto	?	?	$1.94? \times 10^{-5}$	?	?	39.67	249.9

Source: Data based on values given by Whipple (1971). All units normalized to values for earth.

[a] In respect to earth.

[b] The unit of velocity is astronomical units of distance per sidereal year
(1 ft/sec = 6.430×10^{-5} astronomical units per year)

[c] The astronomical unit of distance = 92,956,000 miles = mean distance from the earth to sun
(1 ft = 2.037×10^{-12} astronomical units)

[d] The surface gravity is normalized to the value on earth (32.088 ft/sec²) at the Equator.

[e] The unit of acceleration is astronomical units per (sidereal year)²
(1 ft/sec² = 2029 astronomical units per yr²)

[f] The unit of time is the sidereal year
(1 sec = 3.169×10^{-8} sidereal years)

[g] R in the general expressions for gravitational acceleration is the distance to the center of the body in astronomical units.

The center of the sun is the obvious place for the origin of our coordinate system because it is also the center of mass of the solar system to high accuracy. The only mildly complicated part of the space-travel problem is getting the relative distances and directions correctly specified for the acceleration from the different planets. Fortunately, the planets are widely spaced and we can treat the problem of traveling from one planet to another with pretty good accuracy merely by including the gravitational attraction of the sun and the particular two planets involved. For example, in travelling from the earth to Jupiter, it will be a pretty good approximation to assume that the acceleration on the spaceship is given by

$$\vec{A} = -\frac{39.47\vec{R}}{R^3} + \frac{1.183 \times 10^{-4}(\vec{E}-\vec{R})}{|\vec{E}-\vec{R}|^3} + \frac{0.03915(\vec{J}-\vec{R})}{|\vec{J}-\vec{R}|^3} \tag{71}$$

where $\vec{R}$, $\vec{E}$, and $\vec{J}$ are the locations of the spaceship, the earth, and Jupiter from the origin. Further, because the mass of the spaceship is generally negligible compared to the other masses involved, we can specify the locations of the planets in terms of the time and only have to integrate the equations of motion for the spaceship itself. Assuming that the planets can be regarded as moving in coplanar, circular orbits with the periods shown in Table 3, it is a simple matter to specify the planets in terms of their angular positions at $T = 0$. For example, for the Earth–Jupiter trip,

$$\left.\begin{array}{l} E(1) = COS(A1 * T) \\ E(2) = SIN(A1*T) \end{array}\right\} \text{ where } A1 = 2*3.14159 \tag{72}$$

and

$$\left.\begin{array}{l} J(1) = 5.203*COS(A2*T + A\emptyset) \\ J(2) = 5.203*SIN(A2*T + A\emptyset) \end{array}\right\} \text{ where } A2 = 2*3.14159/11.86 \tag{73}$$

and $A\emptyset$ is the angular position of Jupiter relative to the earth. One must also be careful to put in the right values for the initial position and velocity of the spaceship. For example, if the spaceship leaves an orbit about the earth at $T = 0$, the initial position is given by Eq. (72) plus the relative position of the spaceship in respect to the center of the earth; similarly, the initial velocity is the velocity of the earth at $T = 0$ plus the relative velocity of the spaceship in respect to the center of the earth at that time. Thus, if the spaceship is initially in an orbit 200 miles above the earth in the $R(1)$ direction and leaves the earth at midnight ($T = 0$) with a relative velocity of $V\emptyset$ astronomical units/year, the spaceship's position and velocity at $T = 0$ may be written

$$\begin{array}{l} R(1) = 1 + 4.653 \times 10^{-3} \\ R(2) = 0 \\ V(1) = 0 \\ V(2) = 2*3.14159 + V\emptyset \end{array} \tag{74}$$

On the trip to Jupiter, we merely have to be careful to get the angle $A\emptyset$ specified to correspond to the position of Jupiter in respect to the earth when the spaceship left.

5.13 PROBLEM 27	Write a program to simulate a trip such as that made by Explorer 10 to Jupiter. Let the spaceship leave the earth's position with the initial coordinates given in Eq. (74) and adjust the angle $A\emptyset$ so that you arrive at Jupiter's orbit just after the planet has gone by. If a high-resolution plotter is not available, print the angular lead of the rocket in respect to Jupiter, along with the magnitude of the distance from Jupiter and from the sun. Don't worry about firing rockets; just assume the initial velocity is specified as $(2\pi + 1.8)$ astronomical units/yr.
5.13 RESEARCH PROBLEM	See if you can demonstrate the inverse (comet-capturing) process to the Pioneer 10 journey illustrated in Fig. 5-25.

One of the major triumphs of Newtonian physics was the closed-form solution for the motion of two particles under an inverse-square law, attractive force. The solution was effected by reducing the original two-body problem into two, equivalent one-body problems involving: (1) the motion of one particle located at the center of mass (having a total mass $= M_1 + M_2 =$ sum of the two masses); and (2) the motion of another particle in respect to the center of mass [having an effective mass $= M_1 M_2 / (M_1 + M_2)$]. In this manner, such widely diverse problems as the motion of the earth about the sun in astronomy and the motion of the electron about the proton in the hydrogen atom can be handled in closed form in physics. However, it has not been possible to extend this type of simple, closed-form analysis to the next more complex problem. The motion of two planets about the sun or the motion of two electrons about the nucleus of a helium atom must generally be treated through some sort of perturbation-expansion method. For example, one could start out with the dominant two-body (e.g., the two sun–planet, or the two nucleus–electron) interactions involved and then do a series expansion in terms of the smaller planet–planet (or electron–electron) interactions. Such perturbation methods can be very powerful and, with many problems, the most effective way to use a computer is simply to facilitate evaluation of the expansion process numerically.[23] However, the object of the present discussion is to show how simply the entire problem may be set up from the beginning for numerical solution with a computer.

Although we have already solved some very difficult three-body problems in the present chapter in the discussion of rocket travel, the solutions have, so far, been made with the very important limiting assumption that the spaceship mass was negligible compared to the planetary mass. That assumption is, of course, a very good one in the case of the spaceship problem. However, it would make a very poor assumption in treating something like the collision between Venus and the earth in the Velikovsky hypothesis. Obviously, in that case we would have to include the mutual interaction (effectively Newton's third law) of the two bodies of comparable mass while also under the influence of the sun's gravity. The latter means that we have to integrate the equations of motion simultaneously for each of the planets' coordinates in the problem. If we are careful in the way we set the problem up, the extension from 2 to N planets becomes a simple modification (although one costing proportionately more computer time).

It will be easiest to set up the N-body problem by replacing our previous column arrays for acceleration, position, and velocity with matrices. Specifically, we shall adopt the convention that

$A(J, I) =$ component of acceleration acting on the Jth body in the Ith direction

$V(J, I) =$ component of velocity of the Jth body in the Ith direction

$R(J, I) =$ component of position vector of the Jth body in the Ith direction

where all these quantities are measured in respect to a fixed reference frame whose origin is preferably (although not necessarily) at the center of mass for the entire system. In the case of the solar system, the origin will be the center of the sun.

After defining the interaction coefficients, the initial positions, and velocities for all N bodies, we go on to integrate the equations of motion. It will be instructive first to set up these equations for the solar system without the planet–planet interaction terms. (We shall leave room in the program to introduce these interaction terms at a later point.)

[23] There are several different methods used in practice. For representative reviews of the planetary-perturbation-theory problem, see Kuiper and Middlehurst (1961).

Ignoring the interaction terms, the equations of motion may be integrated in the constant-acceleration approximation in the following manner:

```
300   REM REITERATE TO HERE
400   REM EQNS OF MOTION FOR N PLANETS ABOUT THE SUN
410   FOR J = 1 TO N
420   LET R2 = R(J,1)↑2 + R(J,2)↑2
430   LET R = SQR(R2)
440   LET R3 = R*R2
450   FOR I = 1 TO 2 (assuming coplanar motion)
460   LET A(J,I) = −G0*R(J,I)/R3
470   REM LEAVE SPACE FOR INTERACTION TERMS
...
510   LET R(J,I) = R(J,I) + V(J,I)*T0 + 0.5*A(J,I)*T0*T0
520   LET V(J,I) = V(J,I) + A(J,I)*T0
530   NEXT I
540   NEXT J
550   LET T = T + T0
560   REM PRINT OR PLOT RESULTS
...
570   GOTO 300
```

Using the astronomical units in Table 3, $G0 = 39.47$ for the sun's gravitational attractive acceleration. The program as it stands represents the zeroth approximation to the real problem: we merely get independent elliptical motion for all the N (bound) planets. Although this much of the problem can be solved exactly in closed form, it is worthwhile running this much of the program separately just to make sure that everything is properly defined. Although written for coplanar motion (two dimensions), the necessary modification of lines 420 and 450 to extend the program to three dimensions is trivial; (i.e. line 450 becomes FOR $I = 1$ TO 3 and we add $+R(J, 3)↑2$ to line 420.)

5.14
PROBLEM 28

Write a program to solve the solar system for the first eight planets for which data are summarized in Table 3. Neglect the planet–planet interaction terms. Assume that the motion is coplanar with the same rotation sense and that all planets are in circular orbits and distributed along the x axis ($I = 1$) at $T = 0$. If you have access to a high-resolution plotter, plot the positions of the planets in intervals of $T0 = 0.001$ year for 0.5 year. Otherwise, print the angular position of the planets and distance from the sun at 0.1-year intervals for the same total period of time. (Save your results—or program—to compare with the results of the next problem.)

Next we want to incorporate all the planet–planet interaction terms (see Fig. 5-26). In simplest mathematical form, the interaction terms may be incorporated merely by adding a term to the acceleration acting on the Jth planet in the Ith direction so that the total acceleration becomes

$$A'(J, I) = A(J, I) + \sum_{K \neq J}^{N} \frac{G(K)(R(K, I) - R(J, I))}{|\vec{R}(K) - \vec{R}(J)|^3} \tag{75}$$

where $G(K)$ is the attraction coefficient of the Kth planet (summarized in Table 3) and $R(K, I)$ is the Ith component of the vector, $\vec{R}(K)$, from the origin to the Kth planet. The terms $K = J$ must, of course, be excluded in the summation over all N planets to avoid the singularity that would result in the denominator. (The latter would correspond to a "self-force" on the Kth planet which we, of course, want to omit in the calculation.)

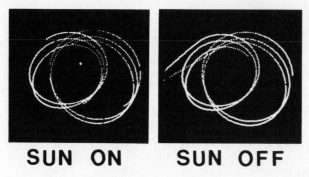

SUN ON   SUN OFF

Fig. 5-26. The three-body problem with and without the interaction from the "third" body. The trajectories on the left correspond to two massive planets interacting with each other and with the sun's gravitational attraction. Without the planet–planet interaction, the two orbits would be ellipses. At the instant the photograph on the left was taken, the sun's attraction was turned off and the continuing trajectory is shown at the right. The two planets then move toward each other as they proceed off the screen to the left. The constants and initial conditions were arbitrarily chosen to give a large observable effect.

Note that the additional terms in Eq. (75) include the action–reaction terms in Newton's third law. It is easiest to keep the signs on these terms straight by treating them directly in terms of accelerations, as done in Eq. (75). However, it should be noted that the corresponding forces ($\vec{F}_{JK} = m_J \vec{a}_K = -\vec{F}_{KJ}$) are indeed equal and opposite.

The solar system (including the sun's motion) could be described entirely by such terms (see Problem 32). However, the motion of the sun is negligible unless perturbed by some external massive object, and including the sun's motion increases the computing time needlessly in most cases of interest.

The terms in the denominator of Eq. (75) are worth computing in advance for each iteration. By storing these denominator terms in a matrix, $D(J, K)$, we may avoid the needless extra computation that would be involved in determining first $|\vec{R}(K) - \vec{R}(J)|$ and then $|\vec{R}(J) - \vec{R}(K)|$. We shall define these matrix elements so that

$$D(J, K) = D(K, J) = \sum_I |(R(K, I) - R(J, I))|^3 \tag{76}$$

These terms may be added to the program before our earlier line 400 in the following manner:

```
300   REM COMPUTE MATRIX OF DENOMINATORS FOR INTERACTION TERMS
310   FOR J = 1 TO N
320   FOR K = 1 TO J − 1
330   LET D2 = (R(K,1) − R(J,1))↑2 + (R(K,2) − R(J,2))↑2
340   LET D = SQR(D2)
350   LET D(J,K) = D(K,J) = D*D2
360   NEXT K
370   NEXT J
```

This program does not define the diagonal terms $D(J, J)$. However, the only place one would really need those would be in a MAT PRINT check of matrix D. For the latter purpose, one need merely initialize the matrix with a MAT $D = IDN(N, N)$ command at the start of the program.

Having stored the matrix of denominators at the start of each reiteration loop, we may then include the interaction terms through the following modification of the previous program:

```
470   FOR K = 1 TO N
480   IF K = J THEN 500
490   LET A(J,I) = A(J,I) + G(K)*(R(K,I) − R(J,I))/D(K,J)
500   NEXT K
```

We, of course, must READ (or otherwise enter) the values for the various planetary interaction coefficients at the start of the program. The latter can be incorporated in a DATA statement made up from appropriate entries in Table 3. For example,

```
900   REM GRAVITATIONAL ACCELERATION DATA NEXT
905   DATA 39.47, 6.549E-6, 0.949E-4, 1.183E-4, 1.263E-5, 3.915E-2
910   DATA 1.165E-2, 1.584E-3, 2.154E-3
```

includes the sun and list of eight planets. Hence the statements

```
10   READ G0
20   FOR I = 1 TO 8
25   READ G(I)
30   NEXT I
```

get the gravitational attraction constants into the program.

Similarly, we can store values for the mean orbit radii and periods (from Table 3) in data statements to get the planets launched with realistic values for their initial positions and velocities. After $T = 0$, of course, they are on their own and their positions will be determined by integrating the equations of motion.

5.14
PROBLEM 29

Modify your program for the previous problem to include gravitational interaction between the various pairs of planets. Using the previous initial conditions, really solve the N-body problem as applied to our solar system. You will need $T0 \leq 0.001$ to get reasonable accuracy. Compute the distance from the earth to the sun for 0.5 sidereal year with and without the planet–planet interaction and see if you can observe a meaningful difference. (Fortunately, our solar system is very stable in the absence of violent external perturbations.)

Suppose that you were to include only the first three planets and were to assume that each had 0.1 times the mass of the sun (still approximating the sun as the center of mass). About how long would it be before the first collision? Suppose there were only the first two planets, each with 0.1 times the solar mass. How long would it be now before the first collision?

5.14
PROBLEM 30

Consider a solar system made of our sun, the planet Venus, the earth, and our moon. Launch them all colinearly at $T = 0$ in coplanar, circular orbits (see Fig. 5-27). How massive does Venus have to be to steal our moon in 0.25 years? Neglect motion of the sun. (If you do not have a high-resolution display, print the time and magnitude of distances from the moon to the two planets involved at ≈ 0.01-year intervals, with $T0 \leq 0.0001$ year.)

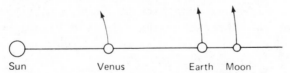

Fig. 5-27

5.14
PROBLEM 31

Consider a solar system made up from a coplanar sun, earth, and moon which are arranged colinearly as shown at $T = 0$ with initial velocities for circular orbits (see Fig. 5-28).

Suppose that at $T = 0$ Tunguska, Siberia, is suddenly hit by an "anti-Mars." From Table 3, 10.7 percent of the earth's mass (hence gravitational attraction) is suddenly converted into radiated energy. For simplicity, assume that the earth's velocity does not change instantaneously but that momentum is conserved by the sudden burst of gamma rays from Siberia. How much effect is there on the earth's and moon's orbits?

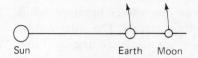

Fig. 5-28

5.14
RESEARCH
PROBLEM

Write a program to investigate the Velikovsky hypothesis. For example, at $T = 0$ consider a coplanar solar system made up with the sun, earth, and Jupiter. Suppose they are colinear at $T = 0$ in the circular-orbit condition and that Venus is fired at $T = 0$ with the escape velocity for Jupiter (given in Table 3) and at an angle θ with the x axis (see Fig. 5-29). By adjusting θ, see if you can get Venus into an orbit about the sun with a mean radius less than 1 astronomical unit.

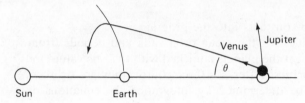

Fig. 5-29

5.14
PROBLEM 32

Modify your program for the solar system to allow for the sun's motion. For example, let $R(1, I)$, $V(1, I)$, and $A(1, I)$ correspond to the sun's position, velocity, and acceleration. Then $G(1) = 39.47$ astronomical units. Our previous program is then made up entirely of "interaction terms" (e.g., we can let $A(J, I) = \emptyset$ on line 46$\emptyset$ and delete lines 42$\emptyset$ through 44$\emptyset$). After making the required modification, try it out on the solar system consisting of the first two planets to make sure it works. Then simulate a collision between the solar system and another star whose mass is equal to that of the sun [i.e., $G(J)$ for the star $= 39.47$]. Take the following initial conditions for the other star:

$$R(J, 1) = -1.5$$
$$R(J, 2) = -0.5$$
$$V(J, 1) = 9$$
$$V(J, 2) = 0$$

For simplicity, just consider the earth bound to the sun at $T = 0$ in a circular orbit with $R(J, 1) = 1$ and $R(J, 2) = 0$. Show that the earth is captured by the other star (see Fig. 5-30). If you do not have a high-resolution display, print out the magnitudes of the distance from the earth to the two suns at intervals of 0.1 year ($T\emptyset \leq 0.001$ year). Next do the same computation for an incident star with 10 times as much initial velocity. Note that the exchange process is most efficient when the incident star velocity is comparable to the planet velocities.

5.14
RESEARCH
PROBLEM

See if you can simulate the creation of a stable solar system by a star-collision model. Because such an investigation will otherwise tend to eat up lots of computer time, it is well worth incorporating the modified Runge–Kutta method discussed in Section 5.17. Among other questions, it would be of interest to estimate the time required for the remaining products of such a collision to settle down into stable circular orbits.

5.14
RESEARCH
PROBLEM

Investigate a classical model of charge-exchange collisions in atomic physics. For example, consider a proton incident on a ground-state hydrogen atom in which the electron is initially in a circular orbit with the Bohr radius (see Fig. 5-30).

Fig. 5-30. Simulating a solar-exchange collision or "planet stealing" (see Problem 32). A star with mass equal to that of our sun is incident from the left at slightly greater than the solar escape velocity and with an impact parameter of 0.5 astronomical unit. The trajectories for the two planets shown correspond to those for Venus and the earth (assumed to be in coplanar circular orbits at $T = 0$). The new sun kicks the old one out and keeps the two planets (in much more elliptic orbits). The process is similar to a resonant charge exchange collision in atomic physics in which, for example, an alpha particle (helium nucleus) would pick off both electrons from a helium atom. The process is roughly resonant when the relative velocity of the incident sun (alpha particle) is comparable to the orbital velocity of the planets (electrons). Note that the exchange collision is somewhat analogous to a nearly head-on collision between two identical billiard balls in which the one initially at rest trades places with the incident one.

The force acting on a particle of electrical charge q in the presence of an electric field $\vec{E}$ is, by definition,

$$\vec{F} = q\vec{E} \tag{77}$$

and, in general, the electric field is calculable from some potential that is in itself determined by solving Maxwell's equations with the appropriate boundary conditions. (In practice, one might merely measure the electrostatic potential corresponding to a given geometry in an electrolytic tank and then fit it empirically to a sensible functional form.)

As long as one confines one's attention to constant voltages applied across infinite parallel-plate condensors, the electric field is uniform and we are faced with a uniform acceleration problem which is essentially the same as that for free fall in a vacuum near the surface of the earth. One could, of course, liven the problem up somewhat by considering charged pith balls moving in glycerine; and so on. However, such problems really would not be any different than those involving wind resistance and other forms of friction that we disposed of earlier in this chapter.

The neat thing about electric fields is that they can be made extremely nonhomogeneous (as long as you do not violate Maxwell's equations). Further, if you run electrons and ions through them in vacuum, extremely large

5.15
Electric Fields: The Quadrupole
Mass Spectrometer[24]

[24] The remaining sections of this chapter are intended primarily for readers with a strong interest in physics. Although the problems discussed all have considerable practical importance, some familiarity with electromagnetic theory on an introductory level will be helpful in understanding this material. The equivalent of a one-year introductory-level college physics course is probably adequate. However, the material will be more readily comprehended by physics and engineering students at the junior or senior level.

accelerations can be obtained without all the massive equipment needed in
something like the space program to produce large accelerations with macros-
copic objects. The acceleration for a nonrelativistic charged particle moving in
an electric field $\vec{E}$ is, of course,

$$\vec{A} = \frac{q}{m}\vec{E} = \frac{\vec{F}}{m} \tag{78}$$

where for an electron [$q \approx 1.6 \times 10^{-19}$ coulomb (c) or $\approx 4.8 \times 10^{-10}$ electrostatic
unit; $m_e \approx 0.91 \times 10^{-27}$ gram (g) $= 0.91 \times 10^{-30}$ kilogram (kg)], an acceleration
$\approx 1.76 \times 10^{11}$ meter (m)/sec$^2 = 1.76 \times 10^{13}$ centimeter (cm)/sec^2 can be obtained
from a field of only 1 volt (v)/m. Another way of putting it is that electrons
that have fallen through a 1-V potential from rest acquire a velocity of
$\approx 0.59 \times 10^8$ cm/sec $= 0.59 \times 10^6$ m/sec. The accelerations can thus be huge; but,
of course, they usually do not act on the particle for very long. Positive atomic
ions (having masses $\approx 1840 A m_e$, where A is the mass number) of course have
proportionately lower accelerations (for longer times) because of their larger
masses.

The quadrupole mass spectrometer (developed by W. Paul and coworkers
at Bonn, West Germany) represents a fairly interesting problem in electrodynamics. At the same time, it has some ominous potential sociopolitical
implications. For many years following World War II, the optimistic outlook
for the future of civilization rested on the belief that small countries would
never be able to solve the technological difficulties involved in separating the
isotopes in uranium on a large-enough scale to permit building nuclear
weapons. The diffusion-separation plants developed in the United States as
part of the fission-weapons program are too huge to conceal and probably
could not be supported economically by small countries. On the other hand,
the exceedingly clever resonance technique developed by Paul and his colleagues (see, e.g., Paul and Raether, 1955) may have eliminated this obstacle.
(More recently developed laser isotope separation methods may have still more
ominous practical implications.)

In the apparatus designed by Paul et al., a symmetric arrangement of four
hyperbolic electrodes is arranged with constant spacing (see Fig. 5-31). The
particular electrode geometry gives rise to a potential

$$\phi = \frac{(U + V_0 \cos \omega t)(x^2 - y^2)}{r_0^2} \tag{79}$$

where $2r_0$ is the spacing between opposite electrodes at closest separation, U
represents a dc potential and V_0 an ac potential at frequency ω applied as
shown in the figure. Noting that the electric field is given in terms of the

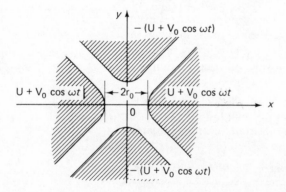

Fig. 5-31. Cross-sectional view of the quadrupole mass filter [after Paul and
Raether (1955)]. The ions travel out of the paper (in the $+z$ direction). Both a dc
and an ac potential are applied with the polarities indicated in the drawing.

potential by

$$\vec{E} = -\vec{\nabla}\phi = -\hat{i}\frac{\partial\phi}{\partial x} - \hat{j}\frac{\partial\phi}{\partial y} - \hat{k}\frac{\partial\phi}{\partial z} \qquad (80)$$

Newton's laws for an ion moving through the apparatus become

$$\vec{F} = m\vec{A} = -q\,\vec{\nabla}\phi \qquad (81)$$

or the acceleration on the ion has the components

$$\frac{d^2R(1)}{dt^2} + \frac{2q(U + V_0\cos\omega t)}{r_0^2} = 0$$

$$\frac{d^2R(2)}{dt^2} - \frac{2q(U + V_0\cos\omega t)}{r_0^2} = 0 \qquad (82)$$

$$\frac{d^2R(3)}{dt^2} = 0$$

By the substitution $T = \omega t/2$, the equations may be rewritten as

$$A(1) + (A + 2Q\cos 2T)*R(1) = 0$$
$$A(2) - (A + 2Q\cos 2T)*R(2) = 0 \qquad (83)$$
$$A(3) = 0$$

where

$$A = \frac{8qU}{mr_0^2\omega^2} \quad \text{and} \quad Q = \frac{4qV}{mr_0^2\omega^2}$$

and

$$A(I) = \frac{d^2R(I)}{dT^2} \qquad \text{for } I = 1, 2, 3 \quad (T = \omega t/2)$$

$$(84)$$

The first two components of Eq. (83) constitute what are known as *Mathieu equations*. Here there are two coupled equations which result in unstable oscillation in either the x or y directions for most arbitrary choices of A and Q. In practice, when the oscillation becomes "unstable," the trajectory rapidly hits the pole face of the apparatus and the ion is lost.

The stability of Mathieu equations has been the subject of theoretical investigation in mathematics. It can be shown that there is a narrow region, roughly as shown in Fig. 5-32, within which the oscillation is stable and outside of which it blows up in one transverse component or the other.

These stability properties may be easily demonstrated through a simple program of the type

```
200   REM REITERATE TO THIS POINT
220   LET V = A + 2*Q*COS(2*T)
230   LET A(1) = −V*R(1)
240   LET A(2) = +V*R(2)
245   FOR I = 1 TO 2
250   LET R(I) = R(I) + V(I)*T0 + .5*A(I)*T0*T0
260   LET V(I) = V(I) + A(I)*T0
270   NEXT I
280   LET T = T + T0
290   REM PRINT OR PLOT HERE
      . . .
```

in which we merely enter different values of A and Q at $T = 0$ and look at $R(1)$ and $R(2)$ as a function of T. There is no point in integrating the z component of the motion, because $A(3) = 0$. The ions just spend the same time in the apparatus for constant V_z ($= V(3)$ in the program).

Because the ratio of A to Q is independent of the mass, ions of different mass fall on a straight line in Fig. 5-32 for particular apparatus parameters. By adjusting the apparatus so that the straight line falls near the top of the stability

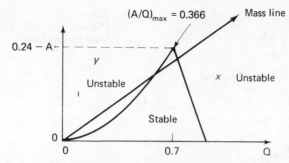

Fig. 5-32. Stability diagram for the mass filter. The particular "mass line" varies with the design parameters of the apparatus. The object is to design the apparatus so that only one isotopic mass of interest falls into the stable region. [After Köhler et al. (1960).]

region for a given isotope, large-resolution $m/\Delta m$) where Δm is the range of mass numbers transmitted) may, in principle, be obtained for very heavy isotopes. In this way, Kohler et al. (1960) obtained an experimental resolution of 8000 for ^{85}Kr ions and anticipated obtaining a resolution of 15,000 for an atomic mass of 200.

The practical advantage of the Paul type of mass filter over most others currently known to man is that $2r_0$ in Fig. 5-31 can be made very large (e.g., 8 cm in the apparatus described by Kohler et al.) and the transmission efficiency at resonance can be very high in practice. By contrast, conventional magnetic mass spectrometers have a resolution that varies inversely with the aperture width. Hence, if the conventional apparatus is designed to separate two isotopes differing by one atomic mass unit at an atomic weight of 235, the transmission efficiency of the apparatus tends to become prohibitively small for processing large quantities of material. This limitation is not present with the Paul type of filter.

The quadrupole mass spectrometer has turned out to be a very convenient device for a wide variety of laboratory research. One should not, however, lose track of its more ominous potential capabilities.

5.15
PROBLEM 33

Write a simple program to investigate the stability of Eqs. (83) in which you merely enter different successive values of the parameters A and Q from the keyboard. For example, take

$$R(1) = R(2) = 20 \quad \text{and} \quad R(3) = 0$$

as the initial position for particles released at $T = 0$ with velocity components

$$V(1) = V(2) = 0 \quad \text{and} \quad V(3) = 2$$

where the generalized units defined in the text have been assumed. Suppose the length of the apparatus is 100 units long (hence the ions take 50 generalized time units to traverse the apparatus in the $R(3)$ direction). Investigate the qualitative nature of the stability diagram shown in Fig. 5-32. For example, arrange your program to stop when either transverse coordinate has reached a maximum excursion of 1000 space units and have it print which coordinate underwent unstable oscillation. (An integration interval of $T\emptyset = 0.5$ generalized time units is adequate to demonstrate the stability characteristics qualitatively. However, as you get near the point $(A/Q)_{max} = 0.366$, much smaller integration time constants are required to demonstrate stability.)

**5.15
PROBLEM 34**
Repeat Problem 33 using a high-resolution plotter or teletype display to show the two transverse components of the motion simultaneously. That is, plot $R(1)$ and $R(2)$ simultaneously as a function of $R(3)$. Displace the two plots by a convenient amount and use the methods of Section 3.2 or 3.3 if you do not have a high resolution random access plotting device. Note that the two transverse components of the motion oscillate independently of each other.

**5.15
PROBLEM 35**
One practical difficulty in making a large enough quadrupole mass filter to permit separating ^{235}U and ^{238}U isotopes of uranium on a practical scale arises from the effects of machining imperfections. (In practice, laboratory versions of the quadrupole mass spectrometer demonstrated by Paul and Kohler et al., have used four round cylinders, rather than the idealized hyperbolic electrodes to which Eq. (79) pertains. A good cylinder is better than a bad hyperbola.) Machining irregularities along the apparatus tend to couple the two transverse oscillations in a real apparatus and can throw the trajectory out of the stable region. Investigate this effect by modifying your solution to either Problem 33 or 34. For example, add statements at the start of each iteration of the type

```
LET F=2*FØ*(RND(1)−.5)+1

LET A=AØ*F

LET Q=QØ*F
```

where $FØ$ is a measure of the average random machining error along the length of the apparatus and $FØ$, $AØ$ and $QØ$ are input from the terminal.

The general force on a particle of charge q moving in combined electric $(\vec{E})$ and magnetic $(\vec{H})$ fields is given by

**5.16
Motion in Combined Electric and Magnetic Fields**

$$\vec{F} = q\vec{E} + q\frac{\vec{V} \times \vec{H}}{[c]} \qquad (85)$$

where the presence of c in the denominator of the second term is unit-dependent.[25]

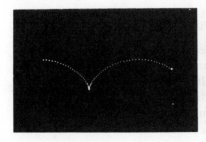

Fig. 5-33. Two examples of cycloidal motion encountered in uniform, crossed $\vec{E}$ and $\vec{H}$ fields. The magnetic field is out of the paper and the electric field is vertical. The magnetic field was increased in going from the left to the right figure.

---

[25] Strictly speaking, the field in the second term should be described as the magnetic induction, $\vec{B}$. However, because we shall only discuss problems involving charged particles moving in free space, we shall not bother with that distinction.

259

If Eq. (85) is specified in cgs units, the term $c =$ velocity of light $\approx$ 3×10^{10} cm/sec is present, the force from the second term is in dynes, the velocity of the particle is in cm/sec, the charge is in electrostatic units, and the magnetic field is in gauss. On the other hand, if mks units are used, the c is omitted from the second term, the force is in newtons, the charge is in coulombs, the velocity is in m/sec, and the magnetic field is in webers (W)/m^2 [1 gauss (G) = 10^{-4} W/m^2]. Some authors compound the confusion by specifying the field in gauss and describing the force in newtons. The units of the first term in Eq. (85) were summarized in the previous section.

The second term in Eq. (85) is commonly known as the Lorentz force and acts in the direction that a right-hand screw would advance if you were to rotate the vector $\vec{V}$ in to $\vec{H}$. It is thus similar in behavior to the approximate force on spinning table-tennis balls discussed previously, except that the law of force here is much more fundamental and precisely defined. Because the Lorentz force is always perpendicular to the velocity, it does no work on the particle. Hence any changes in energy during the particle's motion are entirely the result of the first term in Eq. (85).

For a nonrelativistic particle (i.e., $v \ll c$), the acceleration may be written from Newton's laws in exactly the same manner used in all previous problems discussed in the present chapter. That is, we have

$$\vec{F} = m\vec{A} = m\frac{d\vec{V}}{dt} \tag{86}$$

and therefore

$$\vec{A} = \frac{q}{m}\vec{E} + \frac{q}{mc}\vec{V} \times \vec{H} \tag{87}$$

However, if the fields act long enough to accelerate the particles to relativistic velocities (as measured in one particular nonaccelerated or "inertial" reference frame), the form of the equations changes due to the dependence of particle mass on energy. In the relativistic case, the same equation (85) defines the force, but Newton's laws must be rewritten

$$\vec{F} = \frac{d}{dt}(m\vec{V}) = \frac{dm}{dt}\vec{V} + m\frac{d\vec{V}}{dt} \tag{88}$$

where (Einstein, 1905 and 1907)[26]

$$m = \frac{m_0}{\sqrt{1-(V/c)^2}} \tag{89}$$

The term in the denominator of Eq. (89) prevents the particle from accelerating to unlimited velocities. The total energy of the particle (including the *rest energy*) is then given by

$$E = mc^2 \tag{90}$$

Provided that we can specify the fields in terms of our nonaccelerated reference frame, the solution of Eq. (88) is straightforward. The problem would become more complicated if we were to insist on translating the results of the computation back and forth between our inertial reference and coordinates in other reference frames instantaneously coincident with the moving particle. Then we would need to incorporate Lorentz transformations between pairs of reference frames. However, it is worth emphasizing that such complications are not necessary if you merely want to describe the motion of a relativistic particle in *known* electric and magnetic fields.[27]

---

[26] See the general discussion by Einstein (1954).

[27] The problem of describing the interaction between pairs of relativistic particles is much more formidable.

The only specific relativistic case which we shall consider in the present chapter is that of a particle moving in a general magnetic field. As may be seen by examining Eqs. (85) and (88), the relativistic equations become particularly simple when the electric field is zero (in our reference frame). In that case, because the force is orthogonal to the velocity, we do not have to worry about the term dm/dt in Eq. (88). Hence in that particular case

$$\vec{A} = \frac{d\vec{V}}{dt} = \frac{q}{mc}\, \vec{V} \times \vec{H} = \frac{q}{m_0 c}\sqrt{1-(V/c)^2}\,(\vec{V} \times \vec{H}) \qquad (91)$$

where m is given by Eq. (89) and m_0 is the *rest mass*.

We have at last come to a problem that is prohibitive to solve in the constant-acceleration approximation. We simply have to have solutions for a charged particle moving in a uniform magnetic field in which circular orbits close on themselves within very small fractional errors. The point is that most interesting magnetic-field problems involve motion over a large number of cyclotron orbits. Because the magnetic force is both proportional to the velocity and orthogonal to the velocity, we will get into trouble very fast in the constant-acceleration approximation. In fact, the constant-acceleration approximation is so bad in magnetic-field problems that it is not even worth bothering with as a first-order method—except perhaps for the purpose of illustrating its shortcomings.

We shall, therefore, outline a general program in accordance with the discussion of Section 5.3 for computing the trajectory of a nonrelativistic charged particle in a combined electric and magnetic field of general form. We shall assume that these fields are to be computed from solutions to Maxwell's equations for the particular problem. However, we will not go into the boundary-value problems involved in solving Maxwell's equations here.

It will be easiest to set up this problem in terms of a series of subroutines. First, we shall introduce a subroutine that merely determines the initial conditions for the particle position and velocity. We shall also define the charge-to-mass ratio ($\equiv Q$) for the particle and the time intervals, $T\emptyset$ and $T1$, for the reiterative integration process in this subroutine. The program variables $T\emptyset$ and $T1$ correspond to the time increments t_0 and t_1 discussed in Section 5.3.

Thus this first subroutine will be of the form

5.17
Programming the Modified
Runge–Kutta Bootstrap

```
100   REM SUB FOR INITIAL CONDITIONS ON T,T1,T∅,Q,R(I),V(I)
110   LET T = ∅
120   LET T1 = ...
125   LET T∅ = .1*T1
130   LET Q = ...
140   LET R(1) = ...
145   LET R(2) = ...
150   LET R(3) = ...
160   LET V(1) = ...
165   LET V(2) = ...
170   LET V(3) = ...
190   RETURN
```

Next we shall need a subroutine that computes the current values of the electric and magnetic field at the particle position

```
200   REM SUB COMPUTES E- AND H- FIELDS AS FUNCTION OF X(I)
210   LET E(1) = ...
220   LET E(2) = ...
230   LET E(3) = ...
240   LET H(1) = ...
250   LET H(2) = ...
260   LET H(3) = ...
290   RETURN
```

We shall assume that the magnetic fields defined above include the unit-dependent factor (c) in the denominator of the second term in Eq. (85). Note that the fields are defined in terms of the dummy particle position array, $X(I)$, discussed in more detail below. Also note that if the fields were varying very rapidly as explicit functions of the time, it would be necessary to introduce a similar dummy time variable. (The present problems do not require that modification.)

It is useful to have a separate subroutine that first computes the cross product involved in the acceleration produced by the magnetic field, and then adds the acceleration produced by the electric field. For convenience we shall set this cross-product computation up in terms of a dummy velocity array $U(I)$ which is distinct from the particle velocity array $V(I)$.

```
300   REM SUB COMPUTES ACCEL.C(I) FROM H AND E
310   LET C(1) = Q*(U(2)*H(3) − U(3)*H(2))
320   LET C(2) = Q*(U(3)*H(1) − U(1)*H(3))
330   LET C(3) = Q*(U(1)*H(2) − U(2)*H(1))
340   FOR I = 1 TO 3
350   LET C(I) = C(I) + Q*E(I)
360   NEXT I
390   RETURN
```

We will then need a subroutine to determine the change in position and velocity that would occur in the constant-acceleration approximation over the interval $T0$ ($<T1$). For this purpose we shall use the dummy particle position array $X(I)$ and dummy particle velocity array $U(I)$. The object of this subroutine is to determine the current value of the vector quantity $\vec{b}$ in Eq. (8) of Section 5.3, which will be designated by the array $B(I)$ in the program. We shall determine the change in acceleration starting with the current value stored in $A(I)$.

```
400   REM SUB. FINDS B(I) FROM CONSTANT ACCEL. APPROX. OVER INTERVAL T0
410   FOR I = 1 TO 3
420   LET X(I) = R(I) + V(I)*T0 + .5*A(I)*T0*T0
430   LET U(I) = V(I) + A(I)*T0
440   NEXT I
450   GOSUB 200
460   GOSUB 300
470   FOR I = 1 TO 3
480   LET B(I) = (C(I) − A(I))/T0
490   NEXT I
495   RETURN
```

After having computed the array $B(I)$ corresponding to the current values of $R(I)$, $V(I)$, and $A(I)$, we then need a subroutine to compute new values for these quantities over the large interval $T1$ using Eqs. (3) and (4) of Section 5.1:

```
500   REM SUB COMPUTES R(I),V(I) OVER INTERVAL T1 > T0
510   FOR I = 1 TO 3
520   LET R(I) = R(I) + V(I)*T1 + .5*A(I)*T1*T1 + B(I)*T1*T1*T1/6
530   LET V(I) = V(I) + A(I)*T1 + .5*B(I)*T1*T1
540   NEXT I
550   RETURN
```

Finally, it will be useful to have a subroutine to print or plot results. This one will, of course, depend on the particular problem and instrumentation available.

```
800   REM SUB TO PRINT OR PLOT RESULTS FOR R(I)
  .
  .
  .
890   RETURN
```

Our program then will consist of the following fairly simple set of state-ments

```
20   GOSUB 100      (initial conditions)
30   MAT U = V
40   MAT X = R
50   GOSUB 200      (computes new Ē and H̄ fields)
60   GOSUB 300      [computes local acceleration in C(I)]
70   MAT A = C
80   GOSUB 400      [finds B(I) from constant-acceleration
                     approximation for small interval TØ]
90   GOSUB 500      (finds new R(I) and V(I) over large
                     interval T1]
95   GOSUB 800      (prints or plots results)
96   LET T = T + T1
97   IF...          (conditional statement to halt program
                     after prescribed computation finished)
99   GOTO 30        (reiterate)
```

Then, of course, we need an end statement and whatever initial dimension statements might be required. For example, lines 3Ø, 4Ø, and 7Ø require a DIM $U(3)$, $V(3)$, $X(3)$, $R(3)$, $A(3)$, $C(3)$ statement at the start.

```
999   END
```

Once this initial investment in programming statements has been made, it is relatively straightforward to solve all sorts of general problems through order $T1^3$. One could, of course, go on to add still higher-order corrections. How-ever, the present program is quite adequate for any problems involved in the present chapter.

5.17
PROBLEM 36

Write a general program of the above-modified Runge–Kutta type and try it out on one of the problems encountered earlier in this chapter.† Compare the results and computing time with values involved when you solve the same problem with the constant-acceleration approximation using the same small interval $TØ$ and same large interval $T1$. (To be fair about it, you should really delete all the general statements in the above program which are not needed in the particular problem chosen. For example, if no cross product is needed, you should skip those steps. Similarly, if the original problem is one-dimensional, it would not be fair to compare running times against the more general program working out all three components; and so on.)

5.17
PROBLEM 37

Apply the above modified Runge–Kutta program to the problem of a charged particle moving in a uniform magnetic field. Make sure that you get reasonably good circular orbits. Try doing the same problem with the constant-acceleration approximation and compare the results.

5.17
PROBLEM 38

Apply the above method to the motion of a charged particle moving through uniform, crossed electric and magnetic fields. Note that the motion here is cycloidal (see Fig. 5-33 on p. 259).

† The serious student will probably want to do all the previous problems with this powerful method. However, he or she should be dissuaded—otherwise we'll never get out of Chapter 5!

Ernest O. Lawrence received the Nobel Prize in 1939 for his work on the cyclotron (see, e.g., Lawrence and Cooksey, 1936). At the lowest level of sophistication, the cyclotron seems like one of those simple, but clever,

5.18
Cyclotrons and Similar Devices

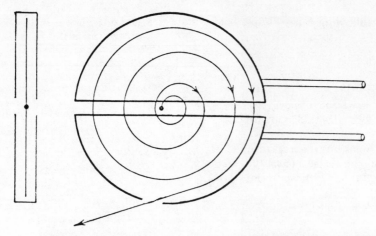

Fig. 5-34. Schematic diagram of a cyclotron. Ions are released at low energy in the gap between the two Dees near the center of the drawing. These are accelerated within the gap region by an oscillating electric field whose frequency is set equal to the orbital frequency for charged particles moving in a uniform magnetic field perpendicular to the Dees. The Dees are hollow, as indicated at the left.

inventions that anyone having successfully completed an introductory course in physics might think of. The basic principle is straightforward enough. Charged particles are released at low energy at a point near the center of the apparatus in the gap between two Dee structures (see Fig. 5-34). The Dees are hollow conducting shells between which an alternating high-frequency voltage

$$E = E_0 \cos \omega t \tag{92}$$

is applied. A uniform magnetic field H is applied perpendicularly to the Dees and would make the charged particles travel in circular orbits in the absence of the oscillating electric field. Because of the shielding from the electric field experienced within the hollow, conducting Dee structures, the charged particles do, in fact, travel in circular orbits most of the time. However, as they cross the gap between the Dees, they are accelerated by the oscillating field.

The frequency ω of the applied voltage is adjusted to match the angular frequency for circular motion in the uniform magnetic field. The latter is, of course, determined by requiring the Lorentz force [second term in Eq. (85)] to provide the centripetal acceleration for circular motion exactly. Hence

$$\frac{V^2}{r} = \frac{qVH}{m[c]}$$

or

$$\omega = \frac{V}{r} = \frac{q}{m[c]} H \tag{93}$$

Here, as previously discussed, the presence of the c in the denominator depends on the choice of units. If the angular frequency determined from Eq. (93) were inserted in Eq. (92), it would then seem that the particles starting out near the center at low energy would remain in phase with the applied voltage and continue indefinitely to pick up an amount of energy equal to qE_0 every time they went through the gap. Eventually, their velocities would become so large that their orbit radii would equal the outer radius of the Dees. Hence at that point the beam of particles would be extracted from the machine as shown schematically in Fig. 5-34.

There are two additional aspects to the problem which make the real situation substantially more complex. The first has to do with the question of the stability of the particle trajectories, and the second has to do with the relativistic effects, which become important as the particle acquires higher and higher velocities. We shall consider the relativistic problem first.

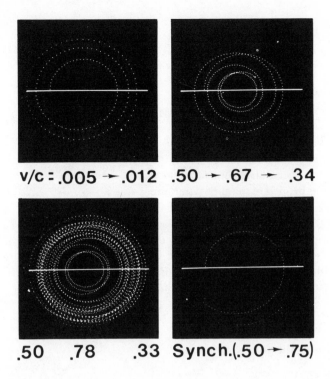

v/c = .005 → .012   .50 → .67 → .34

.50   .78   .33   Synch.(.50 → .75)

Fig. 5-35. Simulation of the motion of a relativistic particle in a cyclotron. A charged particle is released at $T = 0$ from the same position in the same magnetic field. Peak excursions in the values of v/c are shown in each case. The horizontal line denotes the location of the gap between the Dees. In the top left photograph, a fairly nonrelativistic particle is released in phase with the oscillating field at an initial value of $v/c = 0.005$. The program was stopped at $v/c = 0.012$ without significant problems from the relativistic mass increase.

In the top right-hand figure, the particle was injected at $v/c = 0.50$ and accelerates up to $v/c = 0.67$. At that point it gets out of phase with the field and decelerates to $v/c = 0.34$, where the program was halted.

In the lower left-hand picture, the particle starts at $v/c = 0.50$ and was left in the cyclotron for a long period during which the velocity slowly oscillated over the region from $v/c \approx 0.33$ to ≈ 0.78.

The lower right-hand picture is a simulation of a synchrotron. Here it is assumed that the rf voltage is frequency-modulated so as to match the relativistic increase in particle mass.

The main limitation on the maximum energy that can be given to a charged particle with a conventional cyclotron of the type so far described is imposed by the relativistic increase of the particle's mass with velocity [see Eq. (89)]. At some point, the mass m will have increased enough to throw the particle completely out of phase with the oscillating electric field. At this juncture, the field starts slowing the particle down. The particle thus can lose an amount of energy approximately equal to qE each time it goes through the gap and begins to spiral inward. Eventually it slows down enough to get back in phase with the electric field; the particle speeds up and the process repeats. Thus the particle placed in a really big cyclotron would tend to oscillate back and forth in energy. This effect is illustrated by the computed trajectories in Fig. 5-35.

We can simulate the behavior of a relativistic charged particle in a large cyclotron in the following manner. First, take the uniform magnetic field to be in the z direction; i.e.,

$$H(3) = H \quad \text{and} \quad H(1) = H(2) = 0$$

Then the orbital motion occurs in the xy plane and we shall assume that the problem is two-dimensional for the moment. We shall next assume that the electric field is applied in the y direction across a gap of infinitesimal width, occurring along the line $R(2) = 0$. The motion can be described by the simple modified Runge–Kutta procedure discussed in the last section. All we have to do is include the mass dependence on velocity during each iteration and add a subroutine to accelerate the particle when it goes through the gap. The mass dependence can be accomplished by including statements of the type

```
202   LET U2 = U(1)*U(1) + U(2)*U(2)
205   LET M = MØ/SQR(1 − U2/C2)
```

early in subroutine 2ØØ, where $C2$ is the velocity of light squared and $MØ$ is the rest mass.

We then examine the value of $R(2)$ after each iteration to see whether the particle has just gone through the gap. The latter can be done by comparing

SGN($R(2)$) with a stored value from the previous iteration. For example,

Chapter 5
Dynamics

```
91   LET T = T + T1
92   LET S = SGN(R(2))      [determine sign of R(2)]
93   IF S#−S1 THEN 95       [reiterate unless R(2) changed sign]
94   GOSUB 900              (increase the particle energy)
95   GOSUB 800              (print or plot results)
96   LET S1 = S             [store the value of SGN(R(2)) for
                             the next iteration]
99   GOTO 30                (reiterate)
```

accomplishes the desired objectives, provided that we add a subroutine 900 which increments the energy of the particle in an appropriate manner when the particle has just gone through the gap.

We may assume that the particle is traveling in the y direction as it goes through the gap. Hence to simulate the relativistic cyclotron all we need to do is to compute the change, ΔV_y, in particle velocity that occurs (at $y = 0$) due to an increase of energy $\Delta E = qE_0 \cos \omega T$ at the time the particle goes through the gap. Taking the partial derivative of Eq. (89) in respect to V_y, it is seen that

$$\Delta E = \frac{m_0 V_y \, \Delta V_y}{(1 - V^2/c^2)^{3/2}} \qquad (94)$$

This result can be incorporated into our program in the following manner:

```
900   REM RELATIVISTIC CYCLOTRON SUBROUTINE
901   REM E0 IS PREVIOUSLY DEFINED PROPERTY OF CYCLOTRON
905   LET W = (Q/M0)*H(3)
910   LET E1 = (Q/M0)*E0*COS(W*T)
920   LET V2 = V(1)*V(1) + V(2)*V(2)
930   LET V0 = E1*(1−V2/C2)↑1.5/ABS(V(2))
940   LET V(2) = V(2) + V0
950   RETURN
```

where the program variables are defined as follows: $E1$ represents the increment in energy per unit rest mass associated with traversing the gap. $V0$ defined on line 930 is the increment in the velocity $V(2)$ in the y direction which results from this increase in energy in accordance with Eq. (94). W is the resonant angular frequency in the nonrelativistic case corresponding to ω in Eq. (93).

**5.18
PROBLEM 39**

Write a program to simulate the operation of a conventional cyclotron with relativistic particles along the lines of the above discussion.

It is possible to minimize the deleterious effects of the relativistic mass increase by decreasing the frequency of the alternating potential during the particle trajectory. This approach is the basis of the *synchrotron*, or *FM cyclotron* (see Fig. 5-35). It would be difficult in practice to vary the frequency precisely in the manner required. However, we can make a good first-order approximation.

As long as the particle is in phase with the applied electric field, the energy of the particle is increasing in an approximately linear fashion with time. In fact, at the start of the trajectory

$$\frac{dm}{dt} \approx \frac{\Delta E \omega_0}{c^2 \pi} \quad \text{or} \quad m \approx m_0 + \frac{(\Delta E) \omega_0}{c^2 \pi} t \qquad (95)$$

where (ΔE) is the energy gained each time the particle traverses the gap and $\omega_0 = qH/m_0 =$ the initial cyclotron resonance condition. Here, for clarity, we

shall omit the extra unit-dependent factor of c in the denominator of Eq. (85).
Hence, if we change the frequency of the electric field with time in the following simple manner,

$$\omega(t) \approx \frac{qH}{m_0 + [(\Delta E)\omega_0 t/c^2]} = \frac{\omega_0}{1 + [(\Delta E)\omega_0 t/m_0 c^2]} \qquad (96)$$

we should be able to keep the particle in phase with the field over a much longer time and hence obtain much greater output energy.

5.18
PROBLEM 40 Repeat Problem 39 while modulating the cyclotron frequency according to Eq. (96) and compare with the previous results.

A more subtle principle for accelerating particles was incorporated in the betatron (Kerst, 1941, 1942). Here we dispense with the applied electric field altogether and merely increase the magnetic field with time. The device provides one of the nicest demonstrations of Faraday's law of induction that can be imagined. The basic underlying principle is the same one that makes transformers work; namely, the induced electromotive force around a current loop is proportional to the rate of change of magnetic flux through the circuit. Here the flux is changed primarily by increasing the field and the charged particles initially going in a circular orbit about the magnetic field at $T = 0$ play the role of the current loop. The really nice thing about this problem is that one can demonstrate the gain in energy by integrating the equations of motion directly and hence perform a direct check on Faraday's law from other basic principles.

5.18
PROBLEM 41 Write a program to simulate the operation of a betatron. For example, take the magnetic field to be of the form

$$H(3) = H0 + H1*T \qquad H(1) = H(2) = 0$$

and monitor the orbital radius or energy of the relativistic particle as a function of time (see Fig. 5-36). Choose convenient values for the experimental parameters. (It seems more interesting here to see Faraday's law in action than to design an actual betatron.) The modified Runge–Kutta bootstrap is an absolute must in this problem. In fact, it is important to demonstrate that the growth in energy is not just due to systematic integration errors. Hence one should really do the problem twice; once with $H1 = 0$ just to set a limit on computational errors.

Fig. 5-36. Faraday effect as applied to betatron orbits. The magnetic-field variation with time stated in Problem 41 was assumed. Note that while the field is linearly increasing, the orbit radius eventually starts increasing, implying that the charged-particle energy is going up with time. (If the charged-particle energy were constant, the orbital radius would be continually decreasing in the example above.) Note that this type of problem is especially sensitive to computational instabilities of the type discussed in Section 5.2, and that a computational method with equivalent accuracy of the modified Runge–Kutta method is absolutely essential.

Before Lawrence showed them up, a lot of people did not really think the cyclotron would work. The argument was based on taking the concept of a "uniform" magnetic field too seriously. Fortunately, uniform fields do not **5.19**
Magnetic Trapping

really exist in nature. If you really were to build a cyclotron with a precisely uniform field, the beam would tend to hit the top or bottom of the Dee structure very quickly. The point is that during most of the orbit there would be no force that would restore the motion to the median plane. Hence whatever initial velocity the entering ions had in the z direction would ultimately result in their destruction through collision with the walls; that is, $\vec{V}_z \times \vec{H}$ would always be zero and $\vec{V}_{x,y} \times \vec{H}$ would have no component in the z direction.

However, the fields produced by a real magnet with finite dimensions tend to bulge at the median plane, as shown in Fig. 5-37. Consequently, as the particle gets farther away from the median plane, $\vec{V} \times \vec{H}$ tends to have a larger component which restores the particle to the median plane. This is especially true near the edges of the magnet, where the bulge is greatest and the particle velocities are greatest. Hence nature has provided a simple way to keep the beam stable. The particle can be made to oscillate stably back and forth about the median plane without hitting the pole faces for realistic choices of magnet parameters.

Our previous program is quite capable of treating the motion of a relativistic charged particle in a general inhomogeneous magnetic field. The only remaining problem is to specify the functional form of the field itself for inclusion in subroutine 2∅∅.

Although any detailed discussion of the solution of Maxwell's equations is beyond the scope of this chapter, it will be helpful to note the general form that axially symmetric magnetic fields can take. In a charge-free region, time-independent magnetic fields must satisfy the following pair of Maxwell's equations:

$$\vec{\nabla} \cdot \vec{H} = 0 \tag{97}$$

$$\vec{\nabla} \times \vec{H} = 0 \tag{98}$$

where the divergence ($\vec{\nabla} \cdot$) and curl ($\vec{\nabla} \times$) vector operators are used. From the form of Eq. (98) and the vector identity

$$\vec{\nabla} \times (\vec{\nabla} \Phi) = 0 \tag{99}$$

where Φ is any well-behaved scalar function, we may assert that $\vec{H}$ is derivable from such a scalar potential function, Φ. Hence we may define Φ by

$$\vec{H} = -\vec{\nabla} \Phi \tag{100}$$

and note by substituting Eq. (100) in Eq. (97) that Φ must satisfy Laplace's equation

$$\nabla^2 \Phi = 0 \tag{101}$$

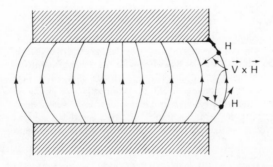

Fig. 5-37. The velocity ($\vec{V}$) of the charged particle is assumed to be out of the paper. The force on the particle is in the direction of $\vec{V} \times \vec{H}$ and hence has a component in the direction of the median plane.

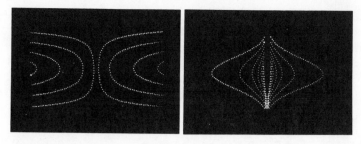

Fig. 5-38. Two extreme cases of axially symmetric fields which are also symmetric about the median plane. The field at the left is a special case for the constricted type given by Eq. (105); the bulging field at the right represents a special case for Eq. (109).

By writing Laplace's equation in cylindrical coordinates, the solutions for axially symmetric fields may be broken down into products of Bessel functions of the transverse coordinates and trigonometric (or hyperbolic) functions of the axial coordinate. There are two separate cases involving symmetry about the median plane $(z=0)$ which simplify considerably—the two limiting cases illustrated in Fig. 5-38, in which the field is either constricted at the median plane or bulges at the median plane.

It may be shown that the most general axially symmetric field which constricts at the origin on the median plane, is symmetric about that plane $(z=0)$, and is finite at $X=Y=0$ can be written as

$$H(1) = H_X = \sum_k H_k \frac{x}{r} J_1(kr) \sin kz$$

$$H(2) = H_Y = \sum_k H_k \frac{y}{r} J_1(kr) \sin kz \qquad (102)$$

$$H(3) = H_Z = \sum_k H_k J_0(kr) \cos kz$$

where $r = \sqrt{x^2 + y^2}$, $J_0(kr)$ is a zero-order Bessel function of the real argument, kr, and $J_1(kr)$ is similarly a first-order Bessel function of the same argument. The quantities k and H_k would generally be determined by boundary conditions in a particular problem. For example, if Eq. (102) were to represent the field from a circular loop of wire of infinitesimal thickness located in the median plane and with radius a, the values of k would be chosen so that the quantities ka corresponded to the successive roots of $J_0(ka)$. The values of J_0 and J_1 can easily be computed from the series

$$J_n(w) = \sum_{m=0}^{\infty} \frac{(-1)^m (w/2)^{n+2m}}{m!(n+m)!} \qquad (103)$$

in a program subroutine. Note from Eq. (103) that the field on the axis is entirely in the z direction and given by

$$H_z(x = y = 0) = \sum_k H_k \cos (kz) \qquad (104)$$

and decreases as we move away from the median plane on the z axis. The transverse components go to zero at $x = y = 0$ and change sign when we go through the median plane. The relative direction of H_z and the transverse field components is such as to produce a field that converges at the origin. However, if we go out radially past the first zero of the J_0 Bessel function (at $w = 2.4048$), the leading term for H_z changes sign and the field will bulge. Hence the expansion is naturally suited for describing fields from current loops, solenoids, or outside of bar magnets (providing the expansion coefficients are all adjusted appropriately).

The leading term in Eqs. (102) may be approximated for small kr by

$$H(1) = H_x \approx H\left(1 - \frac{k^2r^2}{8}\right)\frac{kx}{2}\sin kz$$

$$H(2) = H_y \approx H\left(1 - \frac{k^2r^2}{8}\right)\frac{ky}{2}\sin kz \qquad (105)$$

$$H(3) = H_z \approx H\left(1 - \frac{k^2r^2}{4}\right)\cos kz$$

where again $r = \sqrt{x^2 + y^2}$ and H is now simply the field in the z direction at the origin. Equations (105) satisfy the divergence requirement in Eq. (97) exactly; however, because we have truncated the radial series, there are extra terms of order r^3 in the transverse direction for the curl, and Eq. (98) is not exactly satisfied.

The opposite type of axially symmetric field (which is also symmetric about the median plane) can be obtained mathematically just by replacing k by $-ik$ in Eq (102). That is the general *bulging* field may be written in the form

5.21
Fields That Bulge at the Median Plane

$$H(1) = H_x = \sum_k H_k \frac{x}{r} I_1(kr)\frac{e^{-kz} - e^{+kz}}{2}$$

$$H(2) = H_y = \sum_k H_k \frac{y}{r} I_1(kr)\frac{e^{-kz} - e^{+kz}}{2} \qquad (106)$$

$$H(3) = H_z = \sum_k H_k I_0(kr)\frac{e^{-kz} + e^{+kz}}{2}$$

where I_0 and I_1 are Bessel functions of imaginary argument given by

$$I_0(w) = J_0(iw) = \sum_{m=0} \frac{(w/2)^{2m}}{(m!)^2} \qquad (107)$$

and

$$I_1(w) = -iJ_1(iw) = \sum_{m=0} \frac{(w/2)^{2m+1}}{m!(m+1)!} \qquad (108)$$

Here the field on the z axis increases as we move away from the median plane and the transverse field components have the right orientation in respect to the z component to produce the bulging effect at $z = 0$.

The leading term in Eqs. (106) may be approximated at small kr in this case by

$$H(1) = H_x \approx H\left(1 + \frac{k^2r^2}{8}\right)\frac{kx}{2}\frac{e^{-kz} - e^{+kz}}{2}$$

$$H(2) = H_y \approx H\left(1 + \frac{k^2r^2}{8}\right)\frac{ky}{2}\frac{e^{-kz} - e^{+kz}}{2} \qquad (109)$$

$$H(3) = H_z \approx H\left(1 + \frac{k^2r^2}{4}\right)\frac{e^{-kz} + e^{+kz}}{2}$$

where $r = \sqrt{x^2 + y^2}$ and H is again simply the field in the z direction at the origin. Equations (109) satisfy Maxwell's equations, (97) and (98), within the same approximations as do Eqs. (105). That is, the divergence condition is satisfied exactly and, because the series is truncated, the curl differs from zero by order r^3 in the transverse direction.

Note that although we have restricted kr to small values in the above expressions, kz is not similarly restricted.

**5.21
PROBLEM 42**

Write a program that permits plotting the field lines in the xz plane for the fields described by Eqs. (105) and (109). Note that you can accomplish this objective by starting at some initial coordinates $R(I)$ that correspond to the tail of the arrow on the field line. Then compute the field, take a step in the direction of the field, plot the point, and reiterate. For example,

```
100   INPUT X(1),X(3)
200   REM COMPUTE H(I)
210   LET H(1)=...
220   LET H(3)=...
230   LET H=SQR(H(1)*H(1)+H(3)*H(3))
240   LET X(1)=X(1)+H(1)/H
250   LET X(3)=X(3)+H(3)/H
260   REM PLOT OR PRINT X(1),X(3)
      ...
270   GOTO 200
```

If you do not have a high-resolution xy plotter, print out the successive coordinates on the teletype terminal for a few representative cases.

**5.21
PROBLEM 43**

Write a program to illustrate the stabilization effect that occurs in a cyclotron due to bulging magnetic fields at the median plane. Use Eq. (109) and do not worry about acceleration by the Dees. First, choose a convenient value for k, the velocity of the particle, and the field on the z axis to give a large circular orbit. Add a small velocity component in the z direction at $t=0$ and print t, $r-r_0$, where $r_0 =$ the circular-orbit radius when $v_z = 0$. Note that both the vertical and radial motion oscillate in a coupled fashion about the equilibrium values. [*Note:* It would be appropriate (but not necessary) to expand the $\exp(\pm kz)$ functions to the same order as used in the expansion of the radial functions for this problem.]

The coupled vertical and radial oscillations exhibited in the previous problem lead to disaster in a really large machine because the magnitude of the radial oscillation amplitude can become larger than the extent of the apparatus. The really large synchrotrons, of course, leave out the middle region of the magnetic field and inject the particles at high energy to start with. A clever method to beat the effect of coupled oscillations was originally suggested by a Greek engineer, Nicholas C. Christofilos, who worked for an Athens elevator company.[28] The idea is to make the direction of the field gradient alternate a large, even number of times as the particle goes around in orbit.[29] The radial oscillation at the cyclotron frequency is thus broken up and strong focusing can be provided for both the radial and vertical motion about the desired orbit.

[28] The suggestion that he was an elevator operator was a popular exaggeration of the time. See his obituary in *The New York Times*, in the fall of 1973.

[29] The idea was suggested originally by Christofilos in an unpublished manuscript in 1950. The idea was also conceived independently at a later date by Courant, Livingston, and Snyder at Brookhaven [see Livingston and Blewett (1962, p. 112)].

<table>
<tr><td>

5.21
RESEARCH
PROBLEM

</td><td>

Simulate the stabilization of orbits which is obtained in an alternating gradient synchrotron (AGS). Break the circular orbit up into at least four quadrants. For example, use the bulging field approximation, Eq. (109), in the odd quadrants $[R(1)*R(2)>\emptyset]$ and the converging field approximation, Eq. (105), in the even quadrants $[R(1)*R(2)<\emptyset]$ with the same value of H and k.

Again, do not worry about accelerating electric fields. Just inject the particles with a convenient velocity and choice of field parameters for circular motion when $v_z = 0$ at $T = 0$. Then choose convenient values of k and v_z at $T = 0$ to examine the stabilization effect. However, keep $kr < 1$. Again, print T, z, and $r - r_0$ (where r_0 is the circular-orbit radius when $v_z = 0$ at $T = 0$).

</td></tr>
</table>

The cyclotron stabilization effect seems intuitively reasonable merely from the direction of $\vec{V} \times H$ in the bulging field. After all, the field was carefully chosen to be axially symmetric and centered in respect to the cyclotron orbit. The stabilization effect is therefore not surprising.

A much more surprising phenomenon occurs when relatively low energy charged particles travel in inhomogeneous magnetic fields. By low energy, here, we mean that the radius of curvature for the local cyclotron orbit is small compared to the dimensions over which substantial changes in the field direction take place. For example, we could use the same bulging cyclotron field for the following discussion, but we would have to keep the protons at very low energy.

5.22
Magnetic Bottles, Van Allen Belts, and Solar Flares

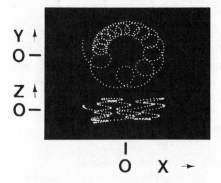

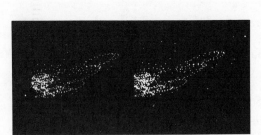

Fig. 5-39. Trajectory for a charged particle trapped in a bulging magnetic field of the type described by Eq. (109), computed with the present modified Runge–Kutta method. The top photograph shows a simultaneous display of the motion in the yx plane and in the zx plane. Note the slowly precessing near-circular orbits projected on the median plane. Also note the oscillatory quasi-helical motion taking place about the median plane in the z direction. The lower figure is a three-dimensional stereoscopic projection of the same trajectory (projected onto the zx plane using the methods discussed in Chapter 3). To view the trajectory in three dimensions, use the method described previously in Chapter 3 (see Fig. 3-9). The gradual buildup in transverse radius of curvature is due to accumulative errors resulting from the particular integration time constants assumed.

The interesting thing about this case is that, although the charged particles tend to follow the field lines in their general motion, the field inhomogeneity produces a coupling between the vertical and radial motion. In particular, the vertical motion oscillates back and forth about the median plane while the projection of the particle motion in the median plane consists of slowly precessing nearly circular orbits. Thus, although the particle gradually migrates over a wide region of the field, it can remain trapped indefinitely.

The effect is illustrated by the computed trajectories shown in Fig. 5-39 in which convenient parameters were arbitrarily chosen and an inhomogeneous field of the type in Eq. (109) was used. The upper portion of the figure shows a simultaneous display of the vertical and transverse projections of the motion, in which both the vertical oscillation and slow precession of the near-circular transverse orbit is apparent. Also shown in that figure is a stereoscopic projection of the motion of the same trajectory computed with the techniques discussed in Chapter 3. The wide extent of the particle migration will be most apparent from the three-dimensional simulation. This particular problem is a good example of the ease with which a computer simulation can be used to provide answers to a real problem that simply cannot be obtained through closed-form analysis without substantial approximation.

The trapping effect is related to a wide variety of phenomena encountered on both the laboratory and astronomical scale. On the laboratory level, the effect has been investigated as a technique in beta spectroscopy and with the object of enhancing positronium formation. At the other terrestrial extreme, it is clearly the mechanism responsible for trapping charged particles above the earth's atmosphere in the Van Allen belts. Charged particles trapped by the earth's magnetic field are also responsible for the polar glow (where the

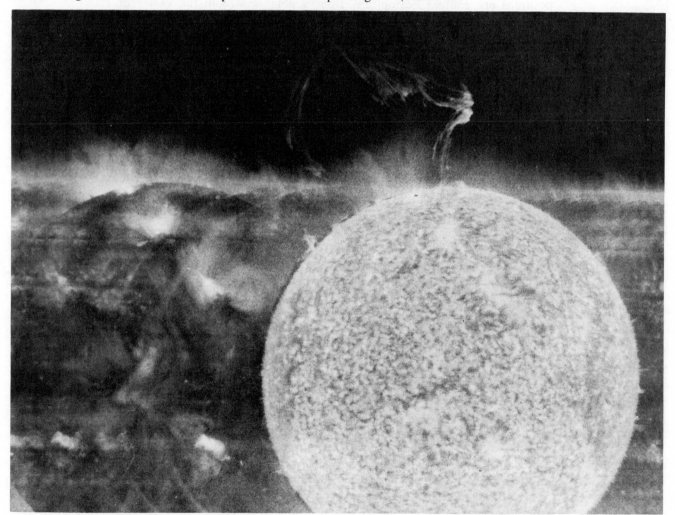

Fig. 5-40. Huge eruption from the surface of the sun seen at 304 angstroms in emission from singly ionized helium. This photograph was taken outside the earth's atmosphere during the Skylab 3 mission and demonstrated that flare eruptions from the sun can stay together for altitudes up to 500,000 miles. (Naval Research Laboratory photograph.)

273

trajectories get into the earth's atmosphere) and for other air-glow emission
bands about the earth. Finally, it is likely to be the primary mechanism involved in recent solar-flare phenomena observed from the outside the earth's atmosphere. Here direct photographs taken on the resonance lines of ionized helium demonstrated that ion trajectories extended outward from the sun by about half the sun's diameter during flare eruptions (see Fig. 5-40).

5.22
PROBLEM 44

An idealistic graduate student wishes to do spectroscopy on excited states of positronium. (Positronium is the bound system of an electron and its antiparticle, the positron. The positronium atom is electronically similar to hydrogen and is, in fact, the only atom that can be solved exactly in relativistic quantum theory.) The experiment will be difficult because the only practical source of positrons will be low-strength radioactive isotopes which emit the particles at high energy. To enhance the formation probability, the student builds an apparatus to produce bulging magnetic fields of the type described by Eqs. (109). The idea is to try to prolong the time that the positrons spend in a small apparatus.

Assume that $k = 0.1$ cm^{-1} and $H = 1000$ G in Eq. (109) and that the positrons are emitted isotropically from a point source in the center of a cylindrical container 10 cm in diameter and 10 cm high.

Write a program to compute the motion of a 250-keV positron ($V = 2.22 \times 10^{10}$ cm/sec at $T = 0$) released from the origin at an angle θ in respect to the vertical axis. Assume that the container is evacuated. Find the minimum angle θ for which the positrons are completely trapped by the field (i.e., the z motion just reverses at the top of the cylinder). For the purposes of this problem, take $T1 = 1$ picosecond (psec) $= 1\emptyset * T\emptyset$. (The particle will eventually escape in your computation due to accumulative errors.)

Note that $q/mc \approx 2.10 \times 10^7$ per G-sec is constant throughout this problem. However, the problem is definitely relativistic ($m \approx 1.195m_0$ and $v/c \approx 0.74$). Note that the positrons will only hit the top or bottom of the cylinder. Hence the particle hits the wall only if

$$ABS(R(3)) > 5$$

for the above conditions.

5.22
RESEARCH
PROBLEM

Investigate the effect of collisions with residual gas atoms in the previous problem.

5.22
PROBLEM 45

The Van Allen "belts"† consist of one fairly continuous region extending from somewhat less than 2 earth radii to more than 8 earth radii in the equatorial plane in which charged particles are trapped by the earth's inhomogeneous magnetic field. The sources of these energetic particles are varied and range from cosmic-ray interactions at one extreme to man-made nuclear explosions at the other. As a specific example, protons at a kinetic energy of ≈ 30 MeV are found within distances of ≈ 2 earth radii at flux densities of 20,000 particles/cm^2-sec. (The energy is ≈ 6 times that for the proton beam from Lawrence's early $27\frac{1}{2}$-inch cyclotron!) Such particles have velocities $\sim 0.247c \sim 7.42 \times 10^9$ cm/sec ≈ 11.6 earth radii/sec and are only slightly relativistic ($m \approx 1.03m_0$).

Suppose that a 30-MeV proton is released 1 earth radius above the

† See Van Allen (1959); Brandt and Hodge (1964, pp. 402–405); and Hess and Greisen (1974).

equator, traveling northeast. At $T = 0$,

$$R(1) = 2 \text{ earth radii}$$
$$R(2) = R(3) = 0$$
$$V(1) = 0$$
$$V(2) = V(3) = 11.6/\sqrt{2} \text{ earth radii/sec}$$

Write a program (using the modified Runge–Kutta procedure) to simulate the motion of the particle. Ignore the earth's gravitational acceleration and all electric field interactions. Show that the particle tends to oscillate back and forth along the field lines in the north–south direction while gradually migrating around the earth. Note that the particle is reflected in regions where the field lines begin to converge appreciably and that the spiraling orbits are compressed where the field lines are compressed and expand where the field lines expand. Roughly, what is the period in seconds for the north–south oscillation with the above initial assumptions? (Take $T1 \leq 0.0005$ sec.) Also, show that if the particle heads directly north at $T = 0$, it tends to come closest to the earth near the North Pole.

If you use a unit of distance equal to 1 earth radius (6.38×10^8 cm) and specify the particle velocities in earth radii/sec, the law of acceleration for motion in a magnetic field becomes

$$\vec{A} = \frac{q}{mc} \vec{V} \times \vec{H} \qquad \text{earth radii/sec}^2$$

where $q/mc = 9260$, ($m \approx 1.03 m_0$), V is in earth radii/sec and H is in gauss. (As a check, note that particles with a velocity of 11.6 earth radii/second moving in a uniform field of 1 G would have a radius of curvature of $\approx 1.25 \times 10^{-3}$ earth radii $\approx 8 \times 10^5$ cm.)

Far from the earth's center, its magnetic field may be approximated by

$$H(1) = H_x = H \frac{3xz}{R^5}$$

$$H(2) = H_y = H \frac{3yz}{R^5}$$

$$H(3) = H_z = H \left(\frac{2z^2 - x^2 - y^2}{R^5} \right)$$

where $H \approx 8 \times 10^{25}$ G-cm$^3 \approx 0.309$ G-earth radii^3.[†] That is, we may regard the field as being the same as that from a magnetic dipole located approximately at the center of the earth.

5.22 RESEARCH PROBLEM

According to the Babcock theory,[‡] sunspots arise when localized magnetic-flux loops burst through the sun's surface from the normal location of flux lines about 0.1 solar radius beneath the surface. The magnetic field above the surface of the sun in the vicinity of the eruption would then presumably be somewhat like the field from the end of a horseshoe magnet (or two oppositely flowing current loops) if the poles (or current loops) were located ≈ 0.1 solar radius below the surface. The motion of helium ions along such a magnetic-field loop is presumably responsible for the spectacular type of trajectory shown in Fig. 5-40.

[†] The numbers assumed in this problem are based on Nagata (1974) and Hess and Greisen (1974).

[‡] Babcock (1961). See also the general discussion of solar magnetic fields in Brandt and Hodge (1964, Chap. 6).

Noting that the sun's radius is $432,500$ miles $\approx 6.96 \times 10^{10}$ cm, the scale of the problem is clearly discernible from the photograph in Fig. 5-40. From the figure, it appears that the lateral separation of the two poles (or current loops) is ≈ 0.4 solar radius and the ion motion extends to a maximum height of about 0.8 solar radius above the sun's surface.

From measurements of Zeeman splitting of spectral lines, it is known that maximum magnetic fields ≈ 4000 G occur in the center of sunspots. The local magnetic fields in these eruptions are enormous compared to the normal average magnetic field at the sun's surface in the absence of such sunspot activity.

See if you can simulate the motion of helium ions under such conditions. (For example, use a superposition of two opposite magnetic dipole field distributions based on the approximation given in Problem 45. However, note that the sharp kinks in the trajectories in Fig. 5-40 suggest the field was time-dependent.)

REFERENCES

BABCOCK, H. W. (1961). "The Topology of the Sun's Magnetic Field and the 22-Year Cycle" *Astrophys. J.*, Vol. 133, p. 572.

BATCHELOR, G. K. (1967). *An Introduction to Fluid Dynamics*. New York: Cambridge University Press.

BAUMEISTER, THEODORE AND L. S. MARKS, eds. (1967), *Standard Handbook for Mechanical Engineers*, New York: McGraw-Hill Book Co.

BRANDT, J. C., AND P. W. HODGE (1964). *Solar System Astrophysics*. New York: McGraw-Hill Book Co.

COUNSILMAN, J. E., (1968). *The Science of Swimming*. Englewood Cliffs, N.J.: Prentice-Hall, Inc.

DAISH, C. B., (1972). *Learn Science Through Ball Games*. New York: Sterling Publishing Co.

DURANT, F. C. (1974a), "Rockets and Missile Systems", *Encyclopedia Britannica Macropedia*, Vol. 15, pp. 924–942.

DURANT, F. C. (1974b), "Space Exploration", *Encyclopaedia Britannica Macropedia*, Vol. 17, pp. 357–375.

EINSTEIN, A. (1905). "Elektrodynamik bewegter Korper." *Ann. Physik*, Vol. 17, pp. 891–921.

EINSTEIN, A. (1954). *Relativity: The Special and the General Theory*. London: Methuen & Company Ltd. First published in 1920.

EMPLETON, B. E., E. H. LANPHIER, J. E. YOUNG, AND L. G. GOFF, eds. (1974). *The New Science of Skin and Scuba Diving*. New York: Association Press.

FEYNMAN, R. P., R. L. LEIGHTON, AND MATTHEW SANDS (1963). *The Feynman Lectures on Physics*. Reading, Mass.: Addison-Wesley Publishing Company, Inc.

FLÜGGE, S., AND C. TRUESDELL, eds. (1959). "Fluid Dynamics," *Handbuch der Physik*, Vol. VIII/1. Berlin: Springer-Verlag. Also see the subsequent Vol. VIII/2 published in 1963 and Vol. IX published in 1960. These volumes contain numerous articles by different authors on both theoretical and experimental work.

HALLADE, J. (1974). "Big Bertha Bombards Paris." *The History of World Wars*, special edition on *The Big Guns* (Artillery 1914–1918), edited by Bernard Fitzsimons (Marshall Cavendish, U.S., 1974), pp. 53–59.

HAMMING, R. W. (1962). *Numerical Methods for Scientists and Engineers.* New York: McGraw-Hill Book Company.

HENRICI, PETER (1964). *Elements of Numerical Analysis.* New York: John Wiley & Sons, Inc.

HESS, W. N., AND K. I. GREISEN (1974). "Van Allen Radiation Belts." *Encyclopaedia Britannica Macropedia*, Vol. 19, pp. 21–23.

HOERNER, S. F. (1965). *Fluid Dynamic Drag.* Published privately by the author, 148 Busteed Drive, Midland Park, N.J. 07432; Library of Congress Catalog Card Number 64–19666.

JACCHIA, L. G., (1974). "A Meteorite That Missed the Earth." *Sky and Telescope*, Vol. 48 (July), pp. 4–8.

KERST, D. W. (1941). "Acceleration of Electrons by Magnetic Induction." *Phys. Rev.*, Vol. 60, p. 47.

KERST, D. W. (1942). "New Induction Accelerator Generating 20 MeV." *Phys. Rev.*, Vol. 61, p. 93.

KÖHLER, R., W. PAUL, K. SCHMIDT, AND U. VON ZAHN (1960). "Preliminary Report on a Quadrupole Spectrometer of High Resolution." *Proceedings of the International Conference on Nuclidic Masses.* Toronto: University of Toronto Press, pp. 507–513.

KUIPER, G. P., AND B. M. MIDDLEHURST, eds. (1961). *Planets and Satellites:* Vol. III, *The Solar System.* Chicago: University of Chicago Press. Reprinted 1971.

KUTTA, W. (1901). "Beitrag zur naherungsweisen integration totaler Differential-gleichunge." *Z. Math. Phys.*, Vol. 46, pp. 435–453.

LAWRENCE, E. O. AND D. COOKSEY (1936). "On the Apparatus for the Multiple Acceleration of Light Ions to High Speeds" *Phys. Rev.*, Vol. 50, pp. 1131–1144.

LEE, D. B., AND W. D. GOODRICH (1972). "The Aerothermodynamic Environment of the Apollo Command Module During Superorbital Entry." *National Aeronautics and Space Administration Technical Note NASA TN-D-6792.* Washington, D.C.: NASA.

LIVINGSTON, N. S., AND J. P. BLEWETT (1962). *Particle Accelerators.* New York: McGraw-Hill Book Company.

McLACHLAN, N. W. (1961). *Bessel Functions for Engineers.* London; Oxford University Press.

MACCOLL, J. W. (1928). "Aerodynamics of a Spinning Sphere." *J. Roy. Aeronaut. Soc.*, Vol. 32, pp. 777–798.

MAGNUS, G. (1853). Poggendorf's *Annalen der Physik und Chemie*, Vol. 88. p. 1.

MOORE, J. E. (1974). *Jane's Fighting Ships, 1973–1974.* London: Jane's Yearbooks.

MORSE, P. M., AND HERMAN FESHBACH (1953). *Methods of Theoretical Physics*, Vol. II. New York: McGraw-Hill Book Company.

NAGATA, TAKESI (1974). "Magnetic Field of Earth." *Encyclopaedia Britannica Mac-ropedia*, Vol. 6, pp. 26–34.

NATIONAL FOOTBALL LEAGUE (1970). *Official Record Book.* New York: Rutledge Books and the Benjamin Co.

NEWTON, SIR I. S. (1686). *Philosophiae Naturalis Principia Mathematica.* London: S. Pepys for the Royal Society.

PAUL, W., AND M. RAETHER (1955). "Das elektrische Massenfilter." *Z. Physik*, Vol. 140, pp. 262–273.

PRANDTL, L. (1952). *The Essentials of Fluid Dynamics.* Glasgow: Blackie & Son Ltd.

RALSTON, ANTHONY, (1965). *A First Course in Numerical Analysis.* New York: McGraw-Hill Book Company.

RAWCLIFFE, R. D., C. D. BARTKY, F. LI, E. GORDON, AND D. CARTA (1974). "Meteor of August 10, 1972." *Nature*, Vol. 247, p. 449.

REYNOLDS, OSBORNE, (1883). "An Experimental Investigation of the Circumstances which determine whether the Motion of Water shall be direct if sinuous and the Law of Resistance in Parallel Channels." *Phil. Trans. Roy. Soc.*, Vol. 174, p. 935.

REYNOLDS, OSBORNE (1886). "On the Theory of Lubrication and Its Application to Mr. Beauchamps Towers' Experiments, Including an Experimental Determination of the Viscosity of Olive Oil." *Phil. Trans. Roy. Soc.*, Vol. 177, p. 157.

REYNOLDS, OSBORNE (1895). "On the Dynamical Theory of Incompressible Viscous Fluids and the Determination of the Criterion." *Phil. Trans. Roy. Soc.*, Vol. 186.

ROUTH, E. J. (1898). *A Treatise on Dynamics of a Particle.* London: Constable and Co. Reproduced by Dover Publications, Inc., New York, 1960.

RUNGE, C. (1895). "Über die numerische Auflösung von Differentialgleichungen." *Math. Ann.*, Vol. 46, pp. 167–178.

RUNGE, C. (1905). "Uber die numerische Auflosung totaler Differentialgleichunger." *Nachr. Gesell. Wiss. Gottingen.*

RUNGE, C., AND H. KONIG (1924). *Vorlesungen über numerisches Rechnen.* Berlin: Springer-Verlag.

SOMMERFELD, ARNOLD (1964). *Mechanics of Deformable Bodies.* Translated by G. Kuerti from second German edition of *Lectures on Theoretical Physics.* New York: Academic Press, Inc.

TENNEKES, H., AND J. L. LUMLEY (1972). *A First Course in Turbulence.* Cambridge, Mass.: The MIT Press.

TODD, JOHN, ed. (1962). *Survey of Numerical Analysis.* New York: McGraw-Hill Book Company.

VAN ALLEN, J. A. (1959), "The Geometrically Trapped Corpuscular Radiation" *J. Geophys. Res.*, Vol. 64, p. 1683.

VELIKOVSKY, IMMANUEL (1950). *Worlds in Collision.* New York: Macmillan Publishing Co., Inc.

VON BRAUN, WERNER, S. A. BEDINI, AND F. L. WHIPPLE (1970). *Moon—Man's Greatest Adventure.* New York: Harry N. Abrams.

WELLS, H. G. (1934). "The First Men on the Moon", *Seven Famous Novels.* New York: Alfred A. Knopf, Inc.

WHIPPLE, F. L. (1971). *Earth, Moon and Planets.* Cambridge, Mass.: Harvard University Press.

Random processes

Except possibly for the final sections on the method of least squares, the material in this chapter should be comprehensible to freshmen in both the sciences and humanities. The material on Poisson and Gaussian distributions in Sections 6.2–6.7 is introduced to clarify the meaning of probability distributions and quantities such as the variance and standard deviation, which are computed from the moments of the distribution. The one-dimensional random-walk problem (Section 6.8) provides a simple introduction to more general diffusion problems. Although the hard-sphere model of atomic diffusion (Section 6.10) may be primarily of interest to students heading toward the physical sciences, this material depends only on simple geometrical relations and provides insight for the later examples involving moth diffusion (Section 6.11) and the spread of disease (Sections 6.12–6.19). The sections on epidemiology (the Martian problem, the treatment of the common cold, and the spread of syphilis) are apt to be the most interesting to humanities students and at the same time illustrate both the power and appeal of Monte Carlo calculations. Sections 6.20–6.22 on the method of least squares will be of most interest to students in the physical sciences and contain the hardest material in the chapter; however, these sections also deal with one of the most important applications of computers in contemporary scientific research.

We shall consider some general properties of random processes in this chapter and illustrate these properties by consideration of specific problems in atomic diffusion, ecology, and epidemiology. Finally, we shall conclude the chapter with a discussion of the method of least squares.

The words "Brownian motion" frequently evoke in one's memory the theory of the effect worked out by Einstein in 1905 rather than the nineteenth-century Scottish botanist, Robert Brown, who first described *Brownian movement.* While investigating the pollen of various plants in solution (using a "simple pocket microscope"), Brown observed a continuous, random motion in these particles which he attributed to a "primitive molecule" of living matter. Brown (1828) commented:

> While examining the form of these particles immersed in water, I observed many of them very evidently in motion; their motion consisting not only of a change of place in the fluid . . . but also not unfrequently of a change of form in the particle. . . . These motions were such as to satisfy me . . . that they arose neither from currents in the fluid, nor from its gradual evaporation, but belonged to the particle itself. (p. 4).

Mixed in with the larger cylindrical-shaped particles present in most samples, he reported observing smaller, spherical particles in very rapid oscillatory motion. Brown concluded that these small spherical particles (about 1/20,000 inch in diameter) represented a simple molecule common to all the organic and inorganic substances that he examined.

> Rocks of all ages including those in which organic remains had never been found, yielded the molecules in abundance. Their existence was ascertained in each of the constituent minerals of granite, a fragment of the Sphinx being one of the specimens examined (*ibid.*, p. 9).

Although it is now known that the particles Brown saw were orders of magnitude larger than the primary molecules of the substances he examined, it is also clear that he was directly observing the effects of molecular collisions on these larger particles. Hence, in a very direct manner, the foundations of modern kinetic theory may be traced to these observations made by Brown during the summer of 1827. One might even read into this early work the visual demonstration that heat is a form of molecular motion.

Some feeling for the importance Einstein attributed to the Brownian motion problem can be obtained by noting that in the same year (1905) in which he published his first paper on special relativity and the photo effect (for which he later received the Nobel Prize), Einstein selected a version of his work on the Brownian motion problem (the determination of molecular dimensions through the speed of diffusion of molecules) for his doctoral dissertation at the University of Zürich (see Fig. 6-1).

An interesting historical summary of work on the problem was provided by Fürth (1956):

> Of the authors who carried out investigations on the Brownian movement before Einstein, we will mention the following: Regnault (1858) thought that the motion was caused by irregular heating by incident light. Chr. Weiner (1863) concluded that it could not have been brought about by forces exerted by the particles on one another, nor by temperature differences, nor by evaporation. Cantoni and Oehl (1865) found that the movement persisted unchanged for a whole year when the liquid was sealed up between two cover-glasses. S. Exner (1867) found that the movement is most rapid with the smallest particles, and is increased by light and heat rays. The idea of Jevons (1870) that the phenomenon is caused by electrical forces was denied by Dancer (1870), who showed that electrical forces had no influence on the

Eine neue Bestimmung der Moleküldimensionen.

Die ältesten Bestimmungen der wahren Grösse der Moleküle hat die kinetische Theorie der Gase ermöglicht, während die an Flüssigkeiten beobachteten physikalischen Phänomene bis jetzt zur Bestimmung der Molekülgrössen nicht gedient haben. Es liegt dies ohne Zweifel an den bisher unüberwindlichen Schwierigkeiten, welche der Entwickelung einer ins einzelne gehenden molekularkinetischen Theorie der Flüssigkeiten entgegenstehen. In dieser Arbeit soll nun gezeigt werden, dass man die Grösse der Moleküle des gelösten Stoffs in einer nicht dissoziierten verdünnten Lösung aus der inneren Reibung der Lösung und des reinen Lösungsmittels und aus der Diffusion des gelösten Stoffes im Lösungsmittel ermitteln kann, wenn das Volumen eines Moleküls des gelösten Stoffs gross ist gegen das Volumen eines Moleküls des Lösungsmittels. Ein derartiges gelöstes Molekül wird sich nämlich bezüglich seiner Beweglichkeit im Lösungsmittel und bezüglich seiner Beeinflussung der inneren Reibung des letzteren annähernd wie ein im Lösungsmittel suspendierter fester Körper verhalten, und es wird erlaubt sein, auf die Bewegung des Lösungsmittels in unmittelbarer Nähe eines Moleküls die hydrodynamischen Gleichungen anzuwenden, in welchen die Flüssigkeit als homogen betrachtet, eine molekulare Struktur derselben also nicht berücksichtigt wird. Als Form der festen Körper, welche die gelösten Moleküle darstellen sollen, wählen wir die **Kugelform.**

EINE NEUE BESTIMMUNG DER MOLEKÜLDIMENSIONEN

INAUGURAL-DISSERTATION

ZUR

ERLANGUNG DER PHILOSOPHISCHEN DOKTORWÜRDE

DER

HOHEN PHILOSOPISCHEN FAKULTÄT
(MATHEMATISCH-NATURWISSENSCHAFTLICHE SEKTION)

DER

UNIVERSITÄT ZÜRICH

VORGELEGT

VON

ALBERT EINSTEIN

AUS ZÜRICH

Begutachtet von den Herren Prof. Dr. A. KLEINER
und
Prof. Dr. H. BURKHARDT

BERN
BUCHDRUCKEREI K. J. WYSS
1905

Fig. 6-1. Title page and abstract of Einstein's PhD dissertation on the molecular diffusion problem. The text of the thesis occupies 16 printed pages; when told by Professor Kleiner that the thesis was too short as originally submitted, Einstein obligingly added one sentence and sent it back in. This technique for handling thesis sponsors probably only works when you have already written three revolutionary papers in your field. Professor Kleiner had already rejected an earlier thesis on thermodynamics submitted by Einstein in 1901 (see Hoffmann, 1972; pp. 35, 55). [The author is indebted to Helen Dukas, trustee of Einstein's literary estate, for permission to reproduce this material.]

motion. In 1877 Delsaux expressed for the first time the now generally-accepted idea that the Brownian movement has its origin in the impacts of the molecules of the liquid on the particles. This point of view was also expressed by Carbonelle.

The first precise investigations we owe to Guoy, who found that the motion is the more lively the smaller the viscosity of the liquid is (as follows also from the theory of Einstein); that very considerable changes of the intensity of illumination had no influence, nor had an extraordinarily strong electromagnetic field. He also ascribed the motion to the effect of the thermal molecular motions of the liquid, and found by measurement the velocity of different particles to be about a hundred-millionth of the molecular velocity.

Ramsay in 1892 disputed the possibility of an electrical origin of the Brownian movement, and affirmed that it must give rise to a pressure, by which certain departures from the established laws of osmotic pressure could be explained. Mäede Bache, in 1894, also accepted Gouy's point of view; while Quincke, in 1898, looked upon the motion as a result of temperature differences in the liquid.

Besides Gouy's work there is only one other investigation of a precise nature before Einstein's treatment of the problem: that carried out by F. M. Exner, who challenged Quincke's assertion, and established that the velocity of the movement decreases with increase of size of the particles and increases with rise of temperature. He expressed also the view that the kinetic energy of the particle must be equal to that of a gas molecule. Since, however, he calculated the former from the observed "velocity" of the particle, which is actually much smaller than the true velocity, his results did not agree. It first became possible to verify this relation by means of measurements of the Brownian motion made according to Einstein's method. (p. 86–88).

6.2 Poisson Distribution

Before treating any specific problems it will be useful to review some properties of random distributions. Consider a counting experiment in which we count f particles per second on the average (from, for example, a radioactive source whose lifetime is infinite compared to the time scale of our experiment). Assuming that the probability of detecting a particle at any instant in time is independent of the time, we shall show that the probability of counting precisely K particles during the large time interval, T, is given by

$$P_{fT}(K) = \frac{(fT)^K e^{-fT}}{K!} \qquad \text{(Poisson distribution)} \qquad (1)$$

Consider breaking up the large time interval T into L small intervals, Δt:

$$L = \frac{T}{\Delta t}$$

(We shall eventually take the limit in our expressions for $\Delta t \to 0$.)

The probability of obtaining 1 count in any small interval Δt is

$$p_{f\Delta t}(1) = f\,\Delta t \qquad (2)$$

(We neglect terms dependent on Δt^2 because they will vanish in respect to those dependent on Δt when we take the limit $\Delta t \to 0$.) The probability of obtaining zero counts in any small interval Δt is therefore

$$p_{f\Delta t}(0) = 1 - p_{f\Delta t}(1) = 1 - f\,\Delta t \qquad (3)$$

Next note that the probability of obtaining zero counts in the large interval T is the product of the L separate probabilities for getting zero counts in each of the small intervals:

$$P_{fT}(0) = p_{f\Delta t}(0) \cdot p_{f\Delta t}(0) \cdots p_{f\Delta t}(0) = (1 - f\,\Delta t)^L$$

(from the binomial theorem)

$$= 1 - \frac{L(f\,\Delta t)^1}{1!} + \frac{L(L-1)(f\,\Delta t)^2}{2!} - \frac{L(L-1)(L-2)(f\,\Delta t)^3}{3!} + \cdots$$

Hence in the limit that $L \gg 1$ (or $\Delta t \to 0$),

$$P_{fT}(0) \to 1 - \frac{(fL\,\Delta t)^1}{1!} + \frac{(fL\,\Delta t)^2}{2!} - \frac{(fL\,\Delta t)^3}{3!} + \cdots = e^{-fL\,\Delta t} = e^{-fT}$$

Therefore,

$$P_{fT}(0) = e^{-fT} \qquad (4)$$

or the case for $K = 0$ in Eq. (1) (note that $0! \equiv 1$).

The probability of obtaining one count in the large interval T is

$$P_{fT}(1) = \frac{T}{\Delta t} P_{f(T-\Delta t)}(0) p_{f\Delta t}(1) \to \frac{T}{\Delta t} e^{-f(T-\Delta t)} f\,\Delta t$$

That is, there are $T/\Delta t = L$ distinct ways of getting one count in a small interval Δt and zero counts in the remaining large time interval, $T - \Delta t$. Therefore, in the limit that $\Delta t \to 0$, we obtain

$$P_{fT}(1) = fTe^{-fT} \qquad (5)$$

or the case for $K = 1$ in Eq. (1).

The probability of obtaining two counts in the large time interval T is

$$P_{fT}(2) = \frac{(T/\Delta t)[(T/\Delta t) - 1]P_{f(T-2\Delta t)}(0)(f\,\Delta t)^2}{2} \to \frac{P_{fT}(0)(fT)^2}{2}$$

as $\Delta t \to 0$. That is, two small intervals must have one count and the remaining $(L - 2)$ have zero; there are $T/\Delta t$ ways to pick the first interval having one count and $(T/\Delta t) - 1$ ways to pick the second small interval having one count; the factor of 2 in the denominator occurs because only half the computed number is distinct (e.g., there is no difference in the total count if the first event occurs in the third Δt interval and the second event occurs in the ninth Δt interval or if the first occurs in the ninth interval and the second in the third.) Therefore, from Eq. (4),

$$P_{fT}(2) = \frac{(fT)^2 e^{-fT}}{2} \qquad (6)$$

as $\Delta t \to 0$, and we get the case for $K = 2$ in Eq. (1).

Similarly, if we consider the probability of obtaining K counts in the large interval T,

$$P_{fT}(K) = \frac{(T/\Delta t)[(T/\Delta t) - 1]\cdots[(T/\Delta t) - K]P_{f(T-K\,\Delta t)}(0)(f\,\Delta t)^K}{K!} \qquad (7)$$

there are $T/\Delta t$ ways to choose the first Δt interval getting one count, $(T/\Delta t) - 1$ ways to choose the second Δt interval getting one count, ..., and $(T/\Delta t) - K$ ways to choose the Kth; but only $1/K!$ of these ways are distinct. Hence (7) goes over to (1) as $\Delta t \to 0$. The form of Eq. (1) is shown in Fig. 6-2 as a function of K for different values of $N = fT$.

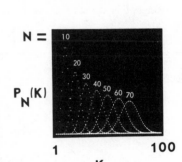

Fig. 6-2. Form of the Poisson distribution, $P_N(K)$, for values of N that range from 10 through 70 in steps of 10. $P_N(K)$ represents the probability of getting K counts when the average number is N.

6.2

PROBLEM 1

Write a program that plots the form of the Poisson distribution on the teletype terminal (or other plotting device) for various input values of $N = fT$ in Eq. (1) over the range $1 \leq K \leq 50$. (Compare with the results shown in Fig. 6-2.)

The average value of K^n over the distribution is defined by

$$\overline{K^n} \equiv \frac{\displaystyle\sum_{K=0}^{\infty} K^n P_{fT}(K)}{\displaystyle\sum_{K=0}^{\infty} P_{fT}(K)} \qquad (8)$$

6.3

Average Values and Moments
of a Poisson Distribution

The main properties of any probability distribution are characterized by the values of these averages, and the first three ($n = 0, 1, 2$) are of primary concern. They determine the normalization constant for the distribution ($n = 0$), the

average number of counts ($n = 1$) that would be recorded in the time interval T
if a counting experiment were done repeatedly, and a quantity (by combination of the results for $n = 1$ and 2) that is related to the average spread from the mean that would be obtained if the experiment were done over and over.

Normalization

Note from Eq. (1) that

$$\sum_{K=0}^{\infty} P_{fT}(K) = e^{-fT} \sum_{K=0}^{\infty} \frac{(fT)^K}{K!} = e^{-fT} e^{+fT} = 1$$

Hence the distribution is normalized to unity and Eq. (8) reduces to

$$\overline{K^n} = \sum_{K=0}^{\infty} K^n P_{fT}(K) \tag{9}$$

The expression in Eq. (9) is called the nth *moment* of the distribution, and it is seen that the nth moment is equal to the average value of K^n when the distribution is normalized.

Average Value of K

From Eq. (9) for $n = 1$,

$$\bar{K} = \sum_{K=0}^{\infty} K P_{fT}(K) = \sum_{K=1}^{\infty} K P_{fT}(K) = \sum_{K=1}^{\infty} \frac{K(fT)^K e^{-fT}}{K \cdot (K-1)!}$$

$$= fTe^{-fT} \sum_{K=1}^{\infty} \frac{(fT)^{K-1}}{(K-1)!} = fTe^{-fT} e^{+fT} = fT$$

Hence the average number of counts that would be measured when the experiment is done over and over for time intervals each equal to T is

$$\bar{K} = fT \tag{10}$$

($=$ average counting frequency times T) and is no surprise.

Average Value of K²

From Eq. (9) for $n = 2$,

$$\overline{K^2} = \sum_{K=0}^{\infty} K^2 P_{fT}(K) = \sum_{K=1}^{\infty} \frac{K^2(fT)^K e^{-fT}}{K \cdot (K-1)!}$$

$$= fTe^{-fT} \sum_{K=1}^{\infty} \left[\frac{K(fT)^{K-1}}{(K-1)!} - \frac{(fT)^{K-1}}{(K-1)!} + \frac{(fT)^{K-1}}{(K-1)!} \right]$$

(where we have subtracted and added the same quantity in the second and third terms for convenience)

$$= fTe^{-fT} \sum_{K=2}^{\infty} \frac{(K-1)(fT)^{K-1}}{(K-1) \cdot (K-2)!} + fTe^{-fT} \sum_{K=1}^{\infty} \frac{(fT)^{K-1}}{(K-1)!}$$

$$= (fT)^2 e^{-fT} \sum_{K=2}^{\infty} \frac{(fT)^{K-2}}{(K-2)!} + fTe^{-fT} e^{+fT} = (fT)^2 e^{-fT} e^{+fT} + fT$$

Therefore,

$$\overline{K^2} = (fT)^2 + (fT) = \bar{K}^2 + \bar{K} \tag{11}$$

(The average of the square equals the square of the average plus the average.)

The variance for any distribution is defined generally by

$$\text{variance} \equiv \overline{K^2} - \bar{K}^2 \tag{12}$$

where $\overline{K^n}$ was defined in Eq. (8), and for a *Poisson distribution* [from Eqs. (10) and (11)],

$$\text{variance} = \bar{K}^2 + \bar{K} - \bar{K}^2 = \bar{K} = fT$$

Hence

$$\text{variance} = \bar{K} = fT \qquad \text{(Poisson distribution)} \qquad (13)$$

Note that the variance is inherently positive (always ≥ 0).

The *standard deviation* is defined generally by

$$\sigma = \sqrt{\text{variance}} \qquad (14)$$

Hence

$$\text{standard deviation} = \sigma = \sqrt{\bar{K}} = \sqrt{fT} \qquad \text{(Poisson distribution)} \qquad (15)$$

We shall show shortly that for $\bar{K}$ large, ≈ 68 percent of the time the measured number of counts will fall within $\pm\sigma$ of the mean. Hence the standard deviation is a good indication of the uncertainty, or *noise level*, in a counting experiment designed to measure the average number of events. Hence the *signal-to-noise ratio* in such an experiment is

6.5 Signal-to-Noise Ratio in a Counting Experiment

$$\frac{\bar{K}}{\sigma} = \sqrt{\bar{K}} \qquad \text{(Poisson distribution)} \qquad (16)$$

If the average number of events determined is 100, the statistical uncertainty is ≈ 10 and the signal-to-noide ratio $\approx 10:1$. Similarly, to get a signal-to-noise ratio of $1000:1$ in a counting experiment, the average number of recorded counts has to be $\approx 10^6$.

If the experiment consists of one in which a voltage is proportional to a signal counting rate, the statistical noise level is proportional to the square root of the voltage. Specifically, if $V = C\bar{K}$, then the limiting signal-to-noise ratio $= \sqrt{\bar{K}} = \sqrt{V/C}$, where C is a constant of proportionality dependent on the apparatus [e.g., see discussion of shot noise in Bennett, Sr., (1960)].

Suppose that we simultaneously have two independent, random sources present in a counting experiment with separate average counting frequencies f_1 and f_2, each satisfying separate Poisson distributions of form (1), and consequently each having separate average counts and variances given by Eqs. (10)–(13). Thus, for the two separate distributions, the averages are

6.6 Addition of Variances for Random and Independent Processes

$$\bar{K}_1 = f_1 T$$
$$\bar{K}_2 = f_2 T$$

and the variances are

$$\text{var}_1 = \bar{K}_1$$
$$\text{var}_2 = \bar{K}_2$$

At the same time, the simultaneous presence of these two random and independent sources will be exactly the same from the point of view of the counting statistics as we would find from *one* source with an average random counting frequency

$$f = f_1 + f_2$$

Hence, we know that the total average count obtained must be

$$\bar{K} = (f_1 + f_2)T = \bar{K}_1 + \bar{K}_2 \qquad (17)$$

and that the total variance must be

$$\text{variance} = \bar{K} = \bar{K}_1 + \bar{K}_2 = \text{var}_1 + \text{var}_2 \qquad (18)$$

Clearly a similar result would have been obtained for the simultaneous presence of any number of random and independent sources.

What we have shown is a special case of a very powerful and general theorem: for the simultaneous presence of a number of random and independent processes, the variance for the sum is the sum of the separate variances and the average of the sum is the sum of the averages. (For formal proofs of this general theorem see specialized texts on statistics such as those by Kolmogorov (1933), Doob (1953), or Fisz (1963).) One should note that the variances are all inherently positive, whereas the average values could be positive or negative, depending on the nature of the process.

For example, if we were looking at the difference between two counting experiments, the average difference count after time T would be

$$\bar{K}_1 - \bar{K}_2 = (f_1 - f_2)T \tag{19}$$

(and could be either positive or negative) whereas the total variance in the difference count would still be the sum of the separate (positive) variances.

Thus the total variance in the difference count[1] $= K_1 + K_2 = (f_1 + f_2)T$ and the standard deviation in the difference count would be the square root of the total variance. Thus the signal-to-noise ratio in the difference count would be

$$\frac{(f_1 - f_2)T}{\sqrt{(f_1 + f_2)T}} \tag{20}$$

Clearly, there could be a considerable noise level in the experiment even if $f_1 = f_2$, and hence the signal, $(f_1 - f_2)T$, were identically zero.

The Poisson distribution is rather cumbersome to handle specifically. Fortunately, the distribution goes over to a Gaussian distribution about the mean (as does the probability distribution for most random processes) at relatively small values for the average.

6.7

Transition from a Poisson Distribution to a Gaussian (or Normal) Distribution

In what follows we shall let $N = \bar{K}$ (the average value for the distribution). The Poisson distribution [Eq. (1)] then takes the form

$$P_N(K) = \frac{e^{-N}N^K}{K!} \tag{21}$$

and represents the probability of getting K counts when the average number is N. Note Stirling's approximation,

$$K! \approx e^{-K}K^K\sqrt{2\pi K} \qquad \text{for } K \text{ large} \tag{22}$$

---

[1] One can derive the above results very specifically (although *very* tediously) by noting that the probability of getting precisely K counts as the difference between the two distributions is

$$P_{(f_1-f_2)T}(+K) = \sum_{j=0}^{\infty} p_{f_1 T}(j+K)p_{f_2 T}(j) = \sum_{j=0}^{\infty} \frac{(\sqrt{f_1 f_2}T)^{2j}(f_1 T)^K}{(j+K)!j!}e^{-(f_1+f_2)T}$$

$$= \left(\frac{f_1}{f_2}\right)^K P_T(-K)$$

where $p_{f_1 T}$ and $p_{f_2 T}$ are the separate Poisson distributions for the two counting frequencies. One can further note that

$$P_{(f_1-f_2)T}(\pm K) = I_{|K|}(\sqrt{f_1 f_2}2T)\left(\frac{f_1}{f_2}\right)^{\pm K/2}e^{-(f_1+f_2)T}$$

where the $I_{|K|}$ are Bessel functions of imaginary argument whose properties permit showing explicitly that

$$\bar{K} = (f_1 - f_2)T \quad \text{and} \quad \overline{K^2} = [(f_1 - f_2)T]^2 + (f_1 + f_2)T$$

Hence the variance in the difference count is

$$\text{variance total} = (f_1 + f_2)T = \text{var}_1 + \text{var}_2$$

Obviously, use of the general theorem on the addition of variances is a much more pleasant and simple way to achieve precisely the same answer.

and let x be the difference in count from the mean for the distribution:

$$x = K - N \tag{23}$$

Putting (22) and (23) in (21),

and let x be the difference in count from the mean for the distribution:

Section 6.7
Transition from a Poisson
Distribution to a Gaussian
(or Normal) Distribution

$$x = K - N \tag{23}$$

Putting (22) and (23) in (21),

$$P_N(K) \approx \frac{e^{-N}N^K}{e^{-K}K^K\sqrt{2\pi K}} = \frac{e^x}{\sqrt{2\pi(N+x)}}\left(\frac{N}{N+x}\right)^{N+x} = \frac{e^x}{\sqrt{2\pi N}}\left(\frac{1}{1+x/N}\right)^{N+x+(1/2)} \tag{24}$$

The last expression in Eq. (24) may be expanded with the binomial theorem. In particular,

$$\left(\frac{1}{1+x/N}\right)^{N+x+(1/2)} \approx e^{-x-(x^2/2N)} \qquad \text{for } N \gg x \text{ and } N \gg 1 \tag{25}$$

The only significant failure of approximation (25) occurs for negligibly small values of the function. Consequently,

$$P_N(K) \to \frac{e^{-x^2/2N}}{\sqrt{2\pi N}} = \frac{e^{-x^2/2\sigma^2}}{\sqrt{2\pi}\sigma} \tag{26}$$

where σ is the standard deviation (see Fig. 6-3). Because in the limit $x/N \ll 1$ the distribution is approximately continuous, one frequently refers to the probability of obtaining x between x and $x + dx$ as

$$P(x)\,dx = \frac{e^{-x^2/2\sigma^2}}{\sqrt{2\pi}\sigma}\,dx$$

Hence a convenient normal form for the distribution is obtained by letting

$$y = \frac{x}{\sigma} \tag{27}$$

(i.e., y is the departure from the mean in units of the standard deviation), for which

$$P(y)\,dy = \frac{e^{-y^2/2}}{\sqrt{2\pi}}\,dy \tag{28}$$

It can be shown that

$$\int_{-\infty}^{+\infty} P(y)\,dy = 1 \tag{29}$$

(the total probability is normalized to 1) and by numerical integration that

$$\int_{-1}^{+1} P(y)\,dy = 0.6826\ldots \tag{30}$$

(the total probability of obtaining a result within 1 standard deviation of the mean ≈ 68.26 percent), and

$$\int_{-2}^{+2} P(y)\,dy = 0.9546\ldots$$

(the total probability of obtaining a result within 2 standard deviations of the mean ≈ 95.46 percent); and so on. Definite integrals of this type are tabulated in various publications and, of course, can be readily computed numerically.

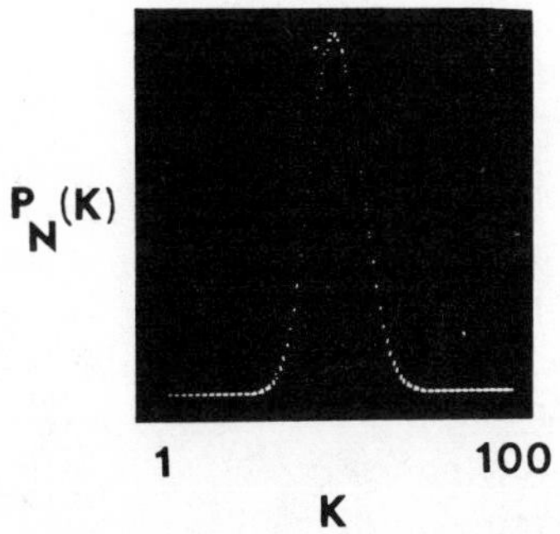

$P_N(K)$

1   100

K

Fig. 6-3. Superposition of Poisson and Gaussian distributions computed for the same standard deviation ($\sqrt{50}$) and ($N = 50$).

6.7 PROBLEM 2	Write a program to investigate the accuracy of approximation (25). For example, for different values of N entered from the keyboard, print out a table of values of $1/(1+X/N)\uparrow(N+X+.5)$ and $EXP(-X-.5*X*X/N)$ as a function of X for $1 \leqslant X \leqslant 20$.
6.7 PROBLEM 3	Write a program to compare corresponding forms of the Poisson and Gaussian distributions. For example, for different values of N entered from the

keyboard, print out a table of values for Eq. (1) and (26) as a function of K. If you have access to a high-resolution plotter, plot a superposition of the two probability distributions (see Fig. 6-3).

6.7
PROBLEM 4

Write a program to evaluate the Gaussian probability integrals of the type given in Eq. (30). (See Chapter 2, Section 2.22.)

6.7
PROBLEM 5

The results of the 1973 draft lottery caused consternation because the lowest two lottery numbers fell on consecutive dates (March 6 and 7).† Although we probably would never be able to convince anyone born on March 7 that the selection was indeed the result of a random process, it is of interest to investigate the nature of the distribution for evidence of unusual bunching. The results of the lottery under question are shown in the form of a DATA statement in Fig. 6-4, where the numbers appear consecutively in the order of

```
999   REM 1973 DRAFT LOTTERY   N.Y.TIMES FEB.3,1972, P.22
1000  DATA 150,328,42,28,338,36,111,206,197,37
1001  DATA 174,126,298,341,221,309,231,72,303,161
1002  DATA 99,259,258,62,243,311,110,304,283,114
1003  DATA 240,112,278,54,68,96,271,154,347,136
1004  DATA 361,26,195,263,348,308,227,46,11,127
1005  DATA 106,316,20,247,261,260,51,186,295,203
1006  DATA 322,220,47,266,1,2,153,321,331,239
1007  DATA 44,244,117,152,94,363,357,358,262,300
1008  DATA 317,22,71,65,24,181,45,21,213,326
1009  DATA 12,108,104,280,254,88,163,50,234,272
1010  DATA 350,23,169,81,343,119,183,242,158,314
1011  DATA 4,264,279,362,255,233,265,55,93,69
1012  DATA 58,275,166,172,292,337,145,201,276,100
1013  DATA 307,115,49,224,165,101,273,98,148,274
1014  DATA 310,333,216,246,122,118,293,18,133,48
1015  DATA 67,15,360,245,207,230,87,251,282,83
1016  DATA 178,64,190,318,95,16,32,91,238,52
1017  DATA 77,315,146,212,61,143,345,330,53,75
1018  DATA 142,39,297,109,92,139,132,285,355,179
1019  DATA 89,202,340,306,305,359,74,199,121,332
1020  DATA 33,5,286,365,324,35,204,60,185,222
1021  DATA 200,253,323,27,3,313,63,208,57,131
1022  DATA 7,249,125,198,329,205,241,19,8,113
1023  DATA 105,162,39,140,302,138,290,76,34,40
1024  DATA 84,182,218,219,17,226,356,354,173,144
1025  DATA 97,364,217,334,43,229,353,235,225,189
1026  DATA 289,228,141,123,268,296,236,291,29,248
1027  DATA 70,196,184,215,128,103,79,86,41,129
1028  DATA 157,116,342,319,171,269,14,277,59,177
1029  DATA 192,167,352,288,191,193,256,9,78,325
1030  DATA 349,327,346,10,107,214,232,339,223,211
1031  DATA 299,312,151,257,159,66,124,237,176,209
1032  DATA 284,160,270,301,287,102,320,180,25,344
1033  DATA 135,130,147,134,170,90,56,250,31,336
1034  DATA 267,210,120,73,82,85,335,38,137,187
1035  DATA 294,13,168,149,80,188,252,155,6,351
1036  DATA 194,156,175,281,164
```

Fig. 6-4. DATA statement summarizing the results of the 1973 draft lottery for use in Problem 5. (See offer in Preface.)

the birthdays. Those born on January 1 received the number 150, those born on January 2 got 328,... those born on December 31 received the number 164, and so on. The March 6 and 7 data are on line 1006. (See offer in Preface regarding DATA statements.)

Compute the distribution function, $N(I)$, representing the number of times that people with consecutive birthdates received lottery numbers differing by $\pm I$. From this distribution function, compute the average value of I, the average of I^2 over the distribution, and the actual standard deviation. To check on typographical errors in entering the data statement, show that the sum of the 365 lottery numbers is $N(N+1)/2$, where $N = 365$.

---

† *The New York Times*, Feb. 3, 1972, p. 1, col. 2; p. 22, cols. 3–5.

The simplest diffusion problem to treat conceptually is the one-dimensional one in which we visualize a drunk staggering along an alley. He or she makes steps of the same length with equal probability in the forward or backward direction. The question is: How far has the drunk diffused after N steps? (That is, what's the standard deviation of the distribution if the experiment is done over and over? Obviously the average displacement from the origin is zero.)

We can simulate this problem easily with the computer in a *Monte Carlo calculation* (i.e., we do the problem repeatedly by using the random-number generator to "shake the dice" for us at each step). For example,

```
 55  LET X = 128
 60  REM WANT RANDOM STEP S = +−1
 80  FOR I = 1 TO 100
 90  LET S = INT(RND(1) + .5)
 91  LET S = 2*S − 1
100  LET X = X + S
110  NEXT I
```

places the drunk initially at the point $X = 128$ (which might be the center of the display on a plotting device) and then makes him take 100 steps chosen randomly to be either ± 1.

In order to see the probability distribution for finding the drunk as a function of X, we have to do the problem over and over and keep track of the number of times that the drunk ends up at position X after 100 steps. We can do the latter by introducing an array of counters $N(X)$ that are all set to zero initially and are incremented each time the drunk ends on X after 100 steps. Note that only integer steps are taken by virtue of the statements on lines 90 and 91. Hence X may be used directly as an array index. Also note that we have deliberately set the problem up so the index can never reach zero or go negative. However, as stated above, the drunk only lands on even values of X.

We store the results of doing the problem over 1000 times by adding the statements

```
 50  FOR J = 1 TO 1000
120  LET N(X) = N(X) + 1
130  REM ONE COULD PRINT OR PLOT X,N(X) HERE
140  NEXT J
```

The note on line 130 is to remind one that a continuous histogram [$N(X)$ vs. X] could be plotted on an analog display device, if available. Otherwise, one has to wait until the end of the J loop to print or display the results of the simulation on a teletype or line printer (see Fig. 6-5).

After doing the experiment a large number (e.g., 1000) of times, one can determine the first ($X1$) and second ($X2$) moments of the actual distribution as follows:

```
200  REM CALC. AV. AND AV-SQUARE OF DISPLACEMENT
210  LET X1 = X2 = N0 = 0
220  FOR X = 1 TO 255
230  LET N0 = N0 + N(X)
240  LET X1 = X1 + N(X)*(X − 128)
250  LET X2 = X2 + N(X)*(X − 128)↑2
260  NEXT X
270  LET X1 = X1/N0
280  LET X2 = X2/N0
290  PRINT "N0 = "; N0, "X1 = "; X1, "X2 = "; X2
300  PRINT "STAND. DEV. = "; SQR(X2 − X1↑2)
305  LET N9 = SQR(X2 − X1↑2)
```

Here $N0$ was used to determine the normalization of the actual distribution obtained, $X1$ was used to determine the average displacement from the

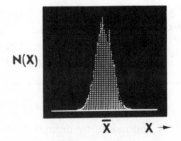

Fig. 6-5. One-dimensional random-walk problem. Superposition of a Gaussian distribution (dotted) with the same standard deviation with a histogram representing the number of times out of 1000 tries that the drunk landed at position X after starting at $\bar{X}$.

289

starting position (128), and *X2* was used to determine the mean-square displacement. These values were then used to compute the standard deviation $= N9 \approx 10 \; (=\sqrt{100})$.

Finally, it is of interest to compare the actual distribution obtained with that of a Gaussian normalized to the same peak height and standard deviation. Such a comparison is shown in Fig. 6-5. As may be seen readily from the figure, the actual distribution has gone over fairly closely to a Gaussian one by the end of 1000 measurements.

One could have estimated the result of the experiment quite accurately in the following manner. Imagine approximating the problem by the simultaneous presence of two Poisson distributions having the same average value $N' = 100/2 = 50$. One distribution function corresponds to the probability of taking positive steps (each of unit magnitude); the other corresponds to taking negative steps. What we want are the moments of the distribution corresponding to the difference between these two functions. From the discussion in connection with Eq. (19), the average value of the difference is zero. (Drunks don't get very far on the average.) However, the variance of the difference distribution is equal to the sum of the separate variances,

$$\text{var}_{\text{total}} = N' + N' = 50 + 50 = 100$$

Therefore, the standard deviation (or noise) for the difference is

$$\sqrt{\text{var}_{\text{total}}} = \sqrt{100} = 10$$

(drunks can be pretty noisy even if they don't get very far on the average). Consequently, one gets a very simple general result for a one-dimensional random-walk problem of the present type: the *root-mean-square* (rms) distance traveled is

$$L \approx \sqrt{N}S \tag{31}$$

where $N = N' + N'$ is the average total number of steps made in both directions combined and S is the step size. Further, the distribution will be approximately Gaussian about the initial location with a standard deviation $= L$.

6.8 PROBLEM 6 Write a program to simulate the one-dimensional random-walk problem. Compute the average displacement and standard deviation for a particular case and show that the distribution can be approximated by a Gaussian distribution in the limit of a large number of steps (see Fig. 6-5).

6.9 Accuracy of Monte Carlo Calculations Performed with RND(X)

It is impossible by definition to compute a truly random series of numbers. One, in principle, could make an endless series of measurements of some random physical process to generate such numbers, or store the results of a long series of such measurements in a table. However, in the interests of economy and simplicity, most computers incorporate a compromise algorithm for generating a sequence of numbers which at least superficially simulates the properties of a real random sequence. Because real computers can only represent numbers with finite accuracy, the approach typically used is to generate a set of integers I falling between zero and some maximum value M, from which the fraction, I/M, falling between zero and 1 is computed and

Chapter 6 / Random Processes

expressed as a floating-point number.[2] Because $I_{n+1} = f(I_n)$ of necessity in the algorithm, the sequence of numbers eventually settles down into a periodically repeating one. The practical usefulness of the sequence depends on the length of the period and that, in turn, increases with the maximum number of bits available to describe integers within the particular computer. Generally, the larger the number of bits per word within the computer, the longer the usable string of simulated random numbers becomes.

It is of interest to use the BASIC RND(X) function to generate a simple distribution whose first and second moments can be easily checked against an ideal random distribution. For example, the statements

```
 30   LET N1 = N2 = Ø
 80   PRINT "ENTER NØ"
 90   INPUT NØ
100   FOR I = 1 TO 255
110   LET N = Ø
120   FOR J = 1 TO NØ
130   LET S = INT(RND(1) + .5)
140   LET N = N + S
150   NEXT J
160   LET N1 = N1 + N
170   LET N2 = N2 + N*N
180   PRINT .5*NØ,N1/I,SQR(.5*NØ),SQR(N2/I−(N1/I)↑2)
190   NEXT I
```

permit making such a comparison. The random-number generator is used on line 13Ø to define a sequence of numbers that should take on the values $S = 0$ or 1 with equal probability. That is, if the average value of RND(1) is indeed 0.5, the integer function assures us that line 13Ø will result in equal numbers of zeros and 1's on the average. The loop on J (lines 12Ø through 15Ø) computes the sum of this sequence for N$\emptyset$ separate numbers. Hence on the average we should find that $N = 0.5*N\emptyset$ after line 15Ø. The loop on I between lines 1ØØ and 19Ø does this calculation 255 separate times and permits keeping running track of the average value of the sum ($N1/I$) and the average square of the sum ($N2/I$). The PRINT statement on line 18Ø prints a running comparison between the expected average value ($0.5*N\emptyset$) and the computed average value ($N1/I$), together with a comparison between the standard deviation ($\sqrt{0.5*N\emptyset}$) of a random distribution having the anticipated average value and the computed standard deviation ($\sqrt{N2/I - (N1/I)\uparrow 2}$) for the actual distribution.

Results obtained from running such a program for the case N$\emptyset = 255$ are shown in Fig. 6-6. Although the average values obtained are quite good, the

---

[2] The most successful randon-number generators appear to be special cases of a method originally introduced by D. H. Lahmer in 1948 [see discussion of random-number generators in Knuth (1969, Vol. 2, Chap. 3)]. The particular machine-language algorithm used in BASIC compilers is equivalent to a subroutine made up of normal BASIC statements of the type

```
REM SUB TO COMPUTE RND(X) ≡ R(X)
REM   I = 1 INITIALLY; J = 2↑15 + 3; M = 2↑31
LET I = J*I − M*INT(J*I/M)
LET R(X) = I/M
RETURN
```

M is a very large integer limited by the number of bits available per word in the computer; the constant integer J is $\approx$ factor 2 less than $\sqrt{M}$ and I is initialized to 1 at the start of the program. The first line computes an integer I from the previous value which amounts formally to the remainder when the product $J*I$ is divided by M (the operation is sometimes written $J*I$ MOD M). Although you can probably generate the first two or three values of RND(X) given by your compiler in the above manner, the fractional accuracy used for floating-point calculations in most compilers will be too small to get very far in the sequence without hitting the repetitive limit. The constants given above are based on a compiler utilizing 32 bits for the RND(X) generator.

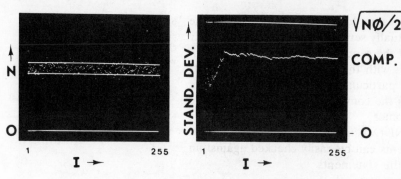

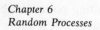

Fig. 6-6. Left: Values of N after line $15\emptyset$ are shown plotted as a function of I for the program discussed in the text. The two horizontal lines represent $\bar{N} \pm \sqrt{N}$, where $\bar{N}$ is the expected average number = 127.5 for the case shown. An ideal random distribution would have ≈ 68 percent of the points within the two parallel lines (i.e., they represent ± 1 standard deviation about the mean). As is visually evident, the distribution function generated from $\text{RND}(X)$ is not quite as noisy as a real random process would be; nevertheless, the average value is quite good.

Right: The dots represent a running computation of the standard deviation for the points shown at the left. The top line represents the standard deviation for an ideal random counting experiment having the same average value. The standard deviation for the simulated random counting experiment has a limiting value that is roughly ≈ 0.70 times that for the ideal random process.

distribution obtained is not as "noisy" as a truly random process should be. That is, the limiting standard deviation computed in a program of the above type is a little (typically ≈ 30 percent) lower than one would expect for an equivalent, purely random distribution. One is usually primarily interested in the average results in Monte Carlo calculations, and the lower noise level is generally not of great practical consequence. However, one should keep the effect in mind before taking computed standard deviations in such calculations too literally.

6.9 **PROBLEM 7**	Write a program using the $\text{RND}(X)$ function to simulate a random counting experiment in which N counts are measured on the average. Compare the average values and standard deviations computed from your program with the expected average (N) and standard deviation $(\sqrt{N})$.
6.9 **PROBLEM 8**	One can devise other statements to substitute in line $13\emptyset$ of the program discussed in the text which result in the same average value for S. In addition to LET $S = \text{INT}(\text{RND}(1) + .5)$, one might try LET $S = \text{INT}(2*\text{RND}(1))$ or LET $S = \text{INT}(\text{RND}(1) + \text{RND}(2))$, where we have introduced two separate values for the dummy argument of $\text{RND}(X)$ in the second case to emphasize that the generator is consulted twice. One *might* intuitively expect that these last two choices would have significantly more noise about the average than the first. (They don't.) Compare the results for the average value and standard deviations for the three choices using a program such as that discussed in the text.
6.9 **PROBLEM 9**	One might expect differences in the average value and standard deviation obtained from different sections of the random-number generator. Try running a program such as the one in the text for substantially different regions of the generator. For example, what happens to the average value and standard deviation if you consult $\text{RND}(X)$ 10,000 times before computing the distribution?

Any quantitative model of atomic diffusion (for example, that used to describe the Brownian motion problem) requires an assumption on the form of the interaction between atoms. You can make the assumption on this interaction as complicated as you like. However, for the purposes of illustration here, we shall assume a hard-sphere (billiard-ball) model and limit the specific treatment to a two-dimensional diffusion problem. We shall assume further that we wish to analyze the diffusion of light atoms through a much larger density of very heavy atoms having the same radius, $R\emptyset$. The situation will be somewhat similar to an occasional helium atom diffusing through a low-pressure gas of xenon atoms.[3]

There will, in general, be a parameter (which we shall define here to be $L\emptyset$), which represents the average distance from a particular light atom to the nearest heavy atom. Generally,

$$L\emptyset^3 = \frac{1}{N}$$

where N = number of heavy atoms per cm^3 (proportional to the pressure).

Because of the randomness of the distribution of atoms in a gas, there will be a random variation in the distance a particular atom goes after the last collision before the next encounter. That distance (D) will generally be enormous compared to the atom's dimensions ($\approx 2R\emptyset$). Hence we shall assume that the scattering interaction at each successive collision is sharply localized to a point a distance D away from the last scattering center, where D is the actual distance the particular atom goes before the next collision. Figure 6-7 illustrates the geometrical relationships assumed in the problem.

For a collision, the angle O is (randomly) distributed over

$$-\frac{\pi}{2} < O < +\frac{\pi}{2}$$

and we shall simulate the randomness by the statement

LET 0 = 3.14159*[RND(1) − 0.5]

(average = 0; peak values $\pm \pi/2$).

Similarly, the randomness in the distance, L, may be simulated by

LET L = L0*2*RND(1)

(average = $L\emptyset$ and L is spread between zero and $2*L\emptyset$).

The *impact parameter* (see Fig. 6-7), B, is obtained from geometry along with the actual distance, D, traveled by the atom along its original velocity direction before the "next" collisions; hence B and D are given by

LET B = L*SIN(0)
LET D = L*COS(0)

Next note that in the hard-sphere model, no collision occurs (scattering angle, S, equals zero) if $|B| > 2R\emptyset$. The angle of incidence (about the normal to the surface of contact) equals the angle of reflection for elastic collisions of the present type. Hence, from geometry and the above discussion we may handle the scattering by the following statements:

IF ABS(B) > = 2*R0 THEN . . . (LET S = 0)

---

[3] We make this assumption merely to avoid obscuring the random-walk concept by the complexity that results from transformations between the center of mass and laboratory reference frames.

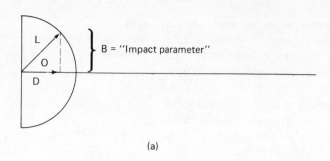

(a)

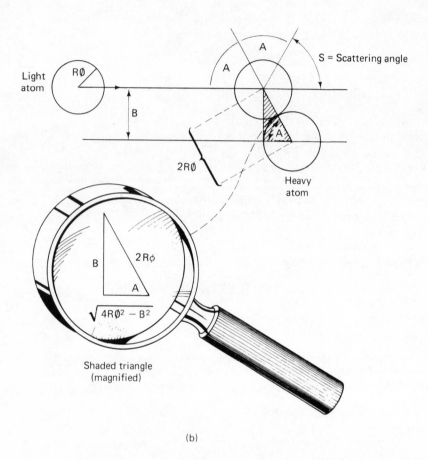

(b)

Fig. 6-7. Geometry used in the atom diffusion problem.

(a) Relation between the quantities L, O, and D and the impact parameter, B. $O \equiv$ angular location of next scatterer, a particular distance L away ($\bar{L} = L\emptyset$); and D = actual distance atom goes (before hitting next atom) in direction of its initial velocity.

(b) Relation between B, $R\emptyset$, A and the scattering angle, S. It is assumed that a light atom enters from the left and undergoes an elastic collision with the heavy atom at the right (both having the same radii, $R\emptyset$).

Otherwise

LET A = ATN(B/SQR(4*R∅*R∅−B*B))

(where we don't have to worry about the quadrant problem because we are only considering the first and fourth quadrants for a collision to occur) and the scattering angle is given by

LET S = 3.14159−2*A

As a specific example, consider the following program for computing the mean time and spread about the mean for light atoms released at the center of a two-dimensional box (255 units on an edge) to diffuse to the walls. After some routine initial statements,

```
15   REM RØ = HARDSPHERE RADIUS, LØ = MEAN-FREE PATH
20   PRINT "ENTER LØ,RØ"
30   INPUT LØ,RØ
40   LET T1 = T2 = Ø
```

we can proceed to calculate 20 separate Monte Carlo trajectories (using the parameter K) in the following manner:

```
50   FOR K = 1 TO 20
55   LET T = Ø
60   LET X = Y = 128
70   REM PLOT OR STORE INITIAL VALUE OF X,Y HERE IF DESIRED
80   LET S = 2*3.14159*RND(1)
```

Line 8Ø starts the light atom off at $T = 0$ with a randomly chosen angle within our two-dimensional diffusion problem from the initial point $X = Y = 128$. We shall assume that the atom velocity is constant. We wish to compute the time for the atom to diffuse to the walls of the box (assumed to be at X and $Y = 0$ and 255, parallel to the X and Y axes) for each Monte Carlo trajectory. The units of time are discussed below. Then by repeating the computation numerous times (the loop on K), determine the mean time ($T1$) and the mean-square time ($T2$) for the diffusion process.

The time, T, to reach the wall during an individual trajectory is obtained through a series of statements, which first choose a random distance L to the next atom (based on the assumed mean distance, $LØ$), choose a direction O for the location of this nearest atom in the forward direction, and then compute the actual distance, D that the incident atom would go (if it did not hit the walls) before hitting the nearest atom (see Fig. 6-7).

```
100   LET L = 2*LØ*RND(1)
110   LET O = 3.14159*(RND(1) − .5)
120   LET B = L*SIN(O)
130   LET D = L*COS(O)
135   LET CØ = COS(S)
136   LET SØ = SIN(S)
```

We have stored the cos S and sin S on lines 135 and 136 to avoid needlessly recomputing these values in the following section of the program.

We next break the path through the distance D to the scattering atom into a large number of small steps (dependent on the resolution required in the calculation) and check to see if the incident atom hits the wall on the way. During each one of the steps, the time is incremented by an amount equal to the step size divided by the incident atom velocity. For simplicity we shall assume both the step size and time increment to be unity here; however, these increments can be easily adjusted to match a particular experiment.

```
140   FOR R = Ø TO D − 1 STEP 1
145   LET T = T + 1
150   LET X = X + 1*CØ
160   LET Y = Y + 1*SØ
170   REM PLOT OR STORE X,Y COORDINATES HERE IF DESIRED
171   IF X > = 225 THEN 300
172   IF Y > = 225 THEN 300
173   IF X < = Ø THEN 300
174   IF Y < = Ø THEN 300
180   NEXT R
```

The conditional statements on lines 171–174 check to see if the atom has hit the walls and, if so, sends the program to line 3ØØ. Otherwise, the program remains within the loop on R until the next scattering atom has been reached. We then compute a hard-sphere scattering angle, S1, using the geometry in Fig. 6-7 and results of our previous discussion. Note that the angle S1 represents an increment to the original angle S. Line 25Ø below performs the increment and the program returns to line 1ØØ, where the next scattering center is located.

```
199   REM HARD SPHERE SCATTERING ANGLE NEXT
200   IF B*B > = 4*RØ*RØ THEN 240
210   LET A = ATN(B/SQR(4*RØ*RØ − B*B))
220   LET S1 = 3.14159 − 2*A
230   GOTO 250
240   LET S1 = Ø
250   LET S = S + S1
260   GOTO 100
```

Eventually, the atom hits the wall (lines 171–174) and the program is sent to line 3ØØ. Here we can print out the time (T) for one diffusion trajectory and increment the variables used to keep track of the average diffusion time (T1) and the average of the square of the time (T2).

```
300   PRINT T
310   LET T1 = T1 + T
320   LET T2 = T2 + T*T
330   NEXT K
```

Closing the loop on K then permits doing the computation 20 times in the program above. Hence the final values for average time and average of the square of the time after 20 trajectories are given by

```
340   LET T1 = T1/20
350   LET T2 = T2/20
```

The results for the mean diffusion time and computed standard deviation about the mean are then printed out by the statements

```
360   PRINT T1, SQR(T2 − T1*T1)
9999  END
```

Hence the calculation not only gives us the average time for the process but an indication of the probable variation about this average. (The computed standard deviation will generally be slightly underestimated, for the reasons discussed in Section 6.9.) A sample trajectory for the problem is illustrated in Fig. 6-8.

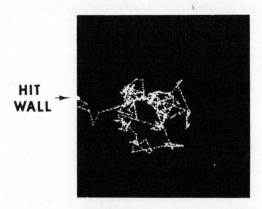

HIT WALL →

Fig. 6-8. Sample trajectory for the two-dimensional hard-sphere diffusion program (computed for $LØ = 3$, $RØ = 0.1$). The box was assumed to be square and to have sides 255 units long and the atom was released from the center at $T = 0$.

The problem, as it is written above, provides information that could be estimated easily in closed-form analysis using the concepts discussed earlier in the chapter. However, only relatively slight differences need be made in the problem to make a closed-form analysis extremely prohibitive. For example, consider light atoms entering from one end of a long rectangular box in which the temperature of the walls has a large and specified variation. The "sticking probability" of the atoms at the wall will be strongly dependent on the wall temperature due to condensation effects. One can introduce a sticking probability function, together with an assumption on the nature of the reflection distribution at the walls, and thereby obtain the spatial variation of light atom density in the region; and so on.

6.10
PROBLEM 10

Consider light atoms entering a pinhole on the axis of a narrow two-dimensional tube 40 units long and 4 units wide. The tube contains heavy atoms of the same size such that the mean distance $(L\emptyset)$ for the light atoms is 3 units and the common radius for the two types of spherical atoms is 0.1 unit. Suppose that the probability is 0.1 per bounce that the light atoms are removed by a chemical reaction at the side walls, and that the ones that are not removed are reflected elastically (angle of incidence equals the angle of reflectance). Assuming hard-sphere collisions, write a program that permits determining the average percent of light atoms which reach the far end of the tube. (The situation described is analogous to that which might be encountered in a liquid air trap, a "getter" pump, or even a catalytic converter.)

6.10
PROBLEM 11

By keeping track of the relative number of times a light atom wanders into each unit area of the tube in the previous problem, it is possible to compute the average relative spatial distribution of light atoms when they enter at a constant rate. For example, one could define a matrix, M, with 4×40 elements which was initially set to zero and then increment the element, $M(I, J)$, at each time increment when the atom is found with coordinates I and J. The normalized distribution may then be plotted on a teletype terminal using the contour-plotting technique discussed in Section 3.5. (The same information could also be conveyed by plotting a probability cloud in the manner of Section 3.4) Write a program to display the average distribution of light atoms in the preceding problem.

6.10
PROBLEM 12

Use the geometry of Problem 10 and the method in Problem 11 to compute the atom density when an untrapped mercury diffusion pump is connected to a tube with a small helium leak at one end. Assume that all wall collisions result in reflecting the atoms back into the (two-dimensional) tube with random direction but that any light atom reaching the pump end is permanently removed. Assume that the heavy-atom density (e.g., mercury) is constant throughout the tube and use the parameters for $L\emptyset$ and $R\emptyset$ in Problem 10. Neglect collisions between the light atoms.

6.10
RESEARCH PROBLEM

It has only been appreciated during the past few years that mankind may well be on the road to self-destruction through the effects of global pollution. Most concern has been for the vulnerability of the stratospheric ozone layer to catalytic destruction by molecules released in aerosol sprays, the exhaust of supersonic transport planes, and the debris of nuclear explosions. The temperature inversion in the stratosphere inhibits convective mixing, and diffusion is the main process for vertical migration of molecules to and from this part of the atmosphere. Consequently, the time constants for pollutants to leave the stratosphere vary from about one year in the lower (15-km) region to many years in the higher (20- to 30-km) regions. The problem is complicated by the variation of densities and temperatures with altitude, the presence of chemical reactions, and the effects of solar and cosmic radiation. Investigate some aspect of the ozone layer depletion problem. (See the review paper by Johnston, 1974.)

Recent infestations of the New England area by large quantities of span-worm and gypsy moths have provided a minor threat to the ecology and a considerable nuisance to the homeowner and farmer. Some authors blame the current difficulty on the reduction of natural predators which has resulted through prolonged use of chemical insecticides; hence an inevitable buildup in moth population took place when the use of such chemical insecticides was recently curtailed.[4]

It therefore appears desirable to investigate nonchemical means for selective destruction of moths. Many moths are attracted strongly by localized sources of light in the evening. (Certainly the latter is true of span-worm moths, although less true of gypsy moths.) It seems probable that, in fact, the main attraction comes in the form of scattered light from other moths (for example, the moth population does not fly off toward the moon in the evening). It would not be surprising to find that this effect is somehow associated with the mating process; most irrational things are. In any event, if we could develop an efficient way to lure moths to their destruction on the basis of scattered light before the mating occurs, we might be able to help the situation without further upsetting the ecological balance.

We therefore shall investigate the following sort of moth trap: consider illuminating a narrow pencil of space in the infestation region with the beam from a laser. Until it stumbles accidentally into the beam, a moth diffuses about with some effective mean free path much like the atomic diffusion problem. Once the moth hits the laser beam, the power can be automatically turned up, thereby cooking the moth and attracting other moths to the same spot through the intense scattered light emitted in the cooking process.

It should be emphasized that this could be accomplished with a minimal expenditure in electrical power per moth. The main expenditure is for the initial cost of the laser. As a numerical example, rough measurements by the author indicate that a power density of $\approx 2 \, W/mm^2$ in the beam at 5145 angstroms (Å) (green) is enough to burn the wings off a span-worm moth in ≤ 1 sec and produce a blinding flash of light. An argon laser costing $\approx \$8000$ initially, with a mean lifetime of ≈ 1000 hours and an efficiency ≈ 0.1 percent, thus costs ≈ 0.2 cent per moth in initial investment and $\approx 5 \times 10^{-4} \, kWh$ per moth to operate (≤ 0.002 cent per moth even with the 1973 Arab embargo on oil).

The arrangement in Fig. 6-9 is probably the easiest to test in practice. We shall assume that the laser beam is normally idling at a very low power level and is only turned up when the signal to the detector is blocked. (It is, of course, advantageous to keep the beam far enough above ground to avoid cooking basketball players and tall farm animals.)

One would, of course, want to measure the moth mean free path and cross section before building a really large system. Nevertheless, we can simulate this problem with a reasonable estimate of the experimental parameters. The problem is, of course, extremely nonlinear in the number of moths and would be very difficult to analyze without a computer.

For illustration, we shall consider a simplified, two-dimensional version of

[4] See, for example, Ehrlich and Holdren (1971).

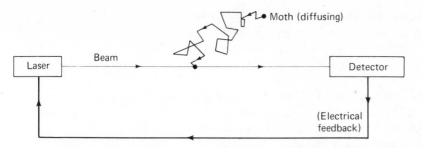

Fig. 6-9. Top view of moth trap. Beam is kept at low idling intensity until moth(s) diffuse into beam. Decreased detector output then turns up laser power, thereby cooking moth(s) and attracting others with scattered light.

the problem in which $N\emptyset$ moths are present at $T = 0$ with randomly specified coordinates X and Y spread over the domain $0 \leqslant X, Y \leqslant 255$. Each moth is flying in a direction randomly distributed in angle A over the region $0 \leqslant A \leqslant 2\pi$.

This much of the problem is accomplished with the following routine statements:

```
  1   REM NONLINEAR MOTH TRAP
 10   DIM X(100),Y(100),A(100)
 20   PRINT "NUMBER OF MOTHS"
 25   INPUT NØ
 30   LET N = NØ
 40   LET T = Ø
 85   REM L = LOCATION AND S = WIDTH OF LASER BEAM
 90   LET L = 128
 95   LET S = 2

100   REM INITIAL RANDOM POSITIONS FOR N MOTHS NEXT
110   FOR I = 1 TO N
120   LET X(I) = 255*RND(1)
130   LET Y(I) = 255*RND(1)
135   REM PLOT OR STORE COORDINATES X,Y HERE IF DESIRED
140   NEXT I
145   REM RANDOM ANGLE EACH MOTH MOVES IN NEXT
150   FOR I = 1 TO N
160   LET A(I) = 6.28318*RND(1)
170   NEXT I
```

Next we want the N moths to execute a two-dimensional random-walk process until one of them stumbles into the laser beam (located at $Y = 128$ with a width of $S = 2$). Assuming the moth mean free path to be 20 units, the random walk may be simulated by the following statements (in which the step size is made equal to S, hence the width of the laser beam).

```
190   REM RANDOM WALK FOR N-MOTHS UNTIL ONE HITS LASER BEAM
200   FOR R = 1 TO 20
205   LET T = T+1
210   FOR I = 1 TO N
230   LET X(I) = X(I) + S*COS(A(I))
240   LET Y(I) = Y(I) + S*SIN(A(I))
250   REM PLOT OR STORE COORDINATES X(I),Y(I) HERE IF DESIRED
255   IF INT(L/S+.5) = INT(Y(I)/S+.5) THEN 300
260   NEXT I
265   NEXT R
270   GOTO 150
```

The unit of time is the time that a moth takes to fly through the laser beam, assuming that all N moths fly with the same velocity. That is, each moth is assumed to move a distance S when T is incremented by 1. If the conditional statement on line 255 is satisfied, it means that the Ith moth is in the laser beam and we move on to a section that cooks the Ith moth and redirects the others toward the intense burst of light. Otherwise, the program iterates to line 15∅, where a new set of randomly chosen angles is defined and we continue the random-walk process.

Once a moth is hit by the beam, the program goes to line 3∅∅, where we store the coordinates of the cooked moth in the variables X and Y, reduce the moth population by 1, and then redirect all remaining moths toward the cooked moth for (up to) one moth mean free path. The last choice is somewhat arbitrary but seemed to be a reasonable assumption in the absence of precise experimental data.

```
300   REM STORE COORDINATES OF BURNING MOTH IN X,Y
305   LET X = X(I)
310   LET Y = Y(I)
315   REM REDUCE MOTH POPULATION BY ONE
320   FOR J = I TO N−1
330   LET X(J) = X(J+1)
340   LET Y(J) = Y(J+1)
350   NEXT J
360   LET N = N−1
370   IF N = 0 THEN 900
```

If the conditional statement on line 37∅ is satisfied, it means that the moths are all gone and it is time to evaluate the results (line 9∅∅). Otherwise, we redirect the remaining moths towards the coordinates X and Y of the last one cooked. This process involves computing the angular directions for each of the remaining N moths. As usual, the only problem involved is in getting the right quadrants for the angles from the arctangent relation and in avoiding singularities when the angles approach $\pm\pi/2$. One way of accomplishing these objectives is as follows:

```
380   FOR J = 1 TO N
385   REM PLOT OR STORE COORDINATES X,Y IF DESIRED
390   REM FIND RIGHT QUADRANTS OF ANGLES TO DIRECT REMAINING MOTHS
395   LET G = X−X(J)
400   LET H = Y−Y(J)
405   IF G#0 THEN 425
410   LET A(J) = −1.57080
415   IF H>0 THEN 435
420   GO TO 440
425   LET A(J) = ATN(H/G)
430   IF G>0 THEN 440
435   LET A(J) = A(J)+3.14159
440   NEXT J
500   GO TO 200
```

[Note that $ATN(X)<\emptyset$, for $X<\emptyset$.] Alternatively, one could determine unit vectors pointing toward the cooked moths and avoid evaluating angles altogether. Line 5∅∅ sends the program back for one more pass through the FOR loop on R, during which the remaining moths fly toward the coordinates of the burnt moth for one mean free path (or until the next moth stumbles into the beam). Finally, after they are all gone, we print (or otherwise evaluate the results) on line 9∅∅:

```
900   PRINT N0;"MOTHS IN TIME ";T;" AV. TIME PER MOTH = "; T/N0
9999  END
```

One could, of course, introduce all sorts of further complications with considerable ease: different burning times, inverse-square-loss, and a threshold sensitivity for the remaining moths to respond to the flash, three-dimensional character of the problem, random variation in path lengths, and so on.

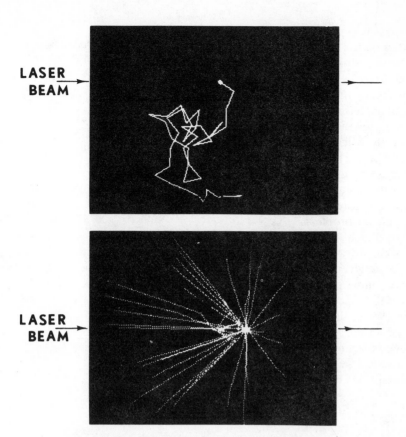

LASER
BEAM

LASER
BEAM

Fig. 6-10. Some results from the moth-diffusion program. Upper figure: 1 moth at $T = 0$; 85 time units to hit beam. Lower figure: 32 moths at $T = 0$; 3.4 time units per moth for destruction. The laser-beam location is indicated by the horizontal lines.

Similarly, one could calculate the mean time per moth and standard deviation as a function of the number of initial moths. The program given above is primarily intended to illustrate the extreme efficiency of the method which occurs at large $N\emptyset$ (see Fig. 6-10).

6.11
PROBLEM 13
Modify the above moth program so that it computes the mean time per moth and standard deviation about the mean for 20 separate calculations. Try it out for $N\emptyset = 10$ and 20 moths at $T = 0$.

Most quantitative studies in the field of epidemiology (the study of the spread of disease) seem largely oriented toward gathering statistical data rather than the development of mathematical models of the contagion problem. For example, many data have been accumulated on the total number of cases of various diseases as a function of time and geographical location, and even a quantity known as the "attack rate" [essentially, $(1/N_0)dN/dt$, where N_0 is the total population and dN/dt is the rate of increase of the number of cases] is frequently tabulated. However, relatively little work seems to have been done on the other side of the equation.[5] The equations are complicated by both severe nonlinearities and random fluctuaations. However, one clearly can simulate the main features of the time development of disease within a given population group using Monte Carlo–type calculations on a high-speed digital computer.

6.12
Epidemiology: The Diffusion of Disease

[5] See, for example, Burton and Smith (1970).

Most diseases have a number of characteristics in common. We shall make the assumption that the transfer of infection occurs only in localized interactions between pairs of individuals and is governed by two probability factors, one sociological (essentially the probability of the encounter per unit time) and the other medical (the probability that the infection is transferred during the encounter). In addition, the net transfer of infection as a result of such an interaction will depend on the previous history of the two individuals. Specifically, was one contagious and the other healthy, but not immune? In the most general form imaginable, the problem would be very difficult (e.g., the spread of bubonic plague by the fleas on rats) because of lack of reliable information on all the necessary probability factors. But it does appear realistic to set up a model for the spread of disease between two separate population groups which at least includes the main features of the general problem.

We shall set up a model of the problem in which we periodically sample the population groups and calculate enough specific "trajectories" for the contagion to determine the average behavior for a given set of initial boundary conditions. The natural unit of time for the sample period will depend on the mean values and variation from the mean of the incubation, cure, and immunity time constants for the particular disease. We shall thus measure these time constants in units of the sample period and adopt a sample period that is at least smaller than the smallest of these time constants.

The average number of infections transferred per sample period between population group N and population group M due to contact between all individuals i and j will then be of the form

$$\sum_{i,j} M(i)P_{soc}(i,j)P_{med}N(j) \tag{32}$$

where j must be contagious and i healthy (and not immune) for the interaction to result in an incubating infection in i; and i must be contagious and j healthy (and not immune) to result in an incubating infection in j.

The medical probability factor, P_{med}, will satisfy

$$P_{med} \leq 1 \tag{33}$$

because it represents the probability per exposure that the disease be transferred between a contagious and a healthy individual in one encounter.

The sociological probability factor, P_{soc}, may be greater than unity because it merely represents the average number of exposures between the i, j pair per sample period.[6]

Although of different origin, the two probability factors may be combined to yield one factor,

$$P_0(i,j) \equiv P_{soc}(i,j)P_{med} \tag{34}$$

which may be greater than unity. If there is a significant difference between the average behavior of the individuals within a group and the average behavior of the group, it is necessary to retain the matrix character of the net probability factors. The matrix is at least symmetric and in many instances could be broken down into a few different elements.

If the average behavior of the individuals within a group is the same as the average of the group, we may say that

$$P_0(i,j) = P_0 \tag{35}$$

where, again, P_0 may be greater than unity. In this instance (which is the only one that we shall treat with specific numerical examples here), one can replace

---

[6] Note that the assumption of pair interactions is equivalent to the two-body collision model used in kinetic theory to treat a dilute gas. The assumption will break down in the "liquid state" (e.g., a crowded subway at Times Square during rush hour).

a systematic scan through the entire population every sample period by a random selection of pairs of individuals which results in every member of the group being sampled once on the average per sample period. The latter situation results in a much greater economy in running time than a systematic scan of the entire population.

Suppose that P_0 is the average probability to transfer contagion per person per exposure and each member of the population is sampled once on the average per sample period in a situation where the average behavior of the individual is the same as the average behavior of his group.

It is helpful to consider constructing a function that takes on the binary values 0 and 1 randomly in such a way as to yield an average value, P_0, for $P_0 < 1$. One choice that *appears* to satisfy this requirement is the BASIC statement

$$\text{LET P} = \text{INT(RND(1)} + \text{P}\emptyset). \tag{36}$$

where $P\emptyset$ is a program variable corresponding to the quantity P_0. Obviously, statement (36) has the desired average value. But, as we will show, it has rather poor statistical properties. A better choice is

$$\text{LET P} = \text{INT(RND(1)} + 2*\text{P}\emptyset*\text{RND(2))} \tag{37}$$

where we have used a different argument in the second random-number generating function to emphasize that there are two different random numbers in statement (37). We can show directly, using a program of the type outlined below, that although the average behavior of (36) and (37) is equivalent, the statistical properties are very different.

```
 80   PRINT "PØ", "MEAN", "STAND. DEV."
 85   FOR PØ = 0 TO 1 STEP .1
 90   LET S1 = S2 = 0
 94   FOR J = 1 TO 100
 95   LET S = 0
100   FOR I = 1 TO 100
110   LET P = INT(RND(1) + PØ)
120   LET S = S + P
140   NEXT I
150   LET S = S*1.00000E − 02
160   LET S1 = S1 + S
170   LET S2 = S2 + S*S
180   NEXT J
190   LET S1 = 1.00000E − 02*S1
200   LET S2 = 1.00000E − 02*S2
210   PRINT PØ,S1,SQR(S2 − S1*S1)
220   NEXT PØ
```

(The program computes the average, average square, and standard deviation in the manner previously discussed.)

Computed results based on the above program are shown below for both probability functions over a range in $P\emptyset$. Note that the standard deviation for statement (37) varies roughly as $\sqrt{P\emptyset}$ even for $P\emptyset > 1$, whereas that for statement (36) goes through maxima at $\approx 0.5, 1.5, 2.5, \ldots$ and is not well behaved even for $P\emptyset < 1$.

	P = INT(RND(1) + PØ)		P = INT(RND(1) + 2*PØ*RND(2))	
PØ	MEAN	STAND. DEV.	MEAN	STAND. DEV.
Ø	Ø	Ø	Ø	Ø
.1	.101099	2.79985E − 02	9.65987E − 02	2.70656E − 02
.2	.193597	3.81789E − 02	.198097	3.91907E − 02
.3	.299996	4.37400E − 02	.297497	4.47164E − 02

.4	.398495	5.18223E−02	.400195	5.32739E−02
.5	.502894	4.73261E−02	.494392	4.77015E−02
.6	.590593	4.98143E−02	.606293	5.15819E−02
.7	.70179	4.14895E−02	.697891	5.99767E−02
.8	.807689	3.98421E−02	.805389	5.82305E−02
.9	.896688	2.83960E−02	.892388	7.64725E−02
1	.999983	4.14320E−03	.992888	6.91879E−02
1.5	1.49728	4.88672E−02	1.50488	.109026
2	1.99997	8.28641E−03	1.98797	.12132
2.5	2.49697	5.06308E−02	2.50437	.154235
3	2.99995	1.31745E−02	3.01006	.154328
3.5	3.49165	4.70172E−02	3.55325	.20756
4	3.99993	1.65728E−02	3.99924	.230775
4.5	4.50375	5.06684E−02	4.51004	.262243
5	4.99992	1.88353E−02	4.94984	.301522

(Note the difference between the two columns for the standard deviation.)

We shall therefore adopt statement (37) in the following treatment.

Also note that the statements

$$\text{LET } P = \text{INT}(\text{RND}(1) + 2*P\emptyset*\text{RND}(2))$$
$$\text{IF } P = \emptyset \text{ THEN} \ldots \text{(reject)} \tag{38}$$

are equivalent to the statements

$$\text{LET } P = \text{RND}(1) + 2*P\emptyset*\text{RND}(2)$$
$$\text{IF } P < 1 \text{ THEN} \ldots \text{(reject)} \tag{39}$$

which take less running time. In the periodic sample of the population we may handle the cases where $P > 1$ by decrementing P at the end of the sample,

$$\text{LET } P = P - 1 \tag{40}$$

and by then sending the program back to the conditional rejection statement in (39) for another run through the population. (The technique will become clearer in the specific cases discussed below.)

**6.14
PROBLEM 14**   Write a program to check the statistical properties of the two probability functions listed in Eqs. (36) and (37). Try it out for $P\emptyset = \emptyset$ to 2 in steps of $\emptyset.2$. Note that differences in the random-number generator (particularly the number of bits used) between compilers may result in slight differences from the results given in the text.

**6.15
State of Health of the Group and Characteristic Time Constants**

Although we shall ignore fluctuations in the total size of the population (e.g., birth, death, migration), we do need to distinguish between at least three states of health: "normal health" (which may include acquired immunity in some cases), "incubating infection," and "recuperating contagion." In addition, we must include average time constants (and fluctuations about the average) for these states of health.

We can handle the bulk of this information with one column array for each population group. For example, the state of health of the Ith member of the group can be largely described by the numerical value of $M(I)$ by choosing $M(I) = 0$ for normal health, $M(I) < 0$ for the infected state, and $M(I) > 0$ for the contagious state. The effect of incubation time constants (T_1) and recuperation time constants (T_2) may be included by adjusting the magnitude of $M(I)$ systematically at the end of each sample period. To handle the effects of immunity induced by previous contagion, and its characteristic time of duration (T_3) after recovery, we shall introduce a second column array, $I(I)$, for the population group. The states of health we shall consider may be summarized as follows:

$M(I) < 0$: I infected; infection incubates for time $T_1 \propto |M(I)|$

$M(I) > 0$: I contagious; contagion recuperates for time $T_2 \propto |M(I)|$ ⠀⠀⠀(41)

$M(I) = 0$: I healthy $\begin{cases} I(I) < 0, \ I \text{ immune for time } T_3 \propto I(I) \\ I(I) \geqslant 0, \ I \text{ is not immune} \end{cases}$

We shall describe the three time constants T_1, T_2 and T_3 with the BASIC variables $T1$, $T2$, and $T3$.

We can *start an infection* in the Ith member of the group with the statement

$$\text{LET M(I)} = -\text{T1} + \text{T1*(RND(1)} - .5) \tag{42}$$

where a random fluctuation of $\pm.5*T1$ is introduced about the mean value, $T1$. Different values for the fluctuation could, of course, be chosen as long as we avoid fluctuations that would make $M(I) = 0$. A clock at the end of the sample period then increments $M(I)$ by 1 until $M(I) \geqslant 0$, at which point we declare $M(I)$ contagious.

We then *start contagion* in the Ith member of the group by the statement

$$\text{LET M(I)} = +\text{T2} + \text{T2*(RND(1)} - .5) \tag{43}$$
$$\text{LET M1} = \text{M1} + 1$$

where a similar random fluctuation is again arbitrarily introduced. (These fluctuations could, of course, be fit more accurately to the characteristics of the particular disease.) The clock at the end of the sample period then decrements $M(I)$ by 1 until $M(I) < 0$, at which point we pronounce $M(I)$ cured by the statements

$$\text{LET M(I)} = \emptyset \tag{44}$$
$$\text{LET M1} = \text{M1} - 1$$

where the statements involving $M1$ in (43) and (44) keep track of the total number of contagious individuals.

If induced immunity is important, we then add the statement

$$\text{LET I(I)} = -\text{T3} + \text{T3*(RND(1)} - .5) \tag{45}$$

after $M(I)$ is cured, where $T3$ is the average time that the individual will remain immune and another random fluctuation about this average has been assumed. The clock at the end of the sample period then increments $I(I)$ by 1. When $I(I) \geqslant 0$, the Ith individual loses his immunity and may be reinfected.

It should be noted that the definitions in (41) *exclude* the possibility that $T1$ or $T2 = 0$. (They may be very small.) However, the statement

$$\text{LET T3} = \emptyset \tag{46}$$

is permissible and means that there is no induced immunity. Natural immunity could be included in the initial boundary conditions by making $I(I)$ suitably negative at $T = 0$.

Also, the *absence* of a cure (either natural or medical) can be incorporated by letting $T2$ be sufficiently large; e.g.,

$$\text{LET T2} = 10000 \tag{47}$$

as done in some of the following specific examples.

It will help to discuss a specific single-population problem next.

The common cold is probably an assortment of different virus diseases. However, they all seem to be characterized by incubation periods ($T1$), natural recovery-time constants ($T2$), and periods of induced immunity ($T3$) which follow recovery from contagion. These time constants typically involve days to weeks in order of magnitude. It further seems reasonable to treat the problem in terms of a single population group in which the average behavior of the group is the same as the average behavior of the individual. We will, therefore, incorporate the notions expressed in the preceding sections in a specific program involving the above assumptions. First we need some routine initial statements:

```
 1   REM TREATMENT OF THE COMMON COLD
 2   REM INFECTION (T1), CURE (T2) AND IMMUNITY (T3) TIME CONST.
 3   PRINT "TIME IN UNITS OF SAMPLE PERIOD"
 4   REM INFECT., CONTAG. STORED IN M(I), IMMUNITY IN I(I)
 7   REM TOTAL # PEOPLE = M; TOTAL # CONTAGIOUS = M1
 8   LET M = 100
10   DIM M(255), I(255)
15   LET T1 = 3
17   LET T2 = 10000
19   LET T3 = 0
```

Although we have set up the dimension statements to handle as many as 255 people (line 10), we have set the total number of people to be 100 on line 8. The last three lines above present a pretty gloomy outlook. Assuming that time is measured in days here, line 15 means that the incubation period is 3 days; line 17 means there is no cure for all practical purposes, and line 19 means there is no induced immunity. We shall continue in this vein by asserting that there is no natural immunity either (line 42 below). However, we shall make all but one member of the population healthy at $T = 0$.

```
34   REM INITIAL CONDITIONS NEXT
35   FOR I = 1 TO M
40   LET M(I) = 0
42   LET I(I) = 0
45   NEXT I
```

We shall choose the one infected member of the group in the following manner:

```
47   LET M1 = 1
50   FOR I = 1 TO M1
60   LET M(I) = T2 + T2*(RND(1) − .5)
70   NEXT I
```

where a random fluctuation in $T2$ has been assigned in accordance with our previous discussion. The statements are set up in a manner that permits changing the initial conditions very easily.

As we shall demonstrate, only one initially contagious member of the population under the above assumptions inevitably results in causing a massive epidemic which infects the entire population in a remarkably short time. The assumptions, for example, permit simulating the demise of the "Martian invaders" in the manner outlined by H. G. Wells in *The War of the Worlds* (1934):

> "And scattered about... in their overturned war-machines... were the Martians—*dead!*—slain by the putrefactive and disease bacteria against which their systems were unprepared;... slain, after all man's devices had failed, by the humblest things that God, in his wisdom, has put upon this earth" (p. 380).

Wells was evidently very fond of this concept and used the common cold to wipe out the creatures living in the moon in another story. There are some fairly profound underlying questions involved here. For example, with the nearly infinite number of different combinations of molecules that could go into the creation of new viruses, it would be remarkable to find that the human species could develop immunity to them all. Are we just living on borrowed time? Have any of the thousands of known, extinct species on earth been wiped out by a virus?... and so on. However, we won't let ayone die in our program. Our main initial objective is to give a realistic quantitative simulation of the rapid spread of something like the common cold when neither cure nor immunity is available.

We shall next make an assumption on the average probability of exposure ($P\emptyset$) per sample period and introduce some PRINT statements that summarize the initial assumptions made.

```
85   REM P0=PROB. CONTAGION PER EXPOSURE (CAN BE>1)
90   LET P0=.5
94   PRINT "T1=INC. TIME="; T1; "T2=CURE TIME="; T2; "T3=IMM. TIME="; T3
95   PRINT "P0="; P0, "M="; M
96   PRINT "TIME", "NO. CONT. PEOPLE"
```

As hinted on line 96, we next want to do a running computation of the number of contagious people in the group as a function of time.

The following portions of the program allow for 51 sample periods (presumably ≈ 1 day each for the common cold), display the results on the computer terminal, and allow for a random exposure within the population group which occurs once every sample period on the average.

```
100  FOR T=0 TO 50
110  REM PLOT OR STORE T, M1 HERE IF DESIRED
200  PRINT T, M1
204  REM I, J RANDOMLY SELECTED AND EXPOSED AV. 1 PER SAMPLE PERIOD
205  FOR K=1 TO .5*M
207  LET P=RND(1)+2*P0*RND(2)
208  IF P<1 THEN 295
210  LET I=(M-1)*RND(1)+1
220  LET J=(M-1)*RND(1)+1
240  IF M(I)>0 THEN 270
245  IF M(J)<=0 THEN 290
250  IF M(I)<0 THEN 290
252  IF I(I)<0 THEN 290
255  REM M(I) INFECTED NEXT
260  LET M(I)=-T1+T1*(RND(1)-.5)
270  IF M(J)#0 THEN 290
275  IF I(J)<0 THEN 290
280  REM M(J) INFECTED NEXT
285  LET M(J)=-T1+T1*(RND(1)-.5)
290  LET P=P-1
292  GOTO 208
295  NEXT K
```

The program chooses 0.5*M (line 2Ø5) random pairs from the total population (M) each sample period. The particular sample pairs (indices I and J) are selected randomly on lines 21Ø and 22Ø. Note that each particular index has an average probability of being chosen of $2/M$ from the combined effects of lines 21Ø and 22Ø. Hence, to ensure that each member of the group is sampled once on the average per sample period, the K loop (lines 2Ø5–295) is traversed 0.5*M times per sample period.

Each time through the K loop, the probability function P on line 2Ø7 is computed to see if an exposure occurs between the I,J pair [see discussion of Eqs. (38)–(40)]. If $P<1$, no exposure occurs that time and the conditional statement on line 2Ø8 sends the program on to the next sample (value of K).

If the program gets past the conditional statement on line 2Ø8, an infectious exposure has occurred at the *K*th sample. The rest of the statements within the *K* loop from 21Ø on run $M(I)$ and $M(J)$ through a "sieve," which results in *J* being infected if *I* is contagious when *J* is normal and not immune, and which also results in *I* being infected when *J* is contagious and *I* is normal and not immune. (Note that the cases where $I = J$ are also thrown out by the sieve.)

Specifically, if the condition on line 24Ø is satisfied, *I* is contagious [$M(I) > Ø$] and the program jumps to line 27Ø to see whether $M(J)$ is healthy [$M(J) = Ø$] and then goes to line 275 to see whether *J* is immune [$I(J) < Ø$]. If the program gets by the conditional statements on lines 27Ø and 275, the *J*th person is healthy and not immune and the *J*th person is then infected on line 285; i.e., $M(J)$ is given a negative value equal to the incubation-time constant plus some arbitrarily imposed random spread about the average value of this time constant. Although infected, *J* is not yet contagious.

The other half of the sieve (from line 245 on) works in exactly the same manner. If the program gets past line 245, *J* is contagious and infects *I* on line 26Ø, provided that *I* is neither already infected [$M(I) < Ø$ on line 25Ø] nor immune [$I(I) < Ø$ on line 252].

Finally, note that when $P > 1$ the combination of lines 29Ø and 2Ø8 merely runs the program back through the same process until $P < 1$ (as discussed in the previous sections). The clock is next advanced by one sample period with the following statements:

```
300   REM CLOCK ADVANCES BY ONE SAMPLE PERIOD
301   REM M(I) = Ø NORMAL, <Ø INFECTED, >Ø CONTAGIOUS
305   FOR I = 1 TO M
310   IF M(I) = Ø THEN 368
315   IF M(I) >Ø THEN 350
319   REM M(I) <Ø MEANS INFECTION INCUBATING
320   LET M(I) = M(I) + 1
325   IF M(I) <Ø THEN 370
328   REM M(I) >Ø MEANS CONTAGIOUS NOW
329   IF M1 = M THEN 334
330   LET M1 = M1 + 1
334   REM START CURE WITH TIME CONSTANT T2
335   LET M(I) = +T2 + T2*(RND(1) − .5)
345   GOTO 370
350   LET M(I) = M(I) − 1
355   IF M(I) >Ø THEN 370
359   REM M(I) < =Ø HERE MEANS M(I) CURED
360   LET M(I) = Ø
362   LET M1 = M1 − 1
363   REM INDUCE IMMUNITY NEXT WITH TIME CONSTANT T3
364   LET I(I) = −T3 + T3*(RND(1) − .5)
365   GOTO 370
368   LET I(I) = I(I) + 1
370   NEXT I
```

Each member of the population is examined. If *I* is normal [$M(I) = Ø$ on line 31Ø], the individual is sent to line 368, where his immunity index in incremented. (When the latter index hits zero, the *I*th member of the group ceases to be immune.) If $M(I) > Ø$ on line 315, *I* is still contagious and is sent to line 35Ø to continue the cure at time constant *T2* [i.e., $M(I)$ is decremented]. If $M(I)$ goes through zero after line 35Ø, *I* is pronounced cured, we subtract one from the contagious population, and start his period of induced immunity (*T3*). If *I* gets as far as line 32Ø, it means that *I* is incubating infection at time constant *T1* and $M(I)$ is incremented. If *I* reaches line 33Ø, $M(I) > Ø$ and *I* is pronounced contagious and counted among the contagious population, *M1*. The cure is then started on line 335 at time constant *T2* (with a random spread about the mean). Finally, the statements

```
500   NEXT T
505   REM PLOT OR STORE T,M1 HERE IF DESIRED
510   PRINT T,M1
9999  END
```

increment time by one sample period until the T loop is completed (line 100). One could add a statement after line 510 to send the computer back to line 35 to do a limited number of Monte Carlo trajectories for the original initial conditions, and it would be easy to add column arrays, which would provide a running account of the average number of cases, the average-square and standard deviation as a function of time. Actually, one obtains a pretty good visual feeling for the average and deviation from average merely by looking at the superposition of solutions on a plotting device. A superposition of several solutions to the Martian problem is shown in Fig. 6-11.

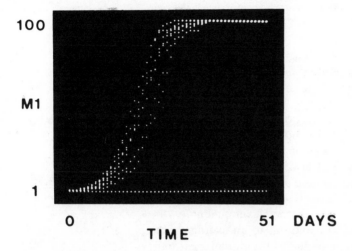

Fig. 6-11. Superposition of seven solutions to the Martian problem assuming $T1 = 3$ days, $T2 = $ infinity, $T3 = 0$, and one contagious person out of a group of 100 at $T = 0$. The average probability of exposure assumed was $P0 = 0.5$ per day. *M1* represents the number of contagious cases out of a total population of 100.

6.16
PROBLEM 15   Write a program that superimposes several solutions to the Martian problem (no cure, no natural immunity) with one infected person out of a group of 100 at $T = 0$. Use the same time constants and time intervals described in the text. If a random-access plotting device is not available, use the technique discussed in Section 3.6 to display the number of contagious people as a function of time on the teletype terminal after computing five Monte Carlo trajectories. If you use a teletype display, normalize the population group to 71 people.

6.16
PROBLEM 16   Write a program to compute the average number of contagious people and standard deviation about the average as a function of time for the above problem.

Solutions obtained with a more optimistic choice of recovery and immunity time constants are of considerable interest. If we allow the possibility of recovery at time constant $T2$, the foreboding results in Fig. 6-11 are circumvented. Here, even if the entire population is contagious at $T = 0$, the majority quickly recovers (see Fig. 6-12). There is one particularly intriguing aspect of

6.17
Effect of Recovery-Time
Constants and Induced
Immunity

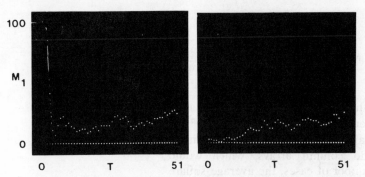

Fig. 6-12. Comparison of two solutions to the common-cold problem. In each case the average probability of contagion per sample period ($P\emptyset$) was assumed to be 0.5 per sample period and the incubation ($T1$) and cure ($T2$) time constants were both assumed to be three sample periods. It was assumed that there was no immunity ($T3 = 0$). In the solution at the left, all 100 people were assumed contagious at $T = 0$. In the solution at the right, only one person was assumed contagious at $T = 0$. Note that both solutions tend toward approximately the same number of contagious people (M_1 in the figure) for $T \gg 0$.

the solutions: for $T \gg 0$, the average number of contagious persons is generally independent of the initial numbers assumed unless the fluctuations are large enough to cause the value of $M1$ to hit zero long enough to put the entire epidemic out completely. This is illustrated in Fig. 6-12, where drastically different assumptions on the initial number contagious at $T = 0$ have been made for the same time constants (here, $T1 = T2$, but immunity has not yet been included). Solutions with increasing amounts of induced immunity (successively larger values of the time constant $T3$) also provide average values which are independent of the initial conditions (see Fig. 6-13). However, in these cases, coherent oscillations at a period roughly equal to the sum of the three time constants ($T1 + T2 + T3$) occur early in the development of the epidemic. Eventually, these oscillations tend to damp out to an average value independent of the initial population assumptions due to the randomness built into the problem (see the superposition of solutions in Fig. 6-13).

At small values of $P\emptyset$, the average tends to be approximately proportional to $P\emptyset$. However, as $P\emptyset$ gets very large, the average tends to approach

$$\left(\frac{M1}{M}\right)_{av} = \frac{T2}{T1 + T2 + T3} \tag{48}$$

That is, the population is in a continuous cycle going from incubation to contagion to induced immunity to incubation without any rest in between.

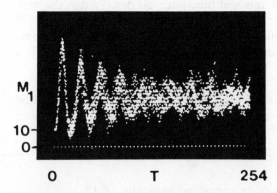

Fig. 6-13. Oscillatory effect that results in the presence of large values for the immunity time constant. Here $P\emptyset = 1$, $T1 = 3$, $T2 = 6$, and $T3 = 9$ with $M1 = 10$ (out of a total population of 100) at $T = 0$. In the figure, M_1 again represents the number of contagious people and is shown plotted as a function of time for a large number of different Monte Carlo trajectories.

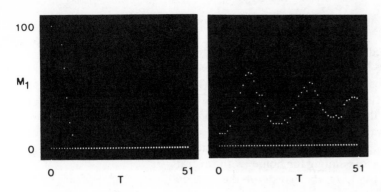

Fig. 6-14. Illustration of a simple cure for the common cold. In each case, it was assumed that $P\emptyset = 1$; $T1 = 3$, $T2 = 6$, $T3 = 9$; and that the total population consisted of 100 people. For the solution at the left, all 100 people were assumed contagious at $T = 0$ and the epidemic goes out completely due to the effects of induced immunity after a relatively short time. For the solution at the right, only 10 percent of the population was assumed contagious at $T = 0$ (the rest had no residual immunity). Here the epidemic goes on forever and the slow oscillation (with a period roughly equal to the sum of the time constants) damps out from the effects of randomness as in Fig. 6-13.

Hence the fraction contagious tends to be merely a fraction of the time occupied by $T2$ on the average, or that given by Eq. (48). However, especially as $T3$ gets to be much longer than $T1$ or $T2$, the oscillatory solutions early in the development of the epidemic can take on extremely large amplitudes. In particular, the excursion in the total number contagious can actually hit zero and remain there long enough to put the entire epidemic out. For example, the results in Fig. 6-14 show two extreme choices in the initial conditions and the same choice for the time constants and contagion probability. In one solution, 10 percent of the population was assumed contagious at $T = 0$ and the epidemic goes on forever. In the other solution, 100 percent of the population was assumed contagious at $T = 0$. In the latter case, the epidemic goes out entirely in a short time (the point being that the entire population tends to be immune at the same time and does not go on reinfecting itself). Although a rather bold approach, and one that would be hard to sell to the general public, we have here what appears to be the first really effective treatment of the common cold!

6.17 **PROBLEM 17**	Consider a population of 100 people with average time constants for incubation and recovery of $T1 = 3$ and $T2 = 6$ days. Suppose that the average probability of exposure per day per person is unity ($P\emptyset = 1$ in the sense discussed in Section 6.13). Compare the number of contagious people after 50 days when 10 percent and 100 percent of the population is contagious at $T = 0$. Make the comparison specifically for the cases where $T3 = 0$ (no induced immunity) and $T3 = 6$ days. Show that for $T3 > 6$, the epidemic always goes out when $M1 = 100$ at $T = 0$. Make the same assumptions on the random spread of the time constants discussed in the text.

Syphilis is, in many ways, an ideal disease to illustrate the two-population problem and we shall develop a computer program to simulate the main features involved in the spread of syphilis within a limited population group.

In the present age when explorers are returning at frequent intervals from outer space, it is particularly relevant to review the early history of this disease

**6.18
Brief History of Syphilis**

311

briefly.[7] In doing so, we can cast some additional light on the historical investigation itself.

It is probable that Columbus discovered syphilis in the fall of 1492 and brought it back to Spain the following year[8] (see Fig. 6-15). Of the original 88 men who sailed with Columbus from Palos, Spain on August 3, 1492, half returned to that port on March 15, 1493, after stopping on March 4 at Lisbon. (Forty-four sailors were left behind after the wreck of the *Santa Maria* on Christmas Eve just prior to the return voyage.) The group initially landed in the Bahamas on October 12 and spent approximately 13 weeks in random contact with natives of the Caribbean area before sailing for home (with several captured natives aboard) on January 16, 1493. In the words of the history books, "the gentle Arawak [Indians] offered the 'men from heaven' all they had"; e.g., tobacco, corn, the hammock, and probably, syphilis. Like most historical conjecture, this last one has been subject to debate.[9] Morison himself summarized the main arguments supporting this conclusion: there is no certain evidence that syphilis existed in Europe prior to 1493, whereas abundant evidence exists of the disease occurring among the American Indians prior to 1492. A Spanish physician, Ruy Diaz de Isla (who published a book on syphilis in 1539) asserted that he personally treated victims of the disease in Barcelona in 1493 when it first appeared (one of these victims was supposedly a sailor with Columbus) and de Isla accordingly assigned the appearance of the disease to the first voyage of Columbus. However, Morison argues against the conclusion on the basis of the "excellent health aboard homecoming *Nina* in 1493, and the absence of evidence to the contrary on *Pinta*." At the same time, Morison thought the argument tenable that the "spirillum was brought to Europe in the bloodstream of Columbus' captive Indians in 1493." (Of the 10 initial natives, one died shortly after landing; three were left in Seville; and Columbus brought the remaining six to the court of Ferdinand and Isabella at Barcelona.) Other historians [e.g., Landstrom (1966), p. 119] do not think it out of the question that Columbus himself might have contracted the disease.

In this connection, it is worth elaborating a little bit on the notion of what is, or is not, highly improbable. As will become abundantly clear in the following computer analysis of the problem, one infected individual returning with Columbus early in 1493 would have been quite adequate to explain what subsequently happened in Europe. In order for the latter event to be highly *im*probable, the average probability of exposure per sailor per week (for the ≈ 50 returning sailors) during their stay in the Carribean area would have had to be $\ll 1/(50*13) \approx 0.0015$. The latter requirement might be satisfied through celibacy by certain dedicated orders of monks; however, the requirement conflicts rather violently with one's intuitive notions regarding the social habits of sailors. The last conclusion, of course, tacitly assumes that most of the

---

[7] At the moment of writing (December 7, 1972), three men and six mice were hurtling toward the moon at $\approx 18,000$ mph!

[8] The basis for the above conjecture is discussed in the text. The suggestion was made at least as early as 1539 by de Isla [see the discussion in Morison (1942)]. It is tempting to speculate that the Viking, Leif Erickson, might actually have discovered syphilis in the year 1003 A.D., but there seems to be no historical evidence to support that possibility. The primary alternative theory is that syphilis evolved bacteriologically from the tropical disease known as yaws and was imported to Spain from Africa in the bodies of captured slaves in the late fifteenth century. The accumulated recorded observations of the time appear to give much greater weight to the Columbus theory. However, in either case, a massive diffusion problem with the same general characteristics was involved which engulfed all of Europe and started in Spain around 1493.

[9] See the discussion by Morison (1942), especially p. 359).

Fig. 6-15. "The Landing of Columbus" (at Watling's Island in the Bahamas on October 12, 1492) by John Vanderlyn. (Reproduced by permission of the Library of Congress from the collection of "the Architect of the Capitol").

native population was infected to begin with. It should, therefore, be noted that it is a general property of the computer solutions to the problem that, if the disease exists at all in a moderately promiscuous society in which neither preventive treatment nor cure is available, essentially the entire community gets it in a very short time (certainly that portion of it which is promiscuous).[10] Hence the most probable interpretation of the events is that Columbus did indeed bring back one or more infected sailors on the first voyage and their medical predicament simply was not noticed. No one seems to dispute the belief that the Spaniards at least contracted the disease from the Indians in subsequent voyages (e.g., Columbus' second voyage in 1493 brought over

---

[10] However, the fraction in the highly infectious state is not so obvious and depends on unknown parameters such as the average life expectancy (probably very short).

313

about 1000 male colonists, and by 1494 Spaniards were roving all over Hispaniola).

The mild outbreak of syphilis in Barcelona in 1493 was followed by a major epidemic of the disease in Naples in 1495 (then under seige by the invading army of Charles VIII of France). This army was largely made up of mercenaries from different parts of Europe and, according to some accounts, even included several of Columbus' former sailors. With the return of the "French" army, the disease swept rapidly across Europe. Similarly, the appearance of the disease in India in 1498 has been accredited to the voyage by Vasco da Gama from Portugal (around the Cape of Good Hope) in May of that year.

According to the sixteenth-century English surgeon, William Clowes, roughly three fourths of the patients admitted to St. Bartholomew's Hospital in London in that period had syphilis. Some feeling for the extent to which the disease spread is given by the report[11] that over half the population of Copenhagen had contracted it by 1885. In retrospect, it seems possible that most of the population on the European continent had the disease during this period—ranging from members of the British Royal Family (starting at least as early as Henry VIII, whose first wife incidentally, was the daughter of Ferdinand of Spain) to the Russian despot, Ivan the Terrible. It has, in fact, become a popular current literary sport to point out that all sorts of famous historical persons had it. Because no cure for the disease was developed until the early 1900s, the only defense against catching it was either abstinence or use of less effective mechanical disease preventative methods. Even then, there was no defense against inheriting the disease from one's parents. It seems probable that the development of Victorian moral standards was largely stimulated by the danger of syphilis. The social stigma associated with the disease has interfered with the collection of accurate data on the rate of infection even through the present time.

The first effective cure for syphilis was discovered by Paul Ehrlich in 1907 (Salvarsan, or Compound 606) and put into use by 1909.[12, 13] The discovery of penicillin by Fleming in 1929 and the investigations of penicillin as a cure for disease by Florey in 1938 and others led to the adoption of penicillin as the established cure for syphilis by 1943. When treated in early stages of the disease, penicillin causes the contagious lesions to heal within about 1 week.[14] Ominously, there is some recent evidence to indicate the development of penicillin-resistant strains of the disease. However, it seems probable that the current epidemic in Connecticut[15] and major cities of the United States is primarily the result of other factors. Governor Meskill's task force says *it's all a moral problem.*[16] A more believable interpretation would include the large-scale adoption of The Pill in place of mechanical methods of birth control, and correspondingly, the enormous increase in the probability of contagion per contact.

It is currently believed that the disease is almost entirely spread by direct contact with the contagious lesions of "early syphilis" during sexual intercourse

---

[11] Blaschke (1910), quoted in Norins and Olansky (1971). (The estimate given in the text was based on an approximate integration of the attack rates given in the reference.)

[12] It is interesting to note that in filming a biography of Ehrlich's life, Hollywood was completely successful in obscuring the nature of the disease that Dr. Ehrlich's "Magic Bullets" were supposed to cure.

[13] There is reason to believe that the early cures (based on the inhalation of mercury vapor) were worse than the disease. Apparently the only real cure prior to 1907 was based on giving the patient malaria. The high fever would kill the spirochete bacillus and, of course, leave the person with malaria.

[14] Burton and Smith (1970) and Norins and Olansky (1971).

[15] Fellows (1972).

[16] *Ibid.*

and with virtually 100 percent probability per exposure. The time development of the disease in individual cases is fairly complicated[17]:

Early syphilis: The primary lesions develop in about 21 days (with a range from 10 to 90); the *untreated* lesion disappears in 4 to 12 weeks. If treated, the primary lesion heals within about 1 week. The secondary lesions begin 6 to 8 weeks later; the *untreated* lesion disappears within 4 to 12 weeks; if treated, the secondary lesion heals within several weeks.

Latent syphilis: Infection is defined as occurring between 2 to 4 years after the initial infection.

Late syphilis: After that. There is no natural immunity ($T3 = 0$), and without treatment the victim eventually dies from the disease, or one of its numerous side effects.[18]

One could build all of this behavior into a computer program. However, we may include the main effects with the following approximations:

1. We shall assume there is just one incubation period characterized by the time constant $T1 = 3$ weeks (with a random variation of $\approx \pm 1.5$ weeks), after which we shall assume the victim is in a continuous state of contagion.
2. We shall assume there is just one time constant, $T2$, characterizing the time required to cure the patient after the disease has been diagnosed. If we assume that ≈ 1 week goes by after reaching the contagious level before treatment is started, $T2 \approx T1 \approx 3$ weeks (± 1.5 weeks), with $T3 = 0$ (no immunity).

These parameters may, of course, be changed easily in the final program. If no medical treatment is provided, $T2 = $ infinity.

We then will avoid interpreting the results of the program too literally over time intervals in excess of about 1 to 2 years (the start of the latent period).

6.19
Two-Population Model
(The Sailor-Prostitute Problem)

One suggestion by the historians is that syphilis was transmitted to "public women in Barcelona" in 1493 by a member of the group returning with Columbus on the first voyage.[19] The fate of northern Europe would then rest on the probability that the prostitute community had generally come down with syphilis in time for the returning French army to spread it about in 1495. We will not worry about the geographical diffusion problem, but will instead concentrate on a more definitely definable problem involving the random interaction between M-men and W-prostitutes, in which one contagious man is introduced at time $T = 0$. We shall assume that there is an average random probability, $P\emptyset$, per week per man for the exposure to occur and then determine the number of contagious men ($M1$) and women ($W1$) as a function of time subject to a reasonably conservative estimate of $P\emptyset$ (e.g., ≈ 0.5), a total male population of 100 (M), and several estimates on the total number of women (W).

It is reasonably straightforward to modify the previous single-population problem to handle the problem of present interest. We merely need to add a second column array $W(J)$ to handle the women, a quantity W to represent the total number, and a quantity, $W1$, to represent the total number that are contagious. We shall assume that the same time constants for incubation ($T1$) and medical cure ($T2$) hold for both population groups and include the possibility of medical cure for generality. We shall omit the immunity indices

[17] Norins and Olansky (1971).

[18] See, for example, the summary of the reports on the infamous "Tuskegee [Ala.] Tests," *The New York Times*, Sept. 12, 1972, p. 23.

[19] Morison (1942) suggests one of the several natives, rather than one of the ≈ 50 sailors.

since no immunity is believed to exist. After some routine initial statements,

```
 1   REM DIFFUSION OF SYPHILIS
 2   REM INCLUDES INFECTION (T1) AND CURE (T2) TIME CONSTANTS
 3   REM STATE OF CONTAGION STORED IN M(I),W(J)
 4   REM NO IMMUNITY!
 5   REM TOTAL # MEN, WOMEN = M,W;  total # CONTAGIOUS =M1,W1
10   DIM M(255), W(255)
```

we enter the initial conditions in essentially the same manner used previously to treat the common cold, except that there are two population groups and no immunity.

```
16   LET M = 100
17   LET W = 100
18   LET T1 = 3
19   LET T2 = 10000
30   FOR I = 1 TO M
33   LET M(I) = 0
35   NEXT I
37   FOR J = 1 TO W
40   LET W(J) = 0
43   NEXT J
45   REM INITIAL CONDITIONS NEXT
47   LET M1 = 1
50   FOR I = 1 TO M1
60   LET M(I) = T2 + T2*(RND(1) − .5)
70   NEXT I
80   LET W1 = 0
```

Lines 30–43 merely assert that everyone is healthy. We then introduce the number of contagious men ($M1$) and contagious women ($W1$) at $T = 0$ in lines 45–80. The assumption on line 19 for $T2$ amounts to the same one used in the Martian problem (i.e., no cure yet).

We then choose some realistic value for the average probability of contagion per exposure per sample period ($P0$) and print out the various quantities assumed.

```
85   REM P0 = PROB. CONTAGION PER EXPOSURE
90   LET P0 = .5
94   PRINT "T1 = INCUBAT. TIME ="; T1; "WKS. T2 = CURE TIME ="; T2; "WKS."
95   PRINT "P0 ="; P0, "M ="; M, "W="; W
96   PRINT "TIME (WKS)", "CONTAG. MEN", "CONTAG. WOMEN"
```

As indicated in lines 94–96, the appropriate unit of time is the week in this problem and we wish to compute the total number of contagious men and women per week in subsequent sections of the program for the initial conditions assumed (1 contagious man and no contagious women at $T = 0$).

We shall next proceed to sample the population at weekly intervals. The method is quite analogous to that discussed in connection with the common-cold problem. For clarity in what follows, we shall use the index I to refer to the Ith sailor [whose health is kept track of in the array $M(I)$] and we shall use the index J to refer to the Jth woman [whose health is monitored in $W(J)$].

```
100   FOR T = 0 TO 50
110   REM PLOT OR STORE T,M1,W1 HERE IF DESIRED
200   PRINT T,M1,W1
204   REM SAMPLING FOR THE SAILOR(I)-PROSTITUTE(J) PROBLEM
205   FOR K = 1 TO M
210   LET I = (M − 1)*RND(1) + 1
212   LET P = RND(1) + 2*P0*RND(2)
215   IF P < 1 THEN 295
```

```
220   LET J = (W − 1)*RND(1) + 1
240   IF M(I) > 0 THEN 270
245   IF W(J) < = 0 THEN 290
250   IF M(I) < 0 THEN 290
255   REM M(I) INFECTED NEXT
260   LET M(I) = −T1 + T1*(RND(1) − .5)
265   GOTO 290
270   IF W(J) #0 THEN 290
280   REM W(J) INFECTED NEXT
285   LET W(J) = −T1 + T1*(RND(1) − .5)
290   LET P = P − 1
292   GOTO 215
295   NEXT K
```

Line 204 is to remind us that the sampling has been arranged in a manner appropriate to the problem under consideration. That is, each man is sampled with equal probability and on the average once per week. However, the Ith man then chooses one woman out of the group W randomly. Thus, although the men are sampled with equal probability and once per sample period on the average, the number of times per sample period the Jth woman is exposed increases with the ratio M/W of the two total populations and the relative probability $P0$. The sociological part of the probability factor, $P0$, is characteristic of only the male population group in this instance. Consequently, in cases where $P0 > 1$, line 292 returns the program to line 215, thus selecting another value of J for the same I. This latter subtlety is not important for the solutions to the problem given below since we assume the average behavior over the male group is the same as the average behavior of each man. However, it would be relatively easy to remove that restriction in the above sample routine merely by introducing a column array $P(I)$ in place of $P0$.

After the Ith man has selected the Jth woman, the rest of the sampling program after line 240 results in: I infecting J (on line 285) if I is contagious and J healthy; or J infecting I (on line 260) if J is contagious and I healthy. If $P < 1$ on line 215, no infection is transferred on that "shake of the dice" and the program goes on to the next value of K. The program also incorporates our previous technique on lines 290 and 292 for handling cases where $P > 1$ per sample period.

We next advance the clock by one week (sample period) separately for the male population group,

```
300   REM CLOCK ADVANCES BY 1 WEEK
301   REM M(I),W(I) = 0 NORMAL, < 0 INFECTED, > 0 CONTAGIOUS
304   REM DO M FIRST
305   FOR I = 1 TO M
310   IF M(I) = 0 THEN 370
315   IF M(I) > 0 THEN 350
319   REM M(I) < 0 MEANS INFECTION INCUBATING
320   LET M(I) = M(I) + 1
325   IF M(I) < 0 THEN 370
329   REM M(I) > 0 MEANS CONTAGIOUS NOW
330   LET M(I) = +T2 + T2*(RND(1) − .5)
333   IF M1 = M THEN 339
335   LET M1 = M1 + 1
339   REM START CURE NOW WITH TIME CONSTANT T2
345   GOTO 370
350   LET M(I) = M(I) − 1
355   IF M(I) > 0 THEN 370
359   REM M(I) < = 0 HERE MEANS M(I) CURED
360   LET M(I) = 0
365   LET M1 = M1 − 1
370   NEXT I
```

and for the female population group:

```
400   REM CLOCK FOR W NEXT
405   FOR I = 1 TO W
410   IF W(I) = 0 THEN 470
415   IF W(I) > 0 THEN 450
419   REM W(I) < 0 MEANS INFECTION INCUBATING
420   LET W(I) = W(I) + 1
425   IF W(I) < 0 THEN 470
429   REM W(I) > 0 MEANS W(I) CONTAGIOUS NOW
430   LET W(I) = + T2 + T2*(RND(1) − .5)
433   IF W1 = W THEN 439
435   LET W1 = W1 + 1
439   REM START CURE NOW WITH TIME CONSTANT T2
445   GOTO 470
450   LET W(I) = W(I) − 1
455   IF W(I) > 0 THEN 470
459   REM W(I) < = 0 HERE MEANS W(I) CURED
460   LET W(I) = 0
465   LET W1 = W1 − 1
470   NEXT I
```

The "clock" section of the program is quite analogous to that discussed before in connection with the single-population-group problem (see Section 6.16). However, the clock is much simpler in the present case because we have removed the effects of natural and induced immunity. [The latter could, in principle, be introduced by the adoption of immunity indices $I(I)$ and $J(J)$ in the manner previously discussed, but would be an unrealistic and unnecessary complication in the present problem.] Note that it would be very easy to introduce different time constants for the two groups.

Finally, we must close the loop on T (time) and print out or display whatever results are desired.

```
500    NEXT T
510    REM PLOT OR STORE T,M1,W1
520    PRINT T,M1,W1
9999   END
```

At this point, one could repeat the solution a number of times and compute the mean and standard deviation about the mean from $M1$ and $W1$ as a function of time. Alternatively, one could merely superimpose solutions for a number of separate Monte Carlo trajectories and visually infer the average behavior and departure from average. The latter technique is illustrated in Fig. 6-16 for a number of solutions to the sailor–prostitute problem. In each instance, $P0$ was taken to be 0.5, and one contagious male (out of 100 males) was introduced at $T = 0$ under conditions where all other members of both population groups were healthy. $T1$ was chosen to be 3 weeks (representative of syphilis), and in order to simulate conditions in Spain in 1493, no cure was assumed ($T2 = $ infinity). The solutions shown correspond to values of $W = 10$, 100, and 200. There is no instance in any one of these solutions where one contagious male at $T = 0$ did not result in bringing essentially the entire group in both populations to the contagious stage within one year. Hence the historical interpretation summarized above appears to make very good sense from a model of the problem containing realistic values of the probabilities involved and values for the incubation time constant ($T1 \approx 3$ weeks) based on current knowledge of the disease.

If one includes the possibility of recovery through medical cure in the above problem, some interesting oscillatory characteristics result which are similar to those encountered with induced immunity in the single-population problem. For example, if we assume that each individual starts medical treatment after

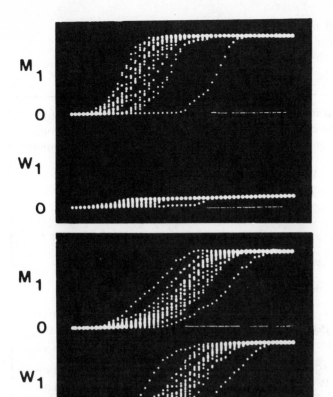

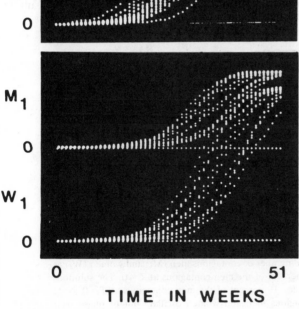

Fig. 6-16. Superposition of Monte Carlo solutions to the sailor–prostitute problem, assuming $P\emptyset = 0.5$ per week per sailor. In each case, one contagious sailor out of a group of 100 was introduced to the prostitute community at time $T = 0$, and all other members of both population groups were assumed to be healthy. Three separate sets of solutions are shown, corresponding to different total numbers of prostitutes: top solution: $W = 10$ ($= M/10$); middle solution: $W = 100$ ($= M$); lower solution: $W = 200$ ($= 2M$). For this problem, the time for the disease to spread increases with W/M. For each case, a superposition of solutions is shown corresponding to the same initial conditions $M_1 = 1$ and $W_1 = 0$ at $T = 0$ with no cure. (M_1 represents the number of contagious males and W_1 represents the number of contagious women.)

reaching the contagious stage without changing his or her social habits, the two population groups tend to give the disease back and forth at a period $\approx T1 + T2$ (where $T2$ is the mean time for cure after reaching contagion). The solutions in Fig. 6-17 were computed to illustrate the effect using representative values for the adjustable parameters. As with the single-population-group problem, the average number of contagious individuals in either group at $T \gg 0$ tends to be independent of the initial number contagious at $T = 0$, unless the fluctuations are large enough to put the epidemic out. Here for $P\emptyset$ large,

$$\left(\frac{M1}{M}\right)_{av} \approx \left(\frac{W1}{W}\right)_{av} \approx \frac{T2}{T1 + T2}$$

319

One can, of course, go on to make more and more specific assumptions on sociological characteristics of the two population groups and introduce appropriate changes in sampling methods. Because the subject is inherently open-ended, we shall leave it here.

**6.19
PROBLEM 18**

Using the method discussed in the text in connection with the sailor–prostitute problem, write a program to compute the mean time for 50 percent of the men to become contagious as a function of the total number of prostitutes, assuming no cure and

$$\left.\begin{array}{l} W1 = 0 \\ M1 = 1 \end{array}\right\} \text{ at } T = 0$$

$$M = 100 = \text{constant}$$

$$T1 = 3 \text{ weeks}$$

$$P\emptyset = 0.5$$

Try values of $W = 10$, 50, and 200.

**6.19
PROBLEM 19**

Suppose that $M = 100$, $W = 10$, $M1 = 1$ and $W1 = 0$ at $T = 0$ in the above problem. How small does $P\emptyset$ have to be so that less than 50 percent of the prostitute community becomes contagious on the average in one year?

**6.19
PROBLEM 20**

What would happen to the solutions shown in Fig. 6-17 if only one population group (for example, the W prostitutes) applied medical treatment? (This situation would not be too dissimilar to that which would be likely to result from some proposals for legalized prostitution.)

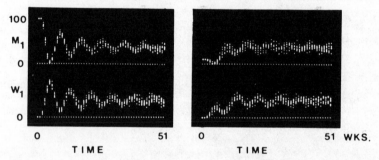

Fig. 6-17. Illustration of oscillatory behavior of the solutions to the sailor–prostitute problem when a cure with time constant $T2$ (after reaching contagion) is introduced. A superposition of solutions is shown for the case $M = W = 100$, $T1 = T2 = 3$ weeks, $P\emptyset = 1$ per sailor per week, and $W1 = 0$ at $T = 0$. The solutions at the left show the number of contagious men (M_1) and women (W_1) as a function of time for 100 percent of the men contagious at $T = 0$. The solutions at the right were computed for 10 percent of the men contagious at $T = 0$. Note that the solutions for contagious men and women oscillate out of phase near $T = 0$, but, owing to the assumed randomness, eventually settle down to average values that are independent of the initial numbers contagious at $T = 0$. As discussed in the text, the solutions assume that the social habits of the individuals do not change when they have the disease.

**6.19
RESEARCH
PROBLEM**

Although the use of one probability to describe the entire population probably is not too bad an approximation for the sailor–prostitute problem, the mere fact that European civilization survived until 1907 implies that different probability factors must be associated with different individuals. Hence if you wanted to make a realistic study of the spread of syphilis in some isolated segment of society (e.g., a hippie commune or a modern coeducational college), it would be necessary to introduce a distribution of average probability factors for the different members of the two population groups.

At the simplest useful level, the additional complexity could be incorporated by introducing two probability arrays (one for the men and one for the women) based on data of the sort contained in the reports by Kinsey and others. One then has to be careful to sample each member from each group once on the average per sample period (e.g., as done in the common-cold problem). The probability for the contagion to spread for a particular pair interaction must somehow involve the product of the separate probabilities. However, the problem is complicated by the fact that the isolated individual probabilities are not directly tabulated in studies of the Kinsey type (what you get out of these studies is the product of individual probabilities for one group integrated over the probability distribution for the other group). One has to unfold these two distributions in some way.

It would be interesting to see how accurately a random-sampling model based on average probable behavior would agree with actual data for a definable problem of this type.

6.20 Method of Least Squares[20]

Application of the Gauss iterative method of least squares to the analysis of data probably represents the most important single use of computers in experimental research which currently exists.

Experimental problems frequently arise in which a theoretical description of the problem is known (or at least thought to be known) but in which the theoretical functional form is too complicated to permit the extraction of key experimental constants within the accuracy of the measurement in any simple, straightforward way. In addition, the individual data points themselves may have considerable statistical noise which arises from random fluctuations in the experiment. The method of least squares provides a reasonably general means to extract the experimental constants in situations of the latter type.

In principle, the method that we are about to derive could be carried out by a hardy soul with a desk calculator. However, the amount of time required to do even the simplest type of least-squares fit by hand is so formidable that most people would prefer to seek out an alternative field of research if it were not for the existence of the computer. The increasing availability of computers (especially the small laboratory type) for the analysis of experimental data has had a major impact. It seems probable, in fact, that anyone who is not familiar with implementing the method of least squares on a high-speed digital computer will be at a serious disadvantage in most areas of experimental research.

We shall limit the present discussion to a fairly rudimentary first-order treatment of the problem and merely shall note that even today people are still publishing large papers on more and more sophisticated methods of approach to the same basic problem formulated by Gauss in the early 1800s.[21]

Suppose that we take a large number N of measurements,

$$y_{\text{measured}}(I) \qquad \text{where } I = 1, 2, 3, \ldots, N \qquad (49)$$

in which the index I can be used to label different values of some independent variable in the experiment. For example, the index I might correspond to different values of the time in a series of measured data points on the decay of

[20] The basic material discussed in this section was first presented by Karl Friedrich Gauss to the Royal Society of Göttingen during the period 1821–1826, in a series of three papers. See, for example, the French translation by J. Bertrand (authorized by Gauss) and published in 1855; or the English translation of the French translation by Hale F. Trotter (1957). We shall, however, use a reasonable amount of individuality in our approach to the problem.

[21] See, for example, Levenberg (1944), Nierenberg (1959), Moore and Zeigler (1960), Ho (1962), and McWilliams et al. (1962).

an excited atomic energy level, or, with equal applicability, the transient decay of a plucked harpsichord string.

Next let us suppose that we have a theory which says that the theoretical value of y for each measured point involves a number J of constant parameters a_i such that

$$y_{\text{theory}} = y_{\text{theory}}(I, a_1, a_2, \ldots, a_J) \qquad \text{where } J < N \qquad (50)$$

(or, better still, $J \ll N$).

What we want to do is to choose the best set of parameters (adjustable constants),

$$a_1, a_2, a_3, \ldots, a_J \qquad (51)$$

so that we get the best fit of the N data points to the theoretical expression.

Specifically, we want to choose the set of adjustable parameters so that the sum of weighted squares,

$$S \equiv \sum_{I=1}^{N} W(I)[y_{\text{meas}}(I) - y_{\text{theory}}(I)]^2 \qquad (52)$$

is a minimum. Obviously, if each data point exactly equaled the theoretical value at that point, the sum (52) would be zero. In practice the sum will never exactly equal zero, and the best one can do is choose the parameters in (51) so that the sum is a minimum. The weighting factor, $W(I)$, is introduced to allow for a variation in statistical accuracy with which successive points are measured. For example, if one point is measured with much greater uncertainty than the others, you clearly want to give it less weight in determining the optimum set of constants. The most reasonable choice for the weighting factor is simply

$$W(I) = \frac{1}{\text{variance of } y_{\text{meas}}(I)} \qquad (53)$$

because the other term in the sum (52) is equivalent to the square of the difference from the mean. We thus expect if the fluctuations are entirely from random processes that $[y_{\text{meas}}(I) - y_{\text{theory}}(I)]^2$ should be smaller than the variance about 68 percent of the time.

However, the relationship of the variance to the value of $y_{\text{meas}}(I)$ itself can vary with the nature of the experiment. If $y_{\text{meas}}(I)$ is simply the number of counts in a constant time interval at different indices (times) I, it is seen from our previous analysis of counting experiments that

$$W(I) = \frac{1}{\text{var}(y_{\text{meas}})} = \frac{1}{|y_{\text{meas}}(I)|} \qquad (54)$$

However, Eq. (54) is a specialized result applying mainly to counting experiments and, if not really applicable, can result in a *worse* fit than would be obtained merely by letting $W(I) = \text{constant}$ (e.g., $= 1$). This point is discussed in more detail below. The great virtue in having an objectively defined weighting factor [as in Eq. (53)] is that you do not have to worry about one "bad" point fouling up the resultant experimental fit. That is, if it is really bad, its weighting factor will attenuate its effect on the final fit. At the same time, by not indulging in the sport of "throwing out bad points" you do not run the risk of producing a major systematic error in the final choice of constants as the result of statistical fluctuations. (On the other hand, no amount of least-squares fitting can undo the damage produced by a systematic experimental calibration error.)

We seek a systematic method to determine the constants a_i in Eq. (51) so that S in Eq. (52) is a minimum. Equation (52) describes a J-dimensional surface that may have more than one "pot hole" in it (for a sufficiently large number of parameters, J, and data points, N). Hence there is no advance assurance that we shall always find the set (51) corresponding to an absolute minimum for Eq. (52). However, the following first-order iterative method works pretty well a large fraction of the time, especially when the number of parameters is small enough to avoid singularities in the matrix inversion process described below (typically, $\leqslant 5$ adjustable parameters when the matrix inversion is done on a machine that computes floating-point numbers to $\leqslant 1$ ppm).

Following the method of Gauss, we shall first make the best guess we can on a trial set of adjustable constants (keeping in mind that this first guess *might* move us from the domain of one pothole to that of another on the surface—or even cause us to fall off the edge of the surface without finding a minimum—if there is an edge). We will then make a systematic correction, Δa_i, to each of the parameters, a_i, chosen in such a way as to land us on a minimum for all a_i if y_{theory} depended linearly on each of the parameter displacements.

That is, we shall expand $y_{\text{theory}}(I, a_1, a_2, \ldots, a_J)$ through first-order terms in a multidimensional Taylor series in the adjustable constants:

$$y_{\text{theory}}(I) \approx y_0(I, a_1, a_2, \ldots, a_J) + \left[\frac{\partial y(I)}{\partial a_1}\right]_0 \Delta a_1 + \left[\frac{\partial y(I)}{\partial a_2}\right]_0 \Delta a_2$$

$$+ \cdots + \left[\frac{\partial y(I)}{\partial a_J}\right]_0 \Delta a_J + \text{terms of order } \Delta a_1 \Delta a_2, \text{ etc.} \quad (55)$$

Here quantities of the type

$$\left[\frac{\partial y(I)}{\partial a_J}\right]_0$$

represent the partial derivative of y in respect to a_J and are evaluated by holding all other parameters except a_J constant while taking the derivative in respect to a_J. The result is then evaluated *numerically* for the initial set of parameters $a_1, \ldots, a_J$. We are going to determine numerical corrections $\Delta a_1, \ldots, \Delta a_J$ to the initial set chosen. Substituting Eq. (55) in Eq. (52),

$$S = \sum_{I=1}^{N} W(I) \left\{ y_{\text{meas}}(I) - y_0(I, a_1, \ldots, a_J) - \left[\frac{\partial y(I)}{\partial a_1}\right]_0 \Delta a_1 - \left[\frac{\partial y(I)}{\partial a_2}\right]_0 \Delta a_2 \right.$$

$$\left. - \cdots - \left[\frac{\partial y(I)}{\partial a_J}\right]_0 \Delta a_J \right\}^2 \quad (56)$$

We next take partial derivatives of (56) in respect to the increments in each of the adjustable constants, and set the derivatives equal to zero (thus defining a minimum for S). This process gives us J simultaneous linear equations:

$$\frac{\partial S}{\partial \Delta a_1} \equiv 0 = \sum_{I=1}^{N} W(I) \left\{ y_{\text{meas}}(I) - y_0(I) - \left[\frac{\partial y(I)}{\partial a_1}\right]_0 \Delta a_1 - \cdots - \left[\frac{\partial y(I)}{\partial a_J}\right]_0 \Delta a_J \right\}$$

$$\times (-2) \left[\frac{\partial y(I)}{\partial a_1}\right]$$

$$\frac{\partial S}{\partial \Delta a_2} \equiv 0 = \sum_{I=1}^{N} W(I) \left[y_{\text{meas}}(I) - y_0(I) - \left[\frac{\partial y(I)}{\partial a_1}\right]_0 \Delta a_1 - \cdots - \left[\frac{\partial y(I)}{\partial a_J}\right]_0 \Delta a_J \right]$$

$$\times (-2) \left[\frac{\partial y(I)}{\partial a_2}\right]_0 \quad (57)$$

$$\vdots$$

$$\frac{\partial S}{\partial \Delta a_J} \equiv 0 = \sum_{I=1}^{N} W(I) \left[y_{\text{meas}}(I) - y_0(I) - \left[\frac{\partial y(I)}{\partial a_1}\right]_0 \Delta a_1 - \cdots - \left[\frac{\partial y(I)}{\partial a_J}\right]_0 \Delta a_J \right]$$

$$\times (-2) \left[\frac{\partial y(I)}{\partial a_J}\right]_0$$

These J linear equations in the unknowns $\Delta a_1, \Delta a_2, \ldots, \Delta a_J$ can be rewritten

323

as one very compact matrix equation through the following substitutions. First we shall define a J-rowed column matrix U given by

$$U = \begin{pmatrix} \Delta a_1 \\ \Delta a_2 \\ \cdot \\ \cdot \\ \cdot \\ \Delta a_J \end{pmatrix} \qquad (58)$$

That is, MAT U contains the new displacements from the last choice in the adjustable constants which will permit determining a new set of adjustable constants nearer to the minimum. We shall store the current values of the adjustable constants in a J-rowed column matrix, A, given by

$$A = \begin{pmatrix} a_1 \\ a_2 \\ \cdot \\ \cdot \\ \cdot \\ a_J \end{pmatrix}$$

Next, we define a column matrix (Q) containing J rows as follows:

$$Q_1 = \sum_{I=1}^{N} W(I)\left(\frac{\partial y}{\partial a_1}\right)_0 [y_{\text{meas}}(I) - y_0(I)]$$

$$Q_2 = \sum_{I=1}^{N} W(I)\left(\frac{\partial y}{\partial a_2}\right)_0 [y_{\text{meas}}(I) - y_0(I)]$$

$$\cdot$$
$$\cdot$$
$$\cdot$$

$$Q_L = \sum_{I=1}^{N} W(I)\left(\frac{\partial y}{\partial a_L}\right)_0 [y_{\text{meas}}(I) - y_0(I)] \qquad (1 \leq L \leq J) \qquad (59)$$

$$\cdot$$
$$\cdot$$
$$\cdot$$

$$Q_J = \sum_{I=1}^{N} W(I)\left(\frac{\partial y}{\partial a_J}\right)_0 [y_{\text{meas}}(I) - y_0(I)]$$

(where Q_L is a generalized term) and finally a square $J \times J$ matrix (S) defined by

$$S_{11} = \sum_{I=1}^{N} W(I)\left(\frac{\partial y}{\partial a_1}\right)_0^2$$

$$S_{12} = \sum_{I=1}^{N} W(I)\left(\frac{\partial y}{\partial a_1}\right)_0 \left(\frac{\partial y}{\partial a_2}\right)_0$$

$$\cdot$$
$$\cdot$$
$$\cdot$$

$$S_{1J} = \sum_{I=1}^{N} W(I)\left(\frac{\partial y}{\partial a_1}\right)_0 \left(\frac{\partial y}{\partial a_J}\right)_0$$

or, in general,

$$S_{LM} = \sum_{I=1}^{N} W(I)\left(\frac{\partial y}{\partial a_L}\right)_0 \left(\frac{\partial y}{\partial a_M}\right)_0 = S_{ML} \qquad (60)$$

where $1 \leq L \leq J$ and $1 \leq M \leq J$. [Note that (S) is symmetric about the diagonal.]

Then note that Eqs. (57) are equivalent to one matrix equation,

$$\begin{pmatrix} Q_1 \\ Q_2 \\ \cdot \\ \cdot \\ \cdot \\ Q_J \end{pmatrix} = \begin{pmatrix} S_{11} & S_{12} & \cdots & S_{1J} \\ S_{21} & S_{22} & \cdots & S_{2J} \\ \cdot & \cdot & \cdots & \cdot \\ \cdot & \cdot & \cdots & \cdot \\ \cdot & \cdot & \cdots & \cdot \\ S_{J1} & S_{J2} & \cdots & S_{JJ} \end{pmatrix} \begin{pmatrix} U_1 \\ U_2 \\ \cdot \\ \cdot \\ \cdot \\ U_J \end{pmatrix} \tag{61}$$

where the individual matrix elements may be identified from the quantities in Eqs. (58), (59), and (60), where use has been made of the standard convention for matrix multiplication. That is, the Kth element of the column matrix representing the product of the square $(J \times J)$ matrix S and the column matrix U is, by definition,

$$Q_K = \sum_{M=1}^{J} S_{KM} U_M \tag{62}$$

After appropriate dimension statements at the beginning of a program and definition of the numerical values for all the elements involved, Eq. (61) may be written in BASIC through one matrix statement,

$$\text{MAT } Q = S * U \tag{63}$$

The programming economy involved in using these matrix statements will become even more apparent in what follows.

The great virtue in transforming the least-squares fitting problem (or any system of simultaneous linear equations) into a set of matrix equations arises from the fact that subroutines are built into the BASIC library for addition, subtraction, multiplication, and, most important, *inversion* of matrices (see the discussion in Chapter 2).

The inverse of matrix S is written S^{-1} and satisfies

$$(S)(S^{-1}) = (S^{-1})(S) = (\mathbf{1}) \tag{64}$$

where $(\mathbf{1})$ is the identity matrix (a square matrix in which all diagonal elements are unity and all off-diagonal elements are zero). Also note that

$$(M)(\mathbf{1}) = (M) = (\mathbf{1})(M) \tag{65}$$

for any appropriately dimensioned matrix M follows as a direct consequence of the general law for matrix multiplication: namely, if $(A) = (B)(C)$, then

$$A_{ij} = \sum_{k} B_{ik} C_{kj} \tag{66}$$

As discussed in Chapter 2, this law is not commutative and one must be careful to observe the correct order of multiplication.

Next we shall restate Eq. (61):

$$Q = SU \tag{67}$$

and multiply from the left by S^{-1}:

$$S^{-1}Q = S^{-1}(SU) = (S^{-1}S)U = (1)U = U \tag{68}$$

Therefore, the set of displacements of the original constants that would land us at the minimum sum of weighted squares in the linear approximation is simply given by

$$U = S^{-1}Q \tag{69}$$

Once we have written statements that specify all the matrix elements needed from the set of data points, a series of BASIC statements of the type

$$\text{MAT } T = \text{INV}(S) \qquad (\text{i.e., } = S^{-1}) \tag{70}$$

$$\text{MAT } U = T * Q \tag{71}$$

yields corrected values for the displacements and the new values for the set of constants is

$$\text{MAT } C = U + A \tag{72}$$

where (A) was the initial set of constants. If each element of $(C) =$ the corresponding element in (A) within some specified accuracy (e.g., 1 ppm), we have (probably) converged on the minimum value for the sum of weighted squares. Otherwise, we use the statements

$$\text{MAT } A = C \tag{73}$$

and calculate new elements for the matrices (S) and (Q) in Eqs. (59) and (60), we then go back to statement (70) and iterate until the solutions agree on successive loops through the program (within an arbitrary numerical criterion).

It can be shown that the variances of the fitted parameters are given by the diagonal elements of the $T \ (=S^{-1})$ matrix when $W(I)$ is given by Eq. (53).

6.21
Specific Example of the Method of Least Squares

Imagine an experiment in which we take data at constant time intervals of the sound from a plucked string. Let us imagine that the string was plucked at $T = 0$ in such a way as to excite only the fundamental frequency, F, and that we have theoretical reasons to believe that the sound will decay at some rate, R, in the form

$$Y(T) = Ae^{-RT} \sin 2\pi FT \tag{74}$$

where T is the time after the string was initially plucked. We take N measurements and would then like to know the best values for the amplitude A, the frequency F, and the decay constant R. We shall also suppose that the problem is further complicated by the presence of random fluctuations on all three of these constants ≈ 10 percent.

In real life we would, of course, go out and get a string, pluck it, and take a lot of data. However, to illustrate what might happen in this case, we shall devise a program that first generates fake data in this form with a specified amount of random fluctuation and then analyze it with a program using the Gauss iterative method.[22]

First we need a few routine statements to remind us what we are doing and define the main terms in the problem. Note, however, that we do not specifically need to put in dimension statements for the matrices and arrays involved provided they have less than 10 rows and columns. (Most computers using BASIC will not be able to invert matrices with as many as 11×11 elements anyway.)

```
2    REM DECAY OF SOUND FROM PLUCKED STRING
3    REM THEORETICAL FORM IN LINE 80
80   REM Y(T) = A*EXP(−R*T)*SIN(2*3.14159*F*T)
85   LET A = 1
90   LET F = 3
95   LET R = 1
```

The values assigned on lines 85–95 are introduced merely for the sake of specific analysis.

The fake data are then "simulated" by the following steps:

```
100  REM GENERATE N FAKE DATA POINTS NEXT
105  LET N = 125
110  PRINT "FRACTIONAL AMPL., FREQ., DECAY RATE FLUCTUATIONS"
```

---

[22] This simulation of data is generally a very useful method for testing least-squares-fitting programs for real laboratory situations. The student, of course, must be honor-bound not to pass off data generated in this manner for the results of a tedious laboratory exercise!

```
115   INPUT A1,F1,R1
120   LET A1 = A1*A
125   LET F1 = F1*F
130   LET R1 = R1*R
135   FOR I = 1 TO N
140   LET T = (I − 1)/(N − 1)
145   LET A2 = A + A1*2*(RND(1) − .5)
150   LET F2 = F + F1*2*(RND(2) − .5)
155   LET R2 = R + R1*2*(RND(3) − .5)
160   LET Y(I) = A2*EXP(−R2*T)*SIN(2*3.14159*F2*T)
165   REM W(I) DEPENDS ON STATISTICS
168   REM EQUAL WEIGHT OBTAINED FOR W(I) = 1
170   LET W(I) = 1
180   REM PRINT OR PLOT I,Y(I) HERE IF DESIRED
190   NEXT I
```

In a real experiment, one could program a computer to take a large number of measurements with a high-speed digital voltmeter hooked to a microphone.

In order to analyze the above data by the method of least squares, we first make an initial guess regarding the three adjustable constants, *A*, *F*, and *R*. The nearer we come on this initial guess, the less reiterative computation is involved and the less likely is it to land in some other pothole than the true minimum we seek. Hence there is a little bit of art to picking the first guess, and one should be on one's toes against the various pitfalls that lurk in this problem. It is helpful, in fact, to be able to watch a few sample iterative solutions on an oscilloscope (or *xy* plotter) just to make sure common sense is not being violated in some gross manner. In the case of the fake data generated above, we, of course, have a pretty good idea what to guess. However, if you were to look at an oscilloscope display of that data initially, you could also make a pretty good estimate of the three constants by eye. Hence we start out the least-squares-fitting method with a guess for each adjustable constant:

```
200   REM INITIAL GUESS ON PARAMETERS NEXT
210   PRINT "ENTER GUESS FOR AMPLITUDE, FREQUENCY, DECAY RATE"
220   INPUT A(1), A(2), A(3)
```

The values of the three adjustable parameters are stored in the column array, *A*. We first set all elements of the matrices *S*, *Q*, and *U* to zero:

```
300   REM LEAST SQUARES FIT OF DATA NEXT
301   LET KØ = 1
305   LET J = 3
310   MAT S = ZER(J,J)
312   MAT Q = ZER(J)
314   MAT U = ZER(J)
```

where *S*, *Q*, and *U* are to be defined by Eqs. (58), (59), and (60). The variable *J* is used to denote the number of adjustable constants in the problem. Hence lines 310–314 automatically give the right dimensions to the matrices, as well as initializing them to zero. The variable *KØ* will be used to count the number of iterations in the program. The program then proceeds as follows:

```
316   LET A = A(1)
318   LET F = A(2)
320   LET R = A(3)
321   PRINT "ITERATION"; KØ
325   FOR I = 1 TO N
330   LET T = (I − 1)/(N − 1)
335   LET YØ = A*EXP(−R*T)*SIN(2*3.14159*F*T)
337   REM PRINT OR PLOT POINTS IF DESIRED
340   REM ADJUST A( = 1), F( = 2) AND R( = 3)
```

327

```
345   LET K1 = EXP(-R*T)
350   LET K2 = SIN(2*3.14159*F*T)
355   LET K3 = COS(2*3.14159*F*T)
357   LET YØ = A*K1*K2
360   REM PARTIAL DERIVATIVES D(L) NEXT
365   LET D(1) = K1*K2
370   LET D(2) = K1*K3*A*2*3.14159*T
375   LET D(3) = -K1*K2*T*A
```

Note that the three partial derivatives needed for a given value of T are stored in $D(1)$, $D(2)$, and $D(3)$. [These are the three derivatives for $J = 3$ that appear in Eqs. (59) and (60).]

The quantities $K1$, $K2$, and $K3$ are used in several different places within the loop on I and have been evaluated separately to minimize computing time.

The elements of the matrices Q and S defined in Eqs. (59) and (60) are computed in a running summation over all the data points by the following lines:

```
380   REM Q(L) AND S(L,M) NEXT
385   FOR L = 1 TO J
390   LET Q(L) = Q(L) + W(I)*D(L)*(Y(I) - YØ)
395   FOR M = 1 TO J
400   LET S(L,M) = S(L,M) + W(I)*D(L)*D(M)
405   NEXT M
410   NEXT L
415   NEXT I
```

After this point in the program we have computed all the matrix elements needed for one particular choice of adjustable constants. We are then ready to invert the S matrix and determine the best set of increments in these adjustable constants to further minimize the sum of squares. The matrix is inverted next and we then check the increments in the constants to see if they are smaller than some arbitrarily prescribed values (i.e., has the reiterative solution converged within that limit yet?).

```
424   REM INVERT S NEXT (=T)
425   MAT T = INV(S)
430   MAT U = T*Q
435   REM CHECK CONVERGENCE NEXT
440   FOR M = 1 TO J
445   IF ABS(U(M)) > 1.00000E - Ø4 THEN 460
450   NEXT M
455   GOTO 470
460   MAT A = A + U
461   PRINT U(1),U(2),U(3), "CORRECTIONS"
462   PRINT A(1), A(2), A(3), "NEW VALUES"
464   LET KØ = KØ + 1
465   GOTO 310
```

If it has not converged within the arbitrary prescription (1×10^{-4}) in line 445, we then go back to line 31Ø and do the calculation again with a corrected set of constants stored in the matrix A.

If it has converged, we then print out the values for the best fit, including their standard deviations [which are given by the square roots of the diagonal elements of the T matrix $= S^{-1}$ if $W(I)$ is given by Eq. (53)].

```
470   PRINT
471   PRINT "PARAMETERS", "BEST FIT", "STANDARD DEVIATION"
472   MAT A = A + U
475   PRINT "AMPLITUDE:", A(1), SQR(T(1,1))
480   PRINT "FREQUENCY:", A(2), SQR(T(2,2))
485   PRINT "DECAY RATE:", A(3), SQR(T(3,3))
```

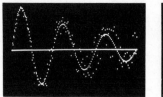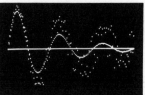

Fig. 6-18. Superposition of best fits and original simulated data for the decaying, plucked string. The results on the left were for the weighting factor $W(I) = 1$ on line 17∅ of the program and those on the right were for $W(I) = 1/Y(I)$ on line 17∅. The fit on the left is obviously much better.

At this point we might also find it useful to do a simultaneous plot of the original data and "best-fit" functional form, or even compute the actual sum of weighted squares for the best fit. However, the primary ingredients in the program are contained in the steps above.

As written above, the sample program (line 17∅) merely assumes that

$$W(I) = 1 \qquad \text{for each } I \tag{75}$$

As previously mentioned, the choice based on Eq. (53) for a *counting* experiment would result [assuming $Y(I)$ proportional to the total number of counts in a constant time interval at I] in[23]

$$W(I) = \frac{1}{|Y(I)|} \tag{76}$$

However, it is easy to see that Eq. (76) is quite inappropriate for the present hypothetical experiment in which the theoretical functional form is given by Eq. (74) and for which comparable, independent random fluctuations are assumed for each of the three adjustable constants, A, F, and R, in the simulation of data (lines 1∅∅–19∅).

The major effect of the weighting factor in Eq. (76) would be to give enormous emphasis to the data points near the zero crossings for Eq. (74) and effectively ignore the values at large amplitude. Hence a factor of this type will give the frequency pretty well but result in a rather poor value for the decay rate.

A comparison of the two weighting factors in Eqs. (75) and (76) is given in Fig. 6-18 for the above program. [In using the factor in Eq. (76) it is helpful to add a small positive term to the denominator in order to avoid singularities when $Y(I) = 0$.] As can be seen immediately by eye in the comparisons between the "data" and the best fits for the two choices of $W(I)$, the results for Eq. (75) are far better with the present simulated data. (Both factors give essentially the same results for the amplitude and frequency.)

The assumptions made in simulating the data in the above experiment are clearly quite different from those upon which the validity of Eq. (76) rests. Assuming that the sources of fluctuation in the amplitude, frequency, and decay rate were all random and independent (which is not obviously a good assumption in the case of a real experiment), and that the variances in these three parameters are

$$(\delta A)^2, \quad (\delta F)^2, \quad \text{and} \quad (\delta R)^2 \tag{77}$$

one may estimate the resultant variance in the measured quantity $Y(I)$ by

[23] Note that if $Y(I)$ results from the difference in two counting measurements involving an average of $S + N$ (signal plus noise) and an average N (noise alone), the total variance would be $S + 2N$; hence $W(I) = 1/(S + 2N)$ in that case.

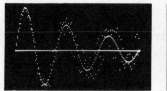

Fig. 6-19. Superposition of best fits and original simulated data for the decaying, plucked string. The results on the left are for the weighting factor given by Eq. (80), and the results on the right are for the weighting factor given by Eq. (79).

taking the partial derivatives of Eq. (74) in respect to these quantities:

$$\text{variance in } Y(I) \approx [\delta Y(I)]^2 \approx \left(\frac{\partial Y}{\partial A}\right)^2 (\delta A)^2 + \left(\frac{\partial Y}{\partial F}\right)^2 (\delta F)^2 + \left(\frac{\partial Y}{\partial R}\right)^2 (\delta R)^2 \quad (78)$$

(See the previous discussion on the addition of variances from independent processes.) Hence, by explicit differentiation of Eq. (74), it is seen that

$$W(I) \approx \frac{1}{\text{var } Y(I)}$$

$$\approx \frac{e^{+2RT}}{A^2\{[(\delta A/A)^2 + (RT)^2(\delta R/R)^2]\sin^2(2\pi FT) + (2\pi FT)^2(\delta F/F)^2 \cos^2(2\pi FT)\}} \quad (79)$$

a result that differs quite substantially from Eq. (76). Although Eq. (79) emphasizes points occurring at late times $T > 0$, it does not weight the points occurring near the zero crossings very heavily in the presence of the δF term. The results of rerunning the same program with the weighting factor in Eq. (79) and the simpler weighting factor,

$$W(I) \approx \frac{e^{2RT}}{A^2} \quad (80)$$

are shown in Fig. 6-19 and agree reasonably well with those obtained by merely letting $W(I) = 1$ as in Eq. (75) (see Fig. 6-18).

In general, one would not know the appropriate factors to include in Eq. (79) without at least having run the program in advance for $W(I) = 1$. The primary moral to the present discussion is that the choice of an inappropriate weighting factor can do much more damage to the goodness of fit than would result merely by assuming it to be constant. Of course, if you do know the values of $W(I)$ experimentally [as, for example, obtained by repeatedly measuring $Y(I)$ at each point I and determining the mean value and variance at each point], those values are most appropriately incorporated in the fitting program. One should also, of course, try to deduce which fluctuations really are random and independent (versus systematic or correlated). For example, in a real plucked-string experiment, it would seem probable that fluctuations in frequency and decay rate would be correlated. However, the presence of random and independent amplitude fluctuations (on top of the other fluctuations) from independent noise sources would be a fairly common state of affairs.

6.22
PROBLEM 21

Write a program to generate fake data for the plucked-string example, as discussed in the text. In a subsequent section of the program, use the method of least squares to extract "best-fit" parameters for the amplitude, decay rate, and frequency. Make a specific comparison of the final best-fit values and minimum sum of weighted squares (starting from the same initial guesses in each case) for the weighting factors in Eqs. (75), (76), and (80).

6.22
PROBLEM 22

Neon atoms in the lower state of the most well-known helium–neon laser transitions decay with time after excitation according to the function

$$N = N_0 e^{-T/19.1} \qquad \text{where } T \text{ is in nanoseconds}$$

Consider an experiment designed to measure this "lifetime" (see Bennett and Kindlmann, 1966). (The "lifetime" is 19.1 nanoseconds in the above equation.) Suppose that 100 atoms are excited at $T = 0$ and the number of states are measured as a function of time at 2-nanosecond intervals for a period of 100 nanoseconds. Also suppose that there is a random background counting rate in the experiment from sources having nothing to do with the excited atoms amounting to 100 counts per nanosecond on the average. (These counts might arise from thermal noise in the photodetection apparatus in a real experiment.)

(a) Assuming that the mean fluctuation in total count as a function of time varies as the square root of the total count on the average, write a program to simulate the experimental data.

(b) Write a least-squares fitting program that permits extracting best-fit values for N_0, the lifetime, and background counting rate together with the standard deviations in these quantities. Compare results obtained using the weighting functions

$$W(I) = 1 \qquad \text{and} \qquad W(I) = \frac{1}{N_{\text{total}}(I)}$$

Note: The theoretical form for the experimental results is

$$N_{\text{total}}(t) = N_0 e^{-T/T_0} + B$$

where N_{total} is measured as a function of time, and one seeks to extract best-fit values of N_0, T_0, and B. ($N_0 = $ total number of atoms at $T = 0$, $T_0 = $ atomic lifetime, and $B = $ background counting rate.) You might find it easiest to do the fit using the decay rate $R \equiv 1/T_0$ as one of the adjustable parameters instead of T_0 directly.]

6.22
PROBLEM 23

Many resonance experiments in physics have transition-line shapes which fit the *Lorentzian function*

$$I(f) = \frac{I_0}{1 + 4[(f - f_0)/\Delta f]^2}$$

where $I(f)$ is the intensity of the line at frequency f, I_0 *is the* maximum intensity at resonance ($f = f_0$), and Δf is the full width at half-maximum response (frequently called the *Lorentz width*).

Consider a spectroscopy experiment in which one counts photons for 1-sec time intervals at uniformly spaced frequencies across the resonance. Suppose that $I_0 = 100$ *counts/sec*, $f_0 = 1{,}000\,\text{MHz}$, $\Delta f = 50\,\text{MHz}$ and that there is a constant average background of $B = 100$ *counts/sec*.

(a) Assuming that the average fluctuation in the measurement is $\sqrt{I(f) + B}$ simulate a set of data points from $f = f_0 - 100$ to $f_0 + 100$ in steps of 5 MHz.

(b) Do a least-squares fit of these simulated data to the Lorentzian form and see how accurately you recover the original constants. Compare the results for the weighting factors $W(f) = 1$ and $1/(I(f) + B)$. Stop the program when the constants agree to within 1 part in 10^3 on successive iterations.

6.22
PROBLEM 24

One question that frequently arises in experiments relying on least-squares-fitting programs regards the certainty with which the theoretical functional form is known itself. For example, there are many resonance experiments in which the data should be fit to a Gaussian function of the type

$$I(f) = I_0 e^{-[(f - f_0)/0.6\,\Delta f]^2} \qquad \text{(a)}$$

instead of the Lorentzian function used in the previous problem. How could you tell which functional form gives the best fit? One approach is simply to see which best-fit solution gives the smallest sum of weighted squares. As a further subtlety, one could compute a limiting obtainable sum of weighted squares from the statistical scatter in the data itself. In particular,

$$S = \frac{N}{N-2} \sum_{I=2}^{N-1} W(I)[y_{\text{meas}}(I) - 0.5(y_{\text{meas}}(I-1) + y_{\text{meas}}(I+1))]^2 \qquad \text{(b)}$$

where $W(I) = 1$ corresponds to Eq. (75) and
$W(I) = 1/y_{\text{meas}}(I)$ corresponds to Eq. (76)

represents such a limiting sum for comparison when the total number of points N is large. That is, Eq. (b) corresponds to the sum of weighted squares that would be obtained from Eq. (52), if the theoretical function were precisely equal to the mean between alternate measured points. If the assumptions for the theoretical form are wrong, the minimum sum in Eq. (52) will generally be much larger than Eq. (b). Conversely, if the minimum sum for Eq. (52) is comparable to Eq. (b), the theoretical form is probably either correct, or at least a good approximation. However, one should be cautious when both sums are excessively large: By adding enough noise to the data, one can get a poor fit to almost any functional form.

Do a least-squares fit of the Lorentzian data generated in the previous problem to both the Lorentzian and Gaussian line shapes. Compare the sum of squares for $W(I) = 1$ for the best fits (e.g., convergence to 1 part in 10^3 on the iterative solutions) in each case with the limiting sum in Eq. (b) based on the intrinsic statistical noise in the data.

REFERENCES

BENNETT, W. R., JR. AND P. J. KINDLMANN (1966). "Radiative and Collision Induced Relaxation of Atomic States in the $2p^5\,3p$ Configuration of Neon." *Phys. Rev.*, Vol. 149 (September), pp. 38–51.

BENNETT, W. R., SR. (1960). *Electrical Noise*, New York: McGraw-Hill Book Co.

BLASCHKE, A. (1910). "Verbreitung der Geschlechtskrankheiten," Vortragsbericht, *Medizinische Reform*, Nos. 4, 5.

BROWN, ROBERT (1828). "A Brief Account of Microscopical Observations Made in the Months of June, July, and August, 1827, On The Particles Contained in the Pollen of Plants; And On The General Existence of Active Molecules in Organic And Inorganic Bodies." Printed privately by Richard Taylor, Red Lion Court, Fleet Street, London.

BURTON, L. E. AND H. H. SMITH (1970). *Public Health and Community Medicine*, Baltimore, Md.: Williams & Wilkins Co.

DOOB, J. L. (1953). *Stochastic Processes*, New York: John Wiley and Sons.

EHRLICH, P. R. AND J. P. HOLDREN (1971). "The Gypsy Moth Backlash." *Saturday Review*, Vol. 54 (Oct. 2), p. 71.

EINSTEIN, ALBERT (1905), "Eine neue Bestimmung der Moleküldimensionen." Inaugural dissertation for the degree of Doctor of Philosophy at the University of Zürich.

FELLOWS, L. (1972). "Venereal Disease an Epidemic in Connecticut." *The New York Times*, Sept. 25, p. 25.

FISZ, MAREK (1963). *Probability Theory and Mathematical Statistics*, New York: John Wiley and Sons.

Fürth, R. (1956). *Investigations on the Theory of the Brownian Movement by Albert Einstein, Ph.D.* Translated by A. D. Cowper. Originally published by Methuen & Co. Ltd. in 1926 and reproduced by Dover Publications, Inc., New York.

Ho, Y. C. (1962). "The Method of Least Squares and Optimal Filtering Theory." *Rand Corporation Memorandum RM-3329-PR.*

Hoffmann, Banesh (1972). *Albert Einstein Creator and Rebel,* New York: Viking Press.

Johnston, H. S. (1974). "Pollution of the Stratosphere," *Environmental Conservation,* Vol. 1, pp. 163–176.

Keen, Benjamin (1959). *The Life of the Admiral Christopher Columbus by His Son Ferdinand.* New Brunswick, N.J.: Rutgers University Press.

Knuth, D. E. (1969). *The Art of Computer Programming:* Vol. 2, *Seminumerical Algorithms.* Reading, Mass.: Addison-Wesley Publishing Company, Inc.

Kolmogorov, A. N. (1933). *Grundbegriffe der Wahrscheinlichkeitsrechnung,* Berlin: Springer-Verlag.

Landstrom, Bjorn (1966). *Columbus.* New York: Macmillan Publishing Co., Inc.

Levenberg, Kenneth (1944). "A Method for the Solution of Certain Non-linear Problems in Least Squares." *Quart. Appl. Math.,* Vol. 2, No. 2, pp. 164–168.

McWilliams, P., W. S. Hall, and H. E. Wegner (1962). "Multichannel Analyzer Data Analysis by a Least Squares Computer Program." *Rev. Sci. Instr.,* Vol. 33, No. 1, pp. 70–73.

Moore, R. H. and R. K. Zeigler (1960). "The Solution of the General Least-Squares Problem with Special Reference to High Speed Computers." *Los Alamos Scientific Laboratory Report LA 2367.*

Morison, S. E. (1942). *Admiral of the Ocean Sea—A Life of Columbus.* Boston: Little, Brown and Company.

Nierenberg, W. A. (1959). "A Method for Minimizing a Function of n Variables." *University of California Lawrence Radiation Laboratory Report UCRL-3816.*

Norins, L. C. and S. Olansky (1971). *Current Diagnosis 3,* edited by H. F. Conn and R. B. Conn, Jr. Philadelphia: W. B. Saunders Company, pp. 223–229.

Trotter, H. F. (1957). *Department of the Army Ordnance Research and Development Project No. PB 2-0001,* Technical Report 5. "Gauss's work (1803–1826) on the Method of Least Squares."

Wells, H. G. (1934). "The War of the Worlds" *Seven Famous Novels.* New York: Alfred A. Knopf, Inc.

333

7

Wave motion and fourier series

The material in this chapter should be comprehensible to freshmen students in both the sciences and humanities. Acquaintance with introductory calculus on the level reviewed in Chapter 2 is required. However, that material can be learned adequately without a formal course in calculus. The main calculus required was developed in Sections 2.4–2.7 and 2.21 and 2.22. If the reader understands the integrals in Eqs. (24)–(28) of Section 7.9, there should be no mathematical difficulty in following the rest of the material. Even with a prior knowledge of calculus, the reader may find it helpful to review the discussion of the trapezoidal rule in Section 2.22. The only other programming difficulties that are likely to arise represent plotting methods discussed in Chapter 3 which are given specific reference where needed.

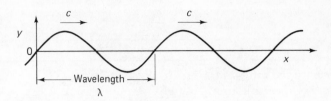

Fig. 7-1.

Historically, the first use of Fourier series was in the solution of the vibrating-string problem (by Daniel Bernoulli). It will, therefore, be helpful to summarize some aspects of wave-motion problems before plunging into a discussion of Fourier series.

Numerous problems in the physical sciences (e.g., ripples on the surface of a pond, light moving through vacuum, sound waves in air, vibration on strings) involve the propagation of periodic disturbances which are either sinusoidal or can be described as the sum of sine and cosine terms. In simplest form, the magnitude of the disturbance (y) would consist of a sine wave running through the medium at a speed c (see Fig. 7-1).

If you were to "freeze" time and examine the disturbance as a function of x, you would find that it repeated itself in a distance λ called the *wavelength*. If you stood at one fixed point and watched the wave go by, you would see f peaks (or cycles) per second, where f is called the *frequency*. (The *period* is the reciprocal of the frequency—i.e., time for one cycle.) The velocity of the wave c is related to the wavelength λ and the frequency f by

$$\lambda f = c \tag{1}$$

In each physical situation, the *disturbance* y (local pressure of the sound wave, electric field in the light wave, size of the ripple on the pond, etc.) satisfies a *wave equation* of the type

$$\frac{\partial^2 y}{\partial x^2} = \frac{1}{c^2} \frac{\partial^2 y}{\partial t^2} \tag{2}$$

where the second derivatives on each side are partial derivatives; that is, in taking $\partial^2 y/\partial x^2$ you hold time constant; and in taking $\partial^2 y/\partial t^2$, you hold x constant. The derivation of the wave equation in each particular case depends on the physical laws involved with the specific problem (e.g., Newton's laws in the case of the vibrating string, Maxwell's equations for the light wave, etc.). The derivation of the wave equation in specific cases is appropriately done in courses on the specific subjects involved (e.g., classical mechanics, fluid mechanics, electromagnetic theory, etc.). We shall merely assume the existence of the wave equation for the present discussion.

Solutions to the wave equation of the type

7.1
Running Waves

$$y \propto \begin{cases} \sin 2\pi\left(\dfrac{x}{\lambda} - ft\right) & (\rightarrow) \\ \text{or} \\ \sin 2\pi\left(\dfrac{x}{\lambda} + ft\right) & (\leftarrow) \end{cases} \tag{3}$$

represent running waves. As indicated by the arrows, the top solution corresponds to a running wave moving in the $+x$ direction; the lower solution represents a running wave moving in the $-x$ direction. You may verify the direction assigned to these two running waves by holding the argument of the sine function constant and determining which way the disturbance moves. For example, if we hold

$$\frac{x}{\lambda} - ft = \text{constant}$$

the disturbance moves at a speed $\partial x/\partial t = +\lambda f$. Hence the top solution in Eq. (3) moves in the positive direction. Similarly, for the lower solution, $\partial x/\partial t = -\lambda f$ for the case where $(x/\lambda) + ft = \text{constant}$. Note at the same time that we have proved that Eqs. (3) correspond to running waves whose frequencies and wavelengths are related to the wave velocity by Eq. (1).

We shall show by direct substitution that Eqs. (3) are really solutions to the wave equation (2).

First, let

$$y = \sin \theta \qquad \text{where} \qquad \theta = 2\pi\left(\frac{x}{\lambda} + ft\right)$$

Holding t constant,

$$\frac{\partial y}{\partial x} = \frac{\partial}{\partial x}(\sin \theta) = \cos \theta \frac{\partial \theta}{\partial x} = \frac{2\pi}{\lambda}\cos \theta$$

Hence

$$\frac{\partial^2 y}{\partial x^2} = \frac{\partial}{\partial x}\left(\frac{2\pi}{\lambda}\cos \theta\right) = -\frac{2\pi}{\lambda}\sin \theta \frac{\partial \theta}{\partial x}$$

or

$$\frac{\partial^2 y}{\partial x^2} = -\left(\frac{2\pi}{\lambda}\right)^2 \sin \theta \tag{4}$$

Next (holding x constant),

$$\frac{\partial y}{\partial t} = \frac{\partial}{\partial t}(\sin \theta) = \cos \theta \frac{\partial \theta}{\partial t} = 2\pi f \cos \theta$$

Hence

$$\frac{\partial^2 y}{\partial t^2} = \frac{\partial}{\partial t}(2\pi f \cos \theta) = -(2\pi f)\sin \theta \frac{\partial \theta}{\partial t}$$

or

$$\frac{\partial^2 y}{\partial t^2} = -(2\pi f)^2 \sin \theta \tag{5}$$

Next, substitute Eqs. (4) and (5) in (2) and note that Eqs. (3) are solutions, provided that

$$(\lambda f)^2 = c^2$$

as claimed in Eq. (1).

You can prove that

$$y = \sin 2\pi\left(\frac{x}{\lambda} - ft\right)$$

is a solution in exactly the same manner.

Similarly, you can show that any of the following quantities or *any linear combination of the following quantities is a solution to Eq. (2)*:

$$y \propto \begin{cases} \sin 2\pi\left(\dfrac{x}{\lambda_n} \pm f_n t\right) \\ \cos 2\pi\left(\dfrac{x}{\lambda_n} \pm f_n t\right) \end{cases} \tag{6}$$

where λ_n and f_n can be anything as long as for each n,

$$\lambda_n f_n = c$$

Running waves will be reflected whenever there is a sharp discontinuity in the medium through which the wave is propagating. The discontinuity also generally results in a different wave velocity, c, in the two media. Thus light is

**7.2
Standing Waves**

337

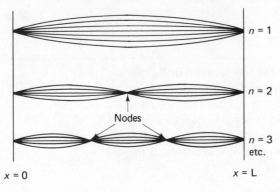

$n = 1$

$n = 2$

Nodes

$n = 3$
etc.

$x = 0$

$x = L$

Fig. 7-2.

(partially) reflected by a transparent window (the velocity of light is slower in the glass than in the air in the room), sound waves are (partially) reflected at the end of an open organ pipe (the velocity of the sound wave is affected by the walls inside the pipe), a pulse sent down a string under tension is reflected at the support; and so on. Similarly, if one matches the wave velocity in the two media (e.g., immersing quartz in carbon tetrachloride), or makes the discontinuity occur very gradually and over many wavelengths (as in certain kinds of horns designed at both audio and radar wavelengths), the reflection at the discontinuity is minimized (e.g., the quartz "disappears"; the horn does not resonate; and so on). If the reflections at opposite ends of the medium are appropriately spaced, the oppositely directed running waves can add up to produce strong standing waves at certain wavelengths.

Suppose that we have two running waves in opposite directions of the form (3):

$$y = \sin 2\pi\left(\frac{x}{\lambda} - ft\right) + \sin 2\pi\left(\frac{x}{\lambda} + ft\right)$$

Noting the trigonometry identity,

$$\sin(A - B) + \sin(A + B) = 2\sin A \cos B$$

we can rewrite the expression for the two running waves as

$$y = 2\sin\frac{2\pi x}{\lambda}\cos 2\pi ft \qquad (7)$$

That is, let $A = 2\pi x/\lambda$ and let $B = 2\pi ft$. This expression results in strong resonances when the right spatial boundary conditions are satisfied. For example, consider the vibrating-string problem, where the string is supported at $x = 0$ and $x = L$ as in Fig. 7-2. The amplitude of the vibration clearly must be zero at the supports, and that boundary condition is satisfied for all wavelengths which let

$$\sin\frac{2\pi x}{\lambda} = 0$$

for *both* $x = 0$ and $x = L$.[1] Hence there will be a series of wavelengths λ_n satisfying the boundary condition requirement given by

$$\frac{2\pi L}{\lambda_n} = n\pi \quad \text{or} \quad \lambda_n = \frac{2L}{n} \qquad n = 1, 2, 3, \ldots \qquad (8)$$

[1] Similarly, solutions of the type $y = 2\cos(2\pi x/\lambda)\cos(2\pi ft)$ are ruled out by the boundary condition at $x = 0$.

with corresponding frequencies f_n given by c/λ_n, or

$$f_n = n\frac{c}{2L} \qquad n = 1, 2, 3, 4, \ldots \qquad (9)$$

For these resonant modes, the variation of the displacement with x (position) and t (time) is obtained by substituting Eqs. (8) and (9) in (7):

$$y_n \propto \sin\frac{n\pi x}{L} \cos\frac{n\pi ct}{L} \qquad (10)$$

Hence, for a given mode, the spatial variation is multiplied by a time-dependent term which oscillates at the frequency given by Eq. (9) (see Fig. 7-2).

The resonant modes for a vibrating string are similar to those in an open organ pipe, or a laser cavity. In the open organ pipe, the pressure in the sound wave is a minimum at both ends (i.e., close to the room pressure). In a laser cavity made from flat metal-coated mirrors, the electric field in the light wave is zero at both ends.

In all three cases, one can enhance one mode at the expense of the others by forcing a node at one point. (A node has zero displacement in the standing wave.) Thus the violinist can make the string oscillate on the second harmonic ($n = 2$) by touching his finger at the midpoint; the organist can suppress the fundamental ($n = 1$) by drilling a hole halfway down the open pipe; the laser cavity designer can favor one mode by introducing a thin (compared to a wavelength of light) conducting film at a node for the particular mode; and so on.

You can also favor certain modes by the way in which you excite the resonances. For example, plucking a string in the middle tends to excite only odd harmonics; placing the hammer on a piano so that it lands on a node for $n = 7$ suppresses the seventh harmonic (which tends to "clash" with the eighth harmonic, hence third octave overtone), and so on.

7.3 Closed Pipe Resonances

The resonant modes in a closed pipe differ from those of an open organ pipe because the normal modes have a maximum pressure at the closed end ($x = L$), but still have a pressure minimum at the open end ($x = 0$) (see Fig. 7-3). From Eq. (7), the resonances are ones for which

$$\sin\frac{2\pi L}{\lambda_n} = \pm 1 \qquad \text{at } x = L$$

Hence

$$\frac{2\pi L}{\lambda_n} = \frac{\pi}{2}, \frac{3\pi}{2}, \frac{5\pi}{2}, \ldots$$

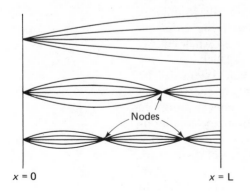

$x = 0$ $x = L$

Fig. 7-3

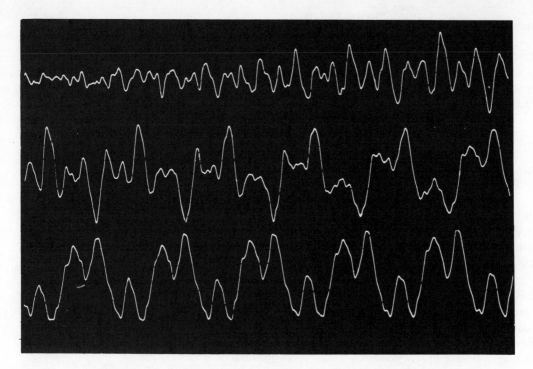

Fig. 7-4. Oscilloscope display of the transient buildup of the sound wave from a closed (quintadena) organ pipe. The air was turned on at the upper left-hand corner and time flows to the right on the successive lines. After ≈ 15 fundamental periods ($\approx \frac{1}{2}$ sec), the waveform is closely periodic at 32.7 Hz. Organists have the curious habit of specifying stops on the basis of the length of an open pipe necessary to give the same frequency. The "16-ft quintadena" (closed pipe) studied was actually only 8 feet tall. Note the odd harmonics (mostly third and first; or as musicians would say, "octave plus a fifth," hence "quint"). (Data taken by the author.) For a discussion of organ pipe construction and voicing, see Audsley (1905).

or

$$f_n = 1\left(\frac{c}{4L}\right), 3\left(\frac{c}{4L}\right), 5\left(\frac{c}{4L}\right), \ldots$$

Thus the resonant frequencies are *odd* harmonics of $c/4L$, a frequency that itself is half the resonant frequency for the fundamental mode of an open pipe of the same length (see Fig. 7-4). Consequently, closed pipes (and single-reed instruments such as clarinets where the reed vibrates in a mode that is closed most of the time) tend to sound something like square-wave oscillators. (As we shall see, the Fourier series for a square wave is made up of only odd harmonics.)

Note that for both open and closed pipes the resonant frequencies increase with c. Thus filling the pipe with helium (in which the velocity of sound is about 2.6 times faster than in air) raises the pitch by more than an octave. Similarly, tightening the violin string increases the velocity of the running waves in the string and increases the pitch of the standing-wave resonances. Analogously, the speaker who has just inhaled helium sounds like Donald Duck.

In general, which modes are specifically excited in a given system will be largely determined by nonlinear processes involving the supply of energy to the cavity; for example, turbulence at the edge of a flue pipe or nonlinear processes in vibrating reeds. In the case of a plucked string, the boundary conditions determine the relative harmonics produced initially; however, this relative distribution rapidly changes with time due to frequency-dependent dissipation. Further, the harmonics radiated acoustically will be differently distributed from those required to describe the spatial distortion of the string at $t = 0$ due to variations in radiation efficiency ("coupling") with frequency.

The field was replete with exciting controversy in its early development.[2]

1. *D'Alembert* solved the vibrating-string problem,

$$\frac{\partial^2 y}{\partial x^2} = \frac{1}{c^2}\frac{\partial^2 y}{\partial t^2}$$

in the form

$$y = \tfrac{1}{2}[f(x+ct)+f(x-ct)] \tag{11}$$

where $f(x)$ was the initial shape of the string at $t=0$.

2. *Daniel Bernoulli* next "shewed" that a formal solution of the vibrating-string problem was also

$$y = \sum_{n=1}^{\infty} A_n \sin\frac{n\pi x}{L}\cos\frac{n\pi ct}{L} \tag{12}$$

that is, a sum of solutions such as those in Eq. (10). He further asserted that this was the *most general solution to the problem possible.* (He was right.)

3. Neither *d'Alembert* nor *Euler* believed Bernoulli and said that such a series could not possibly converge to a function such as $x(L-x)$ at $t=0$, or even worse, the boundary condition on a plucked harpsichord string at $t=0$ (see Problem 12).

4. *Fourier* (1822) proved for the first time that such series *did* converge in a large number of specific cases while discussing his analytic theory of heat.

5. Others (Poisson, Cauchy, Dirichlet, and Bonnet) went on to attempt more general proofs (some of them wrong; according to Whittaker and Watson, the first correct general proof of convergence was given by Dirichlet).

Because the concept of the convergence of a sum of terms such as those in Eq. (12) considered by Bernoulli is of fundamental importance to the usefulness of Fourier series, we shall examine three specific cases graphically.

Case 1: ("sawtooth")

$$\text{Let } Y = \sin X + \frac{1}{2}\sin 2X + \frac{1}{3}\sin 3X + \cdots + \frac{1}{N}\sin NX \tag{13}$$

Case 2: ("square wave")

$$\text{Let } Y = \sin X + \frac{1}{3}\sin 3X + \frac{1}{5}\sin 5X + \cdots + \frac{1}{N}\sin NX \quad (N \text{ odd}) \tag{14}$$

Case 3: ("zigzag" considered by Gibbs)

$$\text{Let } Y = 2\left(\sin X - \frac{1}{2}\sin 2X + \frac{1}{3}\sin 3X + \cdots - \frac{(-1)^N}{N}\sin NX\right) \tag{15}$$

In each of these cases it is helpful to construct a program that computes the shape of the series over one cycle $(0 \leqslant X \leqslant 2\pi)$ through a limiting number of terms, N. The latter can be done easily by defining an array, $Y(I)$, having a suitably large number of rows to illustrate the waveform within the resolution required. For example, the following program would compute the series in case 1, using 255 points over the cycle:

```
10  DIM Y(255)
20  FOR I = 1 TO 255
30  LET Y(I) = 0
40  NEXT I
50  LET A0 = 2*3.14159/254
60  LET N = 1
70  FOR I = 1 TO 255
80  LET X = N*A0*(I − 1)
```

[2] See Whittaker and Watson (1902) for a more extended discussion.

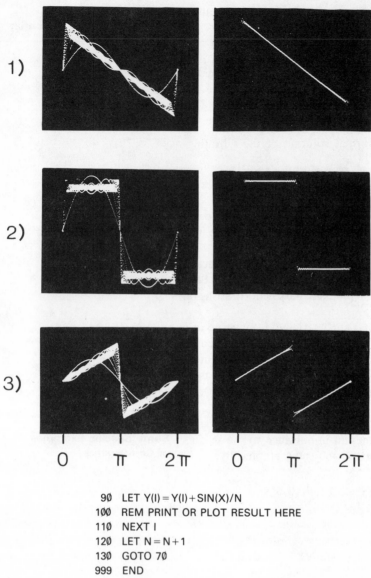

Fig. 7-5. Representation of the Fourier series for a *sawtooth* (1), a *square wave* (2), and the Gibbs *zigzag* (3) by Fourier series. The column at the left shows a superposition of the buildup of the sum through the first 15 terms in each case. The column on the right shows the result after 100 terms in each case. Compare the early development of the square wave with the closed organ pipe waveform in Fig. 7-4.

```
 90    LET Y(I) = Y(I) + SIN(X)/N
100    REM PRINT OR PLOT RESULT HERE
110    NEXT I
120    LET N = N + 1
130    GOTO 70
999    END
```

The program as written keeps going indefinitely until you tell the computer to stop. The results of running such programs for the above three cases are shown in Fig. 7-5, where the superposition of plots of the first few values of N are shown in each case.

If N is taken to be large enough, the final limiting form of the series is obtained within some specifiable limit of error. For example, the results in Fig. 7-5 also show the form of the series obtained in the above three cases when more than 100 terms are summed in each case.

7.5
PROBLEM 1

Write a program to sum the first N terms of one of the series in Eqs. (13), (14), or (15) for ≈50 points over the domain $0 \leq x \leq 2\pi$. Then plot the result on the teletype terminal (or with more points on a high-resolution *xy* plotter). Input N from the keyboard. Try plotting the result for N = 10 and 100.

If you look carefully at the results in Fig. 7-5, you will see evidence of a phenomenon that many people think was first pointed out by a former Yale

7.6
The Wilbraham Effect[3]
(Alias the Gibbs Phenomenon)[4]

[3] Henry Wilbraham (1848).
[4] J. Willard Gibbs, the younger (1899).

physicist, Josiah Willard Gibbs. If you look in the vicinity of $X = 0$ and π in all three cases and the vicinity of $X = \pi$ in cases 2 and 3, you will see that there is one point which stands slightly apart from the straight line(s) made up by the majority of the other points. These "horns" sticking up above the straight line are not computational inaccuracies but are instead manifestations of the *Gibbs phenomenon*. In the limit that N becomes very large, these horns become smaller and smaller in width but approach a finite height (≈ 14 percent higher than the neighboring straight line; see Fig. 7-6). The first mathematical analysis of the effect was given by the Cambridge mathematician Henry Wilbraham for the case of the squarewave and predated Gibbs' contribution to the problem by about 50 years. Gibbs' work on the problem was stimulated by a mild controversy in the literature concerning the nature of the zigzag function, which started with a letter on the subject by Michelson. In fact, Gibbs' first note on the phenomenon was in the nature of an errata to an earlier contribution he had made (quote from Gibbs, 1899):

"I should like to correct a careless error which I made (*Nature*, December 29, 1898) in describing the limiting form of the family of curves represented by the equation

$$y = 2\left(\sin x - \frac{1}{2}\sin 2x \ldots \pm \frac{1}{n}\sin nx\right)$$

as a zigzag line consisting of alternate inclined and vertical portions. The inclined portions were correctly given, but the vertical portions, which are bisected by the axis of X, extend beyond the points where they meet the inclined portions, their total lengths being expressed by four times the definite integral

$$\int_0^\pi \frac{\sin u}{u}\, du\,"$$

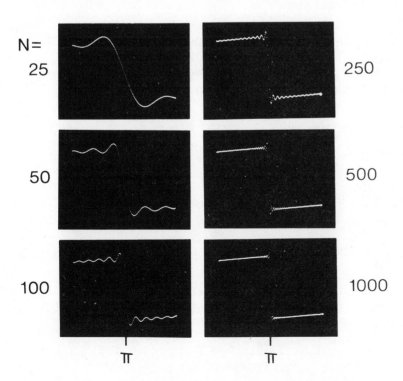

Fig. 7-6. Development of the "horn" in the Wilbraham effect, or Gibbs phenomenon. The region centered about π is shown (magnified) after varying numbers of terms (N) have been added in the Gibbs zigzag.

343

Write a program to display the Wilbraham effect in the vicinity of $\theta = \pi$ for the square wave in Eq. (14). Compute the sum of N terms for ≈ 50 points over the region $0.9\pi \leqslant \theta \leqslant 1.1\pi$, where N is input from the keyboard. Plot the results on the teletype terminal (or high-resolution plotter, if available) for $N = 25$, 100, and 500. If you use an oscilloscope display, choose the storage buffer dimension so that only one set of points is displayed at one time and put in a FOR loop to increment N continuously in integer steps.

**7.7
Fourier Series**

Although an interesting mathematical problem, the "horns" that develop near a sharp discontinuity, such as that found in the cases illustrated in Fig. 7-6, are not of great physical consequence. Most real physical problems are not characterized by such discontinuous changes in the variable. In what follows, we will be concerned with functions that are *well behaved*, in the sense that they are continuous and their derivatives are finite. Any such well-behaved function, $V(\theta)$, which is periodic in 2π,

$$V(\theta + 2\pi) = V(\theta) \tag{16}$$

can be expanded in a series of harmonics of $\sin \theta$ and $\cos \theta$. Thus, for the function illustrated in Fig. 7-7, we can write

$$V(\theta) = A_1 \sin 1\theta + A_2 \sin 2\theta + A_3 \sin 3\theta + \cdots$$
$$+ B_1 \cos 1\theta + B_2 \cos 2\theta + B_3 \cos 3\theta + \cdots$$
$$+ \text{constant} \tag{17}$$

where the terms involving $\sin N\theta$ and $\cos N\theta$ are called the Nth harmonic terms. We could also write the series

$$V(\theta) = \text{constant} + C_1 \sin (1\theta + P_1) + C_2 \sin (2\theta + P_2)$$
$$+ C_3 \sin (3\theta + P_3) + \cdots \tag{18}$$

That is, we may use a phase angle, P_N, for the Nth harmonic which contains the relative amounts of the $\sin N\theta$ and $\cos N\theta$ terms. This permits describing the total contribution of the Nth harmonic through one constant, C_N. From standard trigonometric identities, the Nth terms in (17) match the Nth term in (18) if

$$C_N \sin (N\theta + P_N) = C_N \sin N\theta \cos P_N + C_N \cos N\theta \sin P_N$$
$$= A_N \sin N\theta + B_N \cos N\theta \tag{19}$$

or

$$C_N \cos P_N = A_N$$
$$C_N \sin P_N = B_N \tag{20}$$

Hence squaring and adding the two expressions gives

$$C_N = \sqrt{A_N^2 + B_N^2} \tag{21}$$

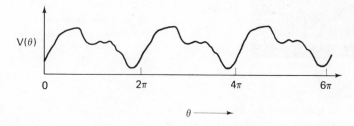

Fig. 7-7.

(because $\sin^2 P_N + \cos^2 P_N = 1$); whereas dividing the two expressions yields

$$\tan P_N = \frac{B_N}{A_N} \qquad \left(= \frac{\sin P_N}{\cos P_N} \right) \tag{22}$$

Thus if we can determine C_N and P_N (the amplitude and phase of the Nth term), we could specify the function by

$$V(\theta) = \text{constant} + \sum_{N=1}^{\infty} C_N \sin(N\theta + P_N) \tag{23}$$

7.8
Analog Spectrum Analysis

Before computers were available, it was generally necessary to rely on analog methods to determine the amplitudes, C_N, in the analysis of experimental data for periodic waveforms. Some of the instruments developed were little short of amazing. For example, Michelson (1903) had a spectrum analyzer made consisting of a large number of vertical rods, each having slightly different resonant frequencies (see Fig. 7-8). Sympathetic resonances resulted in these vertical rods as a horizontal lever was made to trace out the particular curve under analysis. The extent of the vibrations for a given rod was proportional to the Fourier component in the original waveform at the rod's resonant frequency. Michelson used this instrument to unfold complex optical spectra observed interferometrically (i.e., with a "Michelson interferometer").[5]

Modern electronic spectrum analyzers exist which effectively cause a narrow-band filter to be swept through the frequency spectrum present in the input signal and plot the power detected from the filter output as a function of frequency (see Fig. 7-9). Such devices have a number of limitations, which can easily be overcome through methods based on digital computation:

1. The filter has to be swept through the frequency of interest in a time $\gg 1/\Delta f$, where Δf is the frequency resolution required in the measurement; thus analysis of quasi-periodic waveforms in which the amplitudes are changing with time becomes very cumbersome (requires some type of memory device such as tape loops, etc.).
2. The lowest-frequency components that can be analyzed are determined by the filter resonant width. In practice, it is extremely difficult to analyze low-frequency spectra with strong components falling much below ≈ 100 Hz.
3. Usually no phase information (the angles, P_N) is available. In principle, phase information could be provided through more elaborate "lock-in" circuitry.
4. The accuracy of the measurement is limited to errors representative of analog devices (usually not much less than ≈ 1 percent). Extreme dynamic range becomes a difficult thing to obtain because of internal noise levels and circuit nonlinearities.

For these reasons, digital computation of Fourier components is becoming of increasing importance in all sorts of experimental research—experiments ranging from audio to optical frequencies.

We have shown in Section 2.7 that

7.9
Some Useful Integrals
for Fourier Analysis
(Orthogonality)[6]

$$\frac{d}{d\theta} \sin \theta = \cos \theta$$

$$\frac{d}{d\theta} \cos \theta = -\sin \theta$$

---

[5] Michelson's approach remains to this day as a very powerful means for the analysis of far-infrared spectra; recent ramifications of the method have used fast Fourier transforms in computer analysis [see, e.g., Wheeler and Hill (1966)].

[6] Those readers who have not had a formal course in calculus may find it helpful to review the material in Sections 2.4–2.7 and 2.21–2.23 before starting the present section.

Fig. 7-8. Michelson's spectrum analyzer (Michelson, 1903, p. 67). Michelson starts out his description of this amazing contrivance with the comment (p. 68): "It looks very complex; in reality it is very simple." Three figures and five pages later he arrives at the heart of the matter and remarks (p. 73): "The explanation of this process involves so much mathematics that I shall not undertake it here. It will be sufficient to state that the harmonic analyzer ... is ... capable of analyzing such ... curves."[!] (The device is about 6 feet tall and currently resides in the Smithsonian Institution, not far from von Neumann's computer.)

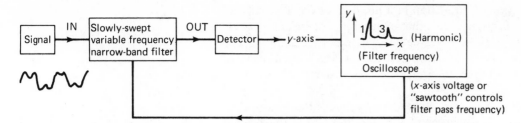

Fig. 7-9. Schematic diagram of an electronic spectrum analyzer. In practice, such devices usually have one very good filter at some fixed high frequency. The filter looks at the sum or difference frequencies produced when the input audio signal is multiplied by a swept, high-frequency oscillator.

Therefore (using the concepts developed in Sections 2.21 and 2.22),

$$\int \cos\theta\, d\theta = \sin\theta + \text{constant} \qquad \text{or} \qquad \int_{\theta_1}^{\theta_2} \cos\theta\, d\theta = \sin\theta_2 - \sin\theta_1$$

and (24)

$$\int \sin\theta\, d\theta = -\cos\theta + \text{constant} \qquad \text{or} \qquad \int_{\theta_1}^{\theta_2} \sin\theta\, d\theta = -(\cos\theta_2 - \cos\theta_1)$$

Next note

$$\int_0^{2\pi} \cos\theta\, d\theta = 0 = \int_0^{2\pi} \sin\theta\, d\theta \tag{25}$$

(The positive and negative areas cancel.) Next, from simple identities in trigonometry, note that

$$\int_0^{2\pi} 2\cos M\theta \cos N\theta\, d\theta = \int_0^{2\pi} \cos(M+N)\theta\, d\theta + \int_0^{2\pi} \cos(M-N)\theta\, d\theta$$

$$= \begin{cases} 0 & \text{if } M \neq N \\ \int_0^{2\pi} (1)\, d\theta = 2\pi & \text{if } M = N \end{cases}$$

(for M and N nonzero and integers) where the only nonzero contribution is from the second integral on the right. Therefore,

$$\int_0^{2\pi} \cos M\theta \cos N\theta\, d\theta = \begin{cases} 0 & \text{if } M \neq N \\ \pi & \text{if } M = N \end{cases} \tag{26}$$

(for M and N nonzero and integers). Similarly, from

$$2\sin M\theta \sin N\theta = \cos(M-N)\theta - \cos(M+N)\theta$$

note that

$$\int_0^{2\pi} \sin M\theta \sin N\theta\, d\theta = \begin{cases} 0 & \text{for } M \neq N \\ \pi & \text{for } M = N \end{cases} \tag{27}$$

(for M and N integers). Next from the identity

$$2\sin M\theta \cos N\theta = \sin(M+N)\theta + \sin(M-N)\theta$$

note that

$$\int_0^{2\pi} 2\sin M\theta \cos N\theta\, d\theta = \int_0^{2\pi} \sin(M+N)\theta\, d\theta + \int_0^{2\pi} \sin(M-N)\theta\, d\theta = 0$$

(for M and N integers) where both integrals on the right vanish identically. Therefore,

$$\int_0^{2\pi} \sin M\theta \cos N\theta\, d\theta = 0 \tag{28}$$

(for all integers M and N). It is customary to speak of functions satisfying a condition such as that in Eq. (28) as being "orthogonal" over the domain of the integral. The reason for the term is that one can regard an expansion such as a

347

Fourier series as the expansion of a function in a multidimensional set of base vectors. As discussed in Section 2.23, the expansion coefficients can be regarded as the projections on these base vectors. The fact that the integral in Eq. (28) is zero is thus equivalent to saying that the $\sin M\theta$ and $\cos N\theta$ base vectors are orthogonal; for example, the only nonzero projection of $\sin M\theta$ is on itself.

We may use the orthogonal properties of the sine and cosine functions to advantage in computing the Fourier coefficients. Let

7.10
Integrals for the Fourier Coefficients

$$V(\theta) = C_0 + \sum_{N=1}^{\infty} A_N \sin N\theta + \sum_{N=1}^{\infty} B_N \cos N\theta \qquad \text{over } 0 \le \theta \le 2\pi \qquad (29)$$

To get the constant, or *d.c.* (for direct-current), *term*, merely integrate (29) over 2π; i.e., take

$$\int_0^{2\pi} V(\theta)\, d\theta = \int_0^{2\pi} C_0\, d\theta$$

Therefore,

$$C_0 = \frac{1}{2\pi} \int_0^{2\pi} V(\theta)\, d\theta \qquad (= \text{average value over one period}) \qquad (30)$$

To get the term A_N, multiply (29) by $\sin N\theta$ and integrate from 0 to 2π:

$$\int_0^{2\pi} V(\theta) \sin N\theta\, d\theta = A_N \pi + 0 \qquad \text{[from (27) and (28)]}$$

Therefore,

$$A_N = \frac{1}{\pi} \int_0^{2\pi} V(\theta) \sin N\theta\, d\theta \qquad (31)$$

To get the term B_N, multiply (29) by $\cos N\theta$ and integrate from 0 to 2π:

$$\int_0^{2\pi} V(\theta) \cos N\theta\, d\theta = B_N \pi + 0 \qquad \text{[from (26) and (28)]}$$

Therefore,

$$B_N = \frac{1}{\pi} \int_0^{2\pi} V(\theta) \cos N\theta\, d\theta \qquad (32)$$

If you wish to express the series (29) as

$$V(\theta) = C_0 + \sum_{N=1}^{\infty} C_N \sin (N\theta + P_N) \qquad (33)$$

merely note that C_0 is given by Eq. (30) and from Eqs. (21) and (22),

$$C_N = \sqrt{A_N^2 + B_N^2} \qquad \text{where } A_N \text{ and } B_N \text{ are given by Eqs. (31) and (32)}$$

and

$$P_N = \arctan \frac{B_N}{A_N}$$

for $N \ge 1$. Therefore, Eqs. (30) through (33) contain all the information we need to compute the Fourier expansion coefficients for periodic functions.[7]

We wish to construct a subroutine to do the integrals in Eqs. (30)–(32) for periodic waveforms. Because there is danger of confusion regarding precisely

7.11
Constructing a Program to Illustrate the Integrals in a Fourier Series[6]

---

[7] It is possible to exploit the symmetry and redundancy of the sine and cosine functions to a much greater extent than we have done in the text. We shall resist this temptation for two reasons: (1) we wish to minimize any unnecessary sources of confusion regarding the properties of the integrals discussed so far; (2) if one wants to do really fast Fourier analysis, it is best to go into machine language with some version of the Cooley-Tukey algorithm. [See, for example, the review of "fast" Fourier transforms by Brigham and Morrow (1967) and the original paper by Cooley and Tukey (1965).]

[8] The reader may find it helpful to review the area interpretation of definite integrals discussed in Sections 2.21 and 2.22.

which curves we are finding the areas under, it is worth laboring the point with some specific examples.

First, let us consider expressing a sine function as a Fourier series in its N harmonics. We know perfectly well that the answer is going to be: $A_1 = 1$ and $A_N = 0$ for $N \neq 1$; $B_N = 0$. However, it will make a good check of our technique.

To start, we need a program to generate a sinewave with P uniformly spaced points covering the range from 0 to 2π. We shall store these initially in an array, $W(I)$. However, we shall want to plot miscellaneous curves computed from the initial data array in later subroutines without losing the contents of $W(I)$. Therefore, we shall also introduce a second array $V(I) = W(I)$ at the start of the program. Hence we can define the sine function by the statements

```
10   INPUT P
20   DIM V(255), W(255)
60   FOR I = 1 TO P
65   LET W(I) = SIN(2*3.14159*(I−1)/(P−1))
75   LET V(I) = W(I)
80   NEXT I
```

where P is an integer ≤ 255 for the particular dimension statements chosen. The constants in the argument of the sine function on line 65 were chosen so that the angle is zero when $I = 1$ and equals 2π when $I = P$.

Next, we wish to display $V(I)$ using a general-purpose plotting subroutine. Hence, we shall introduce the statement

```
90   GOSUB 500
```

where subroutine 500 will depend on the specific equipment available. For example, subroutine 500 could employ a special purpose machine language program to provide a fast oscilloscope display. We want this subroutine to display both the P points in array $V(I)$ and the I axis (line where $V(I) = 0$.) A sample subroutine that accomplishes these objectives with a teletype display is given below.

```
500   REM PLOT P POINTS IN V(I) AND I AXIS ON TELETYPE
505   LET M1 = 1.00000E+36
506   LET M2 = −M1
510   FOR I = 1 TO P
515   IF M1 < V(I) THEN 530
520   LET M1 = V(I)
525   GOTO 540
530   IF M2 > V(I) THEN 540
535   LET M2 = V(I)
540   NEXT I
545   FOR I = 1 TO P
550   LET Y1 = INT(71*(V(I)−M1)/(M2−M1)+1.5)
555   LET Y2 = INT(71*(0−M1)/(M2−M1)+1.5)
560   IF Y1#Y2 THEN 575
565   PRINT TAB(Y1−1);"*"
570   GOTO 595
575   IF Y1 > Y2 THEN 590
580   PRINT TAB(Y1−1);"*"; TAB(Y2−1);"+"
585   GOTO 595
590   PRINT TAB(Y2−1);"+"; TAB(Y1−1);"*"
595   NEXT I
599   RETURN
```

Lines 505 through 540 determine the minimum ($M1$) and maximum ($M2$) values stored in $V(I)$. The array values are normalized to the full teletype scale in the variable $Y1$ on line 550 and the normalized values for the I axis are

Section 7.11
*Constructing a Program
to Illustrate the Integrals
in a Fourier Series*

stored in $Y2$ on line 555. Lines 56Ø through 59Ø cause the teletype machine to plot the symbol * for $V(I)$ and the symbol + for the I axis.

Running the program so far just plots the original sinewave computed on line 65.

7.11
PROBLEM 3
Construct a subroutine starting at line 5ØØ to plot P points stored in the array $V(I)$ and the I axis. Normalize the plot to the full scale of the plotting device used and try it out for the original sinewave defined by line 65. If you use a teletype display, 50 points provides a reasonable upper limit of on P.

Next we wish to construct a subroutine that will find the area under a curve such as that in Fig. 7-10, using the zeroth approximation in Section 2.22. [Note that the first-order correction is $=0$ for $V(1)=V(P)$; hence the following subroutine will give the same answer as the trapezoidal rule in the present case.]

```
600   PRINT"AREA UNDER CURVE =";
610   LET S=Ø
620   FOR I=1 TO P−1
630   LET S=S+V(I)
640   NEXT I
650   LET S=S*2*3.14159/(P−1)
660   PRINT S
670   PRINT
680   RETURN
```

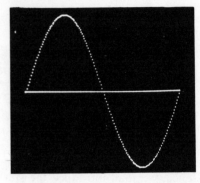

Fig. 7-10. Oscilloscope display of the original sine wave assumed on line 65 of the program.

Note that

$$S = \int_0^{2\pi} V(\theta)\, d\theta$$

where $\theta = 2\pi(I-1)/(P-1)$ from line 65. Hence in line 65Ø, $\Delta\theta = 2\pi\,\Delta I/(P-1) = 2\pi/(P-1)$ because $\Delta I = 1$. The area for the sine wave should, of course, be zero within the errors of the computation. Adding the statement

```
91  GOSUB 6ØØ
```

and running the program for $P=151$ points yields $S = -3.86485 \times 10^{-5}$. The result is small, but not exactly zero. If we divided S by 2π, we would get the constant in Eq. (30) for the Fourier series; that is, $C_0 = -6.15110 \times 10^{-6}$ should be compared to a peak value of 1 for A_1. Hence the error in the zeroth-order computation with 151 points is quite negligible and amounts to only a few parts per million.

Next we wish to examine the nature of the other integrals [Eqs. (31) and (32)] in the Fourier series for the present case [$V(\theta) = \sin\theta$]. The following statements permit *both* plotting the functions to be integrated (i.e., whose areas are to be found) and doing the integration:

```
100   PRINT "CALCULATE FOURIER COEFFICIENTS"
140   PRINT "WHICH HARMONIC";
145   INPUT N
150   PRINT "PLOT V(I)*SIN(";N;"*0)"      [integrand in Eq. (31)]
155   LET AØ=2*3.14159/(P−1)
160   FOR I=1 TO P
162   LET V(I)=W(I)                        [sets V(I) equal to original waveform]
165   LET V(I)=V(I)*SIN(N*AØ*(I−1))        [integrand in Eq. (31)]
170   NEXT I
175   GOSUB 5ØØ                            (plot curve)
176   GOSUB 6ØØ                            [find integral=net area under curve]
180   PRINT "PLOT V(I)*COS(";N;"*0)"       [integrand in Eq. (32)]
```

350

```
185   FOR I = 1 TO P
190   LET V(I) = W(I)                      [set V(I) = original waveform]
195   LET V(I) = V(I)*COS(N*A0*(I - 1))    [integrand in Eq. (32)]
200   NEXT I
205   GOSUB 500                            (plot curve)
206   GOSUB 600                            (compute area)
210   GOTO 140                             (reiterate)
```

The results of running this program for the first five harmonics in the case where $V(\theta) = \sin\theta$ are shown in Fig. 7-11. Note especially that all the integrals ≈ 0, except for A_1. Here, the area under the curve = 3.14152 in the zeroth-order approximation. It should have been $\pi = 3.14159265358979\ldots$ (see Fig. 4-16.)

**7.11
PROBLEM 4**   Write a program that displays the integrands in Eqs. (31) and (32) for the case where $V(\theta) = \cos\theta$. Also compute the integrals and demonstrate the orthogonality of the $\cos\theta$ with $\sin N\theta$ and $\cos N\theta$ for several values of $N \neq 1$ with your program. (The demonstration of course just checks the accuracy of your program.) If you plot the results on a teletype, restrict P to ≈ 25 points.

It is a simple matter to modify the above program to do the same computation for a more general and interesting waveform. For example, instead of defining $W(I)$ to be a sine function on line 65, we could read in P points over one period from a measured waveform whose values have been entered digitally in a series of DATA statements. A series of such DATA statements is contained in Fig. 7-12 for use in a number of problems throughout the remaining chapters. In each of those DATA statements, the number of points (P) over one period $(0 \leq \theta \leq 2\pi)$ is entered on the first DATA line. Consequently, to get the data into our previous program, all we have to do is make the following minor modification:

```
50   READ P
65   READ W(I)
```

(where line 65 is contained within a FOR loop going from $I = 1$ to P). One, of course, must also enter the data statements themselves.

The results of running the same program with one of these more interesting periodic waveforms is shown in Fig. 7-13.

**7.11
PROBLEM 5**   Write a program to display and compute the integrals in Eqs. (31) and (32) for one of the waveforms in Fig. 7-12 (i.e., write a program that produces results of the type shown in Fig. 7-13 for one of the waveforms tabulated in Fig. 7-12).

**7.12
Subroutine to Compute Fourier
Coefficients for Precisely
Periodic Waveforms**

It will be useful to summarize the computation of the coefficients in a Fourier series in one subroutine that we can use again and again in other problems involving periodic waveforms. For the purpose of this subroutine, we shall assume that P points are stored over one period $(0 \leq \theta \leq 2\pi)$ in the column array $V(I)$.

```
400   REM SUB TO CALCULATE FOURIER COEFFICIENTS
401   PRINT "# HARMONICS",
402   INPUT N2
405   LET A0 = 2*3.14159/(P - 1)
```

(Program continued on p. 355)

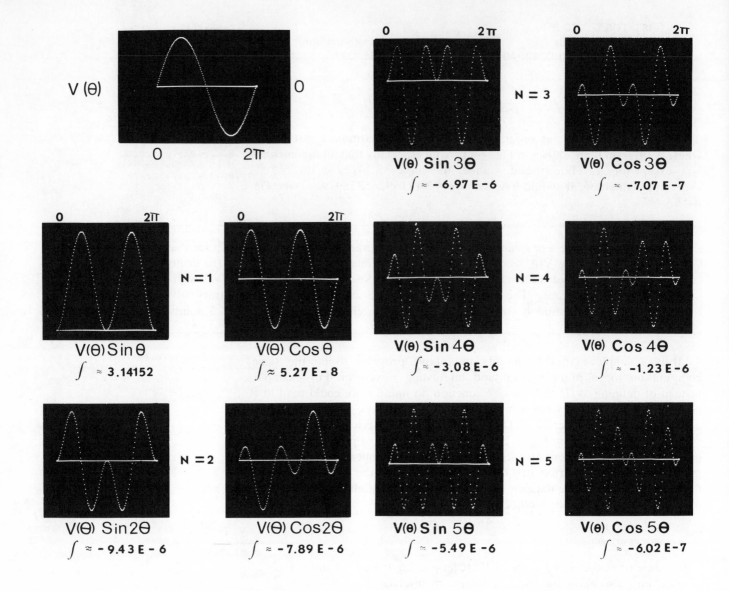

Fig. 7-11. Graphic display of integrals involved in the Fourier expansion coefficients for the periodic function

$$V(\theta) = \sin \theta$$

The function is displayed at the top of the figure and the products $V(\theta) \sin N\theta$ and $V(\theta) \cos N\theta$ which represent the integrands in Eqs. (31) and (32) are displayed for increasing values of N. For the present waveform, the only nonzero integral should be

$$\int_0^{2\pi} V(\theta) \sin \theta \, d\theta = \pi = 3.1415926\ldots$$

All the other integrals for $V(\theta) = \sin \theta$ have equal areas above and below the horizontal axis; the integrals vanish identically and the functions in the integrand are said to be "orthogonal" over the domain 0 to 2π.

The numerical values shown represent the net areas in the figure computed, assuming 250 points over the interval 0 to 2π and the trapezoidal rule. The computer used performed all floating-point operations within a fractional error of ≤ 1 ppm. Note that the nonzero term was found within an error of ≈ 7 parts in 300,000 and that the remaining terms were typically down from the nonzero term by ≤ 1 ppm.

```
999  REM  SERPENT   61.7021 HZ
1000 DATA 203
1001 DATA -5,53,113,167,207,237
1002 DATA 233,223,207,170,140,90
1003 DATA 47,-7,-47,-87,-107,-113
1004 DATA -107,-80,-43,10,73,133
1005 DATA 187,223,250,263,263,250
1006 DATA 223,200,157,130,73,20
1007 DATA -40,-97,-147,-200,-240,-267
1008 DATA -287,-280,-267,-240,-203,-180
1009 DATA -163,-133,-123,-127,-120,-123
1010 DATA -127,-123,-130,-133,-127,-133
1011 DATA -133,-113,-107,-73,-30,37
1012 DATA 103,160,210,237,240,250
1013 DATA 237,207,170,127,90,73
1014 DATA 60,50,40,23,20,-13
1015 DATA -47,-80,-120,-150,-187,-193
1016 DATA -193,-173,-150,-133,-107,-80
1017 DATA -57,-50,-43,0,60,143
1018 DATA 237,323,440,533,620,687
1019 DATA 740,747,640,460,253,20
1020 DATA -353,-737,-1053,-1333,-1497,-1527
1021 DATA -1440,-1273,-993,-667,-327,-20
1022 DATA 210,340,340,260,160,80
1023 DATA -7,-20,50,147,277,420
1024 DATA 553,667,773,853,943,997
1025 DATA 1000,970,927,810,673,500
1026 DATA 273,40,-193,-387,-507,-560
1027 DATA -540,-447,-337,-217,-93,23
1028 DATA 83,130,147,143,140,140
1029 DATA 147,153,167,173,153,117
1030 DATA 77,23,-40,-60,-100,-133
1031 DATA -173,-203,-240,-267,-280,-280
1032 DATA -300,-287,-273,-257,-257,-230
1033 DATA -227,-213,-207,-213,-200,-193
1034 DATA -163,-150,-110,-70,-5


999  REM  F-CORNET   316.075   HZ
1000 DATA 107
1001 DATA -4,44,114,163,212,249
1002 DATA 280,301,311,319,321,321
1003 DATA 311,290,259,223,166,111
1004 DATA 57,5,-47,-83,-106,-122
1005 DATA -124,-119,-98,-83,-67,-52
1006 DATA -41,-47,-62,-83,-109,-150
1007 DATA -192,-231,-259,-285,-301,-303
1008 DATA -293,-269,-228,-166,-96,-13
1009 DATA 78,174,275,370,477,578
1010 DATA 681,777,870,948,995,1000
1011 DATA 974,886,764,617,433,244
1012 DATA 67,-101,-238,-345,-412,-448
```

```
1013 DATA -461,-448,-415,-383,-337,-301
1014 DATA -272,-259,-251,-269,-301,-332
1015 DATA -365,-399,-425,-446,-453,-456
1016 DATA -446,-425,-399,-383,-368,-355
1017 DATA -347,-337,-329,-301,-262,-241
1018 DATA -210,-166,-117,-65,-4


999  REM  FRENCH HORN -LOUD  222.488   HZ
1000 DATA 151
1001 DATA 21,112,188,242,273,318
1002 DATA 356,387,399,394,385,371
1003 DATA 349,309,264,200,133,76
1004 DATA 38,21,17,17,26,52
1005 DATA 67,95,121,147,159,171
1006 DATA 176,166,157,143,140,138
1007 DATA 128,124,124,124,133,143
1008 DATA 147,147,143,140,135,133
1009 DATA 119,105,93,76,62,26
1010 DATA -12,-52,-95,-138,-181,-214
1011 DATA -252,-283,-299,-314,-309,-295
1012 DATA -268,-249,-240,-233,-214,-195
1013 DATA -166,-128,-76,-10,64,121
1014 DATA 176,216,245,273,285,295
1015 DATA 292,292,302,314,333,340
1016 DATA 349,347,347,349,375,428
1017 DATA 508,575,627,656,672,679
1018 DATA 684,684,689,684,670,641
1019 DATA 596,551,508,451,380,304
1020 DATA 214,128,45,-43,-164,-314
1021 DATA -461,-589,-670,-703,-717,-743
1022 DATA -791,-846,-895,-931,-960,-988
1023 DATA -1000,-971,-924,-886,-855,-838
1024 DATA -836,-841,-838,-829,-774,-698
1025 DATA -613,-527,-437,-335,-219,-95
1026 DATA 21


999  REM  OPHICLEIDE   85.1026 HZ
1000 DATA 196
1001 DATA -4,-117,-186,-235,-283,-324
1002 DATA -348,-393,-421,-421,-377,-324
1003 DATA -247,-170,-73,40,126,170
1004 DATA 158,142,113,45,-32,-81
1005 DATA -138,-202,-259,-287,-312,-340
1006 DATA -360,-364,-364,-377,-364,-348
1007 DATA -316,-308,-287,-275,-291,-324
1008 DATA -348,-377,-393,-413,-405,-389
1009 DATA -364,-340,-328,-324,-324,-312
```

Fig. 7-12. Periodic waveforms of musical instruments for use in subsequent problems. Each data statement represents a set of measurements taken over precisely one fundamental period. The instrument is identified in the REM statement on line 999 in each case, along with a precise measurement of the fundamental frequency of the note. Line 1000 in each case indicates the number of measurements over the range $0 \leq \theta \leq 2\pi$. For example, the note for the serpent waveform was at 61.7021 Hz (B natural two octaves below middle C by present standards), and there are 203 data points over the cycle contained in lines 1001–1034 (the points for $\theta = 0$ and 2π are both equal to -5). The data were taken using a high-speed analog-to-digital converter to measure the voltage from a condensor microphone. The sample rate was accurately calibrated against a quartz-crystal oscillator. The data have been normalized and rounded off to integer values in each case over a range that is compatible with the resolution of the 10-bit A-to-D converter used. (It is suggested that these or equivalent DATA statements be made available on punched paper tape, or within a disc file for student use. See the note in the Preface.)

An attempt has been made to collect accurate waveform data here for a number of rather unusual and exotic instruments.

The author is indebted to Richard Rephann (of the Yale University Instrument Collection) and to Robert Sheldon (of the Smithsonian Instrument Collection) for their cooperation in this data-gathering project. The instruments were played by various professional musicians on different occasions (see discussion in Section 7.13).

DATA -291,-259,-259,-259,-267,-287
1011 DATA -291,-283,-279,-247,-170,-73
1012 DATA 49,158,259,372,462,526
1013 DATA 579,607,611,607,575,518
1014 DATA 462,417,401,385,360,332
1015 DATA 308,300,267,235,178,121
1016 DATA 77,32,24,32,61,81
1017 DATA 89,93,109,97,97,105
1018 DATA 134,194,251,255,186,77
1019 DATA -24,-85,-101,-97,-85,-101
1020 DATA -101,-40,40,105,142,142
1021 DATA 154,186,223,271,316,381
1022 DATA 421,421,405,364,328,304
1023 DATA 316,364,421,478,518,514
1024 DATA 486,413,304,142,-89,-348
1025 DATA -632,-911,-1219,-1510,-1741,-1915
1026 DATA -1960,-1911,-1781,-1603,-1381,-1154
1027 DATA -927,-700,-462,-219,28,235
1028 DATA 429,595,749,879,955,996
1029 DATA 1000,1000,972,964,935,866
1030 DATA 777,688,599,514,437,364
1031 DATA 304,255,211,170,158,142
1032 DATA 126,121,130,126,130,142
1033 DATA 142,126,89,-4

999   REM MODE-LOCKED GARDEN HOSE   307.692 HZ
1000   DATA 109
1001   DATA 3,20,43,68,111,176
1002   DATA 273,426,634,861,1000,989
1003   DATA 864,705,563,452,358,273
1004   DATA 199,136,85,45,17,-14
1005   DATA -40,-63,-85,-105,-125,-139
1006   DATA -151,-162,-165,-165,-165,-165
1007   DATA -170,-165,-170,-170,-170,-173
1008   DATA -173,-170,-162,-159,-156,-153
1009   DATA -151,-142,-139,-136,-131,-128
1010   DATA -128,-128,-125,-119,-114,-108
1011   DATA -102,-94,-91,-91,-91,-91
1012   DATA -91,-91,-91,-91,-91,-91
1013   DATA -85,-82,-82,-80,-74,-74
1014   DATA -74,-80,-80,-80,-80,-80
1015   DATA -82,-82,-82,-85,-88,-91
1016   DATA -91,-91,-91,-91,-91,-85
1017   DATA -82,-80,-74,-71,-68,-65
1018   DATA -60,-57,-45,-37,-28,-14
1019   DATA 3

999   REM BACH TRUMPET   597.672   HZ
1000   DATA 168
1001   DATA -5,97,195,280,367,450
1002   DATA 530,610,680,755,807,857
1003   DATA 898,935,967,982,997,1000
1004   DATA 995,987,965,940,910,875
1005   DATA 835,797,742,695,637,585
1006   DATA 527,475,417,357,302,247
1007   DATA 187,130,85,37,-10,-50
1008   DATA -80,-110,-140,-160,-180,-193
1009   DATA -203,-200,-200,-193,-170,-155
1010   DATA -130,-93,-55,-12,35,77
1011   DATA 125,177,227,277,325,367
1012   DATA 408,450,490,517,545,567
1013   DATA 580,587,590,590,580,560
1014   DATA 540,515,485,450,408,367
1015   DATA 327,285,240,190,147,97
1016   DATA 55,15,-35,-65,-100,-133
1017   DATA -155,-180,-200,-215,-230,-233
1018   DATA -245,-245,-242,-245,-242,-240
1019   DATA -238,-235,-238,-235,-235,-242
1020   DATA -253,-260,-265,-282,-300,-320
1021   DATA -343,-363,-390,-413,-440,-463
1022   DATA -490,-513,-535,-557,-583,-603
1023   DATA -623,-643,-660,-680,-690,-715
1024   DATA -733,-753,-773,-793,-810,-830
1025   DATA -845,-857,-873,-875,-875,-882
1026   DATA -873,-870,-857,-835,-810,-785
1027   DATA -755,-720,-673,-623,-563,-500
1028   DATA -433,-355,-272,-193,-110,-5

999   REM FLUTE   262.046   HZ
1000   DATA 192
1001   DATA 18,-54,-75,-101,-134,-165
1002   DATA -178,-247,-281,-291,-335,-376
1003   DATA -428,-425,-464,-438,-446,-425
1004   DATA -402,-412,-330,-299,-250,-160
1005   DATA -82,21,93,180,216,317
1006   DATA 325,358,320,289,255,222
1007   DATA 144,119,111,85,5,26
1008   DATA 5,-34,-52,-57,-106,-67
1009   DATA -64,-75,-34,-34,8,-5
1010   DATA 36,59,101,111,90,119
1011   DATA 119,98,39,57,15,-26
1012   DATA 3,15,0,8,8,-41
1013   DATA -62,-77,-106,-126,-183,-232
1014   DATA -260,-240,-253,-247,-191,-157
1015   DATA -103,-67,-26,28,108,131
1016   DATA 250,340,430,503,595,634
1017   DATA 660,698,675,619,526,448
1018   DATA 369,340,206,124,88,-26
1019   DATA -82,-178,-250,-291,-302,-371
1020   DATA -407,-410,-436,-464,-521,-559
1021   DATA -582,-652,-765,-881,-920,-972
1022   DATA -912,-910,-838,-678,-577,-479
1023   DATA -353,-247,-134,-21,62,121
1024   DATA 155,216,204,193,222,201
1025   DATA 204,216,237,291,376,428
1026   DATA 585,799,840,892,959,1000
1027   DATA 907,747,588,430,222,-46
1028   DATA -289,-376,-518,-598,-655,-655
1029   DATA -621,-526,-459,-327,-188,-26
1030   DATA 90,170,268,361,454,454
1031   DATA 443,485,495,423,407,348
1032   DATA 291,227,144,77,62,18

999   REM KRUMMHORN   192.521   HZ
1000   DATA 174
1001   DATA -59,-91,-157,-216,-100,-78
1002   DATA -162,-176,333,1000,623,-130
1003   DATA -412,-355,-100,422,853,850
1004   DATA 490,-100,-623,-760,-760,-603
1005   DATA -150,255,157,-169,-277,-196
1006   DATA -250,-309,-150,113,206,279
1007   DATA 377,331,108,-74,-51,15
1008   DATA 145,353,510,507,333,164
1009   DATA 93,152,243,341,431,439
1010   DATA 419,373,257,230,186,59
1011   DATA 64,135,201,206,86,-78
1012   DATA -194,-196,-142,-83,47,103
1013   DATA 39,-32,-91,-167,-199,-120
1014   DATA 0,34,27,54,83,118
1015   DATA 125,137,196,230,174,115
1016   DATA 163,20,-120,-316,-471,-412
1017   DATA -277,-81,152,211,47,-137
1018   DATA -267,-353,-319,-176,-69,-25
1019   DATA 10,47,93,100,132,142
1020   DATA 142,162,157,105,27,-44
1021   DATA -78,-110,-118,-110,-78,-44
1022   DATA -32,-51,-74,-98,-103,-137
1023   DATA -137,-110,-78,-88,-113,-123
1024   DATA -78,-34,-5,-20,-88,-196
1025   DATA -353,-451,-453,-512,-534,-578
1026   DATA -534,-446,-397,-324,-306,-358
1027   DATA -306,-245,-140,-61,69,96
1028   DATA 162,152,142,172,213,289
1029   DATA 294,294,309,225,145,-59

999   REM ROHR SCHALMEI   259.674 HZ
1000   DATA 129
1001   DATA 4,-94,-132,-186,-172,-224
1002   DATA -256,-202,-146,-116,-68,-20
1003   DATA -36,-64,-64,-104,-168,-136
1004   DATA -19,-16,82,126,212,158
1005   DATA 158,152,20,-80,-188,-282
1006   DATA -206,720,692,444,1000,648
1007   DATA 694,230,68,-228,-938,-826
1008   DATA -706,-830,-474,-168,126,322

Fig. 7-12. (continued)

```
1009   DATA 376,562,408,280,316,206
1010   DATA 40,16,-44,-96,-178,-168
1011   DATA -170,-194,-242,-402,-568,-488
1012   DATA -584,-754,-604,-410,-378,-32
1013   DATA 144,476,542,678,848,816
1014   DATA 638,272,146,-176,-320,-420
1015   DATA -482,-450,-400,-202,-40,-132
1016   DATA -40,56,-16,0,-36,88
1017   DATA 172,246,414,404,366,430
1018   DATA 364,276,88,-48,-124,-282
1019   DATA -272,-238,-314,-306,-282,-306
1020   DATA -266,-136,-124,12,52,128
1021   DATA 212,166,262,220,192,164
1022   DATA 152,78,4


999    REM PICCOLO   593.877      HZ
1000   DATA 170
1001   DATA -11,34,101,180,218,276
1002   DATA 333,391,451,508,556,590
1003   DATA 631,643,679,695,707,707
1004   DATA 707,695,667,652,631,604
1005   DATA 590,542,525,487,460,422
1006   DATA 388,362,341,326,307,295
1007   DATA 276,269,247,240,247,237
1008   DATA 225,218,192,189,168,151
1009   DATA 134,106,91,74,53,36
1010   DATA 36,14,-10,-29,-34,-62
1011   DATA -77,-86,-115,-115,-125,-129
1012   DATA -139,-146,-149,-146,-153,-146
1013   DATA -146,-137,-137,-127,-127,-118
1014   DATA -108,-89,-72,-55,-38,-10
1015   DATA 24,48,94,125,170,206
1016   DATA 247,285,317,353,388,408
1017   DATA 436,458,460,484,494,477
1018   DATA 482,468,458,451,429,412
1019   DATA 388,369,345,331,321,293
1020   DATA 266,249,216,199,173,161
1021   DATA 115,86,46,22,-14,-70
1022   DATA -120,-182,-245,-317,-386,-480
1023   DATA -556,-616,-686,-751,-815,-859
1024   DATA -897,-935,-959,-981,-993,-990
1025   DATA -990,-1000,-993,-993,-964,-954
1026   DATA -959,-930,-914,-887,-856,-811
1027   DATA -763,-731,-671,-631,-568,-499
1028   DATA -444,-367,-317,-261,-175,-118
1029   DATA -62,-11


999    REM OBOE   259.581      HZ
1000   DATA 194
1001   DATA 2,-181,-397,-581,-717,-809
```

```
1002   DATA -839,-829,-777,-697,-596,-486
1003   DATA -370,-261,-159,-79,-10,45
1004   DATA 82,107,127,149,161,174
1005   DATA 179,179,174,169,156,149
1006   DATA 134,124,104,84,55,15
1007   DATA -35,-79,-112,-144,-159,-164
1008   DATA -161,-159,-154,-151,-159,-161
1009   DATA -164,-169,-159,-144,-114,-84
1010   DATA -50,-10,37,84,127,179
1011   DATA 218,246,261,253,223,176
1012   DATA 127,69,10,-40,-77,-122
1013   DATA -159,-189,-223,-251,-270,-283
1014   DATA -288,-280,-273,-263,-258,-258
1015   DATA -258,-258,-258,-258,-251,-243
1016   DATA -241,-231,-218,-208,-191,-169
1017   DATA -154,-139,-124,-122,-122,-129
1018   DATA -141,-154,-159,-159,-156,-151
1019   DATA -139,-129,-122,-124,-129,-134
1020   DATA -151,-169,-179,-199,-208,-231
1021   DATA -243,-253,-258,-258,-251,-238
1022   DATA -213,-191,-161,-139,-104,-74
1023   DATA -40,-5,27,55,77,89
1024   DATA 97,97,94,87,74,60
1025   DATA 37,15,-20,-60,-104,-156
1026   DATA -213,-280,-347,-409,-474,-526
1027   DATA -566,-588,-586,-558,-499,-422
1028   DATA -330,-221,-109,15,136,256
1029   DATA 377,501,620,739,831,913
1030   DATA 960,993,1000,995,983,963
1031   DATA 938,913,883,856,821,789
1032   DATA 752,715,663,600,496,355
1033   DATA 176,2


999    REM DATA FOR 129.777 HZ   HECKELPHONE WAVEFORM
1000   DATA 138
1001   DATA -8,142,250,308,300,283,262,196
1002   DATA 58,33,42,42,29,-8,-54,-104
1003   DATA -225,-321,-417,-475,-488,-417,-242,0
1004   DATA 217,225,346,608,867,1000,942,642
1005   DATA 25,-50,-108,-267,-475,-650,-667,-471
1006   DATA -217,-204,-167,-25,171,317,417,425
1007   DATA 329,308,229,92,-50,-142,-208,-267
1008   DATA -358,-425,-458,-454,-425,-388,-304,-221
1009   DATA 13,142,262,346,392,425,442,425
1010   DATA 238,158,75,-33,-125,-242,-367,-450
1011   DATA -388,-317,-233,-142,-75,13,112,192
1012   DATA 225,258,292,292,250,175,46,-104
1013   DATA -254,-292,-321,-317,-292,-254,-188,-121
1014   DATA 50,196,396,612,746,725,608,479
1015   DATA 262,167,50,-117,-283,-400,-417,-350
1016   DATA -67,108,258,367,442,475,500,458
1017   DATA -17,-321,-600,-817,-892,-808,-671,-538
1018   DATA -192,-8
```

Fig. 7-12. (concluded)

(Program continued from p. 351)

```
409   PRINT "HARMONIC", "AMPLITUDE", "PHASE REL. TO N=1"
410   FOR N=1 TO N2
415   LET A(N)=B(N)=0
420   FOR I=1 TO P-1
425   LET A(N)=A(N)+V(I)*SIN(N*A0*(I-1))       (main
430   LET B(N)=B[N]+V(I)*COS(N*A0*(I-1))        calculation)
435   NEXT I
436   LET A(N)=A(N)*2/(P-1)       multiply by ΔΘ/π=2/(P-1)
437   LET B(N)=B(N)*2/(P-1)
440   LET C(N)=SQR(A(N)*A(N)+B(N)*B(N))       total amplitude
445   LET P(N)=ATN(B(N)/A(N))                 phase
450   REM GET P(N) IN THE RIGHT QUADRANT
460   IF A(N)>0 THEN 480                       (arctangent problem)
470   LET P(N)=P(N)+3.14159
480   PRINT N,C(N),P(N)-P(1)
485   NEXT N
490   RETURN
```

355

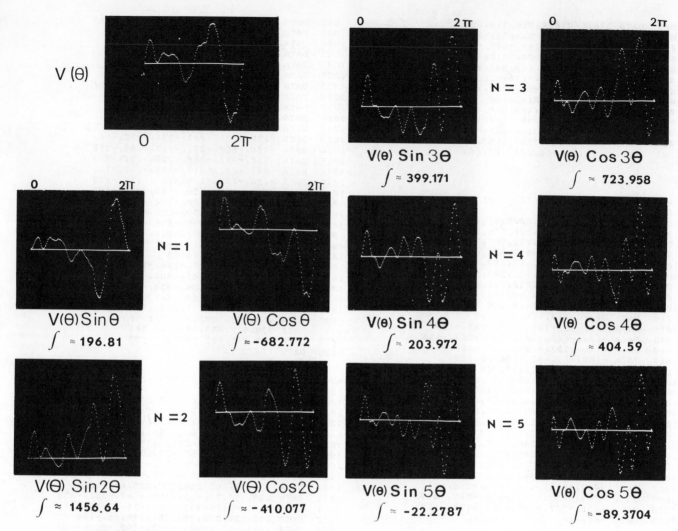

Fig. 7-13. Graphic display of integrals involved in the Fourier expansion coefficients of a complex periodic waveform. The initial waveform, $V(\theta)$, is displayed at the top of the figure over one fundamental period. (The particular waveform shown is for a note at 222.488 Hz on a French horn "played loudly.") The numerical values shown for the net areas were computed using the trapezoidal rule and 151 points over the period, using a computer that performed all floating-point operations within a fractional error of ≈ 1 ppm. Note that just as in the simpler example shown in Fig. 7-11, the cases in which the area above the horizontal axis is approximately equal to the area below the axis result in the smallest Fourier coefficients.

The net amplitude for the Nth Fourier coefficient is stored in array $C(N)$ and the phase angle for the Nth harmonic is stored in the array $P(N)$. Note that, although the phase is simply defined on line 445 by the arctangent of $B(N)/A(N)$, the computer has no way of telling which quadrant the angle should be in from the numerical argument in the $ATN(X)$ function alone. If the argument is positive, the computer puts the angle in the first quadrant; if the argument is negative, the computer assigns the angle to the fourth quadrant (i.e., a negative angle of magnitude $\leq \pi/2$). Hence, to get the phase angles consistently determined, it is necessary to examine the sign of $A(N)$ in the program, as done in lines 45Ø–47Ø. An additional refinement is sometimes useful in real life: before line 445 one might introduce a conditional statement to give the correct limit should $A(N)$ be identically equal to zero. The coefficients $A(N)$ and $B(N)$ are computed from Eqs. (31) and (32) as previously discussed. Note that the above subroutine computes the integrals to the same accuracy obtained from the "trapezoidal rule" when the waveform is precisely periodic [i.e., when $V(1) = V(P)$]. (See the discussion in Section 2.22 for clarification.)

Once the total amplitudes $C(N)$ have been computed, it is useful to be able to portray the spectrum of the Fourier coefficients in visual form as a histogram. The latter can be accomplished using high-speed oscilloscope displays if available. Alternatively, the histogram could be plotted on a teletype machine using the following type of subroutine:

```
700   REM SUB TO PLOT HISTOGRAM OF N2 FOURIER AMPLITUDES C(N)
705   LET M9 = 0
710   FOR N = 1 TO N2
715   IF M9 > C(N) THEN 725
720   LET M9 = C(N)
725   NEXT N
730   FOR N = 1 TO N2
735   PRINT N;
740   FOR I = 1 TO INT(66*C(N)/M9 + .5)
745   PRINT "*";
750   NEXT I
755   PRINT
760   NEXT N
765   RETURN
```

Lines 705 through 725 find the maximum ($M9$) value of $C(N)$. Line 735 prints the numerical value of the harmonic being plotted and lines 740 through 755 draw the histogram starting on the seventh column. A sample histogram of this general type made with a high speed oscilloscope display is shown in Fig. 7-14.

**7.12
PROBLEM 6**

Write a subroutine equivalent to 400 above and try it out on sine and cosine waveforms with ≈100 points over one period. For example, try generating a periodic waveform by adding several specified harmonic terms and then see how accurately your subroutine recovers the coefficients.

**7.12
PROBLEM 7**

Write a subroutine to start at line 700 which displays a histogram of the Fourier coefficients on the teletype terminal. Try it out on the coefficients computed in Problem 6.

**7.12
PROBLEM 8**

Write a program to compute the harmonic coefficients and phases for periodic waveforms of the type tabulated in Fig. 7-12. Display a histogram of the first 15 harmonics. Try the program out on one or two waveforms of your choice.

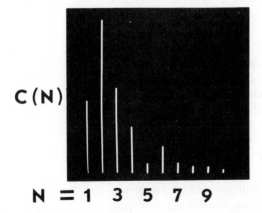

Fig. 7-14. Histogram showing the first 10 Fourier coefficients of the French-horn waveform.

357

One of the great virtues of the digital analysis of waveforms is that we can compute the Fourier coefficients for one period at a time. We can, therefore, catch elusive waveforms "on the fly" and do not have to worry about sustaining the waveform under constant conditions of excitation for long periods of time. Most isolated notes on musical instruments have waveforms that are at least quasi-periodic (i.e., repeat themselves for an appreciable number of fundamental cycles). The validity of expanding such waveforms in harmonics (or in a Fourier series) is clearly justified in something as strongly repetitive as the steady-state waveform from an organ pipe. However, even the transient buildup or decay of such a waveform could be very usefully described by a discrete Fourier series in which the amplitudes and phases are slowly varying with time. The point here is that essentially the same set of harmonically related cavity resonances is excited in the pipe during the transient. Consequently, the same set of discrete frequencies may be used to describe the behavior of the system as a function of time. Thus if you look at the transient buildup of the organ-pipe waveform shown in Fig. 7-4, the wiggles in the waveform are quasi periodic in harmonics of the final steady-state waveform back almost to the point where the pipe was initially turned on. It is also obvious from the picture that the higher harmonics (particularly the fifth) began to build up much earlier than the fundamental. (In fact, the fifth harmonic clearly went through a maximum during the transient in Fig. 7-4.) Similarly, if you look at the transient decay of a plucked string (see Fig. 7-15), you find a waveform that is strongly periodic over a few cycles of the fundamental component. However, there is no such thing as a steady-state waveform in this case. The waveform continuously dies out and the different harmonics die out at different rates. (Some harmonics in Fig. 7-15 actually oscillate in intensity while decaying. Apparently there was an exchange of energy going on between the two sets of strings comprising the 4′ and 8′ stops on the instrument.) Consequently, the relative intensities in the overtones are continuously changing and there is no single set of harmonics that could be said to describe the waveform of a harpsichord. Nevertheless, one could describe the time dependence of this waveform much more economically through the time dependence of 20 harmonic amplitudes and phases than through enough discrete points in time to permit constructing the same waveform with equivalent resolution. Thus, as illustrated in Fig. 7-15 and as is well-known to harpsichordists, the instrumental waveform is best displayed using an *Array mit verschiedenen Veränderungen.*

In studying this type of transient behavior, it is desirable to make as accurate a determination as possible of the fundamental period for the quasi-steady-state waveform first. Having determined the latter, one then merely arranges to sample the waveform at constant, prescribed intervals.

In doing Fourier series in the present chapter, we shall assume in most cases that the system has settled down to a truly periodic, steady-state waveform. However, one should keep in mind that few instrumental waveforms are precisely periodic and that small fluctuations in the relative amplitudes and phases generally occur as a function of time. In fact, it is clear that these variations are the things that produce the "warmth" in tone quality of a real instrument, as opposed to the "mechanical" sound characteristic of the synthesis of such instruments using a reconstruction based on a Fourier series with constant coefficients.

It is reasonably straightforward to design a machine-language subroutine callable from BASIC that will cause a large number of voltage measurements to be taken at high speed and transfer these measurements in floating-point form back to the BASIC compiler. However, there will generally be a nonintegral number of data points taken over the period of the wave being analyzed, and the exact value of that period is not trivial to determine itself in waveforms

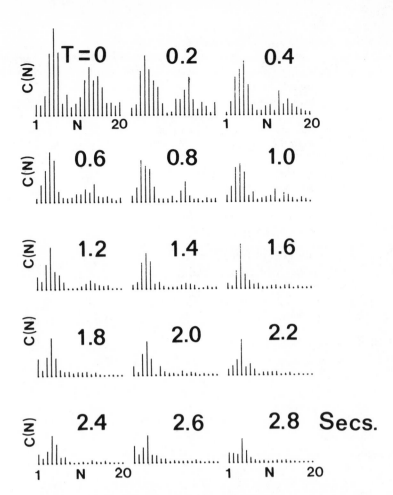

Fig. 7-15. Variation of harmonic coefficients with time in the transient decay of a plucked string. The data were taken at constant time intervals after depressing the low c for the 8-ft stop on a Ruckers harpsichord in the Yale collection. (This particular instrument was restored by Richard Rephann, using crow quills and soft wire according to the original specifications.) Note the unusually large amplitude of the fourth, fifth, and sixth harmonics. (The figure is based on unpublished data by Jean Bennett.)

that are "rich" in harmonics, such as low notes on the bass krummhorn. One effective approach is to determine all zero crossings of the same slope, display the waveform visually on a plotting device, and then allow the operator to choose that particular zero crossing after the first which corresponds to a visually recognizable period. In determining the zero crossings, it will, of course, be necessary to interpolate between the nonzero points of opposite sign.

For example, the following subsection of a program determines zero crossings and their slopes and stores them in the arrays $Z(I)$ and $M(I)$. It is assumed in the program that the digital measurements have already been made, stored in the array $V(I)$ with 254 elements, and displayed to the operator.

```
75   PRINT "# ZERO XING", "ZERO", "SLOPE AT ZERO XING"
80   LET I = 1
90   FOR K = 2 TO 252                    (skip first measurement (K = 1) because of
100  LET Y1 = V(K)                       A-to-D settling-time problems)
120  LET Y2 = V(K + 1)
140  IF SGN(Y2) = SGN(Y1) THEN 178       (examine pairs of points sequentially
142  IF SGN(Y2) #0 THEN 150              and do a linear interpolation to
144  LET K = K + 1                       find crossing point)
```

359

```
146   GOTO 100
150   LET M(I) = Y2 − Y1
160   IF I = 1 THEN 170
165   IF SGN(M(I))#SGN(M(1)) THEN 178
170   LET Z(I) = K − Y1/M(I)
175   PRINT I,Z(I),M(I)
176   LET I = I + 1
178   NEXT K
179   PRINT "NUMBER OF ZERO WITH SAME SLOPE AS Z(1)"
180   INPUT I2
184   LET P = Z(I2) − Z(1)
185   PRINT "ZEROS ";Z(1),Z(I2), "PERIOD = ";P
186   PRINT "SLOPES";M(1),M(I2)
187   PRINT "FUNDAMENTAL FREQUENCY = ";...;"HZ"
```

(reject crossing point if not same slope as first)

(print number of zero crossing, zero-crossing location, and slope at zero crossing)

(you choose which zero crossing was last in period)

(frequency computed from sample rate and P)

After determining the period, P (which is generally not an integer in real life), we would like to do a Fourier series computation for $N2$ harmonics which makes a full first-order (or trapezoidal-rule) correction in the usual situation for which there is not an integral number of points over the period of the waveform (see discussion in Section 2.22). For example,

```
300   REM COMPUTE N2 FOURIER COEFFICIENTS FOR WAVEFORM IN V(I)
302   LET A0 = 2*3.14159/P
304   LET Z1 = INT(Z(1) + .5)
305   LET Z2 = INT(Z(I2) + .5)
307   FOR N = 1 TO N2
309   REM ZEROTH APPROX. 1ST
310   LET A(N) = B(N) = 0
315   FOR I = Z1 TO Z2 − 1
320   LET A(N) = A(N) + V(I)*SIN(N*A0*I)
330   LET B(N) = B(N) + V(I)*COS(N*A0*I)
340   NEXT I
341   REM CORRECTIONS TO ZEROTH APPROX. NEXT
342   LET S1 = V(Z1)*SIN(N*A0*Z1)
343   LET S2 = V(Z2)*SIN(N*A0*Z2)
344   LET C1 = V(Z1)*COS(N*A0*Z1)
345   LET C2 = V(Z2)*COS(N*A0*Z2)
346   LET S3 = S2*(P − Z2 + Z1)
347   LET C3 = C2*(P − Z2 + Z1)
348   LET A(N) = A(N) + .5*(S2 − S1 + S3)
349   LET B(N) = B(N) + .5*(C2 − C1 + C3)
...
```

}(needed because period is not integral number of points)

}(total after first-order correction)

Before closing the loop with a NEXT N statement, the net amplitude and phase should be computed in the manner previously described. One might then want to draw a spectrum of the amplitude coefficients on a logarithmic scale (e.g., expressed in decibels)[9] to correspond to the roughly logarithmic sensitivity of the human ear. However, the logarithmic feature has not been incorporated in the following specific examples. Results obtained for a number of musical instrument waveforms are shown in the following section.

**7.13
PROBLEM 9**
(Those people having access to a high-speed A-to-D converter would probably prefer to skip this problem and do the subsequent research problem instead.) Lay a sheet of transparent graph paper over the organ-pipe waveform shown in Fig. 7-4. Center the time axis so that it divides the waveform into approximately equal areas above and below the axis. Read off values for $V(t)$ for the

[9] The relative intensity in decibels (dB) is given by $10 \log_{10}$ (acoustic power ratio) $= 20 \log_{10}$ (amplitude ratio). One dB is approximately the smallest ratio in loudness that the average human ear can detect.

last two periods of the waveform shown. Using these numbers in a data statement, compute the period (in terms of your graph-paper scale) and do a Fourier analysis over one period of the final steady-state waveform.

(*Optional:* Read off numbers from Fig. 7-4 starting at $t = 0$ so that you can compute the time-dependent behavior of the Fourier coefficients during the transient.

**7.13
RESEARCH
PROBLEM**

Devise a program to do live Fourier analysis of periodic waveforms which are taken digitally by a computer. The exact nature of the program will, of course, be determined by the specific equipment available and the problem of interest. Premedical students might find it interesting to design a computer program to diagnose heart ailments from the Fourier analysis of stethoscope waveforms or electrocardiograms. [For example, see Frome and Frederickson (1974).]

Although any exhaustive survey of the waveforms of musical instruments would be beyond the scope of the present book, there are a few interesting things that we can illustrate very easily with our present program.

As is well known, differences in the relative intensities of the harmonics (or "overtones") in musical-instrument waveforms are the primary characteristics by which the human ear can tell different instruments apart. It is frequently implied that these differences are slight and that a relatively small fraction of the sound intensity is involved in the harmonic content. The truth is quite the opposite: in many instruments a fairly negligible fraction of the total intensity is actually contained in the fundamental and enormous differences in relative harmonic content generally exist between instruments from different families.

The things that make the harmonic series similar in two instruments are common methods of excitation and common scale factors in the resonant cavity dimensions. For example, because the ratio of diameter to length is about the same in a piccolo as it is in a large open (diapason) organ pipe and because both instruments are excited by the production of turbulent vortices across an edge near one end of the instrument, the relative harmonic series for the two waveforms can be quite similar (see Fig. 7-16).

**7.14
Some Musical-Instrument
Waveforms of Unusual Interest**

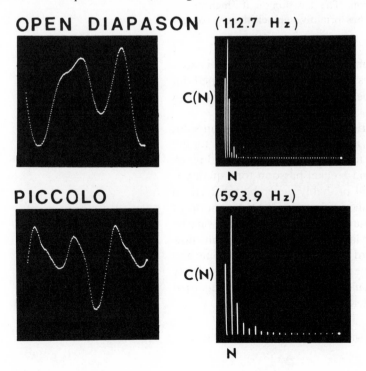

Fig. 7-16. Waveforms and harmonic analysis of a 112-Hz note from a rank of 8-ft open diapason organ pipes and a 593-Hz note on a piccolo (bottom). Although the two instruments are greatly different in length, the *scale* of the instruments (ratio of diameter to length) is roughly the same. Hence it is not too surprising that a similar harmonic structure was excited in the two cases.

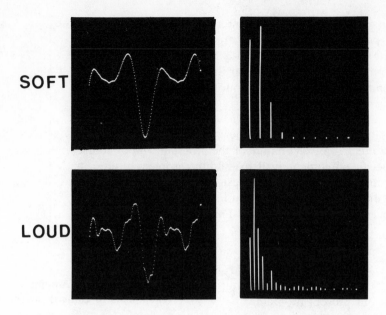

SOFT

LOUD

Fig. 7-17. French-horn waveforms and harmonic analysis. Notice that when the same note (223 Hz) is played loudly, the relative intensity of higher harmonics increases. (The two waveforms have been normalized to the same deflection to illustrate the effect.) Thus the instrument is not only louder; it also has a totally different *timbre*. Similar results are characteristic of nearly all other instruments.

(The author is indebted to James Undercofler for demonstrating most of the brass-instrument waveforms shown in this chapter.)

With essentially all instruments, the importance of higher harmonics increases substantially with increasing intensity. Not only does the sound get louder, but the tonal quality (or *timbre*) changes significantly with loudness. Thus there generally is not any one particular overtone series characteristic of a given note on an instrument (see Fig. 7-17).

There are a few specific waveforms that have had exceptional prominence throughout the history of music that are worth a quick look. For example, the world premiere of Stravinsky's "Le Sacre du printemps" resulted in a riot. Lloyd (1968) comments:

> Its first performance, by Diaghilev's Russian Ballet in Paris in 1913, set off one of the greatest uproars in the history of music and theater. Many in the audience screamed themselves hoarse trying to get the curtain to come down. An equally noisy group demonstrated in favor of the work. . . .
> The ballet begins with a soft introduction. The bassoon in its highest register plays a long, halting melody which has primitive embellishments of grace notes (p. 482).

Camille Saint-Saëns, upon hearing the opening note on the bassoon, is supposed to have exclaimed, "What instrument is that?" and to have stomped out of the concert hall.[10] An analysis of that opening waveform is shown in Fig. 7-18.

It probably is unfair to blame the entire riot on the opening bassoon solo; however, an American bassoonist (seeking anonymity) has confided to the author that it was only a natural reaction to the tone quality of a French bassoon. (The relative merit of the French and Heckel bassoon tone quality is one of those subjective controversies that will probably never be resolved on scientific grounds.) However, the waveform shows that even in the uppermost range of the bassoon, there is a very substantial amount of energy in the overtones. Studies of harmonic spectra in the low register of the bassoon show that the distribution peaks from about the third through the sixth harmonic and that the energy in the fundamental is fairly negligible. Prior to the Stravinsky work, this note on the bassoon (Fig. 7-18) would generally have been regarded as far above the usable range of the instrument.

[10] The Saint-Saëns story was told to the author by the late Professor Roy M. Welch of Princeton University.

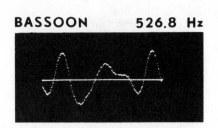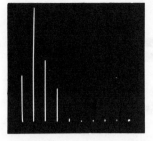

BASSOON   526.8 Hz

Fig. 7-18. Opening solo in "Le Sacre du Printemps" (played on a Heckel bassoon) during a performance by the Yale Symphony (John Mauceri conducting). A similar waveform evidently precipitated a riot in 1913.

There are two remarkable instruments, the krummhorn and the serpent, whose strange sounds have been utilized since about the time of the Spanish Inquisition as punctuation marks within the Catholic Mass. These two instruments produce rather amazing waveforms from both the physical and psychological points of view.

The krummhorn has a double reed which is at least superficially similar to that used on the modern oboe. However, the rest of this J-shaped instrument has a much larger bore than that of the oboe and there is almost no similarity in the sound of these two double-reed instruments. Subjectively, the bass krummhorn sounds like what is known in some circles as the "raspberry." The waveform has an absolutely amazing amount of energy in high harmonics and so many zero crossings within one fundamental period that it becomes something of a feat even to identify its fundamental period (see Fig. 7-19).

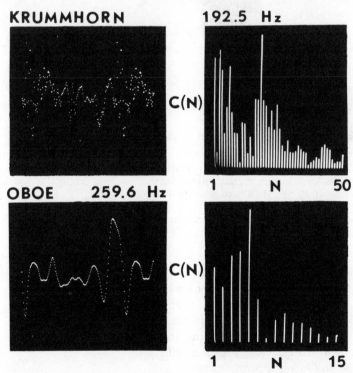

KRUMMHORN   192.5 Hz

C(N)

1   N   50

OBOE   259.6 Hz

C(N)

1   N   15

Fig. 7-19. Comparison of waveforms and Fourier coefficients for a bass krummhorn and an oboe.

In his famous treatise on orchestration, Hector Berlioz (1848) singled out the serpent for the following intriguing comments:

> The truly barbaric tone of this instrument would be much better suited for the bloody cult of the Druids than for that of the Catholic church, where it is still in use—as a monstrous symbol for the lack of understanding and the coarseness of taste and feeling which have governed the application of music in our churches since time immemorial. Only one case is to be excepted: masses for the dead, where the serpent serves to double the dreadful choir of the Dies Irae. Here its cold and awful blaring is doubtless appropriate ... imbued with all the horrors of death and the revenge of an irate God. ...

Fig. 7-20. One of the few operative serpents currently in existence. This instrument was recently restored by Robert Sheldon, for use in the Smithsonian collection in Washington, D.C., and was blown by Mr. Sheldon to generate the waveform shown in Fig. 7-22. It actually sounded much better than we had been led to believe by Berlioz' (1848) remarks. (Photograph courtesy of the Smithsonian Institution.)

It seemed clear that anything which could sound that awful must have a very interesting waveform, and we went to some effort to capture the Fourier series from one of these beasts. A good serpent is very hard to find these days and the only truly operative one that we were able to locate in the United States currently resides in the nation's capital (see Fig. 7-20). The waveform and harmonic spectrum of this instrument are shown in Fig. 7-22, together with those for some related devices discussed in the following section.

There is a very interesting trend in the waveforms shown in Figs. 7-12, 7-17, and 7-22 for the French horn, F-cornet, serpent, ophicleide, and garden hose: as we progress from one extreme to the other, the periodic waveform undergoes a transition from a reasonably smooth shape with just a few important harmonic coefficients to an extremely sharp, repetitive pulse with a nearly Gaussian distribution of harmonic coefficients distributed over a wide range. This transition is roughly correlated with the size of the "coupling hole" in the mouthpiece of the instrument. The bigger the hole, the sharper the

7.15
Acoustic Analog
of the Mode-Locked Laser

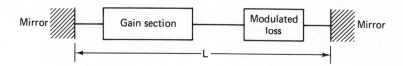

Fig. 7-21. Schematic diagram of a mode-locked laser. The loss element is modulated at the round-trip frequency, $c/2L$ (or integrally related multiple).

waveform becomes; in the case of the garden hose, the "coupling hole" is the same diameter as the resonant cavity itself. It seems clear that this sharpening of the pulse arises from the increased interaction between the open pipe resonances and the nonlinearity represented by the performer's lips. In the case of the garden hose, an exceedingly sharp pulse is produced whose tone quality is reminiscent of that of a trumpeting elephant.[11] The possibility of producing sharp pulses is, of course, further enhanced in the case of the garden hose by its extreme length (the data in Fig. 7-22 were taken for a 50-ft-long, 3/4-inch-bore hose). Hence the normal high-Q open-pipe resonances are at frequencies separated by

$$\frac{c}{2L} \approx 10\,\text{Hz}$$

where c is the velocity of sound ≈ 1043 ft/sec.

There is an interesting analogy between the behavior of the garden hose and that of a mode-locked gas laser.[12] In the latter instance, we have a resonant cavity made from a pair of mirrors separated by some distance, $L \approx 1$ m (see Fig. 7-21). The resonant modes in such a laser are also spaced at $c/2L$, except that $c =$ velocity of light $= 3 \times 10^{10}$ cm/sec. Consequently, the normal resonant modes in such a gas laser with a 1-m mirror separation are spaced at

$$\frac{c}{2L} \approx 150\,\text{MHz}$$

A gain section is introduced in the laser to overcome mirror reflectance loss and oscillation normally occurs independently on a large number of different cavity modes centered about the optical frequency of the transition (typically $\approx 6 \times 10^{14}$ Hz for visible light) but spaced at ≈ 150 MHz. When the system is to be operated in the mode-locked condition, a loss element inside the cavity is modulated at $c/2L$ (or some harmonic or subharmonic of $c/2L$). Because $c/2L$ is the round-trip frequency for light to travel back and forth through the cavity, a steady chain of pulses tends to build up inside the laser at a repetition frequency of $c/2L$. The sharpness of this pulse will increase with the number of modes that can be excited and locked together in phase by the nonlinear loss element. This effect has been used to produce laser pulses as short as 1 psecond (10^{-12} sec) and hence well into a range where direct time-interval measurement by current electronic techniques is impossible. Consequently, pulse widths and pulse shapes from such a laser are usually studied by nonlinear auto-correlation techniques: a fraction of the pulse is extracted with a partially reflecting mirror, delayed (in a device resembling a Michelson interferometer) and then recombined with the rest of the pulse. By looking at the detected output from some nonlinear optical process (e.g., second harmonic generation, two-quantum photoeffect, etc.) in which the measured signal varies as the square of the light intensity (fourth power of the optical electric field), it is possible to deduce the original pulse shape and width indirectly. Some data of that type taken with the two-quantum photoeffect by Bennett et al. (1974) are shown in Fig. 7-22. Also

[11] Unfortunately, our facilities did not permit further investigation of this subjective comparison.

[12] See the general review of picosecond (mode-locked) laser pulses by DeMaria et al. (1969).

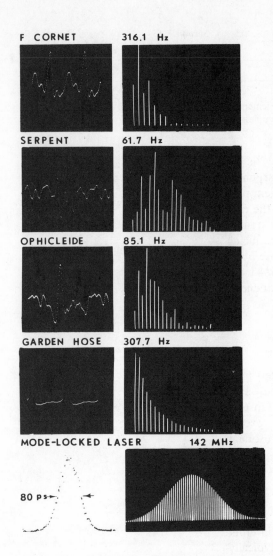

F CORNET   316.1 Hz

SERPENT   61.7 Hz

OPHICLEIDE   85.1 Hz

GARDEN HOSE   307.7 Hz

MODE-LOCKED LASER   142 MHz

80 ps

Fig. 7-22. Waveforms and harmonic spectra for instruments exhibiting varying degrees of "mode locking." Note the gradual increase in sharpness of the circulating pulse in going from the F cornet to the garden hose. The pulse shape and mode spectrum for a mode-locked argon ion laser is shown at the bottom for comparison. In the last instance, the intensity pulse was about 80 picosecond $(80 \times 10^{-12}$ secs) wide and has a roughly Gaussian distribution of modes spaced by $c/2L \approx 142$ MHz about the optical frequency of ≈ 580 THz. With the garden-hose waveform shown, the spectrum of locked modes is also roughly Gaussian. *Note:* The ophicleide is a sort of improved serpent. According to Berlioz (1848), "the sound of these low tones [on the bass ophicleide] is rough ... [and] the highest tones are of a ferocious character." He implied, however, that it was not quite as bad as the serpent. Although the shapes of these two instruments are quite different, the basic method of excitation and length-to-bore ratio are similar. Hence it is not surprising that the two waveforms are similar. [The laser data were taken by Bennett, Carlin, and Collins (1974)].

shown in the figure is the computed mode spectrum in the mode-locked laser. The latter is closely Gaussian in distribution [centered about the optical frequency ≈ 580 terahertz (THz) $= 580 \times 10^{12}$ Hz] over the cavity modes separated by $c/2L \approx 142$ Mhz. The similarity to the garden-hose-mode distribution is startling. The principal difference (other than the medium, frequency range, and specific form of the apparatus) is that the performer on the garden hose can easily produce synchronization of the nonlinear element at very high harmonics of $c/2L$. For example, the garden hose data in Fig. 7-22 involve a fundamental pulse-repetition frequency of 307.69 Hz, or approximately $30(c/2L)$. With the same instrument, the performer was able to produce mode locking at just about any other requested multiple of $c/2L \approx 10$ Hz. For frequencies $\ll 70$ Hz, it becomes difficult for the audience to hear the waveforms clearly.

The garden hose as a musical instrument seems largely to have been advanced by the late English French-horn player,[13] Dennis Brain (see Fig. 7-23), who astonished the audience at one of the Hoffnung Music Festival concerts by performing an entire movement from a concerto by Leopold Mozart on such a device. The waveforms recorded here were produced by the Yale garden-hose expert, William C. Campbell (see Fig. 7-24).

[13] Leonard Brain (private communication) has pointed out that the instrument on which his brother gained most of his fame is actually known in England as the *German* horn; whereas in France and Germany it is simply called *the* horn. Then, of course, there's the *cor Anglais*. ...

Fig. 7-23. Dennis Brain playing the French horn. (Photograph by courtesy of Leonard Brain and Mrs. Yvonne Brain.)

Fig. 7-24. Yale garden-hose and programming expert, William C. Campbell.

7.15 **RESEARCH PROBLEM**	Create a computer model to simulate the buildup of a mode-locked pulse from noise in a system such as that indicated schematically in Fig. 7-21.

Contemporary composers have subjected the modern wind player to a rather astonishing demand in performance: the ability to play double stops and chords. What is even more astonishing is that a number of current soloists seem to be able to do it!

Playing such things on a violin is not so hard because there are four different strings to work with. One could, in fact, give a fairly convincing argument that such a feat should be impossible on common wind instruments such as flutes, clarinets, oboes, and bassoons. The point is that these instruments generally tend to have nonlinear intensity dependent mechanisms which prevent more than one note from oscillating at the same time. As we have seen, these notes can be very rich in harmonic content of one particular fundamental frequency, and it is presumably the same nonlinear mechanism responsible for the generation of harmonics that limits steady oscillation to one "note" at a time. Above oscillation threshold, the available energy tends to be expended in the note requiring the least amount of energy to occur. The situation tends to be similar to that in a homogeneously broadened laser in which the gain is clamped to the threshold loss as the power is turned up above

7.16
Production of Chords on Wind Instruments[14]

[14] The data in this section are from unpublished research by the author's son, William Robert Bennett.

oscillation threshold. To produce more than one nonharmonically related frequency from the same oscillator, one generally needs something analogous to the mechanism in an inhomogeneously broadened gas laser: energy sources for the different frequency components which are roughly independent. To a considerable extent, a multimode gas laser is analogous to a large number of different open-pipe resonators tuned to substantially different frequencies and blown from different sources of air. Equivalently, four different English horn players could simultaneously sound the chord in Fig. 7-25 by each choosing a separate note. The astonishing thing is that one individual player is supposed to hit all four notes simultaneously in the Skrowaczewski (1971) "English Horn Concerto."

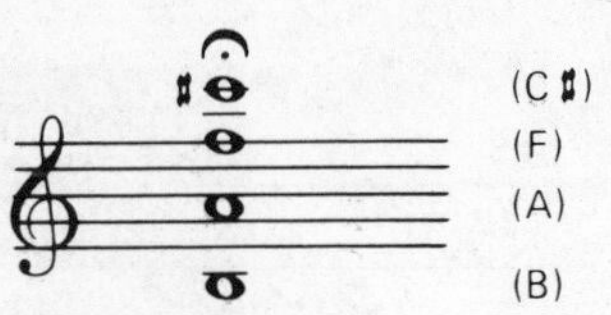

Having convinced ourselves that they cannot do it, we now have to try to understand what it is that the modern wind player really is doing. The instructions given in the score to such a piece are not much help. Generally, the soloist is told to "think in between the notes" and fool around with fingerings until the right sound comes out. Articles have been written in the musicology journals describing such fingerings [e.g., see Heiss, 1966, 1969) and books are now beginning to appear on the subject as well [e.g., Bartolozzi (1967)].

What, in fact, seems to be going on is the production of a single periodic waveform but at a fundamental frequency much lower than the normal range of the instrument. Several periods of the opening chord to the Skrowaczewski concerto are shown in Fig. 7-26 [performed by the English hornist, Thomas Stacy (1972)]. The fundamental period was about 15.5 milliseconds (msec), corresponding to a fundamental frequency of 64.28 Hz. (The skeptical reader may easily verify the periodic nature of the waveform in Fig. 7-26 by marking off one period, T, on a piece of paper and by sliding it along the figure.) The spectrum of the harmonic coefficients for the waveform in Fig. 7-26 is shown in Fig. 7-27 (computed using digital analysis of the waveform on the Stacy recording). The pronounced intensities of the fourth, seventh, eleventh, fourteenth, and eighteenth harmonics are, of course, the things that give the illusion of a chord. The frequencies of these strong harmonics come fairly close to the frequencies on the well-tempered scale for several of the notes in the chord in Fig. 7-25.

Fig. 7-25. First chord in the Skrowaczewski "English Horn Concerto" (transposed here to C).

(C♯)
(F)
(A)
(B)

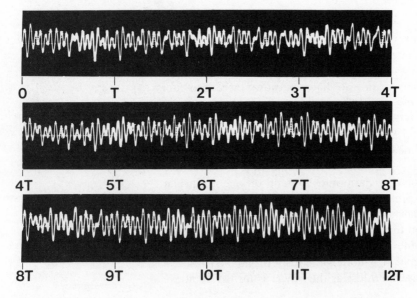

Fig. 7-26. Waveform of the first chord in the Skrowaczewski "English Horn Concerto" (see Fig. 7-25). Note that the waveform is closely periodic in the time interval T (≈ 15.5 msec). (The data were taken by William Robert Bennett from the Stacy (1972) recording.)

368

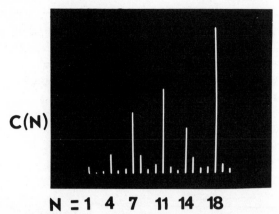

Section 7.17
Reconstruction of the Original
Waveform from the Fourier
Coefficients

C(N)

N = 1 4 7 11 14 18

Fig. 7-27. Computed Fourier coefficients for the periodic waveform shown in Fig. 7-26. The strong harmonics (N = 4, 7, 11, and 18) create the illusion of the chord in Fig. 7-25. Note that the amplitude of the fundamental component (at 64.28 Hz) is small but not completely negligible. The latter would correspond to the fundamental resonant frequency of an 8-ft open pipe—hence about an octave below the normal range of the English horn.

7.16 **PROBLEM 10**	Noting that the frequency ratios in the well-tempered scale are equal to the twelfth root of 2 and are adjusted to $A = 440$ Hz by convention, see how close the strong harmonics in Fig. 7-27 of the fundamental frequency at 64.28 Hz come to the notes of the chord given in Fig. 7-25.
7.16 **RESEARCH** **PROBLEM**	Bartolozzi (1967) has provided a phonograph record of chords played on various woodwind instruments with his book. Investigate the character of these (or similar) waveforms. (At one extreme, the waveforms can be digitized using a high-speed A-to-D converter in the manner discussed in the text; at the other, an oscilloscope record of the waveform could be digitized by hand and fed into a computer through DATA statements.)

It is important to emphasize that it is possible to reconstruct the original waveform to a prescribed accuracy by summing the computed series through some appropriate number of terms. For example, the following section of a program would permit reconstructing the original waveform for N2 harmonics (apart from the dc or constant term).

7.17
Reconstruction of the Original
Waveform from the Fourier
Coefficients

F CORNET 316 Hz

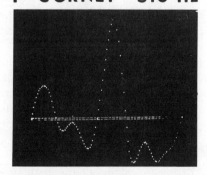

Fig. 7-28. Superposition of an initial waveform and the reconstructed waveform using the first 10 harmonics of the Fourier series. The slight displacement of the time axis in the reconstructed waveform is due to the neglect of the dc term. (A slight dc term was present in the original waveform due to background noise.)

```
800  REM RECONSTRUCT WAVEFORM FROM FOURIER SERIES
801  LET AØ = 2*3.14159/(P − 1)
805  FOR I = 1 TO P
807  LET V(I) = Ø
810  FOR N = 1 TO N2
815  LET V(I) = V(I) + C(N)*SIN(N*AØ*(I − 1) + P(N))
820  NEXT N
821  REM PLOT OR STORE HERE
...
825  NEXT I
850  RETURN
```

An overlap of an original waveform and a reconstructed waveform for 10 harmonics is shown in Fig. 7-28. The slight displacement occurs because we have neglected the dc term; the latter is not identically zero in the data, owing to the presence of background sounds (mostly from the computer) in the auditorium where the measurements were made.

7.17
PROBLEM 11

Using one of the periodic waveforms from Fig. 7-12, compute the first 15 harmonics and phases. Then superimpose the initial waveform and the reconstructed waveform from the Fourier series on one plot. (Use the teletype plotting techniques discussed in Section 3.6 if you do not have access to a high-resolution plotting device.)

7.17
PROBLEM 12

A harpsichord string is distorted by the plectrum as shown in Fig. 7-29. Find the first 20 harmonic amplitudes and phases necessary to represent the shape

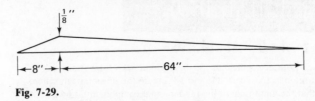

Fig. 7-29.

of the string at $T = 0$ (see Eq. (12); note the minimum at the eighth harmonic). Show that you can reconstruct the original sharply distorted shape of the string by summing the Fourier series. In a real string, the different harmonics would decay with time at different rates (increasing with the frequency). The actual relative sound intensities radiated by the instrument would also be quite different, owing to the variation of acoustic coupling from the string with frequency. The harmonic spectra of the sound waves produced by such a plucked string are shown in Fig. 7-15.

7.18
Fourier Series and the Law

An interesting controversy has recently arisen over the reliability of the Watergate tape recordings of conversations as legal evidence. During the summer of 1973, the Canadian Broadcasting Company reported a series of experiments in which a panel of experts was easily stumped in the challenge to detect edits in tape-recorded conversations. One thing that the experts did not examine at all in this discussion was the change in phase of background sounds which will inevitably result from the editing process. Although the human ear is sensitive to small-intensity fluctuations over a wide range in sound level, it is relatively insensitive to small changes in phase on steady tones. If we assume that background sounds are present in the original recording with phases which are approximately constant over the time interval of a tape splice (typically ≈ 10 msec), it is clear that net phase discontinuities in these Fourier components will be introduced by the splicing process. (Usually a gradual overlap between the two pieces of tape is used to minimize sharp discontinuities. However, even with this gradual overlap, a net phase change must result on constant frequency tones when sections before and after the splice are compared.) Before going on to the digital computation of such phase shifts, it will be useful to consider the difficulties involved in the auditory-phase-discontinuity detection problem.

There are two common situations in which such auditory phase comparisons are made:

1. Time-delay phase shifts are used in everyday life for the binaural location of objects. For example, one can localize the source of a sharp transient or clicking noise as being to the left or right of the head just from the fact that the same signal arrives at one ear before the other. This detection process involves phase comparisons inside the brain between the signals coming separately from the two ears. Interestingly, this sensitivity falls off sharply for time-delay intervals that are much shorter than the width of the human head divided by the velocity of sound in air. Nature has apparently decreed that we have no real need to detect time intervals much shorter than

that (≈ 1 msec). Very real evolutionary implications may lie behind this phenomenon: For example, most people are totally unable to localize the source of sounds while under water (where the velocity of sound is about five times faster than in air and the relative time delays correspondingly smaller).

2. The second common method of auditory phase detection is that practiced by musicians and piano tuners when they adjust two separate notes to the same pitch. Here a "linear" beating effect[15] is used which results merely from adding two sound waves of slightly different frequency and comparable intensity at the same ear. Consider adding sound waves of equal amplitude and different frequencies, f_1 and f_2. The sum will be proportional to

$$\sin A + \sin B = 2 \cos \frac{A-B}{2} \sin \frac{A+B}{2}$$

where $A \equiv 2\pi f_1 t$ and $B \equiv 2\pi f_2 t$ and use has been made of simple trigonometric identities obtained from the formulas for $\sin(x \pm y)$, when $A = x + y$ and $B = x - y$. Note that as $B \to A$ (or $f_2 \to f_1$),

$$\sin A + \sin B \approx 2 \cos \frac{A-B}{2} \sin A$$

and the ear hears a sinewave at frequency $\approx f_1$ which is modulated at half the difference between the two frequencies. Hence, even when the ear cannot tell a difference of pitch when it listens to the two frequencies separately, one can adjust the two frequencies to be closely identical when both waves are simultaneously present. That is, one merely tunes the beat to zero. The phenomenon clearly involves sensitivity to phase in the trigonometric addition of the two sine waves. However, a constant reference tone is needed.

Neither of the above techniques alone is of much help in the auditory detection of the phase discontinuities that would be likely to be present in a skillfully "doctored" tape. (We, of course, assume that the culprit would recopy the tape to eliminate visual detection of splices.) Assuming that it is a monaural recording, both ears are monitoring the same recorded signal and binaural effects would not normally be involved. Further, it would be an unusually cooperative culprit who would add a nice constant-phase sine-wave reference signal to the doctored tape with a frequency close enough to those of steady background tones to produce audible beats.

It is conceivable that one might combine the above two techniques to advantage in the present problem. For illustration, consider a beating experiment in which we feed the two separate sine waves into the separate ears of the individual. The latter can be accomplished easily with a good pair of stereo headphones. In particular, if we arrange things as shown in Fig. 7-30, it is possible (by closing the switch) to make an immediate comparison between the beat heard when both sine waves enter the same ear and that heard when the separate sine waves enter the separate ears. The results of this experiment show that the binaural beat can easily be heard when both frequencies are below about 1 kHz, but cannot be heard at all for frequencies much greater than 1 kHz. That is, the brain loses track of relative phase for signals from the two separate ears when the frequencies are much above ≈ 1 kHz.[16] It is possible

---

[15] Beats are also produced in nonlinear processes. The term "linear" was used here to emphasize the fact that no nonlinear effects are required.

[16] The binaural beat results are based on some unpublished work by the author and his son. A much more sensational way of illustrating this type of effect was recently described by Kubovy et al. (1974), who used computer techniques to generate eight simultaneous and continuous sine waves on each of two channels. By either phase- or frequency-shifting one of the sine waves in respect to its counterpart in the other channel, tones and melodies could be created in the listener's brain which could not be heard separately by either ear alone. Kubovy et al. point out the interesting parallel between this auditory stereophonic detection process and that which goes on with the equivalent visual process (see the discussion of Julesz patterns in Section 3.10).

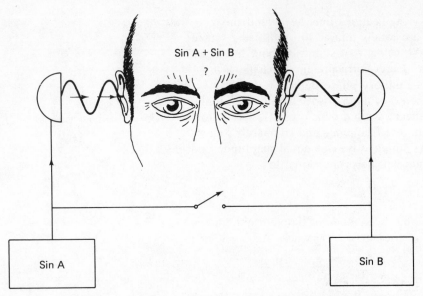

Fig. 7-30. A simple binaural beat experiment (see discussion on p. 371).

that the ability of the brain and ears to detect binaural phase shifts could be used to enhance the auditory detection of tape edits. For example, one could construct a special "stereo" playback head for a tape recorder having two gaps covering the entire width of the recorded track with a time separation of somewhat more than ≈ 10 msec at the tape speed used and feed the two output signals into a pair of stereo headphones. It seems likely that one could adjust the time delay to be small enough so that speech would not be obscured by echo effects and still permit the detection of phase shifts in background signals that would be introduced through the splicing process. To the author's knowledge such a system has never been tried experimentally, and it is certainly far removed from the way in which judges and jurors normally listen to recorded conversations introduced as evidence in court trials.

For these reasons, it is usually easy to fool the human ear in the tape-editing game. You merely pick splice locations where the intensities of background sounds are reasonably constant and ignore the phase changes. On the other hand, the phases of the various Fourier components involved can be computed digitally with great accuracy. In fact, through recent developments in the computer hardware field, and with the use of superfast algorithms (for example, the Cooley–Tukey algorithm), it is possible to obtain nearly continuous computed values for the Fourier components over the entire audio band in real time. It seems highly probable that continuous monitoring of the derivatives of the phase of strong Fourier components would provide a very potent method for the detection of edits in tape recordings. The surprising thing is that none of the experts have so far reported studying this approach to the problem.

In order to test the method, the following experiment was performed by the author.[17] A tape recording was made from the radio broadcast of President Nixon's October 26, 1973, press conference. A constant phase 60-Hz signal was deliberately added to the original recording. The tape was then thoroughly edited and the word order and meaning of the sentences was completely changed in numerous places over a ≈ 20-minute excerpt from the press conference. A total of 57 separate splices was introduced in the tape. A group of students was then asked to determine the number of edits they could detect on the basis of technical flaws in the tape (i.e., not on the basis of obvious changes in word order).

[17] See, for example, B. Davis, "Doctoring Demonstrated—Nixon Confesses Guilt on New Tape," *Yale Daily News*, Nov. 2, 1973, p. 1.

Because there is a tendency for overzealous listeners to detect edits that do not exist, the following experimental safeguard was adopted: a series of timing marks was introduced at 15-second intervals on a second channel of the edited tape. Each member of the audience was supplied with an answer sheet containing rows numbered according to the timing marks. The particular row to be used was then displayed visually (by a monitor listening to the timing mark channel) while the audience concentrated on listening to the edited speech. The results of such an experiment conducted with an audience of 375 people are shown in Fig. 7-31, in which the most probable ("M.P.") and average value ("Av.") are indicated, together with the distribution of audience answers. About five really sloppy edits had been deliberately introduced just to make sure that everyone would be able to get a few correct answers. The distribution of correct and wrong answers is self-explanatory in Fig. 7-31. The most probable number of correctly identified edits was 9.5 (out of 57). No one got more than about half the total number correct and just about everyone identified at least one false edit. The lower part of the figure (labeled "Unreliability Factor") illustrates a severe problem one is likely to have with juries. The number of incorrect identifications made by a given person increases in proportion to the number of correct ones. That is, the lower part of the figure shows a histogram of the number of wrong answers made by persons getting N

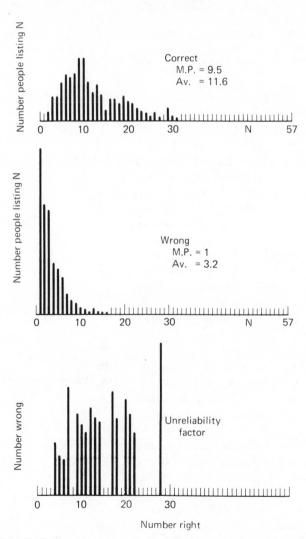

Fig. 7-31. Results of a tape-edit detection experiment for an audience of 375 high school and college-age students (see the discussion in the text).

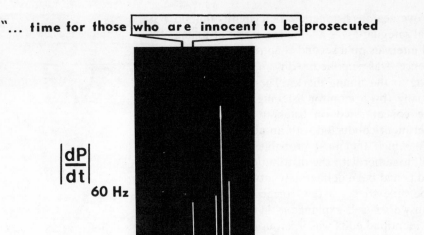

"... time for those who are innocent to be prosecuted

and for those who are guilty to be cleared."

Fig. 7-32. Some results from the tape-editing experiment. The words within the boxes were interchanged by splicing the tape, and an additional splice was introduced after the word "cleared." The computed absolute value of the derivative of the Fourier phase component at 60 Hz (deliberately added to the original tape) is shown plotted against time. The five main splices in the tape show up quite clearly. The sixth "splice" detected by the program (*just* before "who are guilty") was not real. This particular set of splices was usually not detected by the listeners. In fact, some listeners were concentrating so hard to hear tape clicks and other splicing defects that they did not even notice the strange word order.

answers correct. For example, the particular group that actually identified 28 edits correctly also got the largest number of answers wrong.

In contrast, a program that was designed to compute and monitor the absolute value of the rate of change of phase of the 60 Hz signal (deliberately added to the original tape) found about 80 percent of the splices (see example in Fig. 7-32). The fraction missed by the computer program could, in fact, be fully explained by the 20 percent duty cycle of the program (i.e., the program was computing 20 percent of the time and therefore missed 20 percent of the conversation).

In a real situation, one would not know the frequency of constant-phase components in advance, and these signals would, of course, be more difficult to pick out of the noise. However, the fact that one could do the analysis with the entire audio band would be a considerable compensating advantage. (Of course, the technique would not be of much use if the tapes were completely erased or destroyed.)

**7.19
The Watergate Problem**

It is instructive to consider what happens to the phase-discontinuity-detection problem if a strong complex waveform is deliberately added to the original tape recording. The object, of course, would be to obscure the phase discontinuities that would result in the roughly constant Fourier components of background sounds through a tape-editing process. We have called this the "Watergate problem" because the question of detecting such tape-doctoring methods has largely been brought to public attention through coverage of the Watergate matter in the news media. We, of course, do not mean to imply that anyone would actually do such an unscrupulous thing. However, it is worth noting that if such a process were carried out, it would be possible in principle to detect that fact. The detection method, of course, might require more computing time than one would be willing to tolerate in practice.

For a specific example, consider storing a sine wave repetitively in a

250-point column array $V(I)$, using a sinewave period of 50 time units. At the point $T = 100$ we will introduce a phase change of π radians to simulate the effects of a tape splice. The original background sine-wave signal will thus appear as shown in Fig. 7-33. Next we shall add variable amounts of the complex waveform from a heckelphone[18] having a fundamental period of 137 time units. This waveform is rich in harmonics (especially the seventh) and provides strong Fourier components that will surround our original sine wave. We shall refer to this process as "heckeling the tape."

The heckeling can be accomplished in a straightforward manner by computing the sine wave and reading the heckelphone waveform from the data statement in Fig. 7-12. As with the other data in Fig. 7-12, line 1000 contains the number of succeeding points (138) which cover one fundamental period $(0 \leq \theta \leq 2\pi)$ of the instrumental waveform. The maximum amplitude was also normalized to 1000. It is, of course, important to add the heckelphone waveform (multiplied by a constant, S) repetitively without phase discontinuities.

The phase of the Fourier component at the original sine-wave frequency can then be computed through a simple modification of the previous Fourier analysis programs. For example,

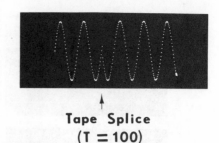

Fig. 7-33. Simulated effect of a tape splice on a constant-frequency sine wave.

```
315    FOR T1 = 1 TO 250
320    LET A = B = 0
330    FOR T = T1 TO T1 + 49
335    IF T > 255 THEN 9999 [stop]
340    LET A = A + V[I]*SIN(A0*(I − 1))
350    LET B = B + V[I]*COS(A0*(I − 1))
360    NEXT T
370    LET C = SQR(A*A + B*B)
380    LET P1 = ATN(B/A)
390    REM GET P1 IN THE RIGHT QUADRANT
400    IF A > 0 THEN 420
410    LET P1 = P1 + 3.14159
420    REM PRINT OR PLOT PHASE, P1
430    NEXT T1
```

where $A0 = 2\pi/50$.

Results from running this program are shown plotted in Fig. 7-34, where the net waveforms and phase angles are shown as a function of time for variable amounts of heckeling. Note that the phase discontinuity is easily recognized for heckelphone amplitudes up to four times greater than the original sine-wave amplitudes (i.e., $S = 4$). For $S > 5$ "false splices" begin to appear in the plot of phase as a function of time, for the 50-point sine wave period assumed. One, of course, could repeat this experiment with greater and greater resolution; for example, with 1024-point sine waves and Fourier transform analysis, and so on. With sufficiently large resolution, the phase discontinuity could always be located, provided no one of the heckeling frequency components were exactly identical to the sine-wave frequency. Eventually, the required resolution would result in prohibitively long computing time. However, it is worth noting that minicomputers are currently available that can do a 1024-point Fourier transform in 15.2 msec. One should further note that by the time the sound from a heckelphone has been added at four times the volume level of the residual constant-phase background sounds, it will not only tend to become conspicuous but will also start to interfere with the intelligibility of speech recorded on the same tape.

[18] The heckelphone, or bass oboe, is named after its inventor, the famous German instrument maker, Wilhelm Heckel (1856–1909). We are indebted to the Yale Concert Band for the loan of one of these rare instruments so that we could analyze its waveform.

375

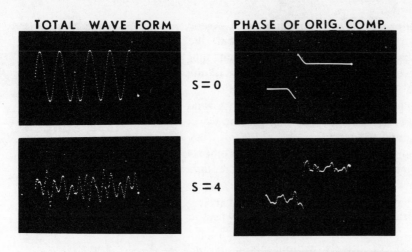

S = 0

S = 4

Fig. 7-34. The Watergate problem with variable amounts of heckeling. The top figure ($S = 0$) corresponds to the original sine wave with a phase discontinuity of π radians introduced by a tape splice (i.e., no heckeling). The next figure ($S = 4$) has four times as much heckelphone waveform peak amplitude as original sine-wave. For much more than five times as much heckelphone amplitude ($S > 5$) as sine-wave amplitude, false tape splices show up in the form of phase discontinuities for the 50-point sine-wave period assumed.

In practice, of course, anyone who would commit such a deliberate deception also could use computer-oriented methods to check his work. For example, monitoring the entire audio band with continuous Fourier transform analysis would permit spotting the residual constant-phase components. Such frequencies could be totally removed before the final tape copy using "notch" filters and prior to the heckeling process. Consequently, a kind of *detente* would probably ensue in practice whose outcome would be difficult to predict. About the only thing that is certain about the outcome is that the fidelity of the recording would get worse and worse and that more and more of the tape would become "unintelligible."

7.19
PROBLEM 13

An important tape recording contains a background sine-wave signal with constant amplitude and a period of 50 time units. The tape was spliced at $T = 100$ time units and a phase change of π radians (rad) inadvertently resulted. The background sine wave thus appears as shown in Fig. 7-34 for $S = 0$. Suppose that a cunning technician seeks to obliterate the telltale phase change in the background signal by adding the sound from one of the instrument waveforms in Fig. 7-12. Assuming that the instrument waveform has a peak amplitude four times that of the sine-wave and instrument waveform are equal, the output waveform from the doctored tape recording will be analogous to that shown in Fig. 7-34 for $S = 4$.

Write a program that computes the phase of the 50 time-unit period Fourier component over 250 time units of heckeled tape and prints the absolute value of the phase change (rounded off to the nearest 0.1 rad) in going from one 50-time-unit period to the next. Note that you do *not* have to calculate the phase change on a point-by-point basis as done in Fig. 7-34. How much greater than the sine-wave peak amplitude must the instrument peak amplitude be before you cannot detect the splice with your program? Suppose that the two waveforms have equal peak amplitude. What is the minimum phase shift in the original sinewave that you detect? Use sample intervals of one time unit (e.g., 51-point sine wave over one period and a 138-point heckelphone waveform).

<table>
<tr>
<td>**7.19**
RESEARCH
PROBLEM</td>
<td>Skillful tape editing in commerical recordings of music has created the illusion of flawless technical proficiency by contemporary recording artists. A feedback effect also occurs in which the young performer feels that he has to outdo the older ones still further. As a result, many recordings are now available that have been done with incredibly brilliant technique, punctuated by rather abrupt and strange changes in tempo and pitch. It might be entertaining to make a study of this phenomenon with computer-oriented methods of Fourier analysis. (Informal comments by professional musicians indicate that the number of splices per recording is actually in the hundreds in some instances.)</td>
</tr>
<tr>
<td>**7.19**
RESEARCH
PROBLEM</td>
<td>Investigate the use of Fourier transforms as a method of analyzing complex spectra. See the references on the Cooley–Tukey algorithm and the review of fast Fourier transforms by Brigham and Morrow (1967).</td>
</tr>
</table>

REFERENCES

AUDSLEY, G. A. (1905). *The Art of Organ Building:* Vol. II, Pipe Construction and Voicing. Reprinted 1965 by Dover Publications, Inc., New York.

BARTOLOZZI, BRUNO (1967). *New Sounds for Woodwind.* New York: Oxford University Press.

BENNETT, W. R., JR., D. B. CARLIN, AND G. J. COLLINS (1974). "Picosecond Time-Interval Measurement and Intensity Correlations Using the Two-Quantum Photo-electric Effect." *IEEE J. Quant. Electron.*, Vol. QE-10, pp. 97–99; Errata Vol. QE-10, p. 498.

BERLIOZ, HECTOR (1848). *Treatise on Instrumentation.* (See translation by T. Front from the 1848 edition, which was edited by R. Strauss and published by E. F. Kalmus, New York, 1948.)

BRIGHAM, E. O., AND R. E. MORROW (1967). "The Fast Fourier Transform." *IEEE Spectrum*, Vol. 4, p. 63. (This is a review paper.)

COOLEY J. W., AND J. W. TUKEY (1965). "An Algorithm for the Machine Calculation of Complex Fourier Series." *Math. Comput.*, Vol. 19, p. 297.

DeMARIA, A. J., W. H. GLENN, JR., M. J. BRIENZA, AND M. E. MACK (1969). "Picosecond Laser Pulses." *Proc. IEEE*, Vol. 57 (January), pp. 2–25.

FOURIER, J. VON (1822). *La Theorie analytique de la chaleur.* Paris. (See Freeman's translation, Cambridge University Press, Cambridge, 1878.)

FROME, E. L., and E. L. FREDERICKSON (1974). "Digital Spectrum Analysis of the First and Second Heart Sounds." *Computers and Biomedical Research.* Vol. 7, pp. 421–431.

GIBBS, J. W. (1898). *Nature, Vol.* 59, p. 200.

GIBBS, J. W. (1899). *Nature,* Vol. 59, p. 606. Two notes on Fourier's series, also reproduced in *The Collected Works of J. Willard Gibbs, Ph.D., LL.D.* New Haven, Conn.: Yale University Press, 1948, pp. 258–260.

HEISS, J. C. (1966). *Perspectives of New Music* (a journal published by the Princeton University Press), Vol. 5, p. 139.

HEISS, J. C. (1969). *Perspectives of New Music* (a journal published by the Princeton University Press), Vol. 7, p. 136.

KUBOVY, MICHAEL, J. E. CUTTING, AND R. M. McGUIRE (1974). "Hearing with the Third Ear: Dichotic Perception of a Melody Without Monaural Familiarity Cues." *Science*, Vol. 186 (October), pp. 272–274.

LLOYD, N. (1968). *The Golden Encyclopedia of Music.* New York: Golden Press. (This volume is not to be confused with the similarly named children's books series.)

MICHELSON, A. A. (1903). *Light Waves and Their Uses.* Chicago: University of Chicago Press.

SKROWACZEWSKI, S. (1971). *"Concerto for English Horn and Orchestra."* New York: Associated Music Publishers.

STACY, T. (1972). With S. Skrowaczewski conducting the Minneapolis Symphony Orchestra, "Concerto for English Horn and Orchestra" by S. Skrowaczewski (Desto Records, New York, Stereo DC-7126A).

WHEELER, R. G. AND J. C. HILL (1966). "Spectroscopy in the 5 to 400 Wavenumber Region with the Grubb Parsons Interferometric Spectrometer." *J. Opt. Soc. America,* Vol. 56 (May), p. 657.

WHITTAKER, E. T. AND G. N. WATSON (1902). *A Course of Modern Analysis.* Cambridge: Cambridge University Press. Reprinted in 1965. See, especially, Chapter IX.

WILBRAHAM, HENRY (1848). "On a Certain Periodic Function," in the *Quarterly Journal of Pure and Applied Mathematics* (Cambridge and Dublin), New Series, Vol. 3, pp. 198–201.

Electronics
and communication

This chapter is intended for students with strong interests in the physical sciences and assumes the material on Fourier series given in Chapter 7 as a prerequisite. Familiarity with calculus on the level reviewed in Chapter 2 is required and the subroutines discussed in Sections 7.11, 7.12, and 7.17 are used without further elaboration. Sections 8.1–8.13 emphasize problems associated with high-fidelity recording and transmission of audio signals. Although the problems can all be formulated using introductory-level electronic circuit theory, nonlinear circuit problems (and methods of "linearizing" nonlinear circuits) are stressed. The material in Sections 8.1–8.13 should be comprehensible to students with a background in introductory calculus and physics at the freshman level. Sections 8.14–8.24 discuss problems in laser physics which start out at the level of a sophomore physics course in optics and gradually increase in difficulty. The final section uses results derived from the Schrödinger theory. Key formulas from the background scientific disciplines are stated and described but are not specifically derived. Thus, although one could do all the problems in the present chapter without having taken background physics or electronics courses, conceptual understanding of the problems really requires such courses as a prerequisite. A common programming method used throughout the entire chapter consists of the reiterative solution of nonlinear and transcendental equations. Finally, it is worth emphasizing that (as throughout the earlier chapters of this book), most of the problems discussed are too difficult to be undertaken in closed-form analysis. Consequently, most of the specific questions examined are seldom treated quantitatively in a standard curriculum. Nevertheless, they all represent important areas of practical application. The material is presented from the point of view of a physicist rather than that of an electronics engineer and is designed to emphasize the underlying physical principles involved in these different application areas.

The great forte of the electrical engineering field has been in the analysis of linear circuits. Linear circuits are particularly susceptible to closed-form analysis in which computers are usually not necessary. Although there are certain areas of linear circuit theory which can be strongly aided by computer analysis, these are areas in which one uses the computer primarily for bookkeeping purposes. For example, the response of a frequency-dependent linear network to a complex periodic waveform can be computed very easily by combining the methods of Fourier analysis and alternating-current circuit theory.[1] However, beyond this general type of analysis, the great power of the digital computer as applied to the electronics world rests in the treatment of nonlinear or transcendental problems of a type that can scarcely be touched through closed-form methods without severely limiting approximation. Consequently, after a brief examination of the bookkeeping type of problem, our main emphasis will be on the analysis of representative nonlinear and transcendental problems of practical consequence in real devices.

Alternating-current (ac) circuit theory provides a simple prescription to relate the input- and output-voltage amplitudes through circuits made up of linear elements when these voltages vary sinusoidally with time at a constant frequency and with constant amplitude. We shall define a *linear circuit* to be one in which the output-voltage amplitude varies linearly with the input voltage amplitude for sinusoidal voltages at a specified frequency. It is further implied by this definition that no spurious components are produced by the circuit at frequencies other than that of the input signal. However, the circuit's effect can differ substantially with the frequency of the input signal: in general, both the output-voltage amplitude and the relative phase of the output signal will vary with frequency in a manner that can be determined from ac circuit theory. Our objective here is not to derive the rules of ac circuit analysis, but rather to show how the results of that analysis may be used to compute the change that a complex waveform will undergo in transmission through the circuit.

8.1
Response of a Filter to a Complex Periodic Waveform

Consider a simple circuit composed of a resistor (R) and capacitance (C), and a driving voltage amplitude, E, at frequency, f, as shown in Fig. 8-1. (We shall assume that any internal impedance of the source is contained in the resistance R and that any subsequent circuitry attached across the output voltage has a negligible effect on the circuit operation.) It may be shown from ac circuit analysis that the output voltage amplitude V is related to the input-voltage amplitude at frequency f by

$$V = \frac{E}{\sqrt{1 + (2\pi f T_0)^2}}$$

and has a phase shift P_0 relative to the input voltage

$$P_0 = \arctan(-2\pi f T_0)$$

where $T_0 \equiv RC$ has the dimensions of time and is called the filter *time constant*. The circuit thus has maximum response at dc (for direct current, or

---

[1] More advanced problems of this general type include the analysis of multiple-loop circuits (in which the computer is used to solve a group of linear simultaneous equations numerically); the reduction of long sequences of four-terminal networks through matrix operations (e.g., see Zelinger, 1963); and analysis of phase (or gain) from general frequency-dependent linear phenomena by numerical evaluation of what the physicists call the *Kramers–Kronig relations* (Kramers, 1927; Kronig, 1926) and the electrical engineers refer to as the *Bode relations* (e.g., see Bode, 1945; Thomas, 1947). These applications represent areas in which the computer can have a very powerful impact; however, they are also areas that require a more advanced knowledge of complex variables than is needed elsewhere in the present book.

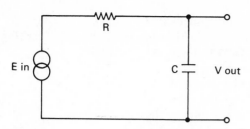

Fig. 8-1.

Section 8.1
Response of a Filter
to a Complete Periodic Waveform

$f = 0$) and falls off as $1/f$ for $f \gg 1/2\pi T_0$. For that reason, the circuit is known as a *low-pass filter*.

One may compute the effects of such a filter on a complex periodic waveform in the following manner:

1. Use the methods of Fourier analysis to determine the relative amplitudes and phases of all the important harmonics of the input waveform.
2. Compute the output voltage from the filter (using the filter equation) for each harmonic amplitude.
3. Compute the output phase for each harmonic adding the filter phase shift.
4. Construct the new time-dependent waveform by summing the modified Fourier series which emerges at the filter output.

Part 1) may be accomplished using the subroutine (4ØØ) described in Section 7.12. Step 4 was discussed in Section 7.17. If one specifies the filter-time constant as a fraction of the fundamental period, the frequency that goes into the filter equation is just the harmonic number for a particular harmonic of the original periodic waveform. The method will be clarified by the following problem.

<table>
<tr><td>**8.1**
PROBLEM 1</td><td>Use the subroutine discussed in Section 7.12 to Fourier analyze the waveform of the French horn played loudly (see DATA statement in Fig. 7-12). Assuming that T_0 is ≈ 13 percent of the fundamental period for the waveform, use the filter equations given above to compute the Fourier coefficients and phases of the output waveform that would occur if the French-horn waveform were fed through the RC filter. (Note that when T_0 is defined in units of the fundamental period, the values for the product fT_0 are just the harmonic numbers.) Finally, reconstruct the time-dependent waveform over one period coming out of the filter. Plot the latter on either a teletype machine or high-resolution device. Compare your results with the original waveform and those given in Fig. 8-2 based on digital filtering in the time domain. Use the first ten harmonics.</td></tr>
</table>

Recent advances in high-speed digital circuitry have made it possible to perform digital filtering throughout the audio band in real time. There are some virtues in this approach to electronics in instances where especially sharp cutoff filters are required.

Our primary concern with digital filtering here will be in the use of a subroutine to remove very high frequency components compared to the desired signal band in several subsequent problems. In these instances, we will mainly be concerned with periodic waveforms which are either computed or "read in" from data statements. In most of these cases it is helpful to store the waveform in two separate column arrays, $V(I)$ and $W(I)$, where I runs from 1 to some large number of points (P) over one period of the waveform. In what follows we will generally retain the original set of data points in $W(I)$. We shall perform various operations on these points and store the results in the array $V(I)$.

As an illustration we shall consider simulating the action of a low-pass RC filter in the time domain. Because the voltage drop across the capacitance $= q/C$ in real time, and $q = \int i \, dt$, where the current i increases with input voltage, the output of an RC filter is roughly proportional to the integral of the input voltage (over a time $\approx T_0 = RC$).

Hence, we shall construct a subroutine to simulate such a low-pass filter by integrating the periodic waveform over an adjustable time constant, $T\emptyset$. In simplest form we merely need to store the sum in $V(I)$ of the previous $T\emptyset$ elements in $W(I)$. Assuming that the waveform data have already been stored in $W(I)$ for one period and that the column arrays $W(I)$ and $V(I)$ have been suitably dimensioned, a low-pass filter subroutine is produced by the statements

```
800   REM DIGITAL FILTER SUBROUTINE
801   PRINT "FILTER TIME CONSTANT";
802   INPUT TØ
810   FOR I = 1 TO P
812   LET V(I) = W(I)
814   FOR J = 1 TO TØ
815   IF I − J < 1 THEN 830
820   LET V(I) = V(I) + W(I − J)
825   GOTO 835
830   LET V(I) = V(I) + W(P − 1 + I − J)
835   NEXT J
840   NEXT I
850   RETURN
```

The filter time constant, $T\emptyset$, is introduced at line 802 from the keyboard and the heart of the filtering action for each point I of the waveform occurs within the J loop between lines 814 and 835. The conditional statement on line 815 is required because we have only stored one period of the original waveform in the array $W(I)$. Hence it is necessary to use the values for the points $P − 1 + I − J$, when $I − J < 1$, where $P − 1 =$ the period of the waveform.

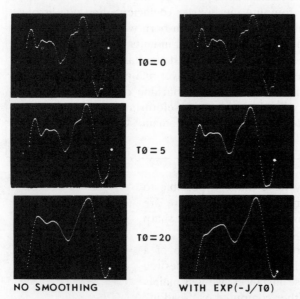

Fig. 8-2. Digital filtering of French-horn waveform for various time constants, with and without the exponential smoothing function. (The waveform period was 150 time units.)

A further refinement can be easily incorporated within the subroutine to avoid the sharp truncation in the integration which results at $J = T\emptyset$. For example, one can multiply $W(I - J)$ on line $82\emptyset$ by an exponentially decaying function of the type given in BASIC by

$$\text{LET F(J)} = \text{EXP}(-J/T\emptyset) \qquad (1)$$

to smooth out the sharp truncation. In this instance, it is necessary to extend the loop on J until the exponential function has decayed to an adequately small value. For example, $5*T\emptyset$ would result in <1 percent error. In most instances the latter refinement is not worth the additional computing time. One should note, of course, that it is only really necessary to evaluate a factor $F = \text{EXP}(-1/T\emptyset)$ before line $81\emptyset$ and then multiply $W(I - J)$ by $F\emptyset$, where $F\emptyset$ is initialized to F before the J loop and cyclically modified by the statement

$$\text{LET F}\emptyset = \text{F*F}\emptyset$$

before

$$\text{NEXT J}$$

That is, we can make use of the fact that

$$e^{-J/T\emptyset} = (e^{-1/T\emptyset})^J$$

(Of course, similar treatment also has to be given to $W(P - \cdots)$ on line $83\emptyset$). A comparison of the two digital filtering methods is given in Fig. 8-2.

High-pass filter subroutines may similarly be constructed using the difference between successive pairs of points in the waveform (i.e., by taking the derivative of the signal rather than the integral).

**8.1
PROBLEM 2**   Compare the results of the sharp-truncation low-pass filter with those obtained using a smoothing function with the same time constant. Use one of the data statements for periodic waveforms in Fig. 7-12. Compare the spectra of the Fourier coefficients for the two results for the first ten harmonics (see Section 7.12).

One frequently needs to use electronic devices that are inherently nonlinear. The reasons nonlinearities exist are deep-rooted in the basic physical phenomena that govern the operation of the device. These reasons may vary from the effects of "collective" processes at small signal levels to the fundamental saturation process based on the conservation of energy which affects nearly every aspect of human life.

**8.2
Nonlinear Distortion**

We therefore wish to consider the operational characteristics of a general device in which the output is a nonlinear function, $f(x)$, of the input, x, and where the input signal itself is a complicated function of the time; i.e., $x = x(t)$.

$$\text{IN} \rightarrow \boxed{\text{DEVICE}} \rightarrow \text{OUT}$$
$$x \qquad\qquad\qquad f(x)$$

The "device" might be anything (e.g., audio amplifier, a microphone or loudspeaker, etc.).

If what comes out of the device is not linearly proportional to what goes in, spurious frequency components will appear in the output waveform that were not present in the input. For example, if $f(x) = x + x^2$, and if the input $= x = \sin \theta$, where $\theta = 2\pi ft$, what comes out of the device is

$$f(\sin \theta) = \sin \theta + \sin^2 \theta$$
$$= \sin \theta + \tfrac{1}{2} - \tfrac{1}{2} \cos 2\theta$$

Although the input was simply a sine wave, what comes out contains a dc term (the constant, $\frac{1}{2}$) and a signal at the second harmonic (the $\cos 2\theta$ term). Hence the device would produce lots of second-harmonic distortion and rectify as well.

This type of effect is easy to illustrate with a computer for complex input waveforms and very general and horrible nonlinear characteristics. We shall use statements of the type outlined before to generate an input waveform (e.g., a sine wave or the waveform from a musical instrument) and use the BASIC function statement to handle the nonlinearity. For example,

```
20   DIM V(255),W(255)
60   FOR I = 1 TO P
65   LET V(I) = W(I) = SIN(2*3.14159*(I−1)/(P−1))
80   NEXT I
```

stores a sine wave with P points (over 0 through 2π) in both $V(I)$ and $W(I)$.

The following statements plot the original sine-wave on a suitable device, Fourier-analyze it (giving just one component for $N = 1$ here) and draw a histogram of the Fourier coefficients using the subroutines discussed in Section 7.12.

```
90   GOSUB 500   (plotting subroutine from Section 7.11)
91   GOSUB 400   (Fourier analysis subroutine, Section 7.12)
92   GOSUB 700   (Histogram plotting subroutine, Section 7.12)
```

We can then look at the input–output characteristic of an assumed nonlinear function using the statements

```
100   REM INTRODUCE NONLINEARITY NEXT
101   DEF FNG(X) = X/(1+ABS(X))
102   PRINT "GAIN CONSTANT, G"
103   INPUT G
105   FOR I = 1 TO P
106   LET X = G*(I−.5*P)/(.5*P)
107   LET V(I) = FNG(X)
108   NEXT I
109   GOSUB 500
```

where the functional form of the characteristic, $FNG(X)$, was assumed arbitrarily on line 101.

Next, we restore $V(I)$ to its original array [from $W(I)$ which has not been altered] and see what the nonlinear characteristic does to the original sine wave:

```
110   FOR I = 1 TO P
115   LET V(I) = W(I)
120   LET V(I) = FNG(G*V(I))
125   NEXT I
130   GOSUB 500
135   GOSUB 400
140   GOSUB 700
```

The results of running lines 90–140 on a 151-point sine wave are shown in Fig. 8-3 (where the gain factor was chosen to be $G = 5$). The spectrum of the Fourier coefficients for the input and output signal is shown at the bottom of the figure and the input and output waveform is shown at the top.

Although the function assumed above on line 101 represents a simple case where the characteristic is linear at very low input amplitudes and saturates at large values of x, it is not really very representative quantitatively of the nonlinearities present in real amplifiers. (As we shall see later, that is a very fortunate state of affairs in that the characteristic in Fig. 8-3 is not very readily "linearized" through the application of negative feedback.) Most physical

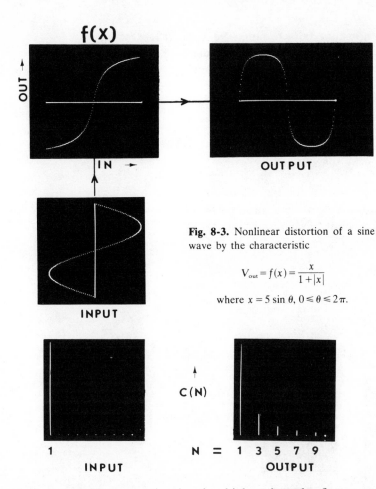

Fig. 8-3. Nonlinear distortion of a sine wave by the characteristic

$$V_{out} = f(x) = \frac{x}{1 + |x|}$$

where $x = 5 \sin \theta$, $0 \le \theta \le 2\pi$.

devices have saturation terms that involve higher than the first power of the input signal. The exact form that occurs obviously depends on the particular device. However, many push–pull transistorized power amplifiers have non-linear characteristics (before application of negative feedback) that can at least be roughly approximated by a characteristic of the type

$$f(x) = \frac{x + x^3}{1 + |x|^3}$$

Any dependence on even powers of x present in the individual transistor characteristics is nearly canceled from the push–pull circuit geometry, and the term $|x|^3$ will give rise to the sharp clipping usually found in such circuits at large input amplitudes, without altering the odd symmetry of the characteristic [i.e., $f(-x) = -f(+x)$]. Odd harmonics will result as distortion products because of the odd symmetry of the nonlinear function; that is, the clipping effect will tend to turn a sine wave into a square wave, which in turn has only odd harmonics. One, of course, could define still other functions to simulate characteristics of a specific device with greater quantitative accuracy.

The following program permits illustrating the effects of the nonlinear characteristic on complex waveforms read in from data statements of the type given in Fig. 7-12.

```
20   DIM V(255),W(255)
25   DIM A(50),B(50),C(50),P(50)
50   READ P
60   FOR I = 1 TO P
70   READ W(I)
71   LET W(I) = 1.00000E − 03*W(I)
75   LET V(I) = W(I)
80   NEXT I
```

Line 71 normalizes the maximum values (previously = 1000) to unity. Next we use previously described subroutines to plot the original waveform, calculate the first 10 Fourier coefficients, and plot a spectrum of the coefficients on a linear scale:

```
90   GOSUB 500      (plot V(I))
91   GOSUB 400      (compute Fourier coefficients for 10 harmonics)
92   GOSUB 700      (plot a histogram of the Fourier series amplitudes)
```

We define the new (or any other) nonlinearity by the statement

```
101  DEF FNG(X) = (X + X↑3)/(1 + ABS(X↑3))
```

and observe the effects of the nonlinear characteristic for different input levels of the complex waveform stored in $W(I)$ (which is now normalized to unity) by the following statements;

```
102  PRINT "GAIN CONSTANT, G"
103  INPUT G
105  FOR I = 1 TO P
106  LET X = G*(I − .5*P)/(.5*P)
107  LET V(I) = FNG(X)
108  NEXT I
109  GOSUB 500                    (plot nonlinear characteristic for given value of G)
```

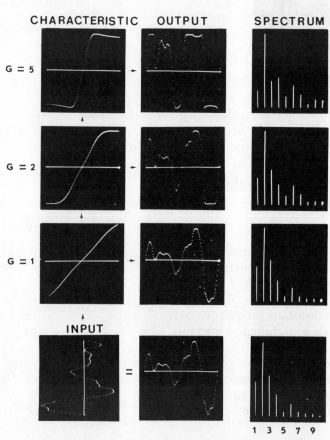

Fig. 8-4. Distortion by a nonlinear amplifier for the case where

$$V_{out} = f(x) \equiv \frac{x + x^3}{1 + |x|^3} \quad \text{and} \quad x = GV_{in}$$

The region of the nonlinear characteristic actually used, the output waveform, and the spectrum of the Fourier coefficients are shown for three different values of the gain parameter. The input waveform (from a French horn) is shown at the bottom, together with its Fourier spectrum. (A linear scale was used for the Fourier coefficients.)

386

```
110   FOR I = 1 TO P
115   LET V(I) = W(I)           (original waveform)
120   LET V(I) = FNG(G*V(I))    (calculate distorted waveform)
125   NEXT I
130   GOSUB 500                 (plot distorted waveform)
135   GOSUB 400                 (calculate Fourier Coefficients)
140   GOSUB 700                 (plot Fourier coefficients)
150   GOTO 102
```

Line 106 was put in merely to facilitate plotting the nonlinear characteristic over the domain $-G \leq X \leq +G$.

Results from the above program are summarized in Fig. 8-4 for various values of G (the nonlinear gain parameter) and the input waveform from a French horn. Clearly, the effect of the nonlinearity (for example in the case $G = 5$) will be to change the output tonal quality considerably.

**8.2
PROBLEM 3**

Assuming the nonlinear characteristic

$$V_{out} = f(x) = \frac{x + x^3}{1 + |x|^3}$$

compute the spectrum of the Fourier coefficients of the output waveform when the input is $x = \sin \theta$. Repeat the calculation for one of the input waveforms in Fig. 7-12. Normalize the peak input amplitude to unity. Compare the input and output Fourier coefficients for the first ten harmonics.

Extraneous sum and difference frequencies (called *beats*) are produced in nonlinear systems. Suppose that we feed $(\sin A + \sin B)$ into a device whose output is proportional to the square of the input:

$$(\sin A + \sin B) \rightarrow \boxed{\text{device}} \rightarrow (\sin A + \sin B)^2$$

The output is

$$\sin^2 A + 2 \sin A \sin B + \sin^2 B$$
$$= (\tfrac{1}{2} - \tfrac{1}{2} \cos 2A) + \cos (A - B) - \cos (A + B) + (\tfrac{1}{2} - \tfrac{1}{2} \cos 2B)$$

**8.3
Beats (or Intermodulation
Distortion) from Nonlinearities**

from trigonometric identities. Hence we get four entirely different frequencies out of the device than we put in: The terms $2A$ and $2B$ are simply (second) harmonic-distortion terms of the type discussed above. However, the terms involving frequencies at $A - B$ and $A + B$ are not harmonically related to the input signal and are sometimes called *intermodulation terms* (i.e., the amplitude of the signal at these new frequencies depends in a multiplicative way on the separate input amplitudes at frequencies A and B). In general, if all degrees of nonlinearity are present in the device (i.e., all powers of the input signal are present in the output), beat frequencies will be obtained at $nA \pm mB$), where $n, m = 0, 1, 2, 3, \ldots$ and A and B are the two input frequencies. Because such intermodulation terms do not generally fall on the normal harmonics of either A or B, they frequently are both more conspicuous and more undesirable than harmonic distortion. However, the generation of difference and sum frequencies can also be of enormous practical value in frequency-measurement applications.

Unless the entire input signal consists of harmonically related frequencies, a Fourier analysis program that simply computes harmonics of the initial fundamental input frequencies will miss the terms generated by sum and difference frequencies. If the sample of the input signal continues long enough, one could determine the presence of these nonharmonic signals by doing a Fourier transform on the entire signal output.

Investigate the production of intermodulation distortion in nonlinear circuits using Fourier transform methods.

One successful method of minimizing distortion in a nonlinear device was discovered by Harold S. Black at the Bell Laboratories. Black (1934) had shown that if one took some of the output of an amplifier and fed it back out of phase (opposite polarity) with respect to the input, the overall gain of the amplifier was much more stable in respect to long-term drift. He also found that a very important fringe benefit resulted: the nonlinear distortion of the amplifier could be greatly reduced at the same time.

Before going into a discussion of the nonlinear case, it will be helpful to review a few properties of the linear negative feedback amplifier.

Consider Fig. 8-5, where the output from the feedback loop is subtracted from the original input signal in the triangular box and the difference fed into an amplifier with multiplicative gain, G. It is easy to solve the linear problem. Obviously,

$$\frac{V_2}{V_1} = \frac{G}{1 + BG} \equiv G_f \tag{2}$$

or the gain in the presence of negative feedback is reduced by the factor $(1 + BG)$ in the denominator. Improvement in stability of the net gain due to fluctuations within the amplifier of amount ΔG is easily seen by differentiating (2) with respect to G. In particular,

$$\frac{\Delta G_f}{G_f} = \frac{\Delta G/G}{1 + BG} \tag{3}$$

where G_f is the total gain with feedback. The fractional gain stability of the original amplifier is improved by the same factor by which the gain is decreased.

Obviously if $BG \to -1$, the feedback amplifier will tend to oscillate. We will not get the infinite output implied by Eq. (2) in a real amplifier because nonlinearities always exist in real life to limit the gain to a finite value.

Owing to phase shifts in real amplifiers, it is possible to have BG effectively approach -1 at some frequency, even when the output of the feedback loop is subtracted from the input signal as shown in Eq. 8-5 [see Nyquist (1932) or, e.g., the discussion of the Nyquist criterion by H. S. Black (1934)]. We shall not treat this aspect of negative feedback amplifiers specifically, except to note later an analogous effect which occurs due to rounding errors in our computing method.

Next we shall introduce a nonlinear gain characteristic, $f(x)$, within our original amplifier in normalized form. For comparison with the previous

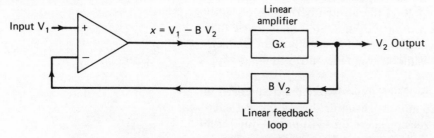

Fig. 8-5. Schematic diagram of a linear negative feedback amplifier. We have used the symbols G (for gain) and B (for feedback) as convenient mnemonic symbols that are also found on the teletype keyboard.

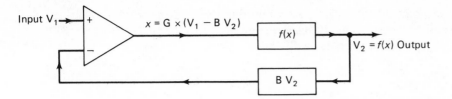

Fig. 8-6. Schematic diagram of a nonlinear amplifier with negative feedback. The amplifier has a multiplicative gain G and a nonlinear characteristic $f(x)$, where $x = G \times (V_1 - BV_2)$. A fraction B of the output is fed back out of phase with the input.

discussion of the linear case, we shall assume that what enters the nonlinear circuit is actually

$$x = G \times (V_1 - BV_2) \tag{4}$$

and that the output is now

$$V_2 = f(x) \tag{5}$$

This approach will permit us to observe the system over varying portions of the nonlinear characteristic by changing the gain constant, G (see Fig. 8-6). Again, V_1 is the original input waveform and V_2 is the final output. We shall ignore phase shifts that might occur in a real amplifier because our main objective is to demonstrate the reduction in nonlinear distortion produced by negative feedback. It should be noted, however, that the methods for handling phase shifts applicable to linear circuits will be of no use in the present instance. In order to include the equivalent of phase-shift effects with a strong nonlinearity present, it is necessary to go back to the fundamental derivative and integral processes which generate phase shifts in normal linear circuits. The latter is not too hard to incorporate in the present type of program but would obscure the main object of the discussion. For the moment, merely note that if such phase-shift effects existed, they would not become important unless $|BG| \geq 1$ for the linear term in $f(x)$.

We shall next write a program to find self-consistent solutions to Eqs. (4) and (5) for general nonlinear functions, $f(x)$. We will solve these equations reiteratively at each instant in time.

Consider the program:

```
215   LET V1 = V(I)
220   LET V2 = E2 = 0
225   LET X = G*(V1 − B*V2)
230   LET V2 = FNG(X)
260   IF INT(100*V2 + .5) = INT(100*E2 + .5) THEN 280
265   LET E2 = V2
270   GOTO 225
280   LET V(I) = V2
```

The input to the amplifier occurs on line 215 for some particular instant in time (index I). Initially we do not know the amplifier output corresponding to this input, so we merely guess a value for $V2 = E2$ on line 220. We then compute the argument (X) of the nonlinear function on line 225 based on the initial guess for $V2$, and then determine the actual output value for $V2$ that would arise from the assumed input. We then compare the new value for $V2$ with the old value stored in $E2$. If these two quantities agree to within some arbitrarily defined criterion, the conditional statement on line 260 sends the program on to the next part of the program after storing the output waveform for that instant of time in $V(I)$ on line 280. Otherwise, we set $E2 = V2$ on line 265 and reiterate to line 225 until the required degree of convergence is satisfied.

Each point in the original waveform can be fed through the above reiterative calculation until the output waveform corresponding to the original input waveform is determined in a point-by-point manner. Thus, after entering the initial waveform in the arrays $V(I)$ and $W(I)$, one may illustrate the effects of negative feedback on a nonlinear amplifier characteristic with the following program:

```
100   REM INTRODUCE NONLINEARITY NEXT
101   DEF FNG(X) = (X + X ↑ 3)/(1 + ABS(X↑3))
203   PRINT "ENTER GAIN, G, AND NEGATIVE FEEDBACK CONSTANT, B";
204   INPUT G, B
210   FOR I = 1 TO P
215   LET V1 = W(I)
220   LET V2 = E2 = G*V1/(1 + G*B)
225   LET X = G*(V1 − B*V2)
230   LET V2 = FNG(X)
260   IF INT(100*V2 + .5) = INT(100*E2 + .5) THEN 280
265   LET E2 = V2
270   GOTO 225
280   LET V(I) = V2
285   NEXT I
290   GOSUB 500        (plot output waveform)
291   GOSUB 400        (calculate Fourier coefficients)
292   GOSUB 700        (plot Fourier coefficients)
310   GO TO 203
```

where the subroutines were described in Sections 7.11 and 7.12. Another slightly better guess for the initial value of $V2 = E2$ has been used above on line 22Ø and the program reiterates as previously described until each point satisfies the criterion introduced on line 26Ø.

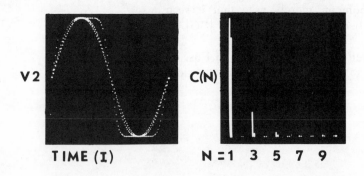

Fig. 8-7. Direct illustration of the reduction of nonlinear distortion produced by application of negative feedback. In both illustrations, a nonlinear amplifier characteristic of the type

$$V2 = \frac{x + x^3}{1 + |x^3|}$$

is shown, where $x = G(V1 − BV2)$, $V2$ is the amplifier output waveform, $V1$ is the input waveform, G is the amplifier gain parameter, and B is the negative feedback parameter. The cases shown were computed for $G = 2$ with and without 40 percent negative feedback (i.e., $B = 0$ and $B = 0.4$).

The left figure shows a superposition normalized to the same peak intensity of the original sine-wave input, as well as the two output waveforms. Note that without negative feedback, the waveform is badly clipped. In contrast, the output closely resembles the input with 40 percent negative feedback.

The right figure shows a superposition (slightly displaced) of the Fourier coefficients for the output waveform under the same two conditions. Without feedback, the saturated waveform has pronounced amounts of odd harmonic distortion. With negative feedback, the gain at the fundamental component $(N = 1)$ is slightly reduced. However, the harmonic distortion is greatly reduced, as can be seen visually for the third and fifth harmonics.

390

It is particularly instructive to superimpose the normalized input waveform and output waveforms for several values of negative feedback and one value of gain. The input waveform can be displayed by going to the plotting subroutine (5ØØ in the above program) prior to the loop on line 21Ø, or by looking at the normalized output waveform on line 29Ø when $G \ll 1$ (i.e., negligible nonlinear distortion for the characteristic assumed on line 1Ø1).

It is also helpful to superimpose the actual Fourier coefficients of the output waveform (slightly displaced in the horizontal direction) for the same value of gain parameter and different values of negative feedback.

Results of this type have been displayed in Fig. 8-7 for a sine-wave input signal and different values of negative feedback. Note the pronounced improvement in both output waveform and spectral purity which results from the application of negative feedback in the cases shown.

8.5
Limitations of the Reiterative Computational Method

The above type of reiterative calculation can go into oscillation for large values of feedback due to truncational errors. The effect is very similar to what happens in real, linear negative feedback amplifiers when you fail to satisfy the *Nyquist criterion*; that is, if the net gain exceeds the loss around the loop and the net phase shifts are such that the output is fed back in phase with the input, the device becomes an oscillator. (See Nyquist, 1932.) The effects of rounding errors in the above type of program are equivalent to the sort of derivative and integration effects in real circuit elements which give rise to phase shifts in inductive and capacitive circuits. In this oscillatory condition, the values of $V2$ and $E2$ are alternately exchanged in the reiterative loop. Precisely where this oscillation will take place depends very much on the computational accuracy of the computer (or more specifically, the number of significant digits retained in the compiler), as well as the form of the nonlinearity assumed. In any event, because this oscillatory behavior can occur at some point in the waveform and generally will occur at large-amplitude input signals rather than small ones, it is useful to put in a print statement such as

```
211  PRINT I;
```

to keep running track of the computational process. Such a statement also makes it easier for you to get control of the computer from the teletype keyboard and stop the program, a consideration that is especially important if you happen to be paying for central processor units when the simulated negative feedback amplifier bursts into oscillation.

8.6
Limitations on the Effectiveness of Negative Feedback

An interesting systematic trend shows up when the program above is used to compute the reduction in nonlinearity that results when negative feedback is applied around hypothetical systems with different forms of nonlinearity. In some instances, a large reduction in nonlinearity is obtained by application of very small amounts of negative feedback. In other instances, a very small reduction in nonlinearity is obtained upon the application of enormous amounts of negative feedback.

In general, negative feedback is very effective in restoring linearity if the nonlinear saturating terms arise through higher-then-first-order terms in the input signal. Also, negative feedback cannot linearize a system in which the first-order terms are identically zero. These are usually not serious restrictions. However, the fact that they exist is not entirely trivial. The magnitude of the effect is illustrated in a few quantitative examples in Fig. 8-8. In each case illustrated, a sine-wave input signal of unit amplitude was assumed. The curves superimposed (normalized to the same peak-to-peak values) represent the output of the nonlinear circuit without negative feedback and the "linearized"

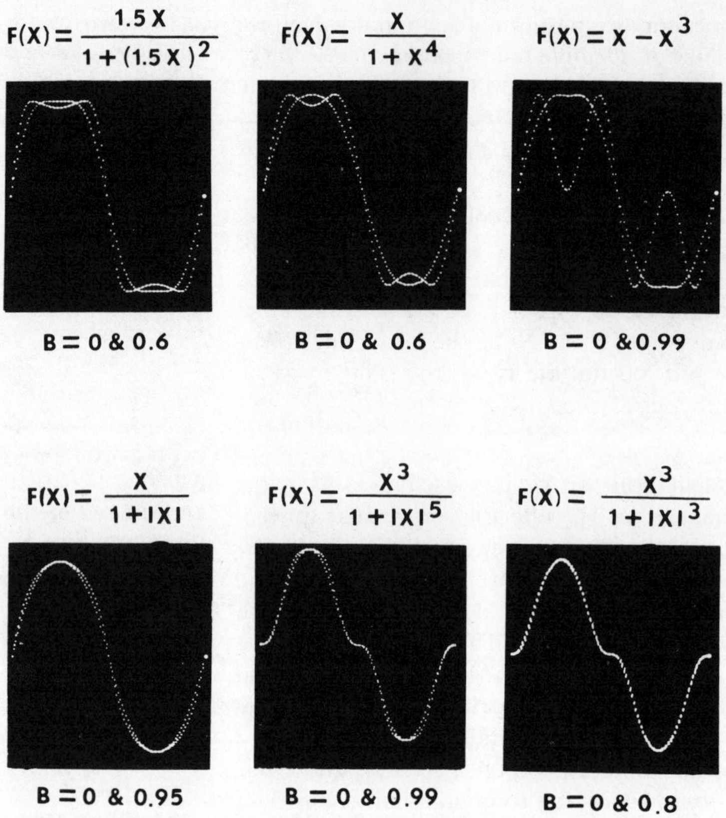

$$F(X) = \frac{1.5\,X}{1 + (1.5\,X)^2}$$ $$F(X) = \frac{X}{1 + X^4}$$ $$F(X) = X - X^3$$

B = 0 & 0.6   B = 0 & 0.6   B = 0 & 0.99

$$F(X) = \frac{X}{1 + |X|}$$ $$F(X) = \frac{X^3}{1 + |X|^5}$$ $$F(X) = \frac{X^3}{1 + |X|^3}$$

B = 0 & 0.95   B = 0 & 0.99   B = 0 & 0.8

Fig. 8-8. Effect of negative feedback in "linearizing" different types of nonlinear characteristics. The types in the top group are substantially improved by relatively slight amounts of feedback, whereas those in the bottom group are only slightly improved by very substantial amounts of negative feedback. The characteristics assumed are indicated above each picture. A unit amplitude input sine wave was assumed and a superposition of the computer output without and with the amount of feedback indicated is given in each case (for $G = 1$). The parameter B denotes the fraction of negative feedback actually applied.

output with the degree of negative feedback specified. The last cases involving x^3 terms on the bottom row have a relationship to nonlinearities in magnetic tape recording which will become apparent from a later discussion; note for the moment that negative feedback would not help much in those instances even if you could apply it.

A final point is worth emphasizing: there seems to be no necessity at all to require the nonlinear characteristic to be monotonic for the negative feedback process to restore linearity. (For example, see the results for the characteristic $x - x^3$.) The function, of course, must not change sign with increasing amplitude over the domain of the input variable. Whether or not effective linearization occurs seems strictly to be a matter of the existence of a linear term in the characteristic and the requirement that the nonlinear terms involve higher than the first power of x. (Various fractional powers of $|x|$ might, of course, be included.)

**8.6
PROBLEM 4**

Consider a nonlinear amplifier for which

$$V_{\text{out}} = f(x) = \frac{x + x^3}{1 + |x^3|}$$

where $x = G * V_{\text{in}}$ and $G = 2$.

Plot the output versus input characteristic of the amplifier. Feed a sine-wave

($V_{in} = \sin \theta$ for $0 \leq \theta \leq 2\pi$) into the amplifier and plot the distorted waveform and harmonic spectrum of the output signal for the first 10 harmonics.

Assuming that 30 percent of the output is fed back negatively to the input in the above amplifier, compute the output waveform and harmonic spectrum. What is the amplifier gain at the fundamental frequency?

8.6
RESEARCH
PROBLEM

Investigate the effects of phase shift on the negative-feedback nonlinear amplifier problem. For example, apply a low-pass digital filter across the amplifier output. Be wary of the computing time expended if the amplifier goes into oscillation.

8.7
Nonlinear Distortion
in Magnetic Tape Recording

Magnetic tape recording is an excellent example of a process that is horribly nonlinear, for inherent physical reasons. The basic notion behind magnetic tape recording is that one may induce a net magnetization (or magnetic moment per unit length) in a thin ferrous oxide layer on one side of the tape and in the direction of a magnetic field (applied parallel to the tape motion). In practice, the magnetic field is usually localized across a very small gap in a wedge-shaped section of a toroidal electromagnet made of high-permeability material (see Fig. 8-9). The magnetization occurs in the tape through reorientation of the discrete magnetic domains.

If a constant magnetic field is applied (due to a constant electric current running through the coil), an approximately constant net magnetization (or magnetic moment per unit length) is transferred to the tape moving in the gap direction. If the direction of the current, hence direction of the magnetic field, is reversed, the direction of the magnetization transferred to the magnetic tape is reversed. One plays back such alternating signals by the inverse procedure: namely, the tape slides past the gap in a similar toroidal head structure where the Faraday effect results in the production of a net voltage across the coil which is proportional to the rate of change of magnetic flux in the gap.

A considerable practical advantage of magnetic tape recording over most other recording media is that one may erase the recorded magnetization by passing the tape across a third "erase" head to which a very high frequency alternating current is supplied. If the high-frequency signal alternates in sign many times during the progress of the tape across the gap, a net depolarization of the magnetic domains on the oxide coating occurs, and the signal is erased. The same effect, of course, is what limits the upper frequency response of the recording medium: as soon as the recorded wavelength on the moving tape becomes comparable to the record-head gap width, self-erasure begins to occur in the recording process itself. The recorded wavelength (λ) is related to the tape velocity (V) and the frequency of the signal (f) by

$$\lambda f = V$$

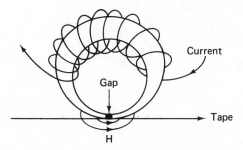

Fig. 8-9. Schematic diagram of a record head in a magnetic tape recorder. The magnetic loop is mainly closed within the tape oxide layer across the gap in the record head. In practice, the head gap is typically a few ten thousandths of an inch wide.

Hence, one can always increase the bandwidth by increasing the tape speed and therefore the ratio of recorded wavelength to gap width. Spreading of the magnetic field outside the physical dimensions of the record head gap occurs at high intensity levels to an extent which tends, in practice, to limit the full dynamic range of the medium to about 15 kHz at 15 inches per second (in/sec) at the present time. Self-erasure effects at "maximum recording level" (defined by convention as that point at which the total rms harmonic distortion from a 400 Hz signal is 3 percent in the system "linearized" by application of high-frequency bias) typically results in about a 10-dB reduction in dynamic range above about 8 kHz at $7\frac{1}{2}$ in./sec in the typical high-quality "home" tape recorder available today.

The practical difficulty with this method of recording lies in the fact that the net magnetization produced on the tape is a highly nonlinear function of the applied magnetic field. The permanent magnetization given to the tape occurs through the orientation of a finite maximum number of magnetic domains per unit length of tape. (This number, of course, increases with the width of the tape "track.") The orientation of individual magnetic domains is affected both by the applied field and by neighboring domains. At low magnetic-field intensities, an interactive effect results in which the net magnetization transferred to a previously unmagnetized tape increases *faster* than the first power of the applied magnetic field. That is, the magnetic fields produced by local magnetic domains inhibit the orientation of neighboring domains at low applied fields. However, as the applied field is further increased, a saturation region is eventually encountered in which most of the finite number of domains per unit length of tape are oriented. Consequently, a nonlinear characteristic of the type shown in Fig. 8-10 is obtained for an initially demagnetized length of tape. In reality, if one tries to re-record over previously magnetized tape, pronounced hysteresis effects are also involved in the characteristic. Because we are primarily concerned in our discussion with methods for reducing nonlinear distortion, we shall ignore such hysteresis effects and assume that a well-defined nonlinear characteristic such as that shown in Fig. 8-10 exists. In practice, this assumption is realistic, provided completely demagnetized tape is used and the tape speed and signal frequency are such that self-erasure is not important.

The distortion that would be produced by such a nonlinear curve would be dreadful (see Fig. 8-11). The net recording characteristic clearly will be odd-symmetric about the origin and has brief linear regions which actually

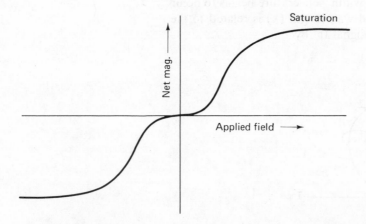

Fig. 8-10. Qualitative representation of a nonlinear characteristic involved in magnetic tape recording. It is assumed that the tape is initially demagnetized and that self-erasure effects are not important. (That is, the hysteresis effects that would be important in recording over an old signal are ignored.)

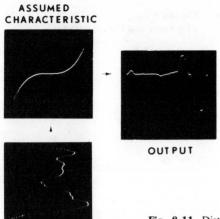

ASSUMED CHARACTERISTIC

OUTPUT

INPUT

Fig. 8-11. Distortion produced by a magnetic tape recording without high-frequency bias. A cubic nonlinear characteristic has arbitrarily been assumed and the distortion produced on the waveform for a French horn is displayed.

represent points of inflection in between the limit of complete saturation and cooperative interaction. One could, of course, apply an average dc magnetic bias and operate at one of these points of inflection. (Some primitive magnetic tape recorders operated on this principle.) However, the latter approach throws away most of the dynamic range of the recording medium and would still be subject to rather substantial amounts of nonlinearity.

The use of negative feedback is quite impractical as a method to reduce nonlinear distortion in this instance: there is simply no realistic way of sampling the net magnetization on the tape while it is still in contact with the record head gap. After the tape has left the record head gap, it is obviously too late to reduce the distortion: it is already there. Further, as discussed in Section 8.6, the particular type of nonlinear characteristic involved is not readily linearized by application of negative feedback anyway.

8.8 Use of High-Frequency Bias to Reduce Nonlinear Distortion

Most contemporary magnetic tape recorders make use of another very simple and powerful technique to linearize the magnetization characteristic.[2] A very high frequency (compared to the audio band) bias of large amplitude is added to the normal signal current applied to the record head. This bias signal sweeps the magnetic field back and forth over the extreme range of the magnetization characteristic at a rate that is fast compared to the highest signal frequency to be recorded. The technique results in an *effective* characteristic that is highly linear for frequency components within the audio band (see Fig. 8-12).

At least two additional, important aspects of the phenomenon can be seen qualitatively from Fig. 8-12. First, the size of the recorded signal for low-amplitude input signals will be greatly increased by the presence of the high-frequency bias (i.e., the net magnetization increases at much faster than the first power of the applied field near the origin). Second, because of the

[2] The history of the discovery of this extremely effective technique is not well documented—probably due to the diverse background of the magnetic recording technology itself: the basic notion of recording electrical signals on magnetized steel was patented as early as 1898 by a Danish inventor named Valdemar Poulsen. Patents were issued in the late 1920s both in the United States and in Germany for rudimentary forms of magnetic recording tape. The development of practical magnetic oxides for this purpose was largely carried out by the Germans during the 1930s and put to wide use in recording Nazi propaganda. This magnetic tape technological advance was disseminated throughout the allied countries after World War II. Somewhere along the line, the beneficial role of high-frequency bias was discovered. The discovery could easily have occurred accidentally by the inadvertent connection of a wire from the *erase* head to the *record* head.

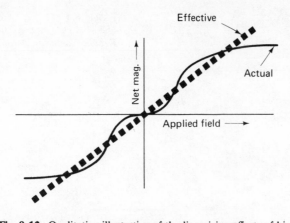

Fig. 8-12. Qualitative illustration of the linearizing effects of high-frequency bias. A large-amplitude, high-frequency bias signal is applied to sweep the magnetization back and forth over the extreme range of the tape characteristic. The low-frequency, small-amplitude input signal then sees an effective linear characteristic, illustrated by the dotted line in the figure. The slope of this effective characteristic can be substantially greater than that of the actual characteristic near the origin. In addition, nonlinearities within the low-frequency band are averaged out.

ultimate saturation at high applied fields, there clearly will be some optimum large amplitude for the high-frequency bias signal. The value of that optimum amplitude will depend on the nature of the magnetic film as well as upon the width of the recorded track. The saturation level is determined by the finite number of magnetic domains within the track width per unit length of tape. Consequently, the optimum bias amplitude will increase as the domain density increases.

An important source of "induced" noise occurs in magnetic tape recording which is closely related to the effect above: large fluctuations in output recorded signal can occur due to minor fluctuations in tape uniformity. This noise source is not present until one actually starts to record on the tape and is not detected merely by listening to or observing the output from a fresh piece of perfectly demagnetized tape with a playback head alone. The noise is induced by the recording process itself and shows up as modulation on the recorded signal. This noise is minimized when the bias amplitude is adjusted to its optimum value because the rate of change of recorded signal with domain density is a minimum at that point. However, significantly away from the optimum bias amplitude, fluctuations in effective track width can give rise to large pulses through modulation of small-amplitude signal components on the recorded tape and these pulses are frequently the predominant source of noise in the medium (commonly ≈ 5 to $10\,\text{dB}$ greater than the rms noise from granularity of the magnetic domain structure for a poorly optimized high-frequency bias amplitude).

Although one can deduce many properties of the system using expansion techniques (in which the signal amplitude is small compared to the bias amplitude), it is much easier to treat the entire problem digitally through computer analysis. Here we do not have to make any approximations and can apply arbitrary bias and signal amplitudes for any definable nonlinear tape characteristic.

First, it is of interest to display the form of the nonlinear tape characteristic assumed. In the following program we assume that some periodic waveform having P points is stored in the column array $W(I)$. The array $V(I)$ is a "working" array which we may use to display the characteristic over the range assumed and to compute the effects of the nonlinearity on the initial waveform. Subroutine 5∅∅ is one that either plots or prints the current values stored in the array $V(I)$ for the set of P points. We have arbitrarily assumed a cubic nonlinear characteristic for FNG(X). However, it is a trivial matter to change the form of this function to include the effects of tape saturation at large signal levels.

```
100   REM INTRODUCE NONLINEARITY NEXT
101   DEF FNG(X) = X*X*X
102   PRINT "NONLINEAR CHARACTERISTIC"          ⎫
105   FOR I = 1 TO P                            ⎪
106   LET X = (I − 5*P)/(5*P)                   ⎬ (display nonlinear characteristic)
107   LET V(I) = FNG(X)                         ⎪
108   NEXT I                                    ⎪
109   GOSUB 500                                 ⎭
110   FOR I = 1 TO P                            ⎫
120   LET V(I) = FNG(W(I))                      ⎬ (display distorted waveform)
125   NEXT I                                    ⎪
130   GOSUB 500                                 ⎭
135   FOR I = 1 TO P                            ⎫
140   LET V(I) = W(I)                           ⎬ (display original waveform)
145   NEXT I                                    ⎪
150   GOSUB 500                                 ⎭
```

The results of running this program are shown in Fig. 8-11 for an input waveform of a French horn (normalized to unity at peak amplitude).

Next we shall demonstrate the linearization effect of a large-amplitude high-frequency bias signal, added to the original input waveform. We shall assume that a high-frequency square wave is added rather than the more usual sine wave, for practicality in plotting and filtering the resultant waveforms. A

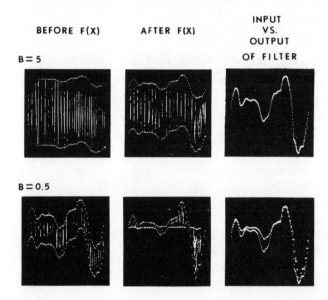

Fig. 8-13. Computer simulation of the reduction in nonlinear distortion produced by the application of a large-amplitude, high-frequency bias signal. The left column represents the sum of the input signal (French-horn waveform) and the high-frequency bias. The middle column shows the corresponding sum after the nonlinear function, $f(X)$. The right-hand column shows a superposition of the original input signal and the output of the digital filter with both waveforms normalized to the same peak-to-peak deflection. The bottom row ($B = 0.5$) shows results where the bias amplitude is half the peak-input-waveform amplitude. The top row ($B = 5$) corresponds to the case where the bias amplitude is five times the peak-input-waveform amplitude. Note the original input signal is almost indistinguishable from the output in the latter case, whereas the distortion is visually obvious for the lower illustration.

397

high-frequency square-wave bias of amplitude B and period 2 time units is added to the original waveform by the following programming steps:

```
200   REM HIGH-FREQUENCY BIAS NEXT
203   PRINT "BIAS AMPL.";
204   INPUT B
205   FOR I = 1 TO P−1 STEP 2
210   LET V(I) = W(I) + B
215   LET V(I + 1) = W(I + 1) − B
220   NEXT I
```

where P should be even.
The addition of a statement such as

```
225   GOSUB 500
```

permits using a standard plotting subroutine to look at the waveform applied to the record head. We then compute the nonlinear magnetization produced prior to the filtering action which results from finite recording bandwidth through statements of the type

```
230   FOR I = 1 TO P
235   LET V(I) = W(I) = FNG(V(I))
240   NEXT I
245   GOSUB 500
```

The bandwidth limitations of the recording tape then filter out the residual components at the bias frequency, a process that can be adequately simulated through use of the digital filter subroutine discussed in Section 8.1 and by adoption of a filter time constant $T\emptyset = 1$ (i.e., the truncating version with $T\emptyset = 1$ identically cancels the residual traces of the high-frequency square wave). Hence the following two statements accomplish the filtering and display the recorded waveform:

```
250   GOSUB 800      (digital filter subroutine)
255   GOSUB 500      (print or display routine)
```

Here P is the period of the modulated waveform in the array $W(I)$ and it is necessary to use the values for the points $P + I - J$ when $I - J < 1$ in line 83$\emptyset$ of the digital filtering subroutine. i.e.

```
830   LET V(I) = V(I) + W(P + I − J)
```

See discussion p. 382. Results of running the above program for a small ($B = 0.5$) and large ($B = 5$) bias amplitude with a French-horn waveform (normalized to a maximum amplitude of 1) are shown in Fig. 8-13. Note from the superposition of input and output waveforms in the large-bias amplitude case that the effects of the nonlinear distortion have been almost completely removed.

One can, of course, be much more quantitative about the reduction in distortion produced by a given bias amplitude by Fourier-analyzing the output and input signal levels and comparing the relative harmonic coefficients.

**8.8
PROBLEM 5**   Using the nonlinear characteristic defined by the BASIC statement DEF FNG(X) = X↑3/(1+ABS(X↑3)) and a sine-wave input waveform with 100 points over the range 0 to 2π, add a subroutine that evaluates the first five harmonic coefficients of the output waveform and investigate the effects of bias

amplitude on the reduction of harmonic distortion. Try bias amplitudes of 0.5, 1, 5, and 10 units with the sine-wave amplitude normalized to 1.

**8.8
RESEARCH
PROBLEM**

Investigate the functional form of the nonlinear characteristic in a real tape recorder. In particular, see if you can provide a quantitatively realistic model of the induced noise pulses described in the text.

Although the use of high-frequency bias is an extremely effective method for reducing total harmonic distortion and intermodulation distortion in magnetic tape recording, the reader should be warned that the presence of the bias frequency can result in the generation of large-amplitude difference frequencies within the audio band (or signal band) due to interaction between high harmonics of the input signal and bias frequency in the nonlinear tape characteristic. It is easy to show through Taylor expansions and trigonometric identities that, for odd-symmetric nonlinear characteristics, the most important source of low-frequency beats occurs through beating of even harmonics of the input signal with the bias frequency. Thus beats at frequencies of the type

**8.9
Extraneous Frequency Spectrum
in Magnetic Tape Recording**

$$(1) \quad f_{bias} - 2f_{signal}$$
$$(2) \quad f_{bias} - 4f_{signal}$$
$$(3) \quad f_{bias} - 6f_{signal} \qquad \text{etc.}$$

will be the most bothersome (in descending order of importance). Terms of type (1) are seldom of concern since almost any tape recorder designed will satisfy the requirement that $f_{bias} \gg 2f_{signal}$. However, terms of type (2) are of important practical consideration in a surprising number of "high-quality" machines. To illustrate, if the bias frequency is 100 kHz, these beats will begin to fall within the audio band when input frequencies exceed 20 kHz. Some musical instruments (for example, the saxophone) have a lot of energy at frequencies $\gtrsim 20$ kHz and can produce different frequencies scattered throughout the entire audio band, owing to the interaction with a 100-kHz bias-oscillation frequency, even when the original signal components themselves are inaudible. Hence, if you must record saxophones with wideband condenser microphones, it pays to choose a bias frequency of at least ≈ 150 kHz (in this case the effect is not pronounced until input frequencies ≈ 30 kHz are of importance). On the other hand, the energy from a fine Stradivarius is generally distributed below ≈ 8 kHz and presents much less of a problem (not to mention other benefits).

One additional, but little recognized, source of extraneous frequencies in magnetic tape recording arises from a phenomenon known as *scrape flutter*. (Normal *flutter* is produced by slight eccentricities in the capstan, which in turn result in frequency modulation of recorded signals at the capstan frequency—typically ≈ 20 Hz at tape speeds of ≈ 15 in./sec.) Scrape flutter arises from the violin-string effect. Although the tape is moving across the head assembly in normal operation, it is nevertheless supported at various discrete points. Consequently, the tape will tend to vibrate resonantly at a frequency determined by the support spacing and the tape tension. (These parameters are usually maintained nearly constant; hence the vibrational resonance frequency is roughly constant.) The scraping motion of the tape against the head assembly tends to excite a low-amplitude vibration in the tape, which, in turn, produces an amplitude-modulation effect on the recorded signal by moving the tape small displacements away from the head gap. The effect produces *sidebands* separated from the recorded signal frequency by the tape resonance frequency (typically a few kHz). The origin of the effect can be seen from the simple

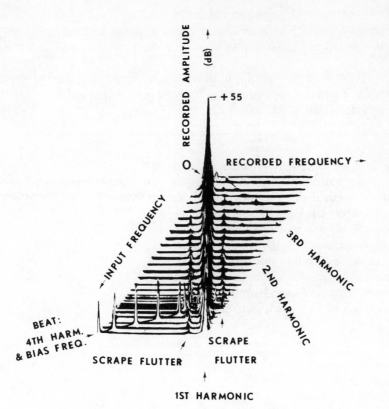

Fig. 8-14. Surface representing the spectrum of extraneous frequencies produced in magnetic tape recording for a sine-wave input signal of variable frequency and constant amplitude at maximum "recommended" recording level. A superposition of output oscillograms obtained from continuous Fourier analysis is shown. The "first harmonic" corresponds to the original sine-wave frequency. The scale is logarithmic: peak third harmonic amplitude is down by ≈55 dB from the peak recorded signal. (An Ampex Type 351 tape recorder was used with a 0.070-in. track width on Ampex 640 series recording tape at 15 in/sec.) The oscillograms have deliberately been lined up in such a way as to emphasize the signals at frequencies different from the input signal frequency; that is, the observer is looking along the ridge created by the desired "first harmonic" signal. The latter was constant within ±1 dB from about 50 to 15 kHz but dropped off rapidly as the input frequency approached 25 kHz. The bias frequency was ≈100 kHz. Note the series of beats between the fourth harmonic of the input signal and the bias frequency. (The recorded beat frequency goes to zero in the figure for an input frequency of 25 kHz = ¼ the bias frequency.) The sidebands, which are due to "scrape flutter," varied considerably in peak amplitude during the course of the measurement and are quite sensitive to tape tension (data taken by the author).

trigonometry identity

$$\sin A \cos B = 0.5 \sin (A+B) + 0.5 \sin (A-B)$$

where we will assume that the angle A is proportional to the time through the original signal frequency and that angle B is proportional to the time through the scrape-flutter frequency. The effect is illustrated very clearly in Fig. 8-14.

Currently available low-noise magnetic recording tape has a useful dynamic range over the audio spectrum (50 to 15 kHz) of about 60 dB on *half-track* (0.070-in. track width) recordings made at 15 in./sec. This range is defined in terms of a maximum recording level at which the total rms harmonic distortion of a 400-Hz tone is 3 percent and the noise level is defined as the total measured noise in the 50- to 15-kHz band on an erased tape which has

8.10
Compression and Expansion:
The Dolby Process

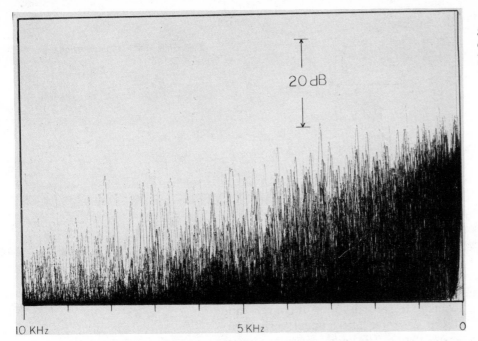

Fig. 8-15. Average power spectrum of an entire performance of "Le Sacre du Printemps" (by the Yale Symphony under the direction of John Mauceri). The data were taken by playing a high-quality recording (made on low-noise $\frac{1}{2}$-in tape at 15 in/sec using a flat frequency characteristic without compression) of the performance repetitively through a scanning, analog spectrum analyzer. Intensity is plotted in decibels vertically as a function of frequency (increasing to the left). The darkening is roughly proportional to the root-mean-square value. Note that although the rms intensity drops off rapidly with frequency, if you wait long enough at almost any frequency within the entire audio band you eventually will find a tone burst comparable to the maximum low-frequency intensity. Hence one really needs the full dynamic range throughout the entire audio band to reproduce a large symphony orchestra without significant distortion. (Data by the author.)

previously been used to record a 400-Hz signal at maximum level.[3] Because the actual dynamic range of a large symphony orchestra can be ≈ 100 dB[4] (see Fig. 8-15), there is some justification in seeking a method that compresses the full orchestral range within the usable tape dynamic range—provided that the distortion added by the compression process does not outweigh the original noise in the recording medium.

The Dolby process[5] is a currently popular version of a fairly old notion in the recording and audio-transmission fields known as the *compander*.[6] The basic notion is that one multiplies the initial signal with a compressive characteristic before making the recording and multiplies the playback signal with the inverse characteristic (see Fig. 8-16). As long as the product of the two characteristics is a straight line (i.e., linear), no distortion is introduced by the compression–expansion process. The method has the disadvantage that the recording itself will contain an amount of harmonic and intermodulation distortion proportional to the degree of compression introduced and is relatively useless unless it can be played back through the inverse process.

[3] Data from Ampex Type 351 Manual TM-2002A (1962) and Type AG-440B Manual 4890301 (1969).

[4] The range in dB is defined as $10 \log_{10}$ (intensity ratio). 1 dB is sometimes thought to be the smallest increment in intensity that can be detected by the human ear; 60 dB represents an intensity ratio of 1 million; 100 dB represents an intensity ratio of 10 billion.

[5] See Dolby (1968) and his first article, which describes the system (Dolby, 1967). See also Ford (1974) and McKenzie (1974).

[6] See, for example, Bennett, Sr. (1970, Sec. 3-3).

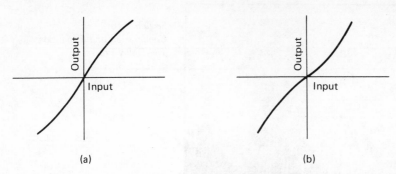

Fig. 8-16. (a) Typical characteristic of a compressor. (b) Typical characteristic of an expander. (See discussion in Bennett, Sr., 1970; Sec. 3-3.)

One, of course, recovers the original dynamic range in the ideal overall system. Although desirable in the production of master tapes, it is not so obviously desirable to seek the original orchestral dynamic range in normal home use. An honest 60-dB range in the living room (in which the volume level is adjusted so that background tape "hiss" is at about the same level as normal background noises) is quite adequate to stop all forms of conversation completely. Whereas the latter may be a desirable effect under certain circumstances, a dynamic range much greater than 60 dB under conditions where certain frequencies may be enhanced by room resonances by perhaps another 30 dB can be distinctly unpleasant.

Some remarkable experiments ("concerts") were conducted at Carnegie Hall in the spring of 1940 by Leopold Stokowski and the Bell Telephone Laboratories in which three-channel stereo recordings (containing a fourth volume compression–expansion channel)[7] of a large symphony orchestra were played back with an additional ≈10 dB dynamic range enhancement (total range ≈110 dB). The peak *acoustic* power produced was about 1500 W over the frequency range from 40 to 15 kHz and was said to be equivalent to an orchestra containing 2000 musicians. According to a *New York Herald Tribune* reviewer[8]:

> The immolation scene from 'Goetterdaemmerung' all but blew the rear end of [Carnegie Hall] ... into Fifty-seventh Street.... The greatest noise of the evening [was] the shout of the crowd when Elijah's appeal to the Lord was answered, which was enhanced until it sounded like a million banshees wailing at once. In a rehearsal of this demonstration Monday night, a woman in the audience doubled up as if kicked by a horse.

Serge Rachmaninoff[9] commented that the "enhanced" music was a "marvelous thing ... from the standpoint of demonstration, but sometimes unmusical because of the loudness. ... Too much enhancing, too much Stokowski."[10] Interestingly, in his later (1943) book, Stokowski states (p. 224) that the optimum dynamic range for typical home listening is 35 dB!

A basic point that should be emphasized here is that real time compression is inevitably accompanied by distortion [i.e., characteristic (a) of Fig. 8-16]. The only tolerable way to accomplish a net compression effect without providing the inverse expansion characteristic is to change the gain of the system *very*

---

[7] Technical details of the recording system were given by Fletcher (1940).

[8] "Super-volume Concert Records Scare Audience," *New York Herald Tribune*, Apr. 10, 1940, p. 27, col. 4

[9] "Sound Waves 'Rock' Carnegie Hall," *The New York Times*, Apr. 10, 1940, p. 27, cols. 6 and 7.

[10] The author is indebted to his wife, Frances Commins Bennett, for her help in tracking down the newspaper references quoted in this chapter.

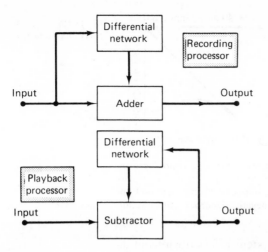

Fig. 8-17. Basic block diagram of Dolby system. During recording, a differential network adds a low-level signal to the straight-through signal. In playback, the low-level component is subtracted. (See Dolby, 1968).

slowly over time intervals which are *very* much longer than the reciprocal of the lowest-frequency components. In practice, such net compression in recorded music requires time delays $\gg 1$ sec, which are difficult to obtain without reliance on other nonlinear processes.

There is some possibility that a realistic means of accomplishing this goal may eventually result in the digital electronics field through incorporation of large numbers of high-speed shift registers. For example, if high-speed sampling could be accomplished with 16-bit accuracy and the digitalized signal shifted from one register to the next at the same rate ($\gtrsim$ twice the required bandwidth, hence $\gtrsim 30$ kHz), a chain of perhaps $\approx 300,000$ 16-bit shift registers would permit compressing an overall dynamic range of ≈ 96 dB to smaller domains through binary division and slowly enough to make the result tolerable. Until such items are economically realistic, the only satisfactory substitute appears to be a musically sensitive human being slowly turning a volume control.

The Dolby system is a split-band compander. The audio band is split into four parts, using four different compression characteristics. The results are then added and recorded. The recording is played back through four separate expanders, and the output of those four circuits is added. Different compander characteristics in different frequency bands permit taking optimum advantage of the tape-noise spectrum and psychological masking effects in the frequency ranges chosen. Representative transfer characteristics are shown in Fig. 8-18, which are said to result in an effective reduction of tape hiss by ≈ 10 dB.

The compression technique is fairly self-evident and is illustrated in Fig. 8-17. A small-amplitude output from a nonlinear "differential" component is added to the original signal. A rough fit of the data published by Dolby on the nature of this nonlinear differential function indicates that it may be approximated by a functional form of the type

$$f(x) \approx \frac{0.9x}{1 + 0.637x^{4/3}} \tag{6}$$

Here we have multiplied the numerator by 0.9 as a matter of convenience to ensure that the differential function is always less than x in magnitude. In the record mode, the input signal to the tape recorder in a particular frequency band is then roughly approximated by

$$x + f(x) \tag{7}$$

where $x < 1$.

403

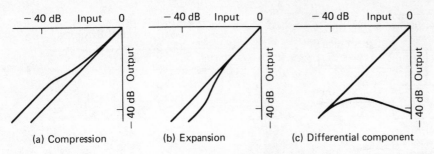

Fig. 8-18. Transfer characteristic curves. Compression curve (a) is produced by adding the differential component (c) to the straight-through signal. The expansion characteristic (b) is formed by subtracting the differential component (c) from the straight-through signal according to the negative-feedback configuration shown in Fig. 8-17. (See Dolby, 1968.)

The playback (inverse) correction in the Dolby system is less obvious in its operation. The output signal from the subtractor is fed back into the input. Indeed, the operation of the playback processor is very similar to that of the negative-feedback amplifier discussed before except that here the nonlinear differential function is placed in the feedback loop, the amplifier is linear, and its gain is unity. Consequently, a reiterative calculational procedure may be used to determine the playback signal which is so literally equivalent to the previous one used to handle the negative feedback amplifier that we may use our previous program with only a few minor changes.

First it is of interest to have a look at the "differential" nonlinear function itself. We can incorporate the latter in a BASIC function definition of the type

$$100 \quad \text{DEF FNF(X)} = .9*X/(1+.637*(X*X)\uparrow.666667) \tag{8}$$

where we have written $X^{4/3}$ as $(X*X)^{2/3}$ to emphasize that the denominator involves the absolute value of X. The form of this nonlinear function may then be evaluated through a program subroutine of the type

```
300   REM SUB TO DISPLAY DOLBY DIFF. FUNCTION
305   PRINT "DOLBY DIFFERENTIAL FUNCTION"
307   LET P = 255
310   FOR I = 1 TO P
320   LET X = (I – 128)*2/255
330   LET V(I) = FNF(X)
340   NEXT I
350   GOSUB 500
360   RETURN
```

where, again, subroutine 500 prints or displays the values stored in array $V(I)$.

The record function may then be defined by

$$105 \quad \text{DEF FNR(X)} = X + \text{FNF(X)} \tag{9}$$

and the results of running a previously stored periodic waveform in array $W(I)$ through the Dolby record process at different amplitude levels (G) are simulated by statements of the type

```
106   PRINT "GAIN CONSTANT, G";
107   INPUT G
110   FOR I = 1 TO P
120   LET V(I) = FNR(G*W(I))
130   NEXT I
140   GOSUB 500        (display subroutine)
150   GOSUB 400        (Fourier series subroutine)
155   GOSUB 700        (plot of Fourier coefficients)
160   GOTO 106
```

The statements on lines 150 and 155 utilize previously discussed subroutines for computing the Fourier coefficients of the periodic waveform and displaying the spectrogram of the Fourier coefficients. The recorded waveform, as discussed above, is now distorted from the original waveform due to the nonlinearity in FNF(X).

The playback waveform may then be reiteratively reconstructed using the approach discussed with the negative feedback amplifier. In doing the reconstruction it is of interest to allow for the possibility that the differential nonlinear function might actually be somewhat different in the playback mode than in the record mode (due to misadjustment of circuit parameters). We will, therefore, define a slightly different function from FNF(X) for use in the playback mode which has provision in it for varying degrees of misadjustment (through the parameter B) to be input from the keyboard. For example,

```
101  DEF FNG(X) = .9*X/(1+.637*(X*X)↑(B*.666667))
```

Here we have arbitrarily assumed that the nonlinear term in the denominator might have a slightly different exponential dependence. The value $B = 1$, of course, makes the two functional forms identical. We may then record and reconstruct the playback signal using various signal levels and varying degrees of circuit misalignment through a program segment of the type

```
203  PRINT "ENTER GAIN, G AND DOLBY MISADJUSTMENT, B"
204  INPUT G,B
205  FOR I = 1 TO P    ⎫
207  LET X = G*W(I)     ⎬  (record)
208  LET V(I) = FNR(X)  ⎭
209  NEXT I
210  FOR I = 1 TO P
211  PRINT I;
215  LET V1 = V(I)
220  LET V2 = E2 = V1
225  LET V2 = V1 – FNG(V2)                               (playback)
260  IF INT(1000*V2+.5) = INT(1000*E2+.5) THEN 280
265  LET E2 = V2
270  GOTO 225
280  LET V(I) = V2
285  NEXT I
290  GOSUB 500    (display)
291  GOSUB 400    (Fourier series calculation)
292  GOSUB 700    (spectrum of Fourier coefficients)
295  GOTO 203
```

The reiterative technique is precisely the same as that discussed in simulating the negative feedback amplifier. For each point I in the periodic waveform we let the input voltage $V1 = V(I)$ on line 215 and make an initial guess for the output voltage $V2$ on line 220. We then compute a new value for the output voltage on line 225 and see if it agrees with the previously obtained output voltage (stored in $E2$) to within a specified numerical accuracy (e.g., 1 part in 1000 on line 260). If the convergence criterion is not met, we reiterate until it is. Otherwise we store the output value in $V(I)$ and go on to the next point in the waveform (NEXT I). It is helpful to print the running value of I (line 211) at least the first time you go through a reiterative program of this type just to make sure that it is not getting hung up at some point in the loop for silly reasons [e.g., if FNG(X) > X this reiterative process will not converge].

Rectifiers are nonlinear circuit elements that have preferential conduction in one direction. An *ideal* rectifier has no backward conductance, but has a perfectly constant resistance in the *forward* direction.

8.11 Rectifiers

No real rectifiers are "ideal." For example, the vacuum-tube diode, in which a cathode (or filament) is heated to a high-enough temperature to "boil off" a significant electron current, has very low conduction in the backward direction (the plate is cold) but a rather nonlinear characteristic in the forward direction. At low currents and high temperatures, the forward current (I) varies roughly as

$$I = I_0 V^{3/2} \tag{10}$$

owing to *space-charge* effects.[11] Here V represents the voltage applied positively to the plate in respect to the cathode and the nonlinear dependence of current on V arises from Coulomb repulsion between like charges in the space between the cathode and plate. (The higher the applied electric field, the more rapidly the individual electrons are transported to the plate and the smaller is the repulsion effect on the net flow of electrons from the cathode. The exact form of the expression follows from Poisson's equation in electromagnetic theory.) The constant I_0 is characteristic of the individual diode.

At high voltages and finite temperatures, the total emission in the forward direction is temperature-limited according to the *Richardson law:*

$$I_{\text{limit}} \propto T^2 e^{-e_0 W/kT} \tag{11}$$

where T is the absolute temperature of the cathode, e_0 is the magnitude of charge on the electron, W is the *work function* of the surface (energy that binds the electrons to the cathode), and k is Boltzmann's constant. The result follows from the application of thermodynamic considerations to the electron "gas" inside the metal cathode. In general, the more grids (wire-mesh structures) or other electrodes placed within the cathode-plate geometry, the more nonlinear the plate circuit characteristic becomes. Triode (amplifier) tubes have a grid that permits modulating the plate current and hence can permit a net voltage

[11] Although the (negatively charged) electrons carry the electrical current in the direction from the cathode to the plate, historic usage forces us to define the current to be positive in the plate-to-cathode direction.

or power amplification in circuits of appropriate design. Because triode plate characteristics are more linear to start with than pentodes, screen-grid tetrodes, or beam-power tubes, they have frequently been used in high-quality linear amplifiers.

Crystal diodes made, for example, by placing a sharp tungsten point ("cat whisker") on a semiconductor (e.g., germanium or silicon) surface, are roughly characterized by a functional dependence of the type

$$I = I_0(e^{AV} - 1) \tag{12}$$

where V is the applied voltage across the crystal, A is a parameter that varies with the spot on the crystal, as well as inversely with the absolute temperature, and I_0 is another semiempirical constant.[12] Although the crystal rectifier conducts more in the forward direction than in the backward direction, the backward conduction can be quite appreciable. In fact, far into the back direction (the *Zener region*) avalanche breakdown can occur within the semiconductor, which results in a very sharp increase in back conduction.

In all the above examples of rectifiers, the conduction characteristic in the forward direction can be linearized by the addition of a series resistance, R. Sometimes, of course, this linearization is done at the expense of front-to-back conduction ratio. The new characteristic, including the resistive term, may then be computed from the old one by noting that the actual voltage across the diode is $V - IR$. For example, in the case of the cat-whisker diode, the new characteristic becomes

$$I = I_0(e^{A(V-IR)} - 1) \tag{13}$$

In the case of the point-contact diode, there is generally a significant resistive term present to begin with which arises from "spreading resistance" on the surface of the semiconductor away from the contact point.

The actual form of the above characteristic is most easily computed by solving the equation for V in terms of I. For example, the equivalent statement in the BASIC language would be

```
LET V = R*I + (1/A)*LOG(1+I/I0)
```

To plot the form of the characteristic, one then pretends that the current through the element is actually the independent variable and computes the various applied voltages which result from a systematic variation over the range of positive and negative current of interest.

Alternatively, one could solve the original characteristic reiteratively. That is, assume that $I = 0$ initially and compute I from V using Eq. (13). By keeping track of the preceding value of I, it is possible to solve the problem reiteratively until some specified level of agreement is obtained on successive solutions. However, it is helpful in such a program to limit the values of I so that $|IR| \leq |V|$.

We shall primarily be interested in the characteristics of such rectifier elements for some amplitude modulation and detection problems discussed below. However, a number of illustrative nonlinear problems of useful practical implication can be formulated just on the basis of the diode characteristics themselves.

---

[12] Point-contact cat-whisker diodes have had an interesting recurrent involvement throughout the history of electromagnetic communication methods. The earliest home radio sets built by amateurs in the 1920s tended to use such point-contact diodes as detectors. Similarly, the earliest detectors and mixers developed in the microwave and millimeter wave range used for radar operation during and after World War II were based on the cat-whisker technique. The field of microwave spectroscopy during the 1950s was largely dependent on such delicate and frustrating circuit elements. More recently, the direct measurement of highly stabilized gas laser frequencies has also relied heavily on ramifications of the old cat-whisker diode to permit determining the most precise value of the velocity of light currently known ($299,792,456.2 \pm 1.1$ m/sec). (See Evenson et al., 1972.)

8.11 **PROBLEM 8**	Compute and plot characteristics of a linearized space-charge-limited thermionic diode and a linearized crystal diode. Let $I_0 = A = 1$ and vary R.
8.11 **PROBLEM 9**	Compare the harmonic generation for the first ten harmonics of thermionic and crystal diodes having $R = 0$ and $A = I_0 = 1$ for $V = \sin \theta$ $(0 \leqslant \theta \leqslant 2\pi)$.

The simplest form of radio communication is based on the notion of amplitude modulation. At one extreme, merely turning the transmitter on and off permits sending messages based on binary codes.[13] At the other extreme, one may continuously vary the amplitude of the rf (radio frequency) "carrier" wave (using a device known as a *modulator*) in proportion to the amplitude of a lower-frequency signal.

It is worth noting at this point that one cannot modulate the rf wave with signal frequencies comparable to or greater than the frequency of the carrier itself. Such a feat would require turning the wave on and off faster than its own frequency. For this reason, the amount of information that can be sent over the carrier is limited by the carrier frequency. For example, human speech needs about a 3-kHz bandwidth for reasonable comprehension. Thus a 1-MHz rf wave might be used to transmit up to ≈ 300 separate voice messages simultaneously—but not much more. The process could be accomplished by *superheterodyning* (or *beating*) the separate voice channels up in frequency to fill the 1-MHz band. Such procedures are currently used to transmit large numbers of messages over a single coaxial cable laid by the telephone company under the North Atlantic.

Increasing the carrier frequency permits increasing the number of potential communication channels that might be transmitted on one carrier. If the carrier were a laser beam operating at $\approx 10^{15}$ Hz, $\approx 10^9$ as much information could be transmitted in principle as that over the 1-MHz radio wave. For example, $\approx 3 \times 10^{11}$ telephone messages might ultimately be transmitted over one laser carrier. This number appears to be within at least an order of magnitude of the total number of telephone conversations that have so far been made in the history of the world.

The modulator adds to the original rf wave a term that is the product of the low-frequency signal and the rf carrier. For reasons that will become apparent, the extent of this modulation is usually chosen to be a fraction of the total rf amplitude which is at least < 1.

At the opposite end of the communication link, the radio wave is received with some form of antenna and ultimately run through a rectifier and low-pass filter to extract the original modulation signal (see Fig. 8-19). There may, of course, be all sorts of other elements in the receiver:[14] rf amplifiers, oscillators that permit shifting the original rf carrier frequency through beating effects in devices known as mixers, if (for intermediate frequency) amplifiers which permit further amplification of the new carrier frequency, and so on. The heart

8.12
Amplitude Modulation and Detection

[13] For reasons not clearly understood by the author, people in the U.S. Navy still communicate from ship to ship using a form of amplitude modulation based upon chopping the output of a searchlight in pulses by use of mechanical, louvered shutters.

[14] Sometimes a specific example is worth a paragraph of generalities: "I was reading your item in R-E August '73 and on page 69 you were wondering aloud why the Philco 39-45 had that weird 1st i.f. transformer with the third winding connected to the suppressor of the 78. I think this circuit was one of the wondrous variable selectivity ideas that were used in those days. The stronger the signal, the wider the pass band and hence the greater fidelity (like the capture ratio effect only different). When the signal strength drops the avc drops and the variable-mu 78 changes in characteristics so the broad (untuned) secondary (third winding) does not predominate the output of the stage." From a letter to the editor of *Radio-Electronics* by S. P. Dow in 1973.

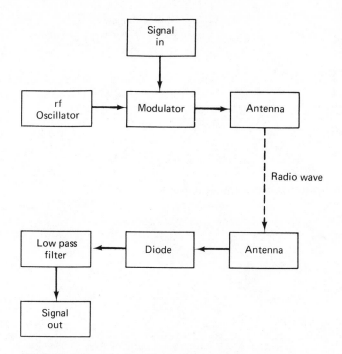

Fig. 8-19. Schematic diagram of an amplitude-modulation communication link.

of the amplitude-modulation (AM) detection process, however, is a rectifying element of some type that permits extracting the modulation envelope on the rf wave.

The AM detection circuitry can be extremely rudimentary. See, for example, Fig. 8-20, where the rectifier could be almost anything. During the mid 1920s when the first high-power radio stations started going on the air, AM detection was reported on a wondrous variety of nonlinear circuit elements: dental fillings, carborundum dust in the eardrums, old bed springs, plumbing fixtures, and "cold" solder joints. A woman from Brooklyn gave a demonstration of her ability to pull in WEAF merely by grabbing an antenna wire in one hand and a good ground in the other ("It's just body induction" explained a radio buff at the scene.[15]) Similarly, a florist in Toronto gained international fame and local hostility because he picked up a radio station at high volume over a water faucet in his shop. When asked if he didn't find the background noise disturbing, he indicated that he certainly did not and that "he often came back to the shop in the evening to hear a good concert."[16]

The main purpose of the *low-pass filter* is to provide a shunt conduction path for the radiowave back to ground. However, it is just as well to keep the rf wave out of the subsequent circuitry. It is of interest to examine some of the common sources of distortion in the AM communication problem. We can simulate the main features of the problem in just a few programming steps. We shall again assume that a periodic waveform with P points has been stored in column array, $W(I)$, and that a working array, $V(I)$, is available with the same dimensions. We also will assume that the previously discussed subroutines for displaying or printing the waveform currently stored in $V(I)$ and for Fourier-analyzing this waveform are available. For example, the statements

```
200   PRINT "ORIGINAL WAVEFORM"
202   GOSUB 500
```

remind us that we are about to display the original signal stored in $V(I)$.

---

[15] *The New York Times*, May 12, 1924, p. 19, col. 2.
[16] *The New York Times*, Nov. 14, 1926, Sec. IX, p. 18, col. 1.

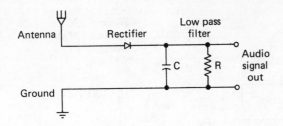

Fig. 8-20.

We can next compute and display an rf waveform amplitude-modulated by the signal through statements of the type

```
203   PRINT "SIGNAL AMPLITUDE"
204   INPUT B
205   FOR I = 1 TO P − 1 STEP 2
210   LET V(I) = 1 + B*W(I)
215   LET V(I + 1) = −(1 + B*W(I + 1))
220   NEXT I
224   PRINT "AMP-MOD. RF CARRIER WAVEFORM NEXT"
225   GOSUB 500      (display)
```

where P should be even.

It is assumed that the original signal is normalized to a peak amplitude of unity. Parameter B represents the modulation depth given to this signal on an rf wave whose peak amplitude is also unity. In real life, the rf wave would be closely sinusoidal and the modulated waveform would be of the type

$$(1 + B*W(t)) \sin (2\pi f_{rf} t)$$

where $W(t)$ is the low-frequency signal. For convenience, we have used a radiofrequency square wave in the above program. No significant errors result from this process, and the computer simulation can be effected in much shorter running time.

We next have to decide what functional form the rectifier element takes at the receiving end. For example, the following statements provide a choice between an ideal rectifier and a crystal diode with zero spreading resistance, and values of unity for the other two constants in Eq. (12).

```
227   PRINT "IDEAL RECT. OR X'TAL RECT.? ANS. 1 OR Ø"
228   INPUT P5
230   FOR I = 1 TO P
231   IF P5 = Ø THEN 235
232   IF V(I) > Ø THEN 240
233   LET V(I) = Ø
234   GOTO 240
235   LET V(I) = EXP(V(I)) − 1
240   LET W(I) = V(I)
244   NEXT I
245   GOSUB 500      (display subroutine)
```

The statement on line 245 calls the subroutine to display $V(I)$ after the rectifier and before the low-pass filter. Next we pass the rectifier output through our previously described digital filter, using a time constant of 1 (half the fundamental rf period) and extract the detected low-frequency-modulation signal.

```
250   GOSUB 800      (filter subroutine)
254   PRINT "OUTPUT LOW PASS FILTER NEXT"
255   GOSUB 500      (display subroutine)
```

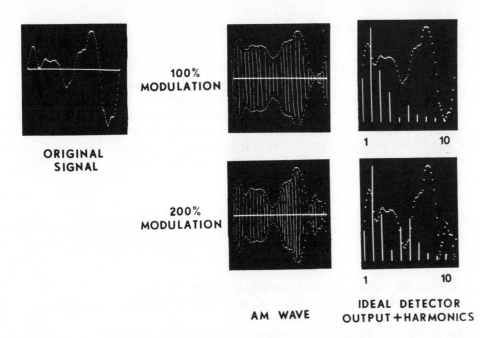

Fig. 8-21. Effect of overmodulation.

Here P is the period of the modulated waveform in the array $W(I)$ and it is necessary to use the values for the points $P+I-J$ when $I-J<1$ in line $83\emptyset$ of the digital filtering subroutine (see p. 398).

Some results based upon the above programming statements are shown in Figs. 8-21 and 8-22.

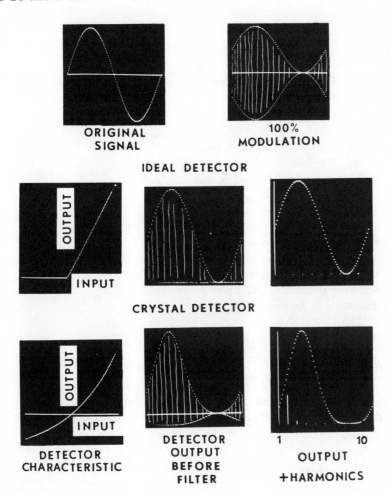

Fig. 8-22. Comparison of ideal and real AM detectors.

411

8.12
PROBLEM 10   Simulate the response of an amplitude modulation detector when the input consists of an rf square-wave which is 100 percent modulated by a low-frequency sine wave. Compute the output waveform after the rf filter from the detector over one period of the sine-wave signal using a sine-wave input waveform with 100 points over the range 0 to 2π. Compute the Fourier coefficients for the first 10 harmonics of the sine-wave frequency and compare results with the bottom illustration in Fig. 8-22. Assume that the detector characteristic is given by Eq. (12) with $A = I_0 = 1$.

8.13
Raudive Voices

An astonishing communication experiment has been publicized recently in the London Press (see Fig. 8-23). It is, of course, the *interpretation* of the experiment that is astonishing. Because the problem has a bearing on several real processes discussed in the present book and because an appreciable number of people apparently take Raudive's interpretation seriously, we shall briefly review the phenomenon.

Konstantin Raudive (a psychologist) has reported identifying a total of 72,000 messages recorded over a period of six years in his laboratory in Bad Krozingen, Germany[17]:

"The voices tell me they come from an anteworld. Anyone with a tape recorder can pick them up. The difficulty is in interpreting them. They speak in a confused mixture of·languages, but seem to favour the native tongue of the experimenter." [Raudive speaks Latvian, Russian, German, Swedish, French, Spanish, and can understand most Slavonic dialects.]

Among the voices identified were those of Hitler, Mussolini, Churchill, Tolstoi, Lenin, Trotski, Nietzsche, Stalin, and the late President John F. Kennedy. As one reviewer of Raudive's book commented, "What is one to think of a 'message' purporting to come from President Kennedy, consisting of three words in Latvian?"[18]

According to the newspaper account, the effect was first discovered by a Swedish ornithologist named Jurgenson when he left a tape recorder running to record birdsong. Jurgenson used a diode (!) rather than a microphone on the input to his tape recorder "to eliminate the possibility of detecting human voices being transported by sound waves over long distances." The possibility that radio signals were being detected was discarded in Jurgenson's early work because he didn't get any recordings of music (!).

In a refinement of the method, Raudive takes the output of a radio receiver tuned to a region of the band in between normally audible signals. He then records the noise output with the gain on his tape recorder turned all the way up and waits.

Anyone who has ever investigated the characteristics of a real tape recorder with any seriousness is, of course, aware that there are numerous sources of

[17] Raudive (1971); quoted from the newspaper account reproduced in Fig. 8-23.
[18] Gaythorpe (1971, p. 70).

412

London, April 3, 1971 | On sale every Thursday | Price 4p | No. 2026 | London, WC2B 5BB

'Voices from the dead' get remarkable Press

HAS SCIENTIST TAPED MESSAGES FROM CHURCHILL AND STALIN?

DID national newspaper reporters hear last week voices from the "dead" electronically recorded on tape?

They attended an intriguing experiment conducted in the Gerrards Cross (Bucks.) home of publisher Colin Smythe in connection with a new book, "Breakthrough."

Published on Monday, it is written by Latvian-born Dr Konstantin Raudive, 60, a psychologist, and former lecturer at Riga and Uppsala Universities, who claims to have recorded thousands of spirit voices.

Alan Whittaker said in the "News of the World" that Peter Bander, connected with the publishing firm, produced a new unusual recording tape still in its sealed container.

This was placed on a tape-recorder. After a while the tape was played back.

The reporter quoted this statement made by Eric Lovelock, a physicist who is a member of the scientific committee of the Churches' Fellowship for Psychical and Spiritual Studies:

Spoke in German

"Voices appeared on the tape which we have not yet identified. They spoke mostly in German."

Later he conducted five hours of further tests.

Also present was David Ellis, who is investigating this phenomenon under a Cambridge university grant.

• • •

Spanish, and can understand most Slavonic dialects.

He said the voices cannot be explained away as chance radio pick-ups. Many messages are personal and addressed directly to living people.

"Despite the difficulties presented by atmospheric interference, I get the impression there are a host of entities wishing to make contact," Raudive told Whittaker.

Patience needed

"In one ten-minute recording I got 200 voices. With patience there is no reason at all why anyone cannot tape the voice phenomena.

"But the experimenter must develop his hearing by constant listening to tapes. What, at first, seems like atmospheric buzzing, is often many voices. They have to be analysed and amplified of course."

The reporter said that Raudive is a Roman Catholic and was a fervent believer in life after death before he began his experiments.

Whittaker asked if any of the transition voices described the transition from life to death. Raudive replied: "There have been hints.

DR KONSTANTIN RAUDIVE, who says, "The voices can be recognised as those of people we once knew."

that the voices of John F. Kennedy and Stalin are also said to be included.

Rose told how a Swedish ornithologist, Friedrich Jurgenson, was the first to stumble on

sound waves, he eliminated the possibility of human voices which had carried over a long distance.

Rose dealt with a suggested explanation that the recorder picked up a scatter of radio signals.

"This was discounted since in the hundreds of recordings made not once was music heard.

"However, that electro-magnetic radio waves were involved in the transmission of the sounds seems proved by the fact that they never occur when recording attempts are made in rooms screened from external radio signals."

Raudive, who was impressed by Jurgenson's sincerity, orderly method and volume of evidence, built a laboratory at Bad Krozingen in Germany.

He equipped it and over six years logged and analysed thousands of recordings.

These include "thousands of bits of speech, many addressed to him by dead people who identify themselves."

Languages are mixed

A gramophone record, produced from Raudive's tapes, revealed the voices were double normal speed, often speaking in a mixture of languages but fairly clear.

Edgar Holt, "Sunday Telegraph" ecclesiastical correspondent, who listened to some of the voices received by Raudive since 1964, wrote:

"Messages received are spoken in either male or female voices and are in a curious mixture of European languages, often two or three in the same sentence.

"Latvian, Dr Raudive's native

the phenomenon — when he left a tape recorder running to record birdsong.

By using a diode, which unlike a normal microphone will receive only radio signals, not

tongue, predominates, but there are also many German, Swedish and Russian words, as well as Spanish, French and English."

Raudive told him: "There are several reasons for believing they are messages from the dead.

"We are given definite self-identification by the owners of the voices. We are addressed by our own names. The voices can be recognised as those of people we once knew."

Robert Chapman in the "Sunday Express" said that the variety of languages, included Latvian, Swedish, German, Russian, French, Italian and English.

Russian is heard

He added that the voice attributed to Churchill was heard to say: "Thank you ... make believe, my dear ... yes..."

A voice which spoke in Russian said: "Stalin is here. Terribly hot. Terrible hurry."

Kennedy, when asked to speak, is said to have made this reply in German: "At night, Kosta ... Damn it all!"

Chapman spoke to David Ellis, who said: "I have listened to the voices and am satisfied that they are voices, not just noises being misinterpreted.

"But this does not mean they are the voices of spirits. You have to take into consideration the possibility of picking up snatches of radio signals not immediately audible to the human ear."

On the whole the publishers must be satisfied with a good Press, though naturally sceptical, for their new book. Seldom has a psychic book achieved so much advance publicity.

Fig. 8-23. Early newspaper account of the "Raudive voice" experiment [reproduced by permission from *Psychic News* (London), Vol. 2026, p. 1, Apr. 3, 1971].

413

nonlinearity present which could potentially serve to detect amplitude modulation on radio signals. The problem is usually one of getting rid of the effect rather than enhancing it. Within the author's own personal experience, the "voices" are usually detected by some mildly nonlinear element within the high-gain microphone preamplifier stage. Whether these nonlinearities are due to "cold solder joints" or transistor characteristics is frequently hard to determine. Because the detector quality is extremely poor in most instances, the "voices" are usually difficult to understand. One fine specimen within the author's personal collection is located on one track of a four-channel stereo recording of the Bach Organ Mass, done at 15 in./sec using $\frac{1}{2}$-in. low-noise Ampex Type 444 tape. The message may well be in Latvian and is certainly hard to understand. Repeated listening suggests that it was most probably something like "Car 43 go to Chapel and Elm." In any event, it was found possible to eliminate the effect by thorough grounding of the microphone preamplifier housing with a large braided copper strap to the main amplifier chassis.

It is of interest to examine Raudive's work from the point of view of the "monkeys at the typewriters" (see Chapter 4). Evidently, a very large volume of material was processed during the 6-year study and the 72,000 messages apparently contain no more than two or three words each (sometimes in as many different languages). However, it seems clear that the probability of random clusters of background noise creating recognizable words could not possibly be large enough without loading the dice in some way.

The probabilities are difficult to estimate in the "voice" identification problem. Anyone who has ever listened to a taxicab radio signal under "good" conditions knows that some people are able to decipher words with almost negligible signal-to-noise ratios and bandwidth. As demonstrated by the *vocoder* experiments conducted at the Bell Telephone Laboratories in the late 1930s, only the low-frequency modulation envelope over a relatively small dynamic range is required to reconstruct recognizable speech. This envelope can be used to modulate other sound formants in the audio range and hence simulate a speaking voice with totally different tonal character. The method was not a great success in the telephone business because people like to recognize who is talking to them and not merely understand what is being said. Probably the main public exposure to the vocoder occurred during the 1940s over commercial radio when the sounds from a steam locomotive were made to advertise a certain headache remedy (thereby creating an increased need for the remedy).

For the sake of quantitative illustration in an optimistic case, let us assume that we only need a 30-Hz modulation bandwidth with a 2-bit amplitude resolution (≈ 10 dB) capability to permit reconstructing speech. If we were to sample at 60 Hz (twice the required bandwidth) the process would require 120 binary bits per second to send the minimum information required to reconstruct words. Suppose that the average word lasts ≈ 0.5 sec and hence requires only 60 binary bits for specification. The binary code could thus identify $\approx 2^{60} \approx 10^{18}$ separate words in a $\frac{1}{2}$-sec interval. Suppose that someone like Raudive knows $\approx 10,000$ words in each of 10 different languages. The probability of his recognizing one word in one 0.5-sec interval due to a random scrambling of the speech envelope would then be ≈ 1 in 10^{13}. At this rate he would only recognize one word every 158,000 years. Because of the exponential dependence involved, small variations in the required number of binary bits can produce large changes in the final probability estimated. Nevertheless, it seems very unlikely that random chance could produce such a high yield of words without some equivalent of the weighting factors discussed in the typewriter problem in Chapter 4. It is much more believable that speech was detected from a modulated radiowave by one of the numerous nonlinear mechanisms in the system. It should also be noted that even if you carefully select a setting on the radio band "in between" stations, there will generally be intermodulation effects (for example, from Doppler shifts in scattering from the ionosphere) which introduce coherent rf signals sporadically.

There is a surprising tendency throughout the history of science for competent and even outstanding scientists to throw "cause and effect" to the winds as they are caught up in the aging process. The paragraph following the quote from Archbishop Tillotson's initial formulation of the "monkey problem" is strangely relevant (Tillotson, 1719; *op. cit.* Chapter 4; p. 11):

> Our Belief or Disbelief of a Thing, does not alter the Nature of the Thing. We cannot fancy Things into Being, or make them vanish into Nothing by the stubborn Confidence of our Imaginations. Things are as sullen as we are, and will be what they are, whatever we think of them ....

8.13
PROBLEM 11

Probably the purest form of the Raudive voice effect would involve the direct use of the tape nonlinearity for detection (and even mixing) and the finite bandwidth of the tape for the low-pass filter in Fig. 8-20. The simplest version would consist of connecting the antenna and ground directly across the record head in Fig. 8-9. Then all we have to do to detect radio waves is bias the record head away from the origin of the tape characteristic in Fig. 8-10 with some residual constant magnetization.†

Simulate this process in the following way: Take the nonlinear tape characteristic to be

$$f(x) = \frac{x^3}{1 + |x^3|}$$

where the input quantity is made up of a constant-bias term ($x_0 \approx -2$) and an rf square wave that is 100 percent amplitude-modulated by a low-frequency sine wave. The bandwidth limitation of the tape may be simulated by the digital filter technique discussed before. Plot the output waveform and spectrum for the Fourier coefficients of the detected signal.

† This is, of course, only one of dozens of methods. Much greater rf sensitivity could be obtained in practice either by applying the "intermediate frequency" output from a superheterodyne receiver to the record head or by doing the superheterodyne mixing (and detecting) directly in the tape with the help of the local high frequency bias oscillator.

The acronym *maser* was coined originally by Gordon et al. (1954) as a term for the first device of its type.[19] It stood for *Microwave Amplification by Stimulated Emission of Radiation*. This definition has introduced some semantic difficulty in extending the technique to the optical domain. Various alternatives have been proposed: *laser* (for *Light Amplification...*), *iraser* (*Infra-Red Amplification...*), *smaser* (*Sub-Millimeter wave Amplification...*), and even *optical maser*. It was suggested at one point that

8.14
Lasers: Meaning of the Acronym

---

[19] It appears that the first published proposal of the "maser principle" was given by J. Weber in *Trans. Inst. Radio Engr.* (Professional Group on Electronic Devices), 1953. However, Weber did not give it a name, nor did he make one work. He did give an interesting summary of early background developments in the field (see Weber, 1965). The possibility of obtaining amplification ("negative absorption") at optical frequencies was evidently noted as early as 1939 by V. A. Fabrikant in his (unpublished) doctoral dissertation at the P. N. Lebedev Physics Institute. (See, Fabrikant *et al*, 1962 and Butayeva and Fabrikant, 1959). The acronym laser was introduced by Gould (1958).

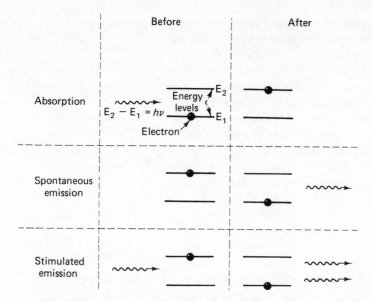

Fig. 8-24. Interaction of light with excited atoms.

the problem should be solved by redefining maser to stand for *Money Acquisition Schemes for Expensive Research.* Fortunately, popular adoption of the acronym laser has spared us from the latter bit of indelicate cynicism.

In almost all laser systems we are concerned with the interaction of light with atoms in one of two energy levels. This interaction is resonant at the frequency, ν, satisfying the Bohr relationship[20]

**8.15
Interaction of Radiation
with Excited Atoms**

$$E_2 - E_1 = h\nu$$

where h is Planck's constant $(\approx 6.61 \times 10^{-27}$ erg-sec) and E_2 and E_1 are the atomic-energy levels involved.

The interaction can take the three main forms illustrated in Figure 8-24:

1. *Absorption:* The atom is initially in the lower state and absorbs one quantum of energy $(E_2 - E_1)$ from the incident light beam by undergoing a transition to the upper level. The intensity of the light beam is attenuated by $E_2 - E_1$.

2. *Spontaneous emission:* The atom is initially in the upper level and no light beam need be present. The atom spontaneously drops to the lower level, emitting its energy as a light quantum with equal probability in all directions. Although there is a characteristic average time for this emission, there is also a random distribution in emission times. Spontaneous emission plays a role in lasers similar to noise in audio amplifiers or oscillators.

3. *Stimulated emission:* The atom is initially in the upper level and the light wave forces the atom to undergo a transition to the lower level. The energy difference, $E_2 - E_1$, is given to the light wave. This amplification process is "coherent": phase, frequency, and direction of propagation are preserved. (Images would be intensified.) Stimulated emission is formally the exact inverse of (stimulated) absorption and its existence was first postulated by Einstein (1917) from symmetry considerations in his analysis of the interaction of "heat" (infrared) radiation with atoms. Einstein showed that the interaction probability per atom for stimulated emission is the same as that for absorption.

[20] Although we used f to stand for frequency so far in this chapter, historic usage makes it impossible to talk about the interaction of light with atoms without introducing the frequency of the light wave through the Greek letter nu (ν).

Consequently, in order to get a net gain out of a medium containing a number of atoms (N_2) in the upper state and a number (N_1) in the lower state, we must have[21]

$$N_2 > N_1 \qquad (14)$$

8.16
Thermal Equilibrium and Detailed Balancing

The argument that led Einstein to postulate the existence of stimulated emission from previously established evidence for absorption is a special case of the *principle of detailed balancing*. In fact, not only can one say that the inverse process must exist, but one also can say how big it is in many instances in relation to the normal process.

For example, consider an electron–atom collision process of the type

$$(\text{energy}) + e + X_1 \rightleftharpoons X_2 + e \qquad (15)$$

Going to the right, reaction (15) means that an energetic electron can result in exciting the atom. Going to the left, reaction (15) means that a slow electron can deactivate the atom and take up the internal energy of the atom as kinetic energy. We could write a pair of equations for the transfer of excitation back and forth between the upper (2) and lower (1) energy levels of the atom. Specifically, if

$N_2 =$ density of atoms in the upper level (energy E_2 in state X_2)

$N_1 =$ density of atoms in the lower level (energy E_1 in state X_1)

then

$$\frac{dN_1}{dt} = -R_{12}N_1 + R_{21}N_2$$
$$\frac{dN_2}{dt} = +R_{12}N_1 - R_{21}N_2 \qquad (16)$$

where the rate coefficients R_{12} and R_{21} are proportional to the number of electrons in the two energy regions and their probability to interact with the atoms in the two levels E_1 and E_2.

The principle of detailed balancing permits one to relate R_{12} and R_{21}: specifically, if the electrons have a thermal velocity distribution (or Maxwellian velocity distribution) corresponding to a temperature T_e, it may be shown quite generally that[22]

$$R_{12} = R_{21}e^{-(E_2-E_1)/kT_e} \qquad (17)$$

where k is Boltzmann's constant ($\approx 1.38 \times 10^{-16}$ erg/deg; $kT \approx 0.0248$ eV at 15°C). Consequently, at steady-state ($dN_1/dt = dN_2/dt = 0$), Eqs. (16) reduce to

$$\frac{N_2}{N_1} = \frac{R_{12}}{R_{21}} = e^{-(E_2-E_1)/kT_e} \qquad (18)$$

and we obtain the irritating (for laser purposes) result that for any system of two interacting particles in thermal equilibrium,

$$N_2 < N_1 \qquad (19)$$

at steady state. Hence we cannot satisfy Eq. (14), there is no gain, and the medium absorbs.

8.17
Population Inversion (Negative Temperatures)

How do you beat the game? The basic answer is that although any one process will tend to lead to a result such as Eq. (18) at thermal equilibrium, the speed with which different processes approach thermal equilibrium varies

---

[21] We shall ignore the statistical weight factors of the levels for simplicity.

[22] For those familiar with Schrödinger theory, the result follows from a quantum-mechanical calculation assuming hermiticity of the perturbing matrix elements in the electron–atom collision problem.

substantially with both the nature of the processes and with the different levels involved. Hence one can play two different processes against each other and obtain a set of steady-state population densities in which neither process has resulted in *thermal* equilibrium. That is, there is no single temperature that can be used to describe the relative amounts of excitation in the different levels of the atom. Under these conditions it is frequently possible to achieve inequality (14) for one pair of levels. That state of affairs is sometimes loosely described through Eq. (18) by postulating a *negative temperature*. That wording is unfortunate, however, since there is generally no thermodynamic equilibrium involved. Hence the concept of temperature loses its meaning. Consequently, the more preferable terminology *population inversion* has generally been adopted to describe instances in which inequality (14) is obtained.

Population inversion in the original ammonia maser (Gordon et al., 1954) was obtained by removing the lower-state molecules bodily: a beam of ammonia molecules was run through a (electric quadrupole) deflection apparatus which caused molecules in the lower state to be deflected out of the beam while letting molecules in the upper state pass through.

The population inversion obtained in the first gas laser (the helium–neon laser)[23] was produced by playing spontaneous radiative decay against an inelastic excitation transfer process of the type[24]

$$He^* + Ne \rightarrow Ne^* + He \tag{20}$$

in which He* is a long-lived (metastable) excited state of helium and Ne* is a short-lived excited state of neon (the upper laser level) in the $4s$ configuration of neon (see Fig. 8-25). Reaction (20) is essentially not reversible in the experiment because the neon state decays through spontaneous emission before the inverse collision reaction occurs. However, as short as it is (≈ 100 nanoseconds) the lifetime of the upper neon laser level is long compared to the lifetime of the lower neon laser level (≈ 20 nanoseconds) in the $3p$ configuration. Consequently, population inversions result in the excited states of neon. It helps, of course, to have an initial excitation process such as reaction (20) which is reasonably selective and efficient.

Because the helium metastables are the lowest excited energy levels in the helium atom, they tend to accumulate much of the excitation in pure helium discharges. When a small partial pressure of neon is added to the discharge, this excitation is efficiently coupled to the neon spectrum. As noted by Headrick and Duffendack (1931): "By the introduction of as little as 0.4 percent neon ... into helium ... the spectrum emitted is changed almost completely from the arc spectrum of helium to that of neon...."

Most *continuously operating* (*cw*, for *continuous wave*) gas laser transitions currently known (the number is in the thousands)[25] involve at least four excited levels of the lasing atom for adequate description of the excitation processes (Fig. 8-26). The upper laser level is generally excited by a collision process in a gas discharge, and the population inversion maintained simply by the inequality

$$A_{21} \ll R_1 \tag{21}$$

where A_{21} is the decay rate from spontaneous emission on the laser transition (sometimes called the *Einstein A coefficient*) from the upper level and R_1 is the total decay rate from the lower level. If there is no direct excitation of the

[23] Javan et al. (1961, 1971); Bennett et al. (1964).

[24] Reactions such as (20) were well known to optical spectroscopists long before the laser. For example, reaction (20) itself had been studied in spontaneous emission for the more important neon laser states by Headrick and Duffendack (1931).

[25] See, for example, the Appendix to Bennett (1965).

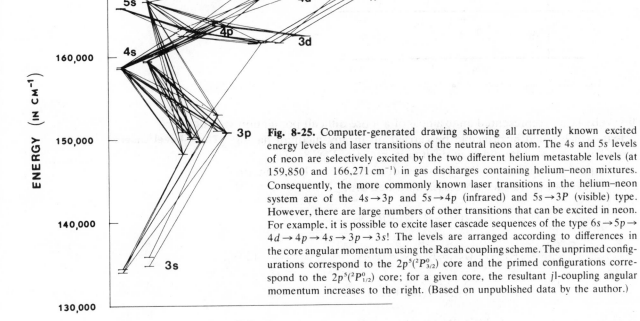

Fig. 8-25. Computer-generated drawing showing all currently known excited energy levels and laser transitions of the neutral neon atom. The 4s and 5s levels of neon are selectively excited by the two different helium metastable levels (at 159,850 and 166,271 cm^{-1}) in gas discharges containing helium–neon mixtures. Consequently, the more commonly known laser transitions in the helium–neon system are of the $4s \to 3p$ and $5s \to 4p$ (infrared) and $5s \to 3P$ (visible) type. However, there are large numbers of other transitions that can be excited in neon. For example, it is possible to excite laser cascade sequences of the type $6s \to 5p \to 4d \to 4p \to 4s \to 3p \to 3s$! The levels are arranged according to differences in the core angular momentum using the Racah coupling scheme. The unprimed configurations correspond to the $2p^5(^2P^0_{3/2})$ core and the primed configurations correspond to the $2p^5(^2P^0_{1/2})$ core; for a given core, the resultant jl-coupling angular momentum increases to the right. (Based on unpublished data by the author.)

lower level, the basis for requirement (21) may be seen by writing an equation for the lower-state density:

$$\frac{dN_1}{dt} = -R_1 N_1 + A_{21} N_2 \qquad (22)$$

(i.e., the formation of lower-state atoms occurs mainly in spontaneous emission at a rate proportional to the upper-state density through the coefficient A_{21}). For $N_2 > N_1$) at steady state ($dN_1/dt = 0$), requirement (21) results from Eq. (22).

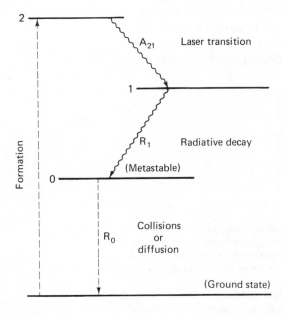

Fig. 8-26. Four-level system characteristic of most gas lasers (see Bennett, 1965).

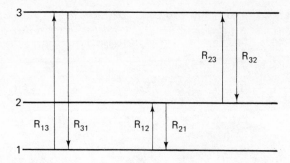

Fig. 8-27. General three-level laser.

The first ruby laser[27] represented an example of a more difficult population-inversion feat, which could in principle be carried off in any medium having three energy levels coupled by different excitation process (Fig. 8-27).

The rate equations describing the densities of these three levels in the presence of the excitation transfer processes indicated are:

8.18
Three-Level Lasers[26]

$$\frac{dN_1}{dt} = -(R_{12} + R_{13})N_1 + R_{21}N_2 + R_{31}N_3$$

$$\frac{dN_2}{dt} = +R_{12}N_1 - (R_{21} + R_{23})N_2 + R_{32}N_3 \tag{23}$$

$$\frac{dN_3}{dt} = +R_{13}N_1 + R_{23}N_2 - (R_{31} + R_{32})N_3$$

At steady state $(dN_1/dt = dN_2/dt = dN_3/dt = 0)$ the three equations in (23) reduce to two distinct equations in the ratios N_2/N_1 and N_3/N_1:

$$-R_{12} = -(R_{21} + R_{23})\frac{N_2}{N_1} + R_{32}\frac{N_3}{N_1}$$

$$-R_{13} = R_{23}\frac{N_2}{N_1} - (R_{31} + R_{32})\frac{N_3}{N_1} \tag{24}$$

Although the three pairs of rate coefficients will always satisfy detailed-balancing relations such as that indicated in Eq. (18), it is possible to find situations in which three different processes are involved at three different "temperatures." That is, one process may couple levels 1 and 2 at temperature T_a and not affect the third level; a second process could couple levels 2 and 3 at temperature T_b and not affect level 1; and finally, a third process could couple levels 1 and 3 at temperature T_c without affecting level 2. Hence from detailed balancing arguments,

$$R_{12} = R_{21} \exp\left(-\frac{E_2 - E_1}{kT_a}\right)$$

$$R_{23} = R_{32} \exp\left(-\frac{E_3 - E_2}{kT_b}\right) \tag{25}$$

$$R_{13} = R_{31} \exp\left(-\frac{E_3 - E_1}{kT_c}\right)$$

[26] The three-level method of achieving population inversion was suggested by Basov and Prokorov (1955). A proposal for producing a three-level solid state (microwave) maser was given by Bloembergen (1956). The first three-level laser was demonstrated by Maiman (1960) in the case of ruby. Possible extensions of the three-level concept to gas discharge lasers were discussed by Bennett (1965) and Gould (1965).

[27] Maiman (1960). This historic paper describing the first successful laser oscillation obtained experimentally was *rejected* by the *Physical Review Letters* in accordance with one of that journal's more quixotic editorial policies.

Note that the limit $T \to \infty$ in any one of these instances means that the two particular rates become equal. (The latter corresponds to the interaction between a pair of levels and an intense laser beam, for example.)

It is easy to see that through suitable choice of the temperatures and rate coefficients in Eqs. (25), it is possible to get a population inversion between any pair of the three levels. In this connection, a solution to (24) with

$$\frac{N_2}{N_1} > 1 \qquad \text{means that the transition } 2 \to 1 \text{ is inverted}$$

whereas

$$\frac{N_3}{N_1} > 1 \qquad \text{means that the transition } 3 \to 1 \text{ is inverted} \qquad (26)$$

and

$$\frac{N_3}{N_1} > \frac{N_2}{N_1} \qquad \text{means that the transition } 3 \to 2 \text{ is inverted}$$

Although not really necessary for the *three*-level problem, it is helpful to consider rewriting Eqs. (24) as one matrix equation,

$$\begin{pmatrix} -R_{12} \\ -R_{13} \end{pmatrix} = \begin{pmatrix} -(R_{21}+R_{23}) & R_{32} \\ R_{23} & -(R_{31}+R_{32}) \end{pmatrix} \begin{pmatrix} \dfrac{N_2}{N_1} \\ \dfrac{N_3}{N_1} \end{pmatrix} \qquad (27)$$

or

$$(E) = (R)(N)$$

Hence the solution for the population ratios is obtained by taking the inverse of the R matrix,

$$\text{MAT } T = \text{INV}(R) \qquad (28)$$

and multiplying that times the matrix E,

$$\text{MAT } N = T*E \qquad (29)$$

The following program solves the above three-level laser problem using the same relative units for the various rate coefficients and the convention that the values of $kT_a \equiv T1$, $kT_b \equiv T2$, and $kT_c \equiv T3$ are measured in the same units as the energy levels, $E1$, $E2$, and $E3$ (see Fig. 8-27). That is, once the rates R_{21}, R_{32}, and R_{31}

```
  1  REM 3-LEVEL LASER PROGRAM
 10  DIM R(2,2), T(2,2)
 20  DIM N(2), E(2)
100  PRINT "ENERGY LEVELS E1, E2, E3"
110  INPUT E1, E2, E3
120  PRINT "DEACTIVATION RATES R21, R32, R31"
130  INPUT R1, R2, R3
140  PRINT "TEMPERATURES T1, T2, T3"
145  INPUT T1, T2, T3
150  LET R(1, 1) = -R1 - R2*EXP((E2 - E3)/T2)
160  LET R(1, 2) = R2
170  LET R(2, 1) = R2*EXP((E2 - E3)/T2)
180  LET R(2, 2) = -R3 - R2
190  LET E(1) = -R1*EXP((E1 - E2)/T1)
200  LET E(2) = -R3*EXP((E1 - E3)/T3)
210  MAT T = INV(R)
220  MAT N = T*E
224  PRINT "GAIN OCCURS IF NUMBERS ARE >1"
225  PRINT "2- ->1", "3→1", "3- ->2"
230  PRINT N(1), N(2), N(2)/N(1)
240  GOTO 140
999  END
```

and the temperatures T1, T2, and T3 for the transfer rates are specified, the inverse rates are determined from detailed balancing [Eq. (25)]. The same technique could, of course, be applied to a large number of levels.

8.18
PROBLEM 12

In an early discussion of the laser potential of ruby, Schawlow (1960) commented (p. 557): "The two strongest lines (at 6919 Å and 6934 Å) go to the ground state, so that they will always have more atoms in their lower state, and are not suitable for maser action." [Maiman (1960) evidently did not believe that argument.] Show, by simulating a three-level laser system and suitable adjustment of the transfer rates and temperatures, that it *is* possible to invert such a system in respect to the ground state. [It should be noted that hindsight is always "20–20." Lots of people *circa* 1960 doubted that it would be possible to obtain laser oscillation on lines terminating in the ground state. Schawlow and his colleagues at the Bell Laboratories were, in fact, a close second in confirming laser oscillation in ruby.]

8.19
Laser Oscillators[28]

In rudimentary form, the laser oscillator consists of a pair of parallel mirrors separated by a medium that amplifies light (through the stimulated emission process).

These mirrors form an optical cavity (a Fabry–Perot interferometer) having resonant frequencies in the optical range, and this cavity provides the positive feedback required to produce oscillation in the amplifying media. The main resonances of the cavity are, in fact, similar to those for the open organ pipe discussed in Chapter 7. (However, the walls are essential in the organ pipe.)

If the gain in the medium is small compared to the loss at the mirrors (or if the mirrors are not there), the excited atoms merely radiate light in all directions through the spontaneous emission process.

However, if the gain in the medium is made large enough to compensate for the loss upon reflection at the ends, light emitted normal to the mirrors will start to grow in intensity and drain energy from the atoms in the medium that would normally be radiated spontaneously in the form of light through the side walls.

Finally, as the intensity continues to increase, a state of saturation is reached in which all the atoms are forced to radiate in the direction perpendicular to the mirrors. Because the mirrors are not 100 percent reflecting and have some nonzero transmission coefficient, a steady output beam is obtained from each end of the laser directly through the mirrors. This switching in direction of emission of the excited atoms as the laser crosses oscillation threshold is one of the most striking aspects of laser radiation.

Above threshold, the preservation of frequency in the stimulated emission process results also in all the atoms emitting at very nearly the same frequency—or on several discrete frequencies corresponding to different cavity resonances spaced (as with the open organ pipe) by $c/2L$, where c is the velocity of the running wave (here, that of light).

8.20
Diffraction

Because the normal cavity modes in a laser arise from diffraction effects, it is worthwhile reviewing some simple, well-known examples of diffraction.

---

[28] The idea of extending maser techniques to the optical domain was suggested by A. L. Schawlow and C. H. Townes (1958) and by Gordon Gould (who introduced the term "laser"). In 1958, Gould submitted a proposal to the Advanced Research Projects Agency to develop lasers for military purposes. The proposal was classified and through one of those strange ironies of fate, Gould himself was denied clearance to work on the problem.

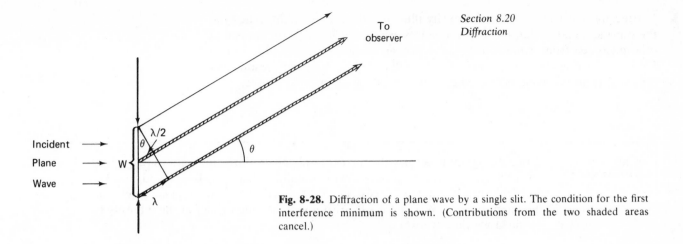

To observer

Incident →

Plane → W {

Wave →

λ/2

θ

θ

λ

Fig. 8-28. Diffraction of a plane wave by a single slit. The condition for the first interference minimum is shown. (Contributions from the two shaded areas cancel.)

Diffraction consists of the constructive and destructive interference of the amplitude of the wave. Thus, in summing up the total contribution at one distant point from an extended source, one must allow both for the $1/R^2$ attenuation of the energy ($1/R$ factor in the amplitude) and the fact that different multiples of the wavelength occur along the separate paths from various regions of the source to the point of observation. The net intensity at a particular point is obtained by squaring the total amplitude.

Thus, if one is infinitely far from a slit illuminated by a coherent plane-wave source, one sees interference minima at angles θ_m such that

$$\sin \theta_m = \frac{m\lambda}{W} \qquad \text{where } m = \pm 1, \pm 2, \pm 3, \dots$$

Here λ is the wavelength and W is the full slit width. The condition for destructive interference is easily understood by noting that for the angles, θ_m, the amplitude contributions to the diffraction integral from opposite halves of the slit cancel in pairs. For example, the two shaded regions shown in Fig. 8-28 for the case $m = 1$ give equal and opposite contributions because the optical path difference is $\lambda/2$. The diffraction integral for a single slit illuminated by a plane wave can be done in closed form in the *far-field case* (observer at infinity, or intensity observed at a constant angle). The result for the intensity as a function of angle θ is[29]

$$I(\theta) \propto \left| \frac{\sin\left[(\pi W/\lambda) \cdot \sin\theta\right]}{(\pi W/\lambda)\sin\theta} \right|^2 \tag{30}$$

where, again, W is the full slit width, λ is the wavelength of a plane-parallel light wave incident on the slit, and θ is the angular direction of the interference pattern with respect to the normal to the plane of the slit. Note that $I(\theta = 0)$ is a maximum because $\lim_{x \to 0}(\sin x / x) = 1$.

The only excuse for using a computer in this instance is to generate the closed-form solutions rapidly and see what they look like on a plotting device.

When a pair of parallel mirrors (Fabry–Perot interferometer) is illuminated by an expanding spherical wave, the resultant constructive interference patterns provide a series of concentric rings when viewed at a great distance (or as a function of angle). These constructive interference rings result for angles such that the wave front upon successive reflections inside the Fabry–Perot differ by integral multiples of the wavelength. Because the situation is symmetric in rotation about the direction of propogation, rings result. A central transmission maximum only occurs if L is a half-integral multiple of the wavelength.

[29] See, for example, Sears (1947, p. 187) for a derivation of Eq. (30).

Because the Fabry–Perot is normally illuminated by a source of light from the outside (i.e., the transmission resonances are similar to the resonances that one might see from a filter being driven by an audio oscillator), the normal Fabry–Perot rings have no simple direct relationship to the cavity resonances obtained from the same device when it is excited by an internal source.

8.20
PROBLEM 13

Write a program to display the far-field, single-slit diffraction pattern [Eq. (30)] on a teletype or other plotting device simultaneously for $W = \lambda$ and $w = 3\lambda$. Note that for $W \gg \lambda$ the fringes get closer together and the angular spread of the intensity narrows about $\theta = 0$. Also note that roughly half of the intensity is confined within $\pm \Delta\theta$ where

$$\Delta\theta \approx \frac{1.2\lambda}{W}$$

when the slit is illuminated by a uniform plane wave.

8.21
Laser Cavity Modes
(Integrodifferential Equations)

Because the actual amplification coefficients from most laser media are fairly small (typically several percent per meter for most gas lasers), it is necessary to use cavities that have a length L such that

$$L \gg \lambda \tag{31}$$

where λ is the wavelength of the light (at frequency c/λ). For visible light $\lambda \approx 5 \times 10^{-5}$ cm. Hence, for $L \approx 1$ m, as in the first gas laser, inequality (31) was well satisfied. (See Fig. 8-29.)

Normal microwave resonant cavities with closed side walls would have so many resonant modes per unit bandwidth as to look essentially like one continuous series of resonances in the limit (31). Consequently, there would not tend to be any *single* cavity resonance in those cases which would win out over all the others in the competition for stimulated emission of excited atoms in the amplifying medium. That is, all the cavity modes (which would represent propagation in all different directions as well as being very closely spaced in frequency) would tend to be excited, and no one of these modes would be able to suppress all the others.

For the above reasons, the open-side-wall structure of the Fabry–Perot interferometer was chosen for the early (and most subsequent) laser experiments.[30] The absence of reflective side walls eliminates the vast majority of resonant modes (of the type which, for example, would be found for sound waves in a living room of rectangular cross section large compared to a wavelength). It was thought on intuitive grounds that there would still be a few resonant modes spaced at $c/2L$ (≈ 150 MHz for $L = 1$ m) which would be analogous to the central transmission maxima in the passive Fabry–Perot interferometer. However, prior to 1960 there was no real evidence that such modes would actually exist.

The minute that the first laser went into oscillation, it was clear from an experimental point of view that such modes existed. However, the earliest theoretical work demonstrating the existence of such modes was done in a series of reiterative computer calculations by Fox and Li (1961) (see Fig. 8-30).

[30] For accuracy it should be noted that many subsequent lasers used a generalized type of Fabry–Perot interferometer containing curved (confocal, or confocal-equivalent) mirrors (see Boyd and Gordon, 1961).

Fig. 8-29. The first (helium–neon) gas laser, invented by A. Javan, W. R. Bennett, Jr., and D. R. Herriott at the Bell Telephone Laboratories in 1960. The discharge was excited by rf leads external to the 15-mm-bore quartz tube. The length of the device was about 1 m. The cw output beam was in the infrared at about 1.15 microns (μm) on five of the $4s \rightarrow 3p$ transitions shown in Fig. 8-25.

By direct numerical integration of the diffraction integral involved in going from one mirror aperture to the next, Fox and Li (1961) showed that the numerical machine solutions for the problem would eventually settle down on successive transits between the mirrors into a self-reproducing mode of the form

$$U_n^{t+1}(x, y) = \gamma_n U_n^t(x, y) \tag{32}$$

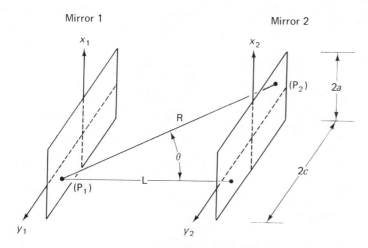

Fig. 8-30. Geometry used by Fox and Li (1961) to treat the diffraction problem between a pair of identical rectangular apertures.

425

where γ_n is a complex constant (eigenvalue)[31] and $U_n^t(x, y)$ represents the optical electric field distribution after the tth transit at the coordinates x and y on the mirror surface. The subscript n is introduced to emphasize that there is, in fact, a whole family of such mode distributions generally produced. The constant, γ_n, includes the diffraction loss in one transit as well as the phase shift (through the imaginary part). The modes have a definite symmetry, and the dominant one (into which most arbitrarily assumed initial field distributions will eventually decay) is even symmetric. Fox and Li (1961) showed that under fairly representative assumptions on cavity geometry, the two-dimensional mirror problem reduces to the product of two separate one-dimensional problems ("infinite-strip" mirrors), for which the form of the diffraction integral becomes[32]

$$U_n(x_2) = \frac{1}{\gamma_n} \int_{-1}^{+1} K(x_2, x_1) U_n(x_1) \, dx_1 \qquad (33)$$

where the term $K(x_2, x_1)$ is given by

$$K(x_2, x_1) \approx \sqrt{N} \, e^{i\pi/4} e^{-i\pi N(x_2 - x_1)^2}$$

and the geometrical phase shift is not included. $N = a^2/L\lambda$ is known as the *Fresnel number*; coordinates x_1 apply to the first aperture and x_2 to the second.

We shall next devise a program to do the integral in Eq. (33) reiteratively and thereby prove the existence of self-reproducing modes in a laser cavity. The only real trick in doing this is in keeping track of the complex quantities involved. That is, we must allow for phase and amplitude variation of the electric field across the aperture. Apart from the constants which may be pulled outside the integral in Eq. (33), the integrand contains a phase angle in the electric field and a phase angle in the diffraction "kernel" $K(x_2, x_1)$. These two phase angles may be lumped together:

$$K(x_2, x_1) U(x_1) = (\sqrt{N} e^{i\pi/4}) E(x_1) e^{i[F(x_1) - \pi N(x_2 - x_1)^2]} \qquad (34)$$

where $U(x_1) \equiv E(x_1) e^{iF(x_1)}$; the field amplitude and phase at the point x_1 are $E(x_1)$ and $F(x_1)$, respectively; and the term $(\sqrt{N} e^{i\pi/4})$ represents a constant that may be taken outside the integral. The integrand of Eq. (33) may then be reduced to the sum of its real and imaginary parts through use of the relation

$$e^{i\theta} = \cos\theta + i\sin\theta \qquad (35)$$

That is, we may rewrite the variable part of (34) as

$$E(x_1) \cos[F(x_1) - \pi N(x_2 - x_1)^2] + iE(x_1) \sin[F(x_1) - \pi N(x_2 - x_1)^2] \qquad (36)$$

We shall use the index I to describe the location across the first aperture and the index J is used to describe the location of the point on the second aperture where the field is specifically being computed. The real (G) and imaginary parts (H) may then be summed separately across the aperture over index I at each point J on the second aperture and the final sums used to calculate one net phase angle through a computer program statement of the type,

$$\text{LET B(J)} = \text{ATN(H/G)} \qquad (37)$$

8.22
Program To Determine the Infinite-Strip Laser Cavity Modes

---

[31] As used here, γ_n is the reciprocal of the Fox and Li eigenvalue.

[32] For a more detailed derivation of the integrals involved in the computer problem see Bennett (1969). Equation (33) will be recognized by the initiated as a "homogeneous integral equation of the second kind." The eigenfunctions for this integrodifferential equation satisfy a non-Hermitian orthogonality relation, and the mathematicians have still not formally demonstrated the existence of solutions to it in a completely general way [see, for example, the discussion in Hildebrand (1965, Chap. 3)].

where one has to be careful to get the quadrant correctly. The modulus of the final integral is then given by

A(J) = SQR(G*G + H*H)

or the square root of the sum of the squares of the real and imaginary parts.

The symmetry properties of the diffraction integral may be used to reduce computing time. As may be seen from Eq. (33), if a wave of definite even- or odd-symmetry is launched at one aperture, that symmetry is preserved at the second aperture. Hence, if we want the dominant even-symmetry mode ($U \equiv +1$), we know that the solutions for the lower half of the aperture will be equal to those for the upper half; if we want the dominant odd-symmetric solution ($U \equiv -1$), we know that the fields for the lower half will be (-1) times those for the upper half. Thus

$$E(-x) = (+1)E(+x) \qquad \text{(even symmetry)}$$
$$E(-x) = (-1)E(+x) \qquad \text{(odd symmetry)}$$

and we only have to integrate numerically over half the aperture. These two symmetry cases may be contained in the single statement

E(-x) = U*E(+x)

by letting $U = +1$ for the even-symmetric case and $U = -1$ for the odd-symmetric case. Hence, after some initial dimension statements to handle the field amplitudes and phases at the first and second apertures,

```
1   REM PROGRAM FOR INFINITE-STRIP MODES
2   DIM E[200], F(200), A(200), B(200)
```

we specify the Fresnel number, N, and symmetry of the modes we want to calculate. The (even) number of numerical integration intervals, P, needed for doing the computation to a given accuracy also is entered, and should be increased roughly as the square of the Fresnel number for a constant fractional error:

```
15   REM SYMMETRIC MODE HAS U = +1, ANTISYMMETRIC MODE HAS U = −1
20   PRINT "ENTER N, P, U"
21   LET T = 0
30   INPUT N, P, U
32   LET P1 = (P/2 + 1)
33   LET P2 = P + 1
40   LET K0 = 3.14159*N*(2/P)↑2
```

Here, *P1* is the midpoint of the aperture and we shall denote the points across the aperture by integers ranging from 1 through *P2*. Specifically,

$$x_1 = (I - 1)2/P - 1 \quad \text{and} \quad x_2 = (J - 1)2/P - 1$$

where *I* and *J* are integers, and $\Delta x_1 = \Delta I \, 2/P = 2/P$.

The constant *K0* is defined to simplify the numerical integration and avoid repeated evaluation of constant quantities within the integration loop.

The initial field distribution across the aperture is then assumed (e.g., constant for $U = +1$, square wave for $U = -1$).

```
50   FOR I = P1 TO P2
60   LET E(I) = 1
65   LET F(I) = 0
70   NEXT I
80   FOR I = 1 TO (P1 − 1)
83   LET E(P1 − I) = U*E(P1 + I)
87   LET F(P1 − I) = F(P1 + I)
90   NEXT I
```

If a convenient plotting device is available, it will be helpful to display the initial choice of the field as a function of aperture position before going on to do the first diffraction integral.

```
100   REM PLOT OR PRINT AMPLITUDE DISTRIBUTION HERE
```

The diffraction integral is then done for point J on the second aperture by summing over points I on the first aperture (and the result could be plotted one point at a time while computing the integral).

```
200   PRINT "LOSS(EIGENVALUE)";"LOSS(FIELD)","PHASE EIGENVAL.(RADIANS)"
300   REM REITERATE TO HERE; INTEGRATE REAL+IMAG.PARTS EQS. (33), (34):
400   FOR J=P1 TO P2
410     LET G=H=0
420     FOR I=1 TO P2−1
430       LET K=K0*(J−I)↑2
440       LET G=G+E(I)*COS(F(I)−K)          [real part of Eq. (36)]
450       LET H=H+E(I)*SIN(F(I)−K)          [imaginary part of Eq. (36)]
460     NEXT I
465   REM TRAPEZOIDAL RULE CORRECTION NEXT
470     LET K1=K0*(J−1)↑2
475     LET K2=K0*(J−P2)↑2
480     LET G=G+.5*(E(P2)*COS(F(P2)−K2)−E(1)*COS(F(1)−K1))
485     LET H=H+.5*(E(P2)*SIN(F(P2)−K2)−E(1)*SIN(F(1)−K1))
490     LET G=G*SQR(N)*2/P
495     LET H=H*SQR(N)*2/P
500     LET A(J)=SQR(G*G+H*H)
505     REM AVOID SINGULARITY (G=0), GET RIGHT QUADRANT, ADD PI/4 EQ. (34)
510     IF G≠0 THEN 530
515     LET B(J)=−1.57080+.785398   ⎫
520     IF H>0 THEN 540             ⎪
525     GOTO 545                    ⎬   [arctangent problem+π/4 from Eq. (34)]
530     LET B(J)= ATN(H/G)+.785398  ⎪
535     IF G>0 THEN 545             ⎪
540     LET B(J)=B(J)+3.14159       ⎭
545     IF B(J)<3.14159 THEN 565    ⎫
550     LET B(J)=B(J)−6.28328       ⎬  (keeps angle from getting too large)
560     GOTO 545                    ⎭
565     REM PLOT OR PRINT A(J),B(J) HERE
570   NEXT J
```

(The indentation in program statements is merely to clarify the operations within the nested loops.) Note that lines 400 through 570 do the diffraction integral for the positive half of the aperture. In this computation, the original field amplitude and phase at the first aperture are stored in $E(I)$ and $F(I)$, respectively, and the new field and phase at the second aperture are stored in $A(J)$ and $B(J)$, respectively. Lines 510 through 540 are used merely to get the quadrant correctly on the phase angle of the computed field and to add the extra $\pi/4$ from the constant exponent in Eq. (34).

We next determine the field on the lower half of the second aperture from symmetry by the statement

```
580   GOSUB 900
```

where subroutine 900 consists of the statements

```
900   REM SUB GETS DIFF. INTEGRAL FOR LOWER APERTURE FROM SYMMETRY
905   FOR J=1 TO P1−1
910   LET A(P1−J)=U*A(P1+J)
920   LET B(P1−J)=B(P1+J)
925   REM PLOT OR PRINT A(P1−J), B(P1−J) HERE
930   NEXT J
940   RETURN
```

This subroutine could be used to plot or print the field distribution across the lower portion of the second aperture on line 925.

Continuing with the main program, we increment the transit counter (T) and find the maximum amplitude (M) of the electric field at the second aperture and the phase (O) at the maximum location:

```
590   LET T = T + 1
600   LET M = A(P1)
610   FOR I = P1 TO P2
620   IF ABS(M) > ABS(A(I)) THEN 640
630   LET M = A(I)
635   LET O = B(I)
640   NEXT I
645   IF U = -1 THEN 660
650   LET O = B(P1)
660   GOSUB 800
```

Subroutine 800 calculates the square of the magnitude of the eigenvalue (L) and the phase of the eigenvalue (Z). (Strictly speaking, the quantity L is only simply related to the eigenvalue after the field settles down to the self-reproducing condition.) The subroutine also computes the total energy loss by direct integration of the square of the electric field across the first and second apertures. The energy loss ($1-L$) computed from the eigenvalue, the energy loss directly computed by integrating the field intensities across the first and second apertures, and the phase (Z) of the eigenvalue are also printed out in subroutine 800 for each transit (T).

```
800   LET L = 0
805   LET W = .5*(E(P1)↑2 - E(P2)↑2)
810   LET Z = 0
815   LET X = .5*(A(P1)↑2 - A(P2)↑2)
820   FOR I = (1 + P1) TO P2
830   LET L = L + (2/P)*(A(I)/E(I))↑2
840   LET Z = Z + (2/P)*(B(I) - F(I))
850   LET W = W + E(I)↑2
860   LET X = X + A(I)↑2
870   NEXT I
880   PRINT 1 - L, 1 - X/W, Z, T
885   RETURN
```

Note that when the field actually settles down to a self-reproducing form, the quantity $\sqrt{L}$ becomes the magnitude of the eigenvalue for the mode and the loss from this eigenvalue ($1-L$) at that point becomes equal to the actual diffraction loss per transit ($1-X/W$), where $\int A^2\, dx / \int E^2\, dx = X/W$ in the program above. Hence one may introduce a simple conditional statement after line 880 to determine whether or not the mode has settled down to self-reproducing form simply by comparing L with X/W. If those two quantities agree within some specified numerical accuracy, the mode has become self-reproducing for the purposes of the program, and the final results can be printed out. Otherwise, one must continue reiteratively solving the diffraction integral.

Continuing with the main program, the statement

```
670   GOSUB 1000
```

sends the program to a subroutine that sets the column array, $E(I)$, used to describe the field over the first aperture, equal to the normalized field, $A(I)/M$, just computed from the diffraction integral and redefines the phase of the field in respect to the phase at the point of maximum amplitude. This normalization of the field and redefinition of the phase serves a dual purpose: it makes it easier to compare the field on successive transits; it also ensures that the field and phase remain within the domain of variables that can be treated by the

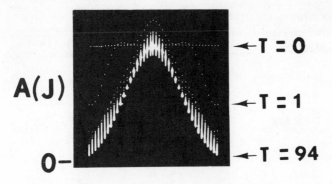

Fig. 8-31. Superposition of field amplitude distribution on successive transits for the infinite-strip-mode problem when a uniform plane wave is launched at $T = 0$. A Fresnel number of unity was assumed, and the amplitude distributions $A(J)$ across the full aperture are shown. The maximum value of the field across the first aperture was normalized to unity in each case, to facilitate the comparison. After a few wildly gyrating distributions (note the case after the first transit, denoted by $T = 1$), the field begins to settle down to a more and more closely self-reproducing form. By the ninety-fourth transit, it is hard to notice any visual difference for the mode distribution in going from one transit to the next.

computer (i.e., otherwise the field amplitude would continue to decrease exponentially and the phase would build up linearly with the transit number).

```
1000   FOR I = 1 TO P2
1010   LET E(I) = A(I)/M
1015   IF E(I) = 0 THEN 1030
1020   LET F(I) = B(I) − 0
1025   GOTO 1040
1030   LET F(I) = 0
1040   NEXT I
1050   RETURN
```

The program then reiterates through statement

```
 680   GOTO 300
9999   END
```

As may be seen by running the program above for different choices of Fresnel number and initial symmetry of the field at $T = 0$, the solutions for the diffraction pattern do eventually settle down into self-reproducing distributions after a large number of transits. Figures 8-31 and 8-32 show a superposition of

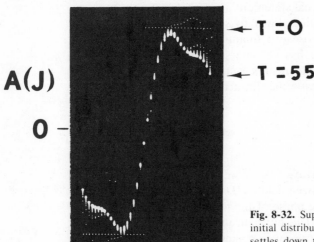

Fig. 8-32. Superposition of successive field distributions when an odd-symmetric initial distribution is launched at $T = 0$ for the conditions in figure. Here, the field settles down to a self-reproducing form much more quickly than in the even-symmetric case.

field amplitudes for successive transits when even- (Fig. 8-31) and odd- (Fig. 8-32) symmetric initial field distributions were launched at $T = 0$.

The wild fluctuations in both figures at the start of the problem are closely associated with the presence of a set of higher-order, more rapidly decaying modes. In both figures we are doing something quite analogous to the expansion of a square wave in a Fourier series. In the present problem we are, in effect, expanding the initial square amplitude distribution at $T = 0$ in the set of self-reproducing modes. Because the higher-order modes (ones having more nodes across the aperture) have higher loss coefficients, they decay more rapidly. The computer solutions will always tend to die down into either the dominant even-symmetric, or dominant odd-symmetric, modes. However, the presence of the fluctuations is a clear indication that other modes exist.

**8.22
PROBLEM 14**

Write a program to compute the dominant-mode eigenvalues and field distributions for even- and odd-symmetric infinite-strip self-reproducing modes. Compute the power loss for these two dominant modes for $N = 1$ and $N = 2$, and compare the results with the loss for a uniform plane wave launched from the same aperture. Use 40 integration points across the aperture.† Assume that the mode is "self-reproducing" when the loss calculated from the eigenvalue agrees within 1 percent of that determined by integrating the field intensity.

**8.22
PROBLEM 15**

Boyd and Gordon (1961) showed that the mode distributions on the mirror surfaces of a square aperture confocal mirror cavity were approximately given by

$$E_{m,n}(x, y) \propto f_m(x) f_n(y)$$

where the functions $f_m(x)$ and $f_n(y)$ are of the form

$$f_m(x) = H_m\left[(2\pi N)^{1/2} \frac{x}{a} \right] \exp\left[-\pi N \left(\frac{x}{a} \right)^2 \right] \qquad \text{(a)}$$

Here $2a$ is the full width of the square aperture in the x and y directions, the $H_m(z)$ are Hermite polynomials, and $N = a^2 / R\lambda$ is the Fresnel number (R is the common radius of curvature of the two mirrors and is equal to the mirror separation). Equation (a) is analogous to the field distribution of the Fox and Li infinite-strip modes found in the plane-parallel mirror geometry.

The most economical way to compute the Hermite polynomials $H_m(z)$ of order m and argument z is through their dependence on the confluent hypergeometric functions. It may be shown that‡

$$H_m(z) = \begin{cases} (-1)^{m/2} \dfrac{m!}{(m/2)!} F\left(-\dfrac{m}{2}, \dfrac{1}{2}, z^2 \right) & \text{for } m = 0, 2, 4, 6, \dots \\[2ex] 2(-1)^{(m-1)/2} \dfrac{m!}{[\frac{1}{2}(m-1)]!} \, z F\left(-\dfrac{m-1}{2}, \dfrac{3}{2}, z^2 \right) & \text{for } m = 1, 3, 5, 7, \dots \end{cases} \qquad \text{(b)}$$

where the confluent hypergeometric functions $F(b, c, z^2)$ are given by the series

$$F(b, c, z^2) = 1 + \frac{b}{c} z^2 + \frac{b(b+1)}{2! c(c+1)} z^4 + \frac{b(b+1)(b+2)}{3! c(c+1)(c+2)} z^6 + \cdots \qquad \text{(c)}$$

which terminates on the first term $= 0$.

---

† The above problem can, of course be done for larger values of Fresnel number (N). However, the number of integration points over the aperture must be increased with N to maintain calculational accuracy, and the running time will increase roughly as N^2. Also note that the

Defining a generalized mirror coordinate, $X1 \equiv (x/a)\sqrt{2\pi N}$, write a program to compute and plot the one-dimensional field distribution $f_m(X1)$ from Eq. (a) over the range $0 \leqslant X1 \leqslant 4$ for m input from the terminal, using subroutines based on Eqs. (b) and (c).

---

properties of a real rectangular aperture will involve the product of two infinite-strip-mode solutions in the orthogonal aperture coordinates. Thus the eigenvalue for a square aperture with $N_x = N_y = 1$ will be given by the product of two separate infinite-strip eigenvalues; in this case, the total field would be the product of the two separate fields. Fox and Li (1961) also treated the circular-aperture problem and showed that these solutions were equivalent to linear combinations of square-aperture modes.

‡ See, for example, Morse and Feshbach (1953); however, there is a misprint in the expression for the odd-order Hermite polynomials in this reference. Also see the discussion in Bennett, Jr. (1969, 1970).

The introduction of gain by the amplifying medium in the laser cavity shifts the oscillation frequency from one of the cavity resonant frequencies (ν_c) to another frequency (ν_0) such that the net phase shift per pass through the cavity is still an integral multiple of π. That is, we still have standing waves generated within the cavity when the laser oscillates (just as within the open organ pipe), but their resonant frequencies are shifted slightly by phase shifts introduced by the amplifying medium.

It may be shown that the oscillation frequency is given by

$$\nu_0 = \nu_c - \frac{\Delta\nu_c}{f}\Delta\phi_m(\nu_0) \tag{38}$$

where $\Delta\nu_c$ is the full width of the cavity resonance in the absence of the medium, $f =$ fractional energy loss per pass, and $\Delta\phi_m(\nu_0)$ is the change in single-pass phase shift at the oscillation frequency introduced by the presence of the amplifying medium. The cavity width is given by standard "Q arguments" through the relation

$$\Delta\nu_c = \frac{f}{\pi}\left(\frac{c}{2L}\right) \tag{39}$$

where $c =$ velocity of light and $L =$ length of the laser cavity.

The gain profile in the absence of oscillation is given by an approximately Gaussian shape,

$$G(\nu) \approx G_0 \exp\left(-\left[\frac{\nu_m - \nu}{0.6\Delta\nu_D}\right]^2\right) \tag{40}$$

which is due to the Doppler shifts resultant from the atoms' thermal velocity distribution. Here $\Delta\nu_D$ is the full width for Doppler broadening and is typically ≈ 2000 MHz at room temperature for transitions in the visible spectrum. G_0 is the gain coefficient at the center of the line ($\nu = \nu_m$).

It may be shown that the phase shift from the Gaussian gain curve in Eq. (40) is given by

$$\Delta\phi_g^{(\nu)} = -\frac{G(\nu)}{\sqrt{\pi}} \int_0^{(\nu_m-\nu)/0.6\Delta\nu_D} e^{x^2} dx \tag{41}$$

At oscillation threshold, $G(\nu) = f$, and the threshold oscillation frequency is given from Eqs. (38), (39), and (40) by letting $\Delta\phi_m(\nu) = \Delta\phi_g(\nu)$. Thus, at threshold, the oscillation frequency is given by the formidable transcendental equation

$$\nu_0 = \nu_c + \frac{\Delta\nu_c}{\sqrt{\pi}} G_0 e^{-[(\nu_m-\nu_0)/0.6\Delta\nu_D]^2} \int_0^{(\nu_m-\nu_0)/0.6\Delta\nu_D} e^{x^2} dx \tag{42}$$

[33] A more detailed discussion of the material in this section has been given by Bennett (1969).

Above threshold, life is still more complicated. Because the region of interaction (approximately equal to what is commonly known as the *Lorentz width* or *natural width*) between the optical field and the excited atoms is much smaller than the Doppler width, localized distortions (*holes*) are burned in the gain curve.

8.24 Hole-Burning Effects

For steady-state oscillation, the actual gain in the presence of the oscillation must be reduced to the fractional energy loss—hence threshold value. (If the gain were less than the loss, the laser would not oscillate. If the gain were greater than the loss, the intensity would keep building up and we would not have reached steady state.) Hence, as was first pointed out by the author (Bennett, 1962), the steady-state requirement in the typical gas laser,

$$G_{\text{actual}}(\nu_{\text{osc}}) = f \equiv \text{cavity loss per pass} \qquad (43)$$

is achieved above threshold by burning a hole in the line. A localized reduction in the original gain coefficient to the threshold value occurs as shown in Fig. 8-33. The direct interaction is, of course, with the atoms in the velocity distribution. However, there is a direct correspondence between distortion in the velocity distribution of the atoms and the resultant distortion in the gain profile.

The actual situation in a single-mode gas laser is somewhat more complicated, owing to the existence of standing waves in the laser cavity. For each resonant frequency there are running waves traveling in opposite directions. If the frequency of the standing wave is detuned from the resonance frequency (ν_m) of the atom at rest, these two running waves interact with different portions of the velocity distribution, owing to the Doppler effect. Specifically, a running wave moving in the $+z$ direction with frequency $\nu > \nu_m$ will interact with atoms with velocity v_z in the vicinity of

$$v_z = +\lambda(\nu - \nu_m)$$

and the running wave with this same frequency moving in the $-z$ direction will

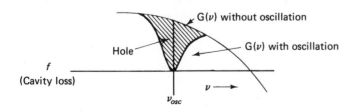

Fig. 8-33. Hole burned in gain curve of Doppler-broadened laser transition to satisfy steady-state requirement above threshold.

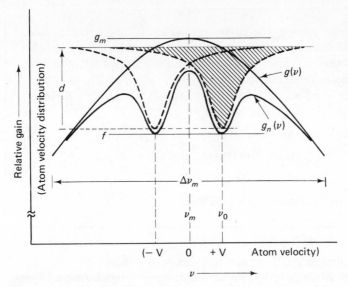

Fig. 8-34. Single-pass gain curve for one oscillation frequency at ν_0 in the limit that the two Lorentzian holes of depth d begin to overlap. Here $g(\nu)$ represents the fractional energy gain per pass in the absence of oscillation, $g_A(\nu)$ represents the actual gain in the presence of the oscillation and f represents the fractional energy loss per pass. The power output in the $+z$ direction is proportional to the shaded area in the diagram for $\nu_0 > \nu_m$. The power can decrease by a factor approaching 2 as the laser is tuned through line center. (From Bennett, 1963.)

interact with atoms with velocity v_z in the vicinity of

$$v_z = -\lambda(\nu - \nu_m)$$

Consequently, there are two holes burnt in the gain curve when the frequency ν is detuned substantially from the center of the line (see Fig. 8-34).

The total reduction in gain at each gain hole is made up by contributions from the two separate interactions. If we let d stand for the depth of the gain hole due to the interaction with *one* running wave alone, the condition for steady state in the standing-wave case (see Fig. 8-34) is given by

$$d\left[1 + \frac{1}{1 + [2(\nu_m - \nu_{osc})/\Delta\nu_L]^2}\right] = G(\nu_{osc}) - f \qquad (44)$$

where $\Delta\nu_L$ is the Lorentz width for the transition. The total power out of the oscillator in each running wave is proportional to d. That is, the gain reduction is accomplished by stimulated emission at the laser frequency. Hence the power out of the single-mode gas laser varies as

$$P \propto d = \frac{G(\nu_{osc}) - f}{1 + \{1 + [2(\nu_m - \nu_{osc})/\Delta\nu_L]^2\}^{-1}} \qquad (45)$$

a result that was presented by the author at the Paris 1963 Conference on Quantum Electronics (Bennett, 1963). This result is precisely the same as that obtained by Lamb from his third-order theory (Lamb, 1964), also described at the Paris conference. That is, the power can go down by a factor approaching 2 as the laser is tuned through line center. The effect is commonly known throughout the laser literature as the *Lamb dip*.[34]

---

[34] The mathematical prediction of this dip was first given by Willis Lamb (private communication to the author in the spring of 1962) and discussed in substantial detail in Lamb (1964). The physical interpretation of the dip based on hole-burning effects was first given by the author in a private communication to Lamb in July 1962. The hole-burning interpretation was described in more detail in Bennett (1962a, 1963, 1969).

The tuning dip was initially reported in experimental observation by McFarlane et al. (1963) using a short magnetostrictively tuned helium–neon laser at 1.15 μm. The dip and its pressure dependence were subsequently studied in considerable detail on this transition by Szöke and Javan (1963, 1966) and it has now become a well-known phenomenon in large ·numbers of gas-laser transitions. Because the width of the dip is much narrower than the full Doppler profile, it has provided a powerful means for the frequency stabilization of gas lasers near the center of the spontaneous emission line.

8.24
PROBLEM 17

The first gas laser had a Doppler width ($\Delta\nu_D$) of ≈ 900 MHz, a cavity loss of ≈ 1 percent per meter, a peak gain of 4 percent per meter, and a pressure-broadened Lorentz width ($\Delta\nu_L$) of ≈ 100 MHz. Compute the shape of the Lamb dip from Eqs. (40) and (45) as ν_{osc} is tuned across the center of the line. Plot the result on the teletype terminal or high resolution display device.

In order to determine the oscillation frequency of the single-mode laser above threshold, one must allow for the changes in phase shift produced by the holes in the gain curve. In particular, for one mode above threshold, Eq. (38) becomes

$$\nu_0 = \nu_c - \frac{\Delta\nu_c}{f}(\Delta\phi_g + \Delta\phi_h) \qquad (46)$$

where the phase-shift coefficient has been broken up into two parts. The first, $\Delta\phi_g$, represents the phase shift due to the original line profile in the absence of oscillation [Eq. (41)]. The other, $\Delta\phi_h$, represents the phase shift produced by the holes in the gain curve. In the limit $\Delta\nu_L \ll \Delta\nu_D$, the holes in the gain profile are Lorentzian and the phase shift produced at frequency ν_0 by a hole at ν may be shown to be of the form

$$\Delta\phi_h(\nu_0) = +\frac{d(\nu - \nu_0)/2\Delta\nu_L}{1 + (\nu - \nu_0)^2/(\Delta\nu_L)^2} \qquad (47)$$

Because this expression is an odd function of the frequency difference from the hole center, there is no phase shift at the center of one gain hole due to itself. That is, the entire contribution to the phase shift from gain holes at one hole location is due to the other (*mirror image*) hole in the limit that $\Delta\nu_L \ll \Delta\nu_D$. Note that the two holes in single-mode operation are spaced by $2(\nu_{osc} - \nu_m)$ (see Fig. 8-34). Hence the phase shift at the oscillator frequency (ν_0) due to the mirror-image hole at $\nu = 2\nu_m - \nu_0$ is

$$\Delta\phi_h(\nu_0) = \frac{(\nu_m - \nu_0)d/\Delta\nu_L}{1 + [2(\nu_0 - \nu_m)/\Delta\nu_L]^2} \qquad (48)$$

Combining Eqs. (44), (46), and (48) yields a still more formidable transcendental equation for the oscillator frequency.

8.24
PROBLEM 18

Using Eqs. (39)–(41), (44), (46), and (48), write a program to compute and print the single-mode frequency-tuning characteristic (ν_0 vs. ν_c) for the helium–neon laser described in Problem 17. Assume that $\Delta\nu_l = 100$ MHz and note that $G_0/f = 4$. [*Hint:* Compute ν_c from ν_0 over the range where $G(\nu)/f > 1$. Use steps of 20 MHz.]

Basov, N. G. and A. M. Prokhorov (1955). "O Vozmozhnie Metodah Poluchenia Aktevnie Molekul Dlia Molekuliarnogo Generatora," *Zhurnal Eksperimentalnoi i Teoreticheskoi Fiziki*, Vol. 28, pp. 249–250. Moscow: Akademia Nayuk.

Bennett, W. R., Jr. (1962a). "Gaseous Optical Masers." *Appl. Optics Suppl. Optical Masers*, pp. 24–61.

Bennett, W. R., Jr. (1962b). "Hole Burning Effects in a He–Ne Optical Maser." *Phys. Rev.*, Vol. 126 (Apr. 15), pp. 580–593.

Bennett, W. R., Jr. (1963). "Relaxation Mechanisms, Dissociative Excitation Transfer and Mode Pulling Effects in Gas Lasers." *Quantum Electronics Paris 1963 Conference*, Vol. 1), edited by Grivet and Bloembergen. New York: Columbia University Press, 1964, pp. 441–458.

Bennett, W. R., Jr. (1965). "Inversion Mechanisms in Gas Lasers," *Chemical Lasers*, pp. 3–33, edited by Shuler and Bennett, Washington, D.C.: Optical Society of America.

Bennett, W. R., Jr. (1969). "Some Aspects of the Physics of Gas Lasers" in *Brandeis Summer Institute in Theoretical Physics (1969)*, *Atomic Physics and Astrophysics*, Vol. 2 (edited by Lipworth and Chretien), New York: Gordon and Breach, pp. 3–201. Also published as *The Physics of Gas Lasers (1977)* by Gordon and Breach.

Bennett, W. R., Jr. (1970). "Theory of Cavity-Mode-Mixing Effects in Internally Scanned Lasers." *Phys. Rev. A:* Vol. 2, pp. 458–490.

Bennett, W. R., Jr. (1964), A. Javan, and D. R. Herriott, U.S. Patent 3,149,290 (Sept. 15), Gas Optical Maser. (Filed, Dec. 1960).

Bennett, W. R., Sr. (1970). *Introduction to Signal Transmission.* New York: McGraw-Hill Book Company.

Black, H. S. (1934). "Stabilized Feedback Amplifiers", *Electronic Engineering*, Vol. 53, pp. 114–120.

Bloembergen, N., (1956). "Proposal for a New Type Solid State Maser," *Physical Review*, Vol. 104, p. 324.

Bode, H. W. (1945). *Network Analysis and Feedback Amplifier Design.* New York: Van Nostrand, Reinhold Company.

Boyd, G. D., and J. P. Gordon (1961). "Confocal Multimode Resonator for Millimeter Through Optical Wavelength Masers." *Bell System Tech. J.*, Vol. 40, p. 489.

Butayeva, F. A. and V. A. Fabrikant (1959). *G. N. Landsberg Memorial Volume*, Moscow, Lebedev Institute, pp. 62–70.

Dolby, R. M. (1967). "An Audio Noise Reduction System" *J. Audio. Eng. Soc.*, Vol. 15, p. 383.

Dolby, R. M. (1968). "Audio Noise Reduction: Some Practical Aspects." *Audio*, June and July.

Einstein, Albert (1917). "Zur Quantentheorie der Strahlung." *Phys. Z.* Vol. 18, pp. 121–128. See English translation in *Laser Theory* edited by F. S. Barnes, New York: IEEE Press; pp. 5–21.

Evenson, K. M., J. S. Wells, F. R. Petersen, B. L. Danielson, G. W. Day, R. L. Barger, and J. L. Hall (1972). "Speed of Light from Direct Frequency and Wavelength Measurements of the Methane Stabilized Laser." *Phys. Rev. Letters*, Vol. 29 (Nov. 6), p. 1346.

Fabrikant, V. A., M. M. Vudynskii, and F. A. Butayeva (1962), "A Method for the Amplification of Elect.omagnetic Radiation," USSR Inventor's Certificate No. 148441 issued June 18, 1951, but not numbered or published until 1962.

FLETCHER, H. (1940). "Stereophonic Reproduction from Film." *J. Soc. Motion Picture Eng.*, Vol. 34, pp. 606–613.

FORD, H. (1974). Reviews of current companders. *Studio Sound* (March), pp. 46–56.

FOX, A. G., AND T. LI (1961). "Resonant Modes in a Maser Interferometer." *Bell System Tech. J.*, Vol. 40, p. 453.

GAYTHORPE, N. (1971). "Breakthrough? 3" *Light* (London), Vol. 91, pp. 69–73.

GORDON, J. P., H. J. ZEIGER AND C. H. TOWNES (1954). "Molecular Microwave Oscillator and New Hyperfine Structure in the Microwave Spectrum of NH_3." *Phys. Rev.*, Vol. 95, p. 282.

GOULD, G. (1958). Unpublished (classified) proposal to ARPA.

GOULD, GORDON (1965). "Collision Lasers," in *Chemical Lasers*, pp. 59–67, edited by Shuler and Bennett, Washington, D.C.: Optical Society of America.

HEADRICK, L. B. AND O. S. DUFFENDACK (1931). "Collisions of the Second Kind and Their Effect on the Field in the Positive Column of a Glow Discharge in Mixtures of the Rare Gases." *Phys. Rev.*, Vol. 37, p. 736.

HILDEBRAND, F. B. (1965). *Methods of Applied Mathematics*. Englewood Cliffs, N.J.: Prentice-Hall, Inc.

JAVAN, A., W. R. BENNETT, JR., AND D. R. HERRIOTT (1961). "Population Inversion and Continuous Optical Maser Action in a Helium Neon Mixture." *Phys. Rev. Letters*, Vol. 6, pp. 106–110.

JAVAN, A., W. R. BENNETT, JR., AND D. R. HERRIOTT (1971). U.S. Patent 3,614,653 (Oct. 19), Optical Maser. (Filed, May 1963.)

KRAMERS, H. A. (1927). *Atti. Congr. Intern. Fisici*, Vol. 2, p. 545; reproduced in *H. A. Kramers: Collected Scientific Papers*, Amsterdam: North-Holland Publishing Co., 1956, "La Diffusion de la lumière par les atomes," pp. 333–345.

KRONIG, R. DE L. (1926). "On the Theory of Dispersion of X-Rays." *J. Opt. Soc. America*, Vol. 12, pp. 547–557.

LAMB, WILLIS E., JR. (1964). "Theory of an Optical Maser." *Phys. Rev.*, Vol. 134, pp. A1429–A1450.

MAIMAN, THEODORE H., (1960). "Stimulated Optical Radiation in Ruby," *Nature* Vol. 187, pp. 493–494.

McFARLANE, R. A., W. R. BENNETT, JR., AND W. E. LAMB, JR. (1963). "Single Mode Tuning Dip in the Power Output of an He–Ne Optical Maser." *Appl. Phys. Letters*, Vol. 2 (May 15), p. 189.

McKENZIE, A. (1974). Reviews of current companders. *Studio Sound* (March), pp. 56–64.

MORSE, P. H. AND FESHBACH, H., (1953). *Methods of Theoretical Physics*. New York: McGraw-Hill Book Company.

NYQUIST, HARRY, (1932). "Regeneration Theory." Bell System Technical Journal, Vol. 11, pp. 126–147.

RAUDIVE, K. (1971). *Breakthrough*. London: Colin Smythe Ltd.

SCHAWLOW, A. L. (1960). "Optical and Infrared Masers" in *Quantum Electronics*, edited by Charles Townes. New York: Columbia University Press, pp. 553–563.

SCHAWLOW, A. L., AND C. H. TOWNES (1958). "Infrared and Optical Masers." *Phys. Rev.*, Vol. 112, p. 1940.

SEARS, F. W. (1947). *Principles of Physics*: Vol. III, *Optics*. Reading, Mass.: Addison-Wesley Publishing Company, Inc.

STOKOWSKI, L. (1943). *Music for All of Us*. New York: Simon and Shuster.

437

SzÖKE, A., AND A. JAVAN (1963). "Isotope Shift and Saturation Behavior of the 1.15 μ. Transition of Ne." *Phys. Rev. Letters*, Vol. 10 (June 15), p. 521.

SzÖKE, A., AND A. JAVAN (1966). "Effects of Collisions on Saturation Behavior of the 1.15 μ. Transition of Ne Studied with He–Ne Laser." Phys. Rev., Vol. 145 (May 6), p. 137.

THOMAS, D. E. (1947). "Tables of Phase of a Semi-infinite Unit Attenuation Slope." *Bell System Tech. J.*, Vol. 26, p. 870.

WEBER, J. (1965). "Introductory Remarks: Lasers and Free Electron Amplifiers." In a special issue on *The Laser* (edited by Leon Goldman and Joseph Weber) in *Ann. N.Y. Acad. Sci.*, Vol. 122, pp. 571–578.

ZELINGER, G. (1963). *Basic Matrix Algebra and Transistor Circuits*. Elmsford, N.Y.: Pergamon Press, Inc.

Appendix

Summary of common BASIC commands and programming statements*

SYSTEM COMMANDS

(entered from terminal and followed by carriage return)

RUN	Computer starts to run program
STOP	Computer stops running program
LIST	Computer lists program on terminal
SCRATCH	Computer erases program

(individual systems have various specialized commands such as

REN	renumber lines in steps of 1∅
REN 2, 1∅, 2∅∅, 3∅∅	renumber lines in steps of 2 from line 1∅ through 2∅∅ and start result as line 3∅∅
LIST, 2∅∅, 25∅	list the lines from 2∅∅ to 25∅.
DEL 2∅∅, 3∅∅	delete lines 2∅∅ through 3∅∅, etc.

plus other specialized commands for reading (PTAPE) and punching (PLIST) programs on tape, reading and writing files on discs, and more powerful editing operations)

(Escape key usually permits telling computer to ignore characters typed prior to carriage return).

COMPUTER REPLIES

READY	computer is ready to accept program statements or RUN in BASIC. *10, 11*
?	computer is waiting for input data plus a carriage return from terminal *6, 13*

(error diagnostic messages that are self-explanatory or follow a simple convention provided by the computer service)

COMMON BASIC PROGRAM STATEMENTS

(entered after the line number, from the terminal and followed by a carriage return; statements are cancelled by typing line number and carriage return).

REM	Remark, ignored by the computer when program runs; useful to remind one of purpose of program or segment *21, 23, 26, 109, 163, 177, 261, 262, 316–18*

---

* Page references supplied for representative use or explanatory comment.

Variable Defining Statements

LET X=3.45E−6	New value of $X = 3.45 \times 10^{-6}$	19, 24
LET X=... (function of variables A, B, C, ...).	New value of the variable at the left (X) is given in terms of the old values for the variables on the right. ("LET" may be omitted with some versions of BASIC)	13, 17
LET X=X+1	New value of X equals old value plus one.	13
LET A(I)=...	defines Ith element of array A. I must be integer such that $1 \le I \le 10$ unless specific dimension statements added	27, 28, 54, 70, 71, 164, 215, 232
LET M(I, J)=...	defines I, J element of matrix M. I, J must be integers such that $1 \le I,J \le 10$ unless specific dimension statements added	54, 57, 82, 83, 149, 251, 252, 328, 421

Arithmetic Statements

LET X=A+B	$X = A + B$	11, 20
LET X=A−B	$X = A - B$	11, 20
LET X=A*B	$X = A \times B$	11, 20, 51, 176
LET X=A/B	$X = A \div B$	11, 20
LET X=A↑B	$X = A^B$	11, 38, 40, 46, 54, 70, 71, 87

Statements in the Function Format Built into BASIC

LET X=SQR(A)	$X = \sqrt{A}$	12, 87, 174, 210, 271, 289, 291, 303, 355, 428
LET X=SIN(X)	$X = \mathrm{Sin}(X)$	12, 43, 44, 80, 81, 83, 96, 231, 232, 342, 350–52, 355, 356, 360, 369, 426
LET X=COS(X)	$X = \mathrm{Cos}(X)$ } X in radians	
LET X=TAN(X)	$X = \mathrm{Tan}(X)$	12
LET X=ATN(Y)	$X = \arctan(Y)$ $(-\pi/2 \le X \le +\pi/2$ for ATN case)	12, 294, 300, 355, 428
LET Y=EXP(X)	$Y = \exp(X)$ or e^X	12, 42, 43, 83, 90, 232, 383, 421
LET Y=LOG(X)	$Y = \log_e(X)$	12, 70, 71, 137, 407
LET Y=ABS(X)	$Y = |X|$	12, 37, 209, 274
LET Y=INT(X)	$Y =$ first integer less than or equal to X.	19, 29, 70, 71, 75, 83, 89, 99, 152, 289, 304
LET Y=SGN(X)	$Y = +1$ if $X > 0$; $Y = 0$ if $X = 0$; and $Y = -1$ if $X < 0$.	48, 266, 359, 360
LET Y=RND(X)	$Y =$ pseudo random number between 0 and 1 (X must be defined but its value does not affect Y).	37, 81, 99, 110–112, 117, 121, 181, 183, 259, 289, 291, 291n, 292, 293, 295, 299, 303–10, 316–20, 327

Functions Defined Within the Program [labelled FNA(X), FNB(X), ... FNZ(X)]

LET Y=FNA(X)	Let $Y =$ value of previously defined function FNA(X) for argument X.	26, 27, 92, 109, 174, 175, 209, 384, 386, 387, 397, 404, 405
DEF FNA(X)=1+X*X	Defines function FNA(X) to be $1 + X^2$	25, 40, 47, 48, 71, 84, 384, 389, 397, 404, 405
DEF FNA(X, Y) LET FNA=... ... FNEND	Format for multiple line function statements (not available on all BASIC compilers)	25

Data-Related Statements

INPUT A, B, C	Computer returns? for each requested variable and waits for operator to enter numerical values from keyboard (followed by carriage return) for A, B, and C.	6, 13, 20, 21, 327
READ D, E, F	Read values for D, E, F sequentially from DATA statements	14
DATA 1.2,4,−1.2E−6,3.56	Data to be assigned (row-wise) in READ statements.	14, 16, 23, 118, 147, 253, 288, 353–55
RESTORE	The next READ statement starts reading entries (row-wise) from the first DATA statement.	14, 172

Print Statements

PRINT X	Print numerical value of X.	*6, 11, 15*
PRINT "X"	Print the character X.	*15, 20, 21*
PRINT X,Y,Z	Print numerical values of X, Y, Z in coarse spacing.	*15*
PRINT X;Y;Z	Print numerical values of X, Y, Z in close spacing.	*15, 177, 357*
PRINT "X", "Y", "Z"	Print the characters X, Y, Z in coarse spacing.	
PRINT "X"; "Y"; "Z"	Print the characters XYZ in adjacent spacing.	*15, 75, 357*
PRINT	Activate carriage return and advance roller.	*15*
PRINT TAB(X);"*"	Print character * on the $(X+1)^{th}$ column.	*16, 76, 77, 82, 89, 165, 349*

String Statements (Not available on some computers)

PRINT CHR$(I);	Prints character corresponding to ASCII code for integer, I, in closely-packed form. (Prints A...Z when $I=65,...,90$).	*31, 32, 84, 99, 109*
INPUT A$	Input string variable from keyboard	*33*
LET V$="ABCD"	Defines V$ to be the string ABCD.	*31, 32*
CHANGE V$ TO V	Stores ASCII integers for characters in string in array $V(I)$; Here $V(1)=65$, $V(2)=66$, $V(3)=67$, $V(4)=68$ and $V(\emptyset)=4=$ length.	*32, 33, 146*

Conditional Statements

IF A=B THEN 75	If A=B, then go to line 75	*16*
IF A>B THEN 75	If A>B, then go to line 75	*16, 17, 24, 77, 78, 109*
IF A>=B THEN 75	If A≥B, then go to line 75 (The order >= is important).	*16, 79, 153*
IF A<B THEN 75	If A<B, then go to line 75	*16, 24, 30, 160, 241*
IF A<=B THEN 75	If A≤B, then go to line 75 (The order <= is important).	*16*
IF A#B THEN 75 } IF A<>B THEN 75 }	If A≠B, then go to line 75	*16, 17* *(see also note on "super BASIC". 78)*

Additional Statements Used in Loops and Branch Points

GOTO 75	computer jumps to line 75 when program is running. (normally used with one of the conditional statements above if GOTO results in a loop)	*16*
FOR I=2 TO 11 STEP .5 ... NEXT I	Sets up loop starting with I=2 and running in increments of 0.5 until I>11. If "STEP .5" is omitted, positive unit steps would be assumed. Start, stop and step size may be computed. Loops may be nested (within limits characteristic of the computer) so long as they do not cross.	*17, 18, 36, 80, 81*
1Ø GOSUB 1ØØ	At line 1Ø computer jumps to subroutine starting on line 1ØØ and continues to the first RETURN statement. It then returns to first program line after 1Ø. GOSUB statements may be nested (within limits characteristic of the computer).	*26, 27, 92, 93, 109, 110, 118, 167, 175, 261–63*
RETURN	denotes end of subroutine. Computer leaves subroutine when first RETURN statement encountered. There can be any number of RETURN statements, so long as they are not encountered before a GOSUB statement.	
END	Normal end statement for program. (Can only be one and must be last line number.)	
STOP	Program jumps to END statement (can be any number).	

Matrix Statements and Dimension Statements* (MAT operations are not available on some computers)

DIM X(15),M(12,3Ø)	Dimension column array X with 15 elements (treated same as matrix with 15 rows and 1 column), dimension matrix M with 12 rows and 3Ø columns. (Dimension statements are not required unless more than 10 rows and columns are used.)	*27, 52, 57, 58, 60, 83, 117, 120, 176*
MAT M=ZER	All elements in matrix M are set equal to zero. (Dimensions must have been explicitly given.)	*52, 327*
MAT M=ZER(11,12)	All elements in M are set to zero and matrix is redimensioned to 11 rows and 12 columns.*	*53, 55, 60, 149, 327*
MAT M=CON	All elements in M are set to one. (Dimensions must have been explicitly given.)	*52, 85, 119*
MAT M=CON(9,11)	All elements in M are set to one and matrix is redimensioned to 9 rows and 11 columns.*	*53*
MAT M=IDN	All diagonal elements set to one, off-diagonal elements set to zero. (M must be square and explicitly dimensioned) M becomes the identity matrix.	*52, 60*
MAT M=IDN(11,11)	M is set equal to an 11×11 identity matrix.*	*53, 252*

* *Note:* the redimensioning statements cannot result in greater dimensions than those contained in the initial DIM statements (or in absence of the latter, 10 rows and 10 columns).

MAT READ M	Read all elements of M row-wise from DATA statements. (Dimensions of M must have been specified.)	*52, 58, 117*
MAT PRINT M	Print all elements row-wise on separate lines.	*52*
MAT PRINT M,	Print all elements row-wise with coarse spacing.	*52*
MAT PRINT M;	Print all elements row-wise with close spacing.	*52, 54*
MAT B=A	B is set equal to A element-by-element. (The dimensions of B and A must be the same and have been specified.)	*56*
MAT C=A+B	C is set equal to A+B, element-by-element. (The dimensions of A, B, C must be the same and have been specified.)	*56, 328*
MAT C=A−B	C is set equal to A−B, element-by-element. (The dimensions of A, B, C must be the same and have been specified.)	*56*
MAT C=(K)*A	C is set equal to A after multiplying each element by the same scalar constant K. (Dimensions of A and C must be the same and specified.)	*55, 85*
MAT C=A*B	C is set equal to the matrix product, A*B, element by element. (Dimensions must have been specified, consistent with matrix multiplication.)	*56–58, 60, 119, 328, 421*
MAT C=TRN(A)	C is set equal to the transpose of A. (Dimensions must have been specified, consistent with the matrix operation.)	*55, 58*
MAT C=INV(A)	C is set equal to the inverse matrix of A. (Dimensions of both must be the same, square and specified.)	*59, 60, 63, 328, 421*

Index

447

One-dimensional random walk, 289, 290
One-dimensional resistance problems, 203
Oneil, H., 187, 197
Open organ pipe, 338, 339
  harmonic coefficient of, 361
  waveform of, 361
Open pipe resonances, 339, 365
Ophicleide, 353 *fig*, 364
  harmonic coefficients of, 366 *fig*
  waveforms of, 366 *fig*
Oppenheimer, J. Robert, 3 *fig*, 34
Optical maser, 415
Optimum bias amplitude, 396
Organ pipe construction, 377
  waveforms of, 340 *fig*, 358, 361 *fig*
Orthogonal functions, 67, 68
Orthogonality, 67, 68, 347 (*see also* Fourier analysis), 426
  non-Hermitian, 426*n*
Orthonormal functions, 67
Oscillation, 391
  frequency, 432, 433
Oscillation frequency of single mode laser above threshold, 435
  at threshold, 432
Oscillator frequency, 435
Oscillatory behavior of sailor-prostitute problem, 320 *fig*
Oscillatory effects of contagion problem, 310 *fig*
Overmodulation, 411 *fig*
Overtones (*see* Harmonic coefficient)
Overtone series, 362
Ozone layer, 297

P

Pth roots, 38, 46
Pair correlation matrix, language identification from, 129, 130
Pair interactions, 302*n*
Palmer Stadium, 213
Parachute, terminal velocity for, 211
Parametric curves, 94
  representation, 79–81
Parentheses, use of, 11
Parkinson's law, 141
Partridge, John F., 213*n*
Pattern identification, 68, 71, 72
Pattern recognition and integration, 67–71
Paul, W., 256 *fig*, 277
Penicillin, 314
Pennemunde, 234
Period, 336, 360
Periodic waveforms, Fourier coefficients for, 351
Petersen, F. R., 436
Phase, 429
  in diffraction, 426
  sensitivity to, 371
Phase angle, 45, 344, 345, 355, 356
Phase change, 376
Phase component, 374 *fig*
Phase discontinuities, 370, 374, 375
Phase shifts, 391, 432
  binaural detection of, 372
  from Gaussian gain curve, 432
  by holes, 435
  sensitivity of brain to, 370
Phase splices, 374
Phillips, Jennifer, 209 *table*
Photoeffect, two quantum, 365

Photoelectric effect, two quantum, 377
Physical Review Letters, 420*n*
Physiologie du marriage, La (*see* H. de Balzac)
Pi, to 5000 places, 182 *fig*
Piccolo, 355 *fig*
  harmonic coefficient of, 361
  waveforms, 361
Pierce, J. R., 197
Ping-pong ball, bouncing, 221–23
  coefficient of restitution, 223
  program for, 219
  spin of, 220 *fig*
  spin-interaction, 223
  trajectories for, 220 *fig*
Pioneer 10 flight past Jupiter, 247, 249
Planck's constant, 416
Planet–planet interaction terms, 251
Planet stealing, 255 *fig*
Playback head, 393
Plotting on the teletype terminal, 74–77
  of field lines, 271
  of N functions, 78
  random points, program for, 84
  a spiral, program for, 85
  surfaces on random access devices, 87, 89
  surfaces on teletype, 86–90
  surfaces without hidden lines, 89
  two functions on the teletype, 77–78
Plucked string, 370
  transient decay, 358, 359 *fig*
Poe, E. A. (*see also* "The Gold Bug"), 123, 128 *fig*, 130 *fig*, 131 *fig*, 140 *fig*, 159, 161, 163, 179, 197
  challenge of, 161
  cipher, 194
  cipher, decoding matrix for, 162
  cipher based on *suaviter in modo, fortiter in re*, 162, 194
  cipher from, 161 *fig*
  literary crypt, 162
  on "Secret Writing," 162
Poisson, 341
Poisson, distribution
  average values and moments, 283, 284
  equation for, 282
  transition from, 286, 287
  variance and standard deviation for, 284, 285
Polar coordinates, parametric representation of, 79, 80
  form, 45
Pollack, Jackson, 124
Population inversion, 417, 418
Portuguese, 129, 130 *fig*, 140 *fig*, 142 *fig*, 170 *table*
  character frequencies for, 131 *fig*
Positronium, 274
Poulsen, Valdemar, 395*n*
Pounds force, 204*n*
Power amplifiers, push-pull transistorized, 385
Prandtl, L., 208*n*, 277
Pratt, Fletcher, 140 *fig*, 155*n*, 157*n*, 187, 197
Prime numbers, 28
Princeton–Dartmouth game of Nov. 25, 1950, 213–16
  program for, 215
  trajectories pertinent to, 216 *fig*
PRINT statements (*see also* Summary in Appendix), 15, 31, 32, 106–9, 165

use of in plotting, 75–79, 82–90, 98–100 (*figs* 76, 86, 88, 98, 100)
Priority of operations, 11
Probabilities, from correlation matrices, 114
Probability clouds, parametric representation of, 80, 81
  program for, 81
Probability function, for contagion, 303, 304
Program, machine language, 5
Programming in BASIC, 10–12
Prohkorov, A. M., 420*n*, 436
Projection plane, 92
  use of variable base vectors for, 93–97
Projections, 91
  coefficients, 68
  of helices and biological molecules, 96
  of straight lines, program for, 93
Psychology of stereoscopic perception, 97–101
Ptolemy III, 141, 144 *fig*, 145
Push-pull transistorized power amplifiers, 385

Q

Quadrant problem, 300, 355, 356, 428
Quadratic equation, 46
Quadratic resistive force, 207 *fig*
Quadrupole mass filter, 256 *fig*, 259
Quadrupole mass spectrometer, 257, 258
Queen Elizabeth I, 190, 191
Queen Mary, 212
Quintadena (*see* Closed organ pipe)

R

Rachmaninoff, Serge, 402
Radiation with excited atoms, interaction of, 416
Raether, M., 256 *fig*, 277
Ralston, Anthony, 202*n*, 277
Ramanujan, Srinivasa, 53
  problem, 53–55
Random access plotting device, 87
Random key, 180, 181
Random number simulator, 37, 123, 291*n*
Random point problem, 84
Random sampling method, 307
Random sequence, entropy for, 181
Random walk, one dimensional, 289
"Raspberry", 363
Rate coefficients, 417
Rate equations, 417, 420
Raudive, Konstantin, 412, 437
Raudive voices, 412–15
  early newspaper account of, 413 *fig*
Rausenberger, Fritz, 217, 224
Rawcliffe, R. D., 245*n*, 246, 278
RC filter, 380, 381, 382
READ statement, 14
READY (computer reply), 10, 11
Real roots or zero crossings, 46
Record head, 393 *fig*
Recorded wavelength, relation to tape velocity, 393
Recovery time constant, 306, 309–11
Rectifiers, 406–7
  ideal, 406
Recuperation time constants, 304
Reentry, 244
  trajectories for, 245 *fig*

457

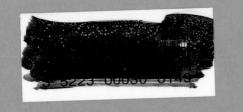